# ARIZONA
## TRAVELER'S
# HANDBOOK

D1324582

# ARIZONA
## TRAVELER'S
# HANDBOOK

### SIXTH EDITION

**BILL WEIR & ROBERT BLAKE**

# MOON
### PUBLICATIONS INC.

# ARIZONA TRAVELER'S HANDBOOK
## SIXTH EDITION

*Published by*
Moon Publications, Inc.
P.O. Box 3040
Chico, California 95927-3040, USA

*Printed by*
Colorcraft Ltd., Hong Kong

ISBN: 1-56691-071-4
ISSN: 1088-0925

*Editors*: Karen Gaynor Bleske and Lisa Stowell
*Copy Editors:* Deana Corbitt Shields and Nicole Revere
*Production & Design:* Rob Warner and David Hurst
*Cartographers:* Bob Race and Brian Bardwell
*Index:* Gina Wilson Birtcil

Cover Photo: Fresh Snow on Vaki Point, South Rim of Grand Canyon National Park, by Kerrick James
All photos by Bill Weir unless otherwise noted.

Distributed in the United States and Canada by Publishers Group West
Printed in Hong Kong

Please send all comments,
corrections, additions,
amendments, and critiques to:

**ARIZONA TRAVELER'S HANDBOOK
c/o MOON PUBLICATIONS, INC.
P.O. BOX 3040
CHICO, CA 95927-3040, USA
e-mail: travel@moon.com**

Printing History
1st edition
    September 1986
2nd edition
    August 1987
    March 1988
    June 1989
3rd edition
    April 1990
    April 1991
4th edition
    June 1992
5th edition
    October 1994
**6th edition
    September 1996**

# CONTENTS

# MAPS

# MAP SYMBOLS

| | | |
|---|---|---|
| ▬▬▬ FREEWAY | INTERSTATE HIGHWAY | ▬ ▬ ▬ NATIONAL BORDER |
| ▬▬ MAIN HIGHWAY | U.S. HIGHWAY | ▬·▬·▬ STATE BORDER |
| ▬ SECONDARY ROAD | ARIZONA HIGHWAY | ▬··▬··▬ OTHER BORDERS |
| ▬ ▬ ▬ UNPAVED ROAD | FOREST ROUTE | O LARGE CITY |
| ▬·▬·▬ FOOT PATH | ▲ MOUNTAIN | ○ MEDIUM CITY |
| ▬▬ RAILROAD | WATER | o SMALL TOWN |
| ▬▬ BRIDGE | | ■ POINT OF INTEREST |
| ⌣ PASS | | Δ CAMPGROUND |

# CHARTS

# SPECIAL TOPICS

# ABBREVIATIONS

a/c—air-conditioning
B&B—bed and breakfast
ca.—circa
d—double
elev.—elevation
F—Fahrenheit
FR—Forest Route
RV—recreational vehicle
s—single
tel.—telephone

# ACKNOWLEDGMENTS

**M**any thanks go to the hundreds of people who assisted in making the *Arizona Traveler's Handbook* as complete and accurate as it is! We are especially indebted to people of the National Park Service, U.S. Forest Service, Bureau of Land Management, U.S. Fish and Wildlife Service, Arizona Game and Fish, and Arizona State Parks, whose high standards make Arizona such a wonderful place to visit. Chambers of commerce, from the tiniest communities to the big cities, supplied valuable ideas, advice, and maps. Extra thanks go to Carol Downey of the research library in the Arizona Capitol and to the staffs of Fort Verde and Jerome state historic parks for generous use of their historic photos. Barton Wright's excellent drawing of the Hopi Reservation, which he kindly gave permission to use in earlier editions, appears on p. 107.

## IS THIS BOOK OUT OF DATE?

Nothing stays the same, it seems. Although this book has been carefully researched, Arizona will continue to grow and change. New sights and services will open while others change hands or close. Your comments and ideas on making *Arizona Traveler's Handbook* more useful to other readers will be highly valued. If you find something new, discontinued, or changed, please let us know so that the information can be included in the next edition. Businesses, too, are most welcome to send a postcard or letter with updates.

Perhaps a map or worthwhile place to visit has been overlooked; please bring it to our attention. All contributions (letters, maps, and photos) will be carefully saved, checked, and acknowledged. If we use your photos or artwork, you will be mentioned in the credits and receive a free copy of the book. Be aware, however, that the author and publisher are not responsible for unsolicited manuscripts, photos, or artwork and, in most cases, cannot undertake to return them unless you include a self-addressed, stamped envelope. Moon Publications will have nonexclusive publication rights to all material submitted. Address your letters to:

*Arizona Traveler's Handbook*
c/o Moon Publications
P.O. Box 3040
Chico, CA 95927 USA

THE EXPLORATION OF THE COLORADO RIVER AND ITS CANYONS

# INTRODUCTION

Few states feature such spectacular and varied terrain as Arizona. Because most of the early travelers who crossed this land kept to the south, traversing the hot desert valleys and plains, these regions form the popular image of Arizona even today. Yet much of the northern and eastern parts of the state feature extensive coniferous forests and rushing mountain streams. Volcanic activity, uplift, faulting, and erosion have formed dozens of mountain ranges and canyons. The Grand Canyon, one of the world's greatest natural wonders, ranks at the top of most visitors' lists, but many other beautiful and intriguing places remain to be discovered. *Arizona Traveler's Handbook* will help you find them. Wilderness areas, early Spanish sites, Indian reservations, old mining towns, bright city lights—they're all here. This book provides practical information for every budget, including that of the oft-neglected low-budget traveler.

## THE LAND

Though geologically complex, the land surface of Arizona can be envisioned as tilting downward to the southwest. More than 90% of the state's drainage flows into the southwest corner via the Colorado River and its tributaries. The river enters Mexico at an elevation of only 70 feet. Mountain ranges rise in nearly every part of Arizona, but they achieve their greatest heights in the north-central and eastern sections. Humphrey's Peak, part of the San Francisco Peaks near Flagstaff, crowns the state at 12,633 feet. Geographers divide Arizona into the high Colorado Plateau Province of the northeast and the Basin and Range Province of the rest of the state. Average elevation statewide is about 4,000 feet. Measuring 335 miles wide and 390 miles long, Arizona is the sixth-largest state in the country.

# ARIZONA LANDFORMS

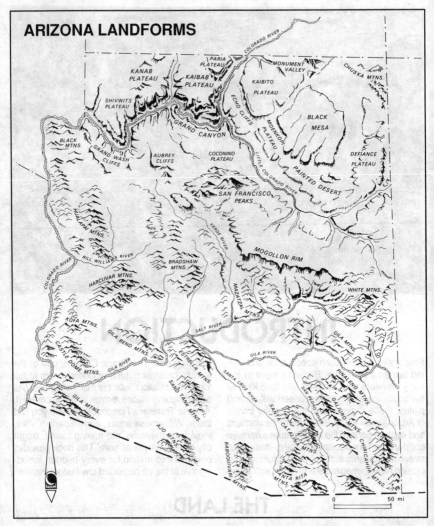

Map labels:
COLORADO RIVER — PARIA PLATEAU — MONUMENT VALLEY — CHUSKA MTNS. — KANAB PLATEAU — KAIBAB PLATEAU — KAIBITO PLATEAU — SHIVWITS PLATEAU — ECHO CLIFFS — MOENKOPI PLATEAU — BLACK MESA — GRAND CANYON — BLACK MTNS. — GRAND WASH CLIFFS — AUBREY CLIFFS — COCONINO PLATEAU — LITTLE COLORADO RIVER — DEFIANCE PLATEAU — PAINTED DESERT — SAN FRANCISCO PEAKS — HUALAPAI MTNS. — BILL WILLIAMS RIVER — VERDE RIVER — MOGOLLON RIM — BRADSHAW MTNS. — HARCUVAR MTNS. — MAZATZAL MTNS. — WHITE MTNS. — KOFA MTNS. — SALT RIVER — GILA MTNS. — CASTLE DOME MTNS. — GILA BEND MTNS. — ESTRELLA MTNS. — GILA RIVER — GILA RIVER — PINALENO MTNS. — COLORADO RIVER — SANTA CRUZ RIVER — SAN PEDRO RIVER — GALIURO MTNS. — SAND TANK MTNS. — SANTA CATALINA MTNS. — CHIRICAHUA MTNS. — GILA MTNS. — OJO MTNS. — BABOQUIVARI MTNS. — SANTA RITA MTNS.

0   50 mi

**Colorado Plateau**

This plateau, a giant uplifted landmass in northeast Arizona, also extends across much of adjacent Utah, Colorado, and New Mexico. Rivers have cut deeply into the plateau, forming the Grand Canyon of the Colorado and other vast gorges. Volcanoes breaking through the surface have left hundreds of cinder cones, such as multicolored Sunset Crater, and larger composite volcanoes, such as the San Francisco Peaks. The most recent burst of volcanic activity in Arizona took place near Sunset Crater about 700 years ago. Most elevations on the plateau range from 5,000 to 8,000 feet. Sheer cliffs of the Mogollon (MUGGY-own) Rim drop to the desert, marking the plateau's southern boundary. To the west, the plateau ends at Grand Wash Cliffs.

*Vista Encantadora on the North Rim*

## Basin and Range Province

Many ranges of fault-block mountains, formed by faulting and tilting of the earth's crust, poke through the desert plains of southern and western Arizona. Several peaks rise above 9,000 feet, creating biological islands inhabited by cool-climate animals and plants. Tucson-area residents can leave the Sonoran Desert and within an hour reach the cool fir and aspen forests of Mt. Lemmon.

## CLIMATE

During any season, some part of Arizona enjoys near-perfect weather. Sunny skies and low humidity prevail over the entire state. Average winter temperatures run in the 50s F in the low desert and the 20s to 30s in the mountains and high plateaus. Desert dwellers endure average temperatures in the 80s and 90s in summer, when high-country residents enjoy averages in the 70s. The highest reading ever recorded in the state is 127° F at Parker, along the Colorado River, on July 7, 1905. Even on a nor-

mal summer day in the low desert, you can expect highs in the low 100s.

## Precipitation

Rain and snowfall correspond roughly to elevation: the southwest corner receives less than five inches annually, while the higher mountains and the Mogollon Rim enjoy about 25 inches. Most precipitation falls either in winter as gentle rains and snow or in summer as widely scattered thundershowers. Winter moisture comes mostly December through March, revitalizing the desert; brilliant wildflower displays appear after a good wet season. Summer afternoon thunderclouds billow in towering formations from about mid-July to mid-September. The storms, though producing heavy rains, tend to be localized in areas less than three miles across. Summer thundershowers make up 60-70% of the annual precipitation in the low desert and about 45% on the Colorado Plateau.

## Storm Hazards

Rainwater runs quickly off the rocky desert surfaces and into gullies and canyons. Flash floods can form and sweep away anything in their paths, including boulders, cars, and campsites. Take care not to camp or park in potential flash-flood areas. If you come to a section of flooded roadway, a common occurrence on desert roads after storms, just wait until the water goes down —usually only an hour or so. Summer lightning causes forest and brush fires, and poses a danger to hikers foolish enough to climb mountains when storms threaten.

# FLORA AND FAUNA

A wide variety of plants and animals finds homes within Arizona's great range of elevations—more than 12,000 feet. Some plants, such as the senita cactus and elephant tree, grow only in southern Arizona and Mexico. Migratory birds often stop by. The colorful parrot-like trogon bird and more than a dozen species of humming-birds fly up from Mexico to spend their summers in the mountains of southeastern Arizona. Canada geese and other northern waterfowl settle in for the winter on rivers and lakes in the low desert.

### Protected Plants
Arizona has many sensitive and endangered species. State law prohibits collecting or destroying most cacti and wildflowers without a permit from the landowner. Offenders can receive a $500 fine and possible prison term. Cacti need time to grow—a saguaro takes 50 years to mature—and cannot survive large-scale collecting. Although the "jumping cactus" is a myth, at least one saguaro has struck back at its oppressor—in February 1982, a man north of Phoenix shot a saguaro twice with a shotgun; a 23-foot section then broke off and crushed him to death.

## LIFE ZONES

To help simplify and understand the different environments of Arizona, some scientists use the Merriam system of life zones. Because plants rely on rainfall, which is determined largely by elevation, each life zone can be expected to occur within a certain range of elevations. The elevation ranges are not exact—south-facing mountain slopes receive more sun and lose more moisture to evaporation than north-facing slopes at the same level. Canyons and unusual rainfall patterns can also

play havoc with classifications. Yet the life zones do provide a general idea of what kind of vegetation and animal life visitors can expect when traveling through the state.

### Lower Sonoran Zone
Arizona's famed desert country of arid plains, barren mountains, and stately saguaro cacti covers about one-third of the state. The south and west sections under 4,500 feet lie within this zone. The big cities and most of the state's population are here, too. With irrigation, farmers find the land good for growing vegetables, citrus, and cotton. Cacti thrive: you'll see the prickly pear, cholla, and barrel, as well as the giant saguaro—its white blossoms are the state flower. The great variety of desert shrubs and small trees includes the palo verde, ocotillo, creosote, mesquite, and ironwood. Flowering plants tend to bloom either after winter rains (the Sonoran or Mexican type) or summer showers (the Mojave or Californian type).

Most desert animals retreat to dens or burrows during the heat of the day, when ground temperatures can reach 150° F. Look for wildlife in early morning, late afternoon, or at night: kangaroo rats, squirrels, mice, cottontails, jackrabbits, skunks, kit foxes, ringtail cats, javelinas, bighorn sheep, coyotes, and the extremely shy mountain lions. Common birds include the cactus wren (state bird of Arizona), Gambel's quail, Gila woodpecker, roadrunner, hawks, eagles, owls, and common raven. Sidewinder and western diamond-back rattlesnakes are occasionally spotted. The rare Gila monster, identified by a beadlike skin with black and yellow patterns, is the only poisonous lizard in the United States; it's slow and nonaggressive but has powerful jaws. Also watch out for poisonous invertebrates, especially the small, slender scorpion—its

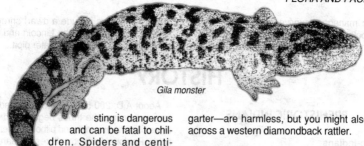

KAY STEPHENSON

*Gila monster*

sting is dangerous and can be fatal to children. Spiders and centipedes can also inflict painful bites. It's a good idea to check for unwanted guests in shoes and other items left outside.

## Upper Sonoran Zone

This zone encompasses 4,500- to 6,500-foot elevations in central Arizona and in widely scattered areas throughout the rest of the state. Enough rain falls here to support grasslands or stunted woodlands of juniper, piñon pine, and oak. Chaparral-type vegetation grows here too, forming a nearly impenetrable thicket of manzanita and other bushes. Many of the animals found in the Lower Sonoran Zone live here as well. You might also see black bear, desert mule deer, white-tailed deer, and the antelope-like pronghorn. Rattlesnakes and other reptiles like this zone best.

## Transition Zone

The sweet-smelling ponderosa pine lives in this zone, at 6,500 to 8,000 feet, where much of the winter's precipitation comes as snow. Ponderosas grow in many parts of the state, but their greatest expanse—the largest in the country—lies along the southern Colorado Plateau, from Williams in north-central Arizona eastward into New Mexico. Gambel oak, junipers, and Douglas fir commonly grow among the ponderosas.

Squirrels and chipmunks rely on the pine cones for food; other animal residents here include desert cottontail, black-tailed jackrabbit, spotted and striped skunks, red fox, coyote, mule deer, white-tailed deer, elk, black bear, and mountain lion. Wild turkeys live in the woods, along with Steller's jays, screech owls, hummingbirds, juncos, and the common raven. Most of the snakes—gopher, hognosed, and

garter—are harmless, but you might also run across a western diamondback rattler.

## Canadian Zone

Douglas firs dominate the cool, wet forests between 8,000 and 9,500 feet, mixed with Engelmann and blue spruce, white and subalpine fir, and quaking aspen. Little sunlight penetrates the dense forests, where the trees function as their own windbreak. Grasses and wildflowers grow in lush meadows amid the forests. You'll find Canadian Zone forests on the Kaibab Plateau of the Grand Canyon's North Rim, the San Francisco Peaks, the White Mountains, and other high peaks. Look and listen for squirrels as they busily gather cones for the long winter. Deer and elk graze in this zone, but rarely higher.

## Hudsonian Zone

Strong winds and a growing season of less than 120 days prevent trees from reaching their potential size at elevations from 9,500 to 11,500 feet. Forests here receive twice as much snow as their counterparts in the Canadian Zone just below. Often gnarled and twisted, the dominant species are Engelmann and blue spruce, subalpine and corkbark fir, and bristlecone pine. This zone appears in Arizona only atop the highest mountains.

On a bright summer day, the trees, grasses, and tiny flowering alpine plants buzz with insects, rodents, and visiting birds. Come winter, most animals move to lower and more protected areas.

## Alpine Zone

In Arizona, this zone is found only on the San Francisco Peaks, where the upper limit of tree growth stands at about 11,500 feet. Freezing temperatures and snow can blast the mountain slopes even in midsummer. About 80 species of plants, many also present in the North American

Arctic, manage to survive on the Peaks despite the rocky soil, wind, and cold. One species of groundsel and a buttercup appear only here.

Seasonal visitors include a dwarf shrew and three species of birds, the Lincoln and white-crowned sparrows and the water pipit.

# HISTORY

## PREHISTORIC INDIANS

### Paleo-Indians

Arizona's first people discovered this land more than 15,000 years ago. They came from a hunting culture that extended across the Great Plains and into New Mexico and eastern Arizona. Spears in hand, tribespeople hunted bison, camel, horse, antelope, and mammoth. Smaller game and wild plant foods completed their diet. About 9000 B.C., when the climate grew drier and grasslands, turned to desert, most of the large animals died off or left. Overhunting may have hastened their extinction.

### Desert Culture Tradition

The early tribes survived these changes by relying on seeds, berries, and nuts collected from wild plants and by hunting smaller game such as pronghorn, deer, mountain sheep, and jackrabbit. Having developed a precise knowledge of the land, the small bands of related families moved in seasonal migrations timed to coincide with the ripening of plants in each area. They traveled light, probably carrying baskets, animal skins, traps, snares, and stone tools. Most likely they sought shelter in caves or built small brush huts. Some Arizona tribes continued a similar nomadic lifestyle until the late 1800s.

### Distinct Cultures Emerge

Between 2000 and 500 B.C., cultivation skills came to the uplands of Arizona from Mexico. Indian groups, though, maintained their seasonal migrations, planting corn and squash in the spring, continuing their travels in search of wild food, and then returning to harvest the fields in autumn. Agriculture became more important about 500 B.C., when beans were introduced. The earliest pottery, for cooking beans and storing other foods and water, emerged at about the same time. The combination of beans, corn, and squash gave the people a nutritious, high-protein diet.

About A.D. 200-500, as they devoted more time to farming, the tribes began building villages of partly underground pithouses near their fields. Regional farming cultures appeared: the Hohokam of the southern deserts, the Mogollon of the eastern uplands, and the Anasazi of the Colorado Plateau in the north.

### Growth and the Great Pueblos

Villages grew larger and more widespread as populations increased from A.D. 500 to 1100. Above-ground pueblo dwellings began to replace the old-style pithouses. Trade among the Southwest cultures and with those in Mexico brought new ideas for crafts, farming, and building, along with valued items such as copper bells, parrots (prized for their feathers), and seashells and turquoise for jewelry. Cotton cultivation and weaving skills also developed.

Major towns appeared between A.D. 900 and 1100, possibly serving as trade centers. Complex religious ceremonies, probably similar to those of the present-day Hopi Indians, were enacted in kivas (ceremonial rooms) and village plazas in the uplands. Ball courts and platform mounds, most often found in the southern deserts, likely served both religious and secular purposes. Desert dwellers also dug elaborate irrigation networks in the valleys of the Salt and Gila rivers.

### Decline and Consolidation

Mysteriously, people began to pack up and abandon, one by one, whole villages and regions throughout Arizona between 1100 and the arrival of the Spanish in 1540. Archaeologists try to explain their disappearance with theories of drought, soil erosion, warfare, disease, and aggression of Apache and Navajo newcomers. Refugees swelled the populations of the remaining villages during this period; eventually, most of these emptied too.

Some Anasazi Indian groups probably survived to become the modern Hopi in northeast-

*petroglyph from the Painted Desert*

ern Arizona. The Mogollon and Hohokam disappeared completely; the modern tribes that replaced them knew nothing of the people who had built the great pueblo structures.

### The Athabaskan Migration

From west-central Canada, small bands of Athabaskan-speaking Indians slowly migrated to the Southwest. They arrived about 1300 to 1500 and established territories in the eastern half of present-day Arizona and adjacent New Mexico. Never a unified group, they followed a nomadic life of hunting, gathering, and raiding neighboring tribes. Some of the Athabaskans, later classified as Navajo on the Colorado Plateau and Apache farther south and east, learned agriculture and weaving from their pueblo neighbors.

## SPANISH EXPLORATION AND RULE

### The Conquistadors

Estévan, a Moorish slave of the viceroy of Mexico, became the first non-Indian to enter what is now Arizona. He arrived from the south in an advance party of Fray Marcos de Niza's 1539 expedition, sent by the viceroy to search for the supposedly treasure-laden Seven Cities of Cíbola.

The first of these "cities" the party entered

was a large Zuni Indian pueblo in present-day New Mexico. There they met their deaths at the hands of the Indians. When Fray Marcos heard the news, he dared view the pueblo only from a distance. Though he returned to Mexico empty-handed, his glowing accounts of this city of stone encouraged a new expedition led by Francisco Vásquez de Coronado.

Coronado departed from Mexico City in 1540 with 336 soldiers, almost 1,000 Indian allies, and 1,500 horses and mules. Instead of gold, the expedition found only houses of mud inhabited by hostile people. Despite hardships, Coronado explored the region for two years, traveling as far north as Kansas. A detachment led by García López de Cárdenas visited the Hopi mesas and the Grand Canyon rim. Another officer of the expedition, Hernando de Alarcón, explored the mouth of the Colorado River in hopes of finding a water route to resupply Coronado. He found the task impossible.

### Missions and Presidios

Nearly 100 years passed after Coronado's failed quest before the Spanish reentered Arizona. A few explorers and prospectors made brief visits, but it was Franciscan missionaries who came to stay. They opened three missions near Hopi villages and had some success in gaining converts, despite strong objections from traditional Hopi.

When pueblo villages in neighboring New Mexico revolted against the Spanish in 1680, the traditional Hopi joined in, killing the friars and many of their followers. Missionary efforts then shifted to southern Arizona, where the tireless Jesuit priest, Eusebio Francisco Kino, explored the new land and built missions from 1691 to 1711. Harsh treatment by later missionaries and land abuses by settlers caused the Pima tribes to revolt in 1751. The Spanish then instituted reforms, meanwhile building a presidio at Tubac to prevent another outbreak. Similar harsh treatment by Spaniards at two missions on the lower Colorado River caused a revolt there in 1781; no attempt was made to reestablish these missions.

### Arizonac

A fantastic silver strike during the Spanish era in 1736 drew thousands to an arroyo known by local Indians as Arizonac, where sheets of native silver weighing 25-50 pounds each were said to cover the ground. The exact location of this extraordinary find is uncertain, but it probably lay west of present-day Nogales. The boom soon ended, but a book published in 1850 in Spain recounted the amazing story. An American mine speculator picked up the tale and used it to publicize and sell mining shares. The name Arizonac, shortened to Arizona, became so well known that politicians later chose it as the moniker governing the entire territory. Or at least that's one theory of how Arizona got its name.

## Mexicans Take Over

This land had always lain on the far fringes of civilization. Politics and the Mexican fight for independence had little effect on Arizona, so when three centuries of Spanish rule came to an end with Mexican independence in 1821, almost nothing changed. In the presidios, a new flag and an oath of loyalty to Mexico marked the transition. Isolation and hostile Apache continued to discourage settlement. Mission work declined as the Mexican government expelled many of the Spanish friars.

# ARRIVAL OF THE ANGLOS

## Mountain Men

Early in the 19th century, adventurous traders and trappers left the comforts of civilization in the eastern states to seek new lives in the West. In 1825, Sylvester Pattie and his son made the first known journey by Anglos to what is now Arizona. The younger Pattie later set down his adventures in *The Personal Narrative of James Ohio Pattie*. Although occasionally suffering attacks by hostile Indians, the Patties and later mountain men coexisted more or less peacefully with the Mexicans and Indians. When U.S. Army explorers and surveyors first visited Arizona in the 1840s and 1850s, they relied on mountain men to show them trails and water holes.

## Arizona Enters America

Anglo traders did an increasingly large business in the Southwest after Mexican independence—their supply route from Missouri was far shorter and more profitable than the Mexicans' long haul from Mexico City. Arizona was of little importance in the Mexican War of 1847-48,

which was ignited by American desire for Texas and California, disputes over Mexico's debts, and Mexican indifference to a political solution. The 1848 Treaty of Guadalupe Hidalgo ceded to the United States not only Texas and California, but everything in between—including Arizona and New Mexico. Still, Arizona remained a backwater, part of the vast New Mexican Territory created by Congress in 1850. The Gadsden Purchase added what's now southernmost Arizona in 1854.

## New Trails

Most early visitors regarded Arizona as nothing but a place to cross on the way to California. The safest routes lay within the lands of the Gadsden Purchase, where Captain Philip Cooke built a wagon road during the Mexican War. Many '49ers, headed for gold strikes in California, used Cooke's road, the Gila Trail. Hostile Indians and difficult mountain crossings discouraged travel farther north, even after Edward Beale opened a rough wagon road across northern Arizona in 1857. Steamboat service on the lower Colorado River, beginning in 1852, brought cheaper and safer transportation to western Arizona.

## Americans Settle In

As the California Gold Rush died down in the mid-1850s, prospectors turned eastward to Arizona. Their first big find here was a placer gold deposit near the confluence of the Colorado River and Sacramento Wash in 1857. More strikes followed. For the first time, large numbers of people came to Arizona to seek their mineral fortunes. Farmers and ranchers followed, cashing in on the market provided by the new mining camps and Army posts.

## Indian Troubles and the Civil War

Mountain men and government surveyors initially maintained good relations with the Indian tribes, but this changed only a few years after first contact. Conflicts between white people and Indians over economic, religious, and political rights, and over land and water, led to loss of land and autonomy for the Indian. Both sides committed heinous atrocities as each sought to drive out the other. Army forts provided a base for troops attempting to subdue the Indians and a refuge for travelers and settlers.

Most Arizonans sided with the Confederacy during the Civil War, but quickly surrendered when large numbers of federal troops arrived. The only Civil War skirmish in Arizona between the North and South occurred at Picacho Pass northwest of Tucson. After several deaths on each side, the Confederates retreated east.

## TERRITORIAL YEARS

Despite the wars and uncertainties of the early 1860s, Arizona emerged for the first time as a separate entity on February 24, 1863, when President Lincoln signed a bill establishing the Arizona territory. Formerly, as part of New Mexico, Arizona had lacked both federal representation and law and order. In 1864, Governor John Goodwin and fellow appointed officials laid out Arizona's first capital at Prescott.

### Continuing Indian Troubles

Control of hostile Indians, especially the Apache and Navajo, proved to be the new territory's most serious problem. Although Arizona's Indians failed to drive out the newcomers, they did succeed in holding back development. Not until the great Apache war leader Geronimo surrendered forever in 1886 did white residents of the territory feel safe.

### Frontier Days End

The arrival of the railroads in the 1870s and 1880s and concurrent discoveries of rich copper deposits brought increasing prosperity. Ranching, farming, and logging grew in importance. By 1890 Arizona no longer needed most of its Army forts. Only Fort Huachuca in southeast Arizona survived as an active military post from the Indian wars to the present.

### Mormon Settlement

Mormons in Utah, seeking new freedoms and opportunities, migrated south into Arizona. They first established Littlefield in the extreme northwest corner of Arizona in 1864. A flood washed out the community in 1867 but determined settlers rebuilt it in 1877. Mormons developed other parts of the Arizona Strip in the far north and operated Lees Ferry across the Colorado River,

ARIZONA STATE ARCHIVES

*When the Warm Springs Apache were moved to San Carlos in 1877, Chief Victorio and a small band escaped. He led a savage campaign against Americans and Mexicans in 1879-80, killing nearly 1,000 people before being shot by a Mexican bounty hunter.*

just upstream from the Grand Canyon. From Lees Ferry, settlers headed as far south as St. David on the San Pedro River in Cochise County. Some settlements were abandoned because of land ownership problems, poor soil, or irrigation difficulties. Mormon towns prospering today include Springerville (founded 1871), Joseph City (1876), Mesa (1878), and Show Low (1890).

## STATEHOOD AND MODERN ARIZONA

After years of political wrangling, on February 14, 1912, President William H. Taft signed a proclamation admitting Arizona as the 48th state. Citizens turned out for parades and wild celebrations; in Phoenix, Governor-elect George W.P. Hunt led a triumphant procession to the Capitol. Arriving in the territory in 1881 as an unemployed miner, Hunt worked his way up to become a successful merchant, banker, territorial representative, and president of Arizona's Constitutional Convention. Hunt's support of labor, good roads, and other liberal causes won him seven terms in the governor's office.

Arizona lived up to its nickname, the Copper State, riding the good times when copper prices were high, as during WW I and the Roaring '20s, and suffering during economic depressions. Water, that all-important resource for farmers and cities, also preoccupied citizens. New dams across the Gila, Salt, and Verde rivers of central Arizona ensured the state's growth.

Over the Colorado River, however, Arizona officials maintained a long-running feud with California and other thirsty states. Arizona pressed for its water rights from the early 1920s until 1944, even calling out the National Guard at one point to halt construction of Parker Dam, designed to supply water to Los Angeles. Wartime priorities finally forced the Arizona Legislature to make peace and join the other river states in the Colorado River Compact.

## WW II and the Postwar Boom

During WW II the Army Air Corps, attracted by good flying weather, arrived in Arizona to build training bases. Army officers, including General Patton, trained their soldiers on the Arizona deserts. Aeronautical and other defense industries built factories; state manufacturing income jumped from $17 million in 1940 to $85 million just five years later. Several POW camps were built for captured Germans and Italians. Japanese-Americans were also interned here; in fact, so many Japanese were herded into the Poston camp south of Parker that for a time it ranked as Arizona's third-largest city.

The war, and the air-conditioning that made low desert summers bearable, changed the state forever. Many of the workers and servicepeople who passed through during the hectic war years returned to Arizona to live. Even some of the German POWs, it is said, liked Arizona enough to return to stay. Much of the industry and many military bases remained as well. Retired people took a new interest in the state's sunny skies and warm winters. Whole towns, such as Sun City, rose just for the older set. Arizona has continued to grow and diversify, yet it retains its natural beauty and Old West heritage.

*President Taft signs the 1912 Valentine's Day gift to Arizonans.*

THE EXPLORATION OF THE COLORADO RIVER AND ITS CANYONS

# ON THE ROAD
## RECREATION AND ENTERTAINMENT

### KEEPING THE "WILD" IN WILDERNESS

As more people seek relief from the confusion and stress of urban life, the use of wilderness areas increases. Fortunately, Arizona contains an abundance of this fragile and precious resource. The many designated wilderness areas are closed to mechanized vehicles—including mountain bikes—to protect the environment and enhance the experience of solitude. Most designated areas lie within national forest or Bureau of Land Management property, where you're normally free to visit anytime without a permit. Other areas, such as the national parks, national monuments, and the Bureau of Land Management's Paria and Aravaipa canyons, require permits.

Suggestions for backcountry travel and camping include these wilderness ethics:

• Before heading into the backcountry, check with a knowledgeable person about weather, water sources, fire danger, trail conditions, and regulations.
• Tell a ranger or other reliable person where you're going and when you expect to return.
• Travel in small groups for the best experience; group size may also be regulated.
• Try not to camp on meadows, as the grass is easily trampled and killed.
• Avoid digging tent trenches or cutting vegetation.
• Use a campstove to avoid marring the land.
• Camp at least 300 feet away from springs, creeks, and trails. State law prohibits camping within a quarter mile of a sole water source.
• Wash away from water sources.
• Don't drink water directly from streams or lakes, no matter how clean the water appears; it may contain the parasitic protozoan *Giardia lamblia,* which causes the unpleasant disease giardiasis. Boiling your water for several minutes will kill *Giardia* as well as most other bacterial or viral pathogens. Iodine chemical treatments usually work too, although they're not as reliable as boiling (see also the special topic "Giardia").

- Bring a trowel for personal sanitation; dig four to six inches deep.
- Bring plenty of feed for horses and mules.
- Leave dogs at home; they foul campsites and disturb wildlife and other hikers. If you do bring a dog, please keep it under physical control at all times.
- Take home all your trash, so animals can't dig it up and scatter it.
- Help preserve Indian and historic ruins.
- A survival kit can make the difference if you're caught in a storm or are out longer than expected. A pocket-sized container can hold what you need for the three essentials: *fire building* (matches in waterproof container and candle), *shelter* (space blanket, knife, and rope), and *signaling* (mirror and whistle).
- If lost, *realize it,* then find shelter and stay in one place. If you're sure of a way to civilization and plan to walk out, leave a note of your departure time and planned route.

**Know before You Go**

Some of the most spectacular and memorable hiking and camping await the prepared outdoors enthusiast. But because Arizona's deserts and canyons are very different from most other parts of the country, even expert hikers can get into trouble. If you're new to these outdoors, read up on hiking conditions and talk to rangers and local hikers. Backpacking stores are good sources of information. Start with easy trips, then work up gradually.

## ARIZONA TRAIL

By the end of this decade the 750-mile Arizona Trail will cross Arizona from Mexico to Utah. Originally planned by a Flagstaff teacher, the trail will provide recreational travel opportunities to hikers, bicyclists (outside the sections designated as wilderness), equestrians, and, in sections at high enough elevations to offer snow part of the year, cross-country skiers and snowshoers. More than 300 miles of the trail are already open and signed with the Arizona Trail logo. Most sections now in use were existing trails, and these sections are still known by their original names and trail numbers. Some sections were primitive roads and parts of these are still legal for motor vehicles.

Many state and federal government agencies helped establish the Arizona Trail and are helping to administer it and to provide information. Call or write Arizona State Parks, 1300 W. Washington, Phoenix, AZ 85007, tel. (602) 542-4174. From south to north, the trail crosses Coronado National Memorial (tel. 366-5515), Coronado National Forest (tel. 670-4552), Empire-Cienega Resource Conservation Area (tel. 722-4289), Saguaro National Monument East (tel. 733-5153), Bureau of Land Management—Phoenix District (tel. 780-8090), Boyce Thompson Southwestern Arboretum (tel. 689-2811), Tonto National Forest (tel. 225-5200), Tonto National Monument (tel. 425-0320), Tonto Natural Bridge State Park (tel. 476-4202), Coconino National Forest (tel. 527-3600), Walnut Canyon National Monument (tel. 526-3367), Kaibab National Forest (tel. 638-2443), Grand Canyon Na-

tional Park (tel. 638-7888 automated switchboard, or 303-297-2757 advance reservations), and the Bureau of Land Management—Arizona Strip District (tel. 801-673-3545).

These agencies should be able to provide information about the trail segments on their terrain and will publish brochures and maps of the sections as they reach completion. (See also the special topic "Arizona Trail: The Grand Canyon Section.")

## Hypothermia

Your greatest danger outdoors is one that can sneak up and kill you with very little warning. Hypothermia, a lowering of the body's temperature below 95° F, causes disorientation, uncontrollable shivering, slurred speech, and drowsiness. The victim may not even realize what's wrong. Unless corrective action is taken immediately, hypothermia can lead to death. This is why hikers should travel with companions and always carry wind and rain protection; close-fitting raingear works better than ponchos.

Remember that temperatures can plummet rapidly in Arizona's dry climate—a drop of 40° F between day and night is common. Be especially careful at high elevations, where summer sunshine can quickly change into freezing rain or a blizzard. Simply falling into a mountain stream while fishing can also lead to hypothermia and death unless proper action is taken.

If cold and tired, don't waste time. Seek shelter and build a fire; change into dry clothes and drink warm liquids. A victim not fully conscious should be warmed by skin-to-skin contact with another person in a sleeping bag. Try to keep the victim awake and drinking warm liquids.

## EVENTS

Arizona offers a full schedule of rodeos, parades, art festivals, historic celebrations, gem and mineral shows, and sporting events. Activities tend to shift between southern Arizona in winter and the north in summer. Stop at a chamber of commerce to see what's coming up. These offices can also provide a statewide *Calendar of Events,* published by the Arizona Office of Tourism.

## Major Holidays

Even though not always mentioned in the text, many museums, parks, and other tourist attractions close on such holidays as Thanksgiving, Christmas, and New Year's Day; call ahead to check.

**New Year's Day:** January 1
**Martin Luther King, Jr.'s Birthday:** January 15; usually observed the third Monday in January
**President's Day:** third Monday in February; honors Washington and Lincoln
**Easter Sunday:** late March or early April
**Cinco de Mayo:** May 5; a Mexican festival celebrated in many Southwest communities
**Memorial Day:** last Monday in May
**Independence Day:** July 4
**Labor Day:** first Monday in September
**Columbus Day:** second Monday in October
**Veterans Day:** November 11
**Thanksgiving Day:** fourth Thursday in November
**Christmas Day:** December 25

# GIARDIA

It can be tough to resist: Picture yourself hiking in a beautiful area by the banks of a crystal clear stream. The water in your canteen tastes stale, hot, and plastic; the nearby stream looks so inviting that you can't resist a cautious sip. It tastes delicious, clean, and cold, and for the rest of your hike you refresh yourself with water straight from the stream.

Days pass and you forget about drinking untreated water. Suddenly one evening after your meal you are terribly sick to your stomach. You develop an awful case of cramps, and feel diarrhea beginning to set in. Food poisoning?

Nope—it's the effects of giardia, a protozoan that has become common in even the remotest of mountain streams. Giardia is carried in animal or human waste that is deposited or washed into natural waters. When ingested, it begins reproducing, causing a sickness in the host that can become very serious and may not be cured without medical attention.

You can take precautions against giardia with a variety of chemicals and filtering methods, or by boiling water before drinking it. The various chemical solutions on the market work in some applications, but because they need to be safe for human consumption, they are weak and ineffective against the protozoan in its cyst stage of life, when it encases itself in a hard shell. Filtering may eliminate giardia, but there are other water pests too small to be caught by most filters. The most effective way to eliminate such threats is to boil all suspect water. A few minutes at a rolling boil will kill giardia even in the cyst stage of life.

# OTHER CULTURES

## VISITING INDIAN RESERVATIONS

Meeting Arizona's Native Americans offers the opportunity to learn about other cultures. Indian lands represent 27% of the state and include some beautiful mountain, canyon, and desert country. Tribes in Arizona, from north to south, are Paiute, Navajo, Hopi, Havasupai, Hualapai, Yavapai, Apache, Mohave, Chemehuevi, Cocopah, Yaqui, Pima, and Tohono O'odham. See descriptions in the individual travel sections for reservation museums, dances, crafts, recreation, food, and accommodations.

On any of the 23 reservations, keep in mind that you're a guest on private land. Most Indians are very private people; ask before taking their photos, and you may need to pay a posing fee. The Hopi prohibit all photography, sketching, and recording in villages—don't even carry a camera there.

Check to see if you need permits before camping, hiking, or leaving the main roads. Usually a small charge applies for these activities. All fishing and hunting on Indian lands require tribal permits, though you won't need Arizona state licenses. Sometimes parts of a reservation are closed to outsiders.

Tribes you might want to visit include: the Hopi, for their exotic kachina dances and ancient pueblo villages; the Navajo, for their remarkable land that includes Monument Valley, Canyon de Chelly, Painted Desert, and other natural wonders; the Havasupai, for their "land of blue-green waters" within the Grand Canyon; and the White Mountain Apache, for their forests, countless trout streams, and many fishing lakes. Several tribes make jewelry; other Indian crafts include Hopi kachina dolls and pottery, Navajo rugs and sandpaintings, Apache beadwork, and Tohono O'odham basketry. Two museums of Indian culture, the Heard in Phoenix and the Museum of Northern Arizona in Flagstaff, provide especially good introductions to the tribes and their crafts.

## VISITING MEXICO

Arizona has always had a close relationship with Mexico. About 16% of Arizona's population is of Spanish descent, and Spanish and Mexican influences are apparent in the state's architecture, food, language, and music.

You may easily visit Mexico via any of the six state border crossings. Most people in the border towns understand English, and shopkeepers happily accept U.S. dollars. Nogales, close to Tucson, offers the best shopping and receives the most visitors. In all the border towns except Sonoita, you can park on the U.S. side and stroll across to the shops and restaurants in Mexico. Sonoita lies two miles beyond the boundary, and you'll probably want to drive there. See individual descriptions of the border towns.

### Permits

United States and Canadian citizens may visit border towns for as long as 72 hours without any formalities; just announce your nationality when returning to the U.S. side. Bring identification—voter's registration, birth or naturalization certificate, passport, or affidavit of citizenship by a notary public. Travelers from other countries should ask for regulations about entering and returning *before* crossing over.

Longer stays or travel to the interior require visitors to carry a tourist card, easily obtainable by U.S. and Canadian citizens at the border with proof of citizenship—a driver's license alone won't work—and usually good for 90 days.

Motorists may drive to the border towns and to Baja California without a permit. To go farther, vehicle permits are necessary; trailers and motorbikes require permits too. To obtain permits, you need to show proof of ownership—title, bill of sale, or registration. If the vehicle belongs to someone else, check requirements with a Mexican consulate.

Most U.S. insurance policies are worthless in Mexico. Unless you have Mexican insurance, the police there might throw you in jail after an accident, even if it wasn't your fault. Buy Mexican insurance, available by the day or longer, in Arizona border towns.

**Information**
Chambers of commerce on the Arizona side (Nogales, Douglas, and Yuma) know about neighboring towns in Mexico; Nogales has an especially good selection of Mexican travel literature. With luck, you might be able to find the chambers of commerce in the Mexican towns too.

# ACCOMMODATIONS AND FOOD

## Motels and Hotels
The busiest seasons, when reservations come in handy, are winter and spring in the southern desert country (Phoenix, Tucson, Yuma), and summer in the high country (Prescott, Flagstaff, Payson, Grand Canyon). Rates fluctuate dramatically with the seasons at the more expensive places, where off-season prices can ofttimes be a bargain. Economy motels either retain the same rates year-round or drop prices only slightly in the off-season.

You'll find the major hotel and motel chains well represented in Arizona. Some of the state's restored historic hotels offer the elegance and romance of the old days. Outstanding historic places, worth a visit to the lobby even if you're not staying there, include the Hassayampa Inn in Prescott, Copper Queen Hotel in Bisbee, El Tovar in the Grand Canyon, and the Gadsden Hotel in Douglas.

## Bed and Breakfasts
Following a European tradition, these private homes or small inns offer a personal touch not found in the usual accommodations. Rates range about $45-150 d. Always call or write for reservations.

You'll find B&Bs in many parts of the state—in cities, in resort towns, and on ranches. Usually they don't advertise; some are listed in these pages or with local chambers of commerce. More complete statewide listings are available from **Bed and Breakfast in Arizona,** 8900 E. Val Vista, Suite 101, Scottsdale, AZ 85258, tel. (602) 860-9338 or (800) 266-7829; **Mi Casa Su Casa,** P.O. Box 950, Tempe, AZ 85280, tel. (602) 990-0682 or (800) 456-0682; and **Arizona Association of Bed & Breakfast Inns,** 3101 N. Central Ave., Suite 560, Phoenix, AZ 85012, tel. (602) 277-0775.

## Hostels
The **Hostelling International** organization offers clean and friendly accommodations for people of all ages. Hostels usually consist of dormitory rooms (separate men's and women's), kitchen, and common room. Some hostels now offer family rooms. Besides being good places for low-budget travelers, they enable you to meet visitors from other countries. Arizona currently offers hostels in Phoenix and Flagstaff; more are planned. Each visitor must bring or rent bed linens and be willing to pitch in to take care of the hostel. Rates run about $10 per night for members; nonmembers usually pay a few dollars more. Some hostels will accept phone reservations made with a credit card.

Membership cards are sold at many hostels and are also available from the national office: Hostelling International, 733 15th St. NW, Suite 840, Washington, D.C. 20005; tel. (202) 783-6161 or (800) 444-6111. One year's membership costs $10 ages 17 and under, $25 ages 18-54, and $15 ages 55 and over. Cards are good at any member hostel in the world; foreign cards are accepted here. In Arizona, Metcalf House, 1026 N. Ninth St., tel. (602) 254-9803, supplies information about the Hostelling International system. The house, between Portland and Roosevelt Streets, is about a mile northeast of downtown. Bus #10 will take you there from the corner of First St. and Washington, near the Phoenix Transit terminal, close to the Greyhound bus station. Get off at the corner of Roosevelt and Ninth Streets. Or call; someone will answer the phone in the early morning or evening but probably not during working hours. You can not make reservations for Metcalf House.

**Independent hostels** in Flagstaff, Tuba City, Williams, Tucson, Page, and other locales offer similar services and rates with fewer rules than HI hostels.

**Guest Ranches**

These ranches feature horseback riding, miles of open country, excellent food, and an informal Western atmosphere. Activities include tennis, swimming, roping and riding instruction, hayrides, cookouts, square dancing, and even the real cowboy chore of working cattle.

Tucson and Wickenburg are the major guest ranch centers, with other ranches scattered about, mainly in the southern half of the state. Rates typically run more than $100 per person

per day and include all meals and activities. Most visitors come in winter, when the desert is at its best; some guest ranches close in summer.

## Campgrounds

The best parts of Arizona lie outdoors, where you can choose among hundreds of campgrounds—federal, state, Indian, or private. Federal government sites, the most common, are offered by the Forest Service, National Park Service, and Bureau of Land Management; sites commonly feature tables, toilets, and drinking water, with fees ranging from free to $12 per night. Many state campgrounds include showers and hookups; they're good values at rates of $7-10 per vehicle per night, or $10-15 w/hookups. Some Indian reservations, most notably the White Mountain Apache and Havasupai, offer primitive campgrounds. Commercial campgrounds possess the most frills—showers, laundromats, hookups, stores, game rooms, sometimes even swimming pools. Rates average about $15 per night; tents may or may not be accepted. Families should be aware that many of Arizona's RV parks cater to retired people—children won't be welcome. Unless otherwise stated, all campgrounds mentioned in these pages do accept families.

Other types of camping are also possible. You're welcome to camp almost anywhere in the national forests; this dispersed style of camping costs nothing and for seasoned campers provides the best outdoor experience. Since

there are no facilities, it's up to you to leave the forest in its natural state. Be very careful with fire—try to use a campstove rather than leave a fire scar. Sometimes high fire danger closes the forests in early summer. The seven national forests in Arizona cover vast expanses of mountain, plateau, and desert country from the state's far south to the far north. Stop at a forestry office for maps and information on camping, hiking, fishing, and back-road travel.

## FOOD

People debate whether Arizona actually has a native cuisine. Even if it doesn't, you'll find a wide selection of appetizing dishes here. South-of-the-border food is quite popular and a Mexican restaurant is never far away. Western-style restaurants dish out cowboy food—beef, beans, and biscuits. You can sample Indian fry bread and the Navajo taco—beans, lettuce, tomatoes, and cheese on fry bread—on or off the reservations. Tucson and Phoenix offer the most cosmopolitan array of ethnic and fine-dining restaurants.

Descriptions in this guide refer to price ranges for dinners (per person) as $: **Inexpensive** (to $8); $$: **Moderate** ($8-15); and $$$ **Expensive** (over $15). Only the sales tax is added to food; you're expected to leave a tip of about 15% for table service.

# TRANSPORT

## BY CAR

Public transport serves the cities and some towns but very few scenic, historic, and recreational areas. Unless on a tour, you really need your own transport. Most people choose cars as the most convenient and economical way to get around; you can easily rent them in any sizable town in Arizona. Phoenix and Tucson offer the largest selection as well as RV rentals. You should consider four-wheel-drive vehicles if you plan extensive travel on back roads. *Arizona Highways* magazine produces the best state

road map; almost any chamber of commerce will have one. The AAA *Indian Country* map provides superb coverage of the Four Corners region, including the Navajo and Hopi Indian reservations. The map is free at AAA offices for members and for sale in stores.

## Driving Hazards

Summer heat in the low desert puts an extra strain on both car and driver. Make sure the cooling system, engine oil, transmission fluid, fan belts, and tires are in top condition. Carry several gallons of water in case of breakdown or radiator trouble. Never leave children or pets in a

*A hole in the radiator knocks out Larry Lipchinsky's car.*

parked car during warm weather—temperatures inside can cause fatal heatstroke in just minutes.

At times the desert has *too much* water—late-summer storms frequently flood low spots in the road. Wait for the water to go down, until you can see bottom, before crossing. Dust storms also tend to be short-lived but can completely block visibility. The best thing to do in a dust storm is pull completely off the road and stop; turn off your lights so as not to confuse other drivers.

Radio stations carry frequent updates when weather hazards exist. With a VHF radio (162.4 and 162.55 MHz), you can pick up continuous weather forecasts in the Phoenix, Tucson, Yuma, Flagstaff, Sedona, Glen Canyon N.R.A., and Las Vegas areas.

If stranded, whether on the desert or in the mountains, stay with the vehicle unless you're *positive* of a route to help; then leave a note detailing your route and departure time. Airplanes can easily spot an obviously stranded car—leave your hood and trunk up and tie a piece of cloth to the antenna—but a person trying to walk out is difficult to see. Emergency supplies can help: blankets or sleeping bags, first-aid kit, tools and jumper cables, shovel, traction mats or chains, flashlight, raingear, water, and food (with can opener).

### Driveaways

These are autos scheduled for delivery to another city. If the auto's destination is a place you intend to visit, a driveaway can be like getting a free car rental. You have to be at least 21 years old and pay a refundable deposit of $75-150. There will be time and mileage limits. Ask for an economy car if you want the lowest driving costs. In a large city—Phoenix or Tucson in Arizona—look in the Yellow Pages under "Automobile Transporters and Driveaways."

### Hitchhiking

Opinions and experiences vary on hitching. It can be a great way to meet people, despite the dangers and long waits. Offer to buy lunch or help with gas money to repay the driver. Often you can arrange rides with fellow travelers at hostels. The ride boards at the University of Arizona (Tucson), Arizona State University (Tempe, near Phoenix), and Northern Arizona University (Flagstaff) list rides available and desired. Highway police tolerate hitchhiking as long as it doesn't create a hazard or take place on an interstate or freeway. Police do routinely check IDs, however. Women should be especially cautious when hitchhiking.

## BY OTHER MEANS

### By Bus

**Greyhound** offers frequent service on its transcontinental bus routes across northern and southern Arizona and between Flagstaff and

Phoenix. Greyhound often has special deals on bus passes and "one-way anywhere" tickets. Overseas residents may buy a Greyhound Ameripass at additional discounts outside North America.

**Nava-Hopi Tours** offers a Flagstaff-Phoenix-Sky Harbor Airport run and connects Grand Canyon National Park (South Rim) with Flagstaff. **Sedona-Phoenix Shuttle** serves Sedona, Cottonwood, Camp Verde, and Phoenix/Sky Harbor. **Citizen Auto Stage** will take you from Tucson to Nogales, just a short walk from Mexico.

**Bridgewater Transport** connects Tucson with the southeastern towns of Sierra Vista, Bisbee, and Douglas, and the airport in Phoenix. Other useful bus services include **White Mountain Passenger Line** from Phoenix to Show Low and other eastern Arizona destinations, and **Navajo Transit System,** which traverses the Navajo and Hopi Indian reservations, but provides no connections with other bus lines in Arizona. Some bus companies give small discounts for roundtrips.

Local bus services are available at Grand Canyon National Park (South Rim), Flagstaff, Phoenix, and Tucson. Service in other towns is usually too infrequent for travelers. Always have exact change ready when taking local buses.

## By Train

**Amtrak** runs two luxury train lines across Arizona. Both connect Los Angeles with New Orleans, Chicago, and other destinations to the east. On the northern route, the Southwest Chief runs daily in each direction with stops in Arizona at Kingman, Flagstaff, and Winslow. On the southern route, the Sunset Limited stops in Yuma, Phoenix, Tempe, Coolidge, Tucson, and Benson, but runs only three times per week in each direction. Amtrak charges more than buses for one-way tickets but has far roomier seating, as well as parlor cars and sleepers. Special fares and roundtrip discounts can often make train travel a good value.

For information and reservations, see a travel agent or call Amtrak toll-free at (800) 872-7245 anywhere in the country. Travel agents outside North America sell USA Railpasses.

## By Air

More than a dozen major airlines fly to Phoenix and Tucson. Fares and schedules tend to change frequently—a travel agent can help you find the best flights. Big-city newspapers usually run advertisements of discount fares and tours in their Sunday travel sections. You'll have the best chance of getting low fares by planning a week or more ahead.

Phoenix serves as the hub for nearly all flights within the state. Destinations from Phoenix include Tucson, Sierra Vista, Yuma, Lake Havasu City, Bullhead City, Prescott, Sedona, Flagstaff, and Page. The cost per mile of these short hops is high but you'll often enjoy excellent views.

## By Bicycle

To be fully alive to the land, skies, sounds, plants, and birds of Arizona, tour on a bicycle. Gliding across the desert or topping out on a mountain pass are experiences beyond words. Some effort, a lightweight touring or mountain bicycle, and awareness of your surroundings are all that's required.

Start with short rides if you're new to bicycle touring, then work up to longer cross-country trips. By learning to maintain and repair your steed, you'll seldom have trouble on the road. An extra-low gear of 30 inches or less will take the strain out of long mountain grades. Arizona's sunny climate offers fine year-round cycling—just adjust your elevation for the desired temperature. Bookstores and bicycle shops provide good publications on bicycle touring. As when hiking, always carry rain and wind gear and plenty of water. Also don't forget to wear a bicycling helmet. Cyclists with the competitive spirit can test themselves in a series of U.S. Cycling Federation-sanctioned races; local bicycle shops have schedules of races and training rides.

## Tours

See your travel agent for the latest on package tours to Arizona. Within the state, local operators offer everything from bus jaunts passing city sights to rafting trips through the Grand Canyon. Gray Line offers the largest selection of bus excursions, ranging from half a day to three days; tours leave from Phoenix, Tucson, and Flagstaff. Smaller companies offer jeep trips to scenic spots inaccessible to passenger vehicles; you'll find jeeps available in Monument Valley, Page, Canyon de Chelly, Sedona, Phoenix, Tucson, and Yuma. You can also hire flightseeing trips from many airports; the Grand Canyon is the most popular destination. The "Transport" sections in each chapter list tour operators; also consult local chambers of commerce.

# INFORMATION AND SERVICES

## Medical Services

In emergencies, use the emergency number listed on most telephones or dial 911. Hospital emergency rooms offer the quickest help, but cost more than a visit to a doctor's office. Hospital care is very expensive—medical insurance is recommended.

## Prices in this Book

Prices of all services mentioned in this book were current at press time. Whenever possible, taxes have been included in the stated cost. You're sure to find seasonal and long-term price changes, however, so *please* don't use what's listed here to argue with staff at motels, campgrounds, museums, or airlines.

You can easily change foreign currency in Phoenix, Tucson, and Grand Canyon Village; anywhere else in the state, it may involve extra delay and expense.

## National Park Passes

Budget-minded travelers, take note: to get the biggest bang for your buck at any national park or monument in the U.S., buy a Golden Passport, available to all U.S. citizens. Seniors age 62 and older can take advantage of the $10 **Golden Age Pass.** Good for a lifetime, it gives you free admittance to any national park or monument. Individuals who receive government benefits because of permanent disabilities should look into the lifetime **Golden Access Pass.** You pay nothing for the pass and are granted unlimited entry to all sites in the national park system. Anyone can buy a **Golden Eagle Pass.** It's good for one year, costs $25, and also means you get in free to all parks and monuments. Drop by any national park or regional office to place an order.

## Measurements

If you ask a rancher how many kilometers to the next town, all you'll receive is a blank stare. Most Arizonans are completely unfamiliar with the metric system, so visitors need to know the Olde English system:

| | |
|---|---|
| one inch | = 2.54 centimeters |
| foot | = 0.305 meter |
| mile | = 1.609 kilometers |
| square mile | = 2.590 square kilometers |
| acre | = 0.405 hectare |
| ounce | = 0.028 kilogram |
| pound (lb) | = 0.454 kilogram |
| quart | = 0.946 liter |
| U.S. gallon | = 3.785 liters |

To figure Centigrade temperatures (C), subtract 32 from Fahrenheit (F) and divide by 1.8.

## Time

Travelers in Arizona should remember that the state is on mountain standard time all year, except for the Navajo Reservation, which goes on daylight saving time—add one hour April to October—to conform with its Utah and New Mexico sections. Note that the Hopi Reservation, completely within Arizona and surrounded by the Navajo, stays on standard time year-round along with the rest of the state. In summer, Arizona runs on the same time as California and

## ARIZONA AREA CODES

In 1995 Arizona added an area-code to become a two-code dialing system.

The Phoenix metro area kept its **(602)** area code. The rest of Arizona changed to **(520).**

In all sections of this book covering metro Phoenix, use **(602)** for any telephone number listed without an area code; any out-of-area numbers are listed with the appropiate area code.

Nevada, and one hour behind Utah, Colorado, and New Mexico. In winter, Arizona is one hour ahead of California and Nevada, on the same time as Utah, Colorado, and New Mexico.

## Postal and Telephone Services

Normal post office hours are Mon.-Fri. 8:30 a.m.-5 p.m. and sometimes Saturday 8:30 a.m.-noon. All telephone numbers within Arizona have a **520 area code** except the metro-Phoenix area, which uses a **602 area code** (use when dialing 1+ or 0+ numbers *inside* as well as outside Arizona). To obtain a local number from Information, dial 1-411; for a number within the state, dial 1-520-555-1212 outside the metro-Phoenix area and 1-602-555-1212 within the metro-Phoenix area; and for a number in another state, dial 1, the area code, then 555-1212. Many airlines, auto rental firms, and motel chains have toll-free 800 numbers; if you don't know the number, just dial 1 (800) 555-1212.

## Free Information

General tourist literature and maps are available from the **Arizona Office of Tourism,** 2702 N. Third St., Suite 4015, Phoenix, AZ 85004; tel. (602) 542-8687 or (800) 842-8257, fax 542-4068. People at the many chambers of commerce in the state will be happy to help. National forest offices and other government agencies also know about outdoor recreation in their respective areas.

THE EXPLORATION OF THE COLORADO RIVER AND ITS CANYONS

# THE GRAND CANYON AND THE ARIZONA STRIP

A collision of the earth's forces—uplifting of the massive Colorado Plateau and vigorous down-cutting by the Colorado River—created the awe-inspiring Grand Canyon and its many tributaries. Neither pictures nor words can fully describe the area. You have to experience the Canyon by traveling along the rim, descending into the depths, and watching the continuous show of colors and patterns as the sun moves across the sky.

The Canyon's grandeur stretches 277 miles across northern Arizona; it measures up to 18 miles wide (with an average width of 10 miles) and one mile deep. Roads provide access to developed areas and viewpoints on both rims. Trails allow hikers and mule riders to descend the precipitous cliffs to the Colorado River, though most of the park remains as remote as ever, rarely visited by humans.

Northward, between the Colorado River and the Utah border, lies the isolated Arizona Strip. This land of forests, desert grasslands, moun-tains, and canyons covers 14,000 square miles, yet supports only 3,200 people. The Grand Canyon presents a formidable barrier between these citizens and the rest of the state; all high-way traffic has to follow a circuitous route around the mighty chasm. To cover 140 miles as the crow flies, residents of Moccasin in the Arizona Strip must drive 357 miles to the Mo-have County seat at Kingman, detouring through Utah and Nevada before reentering Arizona at Hoover Dam.

Historically, the Strip has far more in com-mon with Utah; Mormon pioneers first settled this region. Today, the Strip appeals to those who love wilderness and solitude. Travelers can wander the canyons, back roads, and trails here without meeting another soul. Other at-tractions include fishing and boating on Lake Powell, historic Lees Ferry (15 river miles below Lake Powell), and Pipe Spring National Monu-ment, an early Mormon ranch.

# THE LAND

This is a land of time. Massive cliffs bear limestone composed of animals who lived in long-departed seas, sandstone formed of ancient desert sand dunes, and shale made of silt from now-vanished rivers and shores. Volcanic eruptions have left layers of ash, cinders, and lava. Deeper into the Canyon lie the roots of mountain ranges, whose peaks towered over a primitive land two billion years ago. Time continues to flow in the Canyon with the cycles of the plants and animals that live here, and with the erosive forces of water and wind ever widening and deepening the chasm.

Geologists have a hard time pinpointing the age of the Grand Canyon itself, though it is far younger than even the most recent rock layers —those on the rim, which are about 250 million years old. These lay at sea level 65 million years ago, when the earth's crust began a slow uplift. Somewhere between five and 20 million years ago, the ancestral Colorado River settled on its present course and began to carve the Canyon. Gradual uplift continued, giving the waters even greater power. Today, the South Rim reaches elevations of 7,000 to 7,500 feet, while the North Rim towers about 1,000 feet higher. Still young, the Colorado River drops through the Canyon at an average gradient of 7.8 feet per mile, 25 times the gradient of the lower Mississippi.

## Climate

The Grand Canyon has been compared with an inverted mountain. Temperatures change with elevation as on a mountainside, but with added canyon peculiarities. In winter, the sun's low angle allows only a few hours of sunlight a day to reach the Inner Gorge, creating a cooling effect. The situation is reversed during the summer, when the sun's high angle turns the canyon into an oven. At night, temperatures often drop lower than you'd expect, with cold, dense air on the rims pouring over the edge into the depths.

In one day, a hiker can travel from the cold fir and aspen forests of the North Rim to the hot cactus country of the Canyon bottom—a climate change equal to that between Canada and Mexico. In the Inner Gorge (elev. 2,480 feet at Phantom Ranch), summer temperatures soar, with average highs over 100° F; in early July the thermometer commonly tops 115°. Spring and autumn offer pleasantly warm weather, and are the best times to visit. Winter down by the river can be fine too; even in January, days warm up to the 50s or low 60s and it rarely freezes. Only about seven inches of precipitation make it to the bottom in an average year; snow and rain often evaporate completely while falling through the mile of warm Canyon air.

The South Rim enjoys pleasant weather most of the year. Summer highs reach the mid-80s, cooling to highs in the upper 30s and lower 40s during winter. Winter campers need warm sleeping bags to combat frosty nights when temperatures plunge into the teens. Yearly precipitation at the South Rim's Grand Canyon Village (elev. 6,950 feet) is about 14.5 inches with snow accumulations seldom exceeding two feet.

Although averaging only 1,000 feet higher, the North Rim really gets socked in by winter storms. Snow piles up to depths of 6-10 feet in an average season, and the National Park Service doesn't even try to keep the roads open from early November to mid-May. Summers can be a joy in the cool, fresh air; highs then run in the 60s and 70s. Bright Angel Ranger Station (elev. 8,400 feet) on the North Rim receives about 23 inches of annual precipitation.

Most moisture falls during the winter and late summer (mid-July to mid-September). Summer rains often arrive in spectacular afternoon thunderstorms, soaking one spot in the Canyon and leaving another a short distance away bone dry. The storms are a great show from the rim viewpoints, but you should take cover if the hair on your head stands on end or if you smell ozone. As in mountain areas, the Grand Canyon's weather can change rapidly. Always carry raingear when heading down a trail.

# FLORA AND FAUNA

The seemingly endless variations of elevation, exposure, and moisture allow for an astonishing range of plant and animal communities. The Canyon also acts as a barrier to many nonflying creatures, who live on just one side of the Colo-

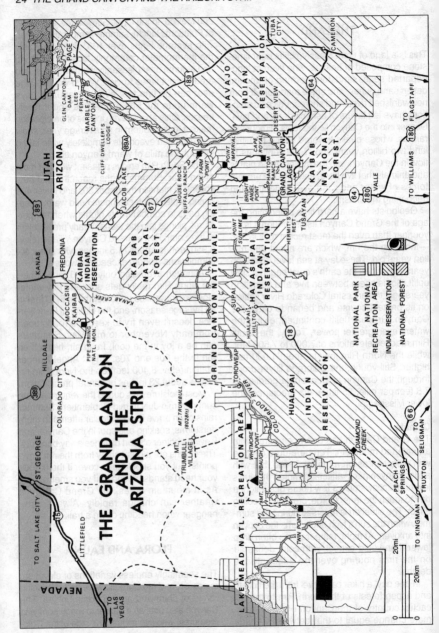

# THE GRAND CANYON AND THE ARIZONA STRIP

NATIONAL PARK

NATIONAL RECREATION AREA

INDIAN RESERVATION

NATIONAL FOREST

rado River or only in the Inner Gorge. Some mammals, such as mountain lion, spotted skunk, cliff chipmunk, and common pocket gopher, evolved into separate subspecies on each rim.

## Spruce-Fir Forest

You'll find dense forests of spruce and fir and groves of quaking aspen on the Kaibab Plateau of the North Rim, mostly above 8,200 feet. Common trees include Engelmann and blue spruce; Douglas, white, and subalpine fir; aspen; and mountain ash. Lush meadows, dotted with wildflowers in late summer, spread out in shallow valleys at the higher elevations.

Animals of the spruce-fir forest include mule deer, mountain lion, porcupine, red and Kaibab squirrel, Uinta chipmunk, long-tailed vole, and northern pocket gopher. The shy Kaibab squirrel, easily identified by an all-white tail and tufted ears, lives only on the North Rim. The Kaibab probably evolved from Abert's squirrels who crossed the Colorado River long ago, perhaps during the Pleistocene epoch. Birds you might see include turkey, great horned owl, saw-whet owl, broad-tailed hummingbird, hairy woodpecker, hermit thrush, Clark's nutcracker, Steller's jay, and mountain bluebird.

## Ponderosa Pine Forest

Stands of tall ponderosas grow between elevations of 7,000 and 8,000 feet on both rims. Mature forests tend to be open, allowing in sunlight for Gambel oak, New Mexican locust, mountain mahogany, greenleaf manzanita, cliffrose, wildflowers, and grasses.

Animals and birds found here include most of those resident in the spruce-fir forests. Abert's squirrel, though common in the Southwest, lives within the park only on the South Rim. This squirrel has tufted ears and a body and tail that are mostly gray with white undersides.

## Piñon-Juniper Woodland

These smaller trees abound in drier and more exposed places between elevations of 4,000 and 7,500 feet. Commonly found with them are broadleaf yucca, cliffrose, rabbit brush, Mormon tea, sagebrush, fernbrush, serviceberry, and Apache plume.

Mule deer, mountain lion, coyote, gray fox, desert cottontail, Stephen's woodrat, piñon

mouse, rock squirrel, cliff chipmunk, lizards, and snakes (including rattlesnakes) make their homes here. Birds include piñon and scrub jays, mourning dove, plain titmouse, Bewick's wren, and black-throated gray warbler.

## Desert Scrub

Except near permanent water, the low-desert country below 4,500 feet cannot support trees. Instead, you'll find such hardy plants as blackbrush, Utah agave, narrowleaf yucca, various cacti, desert thorn, Mormon tea, four-wing saltbush, and snakeweed.

Animals include bighorn sheep, black-tailed jackrabbit, spotted skunk, desert woodrat, antelope ground squirrel, and canyon mouse. Most reptiles hole up during the day, though lizards seem to tolerate higher temperatures than snakes. Chuckwalla, spiny and collared lizard, common king snake, whipsnake, and Grand Canyon rattlesnake live in this part of the Canyon. The shy Grand Canyon or pink rattlesnake, a subspecies of the prairie rattler, lives nowhere else. Birds of the desert scrub have to either look elsewhere for nesting trees or choose a spot in cliffs or on the ground. Species you might see include common raven, turkey vulture, golden eagle, red-tailed hawk, rock and canyon wrens, and black-throated sparrow.

## Riparian Woodlands

Until 1963, seasonal floods of the Colorado River ripped away most vegetation below the high-water mark. Then, when the Glen Canyon Dam was completed upstream, tamarisk (an exotic species originally from the Arabian deserts) began to take over formerly barren beaches. Native cattail, coyote willow, and arrowweed now thrive too. Seeps and springs inside canyons support luxuriant plant growth and supply water for desert wildlife.

Beaver, river otter, ringtail cat, raccoon, Woodhouse's toad, white-footed deermouse, tree lizard, spotted sandpiper, blue grosbeak, and Lucy's warbler make their homes near the streams. Fremont cottonwood trees in the tributaries provide welcome shade for overheated hikers. The cold, clear waters that flow from Glen Canyon Dam have upset breeding patterns of the seven native fish species; they now spawn in warmer waters at the mouths of the Little Colorado River and Havasu Creek. Rainbow trout and 10 other species have been introduced.

## HISTORY

### The First Peoples
Indians knew of this land and its canyons centuries before white people arrived. About 8-10,000 years ago early hunters left behind a Folsom point that was found in the park in 1992. At least 4,000 years ago, a hunting and gathering society stalked the plateaus and canyons of northern Arizona, leaving behind stone spear points and some small split-twig figures resembling deer or sheep. Preserved in caves in the Grand Canyon, these figurines date from approximately 2000 B.C. This culture apparently departed about 1000 B.C., leaving the Canyon apparently unoccupied for the next 1,500 years.

### The Anasazi Arrive
Prehistoric Anasazi came to the Grand Canyon area about A.D. 500. Like their predecessors, they hunted deer, bighorn sheep, jackrabbit, and other animals, while gathering such wild plant foods as piñon nuts and agave. The Anasazi also crafted fine baskets and sandals. At their peak, between 1050 and 1150, the Anasazi grew crops, crafted pottery, and lived in aboveground masonry villages. Toward the end of this period, drought hit the region. By 1150 nearly all the Anasazi had departed from the Grand Canyon, leaving more than 2,000 sites behind. Most likely they migrated east to the Hopi mesas.

### Other Indians Come to the Canyon
While the Anasazi kept mostly to the eastern half of the Grand Canyon (east of today's Grand Canyon Village), another group of hunter-gatherers and farmers, the Cohonina, lived downstream between A.D. 600 and 1150. They adopted many of the agricultural and building techniques and crafts of their Anasazi neighbors. In 1300 the Cerbat, probable ancestors of the modern Havasupai and Hualapai Indians, migrated onto the Grand Canyon's South Rim from the west. They lived in caves or brush shelters and ranged as far upstream as the Little Colorado River in search of game and wild plant foods. The Cerbat also planted crops in areas of fertile soil or permanent springs. It's possible that the Cerbat had cultural ties with the earlier Cohonina.

Nomadic Paiute Indians living north of the Grand Canyon made seasonal trips to the North

Havasupai woman and child, late 1800s

prospector/guide
John Hance
and friends

Rim, occasionally clashing with the Cerbat. The Paiute lived in brush shelters and relied almost entirely on hunting and gathering. They spent their summers on the Kaibab Plateau and in other high country, then moved to lower elevations for the winter. Hopi Indians knew of the Grand Canyon too; they came for religious pilgrimages and to collect salt.

## The Modern Tribes

Today the Havasupai live 35 air miles northwest of Grand Canyon Village in Havasu Canyon, a Grand Canyon tributary, and on lands atop the South Rim. The waterfalls, travertine pools, and greenery of the remote canyon have earned it fame as a Shangri-la. To the west of the Havasupai, the large Hualapai Reservation spreads across much of the Grand Canyon's South Rim. The only road access to the Colorado River within the Canyon goes through their lands. A small band of Paiute Indians lives on the Kaibab Reservation, just west of Fredonia in far northern Arizona.

## Spanish and American Explorers

In 1540, when Francisco Vásquez de Coronado led an expedition in search of the Seven Cities of Cíbola, Hopi Indians told a detachment of soldiers about a great canyon to the west. Hopi guides later took a party of Coronado's men,

led by García López de Cárdenas, to the South Rim but kept secret the routes into the depths. The Spaniards failed to find a way to the river and left discouraged. Franciscan priest Francisco Tomás Garcés, looking for souls to save, visited the Havasupai and Hualapai in 1776 and was well received. Historians credit Garcés with naming the Río Colorado ("Red River").

James Ohio Pattie and other American fur trappers probably came across the Grand Canyon in the late 1820s, but provided only sketchy accounts of their visits. Lieutenant Joseph Ives led the first real exploration of the Colorado River. He chugged 350 miles by steamboat upstream from the river's mouth in 1857-58 before crashing into a rock in Black Canyon. The party then continued overland to the Diamond Creek area in the western Grand Canyon.

Most of the Canyon remained a dark and forbidding unknown until Major John Wesley Powell bravely led a boat expedition through the chasm in 1869. On this trip and a second journey in 1871-72, Powell and his men made detailed drawings and took notes on geology, flora and fauna, and Indian ruins. Powell recorded his experiences in Canyons of the Colorado, now published as The Exploration of the Colorado River and Its Canyons.

## Ranching on the Arizona Strip

Not many pioneers took an interest in the prairie here—the ground proved nearly impossible to plow and lacked water for irrigation. Determined Mormons began ranching in the 1860s despite the constant isolation and occasional Navajo raids. They built Winsor Castle, a fortified ranch, in 1870 as a base for a large church-owned cattle herd. Mormons also founded the towns of Fredonia, Short Creek (now Colorado City), and Littlefield.

Some of these settlers had fled Utah to escape federal laws prohibiting polygamy. About 3,000 members of a polygamous, excommunicated Mormon sect still live in Colorado City and neighboring Hilldale, Utah. Federal and state officials raided Colorado City several times, most recently in 1953, when 27 arrests were made—those charged received one year of probation. Now government policy seems to be "live and let live."

## Miners and Tourists

After about 1880, prospectors entered the Grand Canyon to search for copper, asbestos, silver, and lead deposits. Their trails, many following old Indian routes, are still used by modern hikers.

In 1883, stagecoaches began bringing tourists to the Canyon at Diamond Creek, where J.H. Farlee opened a four-room hotel the following year. Prospectors Peter Berry and Ralph and Niles Cameron built the Grandview Hotel in 1895 at Grandview Point, leading tourists down a trail to Horseshoe Mesa. Other prospectors, such as John Hance and William Bass, also found guiding visitors more profitable than mining. Tourism began on a large scale soon after the railroad reached the South Rim in 1901. The Fred Harvey Company bought Bright Angel Lodge, built the deluxe El Tovar Hotel, and took over from the smaller operators.

As the Canyon became better known, President Theodore Roosevelt and others pushed for greater federal protection. First a forest reserve in 1893, the Grand Canyon became a national monument in 1908, and finally a national park in 1919. The park's size doubled in 1975 when legislation extended the boundaries west to Grand Wash and northeast to Lees Ferry. Grand Canyon National Park now includes 1,892 square miles and receives more than four million visitors annually.

# VISITING GRAND CANYON NATIONAL PARK

Most people head first to the South Rim, entering at either the South Entrance Station near Grand Canyon Village or the East Entrance Station near Desert View. A 26-mile scenic drive along the rim connects these entrances.

The South Rim features great views, a full range of accommodations and restaurants, and easy access—just 60 miles north of I-40 from Williams. Roads and most facilities stay open all year. Attractions include the visitor center, Yavapai Observation Station, Tusayan Pueblo ruin, West Rim Drive to Hermit's Rest (eight miles), and East Rim Drive to Desert View (25 miles). The South Rim also has most of the Canyon's easily accessible viewpoints and trails. It's not surprising, then, that large crowds of visitors, especially in summer, are the main drawback of this part of the Canyon.

The park collects an admission fee of $10 per private vehicle ($4 per pedestrian or bicyclist)

that's good for seven days at the south and east entrances of the South Rim and at the main entrance of the North Rim. Except as noted, the visitor center, museums, programs, and trails are free. Budget travelers can save money by stocking up on groceries and camping supplies at Flagstaff, Williams, or other towns away from the Canyon; prices within the park run up to 25% higher.

Only about one in 10 visitors makes it to the North Rim, but that visitor receives a reward of pristine forests, rolling meadows, splendid wildflower displays, and superb panoramas. Viewpoints here provide a perspective of the Canyon dramatically different from that of the South Rim, lower than the North Rim by 1,000 feet. The North Rim area offers lodging, dining, and camping facilities similar to the South Rim's, though on a smaller scale. Unless you want to ski in (backcountry permit required), the North Rim is open

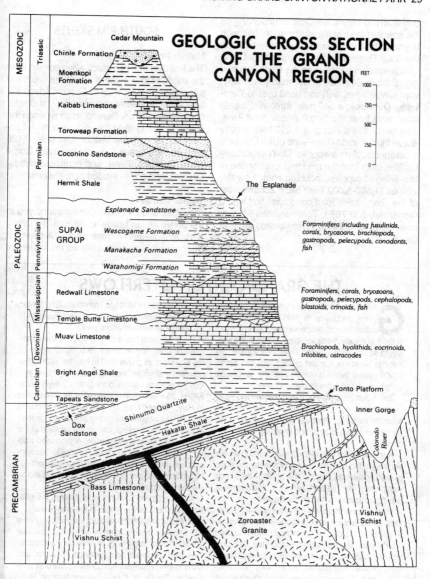

# GEOLOGIC CROSS SECTION OF THE GRAND CANYON REGION

**MESOZOIC**

**Triassic**
- Cedar Mountain
- Chinle Formation
- Moenkopi Formation

**PALEOZOIC**

**Permian**
- Kaibab Limestone
- Toroweap Formation
- Coconino Sandstone
- Hermit Shale

The Esplanade

**SUPAI GROUP**

**Pennsylvanian**
- Esplanade Sandstone
- Wescogame Formation
- Manakacha Formation
- Watahomigi Formation

*Foraminifera including fusulinids, corals, bryozoans, brachiopods, gastropods, pelecypods, conodonts, fish*

**Mississippian**
- Redwall Limestone

**Devonian**
- Temple Butte Limestone

*Foraminifers, corals, bryozoans, gastropods, pelecypods, cephalopods, blastoids, crinoids, fish*

**Cambrian**
- Muav Limestone
- Bright Angel Shale
- Tapeats Sandstone

*Brachiopods, hyolithids, eocrinoids, trilobites, ostracodes*

Tonto Platform

Inner Gorge

**PRECAMBRIAN**
- Dox Sandstone
- Shinumo Quartzite
- Hakatai Shale
- Bass Limestone
- Zoroaster Granite
- Vishnu Schist

Colorado River

FEET
1000
750
500
250
0

only from mid-May to late October depending on the arrival of the first big winter storm. Although the rims stand just 10 miles apart, motorists on the South Rim must drive 215 miles to get here.

Adventurous travelers on the North Rim willing to tackle 61 miles of dirt road (each way; impassable when wet) can head over to **Toroweap Overlook,** a 140-mile, three and a half-hour drive from the Bright Angel Point area. This perch sits a dizzying 3,000 feet directly above the Colorado River—one of the Canyon's most spectacular viewpoints. Don't expect any facilities other than the road and an outhouse or two. Bring all supplies, including water. Low elevations (4,500-5,000 feet) allow access most of the year; check road conditions first with a ranger, tel. 638-7888. Toroweap lies 91 river miles downstream from the developed areas of the park.

## SOUTH RIM SIGHTS

### Mather Point
The first overlook you reach when coming from the south, Mather Point is where the south entrance road curves west to Grand Canyon Village. Stephen Mather served as the first director of the National Park Service, in office when the Grand Canyon joined the park system on February 26, 1919. Below Mather Point (elev. 7,120 feet) lie Pipe Creek Canyon, the Inner Gorge of the Colorado River, and countless buttes, temples, and points eroded from the rims.

### Visitor Center
Dioramas and other exhibits introduce you to the park's Indian residents, miners, explorers, early tourists, and natural history. A riverboat display in the courtyard shows the variety of

# THE GRAND CANYON OVERFLOWS

Grand Canyon National Park suffers from extreme popularity. In 1995 an estimated five million visitors descended on the park, most of them in private motor vehicles. Although the park would seem large enough to accommodate this number all at once, most of its 1,218,376 acres (1,904 square miles) is remote from the developed visitor areas and not suitable for crowds.

The worst problem is parking. During the peak summer season, more cars, trucks, and buses often enter the park than there are parking spaces at the scenic overlooks, lodges, and shopping areas combined.

A shuttle for the West Rim Drive (closed to private vehicles in the summer) has only shaved the edge of the problem as most of the shuttle users park within the park. The park service is seeking more drastic measures to lessen the crowding.

Most of these ideas are still in the planning stage. One would require visitors to make a reservation to drive into the park. A second proposal is to build a large parking area inside or outside the park, possibly in Tusayan. A shuttle would bring visitors into the park and other shuttles would move them within the park. The park service might offer parking permits to guests at lodges and to hikers needing to reach remote trailheads. It even proposes to use a

railroad shuttle to Maswik Transportation Center, adjacent to Maswik Lodge, to connect Tusayan to the shuttle system within the park.

Even Tusayan has growth problems; the airport terminal often has as many as a dozen times as many visitors as it was built to handle. Although a new terminal will be built at Tusayan, the park service might route visitors to the Grand Canyon Valle Airport, 25 miles south of the park at the intersection of Hwy. 180 and Hwy. 64. The airport, built during WW II, has been reopened to relieve congestion at the Tusayan terminal and as the location of the **Planes of Fame Air Museum.** A proposed train terminal at Valle would shuttle visitors to Tusayan and into the park. Visitors waiting for a scheduled train ride or airplane or helicopter tour could examine the museum's vintage planes.

Call the Grand Canyon Valle Airport, tel. 638-0116, to check on the status of these proposals.

Grand Canyon National Park's visitation system will undergo many changes within the next few years. Visitors might wish to write for the latest information on lodges, campgrounds, RV parks, and parking and shuttle service. Send for the park publication, *The Guide,* Grand Canyon National Park, P.O. Box 129, Grand Canyon, AZ 86023.

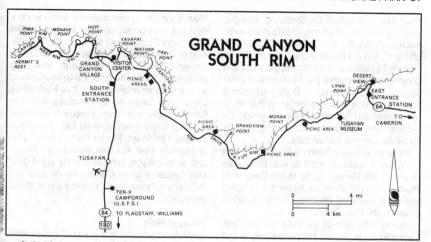

# GRAND CANYON SOUTH RIM

craft that have run the Colorado. Oldest is a 1909 cataract boat used by the Stone Expedition, which put in at Green River, Wyoming, on September 12, 1909, and came out 37 days and 1,300 miles later at Needles, California.

Short movies and slide presentations illustrate the park and suggest ways to see it. A bulletin board in the lobby lists ranger-guided rim walks, Canyon talks, and evening presentations. A ranger at the desk will answer your questions and provide maps and brochures. A bookstore offers a good selection of Canyon-related books, posters, topographical maps, slides, videos, and postcards. The visitor center is open daily 8 a.m.-5 p.m., extended in summer. Call 638-7888 to reach the automated switchboard with recording of scheduled programs and other park information, or 638-7805 for TDD information for people with hearing impairments. The center is on the east side of Grand Canyon Village, three miles in from the South Entrance Station.

## Yavapai Observation Station

Set on the brink of the Canyon, this geologic museum illustrates the long history of the rock layers revealed below. Panels identify the many buttes, temples, points, and tributary canyons seen through the windows. It's open daily 8 a.m.-5 p.m., with extended summer hours. Books, maps, slides, videos, and postcards can be purchased. Yavapai Observa-

tion Station is 0.8 mile northeast of the visitor center by road or one mile by foot trail.

## South Rim Nature Trail

People of all ages can enjoy a walk along this easy trail. The 2.7-mile section from the Yavapai Observation Station past the El Tovar Hotel to Maricopa Point is paved and nearly level. Pick up biology and geology brochures (25 cents each) for the self-guided trail at the visitor center, at Yavapai Observation Station, or outside Verkamp's Curios, next to El Tovar Hotel. Start anywhere along the way; there are no keyed trail numbers. You'll enjoy views from many different vantage points.

The Rim Trail continues west 6.7 miles as a dirt path to Hermit's Rest, at the end of West Rim Drive. Another unpaved segment heads east a half mile from Yavapai Observation Station to Mather Point. The free Canyon shuttle bus operates in summer, running about every 15 minutes, stopping at eight places along the Rim Trail.

## West Rim Drive

The Santa Fe Railroad built this eight-mile-long road from Grand Canyon Village to Hermit's Rest in 1912. Pullouts along the way allow drivers to stop and enjoy the views. Your map will help you pick out Canyon features: Bright Angel Trail switchbacking down to the grove of trees at Indian Garden; Plateau Point at the end of a short trail from Indian Garden; long, straight, Bright Angel Canyon on the far side of the river; the many majestic temples rising to the north and east; and the rapids of the Colorado River.

Hermit's Rest—with restrooms, gift shop, and drinking water—marks the westernmost viewpoint and end of the drive. During summer a free shuttle bus runs the length of the drive; other times you can take your own vehicle. Bicyclists enjoy this drive too, and aren't affected by the summer ban on cars.

If you've walked to Hermit's Rest on the Rim Trail, you'll probably want to rest too. Louis Boucher, the Hermit, came to the Canyon in 1891 and stayed 21 years; he lived at Dripping Springs and built the Boucher Trail to his mining claims in Boucher Canyon.

Hermit Trail, built by the Fred Harvey Company after Louis Boucher departed, begins just beyond Hermit's Rest at the end of a gravel road. The trail descends to the Tonto Trail and on to the river at Hermit Rapids. Visitors taking this trail between 1912 and 1930 could stay at a tourist camp partway down on the Tonto Platform; only foundations remain today. A branch in the upper trail goes to Dripping Springs and Boucher Canyon.

### East Rim Drive

Outstanding overlooks line this 25-mile drive between Grand Canyon Village and Desert View. Each has its own character and is worth a stop, but many people consider the aptly named Grandview Point one of the best. It's 12 miles east of Grand Canyon Village (14 miles before Desert View), then 0.8 mile north. Sweeping panoramas take in much of the Grand Canyon from this commanding site above Horseshoe Mesa. The vastness and intricacies of the Canyon show themselves especially well here.

Other major viewpoints on East Rim Drive include Yaki Point, Moran Point, Lipan Point, and Desert View. At Lipan, by looking both up-and down-canyon, you can see the entire geologic sequence of the Canyon. Hiking trails into the Canyon leave from or near each of these overlooks.

### Tusayan Ruin

Prehistoric Anasazi Indians built this pueblo about A.D. 1185. Perhaps 30 people lived here, contending with poor soil, low rainfall, and scarce drinking water. After staying about 20 years, they moved on. Archaeologists who excavated the site in 1930 named it Tusayan, a Spanish term for Hopi Indian territory.

A small museum introduces the Anasazi culture with artifacts and models of dwellings; exhibits describe modern tribes of the region. Outside, a short, self-guided trail leads to the plaza and ruins of living quarters, storage rooms, and two kivas. A leaflet (pick up at the museum, 25

Tusayan Ruin

cents) describes how the Anasazi farmed and obtained some of their wild foods. You can also take a free, guided 30-minute tour, scheduled several times daily.

The museum is open daily 9 a.m.-5 p.m., with summer hours possibly extended. It's on the East Rim Drive, 23 miles east of Grand Canyon Village and three miles west of Desert View, tel. 638-2305.

### Desert View

This overlook offers a stunning view at the end of East Rim Drive. Although the surrounding piñon pines and junipers suggest a lower elevation, this is the highest viewpoint on the South Rim (elev. 7,500 feet). Far to the east lies the multihued Painted Desert that gave the viewpoint its name. Below, to the north, the Colorado River flows out of Marble Canyon, then curves west.

The strange-looking Desert View Watchtower, designed by Mary E. J. Colter, incorporates design elements from both prehistoric and modern Indian tribes of the region. The Fred Harvey Company built the 70-foot structure in 1932, using stone around a steel frame. The interior (25 cents admission) contains reproductions of a Hopi altar, wall paintings, and petroglyphs; stairs lead to windows at the top.

Desert View has a small visitor center, snack bar, general store, service station, and campground; the visitor center, campground, and some services close during the off-season. A short nature trail loops around the point. Energetic hikers can head cross-country to Zuni and Papago points off East Rim Drive, or take the long 12-mile roundtrip route to Comanche Point north of Desert View; ask a ranger at Desert View for directions. Highway AZ 64 continues east from Desert View for about 20 miles to two overlooks of the Little Colorado River Gorge—signed Scenic View—on the Navajo Indian Reservation, then another 10 miles to Cameron on US 89.

## SOUTH RIM ACCOMMODATIONS

The Grand Canyon offers too much to see in one day. In Grand Canyon Village you can stay right on the rim at **Bright Angel Lodge, Thunderbird Lodge, Kachina Lodge,** or **El Tovar** **Hotel.** Other lodges lie back in the woods. The town of Tusayan, just outside the park, nine miles south of Grand Canyon Village, has additional places to stay. Reservations are essential in the busy summer season and a good idea the rest of the year.

### Grand Canyon Village

**Grand Canyon National Park Lodges** operates all the lodges here, as well as **Moqui Lodge** just outside the South Entrance Station. Make reservations at Box 699, Grand Canyon, AZ 86023, tel. (303) 297-2757 (advance reservations) or 638-2631 (same-day reservations), fax 638-9247.

One of the grand old hotels of the West, **El Tovar** has offered the Canyon's finest accommodations and food since 1905. This national historic landmark offers 14 styles of rooms with all modern conveniences, yet retains an old-fashioned ambience. Several suites have canyon views; room rates run $116.66-176 s or d and suites run $193-287.40.

**Kachina** and **Thunderbird** lodges, also on the rim, offer deluxe modern rooms for $101.80 park-side or $112.41 canyon-side, s or d. Historic **Bright Angel Lodge** sits on the rim a short distance from the Bright Angel trailhead. The lobby, patio, restaurant, and lounge are popular gathering spots for hikers and other visitors. Rates for cabins are $56.20-117.71 s or d; rooms in the lodge cost $40.29 and $46.66 s or d with the shower down the hall or $57.26 with bath. The Bright Angel History Room displays memorabilia from early tourist days and a "geological fireplace" in which Canyon rocks have been laid, floor to ceiling, in the proper stratigraphic sequence. The transportation desk in the lobby organizes scheduled bus service, bus and air tours, mule trips, and accommodations at Phantom Ranch at the bottom of the Canyon.

**Maswik Lodge,** two blocks south of Bright Angel Lodge, has cabins for $50.91 s or d and rooms for $73.15 s or d in the south section, $109.23 s or d in the north section, and a cafeteria. **Yavapai Lodge's** modern rooms cost $83.78 in the west section or $94.38 in the east section s or d; there's also a cafeteria. It's near the visitor center, one mile east of Bright Angel Lodge, and closed Nov.-Feb., except open holidays.

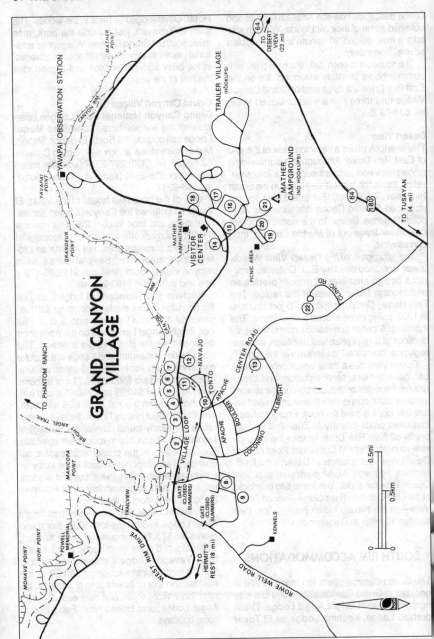

## GRAND CANYON VILLAGE

1. Bright Angel Trailhead; Kolb Studio
2. Bright Angel Lodge and Restaurant
3. Thunderbird Lodge
4. Kachina Lodge
5. El Tovar Hotel and Restaurant
6. Hopi House (souvenirs)
7. Verkamp's (souvenirs)
8. Maswik Lodge and Cafeteria
9. Maswik Transportation Center
10. ranger office
11. historic railroad station
12. public garage
13. Albright Training Center
14. Shrine of the Ages
15. RV dump station
16. store, post office, bank
17. Yavapai Lodge and Cafeteria
18. service station
19. Backcountry Office (BO)
20. showers, laundromat
21. Sage Loop Campfire Circle
22. Grand Canyon Health Center (clinic, dentist, pharmacy)

### Tusayan

**Moqui Lodge,** just outside the South Entrance Station and one mile north of Tusayan, offers rooms at $94.38 s or d (breakfast incl.) from March 16 to October 31, with reduced rates off-season, and closes in January and February; tel. 638-2424. The lodge has a restaurant, an information desk where you can arrange tours and horseback riding, a gift shop, and a service station. **Red Feather Lodge,** nine miles south from Grand Canyon Village in Tusayan, is open year-round with standard rooms at $114.53 s or d and deluxe rooms at $135.74 s or d (May 1 to October 31, less off-season), a restaurant, and gift shop; tel. 638-2414 or (800) 538-2345. **Holiday Inn Express,** next to the Red Feather, is open all year with a free continental breakfast bar. Rooms rent for $135.74 s or d; tel. 638-3000 or (800) HOLIDAY. **Quality Inn-Grand Canyon,** behind the Red Feather, is open all year with a restaurant, swimming pool, jacuzzi, and gift shop. Rates are $103.93-146.35 s or d from March 25 to October 31, less off-season; tel. 638-2673 or (800) 221-2222.

**Seven Mile Lodge** has rooms at $84.84 s or d in summer, less in winter; tel. 638-2291. The nearby **Grand Canyon Squire Inn** (Best Western) features standard rooms at $106.05 s or d, deluxe rooms at $132.56 s or d, and suites at $159.08 s or d high season with lower rates the rest of the year; amenities include a restaurant, swimming pool, jacuzzi, sauna, exercise room, tennis courts, bowling alley, beauty salon, and gift shop; tel. 638-2681 or (800) 6-CANYON.

### Valle

Highways US 180 from Flagstaff and AZ 64 from Williams meet at this road junction 24 miles south of Grand Canyon Village. Stay at **Grand Canyon Inn** ($103.93 s or d) or the nearby **Grand Canyon Motel** ($79.54 s or d). The phone number for both is 635-9203. Both close January to mid-February. The Inn offers a restaurant serving breakfast, lunch, and dinner daily, and a gift shop. Visit the **Planes of Fame** air museum at the Valle Airport to see restored vintage planes, many kept in flying shape, plus replicas of planes from both world wars. A few highlights include a Lockheed Constellation named "Bataan" and used by General Douglas MacArthur, a Fuji Ohka 11 piloted suicide rocket, a Messerschmitt Bf 109G Gustav fighter plane, a P-51 Mustang, a 1928 Ford Trimotor, and more. The museum is open daily except Thanksgiving and Christmas; adults $5, children ages 5-12 $1.95, free under five years of age; tel. 635-1000. The airport, at the south end of Valle, also serves private planes but hopes to add airplane and helicopter tours to relieve the pressure at the Tusayan terminal; tel. 638-0116.

### South Rim Campgrounds

Campgrounds tend to be crowded in the warmer months. If you don't have a reservation, it's best to arrive before noon to look for a site. Rangers enforce the No Camping Outside Designated Sites policy with stiff fines. Backpackers inside the Canyon need free permits from the Backcountry Office.

**Mather Campground** is conveniently located south of the visitor center in Grand Canyon Village; tel. 638-7851. It's open early April to end of November, though one loop stays open year-round. Sites have drinking water but no hookups, and run $10 per night, $5 with a Golden Age pass. Backpackers and bicyclists can camp at a walk-in area for $2 per person, no reservations needed. When the campground is signed "FULL" the walk-in area may still have space. Showers, laundromat, and ice are available for a small charge near the campground. Reservations for family and group sites can be arranged one day to eight weeks in advance through Mistix; tel. (800) 365-CAMP.

**Trailer Village,** just east of Mather Campground, offers RV sites for $18.05 w/hookups all year; make reservations with Grand Canyon National Park Lodges (Box 699, Grand Canyon, AZ 86023); tel. 638-2401 (advance reservations), 638-2631 (same-day reservations).

**Desert View Campground,** near the East Entrance Station (25 miles east of Grand Canyon Village), has sites with drinking water but no hookups; it's open mid-May to the end of September, costing $10 a site with no reservations taken.

**Grand Canyon Camper Village** in Tusayan (nine miles south of Grand Canyon Village) has sites for tents back in the trees ($15), for RVs ($18-22 w/hookups), and for tepee tents (warmer months only, $18). The village includes coin showers; stores and restaurants are nearby. Write Box 490, Grand Canyon, AZ 86023, or phone 638-2887. **Ten X Campground** in the Kaibab National Forest has drinking water but no hookups; it's open May 1 to September 30 for $10 a site. Amphitheater programs take place many nights, while a half-mile nature trail provides an introduction to the natural history of the area. To reach Ten X from Tusayan, go south three miles to the turnoff (between Mileposts 233 and 234), then east a quarter mile; tel. 638-2443.

**Flintstone Bedrock City** campsites in Valle, 24 miles south of Grand Canyon Village, cost $12.66 for tents or RVs ($16.88 w/hookups); it has coin showers, store, snack bar, Fred's Dinner Restaurant, and theme park. The campground is open Easter to the end of October; self-contained vehicles can park there in the winter; tel. 635-2600.

Dispersed camping in the Kaibab National Forest just south of the park is another possibility—just practice no-trace camping, carry your own drinking water, and stay at least a quarter mile from the nearest paved road and a quarter mile from any surface water. Check with the ranger station to learn whether campfires are permitted. The Forest Service office (across from Moqui Lodge) north of Tusayan can make suggestions; the Kaibab Forest map shows the back roads.

# SOUTH RIM FOOD

### Grand Canyon Village Area

**El Tovar Hotel** offers elegant dining daily for breakfast, lunch, and dinner; tel. 638-2631 Prices are moderate to expensive, and dinner reservations are recommended. **Bright Angel Lodge** features two moderately priced restaurants: the Bright Angel Restaurant serving breakfast, lunch, and dinner daily, tel. 638-2631; and the Arizona Steakhouse, offering steaks, fish, chicken, and ribs for dinner daily, tel. 638-2631. **Maswik Lodge,** two blocks south of Bright Angel Lodge, has a large cafeteria open daily for breakfast, lunch, and dinner. **Yavapai Lodge,** near the visitor center, features a smaller cafeteria open daily for breakfast, lunch, and dinner from March to October and winter holidays.

**Babbitt's,** near the visitor center, includes a deli counter and tables. **Bright Angel Fountain** serves ice cream and other snacks on the Canyon rim behind Bright Angel Lodge; it's closed in the winter. You can buy groceries at **Babbitt's,** with stores in Grand Canyon Village, Desert View, and Tusayan.

### Tusayan

**Moqui Lodge** has a Mexican-American restaurant, open daily for breakfast and dinner only; closed January and February; tel. 638-2424. You'll also find restaurants at the **Red Feather Lodge,** tel. 638-2150, **Quality Inn-Grand Canyon,** tel. 638-2673, and **Grand Canyon Squire Inn,** tel. 638-2681. **The Steak House** features mesquite-grilled steaks and other fare daily for dinner; tel. 638-2780. **We Cook Pizza, Etc.** offers Italian sandwiches and dinners as well as pizza daily for lunch and dinner; tel. 638-2278. One of the newer eateries features several restaurants and a movie theater in a group of domes at the south end of Tusayan called the **Grand Canyon Experience,** tel. 638-2180, which houses the **Arizona BBQ Kitchen** (barbecued chicken and beef served daily at lunch and dinner for $5.50-14.95), **Red Canyon Cafe** (fast food American or Mexican style, mostly with chips or beans, for lunch and dinner daily at $3.95-12.95 plus a ranch breakfast), and **Canyon Steakhouse** (outdoor dining priced $6.50-12.95). The **Taco Bell** in the Grand Canyon IMAX Theatre complex is about to be joined by a **Pizza Hut. Burger King** was also considering a move to Tusayan.

There's a **McDonald's** in town too, but don't expect it (or any other isolated fast-food restaurant, for that matter) to have the same prices as at home; the staff will happily give you a handout explaining why the costs are so high.

## SOUTH RIM SERVICES

### Entertainment

The **Grand Canyon IMAX Theatre** in Tusayan projects an impressive movie, *The Grand Canyon—The Hidden Secrets,* on a 70-foot screen with six-track stereo sound. Seventy-millimeter film projects very fine images. The 34-minute presentation briefly covers Canyon history and wildlife, with sections on river-running, flying, and scenic viewpoints. Showings take place hourly 8:30 a.m.-8:30 p.m. every day, with reduced hours in winter. Cost: $7 adults, $4 children 3-11; tel. 638-2468/2203.

For **nightlife** in Grand Canyon Village, try the El Tovar cocktail lounge for piano music, the Bright Angel Lodge cocktail lounge for varied live music, or the Maswik Lodge for big-screen TV.

Rangers present **evening programs** year-round; check the bulletin board at the visitor center to find out what's on and where.

### Shopping

The **visitor center** includes a good bookstore that sells topographical maps. **Babbitt's,** at Desert View, Tusayan, and just south of the visitor center, sells groceries, camping and hiking supplies, clothing, books, maps, and souvenirs. **Lookout Studio,** on the rim near Bright Angel Lodge, features beautiful rock, mineral, and fossil specimens. Indian crafts, postcards, and other souvenirs can be purchased at **El Tovar Hotel, Bright Angel Lodge, Hopi House,**

**Verkamp's Curio, Hermit's Rest, Desert View Lookout Tower,** and **Gallery at the Grand Canyon** (Tusayan).

### Other Services

You'll find a **bank** and **post office** south across the road from the visitor center; the bank includes an ATM and can cash traveler's checks, exchange foreign currency, send and receive wire transfers, and give cash advances on Visa and MasterCard. It cannot cash out-of-town checks. **Babbitt's** in Tusayan also includes a **post office. Grand Canyon Health Center** offers medical (tel. 638-2551) and dental (tel. 638-2395) services and a pharmacy (tel. 638-2460). For an ambulance or other emergency, call 911 or 638-7888.

National Park Service staff provide wheelchairs, an accessibility guide, Braille literature, sign-language interpreter, and other services; ask at the visitor center or write ahead to the park. **Reservations** can be made via **South Rim Travel** for rooms, flights, tours, charters, and mule rides by calling (800) 682-4393. The service is free.

**Theft** has become a problem in the Canyon—be sure to keep valuables hidden or take them with you. Park rangers patrol the park, serving as law enforcement officers and firefighters; see them if you have difficulties. **Pets** won't be welcome in the lodges or permitted on the inner-canyon trails, but they can stay in the kennels at Grand Canyon Village. Next to Mather Campground you'll find a laundromat and coin operated showers—a welcome sight to any traveler who's been a long time on the road or trail.

## SOUTH RIM INFORMATION

The **visitor center** has exhibits, slide shows, movies, bookshop, bulletin board of scheduled events, and information desk; it's open daily 8 a.m.-5 p.m., extended in summer. Look for it on the east side of Grand Canyon Village, three miles north of the South Entrance Station. Pick up a copy of the *Guide* newspaper for the latest visitor information. Stop at the **Backcountry Office,** south of the visitor center, for information about hiking and backcountry camping permits (day-hikers don't need a permit); it's open daily 8 a.m-noon; tel. 638-7888. Call between 1 and 5 p.m. to speak with someone in person. The **park address** is Box 129, Grand Canyon, AZ 86023.

You can obtain a **weather forecast** and many other recordings and reach all park offices through the **automated switchboard,** tel. 638-7888. **Hearing-impaired** people can use the TDD number for park information, tel. 638-7804.

The **Kaibab National Forest,** often ignored in the shadow of Grand Canyon National Park, offers both developed and primitive camping. Stop at the **Tusayan Ranger Station** for a map and information. Staff can also provide directions for hiking the Red Butte Trail, a 2.4-mile roundtrip climb up a prominent butte 12 miles south of Tusayan, as well as 22 miles (one-way) of the Arizona Trail just south of the park. In winter, cross-country skiers can glide along a section of the Arizona Trail from the Grandview Lookout. The station, open Mon.-Fri. 8 a.m.-5 p.m., is in the Tusayan Administrative Site, across from Moqui Lodge just outside the South Entrance Station; Box 3088, Grand Canyon, AZ 86023; tel. 638-2443.

## SOUTH RIM TOURS

### Mule Rides
Sure-footed mules have carried prospectors and tourists in and out of the Canyon for more than a century. These large animals, a cross-breed of female horses and male donkeys, depart daily year-round on day and overnight trips. Although easier than hiking, a mule ride should still be considered strenuous—you need to be able to sit in the saddle for long hours and control your mount.

Day-trips proceed down the Bright Angel Trail to Indian Garden and out to Plateau Point, a spectacular overlook directly above the river; the 12-mile, seven-hour roundtrip costs $105.50. On the overnight trip you follow the Bright Angel Trail all the way to the river, cross a suspension bridge to Phantom Ranch, spend the night in a cabin, then come out the next day via the South Kaibab Trail. The cost: $261.77 ($467.32 for two, $216.70 each additional person), including meals and cabin. Three-day, two-night trips offered mid-November to March 31 cost

$366.60 ($620.79 for two, $276.46 each additional person).

These trips are definitely not for those afraid of heights. If you're in doubt, Fred Harvey Movies (Box 699, Grand Canyon, AZ 86023) will send a videotape or Super-8 movie for $16 postpaid showing what it's like in the saddle.

Enforced requirements for riders include good health, weight under 200 pounds (91 kilograms), fluency in English, height over four feet seven inches (140 cm), and ability to mount and dismount without assistance. No pregnant women are allowed. A hat, tied under the chin, long pants, a long-sleeved shirt, and sturdy shoes (no open-toed footwear) are necessary. Don't bring bags, purses, or backpacks; you can carry a canteen and a camera or binoculars.

Reservations should be made 9-12 months in advance for summer and holidays. Also be sure to claim your reservation at least one hour before departure. Without a reservation, there's a chance of getting on via the waiting list, especially off-season; register between 6 and 10 a.m. the day before you want to go.

Mules will also carry hikers' overnight gear to Phantom Ranch, $43.60 in or out (30 pound limit). For information, reservations, and standbys see the Bright Angel transportation desk, tel. 638-2631, or contact Grand Canyon National Park Lodges, Reservations Department, Box 699, Grand Canyon, AZ 86023; tel. 638-2401 (advance reservations).

### Horse Rides
**Apache Stables** offers short rides through the Kaibab National Forest ($23.21 for one hour, $38 for two hours), four-hour trips to the South Rim ($60.66), and other excursions. The season lasts March 1 to December 31, depending on the weather. Make reservations at Moqui Lodge, one mile north of Tusayan; tel. 638-2891.

### Bus Tours
**Fred Harvey Transportation Co.** will show you the sights of the South Rim and narrate the Canyon's history, geology, and wildlife. Hermit's Rest Tour visits viewpoints of West Rim Drive (two hours, $11). Desert View Tour travels along East Rim Drive (3.75 hours, $17, or $20 including Hermit's Rest Tour). Sunset Tour goes over to Mohave or Yaki points (1.5 hours,

$7.50, May-Oct. only). Anasazi Indian Adventure visits Wupatki, Sunset Crater, Walnut Canyon, and the Museum of Northern Arizona (11 hours, $80). Monument Valley Expedition visits the striking landscape of buttes and sand dunes on the Navajo Indian Reservation (11-13 hours; $80).

A River Raft Excursion runs the smooth-flowing Colorado River in Marble Canyon above Lees Ferry; stops on the drive there take in highlights of East Rim Drive and Navajo Indian Reservation (12 hours, $80, April to early November). Tours in the park leave daily (twice a day in summer for the Hermit's Rest and Desert View tours); check departure days for tours outside the park. Get tickets at Bright Angel, Maswik, or Yavapai Lodge transportation desks; children under 16 (under 12 for tours out of park) go at half price. No reservations needed, though you could make them for the Anasazi, Monument Valley, and River Raft tours; Box 699, Grand Canyon, AZ 86023; tel. 638-2401.

## Jeep Tours

**Grand Canyon Jeep Tours** offers a 2-2.5 hour **Canyon and Forest Tour** through Kaibab National Forest and to the Grand Canyon at $50 adult and $32 child (12 and younger), and a **Cave Paintings Tour** in Kaibab National Forest at $25 adult and $15 child (12 and younger). Make reservations and meet your tour at McDonald's in Tusayan; tel. 638-2922 or (800) 320-JEEP.

## Air Tours

Flights over the Canyon provide breathtaking views and a look at some of the park's more remote areas. About 40 scenic flight companies operate helicopters or fixed-wing aircraft here. The 50,000-plus flights a year sometimes detract from the wilderness experience of backcountry users—Tusayan's airport is the third-busiest in the state. However, restrictions on flight routes and elevations help minimize the noise.

Scenic flights depart all year from Tusayan Airport, while **Papillon Grand Canyon Helicopters** and **Kenai Helicopters** leave right from the village of Tusayan. Transport from lodges to terminals is available. Rates listed are per adult; children under 12 usually fly at a discount.

**Grand Canyon Airlines** started flying here in 1927 with Ford Trimotors. Today the company uses high-wing, twin-engine planes on 45- to 55-minute flights over both rims of the Canyon ($50); tel. 638-2407 or (800) 528-2413 out of state.

**Air Grand Canyon's** high-wing Cessnas offer three loops: a 30- to 40-minute flight over the Canyon ($55.95), a 50- to 60-minute trip over the eastern Canyon ($65.95), and a 90- to 100-minute grand tour of both Havasu and Grand canyons ($135.95). Charters and other tours can be arranged, too; tel. 638-2686 or (800) 247-4726.

**Windrock Airlines** flies high-wing Cessnas to many destinations; Grand Canyon trips range 20-30 minutes ($50) over the main gorge, to 90 minutes ($136) over both the east and west sections of the Canyon. Other flights journey to Monument Valley, Bryce Canyon, Zion, Lake Powell, Sedona, Prescott, Bullhead City, and Flagstaff; tel. 638-9591/9570 or (800) 24-ROCKY.

**Papillon Grand Canyon Helicopters** flies across the Canyon (30 minutes, $90) and over the eastern Grand Canyon (50 minutes, $165); you can also arrange to land at Supai village in Havasu Canyon and visit the waterfalls on daytrips; tel. 638-2419.

**Kenai Helicopters** heads across the Canyon (25-30 minutes, $90) and over the eastern Grand Canyon (45-60 minutes, $160); tel. 638-2412 or (800) 541-4537.

**AirStar Helicopters** will take you across the Canyon (25-30 minutes, $80) and around the eastern Grand Canyon (40-45 minutes, $120), from the airport; tel. 638-2622 or (800) 962-3869 in state.

**Airstar Airlines** has a flight over the eastern part of the Canyon and the Little Colorado River (50 minutes, $60); tel. 638-2139 or (800) 962-3869.

# SOUTH RIM TRANSPORT

## Shuttle Services

The park service runs two free shuttle services from Memorial Day to early autumn to reduce traffic congestion. During this period the West Rim Drive is closed to private vehicles. The **Vil-**

lage **Loop Shuttle** connects the visitor center, Yavapai Observation Station, campgrounds, lodges, shops, and offices of Grand Canyon Village; service operates daily every 15-20 minutes from early morning to late at night.

The **West Rim Drive Shuttle** leaves from the West Rim Interchange near Bright Angel Lodge and goes to Hermit's Rest, with stops at eight overlooks; it operates daily every 15 minutes from about 7:30 a.m. to 6:45 p.m. Two "Hiker's Specials" leave in the morning from the Backcountry Office for the South Kaibab trailhead. In the off-season, Fred Harvey Co. runs a shuttle to the South Kaibab trailhead for a charge.

**Tusayan-Grand Canyon Shuttle** connects Bright Angel Lodge and other places in Grand Canyon Village with Tusayan and the airport all year for a small charge; check schedule with lodge transportation desks or call 638-0821.

**Trans Canyon** offers daily roundtrip van service to the North Rim from May 15 to October 23, by reservation the rest of the year; Box 348, Grand Canyon, AZ 86023. Contact any lodge transportation desk or call 638-2820. Trans Canyon does not run when the trail system across the canyon is closed. If you still need a shuttle check with **River-Runner Shuttle** in the office at the south end of Babbit's in Tusayan or call 638-2748 or (800) 682-4393.

**Auto Rentals and Taxi**
You can rent cars from **Budget**, tel. 638-9360, or **Dollar Rent-A-Car**, tel. 638-2625, at Tusayan Airport. For a taxi, call **Fred Harvey Transportation Dispatch** at 638-2822.

**Bus**
**Nava-Hopi** buses connect Bright Angel Lodge with Flagstaff; fares are $12.50 one-way, $25 roundtrip. See lodge transportation desks for schedules, no reservations needed; tel. 774-5003 (Flagstaff) or (800) 892-8687.

**Train**
Passenger trains rolled into the railroad station at the Grand Canyon from 1901 to 1968. Twenty-one years later, in 1989, the **Grand Canyon Railway**'s trains again began to provide service from downtown Williams to the historic log depot in Grand Canyon Village.

Trains are scheduled daily except December 24th and 25th. Roundtrip fare is $57.17 adults ($4 more for park admission per person aged 17-61); children's fares (ages 3-16) are $20.62. Call (800) THE-TRAIN.

**Air**
Scenic Airlines and Air Nevada fly to Las Vegas. **Scenic Airlines** offers five to 14 flights out daily, $119 one-way, $169 roundtrip. A "K-class" fare of $59 and "Q-class" of $30 are offered on the first flights out and the last in. Make reservations at least two weeks ahead in summer and two days in advance in winter; tel. 638-2617 (Grand Canyon), (702) 739-1900 (Las Vegas) or (800) 634-6801 (toll-free). **Air Nevada** features a similar service with three to five flights daily, $109 one-way, $159 roundtrip, $59 K-class, and $29 standby; tel. (702) 736-8900 or (800) 634-6377. Flights between Las Vegas and the Grand Canyon often feature a narrated tour over the Canyon, an added bonus.

**Tri-Star Airline** offers flights from Tusayan to Las Vegas (from $49-99), Los Angeles (from $99), and San Francisco (from $99) as well as from those cities to Tusayan; city to city and vacation packages are also available; tel. 638-3010 or (800) 218-8777.

## NORTH RIM SIGHTS

The North Rim offers an experience very different from that of the South Rim. Elevations 1,000 to 1,500 feet higher result in lower temperatures and nearly 60% more precipitation. Rain and snowmelt have cut deeply into the North Rim: it is now about twice as far from the Colorado River as the South Rim. Dramatic vistas from the north inspired early explorers to choose names like Point Sublime, Cape Royal, Angel's Window, and Point Imperial.

Even away from the viewpoints, the North Rim is a place of great beauty. Spruce, fir, pine, and aspen forests thrive in the cool air. Wildflowers bloom in blazes of color in the meadows and along the roadsides.

You'll find visitor facilities and major trailheads near Bright Angel Point, a 45-mile drive south on Hwy. 67 from Jacob Lake in the far north of Arizona. The road to Bright Angel Point opens in mid-May, then closes after the first big winter storm, anytime from early October to the end of November.

## Bright Angel Point

Park at the end of the highway, near Grand Canyon Lodge, and follow the paved foot trail to the tip of Bright Angel Point, an easy half-mile roundtrip walk. Roaring Springs Canyon on the left and Transept Canyon on the right join the long Bright Angel Canyon below. John Wesley Powell's expedition camped at the bottom of this canyon and gave the name Bright Angel Creek to its crystal-clear waters. Listen for Roaring Springs far below on the left, and look to see where the springs shoot out of the cliff. A pumping station at the base supplies drinking water to both North and South rims. Roaring Springs makes a good day-hike or muleback-ride destination via the North Kaibab Trail (see "Maintained Trails of the Inner Canyon," below).

You can enter Transept Canyon, which usually has only a small flow, from the North Kaibab Trail; it's best attempted on an overnight trip, though you must camp elsewhere—there's no camping in Transept Canyon. Up on top, Transept Trail (1.5 miles one-way) winds along the canyon rim between Grand Canyon Lodge and the campground.

## Cape Royal Scenic Drive

Paved roads lead to some of the North Rim's most spectacular viewpoints. **Point Imperial** (elev. 8,803 feet) offers the highest vantage point from either rim. Views encompass impressive geology in the park's eastern end. You can see Nankoweap Creek below, Vermilion Cliffs on the horizon to the north, rounded Navajo Mountain on the horizon in Utah to the northeast, the Painted Desert far to the east, and the Little Colorado River Canyon to the southeast. Hikers can descend to Nankoweap Creek and the Colorado River on the difficult Nankoweap Trail (see "Unmaintained Trails of the Inner Canyon," below); the trailhead lies northeast of here near Saddle Mountain. Point Imperial is 11 miles from Grand Canyon Lodge; go north three miles from the lodge, turn right 5.3 miles on Cape Royal Drive, then left 2.7 miles to the parking area.

Cape Royal Drive continues beyond the Point Imperial turnoff past **Vista Encantadora, Walhalla Overlook,** and other viewpoints to a park-

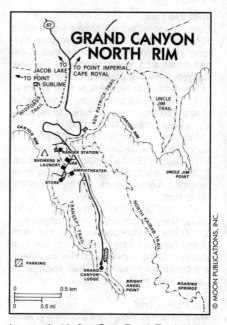

ing area just before Cape Royal. Total driving distance from Grand Canyon Lodge is 23 miles one-way. A trail continues south 0.6 mile from the parking lot to Cape Royal. On the way you'll see **Angel's Window,** a massive natural arch. A short side trail actually traverses the top of the arch. **Cape Royal** is the southernmost viewpoint of the North Rim in this part of the Grand Canyon: Freya Castle lies to the southeast, nearby Vishnu Temple and Creek and the distant San Francisco Peaks are to the south, and a branch of Clear Creek Canyon and flat-topped Wotans Throne lie to the southwest.

A short hike on **Cliff Spring Trail** winds through some pretty scenery. The one-mile roundtrip trail descends into a forested ravine, passes a small Indian ruin, and travels under an overhang to the spring. The canyon walls open up impressively as you near the spring. It's possible to continue on a rougher trail another half mile for more canyon views. Cliff Spring Trail begins from Angel's Window Overlook, a small pullout on a curve of Cape Royal Drive, 0.9 mile past Walhalla Overlook and a half mile before road's end.

## Widforss Trail

Gently rolling terrain, fine canyon views, and a variety of forest types attract hikers to the Widforss Trail. From the edge of a meadow, the trail climbs a bit, skirts the head of Transept Canyon, then runs across a plateau covered by ponderosas to an overlook near Widforss Point. The trail and point honor Swedish artist Gunnar Widforss, who painted the national parks of the West between 1921 and 1934.

Haunted Canyon lies below at trail's end, flanked by The Colonnade on the right and Manu Temple, Buddha Temple, and Schellbach Butte on the left; beyond lie countless more temples, towers, canyons, and the cliffs of the South Rim.

Widforss Trail is 10 miles roundtrip; allow five hours. Many people enjoy going just partway. You'll often see mule deer along the trail. From Grand Canyon Lodge, go 2.7 miles north on the highway, then turn left and drive one mile on a dirt road; the turnoff is 0.3 mile south of the Cape Royal turnoff.

## Ken Patrick Trail

The 9.9-mile trail offers forest scenery and views across the headwaters of Nankoweap Creek. From Point Imperial, the Ken Patrick winds about three miles along the rim to Cape Royal Rd., then continues seven miles through forest to the North Kaibab trailhead; you drop 560 feet in elevation. A section of switchbacks about halfway along is sometimes overgrown. Allow six hours for the entire hike, one-way.

Trailheads lie near the south end of the Point Imperial parking area; on Cape Royal Rd. one mile east of the Point Imperial junction; and at the upper end of the North Kaibab trailhead parking area, two miles north of Grand Canyon Lodge.

Ken Patrick worked as a ranger on the North Rim for several seasons in the early 1970s. He was shot and killed by escaped convicts while on duty at California's Point Reyes National Seashore in 1973.

## Uncle Jim Trail

The first mile follows the Ken Patrick Trail—from the North Kaibab trailhead—then turns southeast to Uncle Jim Point. Allow three hours for the five-mile roundtrip. Views from the point

*Mt. Hayden, from Point Imperial*

include Roaring Springs Canyon and North Kaibab Trail. James "Uncle Jim" Owens served as the Grand Canyon Game Reserve's first warden from 1906 until establishment of the national park.

## Point Sublime

A 17-mile dirt road, negotiable only by high-clearance vehicles or by hiking, leads to this overlook and picnic area west of Bright Angel Point. The route is bumpy and not always passable; check at the North Rim Backcountry Office or the Grand Canyon Lodge information desk. Views take in an impressive amount of the Canyon, truly sublime.

**Tiyo Point** is closed to driving but is accessible by hiking. Turn south 6.3 miles from Point Sublime Rd. at a large meadow, 4.2 miles in from AZ 67. You can camp at either point with a permit from the North Rim Backcountry Office, located in the ranger station. The drive/hike to Point Sublime or Tiyo Point begins 2.7 miles north of Grand Canyon Lodge; turn west onto the road signed Widforss Point Trailhead. Other scenic vistas on the North Rim can be reached on back roads; consult with a ranger for suggestions.

## Fire Point

The Fire Point panorama takes in Tapeats Amphitheater, Steamboat Mountain, and Powell Plateau; Great Thumb Mesa lies across the river. Careful drivers can negotiate the roads in good weather.

From the AZ 67 turnoff in De Motte Park, 0.8 mile south of the North Rim Country Store, turn west and drive two miles on Forest Route 422, south two miles on Forest Route 270, then west 13 miles on Forest Route 223 to the end of the road. The last mile is within Grand Canyon National Park and may be closed to vehicles; in the future, this road may be closed to motor vehicles altogether. Forest roads in the area also lead to Timp, Parissawampitts, Crazy Jug, and Big Saddle points.

## East Rim Viewpoint

Expansive vistas across the Marble Canyon area greet visitors at this overlook on the east edge of the Kaibab Plateau. The site (elev. 8,800 feet) is on Kaibab National Forest land several miles north of Grand Canyon National Park. From the AZ 67 turnoff in De Motte Park, 0.8 mile south of the North Rim Country Store, turn east and drive five miles on Forest Route 611, following signs. Cars can easily travel the gravel roads in good weather. East Rim View is a great spot to watch sunrises—colors reflect off the distant Vermilion Cliffs and Painted Desert at sunset. Good places for primitive camping lie in the conifer and aspen forests nearby; the Forest Service offers a pair of outhouses but no other facilities. No camping permit or fee is required.

Hikers can wander some of the Arizona Trail from here or descend into North Canyon in the Saddle Mountain Wilderness. **Marble Viewpoint,** to the south of East Rim View, offers another perspective; it's reached from De Motte Park via Forest Routes 611, 610, and 219 in about 11.5 miles.

## House Rock Valley

Here, rolling hills of grasslands and piñon-juniper woodlands separate cliffs of the Kaibab Plateau and Marble Canyon. Viewpoints provide intimate and detailed views of Marble Canyon. Turn off US 89A, 20 miles east of Jacob Lake and 21.5 miles west of Marble Canyon Lodge, onto House Rock Buffalo Ranch Rd. (Forest Route 445). About 90 **buffalo** roam freely across 67,000 acres of the valley; you're most likely to see them in summer, least likely during hunting season in autumn. (Yes, some people still shoot them.) For **Buck Farm Overlook,** head south 23.5 miles to a fork; take the left fork east two miles, then turn left on Forest Route 445H and drive three miles to its end.

**Triple Alcoves Overlook** features a different panorama; go 2.5 miles south on Forest Route 445 from the 445-445H junction, then hike east a half mile on an old jeep road to the overlook. Signs mark the trailhead. House Rock Buffalo Ranch Rd. provides nearly year-round access to these and other viewpoints, as well as to Saddle Mountain Wilderness. Drivers with high-clearance vehicles can traverse the steep and winding East Side Game Rd. (Forest Route 220) and Forest Route 213 between the Kaibab Plateau and House Rock Valley.

Kaibab National Forest contains many other viewpoints, scenic drives, and trails. The visitor center in Jacob Lake or ranger station in Fredonia—as well as the information desk in Grand Canyon Lodge—should stock forest maps and the *Recreation Opportunity Guide* for the North Kaibab Ranger District.

Visitors may wish to inquire about the new **Rim Trail,** currently under construction. The trail starts at Big Saddle Camp at the junction of Forest Routes 292 and 272 and goes as far as Fence Point. As yet, no signs are posted so be sure to obtain additional information. Not all Forest Service personnel are familiar with the Rim Trail, so it may take a while to find someone with the information you need.

## Winter Activities

In winter, a deep blanket of snow covers the Kaibab Plateau's rolling meadow and forest country. The snow cover is typically packed to a depth of four to 10 feet and during the winter of 1994-95 reached a depth of more than 19 feet. Cross-country skiers and snowshoers find the conditions ideal. The **Canyoneers** operates cross-country ski runs and offers tours, accommodations, and food in the Kaibab National Forest north of the park. Canyoneers provides SnowVan transportation to Kaibab Lodge, or you can ski in. Contact the Canyoneers at Box 2997, Flagstaff, AZ 86003; tel. (800) 525-0924 for reservations out of state, 526-0924 for reservations in Arizona, or 638-2389 for Kaibab Lodge.

The **North Rim Nordic Center at Kaibab Lodge** provides rentals, instruction from beginner to advanced, tours, set track, groomed trails, and unlimited backcountry skiing from mid-December to mid-April; it's 26 miles south of Jacob Lake off AZ 67. **Kaibab Lodge** offers rustic accommodations and a restaurant year-round; winter visitors can use the hot tub. You have a choice of bunks in yurts or private cabins; ask about winter package programs.

The park itself has no facilities open on the North Rim in winter; you can camp there, however, with a permit from the Backcountry Office.

## NORTH RIM PRACTICALITIES

The road from Jacob Lake to the Rim is usually open earlier in the spring and later in the fall than Grand Canyon Lodge, restaurants, gas station, and campground. A sign at Jacob Lake near the turnoff for the North Rim lists the services available.

### Accommodations

**Grand Canyon Lodge,** overlooking Transept Canyon near Bright Angel Point, offers the only park accommodations on the North Rim. Lodging comes in four types: Frontier Cabins, $55.92 s or d; Western Cabins, $86.51 s or d; Pioneer Cabins, $75.96-81.24 four or five people only; and modern motel rooms, $67.52 s or d. Four cabins are close enough to the edge to permit canyon viewing from the porch, $93.90 s or d. Each additional person costs $5.28 in both cabins and rooms. It's open mid-May to late October, with reservations and deposit recommended. Contact TWA Services, Box 400, Cedar City, UT 84721; tel. (801) 586-7686.

**North Rim Campground,** 1.5 miles north and west of Grand Canyon Lodge, provides drinking water but no hookups. It's open mid-May to mid-October; $10 per night, $5 with Golden Age pass; reservations are required. Backpackers and bicyclists can camp at a walk-in area for $2 per person. A "FULL" sign at the campground means that all drive in spaces are taken but spaces may still be available for walk-ins. Coin-operated showers, laundromat, store, and ice are available next to the campground. Reservations for family and group sites can be made one day to eight weeks in advance through Mistix; tel. (800) 365-CAMP.

**Kaibab Lodge,** 18.5 miles north of Bright Angel Point, offers cabins ($68.58 and 72.80 s or d and up in summer) and a restaurant; see "Winter Activities," above. Across the highway, **North Rim Country Store** sells groceries, camping and auto supplies, and gas and diesel; open mid-May to mid-November. **Jacob Lake Inn,** open all year, lies 45 miles north of the North Rim at Jacob Lake on US 89A; it has an Indian crafts shop, groceries, gas station, restaurant, and basic motel rooms ($79.54 s or d and up) and cabins ($62.57 and up April-Nov. only); tel. 643-7232.

**De Motte Forest Camp,** 18.5 miles north of Bright Angel Point, is open early June to late September, with drinking water but no showers or hookups; $10 per night.

**Jacob Lake Forest Camp,** at Jacob Lake, has drinking water but no showers or hookups; open mid-May to late October; $10 per night; reservations available by calling (800) 280-CAMP. **Jacob Lake RV Park,** just three-quarters of a mile off AZ 67 south of Jacob Lake, is open May 1 to October 31 (depending on weather) with tent spaces ($10) and RV sites ($20-22 w/hookups) but no showers; reservations via Jacob Lake, AZ 86022; tel. 643-7804.

### Food and Services

**Grand Canyon Lodge** serves moderately priced breakfast, lunch, and dinner in a huge rustic dining room with Canyon views; open daily mid-May to late October; reservations are suggested for breakfast and required for dinner; tel. 638-2611. A cafeteria style **snack bar,** also part of the lodge, offers faster service and lower prices but no atmosphere; it's open in season (may-Oct.) for breakfast, lunch, and dinner. The lodge also contains the **Saloon,** which serves gourmet coffees as well as more potent beverages.

You'll find a **post office** and **gift shop** in Grand Canyon Lodge. A **service station** is near the campground, along with a small **general store and snack bar** offering camping supplies, groceries, and cooked food. In **emergencies,** see a ranger or call 911. For recorded **weather forecasts,** dial 638-7888.

### Information

Rangers staff the **information desk** in the Grand Canyon Lodge lobby daily 8 a.m.-8 p.m.; tel. 638-7864. They'll provide times of nature walks and Canyon lectures. Obtain backpacking permits and information from the **Backcountry Office** (Box 129, Grand Canyon, AZ 86023) on the South Rim or at the ranger station on the North Rim (turnoff from the highway is a quarter mile north of the campground turnoff). The North Rim Backcountry Office is open daily in season 8 a.m-noon. The park's automated switchboard has recorded information and will connect you to any office; tel. 638-7888.

### Mule Rides, Tours, and Transport

Mule rides take you along the rim and into the Canyon. One-hour rim rides cost $12 (minimum age six), half-day trips down the North Kaibab Trail to the tunnel are $35 (minimum age eight), and full-day rides to Roaring Springs are $85 including lunch (minimum age 12). For further information, visit the mule rides desk in the Grand Canyon Lodge lobby. Requirements for riders are similar to those for South Rim trips. Reservations are a good idea; phone 638-9875 at the lodge, or (801) 679-8665 before June 1.

Narrated **bus tours** pass by Cape Royal, Point Imperial, and other North Rim highlights (three hours, $20 adults, $10 children ages 4-12); make reservations at the Grand Canyon Lodge mule rides desk.

**North Rim Hikes and Tours,** operated by the Canyoneers at Kaibab Lodge, 18.5 miles north of Bright Angel Point and 26 miles south of Jacob Lake, offers a variety of guided hikes and mountain bicycle rides in the Grand Canyon area. In winter, the **North Rim Nordic Center at Kaibab Lodge** offers cross-country ski trails, tours, and accommodations; see "Winter Activities."

**Trans Canyon** offers daily roundtrip van service to the North Rim May 15 to October 23, and by reservation the rest of the year; Box 348, Grand Canyon, AZ 86023; tel. 638-2820.

## TOROWEAP

This seldom-visited area of the North Rim lies between Kanab Canyon to the east and the Pine Mountains (Uinkaret Mountains) to the west. An overlook (elev. 4,552 feet) provides awesome Canyon views from sheer cliffs that drop nearly 3,000 feet to the river below. Toroweap, also known as Tuweap or Tuweep, lies 140 road miles west from the developed North Rim area of Bright Angel Point. The views, many hiking possibilities, and solitude reward those visitors who make it here.

**Sinyala Butte,** 25 miles east of the overlook, marks the mouth of Havasu Canyon. Most of the Havasupai Indians who live on the reservation dwell in Supai village, 11 miles up Havasu Canyon. The **Hualapai Indian Reservation** lies directly across the Colorado River from the overlook. Lava Pinnacle, also known as Vulcan's Forge or Thor's Hammer, sits in the middle of the river directly below. This 50-foot-high lava neck is all that remains of an extinct volcano.

**Lava Falls,** visible downstream, roars with a vengeance. Debris from Prospect Canyon on the South Rim forms the rapids, perhaps the roughest water in the Grand Canyon. Water flowing between 12,000 and 20,000 cubic feet per second drops abruptly, then explodes into foam and spray. River-runners commonly rate these rapids a 10-plus on a scale of 1-10. The steep Lava Falls Route leads down to the rapids from a nearby trailhead (see "Inner Canyon Hiking," below).

**Vulcan's Throne,** the 600-foot-high rounded hill just west of the overlook, is one of the youngest volcanoes in the area. Between 30,000 and 1.2 million years ago, eruptions of red-hot lava built about 60 volcanic cones here, even forming dams across the Colorado River. One of the dams towered nearly 500 feet, but the river washed it away long ago.

Forests cover **Mt. Trumbull** (elev. 8,028 feet) to the north. Mormons logged trees here to build their temple in St. George, Utah. John Wesley Powell named the rounded peak for a Connecticut senator.

Piñon pine, juniper, cactus, and small flowering plants cover the plateau. Watch for rattlesnakes. Hikers can indulge in many easy ram-

*view upstream from Toroweap Overlook*

bles across the plateau near the overlook or scramble up Vulcan's Throne. More adventurous hikes in the area include Lava Falls Route or Tuckup Trail (see "Inner Canyon Hiking").

### On the Road

A camping area (two-site limit) sits close to the overlook at the end of the road; sleepwalking isn't recommended here. More sheltered spots are available in the main campground farther back from the rim. There's no camping charge, no reservations accepted, and no permit needed for the established sites; ask a ranger about alternative areas if all campsites are full. Bring water, extra food, and camping gear.

From AZ 389, nine miles west of Fredonia, turn south at the sign reading Mt. Trumbull 53 Miles. The road to Toroweap, 60 miles one-way, is dirt, in good condition when dry. Watch for livestock and take it slow through washes and cattleguards. The last few miles are a bit rocky, but careful drivers should make it okay. The Tuweep Ranger Station is on the left 6.2 miles before the overlook. Beyond the ranger station, Toroweap Point (summit elev. 6,393 feet) towers on the left; dumpy Vulcan's Throne (summit elev. 5,102 feet) sits on the right.

You can also drive to Toroweap on a 90-mile dirt road from St. George or a 55-mile road from Colorado City. Avoid driving these roads after heavy rain or snow, especially the route from Colorado City. Snows usually block the road from St. George between October and May. Water, food, and gas are not available in this country. Bring a map, as signs may be missing at some junctions. Obtain hiking information and emergency help at the Tuweep Ranger Station, open all year.

# INNER CANYON HIKING

Hiking in the Canyon is the best way to see and appreciate the wonders within. Just remember the Inner Canyon is a wilderness area, subject to temperature extremes, flash floods, rock slides, and other natural hazards. Careless hikers have ruined many a Canyon trip by hiking without water or indulging in other foolish acts.

Always carry—and drink—water. All too often people will walk merrily down a trail without a canteen, then suffer terribly on the climb out. Only the Bright Angel and North Kaibab trails pass sources of treated water. In summer, carry one quart or liter of water for each hour of hiking; half a quart per hour should be enough in the cooler months. Also consider such electrolyte-replacement drinks as the Gookinaid E.R.G. brand.

Canyon trails offer little shade—you'll probably want a hat, sunglasses, and sunscreen. Footgear should have good traction for the steep trails; lightweight boots work well. Instep crampons—metal plates with small spikes—are helpful on icy trails in winter and early spring at the higher elevations. Raingear will keep you dry during rainstorms; ponchos, on the other hand, provide poor protection against wind-driven rain. Be careful when rock-scrambling—soft and fractured rocks predominate in the Canyon. Don't swim in the Colorado River; its cold waters and swift currents are simply too dangerous.

### Permits

You'll need a free permit for all overnight camping trips, but not for day-hikes or stays at Phantom Ranch. Obtain permit information from rangers at the Backcountry Office (BO) on the South Rim, next to Mather Campground; North Rim BO at the Ranger Station, reached via a turnoff from the highway a quarter mile north of the campground; or Tuweep Ranger Station in the Toroweap area of the North Rim. Ask for the *Backcountry Trip Planner,* which includes regulations, a map, and a permit request form.

The park service limits the number of campers in each section of the Canyon to provide visitors with a quality wilderness experience and to protect the land from overuse. Try to request permits as early as possible, especially for holidays and the popular months of March to May. Permits can be requested through the Backcountry Office, Grand Canyon National Park, P.O. Box 129, Grand Canyon, AZ 86023. Permits will be sent through the mail so be sure to make your request early, though requests are not accepted more than four months in advance starting with the first day of the month of that four month period.

Permits can sometimes be obtained from rangers on duty at Tuweep, Meadview, and Lees Ferry Ranger Stations. However, these

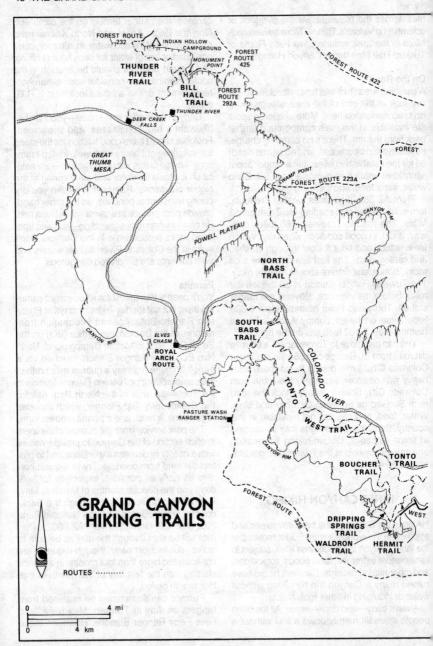

GRAND CANYON
HIKING TRAILS

ROUTES  ............

0          4 mi
0          4 km

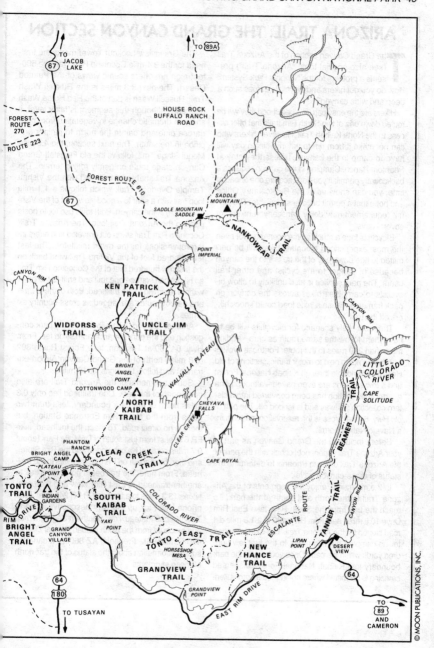

# ARIZONA TRAIL: THE GRAND CANYON SECTION

The Grand Canyon section of the Arizona Trail (see also special topic "Arizona Trail") presents a problem for the National Park System. How do you get hikers and bicyclists across such a deep and wide canyon?

Hikers are the easy part. In all likelihood they will be routed down one of two South Rim trails that offer access to the North Kaibab Trail. However, hikers who can not make it from rim to rim in a single day will have to camp in the canyon, unless they stay at Phantom Ranch. Camping in the canyon requires a backcountry permit; if you don't acquire one ahead of time, you can show up at the Backcountry Office and hope that a permit becomes available. The permit requirement may delay transcanyon hikers for several days.

Bicyclists face a much worse scenario. Not even the most experienced mountain biker will be permitted to ride down any of the trails into the canyon because of danger to the cyclist and other trail users. The park service is also unlikely to allow bicyclists to carry their bikes across the canyon on pack frames because a wide load could knock hikers off the trail.

The most likely scenario for bicyclists will be to have them follow the same route as cars—adding more than 200 miles to the route. For those cyclists who dislike riding next to motor traffic, sections of old Hwy. 64 are ridable through Kaibab National Forest and a few sections are even paved—although one quarter-mile section has been converted into a cistern collection spillway and is fenced off. The part of old Hwy. 64 that crosses the reservation may require a Navajo Nation permit.

Before including the Grand Canyon as part of your Arizona Trail experience, check with the park or the Arizona Trail office in Phoenix to determine the status of cross-canyon travel.

In the meantime, enjoy the segments of the Arizona Trail to the north and south of the park. To reach the trail from the South Rim, take East Rim Drive 10.8 miles east from Hwy. 180 to a 1.3-mile dirt road signed for the Arizona Trail. The road is tagged for no camping but this refers to the first few hundred yards within the park. Once you're past the park boundary into Kaibab National Forest, dispersed camping is permitted where not tagged as prohibited.

The Grandview Lookout Tower marks the trailhead for the 9.4-mile Coconino Rim Trail; the 500-foot-high rim offers scenic views of the Painted Desert. The next 8.3 miles is the Russell Wash Trail; Russell Wash is part of the Red Horse Wash drainage. Although this segment is fairly level, it shows a dramatic change in vegetation from ponderosa pine and oak in the north to juniper and piñon in the south. The next section, the 4.6-mile Moqui Stage Trail, follows the old Flagstaff-Grand Canyon stage route on gently rolling terrain. The Arizona Trail shares its trailhead with the Vishnu Temple Overlook Trail, which follows a 1.1-mile loop trail with a spur to a good viewpoint of the Vishnu Temple in the canyon. Both trails use route posts bearing the Arizona Trail logo. The Arizona Trail/Coconino Rim Trail starts out graveled and offers interpretive signs for the dwarf mistletoe. The last few hundred feet of the Vishnu Trail wind back on the first few hundred feet of the Coconino Rim Trail so hikers can start on one trail and shift to the other without returning to the trailhead. Both of these trails and nearby routes are tagged as cross-country ski routes.

Another route to this trailhead avoids park congestion and the park entrance admission fee. From Hwy. 64/180 at Tusayan, take Forest Route 302 (0.8 miles north of the Grand Canyon Airport entrance) and follow the signs for 16 miles.

Some segments of the Arizona Trail are also open north of the park. One trailhead lies only 0.3 miles north of the park boundary, less than two miles from the North Rim Entrance Station, but there is no direct road. To reach the trailhead, take FR 611 east from just south of DeMotte Park (about 0.7 miles south of Kaibab Lodge and the Rim Store), and then bear south on FR 610 six miles to the trailhead. From here, the trail bears north 7.3 miles to another trailhead at East Rim View and then continues 13.3 miles to a trailhead at FR 241 near Telephone Hill. Pick up the very descriptive Arizona Trail, Kaibab Plateau Trail, Southern Segment map and brochure from the North Kaibab Ranger District, 430 S. Main St., Fredonia, AZ 86022. It can also supply information about the status of the trail north of these segments.

rangers are often hard to find because patrol duties have priority. Do not depend on being able to obtain a permit on a walk-in basis.

If you arrive without a permit, show up at the Backcountry Office by 8 a.m. to find out what's available. Your chances are slim—especially in peak season—though a waiting list is kept.

### Hiking Information

Several guidebooks contain Canyon trail descriptions. The most current is the *Official Guide to Hiking the Grand Canyon* by Scott Thybony. However, the best source of up to the minute information is the **Backcountry Office (BO)** on the South Rim; it's open 8 a.m.-noon all year. **Backcountry Information Line** is open Mon.-Fri. 1-5 p.m.; tel. 638-7888. Rangers staff the Backcountry Office at the North Rim Ranger Station daily 7 a.m.-noon from mid-May to late October. Topo maps and hiking guides are sold at the visitor center bookstore and other shops in Grand Canyon Village and Tusayan.

## MAINTAINED TRAILS OF THE INNER CANYON

You have the option of three types of hikes in the Inner Canyon. You can follow maintained trails, unmaintained trails, or routes. Park Service rangers usually recommend first-time visitors try one of the maintained trails to get the feel of Canyon hiking. These trails are wide and well-signed. Rangers and other hikers will be close by in case of problems.

Camping along maintained trails is restricted to established sites at Indian Garden, Bright Angel, and Cottonwood. Mice and other small varmints at these campgrounds have voracious appetites for campers' food—keep yours hung from a cord off a high tree branch or risk losing it.

**Phantom Ranch,** on Bright Angel Creek at the bottom of the Canyon, offers dormitory beds ($21.06), cabins ($56.21 s or d, $11.14 each extra person), meals (breakfast $11.14, box lunch $5.04, stew dinner $18, steak dinner $29.43), drinks, and snacks. You must make advance reservations for meals and accommodations with the Bright Angel Lodge transportation desk or with Grand Canyon Lodges, Box 699, Grand Canyon, AZ 86023; tel. 638-2401/

*Descending Bright Angel Trail in the early 1900s. That's Teddy Roosevelt riding up front.*

GRAND CANYON NATIONAL PARK (NEG. #5130)

2631. If you'd rather have your gear carried by someone else, mules are available for $43.60 in or out with a weight limit of 30 pounds. Mules will carry you, too (see "South Rim Tours," above).

### Bright Angel Trail

Havasupai Indians used this route from the South Rim to reach their fields and the spring at Indian Garden. Prospectors widened the trail in 1890, later extending it to the Colorado River. Now it's the easiest and most popular trail into the Canyon.

The trailhead lies just west of Bright Angel Lodge in Grand Canyon Village. Resthouses 1.5 and three miles below the rim include emergency telephones and usually offer water from May 1 to September 30. One-way distances from the top are 4.6 miles to Indian Garden (campground, water, and ranger station), 7.8 miles to the Colorado River, and 9.3 miles to Bright Angel Creek (campground, water, ranger station, and Phantom Ranch). Allow four to five hours for the descent to the river and 8-10 hours coming out (elevation change 4,500 feet).

**Plateau Point** is a good all-day hike. Perched 1,300 feet directly above the swirling Colorado River, you'll enjoy a 360-degree panorama of the Canyon. To reach Plateau Point, take the Bright Angel Trail to Indian Garden, then follow the signs. This strenuous day-hike is 12.2 miles roundtrip from the rim; elevation change is 3,080 feet.

### River Trail
This short, 1.7-mile trail parallels the river in the twisted rocks of the Inner Gorge, connecting the bottoms of the Bright Angel and South Kaibab trails. Two suspension bridges cross the river to Bright Angel Creek.

### South Kaibab Trail
On this trail, hikers will enjoy sweeping views up and down the Canyon. From the trailhead near Yaki Point, 4.5 miles east of Grand Canyon Village, the South Kaibab drops steeply, following Cedar Ridge toward the river and Bright Angel Creek (6.4 miles one-way). There's an emergency telephone at the Tipoff, 4.4 miles below the rim, where the trail begins to descend into the Inner Gorge.

Lack of shade and water and the steep grade make this trail especially difficult in summer. Allow three to five hours for the descent and six to eight hours coming out (elev. change 4,800 feet). Cedar Ridge, partway down, makes a good day-hike destination—three miles roundtrip and an elevation change of 1,160 feet. Strong hikers enjoy continuing down to the nearly level Tonto Trail (4.4 miles from the rim), turning left 4.1 miles on the Tonto to Indian Garden, then 4.6 miles up the Bright Angel Trail. A car shuttle is needed for this 13.1-mile hike. Very strong hikers can make it all the way from rim to river and back in one day. During summer, however, this is grueling and dangerous for *anyone* and isn't recommended.

### North Kaibab Trail
Few other Canyon trails compare in the number of interesting side trips and variety of scenery. Hikers on this trail start in the cool forests of the North Rim, descend through the woods into Roaring Springs Canyon, then follow rushing Bright Angel Creek all the way to the Colorado River. Look for the trailhead at the lower end of the parking lot, two miles north of Grand Canyon Lodge. Snows close the road from some time in October or November until mid-May, but you can reach the North Kaibab year-round on trails from the South Rim. A long section of trail between the rim and Roaring Springs has been cut into sheer cliffs; waterfalls cascade over the rock face in spring and after rains. A picnic ground near Roaring Springs is a good destination for day-hikers (9.4 miles roundtrip from the North Rim; elev. change 3,160 feet).

**Cottonwood Campground,** 6.9 miles below the rim, is a good stopping point for the night or a base for day-trips—it has a ranger station, and water in summer. Winter campers must purify water from the creek. **Ribbon Falls** pours into a miniature paradise of travertine and lush greenery, nestled in a side canyon 1.5 miles downstream from Cottonwood Campground.

The North Kaibab Trail continues downstream along Bright Angel Creek, entering the dark contorted schists and other rocks of the ancient Vishnu Group. Near the bottom you'll walk through Phantom Ranch, then Bright Angel Campground. Most people can descend the 14.2-mile North Kaibab in eight to nine hours of steady hiking (elev. change 5,700 feet). Climbing out requires 10-12 hours, and is best attempted over two days. Anglers are often successful in pulling rainbow trout from Bright Angel Creek, especially in winter.

## UNMAINTAINED TRAILS OF THE INNER CANYON (SOUTH RIM)

These trails lead to some beautiful corners of the park, offering solitude and new Canyon perspectives. Hikers must be self-reliant on unmaintained trails—know where water sources are, how to use map and compass, and how to handle emergencies. Most trails follow prehistoric Indian routes or game trails that miners improved in the late 1800s. Conditions vary widely; some trails are in excellent condition, while others are dangerous or require careful map reading. Although the Park Service calls these trails "unmaintained," it sometimes performs trail work on sections that have become

VISITING GRAND CANYON NATIONAL PARK 53

impassable. Hermit Trail and parts of the Tonto Trail feature designated camping areas you're required to use.

The following trails are listed from west to east.

## Tonto Trail

Hikers in a hurry will find the Tonto frustrating: winding in and out of countless canyons, this 92-mile trail contours along the Tonto Plateau, connecting most of the South Rim trails between the mouth of Red Canyon at Hance Rapids and Garnet Canyon far downstream. The view continually changes as you walk along, sometimes revealing spectacular panoramas from the edge of the Inner Gorge. Most of the hike is gently rolling, with an average elevation of 3,000 feet. You might lose the trail occasionally, but with attention to rock cairns and the map, you'll soon find it again. The sun bears down relentlessly in summer, when it's best to avoid this hike.

## South Bass Trail

William Bass learned about this route from the Havasupai Indians in the 1880s, using it to start a small tourist operation. Bass also built a trail up to the North Rim, crossing the river by boat and later by a cage suspended from a cable. No such crossing exists today.

The South Bass Trail is generally in good condition and easy to follow. It drops to the Esplanade, a broad terrace, then down to the river. You'll need a high-clearance vehicle to reach the trailhead, four miles north of Pasture Wash Ranger Station; ask at the Backcountry Office for directions. Hiking the nine-mile trail to the river takes about five hours down and nine hours up, with an elevation change of 4,400 feet. No reliable water is available before the river.

## Boucher Trail

Louis Boucher, the Hermit, came to the Canyon in 1891, mining copper along the creek that bears his name until 1912. Steep terrain and rock slides can make the trail difficult—it's best for experienced hikers with light packs.

Take Hermit and Dripping Springs trails to Boucher Trail. The Boucher contours along the base of the Hermit Shale, high above the west side of Hermit Canyon, affording excellent views. You'll reach Tonto Trail just before Boucher Creek. The route down the creek to Boucher Rapids on the Colorado River is an easy 1.5 miles. From the Hermit trailhead on West Rim

*Louis Boucher, "The Hermit" (far left), at his mine*

GRAND CANYON NATIONAL PARK (NEG. #5563)

Drive, it's 11 miles to Boucher Creek; allow seven to eight hours down and nine to 10 hours coming up, with an elevation change of 3,800 feet. The Boucher, Tonto, and Hermit trails make a fine three- or four-day loop hike. Boucher and Hermit creeks have water year-round.

## Hermit Trail

Although named for Boucher, the trail was actually built for tourists by the Santa Fe Railroad in 1912. Visitors took this route to Hermit Camp, which operated until 1930. Most of Hermit Trail is in good condition; the few places covered by rock slides can be easily crossed. The trail begins just beyond Hermit's Rest, at the end of eight-mile West Rim Drive. Water is available at Santa Maria Spring (two miles one-way) and Hermit Creek (seven miles one-way). To reach Hermit Rapids on the Colorado River requires an easy 1.5-mile walk down the bed of Hermit Creek; a sign on the Tonto Trail points the way down to Hermit Creek. Elevation change from rim to river is 4,300 feet: allow five to six hours going down and eight to 10 hours climbing out.

Hermit Trail also connects with Waldron, Dripping Springs, and Tonto trails. Day-hikers can head to Dripping Springs, a six-mile roundtrip hike requiring four to six hours with an elevation change of 800 feet. Descend the Hermit Trail 1.5 miles, then turn left 1.5 miles on Dripping Springs Trail. Carry water for the entire trip, as the springs offer only a tiny flow. Hikers with high-clearance vehicles can also reach the upper ends of Waldron and Dripping Springs trails; consult a topo map. The 22.5-mile Hermit Loop hike, which follows the Hermit, Tonto, and Bright Angel trails, is quite popular. Water is available on this loop year-round at Monument Creek and Indian Garden and seasonally at Salt and Horn creeks. Hikers can easily descend the bed of Monument Creek to Granite Rapids, 1.5 miles one-way.

## Grandview Trail

Day-hikers frequently use this steep but scenic trail to Horseshoe Mesa. The trailhead lies at Grandview Point on the East Rim Drive. Miners improved an old Indian route in 1892 so they could bring out high-grade copper ore from Horseshoe Mesa. Mining ceased in 1907, but

mine shafts, machinery, and ruins of buildings remain.

**Cave of the Domes,** a limestone cavern on the west side of the mesa, has some good passages; look for a trail fork west of the butte atop the mesa. Three trails descend Horseshoe Mesa to the Tonto Trail. Bring water, as the springs are either unreliable or difficult to reach. Allow six hours for the six-mile roundtrip hike to Horseshoe Mesa, with an elevation change of 2,600 feet.

## New Hance Trail

John Hance, one of the first prospectors to switch to the tourist business, built this trail down Red Canyon in 1895. The unsigned trailhead lies about one mile southwest of Moran Point turnoff on the East Rim Drive; obtain directions from a ranger. Suited for more experienced hikers, the trail descends steeply—poor footing in places—to the river at Hance Rapids. Most of the trail is easy to follow, especially when you're descending. No reliable water is available before the river. The eight-mile trail takes about six hours to descend and eight to 10 hours to ascend, with an elevation change of 4,400 feet.

## Tanner Trail

Seth Tanner improved this Indian trail in the 1880s to reach his copper and silver mines along the Colorado River. Although in good condition and easy to follow, the Tanner Trail is long—10 miles one-way—and dry, and best attempted in the cooler months. Hikers often cache water partway down for the return trip.

The trailhead lies about 100 yards back down the road from Lipan Point parking lot, off East Rim Drive. Allow six to eight hours for the descent and an 8-10-hour return, with an elevation change of 4,700 feet.

## Beamer Trail

This slim path begins at Tanner Canyon Rapids (lower end of Tanner Trail) and follows the river four miles upstream to Palisades Creek, then climbs to a high terrace for the remaining five miles to the Little Colorado River confluence. No camping is allowed within a half mile of the confluence.

## UNMAINTAINED TRAILS OF THE INNER CANYON (NORTH RIM)

### Whitmore Wash Trail

Although little known or used, this three-quarter-mile-long trail offers the park's easiest hike from trailhead to river. The trick is reaching the trailhead; you'll need a high-clearance 4WD vehicle. Follow dirt roads on the Arizona Strip from Toroweap, Fredonia, Colorado City, or St. George to Mt. Trumbull Village junction (marked by an old schoolhouse), then turn south 23.5 miles to road's end. The last 7.5 miles are rough, as the road crosses lava flows from Mt. Emma. This lava acts as a ramp for the road to descend deep into the Grand Canyon. The trail appears to drop off the rim where the road ends, but that's not the real trail. Instead, climb up above the barbed-wire fence to the trail.

You'll drop about 850 feet as the trail switchbacks, then skirts the base of a massive cliff of columnar basalt before ending on a sandy beach. Lava remnants of ancient dams can be seen on both sides of the river. A small trail near the bottom leads a half mile downstream to Whitmore Rapids and lower Whitmore Canyon, which you can explore for about a half mile upstream.

### Lava Falls Route

The Colorado River explodes in a fury of foam and waves at Lava Falls, reached by this short but steep route from the Toroweap area of the North Rim. Cairns mark the way down a lunarlike landscape of volcanic lava. Barrel cacti thrive on the dark, twisted rock. Although the route is only 1.5 miles one-way, it's considered difficult because of steep grades and poor footing. Summer temperatures get *extremely* hot; elevation at the river is only 1,700 feet. Summer hikers should start at dawn and carry plenty of water.

From Toroweap Overlook, backtrack on the road 2.5 miles and look for a dirt track on the left (3.5 miles south of Tuweep Ranger Station); follow it 2.5 miles across normally dry Toroweap Lake and around the west side of Vulcan's Throne. The route is too rough for cars and impassable for any vehicle when the lake contains water. At road's end, the route descends to a hill of red cinders about two-thirds of the way down; the last part of the descent follows a steep

*Inner Gorge*

gully. Lava Falls lies 0.3 mile downstream. Camping is possible along the river with a permit. Allow two hours going down and two and a half to four hours coming out, with an elevation change of 2,500 feet.

### Tuckup (Tuweep) Trail

Experienced canyon hikers looking for solitude and expansive vistas can try this faint trail. It follows the Esplanade of the North Rim for more than 70 miles between the Toroweap Point area and Hundred and Fifty Mile Canyon. Back roads lead to trailheads near these two areas and to upper Tuckup Canyon, about the halfway point on the trail.

The Toroweap trailhead is reached by a 3.5-mile jeep road; turn east at a fork 4.6 miles south of the ranger station, 1.6 miles north of the overlook. You can wander off on a variety of jaunts in this remote area; hikers have followed the Tuckup Trail from Toroweap Point to Cottonwood Canyon, descended Cottonwood and Tuckup canyons to the Colorado River (rope needed), hiked the shore downstream to Lava Falls

Route, and ascended back to Toroweap in a week or so of travel. Springs of varying reliability provide water along the Tuckup Trail. Talk with rangers knowledgeable about the area for trailhead, spring, and hiking conditions.

## Thunder River Trails

Thunder River blasts out of a cave in the Muav Limestone, cascades a half mile, then enters Tapeats Creek. It's not only the world's shortest river but suffers the humiliation of being a tributary to a creek.

Deer Creek Falls, another area attraction, plummets more than 100 feet onto the banks of the Colorado River. Cottonwood trees, willows, and other cool greenery grace the banks of Thunder River and both creeks. Trails are generally good and easy to follow, though spring runoff and rains can make Tapeats Creek too high to cross safely.

Two trails descend from the North Rim: the **Thunder River Trail** from Indian Hollow Campground at the end of Forest Route 232, and the **Bill Hall Trail** from the east side of Monument Point at the end of Forest Route 292A. The Bill Hall Trail saves five miles of walking but the steep grade can be hard on the knees.

Reach the trailheads by turning west on Forest Route 422 from AZ 67 in De Motte Park, one mile south of Kaibab Lodge and 17.5 miles north of Bright Angel Point; see the Kaibab National Forest map (North Kaibab Ranger District). It's about 35 miles of dirt road from the highway to either trailhead. Cars can negotiate the roads in good weather, but winter snows bury this high country from about mid-November to mid-May. Thunder River and Bill Hall trails both drop steeply to the Esplanade, where they meet. Thunder River Trail then switchbacks down to Surprise Valley, a giant piece of the rim that long ago slumped thousands of feet to its present position. Surprise Valley is an oven in summer and lacks water.

**Deer Creek Trail,** marked by a large cairn in Surprise Valley, splits off to the west for Deer Creek, 3.5 miles away. A short walk down Deer Creek leads to the falls and a trail to the river just west of the falls.

**Thunder River Trail** goes east across Surprise Valley, drops to Thunder River, and follows it to Tapeats Creek. Except at high water,

Tapeats Creek can be followed 2.5 miles upstream to its source in a cave. The Colorado River is a 2.5-mile hike downstream from the junction of Thunder River and Tapeats Creek. Camp at the designated sites near this junction, downstream on the Colorado River, or along upper Deer Creek. Good fishing attracts anglers to Tapeats Creek and perhaps always has—prehistoric Cohonina Indians left ruins along this creek. The trek from Bill Hall trailhead at Monument Point to Tapeats Rapids is about 12 miles one-way, with an elevation change of 5,250 feet; figure seven hours to reach the upper campsite on Tapeats Creek and nine hours to hike all the way to Tapeats Rapids. Thunder River, nine miles from the Bill Hall trailhead, is the first source of water.

## North Bass Trail

This difficult trail drops from Swamp Point on the North Rim to Muav Saddle, where there's a 1925 Park Service cabin. It makes a sharp left toward Muav Springs, drops steeply to White Creek in Muav Canyon, follows a long bypass to a safe descent through the Redwall, winds down White Creek to Shinumo Creek, continues to Bass Camp, then cuts over a ridge to the left and drops down to a fine beach on the Colorado River. The trail reaches the Colorado about 0.3 mile below where the South Bass Trail comes down on the other side. No crossing exists today, though people occasionally hitch rides to the far shore with river-rafters. A waterfall blocks travel down Shinumo Creek just before the river, so the trail climbs over the ridge.

Once at the Colorado River via the main trail, you can loop back to Bass Camp on another trail, which begins at the downstream end of the beach; it crosses over to lower Shinumo Creek, which you can then follow upstream back to Bass Camp and the North Bass Trail.

The Muav and Shinumo drainages very much create their own canyon worlds—you're not really exposed to the Grand Canyon until reaching the ridge above the Colorado River near trail's end. Muav Saddle Springs offers water just off the trail. White Creek has intermittent water above and below the Redwall. Shinumo Creek's abundant flow supports some small trout. Shinumo can be difficult to cross in spring and after summer storms; other times rocks provide a way to hop across. Allow three to four days for the 28-mile roundtrip to the river, with an elevation change of 5,300 feet; only experienced hikers should tackle this long and faint trail.

Many routes off the North Bass Trail invite exploration, such as the Redwall Narrows of White Creek above the trail junction, Shinumo Creek drainage above White Creek, and Burro Canyon. With a high-clearance vehicle you can reach the trailhead at Swamp Point from AZ 67 in DeMotte Park via Forest Routes 422, 270, 223, 268, 268B, and Swamp Point Road. Navigation isn't improved using the North Kaibab Forest map, which doesn't show 268B going across the park boundary to the Swamp Point Road. Route 223A no longer goes through to Swamp Point Road, though you can hike or bike the old route. The drive from DeMotte Park to Swamp Point takes nearly two hours due to the rough condition of Swamp Point Road.

**Powell Plateau Trail**

A good trail from Swamp Point connects this isolated "island" within the vast reaches of the Grand Canyon. Once part of the North Rim, the plateau has been completely severed from the rim by erosion, except for the Muav Saddle connection. The trail is about 1.5 miles one-way; you drop 800 feet to Muav Saddle on the North Bass Trail, then continue straight across the saddle and up another set of switchbacks to a ponderosa pine forest on the Powell Plateau. Here the trail fades out. Many places on the seven-mile-long plateau offer outstanding views. Travel is cross-country, so you'll need map and compass; expect to do some bushwhacking.

The easiest viewpoint to reach lies to the northwest; just follow the northern edge of the plateau (no trail) to a large rock cairn about one mile from where the trail from Swamp Point tops out on the plateau. You can camp on the Powell Plateau with a backcountry permit; all water must be carried in from the trailhead or Muav Saddle Springs. See "North Bass Trail" for directions to Swamp Point.

**Clear Creek Trail**

This trail, in very good condition and easy to follow, is the North Rim's version of the Tonto Trail. It begins 0.3 mile north of Phantom Ranch and climbs 1,500 feet to the Tonto Plateau,

winding in and out of canyons until dropping at the last possible place into Clear Creek, nine miles from Phantom Ranch. Carry water—there's no source before Clear Creek—and be prepared for very hot weather in summer. The best camping sites lie scattered among the cottonwood trees where the trail meets the creek.

Day-hikers enjoy the first mile or so of Clear Creek Trail for its scenic views of the river and Inner Gorge. Strong hikers can walk all the way to Clear Creek and back in a long day. Better still would be a trip of several days.

To reach **Cheyava Falls,** the highest falls in the Canyon, requires a six- to eight-hour roundtrip journey up the long northeast fork of Clear Creek. The falls put on an impressive show only in spring and after heavy rains. Other arms of the creek offer good hiking as well; the creek, branching east about a half mile downstream from the end of Clear Creek Trail, flows through a narrow canyon of quartzite. You can also walk along Clear Creek to the Colorado River, a five- to seven-hour roundtrip hike through dark and contorted schist and granite. You can bypass a 10-foot-high waterfall a half mile from the river by clambering around to the right.

**Nankoweap Trail**

Dangerous ledges on the Nankoweap Trail should discourage hikers afraid of heights. But if you don't mind tiptoeing on the brink of sheer cliffs, this trail will open up a large section of the park for your exploration. The trailhead lies at Saddle Mountain Saddle, 2.4 crow-flying miles northeast of Point Imperial. You can't drive to the trailhead, however; it must be approached on foot, either three miles one-way from House Rock Buffalo Ranch Road (south from US 89A), or three miles one-way from the end of Forest Route 610 (east off AZ 67). Both access roads are dirt, passable by cars, but House Rock Buffalo Ranch Road lies at a lower elevation and is less likely to be snowed in.

The Nankoweap Trail drops several hundred feet, then contours along a ledge all the way to Tilted Mesa before descending to Nankoweap Creek. Some care in route-finding is needed between Tilted Mesa and the creek. Nankoweap Creek, 10 miles from the trailhead, is the first source of water; you may want to cache water partway down to use on your return. The remaining four miles to the river are easy. Allow three to four days for a roundtrip journey, with an elevation change of 4,800 feet.

## ROUTES OF THE INNER CANYON

The Canyon offers thousands of possible routes for the experienced hiker. Harvey Butchart, master of Canyon off-trail hiking, describes many routes in his three books (see the Booklist). The Backcountry Office will suggest interesting routes as well, plus give you an idea of current conditions. You'll no doubt come up with route ideas of your own through hiking in the Canyon and studying maps.

Just keep in mind that much of the Canyon's exposed rock is soft or fractured—a handhold or foothold can easily break off. The Colorado River presents a major barrier, as the water is too cold, wide, and full of treacherous currents to cross safely.

### Royal Arch Loop

The rugged trip to Royal Arch and Elves Chasm is regarded as "fantastic" by experienced hikers. The route follows parts of the South Bass and West Tonto trails in making a long loop with the Esplanade Route and Royal Arch Canyon. Allow a minimum of five days for this one; be prepared for plenty of rough spots. Fewer than half the people who attempt this loop, it is said, actually make it without turning back.

Sections of the route are quite difficult to follow. The Royal Arch-Colorado River section is very exposed and requires a 50-foot rope. An easier hike takes the Tonto Trail to its end at Garnet Canyon, descends to the Colorado, and follows the river to Elves Chasm; return is by the same way. Royal Arch is just a half mile upstream from Elves Chasm, but you'll need to backtrack one mile up the Colorado River to the well-trod route used for reaching the arch. A 15-foot section of travertine takes some skill to climb. Carry a 50-foot rope; existing ropes will have weathered and may be unsafe.

### Escalante Route

The Tonto Trail's upper end gives out at Hance Rapids, but you can continue upstream to Tan-

ner Rapids and the Tanner Trail. Cairns mark the 15-mile Escalante Route. Expect rough terrain and difficult route-finding in some sections. The Colorado River, easily accessible only at the ends of the route, provides the only reliable source of water. The route is somewhat easier to hike in the downstream direction, Tanner to Hance.

## RUNNING THE COLORADO RIVER

Running the Colorado River through the Grand Canyon provides the excitement of roaring rapids and the tranquility of solitude. Although explorers of 100 years ago feared this section of the river, rendering it in dark and gloomy drawings, boating the Canyon today is a safe and enjoyable experience. Running the Colorado opens up some of the most beautiful and remote corners of the Canyon. River parties make frequent stops to explore the twisting side canyons, old mining camps, and Indian ruins along the way. Within the Grand Canyon, the Colorado River flows 277 miles, drops 2,200 feet, and thunders through 70 major rapids.

### River Tours

Sixteen companies offer a wide variety of trips through the Canyon, ranging from one-day introductions to adventurous 20-day expeditions. Write Grand Canyon National Park for a list of companies (Box 129, Grand Canyon, AZ 86023) or ask at the visitor center. If possible, make reservations (with deposit) six months in advance. **Rivers and Oceans** can supply additional information about companies offering river trips and make reservations at no additional cost to you; P.O. Box 40321, Flagstaff, AZ 86004; tel. 526-4575 or (800) 473-4576.

All but one of the tour companies use rafts of various sizes; the exception is **Grand Canyon Dories,** which employs sturdy boats. Both oar-powered and motorized craft run the river. The oar- or paddle-powered trips provide a more natural and quiet experience but take half again as much time. Motor-powered rafts can zip through the entire Canyon in six days, or zoom from Lees Ferry to Phantom Ranch in two days. River-running season normally lasts from April to October, though only oar-powered craft depart mid-September to mid-December. Most tours put in at Lees Ferry, just upstream from the park, and end downstream at Diamond Creek or Lake Mead. Shorter trips are possible using hiking trails or helicopters.

If you'd like just a taste of river-running, take a one-day trip from Glen Canyon Dam to Lees Ferry with **Wilderness River Adventures,** based in Page (see Page "Tours," later in this chapter), or raft the lower Grand Canyon with **Hualapai Tribal River Runners,** based in Peach Springs (see "Visiting the Hualapai Indian Reservation," under Havasupai).

Typical commercial oar trips include: 12 days from Lees Ferry to Diamond Creek covering 226 miles; five or six days from Lees Ferry to Phantom Ranch, 87.5 miles; and eight or nine days from Phantom Ranch to Diamond Creek, 138.5 miles. Equivalent motorized trips occupy eight days from Lees Ferry to Diamond Creek; three or four days from Lees Ferry to Phantom Ranch; and five days from Phantom Ranch to Diamond Creek. Many other combinations are available. Expect to pay $200 or more per day; discounts may be available for groups, children under 14, early booking, and off-season journeys.

If you've children in tow, check for minimum age requirements; sometimes this is left up to the passenger, other times operators require minimum ages of anywhere between 8 and 16 years. Trips usually include land transportation; most depart from Flagstaff, Page, St. George, or Las Vegas. Meals, camping gear, and waterproof bags are usually included in the price. Experienced kayakers can tag along with many tours, paying a lower rate. You can also organize your own Canyon expedition, but you must plan far in advance and meet all Park Service requirements; contact the **River Permits** office, tel. 638-7843. If you need a shuttle for your party and raft to or from the river contact **River-Runner Shuttle;** tel. 638-2748 or (800) 682-4393.

### Canoeing the Lower Grand Canyon

Canoes in the Grand Canyon? Yes indeed, in the last 40 miles within the park. A powerboat is needed to carry the canoes from Lake Mead to Separation Canyon (Mile 240 on the river). Most of the southern shore on this trip belongs to the Hualapai Indians; obtain tribal permits if you plan to camp or hike on their land.

*rafting through Marble Canyon*

# HAVASUPAI AND HUALAPAI INDIAN RESERVATIONS

## VISITING HAVASU CANYON

Havasu Canyon is a land of towering cliffs, blue-green waters, breathtaking waterfalls, and lush vegetation. Havasu Creek rushes through the canyon past the Indian village of Supai before beginning its wild cascade down to the Colorado River. The canyon and its creek, about 35 air miles northwest of Grand Canyon Village, belong to the Havasupai Indians (*havasu* means "blue," and *pai* means "people").

Havasupai lived here long before the first white people arrived. The tribe farmed the fertile canyon floor during the summer, moving to the plateau after harvest. The Havasupai wintered atop the plateau, gathering abundant wild foods and firewood. Spanish missionary Francisco Garcés visited the Havasupai in 1776, finding them a happy and industrious people. Though a peaceful tribe, the Havasupai suffered the usual fate of American Indians: confined to a tiny reservation while white people grabbed their lands. The Havasupai protested, but it wasn't until 1975 that the tribe's winter homelands were returned. The Havasupai Reservation now spans 188,077 acres; most of the 500-600 tribal members on the reservation live in Supai village.

### Getting There

The tribe decided against allowing road construction in the canyon, so most residents and tourists arrive by mule, horse, or on foot. Helicopters provide another option, though the noisy machines seem out of place here.

The eight-mile trail from Hualapai Hilltop to Supai is the usual way in. From Seligman on I-40, take AZ 66 northwest for 28 miles, then turn right 63 miles on a signed road, paved all the way to Hualapai Hilltop. If coming from the west, take AZ 66 northeast out of Kingman for 60 miles, then turn left and drive 63 miles. Fill up with gas before leaving AZ 66; no water, supplies, or stores are available after the turnoff.

The road to Hualapai Hilltop climbs into forests of ponderosa pine that give way to piñon and juniper, then desert grasslands close to the rim. Hualapai Hilltop offers parking areas and stables. Various dirt road shortcuts to Hualapai Hilltop suffer from poor signing and rough surfaces.

### Hiking In

You *must* obtain reservations to camp or to stay in the lodge. From Hualapai Hilltop (elev. 5,200 feet), the trail descends at a moderate grade into Hualapai Canyon for the first 1.5 miles, then levels off slightly for the remaining 6.5 miles to Supai village (elev. 3,200 feet). About 1.5 miles before the village, the trail joins the sparkling waters of Havasu Canyon. Avoid the heat of the day in summer when temperatures soar past 100° F, and always carry drinking water. All visitors must pay a $15 entrance fee ($12 in winter) on arrival at Supai. The tribe asks you to leave pets, alcohol, and firearms at home. To preserve the canyon floor, no fires or charcoal are allowed; campers need to bring stoves if planning to cook.

### Sights

The famous sights of the canyon begin 1.5 miles downstream from Supai. Four waterfalls plunge over cliffs of Redwall Limestone in a space of just two miles.

You'll first come to 75-foot-high **Navajo Falls,** featuring several widely spaced branches. It's named after a 19th-century Havasupai tribal chief kidnapped by Navajo Indians as an infant and raised as a Navajo. Not until he grew to manhood did he learn of his true origin and return to the Havasupai.

Spectacular **Havasu Falls** drops 100 feet into a beautiful turquoise-colored pool rimmed by travertine deposits. Clear, inviting waters make this a perfect spot for swimming or picnicking.

**Mooney Falls,** most awe-inspiring of all, plummets 196 feet into a colorful pool. The Havasupai named this most sacred of waterfalls Mother of the Waters. The present name comes from a prospector who died here in 1880. Assistants were lowering Daniel Mooney down the cliffs next to the falls when the rope jammed. Mooney hung helpless as the rope frayed and broke. He fell to his death on the rocks below, and 10 months passed before his companions could build a wooden ladder down the falls to reach and bury the travertine-encrusted body. A rough trail descends beside the falls along the same route hacked through the travertine by miners in those months after Mooney's death. You'll pass through two tunnels and then ease down with the aid of chains and iron stakes. At the bottom—as soon as your knees stop shaking—you can enjoy a picnic or swim in the large pool. Holes high on the canyon walls were drilled by miners extracting silver, lead, zinc, and vanadium.

**Beaver Falls,** two miles downstream from Mooney, is a good day-hike from the campgrounds or Supai village. You pass countless inviting travertine pools and small cascades, of which Beaver Falls is the largest. The trail, rough in places, crosses the creek three times, climbs high up a cliff, then descends and crosses a fourth time below Beaver Falls. The trail continues downstream along Havasu Creek four more miles to the Colorado River. Travel fast and light if going to the river, as camping is prohibited below Mooney Falls. Photographing the falls can be a challenge; the best time to snap them in full sunlight is May, June, and July.

### Havasu Campground

Most visitors prefer to camp, listening to the sounds of the canyon and enjoying the brilliant display of stars in the nighttime sky. Havasu Campground begins a quarter mile below Havasu Falls (or 10.75 miles from Hualapai Hilltop), and features spring water, picnic tables, litter barrels, and pit toilets. What most campers don't realize is that the campground extends three-quarters of a mile along Havasu Creek to the brink of Mooney Falls. You'll enjoy more solitude if you walk to the far end. Theft is a serious problem in the campground, so don't leave valuables in your tents or lying around.

You must obtain reservations and pay $10 per night per person ($9 in winter) to camp. Camping outside the established campground is

*down the steep slope
to the base of Mooney Falls*

prohibited. Call 448-2121 or write Havasupai Tourist Enterprise, Supai, AZ 86435. Pay on arrival at Supai. Try to make reservations far ahead, especially for holidays, weekends, and all of May, June, and July.

### Accommodations and Food

The village of Supai offers the modern **Havasupai Lodge,** featuring rooms with air-conditioning, two double beds, and private bath for $78.75 s, $84 d, $8.40 each additional person (in winter, November 1 to March 31, rates drop to $47.25 s, $52.50 d, $8.40 each additional person). Obtain the required reservations from Havasupai Lodge, Supai, AZ 86435; tel. 448-2111. A cafe nearby serves breakfast, lunch, and dinner daily 7 a.m.-6:30 p.m. Try the Indian taco—red beans, beef, cheese, onion, and lettuce on Indian fry bread. Ice cream prices are high, though not incredibly so when you consider what it takes to move ice cream to such a remote area. The other prices aren't bad. A store across the street sells meat, groceries, and cold drinks daily 7 a.m.-6 p.m.

## Services

Send your postcard home via pack train—the only such mail service in the country—with a postmark to prove it. The **post office** is open weekdays 9 a.m.-4 p.m., next to the store.

If you'd rather ride than walk, local families will take you and your gear on **horses** or **mules** from the parking lot at Hualapai Hilltop to Supai ($57.75 one way or $115.50 roundtrip). Try to get an early start from Hualapai Hilltop, especially in the warmer months; a small surcharge is added for departures after 9 a.m. A sightseeing trip from Supai to the falls and back costs $40 by horse or mule, depending on what's available.

You must make reservations—at least six weeks in advance—and pay a 50% deposit to Havasupai Tourist Enterprise, Supai, AZ 86435; tel. 448-2121. Always call one day before arrival to make sure your animal is available. Visitors may also bring their own horses if they take along feed and pay a $15 trail fee. A **health clinic** in Supai provides emergency medical care.

## VISITING THE HUALAPAI INDIAN RESERVATION

The Hualapai (Pine-tree People) once occupied a large area of northwestern Arizona. In language and culture, they're closely tied to the Havasupai and Yavapai tribes. Early white visitors enjoyed friendly relations with the Hualapai, but land seizures and murders by the newcomers led to warfare. Army troops defeated the Hualapai and herded them south onto the Colorado River Reservation, where many died. Surviving Hualapai fled back to their traditional lands, part of which later became the Hualapai Indian Reservation. About half of the 1,500 tribal members live on the 993,000-acre reservation. Much of the lower Grand Canyon's South Rim belongs to them.

## Peach Springs

This small town, 54 miles northeast of Kingman on AZ 66, is the only town on the reservation. Peach Springs offers neither charm nor anything to see, but it's the only place to obtain permits for reservation recreation and back-road trips. One office organizes one- and two-day rafting trips through the lower Grand Canyon.

There's no place to stay in Peach Springs (a motel is planned), but nearby Truxton (nine miles southwest) features two motels along with RV spaces. Peach Springs does have a cafe serving basic short-order items. There's also a grocery store.

## Diamond Creek Road

This scenic 21-mile gravel road travels north from Peach Springs to the Colorado River at Diamond Creek, providing the only road access to the river within the Grand Canyon. The road is suffering from overuse, and the tribe prefers that traffic cease. But if you do choose to go, you'll see fine canyon views, though not as spectacular as those at the developed areas of Grand Canyon National Park. Except for river-runners, who use the road to take out or put in boats, few people visit this spot. Yet the very first organized groups of tourists to the Canyon bounced down the road to Diamond Creek in 1883. A hotel built here and used 1884-89 was the first such structure in the Grand Canyon.

During dry weather, cars with good ground clearance can traverse the road. Summer rains in July and August necessitate use of a truck. Except for some picnic tables and an outhouse or two, the area is undeveloped. Hikers can explore Diamond Creek and other canyons; see Stewart Aitchison's *A Naturalist's Guide to Hiking the Grand Canyon.* Before attempting to travel Diamond Creek Rd. you should stop at the Hualapai River Runners office to obtain permits and information on road conditions. Sightseeing permits cost $4 per day per person (ages 6 and over). Camping is $7 per day per person, and includes the sightseeing fee. Diamond Creek Road parts from AZ 66 beside the River Runners office in town.

## Grand Canyon West Tours

The Hualapai tribe offers a tour of 4.6 miles of the rim of Grand Canyon West to Guano Point, where visitors enjoy views of the Grand Canyon uncluttered by development; participants are fed mesquite barbecued beef and chicken, tortillas, corn on the cob, beans, and rolls. The tour and meal runs $27.50 per person with children under age five free. For information contact Grand Canyon West; P.O. Box 359, Peach Springs, AZ 86434.

*Farlee Hotel near Diamond Creek; built in 1894 and in ruins when this picture was taken, circa 1914*

**River-Running**

**Hualapai River Runners** offers one- and two-day motorized-raft trips down the lower Grand Canyon between Diamond Creek and Pearce Ferry on Lake Mead at $257-384 per person. Rates cover food, accommodations (including a room the nights before and after the trip), waterproof bag use for personal effects, and transportation from Peach Springs. The season lasts from May 1 to October 31; write for the schedule well in advance so you can make reservations with Hualapai River Trips, Box 246, Peach Springs, AZ 86434; tel. 769-2219, 769-2210, or (800) 622-4409. The office is open daily during the season and Mon.-Fri. 8 a.m.-5 p.m. the rest of the year. Look for the office at the corner of AZ 66 and Diamond Creek Road in town next to the Cash and Carry Market.

# PAGE

Before 1957, only sand and desert vegetation lay atop Manson Mesa. In that year the U.S. Bureau of Reclamation decided to build a giant reservoir in Glen Canyon on the Colorado River. Glen Canyon Dam became one of the largest construction projects ever undertaken, the 710-foot-high structure creating a lake covering 250 square miles with a shoreline of nearly 2,000 miles. Workers hastily set up prefabricated metal buildings for barracks, dining hall, and offices. Trailers rolled in, one serving as a bank. And thus was born the town of Page, occupying a site 130 miles north of Flagstaff. The Bureau of Reclamation named the place for John C. Page, who served as the bureau's commissioner from 1937 to 1943.

The remote desert spot gradually turned into a modern town with schools, businesses, and churches. Streets were named, grass and trees were planted, and Page took on the appearance of an American suburb. Today, the town still looks new and clean. Though small (pop. 8,200), it's the largest community in far north Arizona and offers travelers a variety of places to stay and eat.

Wedged between the Arizona Strip to the west, Glen Canyon National Recreation Area to the north, and the Navajo Reservation to the east and south, Page is a useful base for visiting each of these areas. The townsite (elev. 4,300 feet) overlooks Lake Powell and Glen Canyon Dam; the large Wahweap Resort and Marina lies just six miles away. Unless you take a commercial flight in, you'll need your own transport to get here.

**Powell Museum**

This collection honors scientist and explorer John Wesley Powell. In 1869 Powell led the first expedition down the Green and Colorado River gorges, running the rivers a second time in 1871-72. It was Powell who named the most splendid section the Grand Canyon.

Old drawings and photographs illustrate

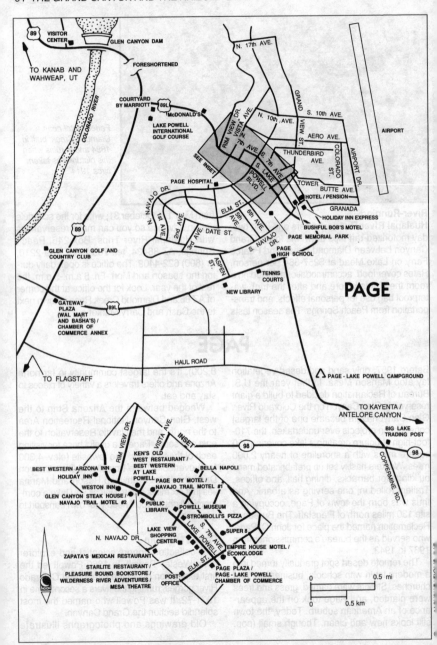

# PAGE

**89** VISITOR CENTER
GLEN CANYON DAM
TO KANAB AND WAHWEAP, UT
FORESHORTENED
COLORADO RIVER
COURTYARD BY MARRIOTT
**89L**
McDONALD'S
LAKE POWELL INTERNATIONAL GOLF COURSE
SEE INSET
PAGE HOSPITAL
**89**
N. NAVAJO DR.
1st AVE.
2nd AVE.
3rd AVE.
ELM ST.
DATE ST.
RIM VIEW DR.
VISTA IN.
7th AVE.
S. 7th AVE.
S. LAKE POWELL BLVD.
N. 17th AVE.
N. 10th AVE.
S. 10th AVE.
GRAND VIEW ST.
AERO AVE.
COLORADO ST.
AIRPORT DR.
AIRPORT
THUNDERBIRD AVE.
TOWER
BUTTE AVE.
GRANADA
HOTEL / PENSION
HOLIDAY INN EXPRESS
BUSHFUL BOB'S MOTEL
PAGE MEMORIAL PARK
5th AVE.
6th AVE.
S. NAVAJO DR.
PAGE HIGH SCHOOL
ASPEN ST.
TENNIS COURTS
NEW LIBRARY
GLEN CANYON GOLF AND COUNTRY CLUB
GATEWAY PLAZA (WAL MART AND BASHA'S) / CHAMBER OF COMMERCE ANNEX
**89L**
TO FLAGSTAFF
HAUL ROAD
PAGE - LAKE POWELL CAMPGROUND
TO KAYENTA / ANTELOPE CANYON
BIG LAKE TRADING POST
COPPERMINE RD.
**98**
**98**

### INSET
RIM VIEW DR.
VISTA AVE.
KEN'S OLD WEST RESTAURANT / BEST WESTERN AT LAKE POWELL
BELLA NAPOLI
BEST WESTERN ARIZONA INN
HOLIDAY INN
WESTON INN
GLEN CANYON STEAK HOUSE / NAVAJO TRAIL MOTEL #2
PAGE BOY MOTEL / NAVAJO TRAIL MOTEL #1
POWELL MUSEUM
STROMBOLLI'S PIZZA
PUBLIC LIBRARY
SUPER 8
LAKE VIEW SHOPPING CENTER
N. NAVAJO DR.
S. 7th AVE.
LAKE POWELL
EMPIRE HOUSE MOTEL / ECONOLODGE
ZAPATA'S MEXICAN RESTAURANT
STARLITE RESTAURANT / PLEASURE BOUND BOOKSTORE / WILDERNESS RIVER ADVENTURES / MESA THEATRE
POST OFFICE
ELM ST.
PAGE PLAZA / PAGE - LAKE POWELL CHAMBER OF COMMERCE

0    0.5 mi
0    0.5 km

Powell's life and voyages. Fossil and mineral displays interpret the thick geologic sections revealed by the canyons of the Colorado River system. Other exhibits contain pottery, baskets, weapons, and tools of Southwestern Indian tribes, as well as memorabilia from early pioneers and the founding of Page. Travel info, Lake Powell boat tours, all day and half-day float trips, ground tours, scenic flights, and regional bookstore are available.

The museum offers **Destiny Adventures** hiking tours to nearby natural wonders and also climbing and rappelling gear and instruction. Summer hikes are early morning and late afternoon from two hours to all day; cooler months offer even more hiking opportunities. For more information call the museum or write to Destiny Adventures, Box 1711, Page, AZ 86040.

It's open May to September Sunday 10 a.m.-6 p.m. and Mon.-Sat. 8 a.m.-6 p.m. April and October hours are Mon.-Sat. 8 a.m.-5 p.m.; mid-February, March, and November to mid-December hours are Mon.-Fri. 9 a.m.-5 p.m.; it's closed mid-December to mid-February; tel. 645-5258/9496. The museum is in downtown Page at the corner of Lake Powell Blvd. and N. Navajo Drive.

## Rattlesnake Alive Museum and Zoo

This new museum offers visitors a chance to see live rattlesnakes, a giant iguana, tarantulas, scorpions, and other creepy crawlies. It's just three doors from the Powell Museum, open daily 10 a.m.-10 p.m. with $3.50 admission; no phone.

## Diné Bí Keyah Museum (Big Lake Trading Post)

This small collection of modern and prehistoric Indian artifacts is on the second floor, and open daily 6 a.m.-9 p.m.; free admission; tel. 645-2404. Big Lake Trading Post lies 1.3 miles southeast of town on AZ 98. The post features Indian crafts and groceries for sale.

## Corkscrew Canyon

You can visit Antelope Wash to see this beautifully contoured red rock slot canyon by driving southwest on Hwy. 98 one mile past Big Lake Trading Post. Turn right into the parking area where $5 per person is collected for a tribal hiking permit plus $10 per person shuttle charge for the 3.5 mile drive into the trailhead area; no walk-ins or private drive-ins are permitted.

## Accommodations

All Page motels lie on or near Lake Powell Blvd., a 3.25-mile loop designated US 89L that branches off the main highway. The summer rates listed here drop substantially in winter.

**Lake Powell International Hostel** at 141 Eighth Ave. offers the lowest rates in Page; dorm rooms run $12-15 ($10 in winter) while private rooms cost $35-45; tel. 645-3898.

**Lake Powell International Pension** at 115-119 Eighth St. charges $30-60; tel. 645-3898.
**Bashful Bob's Motel** at 750 S. Navajo Dr. offers mostly two bedroom apartments, many with kitchens, at $38.52 s, $42.92 d; tel. 645-3919.
**EconoLodge**, 121 S. Lake Powell Blvd., tel. 645-2488, offers rooms for $77.05-99.05 s or d. **Weston's Empire House Motel,** with coffee shop and swimming pool at 107 S. Lake Powell Blvd., features rooms for $57.23 s, $70.43 d; tel. 645-2406.

**Super 8 Motel,** at 75 S. Seventh Ave. behind Taco Bell, furnishes accommodations for $75.80 s, $80.20 d; tel. 645-2858. **Page Boy Motel** and its swimming pool can be found at 150 N. Lake Powell Blvd.; $39.62 s, $48.43 d; tel. 645-2416. **Navajo Trail Motel** has rooms at 800 Bureau for $42.86 s or d, tel. 645-9508; and nearby at 630 Vista, behind Glen Canyon Steak House, for $49.86 s or d, tel. 645-9510.

The **Weston Inn** (Best Western) offers a swimming pool at 207 N. Lake Powell Blvd.; $78.14-81.43 s, $89.14-100.15 d; tel. 645-2451. **Best Western at Lake Powell** has a heated pool and spa at 208 N. Lake Powell Blvd.; $86.94-115.55 s or d; tel. 645-5988 or (800) 528-1234. **Holiday Inn** features a swimming pool, restaurant, and views over Lake Powell from 287 N. Lake Powell Blvd.; $101.25 s, $108.95 d; tel. 645-8851 or (800) 232-0011. The **Best Western Arizona Inn** provides fine views, swimming pool, and adjacent restaurant; $75.76-79 s, $75.93-101.25 d at 716 Rim View Dr. and Lake Powell Blvd. (across from Holiday Inn); tel. 645-2466 or (800) 826-2718. **Courtyard by Marriott** offers great views, a restaurant, a pool, whirlpool, and adjacent 18-hole golf course at 600 Clubhouse Dr. for $156.27 s or d; tel. 645-5000 or (800) 321-2211.

Page also has several charming, if small, bed and breakfast inns. Call the Chamber of Commerce or Bob at Bashful Bob's Motel for more details.

**Page-Lake Powell Campground** offers sites for tents and RVs, $16.51 no hookups, $18.71 w/hookups; showers available. The campground is 0.7 mile southeast of town on AZ 98; tel. 645-3374. Other campgrounds, an RV park, and motels are in the Wahweap area (see "Wahweap" under "Glen Canyon National Recreation Area").

## Food and Entertainment
**Glen Canyon Steak House** serves American food daily for breakfast, lunch, and dinner; specialties include steak, seafood, ribs, and chicken; enjoy karaoke 9 p.m.-1 a.m. nightly except Wednesday. The Steak House is at 201 N. Lake Powell Blvd.; tel. 645-3363, fax 645-5959. **Ken's Old West Restaurant** offers steak, prime rib, and seafood; open daily for dinner, with country-western bands providing music Mon.-Sat.; 718 Vista Ave.; tel. 645-5160. **Family Tree Restaurant** in the Holiday Inn offers a varied menu and is open daily for breakfast, lunch, and dinner; 287 N. Lake Powell Blvd.; tel. 645-8851.

**Butterfield Stage Restaurant** serves American food daily for breakfast and dinner at 704 Rim View Dr. next to Best Western Arizona Inn at Lake Powell; tel. 645-2467. The **Canyon Bowl Bistro** serves breakfast, lunch, and dinner daily, including steak, swordfish, and chicken, at 24 N. Lake Powell Blvd.; tel. 645-2682. **Pepper's Restaurant** at the Courtyard by Marriott offers American-continental cuisine with a Southwestern flair and is open daily for breakfast, lunch, and dinner at 600 Clubhouse Dr.; tel. 645-5000.

Chinese food is available at **Starlite,** open Mon.-Fri. for breakfast, lunch, and dinner and Saturday for lunch and dinner only; 46 S. Lake Powell Blvd.; tel. 645-3620. **Zapata's Mexican Restaurant** is open daily for dinner only; 614 N. Navajo Dr.; tel. 645-9006. **Dos Amigos Mexican Restaurant** is open daily for lunch and dinner at 610 Elm St.; tel. 645-3036. **Bella Napoli** offers fine Italian cuisine Mon.-Sat. for dinner in spring, then opens daily for dinner until mid-autumn; closed in winter; 810 N. Navajo Dr.; tel. 645-2706. Pizza, spaghetti, and other Italian

fare are served daily for lunch and dinner by **Strombolli's Pizza,** 711 N. Navajo Dr., tel. 645-2605, **Pizza Hut,** Lake View Shopping Center, tel. 645-2455, and **Little Caesar's,** carry-out only, Page Plaza, tel. 645-5565.

You can buy **groceries** at Safeway (Page Plaza at corner of Lake Powell Blvd. and Elm St.), Basha's (Gateway Plaza), or at Mrs. C's Health Food Center (32 S. Lake Powell Blvd.). Catch movies at **Mesa Theatre,** 42 S. Lake Powell Blvd., tel. 645-9565.

## Events
**January:** Hole-in-Rock Commemoration on Lake Powell celebrates the 1880 crossing of the Colorado River by Mormon pioneers; historic programs and tours take place at Wahweap and Bullfrog marinas. The Striper Derby continues at Lake Powell (see "November").

**February:** Striper Derby continues at Lake Powell.

**March:** A Hot Air Balloon Regatta occurs over the Page area on the last weekend of the month. In the Bullfrog Open, prizes are awarded for the biggest largemouth bass.

**April:** The Lake Powell Marathon takes place on the last weekend of the month.

**May:** Catch the 4-H Horse Show or the Page Open Rodeo.

**July:** July 4th celebration with food, games, and fireworks at Page Memorial Park.

**August:** Halls Crossing-Bullfrog Swim is an early morning swimming race between the two marinas.

**September:** Northern Arizona Fall Roundup Rodeo takes place. Rod Run, a custom and antique car show, occurs on the third weekend of the month. The Lake Powell Triathlon gets under way at Bullfrog Marina.

**October:** Air Affair lifts off over Page with hot air balloons, airplane aerobatics, and parachutists.

**November:** Anglers compete for the biggest striped bass in the Striper Derby, lasting through February at Lake Powell. Bullfrog's Festival of Lights Parade takes place.

**December:** Check out the Here Comes Santa Parade in Page and Wahweap Festival of Lights Parade on Lake Powell. Striper Derby continues at Lake Powell.

For more information on Lake Powell events,

contact Lake Powell Resorts and Marinas, tel. (800) 528-6154, (602) 278-8888 in greater Phoenix. To learn about other events, contact Page/Lake Powell Chamber of Commerce, tel. 645-2741, fax 645-3181.

## Services and Recreation

The **post office** is at 615 Elm St.; tel. 645-2571. **Page Hospital** is at the corner of Vista Ave. and N. Navajo Dr.; tel. 645-2424. In **emergencies**—police, fire, medical—dial 911.

Page High School features an indoor **swimming pool,** open all year, near the corner of S. Lake Powell Blvd. and AZ 98; tel. 608-4100. Play **tennis** at the courts on S. Lake Powell Blvd. (Church Row). **Glen Canyon Golf and Country Club** has a nine-hole golf course west of town on US 89; tel. 645-2715. **Lake Powell National Golf Course** offers an 18-hole championship golf course at Hwy. 89 and Loop 89 adjacent to the Courtyard by Marriott; tel. 645-2023. **Twin Finn Diving Center** offers a variety of diving activities and classes and rents diving equipment and kayaks at 828 Vista Ave.; tel. 645-3114. **Rope and Saddle Promotions** offers horseback riding at Vermilion Downs on Haul Rd.—the first right turn off Hwy. 98 after descending the hill; first hour $26.75, $16.05 each additional hour. There are half a dozen places to rent boats in Page and nearby; consult the yellow pages of the phone book.

## Information

The **Page/Lake Powell Chamber of Commerce** offers information about area sights and services and books lake and river tours and scenic flights; open daily 7 a.m.-7 p.m. from May 16 to October 16, then Mon.-Sat. 8 a.m.-5:30 p.m. the rest of the year. The office is in Page Plaza on the side facing the road, around the corner from Safeway (Box 727, Page, AZ 86040); tel. 645-2741. The **public library** is open daily except Sunday at the corner of 697 Vista Ave. and N. Lake Powell Blvd. (the library plans to relocate to 457 S. Lake Powell Blvd.); tel. 645-2231. **Pleasure Bound Bookstore** has regional titles and general reading at 48 S. Lake Powell Blvd. in Adkinson Mall; tel. 645-5333.

## Tours

**Lake Powell Jeep Tours** (tel. 645-5501/3142) offers back-road drives to Corkscrew Canyon in Antelope Wash and other area destinations. Tours go daily all year including holidays unless weather cancels the tours. You can make reservations through the Powell Museum and Page/Lake Powell Chamber of Commerce. **Rogers Photographic Tours** goes to similar destinations in a ninety minute-two hour tour at $26.50 and a four to six hour photographic tour at $42.63; tel. 645-8579 or (801) 675-9109.

**Wilderness River Adventures** offers raft trips down the Colorado River from just below Glen Canyon Dam to Lees Ferry, traveling over 15 miles of smooth-flowing water. Fees are $40 adults, $35 children under 12; leaving once or twice daily March 1 to October 31, weather permitting; all-day trips are also available as well as Grand Canyon raft trips of 3-12 days. Contact the company at 50 S. Lake Powell Blvd. in Lake View Shopping Center; mailing address Box 717, Page, AZ 86040; tel. 645-3279, (800) 528-6154.

**Scenic Airlines** offers a number of flightseeing trips, including journeys over Lake Powell and Rainbow Bridge (half-hour, $61), Grand Canyon (1.5 hours, $149), Monument Valley (1.5 hours, $140, $180 with ground tour), and Bryce Canyon (1.5 hours, $139); a two-person minimum applies to most tours; children 12 and under fly for 20% off. Charter flights to Flagstaff, Phoenix, Las Vegas, Salt Lake City, and Grand Junction can also be arranged; tel. 645-2494 or (800) 245-8668. Boat tours to Rainbow Bridge and other destinations leave from nearby Wahweap Marina; see "Glen Canyon National Recreation Area."

## Transport

Wahweap Lodge operates **Page Shuttle** frequently to Page and the airport; tel. 645-2433. Most area motels also provide transportation for guests to and from the airport. From the Page Airport on the east edge of town, **Sky West Airlines** flies three times daily (one-way fares) year-round to Phoenix ($89); in summer, planes leave daily for St. George ($49), Salt Lake City ($139), Las Vegas ($134), and other destinations; tel. 645-9200 or (800) 453-9417.

You can rent cars at the airport from **Avis,** tel. 645-2024, or **Budget,** tel. 645-3977.

# GLEN CANYON NATIONAL RECREATION AREA

This vast recreation area covers 1.25 million acres, most of which spreads northeast into Utah. Lake Powell is the centerpiece, surrounded by beautiful canyon country. Just a handful of roads approach the lake, so the visitor must boat or hike to truly explore this unique land of water and rock. The recreation area also includes a beautiful remnant of Glen Canyon in a 15-mile section of the Colorado River from Glen Canyon Dam to Lees Ferry.

## LAKE POWELL

Conservationists deplored the loss of remote and beautiful Glen Canyon, buried today beneath Lake Powell. Only words, pictures, and memories remind us of its lost wonders.

Lake Powell is the second-largest artificial lake in the United States. Only Lake Mead, farther downstream, has a greater water-storage capacity. Lake Powell boasts a shoreline of 1,960 miles and holds enough water to cover the state of Pennsylvania a foot deep. Bays and coves offer nearly limitless opportunities for exploration by boaters. Only the lower portion—Glen Canyon Dam, Wahweap Resort and Marina, Antelope and Navajo canyons, and the lower parts of Labyrinth, Face, and West canyons—extend into Arizona. Surface elevation fluctuates an average 20-30 feet through the year (fluctuation has reached 59 feet), peaking in July; Lake Powell reaches 3,700 feet when full. The Carl Hayden Visitor Center, perched beside the dam, offers tours of the dam, related exhibits, and an information desk covering the entire Glen Canyon National Recreation Area.

### Climate

Summer, when temperatures rise into the 90s and 100s F, is the busiest season for swimming, boating, and waterskiing. Visits during the rest of the year can be enjoyable too, though more conducive to sightseeing, fishing, and hiking. Spring and autumn are the best times to enjoy the backcountry. Winter temperatures drop to highs in the 40s and 50s, with freezing nights and the possibility of snow. Lake surface temperatures range from a comfortable 80° in August to a chilly 45° in January. Chinook winds can blow day and night from February to May. Thunderstorms in late summer bring strong, gusting winds with widely scattered rainshowers. Annual precipitation averages about seven inches.

### Geology, Flora, and Fauna

The colorful rock layers rising above the lake's surface constitute the remains of ancient deserts, oceans, and rivers. Uplift of the Colorado Plateau beginning about 60 million years ago started a cycle of erosion that has carved canyons and created delicately balanced rocks and graceful natural arches and bridges.

The desert comes right to the edge of the water, because fluctuating lake levels prevent growth along the shore. Common plants of this high-desert country include prickly pear and hedgehog cacti, rabbitbrush, sand sagebrush, blackbrush, cliffrose, mariposa and sego lilies, globemallow, Indian paintbrush, evening primrose, penstemon, and Indian rice grass. Piñon pine and juniper trees grow on the high plateaus. Springs and permanent streams support sandbar willow, tamarisk, cattail, willow, and cottonwood. Look for hanging gardens of maidenhair fern, columbine, and other water-loving plants in small alcoves high on the sandstone walls.

Most animals are secretive and nocturnal; you're most likely to see them in early morning or in the evening. Local mammals include pronghorn, mule deer, mountain lion, coyote, red and gray foxes, ringtail cat, spotted and striped skunks, bobcat, badger, river otter, beaver, prairie dog, Ord kangaroo rat, black-tailed jackrabbit, several species of squirrels and chipmunks, and many species of mice and bats. Lizards you might spot sunning on a rock include collared, side-blotched, desert horned, and chuckwalla. Snake species include common kingsnake, gopher, striped whipsnake, western rattlesnake, and western diamondback rattlesnake.

Birds stopping by on their migratory routes include American avocet, Canada goose, and teal. Others, such as blue heron, snowy egret, and bald eagle, come for the winter. Birds in residence all year are American merganser, mallard, canyon wren, piñon jay, common raven, red-tailed and Swainson's hawks, great horned and long-eared owls, peregrine and prairie falcons, and golden eagle.

## Recreation at Lake Powell

If you don't have your own craft, Wahweap and other marinas will rent you a boat for fishing, skiing, or houseboating. Boat tours visit Rainbow Bridge—the world's largest natural bridge—and other destinations from Wahweap, Bullfrog, and Halls Crossing Marinas. Sailboats find the steadiest breezes in Wahweap, Padre, Halls, and Bullfrog Bays, where spring winds average 15-20 knots. Kayaks and canoes can be used in the more protected areas. All boaters need to be alert for approaching storms that can bring wind gusts up to 60 mph. Waves on open expanses of the lake are sometimes steeper than ocean waves, exceeding six feet from trough to crest. Marinas and bookstores sell Lake Powell navigation maps.

You'll need an Arizona fishing license for the southern five miles of the lake and a Utah license for the rest of Lake Powell. Licenses and information can be obtained from marinas on the water or sporting goods stores in Page. Anglers catch largemouth, smallmouth, and striped bass; northern and walleye pike; catfish, crappie, and carp. Smaller fish include bluegill, perch, and sunfish. Wahweap has a swimming beach (no lifeguards), and boaters can find their own remote spots. Scuba divers slip underwater to swim with the sizable bass.

Hikers can choose between easy day-trips or long wilderness backpack treks. The canyons of the Escalante in Utah rate among America's premier hiking areas (see Moon's *Utah Handbook*). Other good hiking areas within or adjacent to Glen Canyon N.R.A. include Rainbow Bridge National Monument, Paria Canyon, Dark Canyon (see *Utah Handbook*), and Grand Gulch (see *Utah Handbook*). National Park Service staff at the Carl Hayden Visitor Center and the Bullfrog Visitor Center can suggest trips and supply trail descriptions. Several guidebooks to Lake Powell offer detailed hiking, camping, and boating information. Most of the canyon country near Lake Powell remains wild and little explored—hiking possibilities are limitless. As always, be sure to carry plenty of water.

skimming the waters of Lake Powell

ARIZONA OFFICE OF TOURISM

## GLEN CANYON DAM

Construction workers labored from 1956 to 1964 to build this giant concrete structure. It stands 710 feet high above bedrock, the top measuring 1,560 feet across. Thickness ranges from 300 feet at the base to just 25 feet at the top. As part of the Upper Colorado River Storage Project, the dam provides water storage (its main purpose), hydroelectricity, flood control, and recreation on Lake Powell. Eight giant turbine generators churn out a total of 1,150,000 kilowatts at 13,800 volts. Vertigo victims shouldn't look down when driving across Glen Canyon Bridge, just downstream of the dam; the cold, green waters of the Colorado River glide 700 feet below.

### Carl Hayden Visitor Center

Photos, paintings, movies, and slide presentations in the visitor center present various features of the Glen Canyon National Recreation Area, including Lake Powell and the construction of the dam. A giant relief map helps you visualize the rugged terrain surrounding the lake; look closely and you'll spot Rainbow Bridge. Guided tours inside the dam and generating room depart daily in summer. You can take a self-guided tour daily 7 a.m.-6 p.m. in summer, 8 a.m.-4 p.m. the rest of the year.

National Park Service staff operate an information desk where you can find out about boating, fishing, camping, and hiking in the immense Glen Canyon National Recreation Area, or you can write Box 1507, Page, AZ 86040; tel. 608-6404 or 608-3000 (emergencies only). The ranger staff also offers short talks on a variety of topics relevant to the Glenn Canyon area. The Glen Canyon Natural History Association sells a variety of books on the recreation area and its environs. A Navajo rug exhibit illustrates one of the many different weaving patterns used. An exhibit depicts prehistoric mammals roaming Glen Canyon during the Ice Age. Souvenirs, snacks, and postcards are available at a gift shop in the visitor center building.

The Carl Hayden Visitor Center is open daily 7 a.m.-7 p.m. in summer and 8 a.m.-5 p.m. the rest of the year. Tours, exhibits, and movies are free. In summer, you can attend a campfire program several nights a week at nearby Wahweap Campground amphitheater.

## MARINAS

The **National Park Service** provides public boat ramps and ranger offices at most of the marinas. Rangers know current boating and back-road conditions, primitive camping areas, and good places to explore. **Lake Powell Resorts & Marinas** operates marina services, boat rentals, boat tours, accommodations, RV parks, and restaurants; for information and reservations (strongly recommended in summer) write P.O. Box 56909, Phoenix, AZ 85079; or call (800) 528-6154 (602-278-8888 in greater Phoenix), fax 331-5258. To make reservations seven days or fewer in advance, contact each marina or resort directly. All the marinas stay open year-round; you can avoid crowds and peak prices by arriving in autumn, winter, or spring. Private or chartered aircraft can fly to Page Airport and airstrips near Bullfrog and Halls Crossing Marinas.

### Wahweap

The name means Bitter Water in the Ute Indian language. Wahweap Lodge and Marina, Lake Powell's largest, offers complete boaters' services and rentals, guided fishing trips, deluxe accommodations, an RV park, and fine dining. Wahweap lies seven miles northwest of Page, five miles beyond the visitor center.

**Wahweap Lodge** offers several types of rooms starting at $115.59 s, $147.41 d in summer (April 1 to October 31); $75.30 s, $97.57 d in winter (November 1 to March 31). Guests enjoy lake views, restaurants, and, in summer, live entertainment and dancing. Contact Lake Powell Resorts & Marinas for reservations at P.O. Box 56909, Phoenix, AZ 85079; tel. (800) 528-6154 (602-278-8888 in greater Phoenix), fax 331-5258. You can also reach Wahweap Lodge & Marina at Box 1597, Page, AZ 86040; tel. 645-2433.

**Lake Powell Motel** features less expensive rooms at nearby Wahweap Junction, four miles northwest of Glen Canyon Dam on US 89; $74.24 s, $85.37 d in summer; closed in winter. Call 645-2477 or contact Lake Powell Resorts & Marinas for reservations.

An **RV park** with coin showers and laundry costs $23.76 w/hookups ($16.37 in winter). **Wahweap Campground** is operated first-come, first-served by the concessionaire; the $8.50 sites have drinking water but no showers or hookups. Campers may use the pay showers and laundry at the RV park. The campground, RV park, and a picnic area are between Wahweap Lodge and Stateline.

Primitive camping—no water or fee—is available at **Lone Rock** in Utah, six miles northwest of Wahweap off US 89. Boaters may also camp along the lakeshore, but not within one mile of developed areas. A free picnic area and fish-cleaning station are just west of Wahweap Lodge. You'll find public boat ramps adjacent to the lodge and at Stateline, 1.3 miles northwest of the lodge. During summer (June 1 to September 30), you can obtain maps and brochures from the **Wahweap Ranger Station** near the picnic area; at other times see the staff at Carl Hayden Visitor Center.

The marina offers six **lake tours,** ranging from an hour-long paddle-wheel cruise around Wahweap Bay ($9.50 adults, $6.80 children) to an all-day trip to Rainbow Bridge, 50 miles away ($75.96 adults, $41.15 children). Half-day trips to Rainbow Bridge cost $58.78 adults, $32.70 children. **Boat rentals,** at Stateline, include a 16-foot skiff with 25-h.p. motor, $66 per day; an 18-foot powerboat with 120-h.p. motor, $195.80 per day; and three sizes of houseboats starting at $721.40 for three days. You can rent water toys, fishing gear, and waterskis, too. Rental and some tour rates drop as much as 40% in the off-season.

### Dangling Rope

This floating marina lies 42 miles uplake from Glen Canyon Dam. The only access is by boat. Services include a ranger station, store, minor boat repairs, gas dock, and sanitary pump-out station. A dangling rope left behind in a nearby canyon, perhaps by uranium prospectors, prompted the name. The Rainbow Bridge dock lies 10 miles farther uplake in Bridge Canyon, a tributary of Forbidding Canyon.

### San Juan

You can hand-launch boats at **Clay Hills Crossing** at the upper end of the San Juan Arm. An unpaved road that requires high clearance branches 11 miles southwest from UT 276 to the lake; don't attempt the road after rains. River-runners on the San Juan often take out here; no facilities provided. Access to the lake by boat is sometimes blocked at low water by a bar of sediment dropped by the San Juan River as it enters Lake Powell. At high water the bar is covered.

### Halls Crossing-Bullfrog Ferry

The *John Atlantic Burr* ferry can accommodate vehicles of all sizes and passengers for the short 20-minute crossing between these marinas. Halls Crossing and Bullfrog Marinas lie on opposite sides of Lake Powell about 95 lake miles from Glen Canyon Dam, roughly midway up the length of the lake. Sections of paved highway UT 276 connect each marina with UT 95. The ferry's daily schedule includes six roundtrips from May 15 to September 30, then four roundtrips the rest of the year; no reservations needed. You can pick up a schedule at either marina. Service is suspended for a brief time annually, usually in November, for maintenance; signs at the UT 276 turnoffs warn you when the ferry is closed.

### Halls Crossing

In 1880, Charles Hall built the ferry used by the Hole-in-the-Rock pioneers, who crossed the river to begin settling in southeast Utah. The approach roads were so bad, however, that in 1881 he moved the ferry 35 miles upstream to present-day Halls Crossing. Business remained slow, and Hall quit running the ferry in 1884.

Arriving at Halls Crossing by road, you first pass a small store offering **housekeeping units** ($125.06 d in summer, $75.04 d in winter), an **RV park** ($25 w/hookups in summer, $17.24 in winter), and gas pumps. The store may close in winter, but services are still available—ask at the trailer office next door. Coin-operated showers and laundry at the RV park are also open to the public. The separate campground just beyond and to the left offers sites with good views of the lake, drinking water, and restrooms for $8.50. A half mile farther down the main road are the boat ramp and **Halls Crossing Marina.** The marina features a larger store (groceries and fishing and boating supplies), tours to Rainbow Bridge, a boat rental office, a gas dock, slips, and storage. The ranger station is nearby, though rangers are usually out on patrol; look for ranger vehicles in the area if the office is closed.

Contact Lake Powell Resorts & Marinas for accommodations, boat rental, and tour reservations at P.O. Box 56909, Phoenix, AZ 85079; tel. (800) 528-6154 (602-278-8888 in greater Phoenix), fax 331-5258. The marina can also be reached at Hwy. 276, Lake Powell, UT 84533; tel. (801) 684-2261.

Stabilized Anasazi ruins at **Defiance House** in Forgotten Canyon make a good boating destination 12 miles uplake; a sign marks the beginning of the trail to the ruins.

## Bullfrog

Before the days of Lake Powell, Bullfrog Rapids offered boaters a fast and bumpy ride. Today, Bullfrog Marina rivals Wahweap in its extensive visitor facilities. When driving on the highway, you'll come first to the **visitor center,** on the right, open daily 8 a.m.-5 p.m. (may be closed in winter); tel. (801) 684-7400. The **clinic** is here too; it's open mid-May to mid-October 9:30 a.m.-6 p.m.; tel. (801) 684-2288. Next, you'll see a large **campground** on the left; the $8.50 sites include drinking water and restrooms. Continue on the main road to a junction, where a service station offers repairs and supplies. Continue straight at the junction for a picnic area and the boat ramp; turn right at the service station for Defiance House Lodge and Restaurant, Trailer Village, Bullfrog Painted Hills RV Park, and Bullfrog Marina.

**Defiance House Lodge** offers luxury accommodations and the **Anasazi Restaurant** (open daily for breakfast, lunch, and dinner). The front desk at the lodge also handles **housekeeping units** (trailers) and an **RV park,** both nearby with rates similar to those at Halls Crossing, and **tours** to Rainbow Bridge and Defiance House. Showers, laundry, convenience store, and post office are at **Trailer Village.** The RV park also has showers. Ask rangers for directions to primitive camping areas elsewhere along Bullfrog Bay.

All-day **Rainbow Bridge tours** usually leave daily from April 15 to October 31 and stop on request to pick up passengers at Halls Crossing Marina; call for dates in winter. Costs: $76.95 adults, $42.54 children. **Canyon Explorer tours**

spend 2.5 hours in nearby canyons during the same season; $23.74 adults, $16.40 children. **Bullfrog Resort & Marina** offers boat rentals, gas dock, slips, storage, and a store. Contact Lake Powell Resorts & Marinas for accommodations, boat rental, and tour reservations at P.O. Box 56909, Phoenix, AZ 85079; tel. (800) 528-6154 (602-278-8888 in greater Phoenix), fax 331-5258. Bullfrog Resort & Marina can also be reached at Box 4055-Bullfrog, Lake Powell, UT 84533; tel. (801) 684-3000.

## Hite

In 1883, Cass Hite came to Glen Canyon in search of gold. He found a few nuggets at a place later named Hite City, setting off a small gold rush. Cass and a few of his relatives operated a small store and post office, the only services available for many miles.

Travelers wishing to cross the Colorado River here faced the difficult task of swimming their animals across. Arthur Chaffin put through the first road and opened a ferry service in 1946. The Chaffin Ferry served uranium prospectors and adventurous motorists until the lake backed up to the spot in 1964. A steel bridge now spans the Colorado River far upstream; Cass Hite's store and the ferry site lie underwater about five miles downlake from Hite Marina.

The uppermost marina on Lake Powell, Hite lies 141 lake miles from Glen Canyon Dam. From here boats can continue uplake to the mouth of Dark Canyon in Cataract Canyon at low water or into Canyonlands National Park at high water. Hite tends to be quieter than the other marinas and is favored by anglers. The turnoff for the marina from UT 95 lies between Hanksville and Blanding. On the way in, you'll find a small **store** with gas pumps, **housekeeping units** (trailers, same rates as at Halls Crossing), and a primitive **campground** (no drinking water, free). Primitive camping is also available nearby off UT 95 at Dirty Devil, Farley Canyon, White Canyon, Blue Notch, and other locations. **Hite Marina,** at the end of the access road, features boat rentals (fishing, ski, and houseboat), slips, storage, gas dock, and a small store. Hikers can make arrangements with the marina for dropoffs and pickups at Dark Canyon. A **ranger station** (tel. 801-684-2457) is occasionally open.

Contact Lake Powell Resorts & Marinas for accommodations and boat rental reservations at P.O. Box 56909, Phoenix, AZ 85079; tel. (800) 528-6154 (602-278-8888 in greater Phoenix), fax 331-5258. Hite Marina can also be contacted at Box 501, Lake Powell, UT 84533; tel. (801) 684-2278.

# THE ARIZONA STRIP

Lonely and vast, the Arizona Strip lies north and west of the Colorado River. Phoenix and the rest of the state seem a world away, cut off by the Grand Canyon. The Arizona Strip's history and geography actually tie it more closely to Utah.

Some beautiful canyon and mountain country await the adventurous traveler. In addition to Grand Canyon National Park and Glen Canyon National Recreation Area, nine designated wilderness areas totaling nearly 400,000 acres protect some of the most scenic sections. Several tiny communities in the Arizona Strip offer food and accommodations; more extensive facilities lie just outside the region, in Page across the river and to the east, and at Kanab and St. George across the Utah border to the north. For most visitors, the new Navajo Bridge, near Lees Ferry, serves as the gateway to the Arizona Strip. Local information is available at the old Navajo Bridge, which is now used by pedestrians to view the river 470 feet below.

## LEES FERRY

The Colorado River cuts one gorge after another as it crosses the high plateaus of southern Utah and northern Arizona. Settlers and travelers found the river a dangerous and difficult barrier until well into this century. A break in the cliffs above Marble Canyon provided one of the few places where a road could be built to the water's edge. Until 1929, when Navajo Bridge finally spanned the canyon, vehicles and passengers had to cross by ferry. Zane Grey expressed his thoughts about this crossing, known as Lees Ferry, in *The Last of the Plainsmen* (1908):

*I saw the constricted rapids, where the Colorado took its plunge into the box-like head of the Grand Canyon of Arizona; and the deep, reverberating boom of the river, at flood height, was a fearful thing to hear. I could not repress a shudder at the thought of crossing above that rapid.*

The Dominguez-Escalante Expedition tried to cross at what's now known as Lees Ferry in 1776, but without success. The river proved too cold and wide to swim safely, and winds frustrated attempts to raft across. The Spaniards traveled 40 miles upriver into present-day Utah before finding a safe ford.

About 100 years later, Mormon leaders eyed the Lees Ferry crossing as the most convenient route for expanding Mormon settlements from Utah into Arizona. Jacob Hamblin led a failed rafting attempt in 1860; he returned four years later and this time made it safely across.

Although Hamblin was the first to recognize the value of this crossing, it now bears the name of John D. Lee. This colorful character gained notoriety in the 1857 Mountain Meadows Massacre. One account of this unfortunate chain of events relates that Paiute Indians, allied to the Mormons, attacked an unfriendly wagon train; Lee and fellow Mormons then joined in the fighting until all but the small children, too young to tell the story, lay dead.

When a federal investigation some years later uncovered Mormon complicity in the slaughter, the Mormon Church leaders, seeking to move Lee out of sight, asked him to venture to Arizona to start a regular ferry service on the Colorado River. This he did in 1872. One of Lee's wives remarked on seeing the isolated spot, "Oh, what a lonely dell," and thus Lonely Dell became the name of their ranch. Lee managed to succeed with the ferry service despite boat accidents and sometimes hostile Navajo, but eventually his past caught up with him. In 1877, authorities took Lee back to Mountain Meadows, where a firing squad and casket awaited.

Miners and farmers came to try their luck along the Colorado River and its tributaries. The

# ARIZONA STRIP WILDERNESS AREAS

ferry service continued too, though it suffered fatal accidents from time to time. The last run took place in June 1928, while the bridge went up six miles downstream. The ferry operator lost control in strong currents and the boat capsized; all three people aboard were lost. Fifty-five years of ferryboating had come to an end. Navajo Bridge opened in January 1929, an event hailed by the Flagstaff *Coconino Sun* as the "Biggest News in Southwest History."

Today, the Lees Ferry area and the canyon upstream are included in the Glen Canyon National Recreation Area. Grand Canyon National Park begins just downstream. Rangers of the National Park Service administer both areas.

## Lonely Dell Ranch and Lees Ferry
You can tour old buildings, trails, mining machinery, and a wrecked steamboat in these historic districts. A self-guided tour booklet, available on site, as well as at the Carl Hayden Visitor Center, identifies historic features and traces their backgrounds. A log cabin thought to have been built by Lee, root cellar, blacksmith shop, ranch house, orchards, and cemetery occupy Lonely Dell Ranch, a short distance up the Paria River. Historic buildings near the ferry crossings include Lees Ferry Fort, built in 1874 to protect settlers from possible Indian attack, but used as a trading post and residence. A small stone post office, in use 1913-23, and structures occupied by the American Placer Company and the U.S. Geological Survey are also nearby.

Charles Spencer, manager of the American Placer company, brought in sluicing machinery, an amalgamator, and drilling equipment. In 1910 his company tried mule trains to pack coal from Warm Creek Canyon, 15 miles upstream. When this didn't work, company financiers shipped a 92-foot-long steamboat, the *Charles H. Spencer,* in sections from San Francisco. The boat performed poorly, burning almost its entire load of coal in just one roundtrip, and was used only five times. The boiler, decking, and hull can still be seen at low water on the shore upstream from the Lee's Ferry historic buildings. Although Spencer's efforts to extract fine gold particles proved futile, he continued to prospect in the area as late as 1965 and made an unsuccessful attempt to develop a rhenium mine.

A paved road to Lees Ferry turns north from US 89A just west of Navajo Bridge. Follow the road in 5.1 miles and turn left 0.2 mile for Lonely Dell Ranch Historic District or continue 0.7 mile on the main road to its end for Lees Ferry Historic District.

## Spencer Trail
Energetic hikers climb this unmaintained trail for fine views of Marble Canyon from the rim

1,500 feet above the river. The ingeniously planned route switchbacks up sheer ledges above Lees Ferry. It's a moderately difficult hike to the top, three miles roundtrip; carry water. From Lees Ferry parking lot at the end of the road, follow the path through the historic district to the steamboat wreck, then take the unmaintained trail leading to the cliffs.

### Cathedral Wash Route

This 2.5-mile roundtrip hike follows a narrow canyon to Cathedral Rapid and back. Park at the second pullout, overlooking the wash, on the

*Marble Canyon*

road to Lees Ferry, 1.4 miles in from US 89A and three miles before the campground.

### Boating and Fishing

There's a fish-cleaning station and parking area on the left just before the launch areas. At road's end, a paved upriver launch site is used by boaters headed toward Glen Canyon Dam; Grand Canyon river-running groups use the unpaved downriver launch area. Powerboats can travel 14.5 miles up Glen Canyon almost to the dam. The Park Service recommends a boat at least 16 feet long with a minimum 25-h.p. motor; currents are swift. Boating below Lees Ferry is prohibited without a permit from Grand Canyon National Park. Rainbow trout flourish in the cold, clear waters released from Lake Powell through Glen Canyon Dam. Anglers should be able to identify and must return to the river any of the endangered native fish—the Colorado squawfish, bonytail chub, humpback chub, and razorback sucker.

### Campground

The $8 sites at Lees Ferry Campground have drinking water but no hookups or showers—showers are available next door to Marble Canyon Lodge. From US 89A, take Lees Ferry Rd. in 4.4 miles and turn left at the sign. The ranger station is just past the campground turnoff; obtain boating, fishing, and hiking information here (open irregular hours) or look for a ranger; tel. 355-2234. The National Park Service allows boat camping on the Colorado River above Lees Ferry only at the several developed campsites. These sites lack piped water but are free. Remember to purify river water before drinking and pack out what you pack in.

## MARBLE CANYON TO FREDONIA ON US 89A

### Marble Canyon Lodge

John Wesley Powell named the nearby section of Colorado River canyon for its smooth, marblelike appearance. The lodge, on US 89A at the turnoff for Lees Ferry, offers motel rooms and kitchenettes ($47.72 s, $58.33 d and up, less in winter), restaurant (American food for breakfast, lunch, and dinner daily), store (groceries, camping supplies, and Indian crafts), post office, laundromat, coin showers, gas station, and paved airstrip; tel. 355-2225 or (800) 726-1789.

### Lees Ferry Lodge
The lodge has motel rooms ($42.40 s, $47.70 d), a restaurant (American food for breakfast, lunch, and dinner daily), gift shop, and sporting goods store. Located on US 89A, three miles west of Marble Canyon and 38 miles east of Jacob Lake; tel. 355-2231.

### Cliff Dweller's Lodge
About 1890, white traders built an unusual trading post underneath a giant boulder. The old buildings are still visible along the highway beside modern Cliff Dweller's Lodge. The lodge offers rooms ($60.45 and $71.05 s or d, less in winter), a restaurant (American food for breakfast, lunch, and dinner), small store, and gas station. Located on US 89A, eight miles west of Marble Canyon and 33 miles east of Jacob Lake; tel. 355-2228.

### San Bartolome Historic Site
Markers tell the story of the Dominguez-Escalante Expedition, which camped near here in 1776. Returning from a failed attempt to reach Monterey, California, the group struggled to find a route through the rugged terrain to Santa Fe. The site is signed on the north side of US 89A about midway between Marble Canyon and Jacob Lake.

### Vermilion Cliffs
These sheer cliffs, a striking red, appear to burst into flames at sunset. The cliffs dominate the northern horizon for many miles; a hilltop pullout 11 miles east of Jacob Lake on US 89A offers the best view.

### Jacob Lake
High in the pine forests (elev. 7,925 feet), this tiny village is on US 89A at the AZ 67 turnoff

## DON'T LOOK DOWN

A new wider bridge for traffic has replaced the old Navajo Bridge across the Marble Canyon Gorge, and the old bridge has been left for pedestrians. You'll find parking at both ends of the bridge and interpretive signs and a visitor center on the west end. Pedestrians can enjoy a 909-foot walk 470 feet above the water. Do not throw anything off the bridge as even a small object can pick up lethal velocity from such a height and rafts full of people pass under the bridge.

for the Grand Canyon North Rim. The nearby lake honors Mormon missionary and explorer Jacob Hamblin.

**Jacob Lake Inn** offers basic motel rooms ($79.54 s or d and up), cabins (April to November only, $62.57 and up), restaurant (American food for breakfast, lunch, and dinner), grocery store, Indian crafts shop, and service station; open all year, tel. 643-7232. **Jacob Lake Forest Camp** has sites with drinking water but no hookups or showers; open mid-May to late October; $10 per night.

**Jacob Lake RV Park,** three quarters of a mile off AZ 67 just south of Jacob Lake, is open May 1 to October 15 (depending on weather) with tent spaces ($10) and RV sites ($20-22 w/hookups), but no showers; Jacob Lake, AZ 86022, tel. 643-7804. The Forest Service's **North Kaibab Visitor Center** is near Jacob Lake Inn; it is open daily about May 1 to October 1, offering new interpretive displays.

**Canyoneers** offers cross-country ski facilities in winter at Kaibab Lodge, 26 miles south of Jacob Lake off AZ 67. Kaibab Lodge has rustic accommodations and food year-round; Canyoneers provides SnowVan transportation in winter. Contact Canyoneers at Box 2997, Flagstaff, AZ 86003; tel. (800) 525-0924 for reservations out of state, 526-0924 for reservations in Arizona, 638-2383 for North Rim Winter Camp, or 638-2389 for Kaibab Lodge.

### Fredonia
Though just a tiny town (pop. 1,220), Fredonia is the largest community on the Arizona Strip. Mormon polygamists, seeking refuge from federal agents, settled here in 1885. They first called the place Hardscrabble but later chose Fredonia, perhaps a contraction of the words "freedom" and "doña" (Spanish for wife).

Five modest motels lie along Main St. (US 89A). **Crazy Jug Motel** is at 465 S. Main St. rates are $38 s, $49 d; tel. 643-7752. The **Blue Sage Motel and RV** is located at 330 S. Main

St.; $10.80 RV w/hookups, $32.40 s, $37.80 d; may close in winter; tel. 643-7125. The **Ship Rock Motel (National 9)** is across the highway at 337 S. Main St.; rates are $32.45 s, $34.60 d; may close in winter; tel. 643-7355. The **Grand Canyon Motel** at 175 S. Main St. charges $32.45 s, $37.75 d, extra for kitchenettes; tel. 643-7646. **Jackson House B&B** no longer supplies breakfast but does offer use of the kitchen; it's at 90 N. Main St.; rates are $32.43 and $37.83 s or d, $43.23-64.83 for three to eight persons; tel. 643-7702. **Wheel-Inn RV Park** offers spaces for RV's only at $8 no hookups, $12 w/hookups, no showers; register at the Sinclair station at the corner of Hwy. 389 and Hwy. 89A; tel. 643-7089. For a much larger selection of accommodations (including a hostel), restaurants, shopping, and recreation, the town of Kanab is a ten minute drive north.

For Mexican and American food, dine at **Nedra's Cafe,** 165 N. Main St., open daily for breakfast, lunch, and dinner but closes in winter; tel. 643-7591. **Traveler's Inn Restaurant** serves steak, seafood, and other fare three miles north of town Mon.-Sat. for dinner with reduced service in winter; tel. 643-7402.

The **public library** is at 118 N. Main Street. The **city park** offers picnic tables, playground, and outdoor pool; turn two blocks east on Hortt from N. Main. The **post office** is at 85 N. Main Street.

**Cowboy Aviation** will take you on a 40-minute flight over the scenic Kaibab Plateau at $79 each (minimum two people, reduced rates for three or more) and on an 85-minute flight over the Grand Canyon at $109 each (two person minimum, reduced rates for three or more); flights leave from the airport four miles north of town on Hwy. 89A; tel. (801) 644-2299. **Color Country Tours** offers three- to four-hour backcountry 4WD trips on (mostly) private land to see an Anasazi ceremonial cave and canyon, Jurassic dinosaur tracks, and both slot and maze canyons at $40 adults, $20 children age 10 and younger from 145 North 100 East; tel. 643-7509. **Hunt's Car and Jeep Rentals** can supply a motor vehicle suitable for on road or off road touring; their office is in Kanab but they can deliver the vehicle in Fredonia; tel. (801) 644-2370 or (520) 643-7029 (after hours).

Fredonia is building a welcome center at the north end of town at 800 N. Hwy. 89A to offer in-

*visiting Winsor Castle*

formation about the town, the Vermilion Cliffs (scenic) Highway, and a local scenic loop. To contact the welcome center call the town office at 643-7241; weekends, call 643-7207. Folks at the **North Kaibab Ranger District** office will tell you about hiking, Grand Canyon viewpoints, and the back roads of the national forest north of the Grand Canyon; a North Kaibab Forest map costs $3 (a new waterproof version is expected to go for $4). It's open weekdays 7 a.m.-5 p.m. and Saturday 8 a.m.-4 p.m. from mid-May to mid-October and Mon.-Fri. 7:30 a.m.-5 p.m. in winter; 430 S. Main St. (Box 248, Fredonia, AZ 86022); tel. 643-7395. This ranger district is developing North Rim Trail No. 10 for hiking and riding along the rim of Grand Canyon overlooking Tapeats Amphitheater. The 23-mile trail offers spectacular views of a part of the canyon seldom seen by visitors and with less restrictions than in the park. Though work on the trail began with flagging in 1981, the trail needs signing, brush clearing, treadwork, and waterbars before visitors will be directed to it. If you would like to use this trail, please consult rangers at the North Kaibab Ranger District before planning a hike.

# PIPE SPRING NATIONAL MONUMENT

Excellent exhibits in Winsor Castle, an early Mormon ranch southwest of Fredonia, provide a look into frontier life. The abundant spring water here first attracted prehistoric Basket Maker and Pueblo Indians, who settled nearby more than 1,000 years ago, then mysteriously departed. Nomadic Paiute Indians arrived more recently, and now live on the surrounding Kaibab-Paiute Indian Reservation. Mormons discovered the springs in 1858 and began ranching five years later. Navajo raiding parties occasionally stole some stock and were suspected of having killed two Mormon men who tried to pursue them. A treaty signed in 1870 between the Mormons and Navajo ended the raids and opened the land to development.

Mormon leader Brigham Young then decided to move the church's southern Utah cattle herd to Pipe Spring. A pair of two-story stone houses went up with walls connecting the ends to form a protected courtyard; workers added gun ports just in case, but the settlement was never attacked.

The structure became known as Winsor Castle—the ranch superintendent, Anson P. Winsor, possessed a regal bearing and was thought to be related to the English royal family. Winsor built up a sizable herd of cattle and horses and oversaw farming and the ranch dairy.

A telegraph office—the first in Arizona—opened in 1871, bringing Utah and the rest of the world closer together. Eventually, so many newlyweds passed through after marriage in the St. George Temple that the route became known as the Honeymoon Trail. In the 1880s, the Mormon Church came under increasing assault from the U.S. government, and, fearing the feds would soon seize church property, the church sold Winsor Castle to a non-Mormon.

President Harding proclaimed Pipe Spring a national monument in 1923 "as a memorial of Western pioneer life." Today, National Park Service staff keep the frontier spirit alive by maintaining the ranch much as it was in the 1870s. Activities such as gardening, weaving, spinning, quilt-making, cheese making, and butter churning still take place, albeit on a smaller scale. At times you can hear a real cowboy or a Paiute speaker tell of life on the Arizona Strip. You can take a short tour of Winsor Castle or explore the restored rooms and outbuildings on your own. A half-mile loop trail climbs the small ridge behind the ranch to a viewpoint; signs describe the history and geology of the area.

## Visitor Center

Historic exhibits are open daily 8 a.m.-4 p.m. year-round; $2 admission; tel. 643-7105. A short video introduces the monument. Produce from the garden is ofttimes given away. A gift shop offers regional books and Southwestern Indian arts and crafts. The snack bar menu includes such delicacies as cowboy beans and beef, similar to the food consumed here 100 years ago.

The Paiute tribe operates **Pipe Spring Casino** a quarter mile northeast of the monument. In addition to slot machines and video keno and poker there is an RV park at the south end of the casino building. Sites stay open all year; no showers; $3 tent or RV no hookups, $5 w/hookups; tel. (801) 559-6537. The nearest grocery stores, restaurants, and motels are in Fredonia.

Pipe Spring National Monument lies just off AZ 389, 14 miles southwest of Fredonia.

# PARIA CANYON-VERMILION CLIFFS WILDERNESS

The wild and twisting canyons of the Paria River (sometimes spelled Pareah) and its tributaries offer a memorable experience for experienced hikers. Silt-laden waters have sculpted the colorful canyon walls, revealing 200 million years of geologic history. You can enter the 2,000-foot-deep gorge of the Paria (Paiute for Muddy Water) in southern Utah, then hike 38 miles downstream to Lees Ferry in Arizona, where the Paria empties into the Colorado River. Besides the canyons, this 110,000-acre wilderness area protects colorful cliffs, giant natural amphitheaters, sandstone arches, and parts of the Paria Plateau. Wonderful swirling patterns in sandstone hills enthrall visitors on top of the plateau. The 1,000-foot-high, rosy-hued Vermilion Cliffs meet the mouth of Paria Canyon at Lees Ferry.

Ancient petroglyphs and campsites indicate that Pueblo Indians traveled the Paria more than 700 years ago. They hunted mule deer and bighorn sheep while using the broad, lower end of the canyon to grow corn, beans, and squash.

The Dominguez-Escalante Expedition stopped at the mouth of the Paria in 1776; they were the first white people to gaze upon the Paria River. After John Lee began his Colorado River ferry service in 1872, he and others farmed the lower Paria Canyon. Though prospectors came in search of gold, uranium, and other minerals, much of the Paria Canyon remained unexplored.

In the late 1960s, the Bureau of Land Management (BLM) organized a small expedition; its research led to protection of the canyon as a primitive area. The Arizona Wilderness Act in 1984 designated Paria Canyon a wilderness, together with parts of the Paria Plateau and Vermilion Cliffs.

Allow four to six days to hike Paria Canyon—there are many river crossings and you'll want to take side trips up some of the tributary canyons. The hike is considered moderately difficult. Hikers should have enough backpacking experience to be self-sufficient, as help may lie days away. Flash floods can race through the canyon, especially from July to September. Rangers close the Paria if they think danger exists. The upper end contains the more narrow passages, particularly between Miles 4.2 and 9.0. Rangers suggest all hikers obtain up-to-date weather information.

You must register at one of the four trailheads—White House, Buckskin, Wire Pass, or Lees Ferry. You should check to see if the planned trail permit system has been implemented. Weather forecasts and up to date information is available from BLM rangers at the Paria Information Station near the trailhead (open daily 8:30 a.m.-5 p.m. March to October and then intermittently the rest of the year) and from the Kanab Area Office, 318 N. 100 East in Kanab, Utah 84741, tel. (801) 644-2672 (open Mon.-Fri. 7:45 a.m.-4:30 p.m. year-round). The Paria

inside Paria Canyon

Information Station posts weather forecasts and offers drinking water.

All visitors need to take special care to minimize impact on this beautiful canyon. Check the BLM "Visitor Use Regulations" before you go. These include no campfires in the Paria and its tributaries, a pack-in/pack-out policy (including toilet paper), and latrine location of at least 100 feet away from river and campsites. Hiking parties may contain 10 people maximum.

The best times to travel along the Paria include mid-March to June, and late September to November. May, especially Memorial Day weekend, tends to be crowded. Winter hikers often complain of painfully cold feet. Wear shoes suitable for frequent wading; light fabric and leather boots or jungle boots work better than heavy leather hiking boots.

You can draw good drinking water from springs along the way—see the new BLM booklet *Hiker's Guide to Paria Canyon.* It's best not to use river water because of possible chemical pollution from farms and ranches upstream. Normally the river flows only ankle deep, but can rise to waist-deep levels in the spring or after rainy spells. During thunderstorms, the river can roar up to 20 feet deep in the Paria Narrows, so heed weather warnings. Quicksand, most prevalent after flooding, is more a nuisance than a danger—usually it's only knee deep. Still, many hikers carry a walking stick for probing the opaque waters before crossing.

### Wrather Canyon Arch

One of Arizona's largest natural arches lies about one mile up this side canyon. The massive structure has a 200-foot span. Veer right (southwest) at Mile 20.6 on the Paria hike. The mouth of Wrather Canyon and other points along the Paria are unsigned; you need to follow your map.

### Trailheads

The BLM Paria Information Station is in Utah, 30 miles northwest of Page on US 89 near Milepost 21, on the south side of the highway, just east of the Paria River. The actual trailhead lies two miles south on a dirt road near an old homestead site called White House Ruins. There is a parking area near the trailhead with pit toilets and picnic tables. When the canyon is open for hiking you may camp here, but when the two mile road to the trailhead is locked when the canyon is closed because of flood danger you must camp elsewhere. The exit trailhead is at Lonely Dell Ranch near Lees Ferry, 44 miles southwest of Page via US 89 and 89A.

### Shuttle Services

This hike requires a 150-mile roundtrip car shuttle. You can make arrangements for someone else to do it for you, using either your car (about $50-90), or theirs (about $100-150). Contact: Cathy Martinez (tel. 355-2295), Sharon Rogers (tel. 355-2254), Ken Berlin (tel. 355-2286), Richard Clark (tel. 355-2281), or Rona Levein (tel. 355-2262); all can be reached at Marble Canyon, AZ 86036. Rangers at the BLM Kanab Resource District can supply you with an up to date list of shuttle services.

### Buckskin Gulch

This amazing Paria tributary features convoluted walls hundreds of feet high, yet narrows to as little as four feet in width. In some places the walls block out so much light you'll think you're

walking in a cave. Be *very* careful to avoid times of flash floods. Hiking can be strenuous, with rough terrain, deep pools of water, and log and rock jams that sometimes require the use of ropes.

You can descend into Buckskin from two trailheads, Buckskin and Wire Pass, both approached by a dirt road not always passable by cars. The hike from Buckskin trailhead to the Paria River is 16.3 miles one-way and takes 12 or more hours. From Wire Pass trailhead it's 1.7 miles to Buckskin Gulch, then 11.8 miles to the Paria. You can climb out to a safe camping place on a hazardous (extremely hazardous if you're not an experienced climber) route about halfway down Buckskin Gulch. Carry enough water to last until the mouth of Buckskin Gulch.

## OTHER ARIZONA STRIP WILDERNESS AND SCENIC AREAS

Nine areas on the Arizona Strip have been designated as wilderness areas under the 1984 Arizona Wilderness Act. For hiking and access information to BLM and Forest Service land on the Arizona Strip and into Utah, contact the **Interagency Information Office,** 345 E. Riverside Dr., St. George, UT 84770; open Mon.-Fri. 7:45 a.m.-5 p.m. and weekends 9 a.m.-5 p.m. tel. (801) 628-4491.

The BLM **Kanab Resource Area** office takes care of the Paria Canyon-Vermilion Cliffs Wilderness at 318 N. 100 East, Kanab, UT 84741; open Mon.-Fri. 7:45 a.m.-4:30 p.m.; tel. (801) 644-2672.

The U.S. Forest Service manages Saddle Mountain Wilderness and part of Kanab Creek Wilderness area; the **North Kaibab Range District** office, at 430 S. Main St. in Fredonia (Box 248, Fredonia, AZ 86022), is open Mon.-Fri. 7 a.m.-5 p.m., tel. 643-7395. The BLM *Arizona Strip District* map details strip topography, roads, and land ownership. To obtain this map call the St. George Interagency Office, Kanab Resource Area Office, or the North Kaibab Ranger District; you can order the map through the mail ($6, plus $2 shipping). Some hikers may prefer the more detailed USGS 1:100,000 and 1:24,000-scale topo maps.

## Exploring the Arizona Strip

High-clearance, 4WD vehicles are recommended in most of this remote and rugged land. Drivers of other vehicles need to take extra care not to become stuck on steep or washed-out roads. All visitors must respect the remote location, lack of water, and absence of facilities here. Be sure to carry camping gear, extra food and water, tools, and a first-aid kit in case of breakdown. Distances can be great—make sure you have enough gas. Some roads shown on maps will be very difficult, hazardous, or completely closed; learn of current conditions from the BLM or Forest Service. Leave an itinerary with a reliable person in case you don't emerge on time. A small number of ranches run cattle on the strip; gates should be left as you found them.

## Saddle Mountain Wilderness

Much of this 40,600-acre wilderness covers the densely forested Kaibab Plateau. Mountain lion, bear, and mule deer roam the area. North Canyon Wash is noted for its pure strain of native Apache trout. Saddle Mountain (8,424 feet) is northeast of the Bright Angel Point area on the Grand Canyon's North Rim; you can see Saddle Mountain from the Point Imperial viewpoint. A network of trails provides access to hikers and horseback riders.

## Kanab Creek Wilderness

This is the largest canyon system on the Grand Canyon's North Rim. Headwaters lie 100 miles north on the Paunsaugunt Plateau in Utah. The wilderness area protects 77,100 acres along the Kanab and its tributaries. Springs in Kanab Canyon nourish large cottonwood trees and lush growths of desert willow, tamarisk, maidenhair fern, and grass. From Hack Canyon, a popular entry point, hikers can descend 21 miles down Kanab Creek to the Colorado River; allow three days for the one-way trip. You'll need a Grand Canyon backcountry permit to camp below the junction with Jumpup Canyon.

## Mount Trumbull Wilderness

This 7,900-acre wilderness includes the wooded slopes of Mt. Trumbull (8,028 feet), a large basalt capped meadow. Oak, piñon pine, and juniper woodlands cover the lower slopes. Higher and more protected areas support ponderosa pine and some aspen. Kaibab squirrels, introduced in the early 1970s, flourish in the forests.

A 2.7-mile trail leads most of the way to the summit; the last mile is cross-country. Mormon pioneers built a steam-powered sawmill near the trailhead in 1870 to supply support timbers for the St. George Temple. Water from Nixon Spring, higher on the slopes, once supplied the sawmill and is usually still available. You can reach the trailhead by dirt roads from Toroweap, Fredonia, Colorado City, or St. George; careful drivers can negotiate these roads in dry weather.

## Mount Logan Wilderness

Scenic features of this 14,600-acre volcanic region include Mt. Logan (7,866 feet), parts of the Uinkaret Mountains, and a large natural amphitheater known as Hell's Hole. Geology, forests, and wildlife are similar to those of Mt. Trumbull, a short distance to the northeast. A road approaches the east side of Mt. Logan; hikers can climb to the summit via abandoned roads and a cross-country route; the hike is about 0.5 mile one-way. Mount Logan and nearby Mt. Trumbull lie north of the Toroweap area of the Grand Canyon. John Wesley Powell named both peaks after U.S. senators.

## Whitmore Wash Road

Lava flows from Mt. Emma in the Uinkaret Mountains make it possible to drive a high-clearance, 4WD vehicle deep into the Grand Canyon though the route is very rough. A short trail at road's end leads down to the Colorado River. See "Whitmore Wash Trail" under "Visiting Grand Canyon National Park" for directions and hiking information.

## Whitmore Point

Spectacular views of the Grand Canyon, Parashant Canyon, Mt. Logan, and Uinkaret Mountains are available to those who ascend this 5,500-foot perch. Volcanoes and massive lava flows between here and the Toroweap area to the east can be seen clearly. There are plenty of good places to camp, with no permit needed.

From Mt. Trumbull Village, marked by a restored historic schoolhouse, head west, then south 22.2 miles. Some junctions feature signs,

*Kanab Creek*

but you'll need to refer to a map frequently. At 9.9 miles in, a jeep road to the right heads down Trail Canyon to Parashant Canyon, a good area for adventurous hikers. Continue straight (south) for Whitmore Point. As with most roads on the Arizona Strip, conditions get rougher as you move closer to the Grand Canyon; a high-clearance vehicle is necessary. Whitmore Point and other areas north of the western Grand Canyon are the responsi-bility of the Lake Mead National Recreation Area; the agency could improve its road maintenance and signing efforts, as you'll see.

### Mount Dellenbaugh

This small volcano atop the Shivwits Plateau offers a great panorama of the Arizona Strip. Vast forests of juniper and piñon and ponderosa pine spread across the plateau. A long line of cliffs marks the Grand Canyon to the south. Beyond rise the Hualapai Mountains near Kingman. You can see other mountain ranges in Arizona, Nevada, and Utah as well.

From Mt. Trumbull Village, go north 10.2 miles to Parashant Rd.—*not* the road into Parashant Canyon—and turn southwest 42 miles, following signs. From St. George, Utah, it's 46 miles to the junction, then 42 miles to Mt. Dellenbaugh. The last five miles can be negotiated only when dry; high-clearance vehicles recommended. The trailhead lies just past the BLM's Shivwits Ranger Station; follow an old jeep road, now closed to motor vehicles. The trail is an easy four miles roundtrip, climbing 900 feet to the 7,072-foot summit.

## Twin Point

The beautiful views here take in the lower Grand Canyon, Surprise Canyon, Burnt Canyon, and Sanup Plateau. Follow Parashant Rd. south 37 miles, keep straight where the road to Mt. Dellenbaugh turns left, and continue south another 14 miles. You'll pass Parashant Field Station on the left; it's another two miles beyond the Mt. Dellenbaugh turnoff. Ponderosa pine gives way to juniper and piñon pine as you near the point. Stay left at a fork three miles past the field station—the right fork goes one mile to an overlook of upper Burnt Canyon, perhaps named for the colorful yellow and red rock layers. The main road continues south 2.7 miles, then skirts the west rim, offering many fine views into Burnt Canyon. Just before the road ends, it forks left for Twin Point and right for a trailhead to Sanup Plateau. Ranchers run cattle down this trail for winter grazing. Twin Point offers plenty of places to camp; no permit needed. Maps indicate a road to Kelly Point, east of Twin Point, but road conditions have deteriorated to such an extent that the route is now nearly impassable.

## Grand Wash Cliffs Wilderness

Grand Wash Cliffs mark the southwest edge of the Colorado Plateau, forming a major landmark of the western Grand Canyon. The wilderness protects 36,300 acres along a 12-mile section of the cliffs in an extremely remote portion of Arizona. Desert bighorn sheep and raptors live in the high country; desert tortoises forage lower down. Hikers can use an abandoned mining

road, now closed to vehicles, along the base of the cliffs to explore rarely visited side canyons. An exceptionally scenic jeep road through Hidden Canyon crosses the Grand Wash Cliffs north of the wilderness.

To reach the eastern end of this drive, follow Parashant Rd. south 16.6 miles, then turn right at the sign for Hidden Canyon. Small canyon cliffs appear four miles on, then become higher and higher as the road winds downstream along the canyon floor, repeatedly crisscrossing the normally dry streambed. Juniper and piñon pine on the Shivwits Plateau in the upper canyon give way to Joshua trees in the desert country below.

After about 20 miles, you leave the canyons. Roads turn south for the west face of the Grand Wash Cliffs Wilderness and Grand Wash Bay of Lake Mead. Other roads continue north to the Virgin Mountains and Paiute Wilderness. Due to numerous sandy washes, a high-clearance, 4WD vehicle is required for Hidden Canyon and most other roads in the Grand Wash Cliffs area.

## Paiute Wilderness

This 84,700-acre wilderness is in the extreme northwest corner of Arizona, south of I-15 and the Virgin River. The jagged Virgin Mountains contain a wide variety of plant and animal life, from desert country at 2,400 feet to pine and fir forests atop Mt. Bangs, 8,012 feet high.

Several hiking trails wind through the rugged terrain. Sullivan Trail, a rough route, begins 1.5 miles downstream and across the Virgin River from Virgin River Campground, near I-15, 20 miles southwest of St. George. The trail climbs through Sullivan Canyon to Atkin Spring and on to the summit of Mt. Bangs, a strenuous 12-mile hike one-way. You can also reach Sullivan Trail via the Cougar Springs Trailhead just off the Black Rock Road (no. 1004) below Mt. Bangs. If the water is high at the crossing of the Virgin River, check the water depth carefully and turn back if the water is too high to cross safely.

## Beaver Dam Mountains Wilderness

This 19,600-acre wilderness includes alluvial plains and the rugged mountains of extreme northwestern Arizona and part of adjacent Utah. Desert bighorn sheep, desert tortoise, raptors, the endangered woundfin minnow, Joshua trees, and several rare plant species live here. No trails, but hikers enjoy traveling cross-country through the beautiful Joshua tree forest at the lower elevations. Cedar Pocket Rest Stop on I-15, 20 miles southwest of St. George, is a good starting point.

## Cottonwood Point Wilderness

The 6,500-acre wilderness contains multicolored 1,000-foot cliffs, jagged pinnacles, and wooded canyons. Springs and seeps in the main canyon east of Cottonwood Point support a world of greenery, an oasis surrounded by desert. The wilderness lies on the Utah border near Colorado City, west of Fredonia. Dirt roads from AZ 389 provide access.

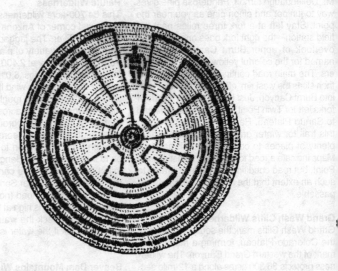

# NORTHEASTERN ARIZONA

This is Indian country, a place made special by the ancient cultural traditions of Native Americans—traditions that have survived to the present. The hardworking Hopi have lived here longest. Ruins, occupied by their ancestors as long ago as 1,500 years, lie scattered over much of northeastern Arizona and adjacent states. The once warlike and greatly feared Navajo came relatively late, perhaps 500-700 years ago. Today, Native Americans welcome visitors who respect tribal customs and laws. Here you'll have an opportunity to glimpse a unique way of life in a land of rare beauty.

## THE LAND

Multihued desert hills, broad mesas, soaring buttes, vast treeless plains, and massive mountains give an impression of boundless space. Northeastern Arizona sits atop the Colorado Plateau, ranging in elevation from 4,500 to 7,000 feet. Several pine-forested ranges rise above the desert near Arizona's borders with Utah and New Mexico. Navajo Mountain, just across the

border in Utah, ranks as the highest peak in the area at 10,388 feet. Nearby you'll find Rainbow Bridge, the world's highest natural stone span over water. You can reach the bridge by boat on Lake Powell or by a spectacular 26- to 28-mile roundtrip hike. The beautiful canyons in Navajo and Canyon de Chelly national monuments also offer excellent scenery and hiking.

## Climate

Expect warm to hot summers and moderate to cold winters. Spring to autumn is the ideal time to visit, though winds in March and April can kick up dust and sand. The rainy months are July through September. Storms usually pass quickly, but flash floods pose a danger in low-lying areas.

## HISTORY

### The Hopi

Legends and long-abandoned pueblos indicate Native American peoples lived here many hundreds of years. Old Oraibi, a Hopi village dat-

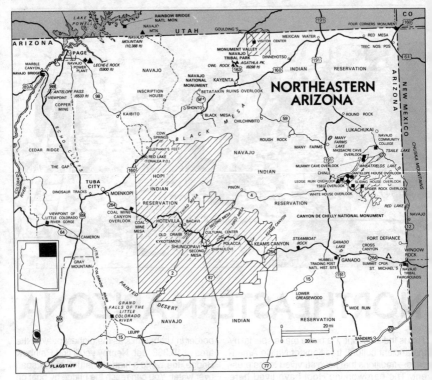

ing from at least A.D. 1150, is thought to be the oldest continuously inhabited settlement in the United States, and some Hopi identify even older village sites as the homes of their ancestors.

Spanish explorers began to arrive in the 1500s, looking for gold and treasure; they left empty-handed. Desiring to save Hopi souls, Spanish friars arrived about 1630 and had some success. But traditional Hopi leaders, fearing the loss of their own culture, joined with the New Mexico Pueblo Indians in a revolt against the Spanish in 1680. Hopi killed any foreigner unable to escape, massacred many of their own Christian followers, and tore down the mission buildings. During the 1800s, American frontierspeople arrived seeking mineral wealth and fertile lands, but they too usually met with disappointment. So the Hopi continued to farm in relative peace, raising crops of corn, squash, and beans.

## The Navajo
The seminomadic Navajo, relatives of the Athabaskans of western Canada, wandered into the area between A.D. 1300 and 1600. This adaptable tribe learned agriculture, weaving, pottery, and other skills from its Pueblo neighbors and became skilled horsemen and sheepherders with livestock obtained from the Spanish.

The Navajo habit of raiding neighboring tribes —this time, white people—almost caused the tribe's downfall. In 1863-64 the U.S. Army rounded up all the Navajo it could find, forcing the survivors to make "The Long Walk" from Fort Defiance in eastern Arizona to a bleak camp at Fort Sumner in eastern New Mexico. This attempt at forced domestication failed dismally, and the Navajo were released four years later to return to their homeland.

## Indian Reservations

In 1878 the federal government began ceding to the Navajo land that has since grown into a giant reservation spreading from northeast Arizona into adjacent New Mexico and Utah. The Navajo Nation, with more than 200,000 members, ranks as the largest Native American tribe in the country. In 1882 the federal government also recognized the Hopi's age-old land rights and began setting aside land for them. Approximately 10,000 Hopi live today on a reservation completely surrounded by Navajo land. Government officials have redrawn the reservation boundaries of the Navajo and Hopi many times, never to the satisfaction of all parties. In 1978, congressional and court decisions settled a major land dispute between the two tribes in favor of the Hopi. The victorious Hopi regained part of the territory previously designated for joint use but largely settled by Navajo. To the Hopi this was long-overdue justice, while the Navajo called it The Second Long Walk. The Navajo and Hopi Indian Relocation Commissioners are trying to negotiate a multimillion dollar resettlement of families in the respective reservations.

## INDIAN CULTURES

White people have always had difficulty understanding Arizona's Indians, perhaps because the Native American cultures here emphasize very different spiritual values. The Hopi and Navajo exist in accord with nature, not against it, adapting to the climate, plants, and animals of the land. Yet when visiting Native American villages, outsiders often see only the material side of the culture—the houses, livestock, dress, pottery, and other crafts. The visitor has to slow down and look deeper to gain even a small insight into Indian ways.

The Hopi and Navajo differ greatly in their backgrounds. The Hopi usually live in compact villages, even if this means a long commute to fields or jobs. The Navajo spread their houses and hogans across the countryside, often far from the nearest neighbor.

## Ceremonies

Religion forms a vital part of both Navajo and Hopi cultures. Most Navajo ceremonies deal with healing. If someone is sick, the family calls in a healer who uses sandpaintings, chants, and dancing to effect a cure. These events, often held late at night, aren't publicized. If you're driving at night and see large bonfires outside a house, it's likely there's a healing ceremony going on. Don't intrude on any ceremony unless invited.

The Hopi have an elaborate, almost year-round schedule of dances in their village plazas and kivas (ceremonial rooms). Some, such as those in the kivas, are closed to outsiders, but others are open to the public. Nearly all Hopi dances are prayers for rain and fertile crops. The elaborate and brilliant masks, the ankle bells, the drums and chanting—all invite the attention of the supernatural spirits (kachinas) who bring rain. Men perform these dances; while they're dancing, they are kachinas. At the end of the line of dancers, you might see boys who are learning the ritual; dance steps must be performed very precisely. When watching, remember that this is a religious service. Dress respectfully, keep clear of the performers, be quiet, and don't ask questions. Hopi ceremonies generally take place on the weekends; call or ask at the Hopi Cultural Center or the Hopi Tribe Office of the Chairman.

## Arts and Crafts

The strength of the Navajo and Hopi cultures is evident in their excellent arts and crafts. The best work commands high prices but can be fine mementos of a visit to the Native American lands. Trading posts and Indian crafts shops on and off the reservations offer large selections of goods. To learn what to look for in Indian art, drop in at the Heard Museum in Phoenix or the Museum of Northern Arizona in Flagstaff.

The Navajo have earned fame for silver jewelry and woven rugs. Sometimes at trading posts you can buy the colorful velveteen blouses and long, flowing skirts worn by Navajo women. The style was adopted during the Navajo's stay at Fort Sumner in the 1860s; it was what U.S. Army wives were then wearing.

The Hopi make basketry, silverwork, pottery, and exotic kachina dolls carved from cottonwood. Artists of both tribes create attractive paintings and prints with Indian motifs.

Be careful when shopping; wherever there are tourists, there may be tourist junk. Indians know what their crafts are worth, so bargaining is not normally an option—though there's no law against it either. Prices often come down at the end of the tourist season in September and October.

## Visiting the Reservation

Learning about Native American cultures on the reservation can reward visitors with new insights. It's easy to visit Indian lands; the tribes ask guests to follow only a few simple rules.

Hordes of eager photographers besieged Hopi villages from the late 1800s until early in this century, when the Hopi cried "No more!" And that's the way it is now—photography is generally forbidden in all Hopi villages. Even the sight of a camera will upset some tribal members. The Navajo are more easygoing about photos, but you should always ask first. Expect to pay a posing fee unless attending a public performance.

Reservation land, though held in trust by the government, is private property; obtain permission before leaving the roadways or designated recreational areas. Don't remove anything. A few feathers tied to a bush may make a tempting souvenir, but they're of great religious importance to the person who put them there. Normal good manners, respect, and observance of posted regulations will make your visit pleasurable for both you and your hosts.

# ON THE ROAD IN NORTHEASTERN ARIZONA

## Accommodations and Food

Because of the distances involved, visitors usually want to stay overnight on or near the reservation. Most towns have a motel or two that can quickly fill up in the tourist season; bookings are a good idea. Most campgrounds offer minimal or no facilities; only some have water. Few RV parks exist. Accommodations in towns outside the reservations—Flagstaff, Winslow, Holbrook, Page—are another possibility.

Indians enjoy American and Mexican dishes as well as the ever-present fast foods. Try the Navajo taco, a giant tortilla smothered with let-

tuce, ground beef, beans, tomatoes, chilies, and cheese. The Hopi Cultural Center restaurant on Second Mesa has many Indian specialties, but chances are the Hopi family at the next table will be munching on hamburgers. No alcohol is sold or permitted on the Navajo and Hopi reservations; you won't find much nightlife, either.

## Information

Not always easy to get. Motels and trading posts can be helpful; tribal police know regulations and road conditions. Try the museums run by the Navajo at Window Rock and Tsaile and by the Hopi on Second Mesa. Local newspapers report on politics, sports, and social events, but not religious ceremonies. The **Navajo Nation Tourism Department** office provides literature and information for visitors to the Navajo Indian Reservation; it's open Mon.-Fri. 8 a.m.-5 p.m. in the Economic Development Building, 2.5 miles west of Window Rock on AZ 264; Box 663, Window Rock, AZ 86515; tel. 871-6436 or (800) 806-2825, fax 871-7381.

Fishing and hunting on the Navajo Reservation require tribal permits from **Navajo Fish and Wildlife,** Box 1480, Window Rock, AZ 86515; tel. 871-6451/6452. Arizona Game and Fish has no jurisdiction; you need only tribal permits. For hiking and camping information and permits on Navajo lands, contact the **Navajo Parks and Recreation Department** at Box 9000, Window Rock, AZ 86515; tel. 871-6647/6635/6631. All photography with commercial intent must be cleared with the **Office of Broadcast** at Box 2310, Window Rock, AZ 86515.

The **Hopi Tribe Office of the Chairman** provides information for visitors to the Hopi Indian Reservation; the office is in Kykotsmovi, one mile south of AZ 264 in the Tribal Headquarters building; Box 123, Kykotsmovi, AZ 86039; tel. 734-2441, ext. 102. The **Hopi Cultural Center** on Second Mesa has a museum, motel, campground, and restaurant; Box 67, Second Mesa, AZ 86043; tel. 734-2401. People at either place can tell you about upcoming dances open to the public. The Hopi generally don't allow outsiders to hike, fish, or hunt.

## What Time is It?

This must be the question most frequently asked by reservation visitors. While most of the United States goes on daylight saving time from early April to late October, most of Arizona stays on mountain standard time. The big exception is the Navajo Reservation, which goes on daylight saving time to keep in step with its New Mexico and Utah territories. Keep in mind the time difference on Navajo land during daylight saving time or you'll always be one hour late. The Hopi, who rarely agree with the Navajo on anything, choose to stay on standard time.

### Getting Around
Your own transport is by far the most convenient, but tours of Indian country do leave from major centers (see the "Tours" descriptions in the Grand Canyon, Flagstaff, Phoenix, and Tucson sections).

**Navajo Transit System** (based in Fort Defiance, tel. 729-4002) offers bus service across the Navajo and Hopi reservations from Fort Defiance and Window Rock in the east to Tuba City in the west, Mon.-Fri. in each direction, $13.05 one-way. Stops on this route (east to west on AZ 264) are Window Rock (Basha's

parking lot), St. Michaels, Ganado Post Office, Burnside Thriftway Store (near junction of US 191), Standing Rock, Steamboat Trading Post, Toyei School, Keams Canyon Trading Post, Polacca Circle-M store, Second Mesa Trading Post, Hopi Cultural Center, Kykotsmovi turnoff, Hotevilla turnoff, Coal Mine Mesa, and Tuba City (Truck Stop Restaurant, Community Center, and PHS Hospital).

Navajo Transit System also heads north from Window Rock and Fort Defiance to Kayenta, Mon.-Fri., $11.85 one-way, with stops at Fort Defiance 7 Eleven Store, Window Rock (Basha's parking lot), Navajo (in New Mexico), Navajo Community College at Tsaile, Chinle (Baldwin's Market, Shopping Center, PHS Hospital), Many Farms, Rough Rock junction, Chilchinbito junction, and Kayenta (7 Eleven store and police station). Navajo Transit leaves Fort Defiance and Window Rock Mon.-Fri. for the New Mexico towns of Crownpoint and Gallup.

You'll often see Indian people hitchhiking, and you can too. Be prepared for long waits—traffic is light—and rides in the backs of pickups.

# WESTERN NAVAJO COUNTRY

## CAMERON

The **Cameron Trading Post,** built in 1916 beside the Little Colorado River, commemorates Ralph Cameron, Arizona's last territorial delegate before statehood. The trading post's strategic location near the Grand Canyon makes it a popular stopping point. Facilities include a motel ($69 s, $79 d, less in winter), RV park ($14 w/hookups, no tents, no showers), restaurant (open daily for breakfast, lunch, and dinner—try the Navajo taco), cafeteria, grocery store, Indian crafts shop and art gallery, post office, and service station. For information and reservations, contact Cameron Trading Post, Box 339, Cameron, AZ 86020; tel. 679-2231 or (800) 338-7385.

Cameron is on US 89, one mile north of the junction with AZ 64 and 54 miles north of Flagstaff.

### Vicinity of Cameron
The colorful hills of the **Painted Desert** lie to the north and east. To the west, the high, sheer walls of the **Little Colorado River Canyon** are an impressive sight, even with the Grand Canyon so near. Viewpoints are nine and 11 miles west on AZ 64, about halfway to Desert View in Grand Canyon National Park. You'll also have a chance to shop for Navajo jewelry at the many roadside stands in the Cameron area.

Drop in at the **Cameron Visitor Center,** at the US 89-AZ 64 junction, for information about the Navajo Reservation; you can buy hiking and camping permits for the reservation here, too; the center is open Mon.-Fri. and summer weekends 8 a.m.-5 p.m. **Navajo Arts & Craft Enterprise** sits next door, with a good selection of Indian crafts. **Grand Canyon Junction RV Park,** across US 89, is open all year, with a store, sites for tents ($8.50) and RVs ($14.50 w/hookups), and $1.50 showers; tel. 679-2281.

**Gray Mountain Trading Post,** 10 miles south of Cameron on US 89, features Gray Mountain Anasazi Inn, Whiting Bros. Motel, restaurant (open daily for breakfast, lunch, and dinner), Indian crafts shop, and grocery store. The **Anasazi Inn** has a pool and playground; rates run from $74.22 s or d; Box 29100, Gray Mountain, AZ 86016, tel. 679-2214.

## TUBA CITY

This administrative and trade center for the western Navajo has nothing to do with tubas and is not much of a city. The town (pop. 7,612, elev. 4,936 feet) commemorates Chief Tuba of the Hopi tribe. An oasis of green lawns and shade trees, Tuba City contrasts with the surrounding desert. The springs nearby attracted Mormons, who founded a settlement in 1877. They could not gain clear title to the land, however, and the U.S. Indian Agency took it over in 1903. Besides the U.S. government offices, the town has a hospital, schools, and a bank. Tuba City is near the junction of AZ 264 to the Hopi mesas and US 160 to Monument Valley.

### On the Road in Tuba City
**Greyhills Inn** provides the only inexpensive place to stay on the reservation; students of Greyhills High School operate the motel and youth hostel as part of a training program. Rates are $42.12 s, $47.52 d; people with hostel cards (American or international) can stay in shared rooms for $16.20. The bath is down the hall, there's a kitchen available, and credit cards are not accepted. It's open 24 hours. You can make reservations by phone or mail with the Hotel Management Program, Greyhills High School, Box 160, Tuba City, AZ 86045; tel. 283-6271, ext. 141/142. From the junction of US 160 and AZ 264, go northeast a half mile on US 160 to just past the pedestrian overpass, turn left 0.15 mile, turn right, then make the first left to the Inn's parking lot. **Tuba City Motel** sits in the center of town, one mile north of the highway junction. Rooms cost $102.65 s, $91.24 d, less in winter; tel. 283-4545.

**Pancho's Family Restaurant,** next to the Tuba City Motel, serves Mexican-American food at moderate prices; it's open daily for breakfast, lunch, and dinner. Buffets are available at all meals.

The unusual octagonal **Tuba City Trading Post** next door sells Indian crafts and offers groceries next door to that. **Kate's Cafe,** a half block east of the trading post, serves American and pasta dishes; it's open Sunday for breakfast and lunch, Mon.-Sat. for breakfast, lunch, and

*Navajo camp, early 20th century*

dinner. Several fast-food places and grocery stores line the road into town. **The Truck Stop Cafe** is on the highway at the turnoff for Tuba City. **Toh Nanees Dizi Shopping Center,** a half mile northeast on US 160, offers Village Inn Pizza, a supermarket, a movie theater, and other shops.

The motel and trading post may have information on Indian dances or events, both Navajo and Hopi. **Van Trading Co.,** west of town on US 160, sells Indian crafts, groceries, and most everything else. The **Western Navajo Fair,** held in October, features a rodeo, arts and crafts, dance performances, and other entertainment.

## VICINITY OF TUBA CITY

### Dinosaur Tracks

Distinct footprints are visible 5.5 miles west of Tuba City off US 160, about midway between Tuba City Junction and US 89. Look for a small sign on the north side of the highway between Mileposts 316 and 317. If that sign is down, find the Moenave turnoff. Some Navajo jewelry stalls will probably stand on site. Scientists think carnivorous biped reptiles about 10 feet tall made these tracks, now preserved in sandstone. **Elephant's Feet,** a pair of distinctive sandstone buttes, stands near Red Lake, 21 miles northeast of Tuba City on US 160.

# NORTHERN NAVAJO COUNTRY

## NAVAJO NATIONAL MONUMENT

Navajo National Monument preserves three spectacular prehistoric Indian cliff dwellings, last occupied about 700 years ago. The now-vanished Anasazi—a Navajo word for Alien Ancient Ones—who once lived here probably are ancestors of the present-day Hopi. Of the three sites, Betatakin is the most accessible; you can see it from a viewpoint near the visitor center. Rangers lead groups into Betatakin during spring, summer, and autumn.

**Keet Seel,** to the northeast, is the largest cliff dwelling in Arizona. It is approached by a 16-mile roundtrip hike or horseback ride. Inscription House, to the west, is the smallest of the three ruins, and is closed to the public. Inscription House Trading Post should not be confused with the ruins, which lie some distance away.

You can reach the monument's headquarters and visitor center by following US 160 northeast 52 miles from Tuba City—or southwest 22 miles from Kayenta—then turning north nine miles on AZ 564 at Black Mesa Junction.

### Visitor Center

The Anasazi left many questions behind when they abandoned this area. You can learn what is known about these people, and ponder the mysteries, on a tour of the visitor center. Exhibits of prehistoric pottery and other artifacts attempt to piece together what life was like for these early people. An excellent 25-minute movie on the Anasazi is shown hourly; a five-minute slide show is available on request. You can peek into an old-style Navajo forked-stick hogan and a sweathouse behind the center. Rangers answer questions and offer books and maps for sale. A gift shop offers Navajo crafts and Hopi, Navajo, and Zuni jewelry. The shop usually closes in the winter.

The visitor center is open daily 8 a.m.-6 p.m. in summer and 8 a.m.-5 p.m. in winter except Thanksgiving, Christmas, and New Year's Day. Contact monument personnel at HC 71, Box 3, Tonalea, AZ 86044-9704; tel. 672-2366.

### Sandal Trail

This easy trail begins behind the visitor center and winds through a piñon pine and juniper forest to Betatakin Point Overlook. The paved trail is one mile roundtrip and drops 160 feet to the overlook. Labels along the way identify native plants and describe how they were used by Native Americans. Bring binoculars or use the free telescope to see details of the ruins. **Aspen Forest Overlook Trail** branches off Sandal Trail, traveling about one-third of a mile and dropping 300 feet to a canyon viewpoint; the trail offers no ruin view or access.

### Visiting Betatakin

The Betatakin (Navajo for Ledge House) ruins lie tucked in a natural alcove on the far side of a canyon. The alcove measures 452 feet high, 370 feet across, and 135 feet deep. It contains 135 rooms and one kiva. Inhabitants built and abandoned the entire village within two generations, between A.D. 1250 and 1300.

You may visit the ruins only with park rangers, who lead one or two trips a day from May to September. Groups are limited to 25 people so sign on early. Starting from the visitor center, the five-mile roundtrip trail is well-graded but drops 700 feet, which you have to climb on the way back. After passing through an aspen grove on the canyon floor, the trail climbs a short distance to the ruins. Allow five to six hours for the hike and a look around the ancient dwellings. Trailhead elevation is 7,300 feet. Thin air can make the hike very tiring—people with heart or respiratory problems shouldn't attempt it.

### Visiting Keet Seel

This isolated cliff dwelling is one of the best preserved in the Southwest. Keet Seel (Navajo for Broken Pottery) features 160 rooms and four to six kivas. The site, eight miles away by trail from the visitor center, is open from the end of May to early September. A permit is required, and there's a limit of 20 people per day. Visitors must make reservations at least one day in advance, but not more than two months ahead, with Navajo National Monument, H.C. 71, Box 3, Tonalea, AZ 86044-9704; tel. 672-2366. Pick up your permit before 9 a.m. (daylight saving time) on the day of your hike or you'll lose your space.

The hike's first 1.5 miles run along the rim on a dirt road to Tsegi Point. There the trail descends 1,000 feet to the canyon bottom, travels downstream a short distance, then heads upstream into Keet Seel Canyon. You may have to do some wading. Carry water; the streams are polluted by livestock. The ruins look as though they were abandoned just a few years back, not seven long centuries ago. Visitors may not enter the site without a ranger, stationed nearby. Backpackers can stay in a primitive campground (free, one-night limit) near Keet Seel. You can rent horses for the trip from a local Navajo family for about $55 per person. Some riding ex-

perience is advised, and riders must be at least 12 years old. Make reservations through monument personnel.

### Accommodations and Food

A free **campground** with restrooms and water lies near the visitor center, open mid-May to mid-October. The rest of the year it's open, but there's no water. **Anasazi Inn** ($86.43 s, $97.14 d, less in winter) and its cafe (open daily for breakfast, lunch, and dinner—try the Navajo taco) lie 20 miles away on the road to Kayenta; tel. 697-3793. Kayenta, an additional nine miles, offers two motels and several restaurants.

**Black Mesa Shopping Center,** nine miles south of the monument at the junction of AZ 564 and US 160, offers the closest cafe, grocery store, and service station. The road south goes to the coal mines of the Peabody Coal Company, a major place of employment for the Navajo.

### Shonto

This Navajo settlement sits in a small canyon southwest of the monument. A trading post offers groceries and Navajo crafts. The shaded park in front is a good spot for a picnic. A chapter house and Bureau of Indian Affairs (BIA) boarding school lie nearby. Shonto is 10 miles from the monument on a sandy road not recommended for cars (except during the school year when it is kept graded), or 33 miles via US 160 on paved roads.

## RAINBOW BRIDGE NATIONAL MONUMENT

Rainbow Bridge forms a graceful span 290 feet high and 275 feet wide; the Capitol building in Washington, D.C., would fit neatly underneath. The easiest way to Rainbow Bridge is by boat tour on Lake Powell from Wahweap, Bullfrog, or Halls Crossing marinas.

The more adventurous can hike to the bridge from the Cha Canyon Trailhead (just north across the Arizona-Utah border on the east side of Navajo Mountain) or from the Rainbow Lodge ruins (just south of the Arizona-Utah border on the west side of Navajo Mountain). Rugged trails from each point wind through highly scenic canyons, meet in Bridge Canyon, then continue

*Rainbow Bridge*

two miles to the bridge. The hike on either trail, or a loop with both (car shuttle needed), is 26-28 miles roundtrip. Hikers must be experienced and self-sufficient; these trails cross wilderness. Because the trails are unmaintained and poorly marked, hikers should consult a Navajo Mountain (Utah) 15-minute topo map or the newer 7.5-minute Navajo Begay and Chaiyahi Flat maps.

No camping is allowed at Rainbow Bridge and no supplies are available. You may camp a half mile east of the bridge at Echo Camp. The Dangling Rope Marina and National Park Service ranger station are 10 miles away, by water only. The best times to go are April to early June, September, and October. Winter cold and snow discourage visitors, and summer is hot and brings hazardous flash floods. The National Park Service offers "Hiking to Rainbow Bridge" trail notes; Glen Canyon N.R.A., Box 1507, Page, AZ 86040; tel. 608-6404.

The National Park Service cannot issue hiking permits to Rainbow Bridge. Obtain the required tribal hiking permit ($5 one person, $10 group of 2-10, $20 group of 11 or more) and camping permit ($2 per person per night) from the Cameron Visitor Center (not always open) or Navajo Parks Department, Box 9000, Window Rock, AZ 86515; tel. 871-6635/6636/6647. Both offices are open Monday to Friday about 8 a.m.-5 p.m.; the Cameron office is also open weekends from April to September.

The only road access to the Navajo Mountain area is Indian Route 16 from AZ 98, between Page and Kayenta. To reach the east trailhead, drive north 32 miles on Indian Route 16 past Inscription House Trading Post to a road fork, and then turn right six miles to Navajo Mountain Trading Post. Continue on the main road 6.5 miles (go straight at the four-way junction) to an earthen dam. Drive straight across the dam, take the left fork after a half mile, and then go 1.6 miles to Cha Canyon Trailhead at the end of the road.

You can reach the west trailhead by driving north 32 miles on Indian Route 16 and turning left and driving about six miles at the road fork to the Rainbow Lodge ruins. Always lock vehicles and remove valuables at trailheads. Because Navajo Mountain is sacred to the Navajo, you need permission to climb from the Navajo Parks Department.

# KAYENTA

The "Gateway to Monument Valley" is Kayenta, a town of 5,200 in a bleak, windswept valley (elev. 5,660 feet). Its name is loosely derived from the Navajo word Teehindeeh, meaning "boghole," as there were once shallow lakes here. Kayenta, a handy stop for travelers, offers two good motels and several restaurants.

## Accommodations

**Wetherill Inn** lies in the center of town on US 163, one mile north of US 160. Its name honors John Wetherill, an early trader and rancher in the region who discovered Betatakin, Mesa Verde, and other major Anasazi sites. Rooms cost $78.48 s, $85.02 d in summer; tel. 697-3231. The **Holiday Inn,** on US 160 at the turnoff for Kayenta, features rooms ($117.72 s, $128.52 d in summer), restaurant, and pool; tel. 697-3221 or (800) HOLIDAY. The **Coin-Op Laundry** in town offers tent and RV spaces for $9.50 w/hookups; showers are also available for non-campers at $2.25; tel. 697-3738.

## Food

The Holiday Inn's **Wagon Wheel Restaurant** features good Navajo tacos and standard American fare; it's open daily for breakfast, lunch, and dinner. **Amigo Cafe** serves Mexican and American food; it's open daily for breakfast, lunch, and dinner. You'll find it on US 163 between the Kayenta turnoff and town. **Golden Sands Cafe,** near the Wetherill Inn, offers American food daily for breakfast, lunch, and dinner. For pizza, try **Pizza Edge,** next to the Teehindeeh Shopping Center. Nearby is the **Blue Coffee Pot Cafe,** which serves Mexican and American food weekdays; it's open for breakfast, lunch, and dinner. Buy groceries at the supermarket in the shopping center or at the Kayenta Supermarket behind the Wetherill Inn.

## Shopping and Services

Look for Indian crafts at both motels, **Lee's Trading Co.** (in the shopping center), and **Burch's Indian Room** (near Wetherill Inn). The **Navajo Nation Visitor Center** near the shopping center was built to offer Navajo arts and crafts for sale, to serve as a gallery, and to pro-

vide a location for dances and story telling; it's open Mon.-Fri. 10 a.m.-7 p.m.; tel. 697-3572.

Tours in 4WD vehicles to Monument Valley and the surrounding country can be arranged at the motels or at **Crawley's Monument Valley Tours** on Hwy. 160 just east of the Hwy. 163 junction; tel. 697-3463. Charges start at about $30 half day or $60 full day with minimums of four or six people.

# MONUMENT VALLEY

Towering buttes, jagged pinnacles, and rippled sand dunes make this an otherworldly landscape. Changing colors and shifting shadows add to the feeling of enchantment. Most of the natural monuments are remnants of sandstone eroded by wind and water. Agathla Peak and some lesser summits are roots of ancient volcanoes; the dark rock contrasts with the pale yellow sandstone of the other formations. The valley lies at an elevation of 5,564 feet in the Upper Sonoran Zone; annual rainfall averages about 8.5 inches.

In 1863-64, when Kit Carson was ravaging Canyon de Chelly, rounding up Navajo, Chief Hoskinini led his people to the safety and freedom of Monument Valley. Merrick Butte and Mitchell Mesa commemorate two miners who discovered rich silver deposits on their first trip to the valley in 1880. On their second trip both were killed, reportedly by Paiute Indians. Hollywood movies made the splendor of Monument Valley known to the outside world. Stagecoach, filmed here by John Ford in 1938, was the first in a long series of movies shot in the valley. Hollywood's fascination with the locale continues to this day; warriors from John Wayne to Susan Sarandon have ridden across these sands.

The Navajo have preserved the valley as a tribal park with a scenic drive, visitor center, and campground. From Kayenta, go 24 miles north on US 163 and turn right 3.5 miles.

## Visitor Center

The information desk, exhibits, and Indian crafts shop are open daily about 7 a.m.-8 p.m. from May to September, then daily 8 a.m.-5 p.m. the rest of the year; tel. (801) 727-3353. Visitors pay a $2.50 fee ($1 ages 60 and over, free ages six and under) collected on the entrance road.

## Monument Valley Drive

A 17-mile, self-guided scenic drive begins at the visitor center and loops through the heart of the valley. Overlooks provide sweeping vistas from several different vantage points. The dirt road is normally okay if you drive cautiously. Avoid stopping and becoming stuck in the loose sand that sometimes blows across the road. Allow one and a half hours for the drive, open 7 a.m.-7 p.m. in summer, 8 a.m.-5 p.m. the rest of the year. No hiking or driving are permitted off the signed route. Water and restrooms are available only at the visitor center.

## Valley Tours

Take one of the guided tours leaving daily year-round from the visitor center—visit hogans, cliff dwellings, and petroglyphs in areas beyond the self-guided drive. The trips last two and a half to three hours and cost $15 per person. Shorter trips of one and a half hours cost $12 per person. Guided horseback rides from near the visitor center run $20 for one and a half hours; longer day and overnight trips can be arranged too. Tours may be unavailable in winter. If you'd like to hike in Monument Valley, you must hire a guide; hiking tours of two hours to a day or more can be arranged at the visitor center.

## Accommodations

Sites at **Mitten View Campground** near the visitor center cost $10; hot showers are available at an extra charge. The season is early April to mid-October. Tent campers must often contend with pesky winds in this exposed location. Goulding's Lodge offers the nearest motel, restaurant, and store. You'll also find motels at Kayenta in Arizona and at Mexican Hat and Bluff in Utah.

## Goulding's Lodge and Trading Post

Harry Goulding and his wife, Mike, opened this trading post in 1924 two miles west of the US 163 Monument Valley turnoff, just north of the Arizona-Utah border. **Goulding's Museum,** in the old trading post building, displays prehistoric and modern Native American artifacts, movie photos, and Goulding family memorabilia. It's open daily, may close in winter; donation requested. Motel rooms start at $115 s or d in summer, less in the off-season. Guests can enjoy a small indoor pool. A gift shop sells souvenirs, books, and high-quality Indian crafts. The nearby store has groceries and gas pumps.

The lodge's Monument Valley tours operate year-round. Rates are $30 half day, $60 full day with a six-person minimum; children under 12 are charged $18 half day, $45 full day. The lodge stays open all year. For accommodation and tour info, write Box 360001, Monument Valley, UT 84536; tel. (801) 727-3231 or (800) 874-0902.

**Monument Valley Campground** offers tent and RV sites a short drive west; rates are $15.26 tent, $23.98 w/hookups. It's open March 15 to October 15; tel. (801) 727-3235 or (800) 874-0902. The Seventh-day Adventist Church runs a hospital and mission nearby.

# FOUR CORNERS MONUMENT

An inlaid concrete slab marks the place where Utah, Colorado, New Mexico, and Arizona meet. This is the only spot in the United States where you can put your finger on four states at once. It is said that more than 2,000 people a day stop at the marker in the summer. Average stay? Seven to 10 minutes. On the other hand, five national parks and 18 national monuments lie within a 150-mile radius of this point. Navajo, and occasionally Ute and Pueblo, set up dozens of craft and refreshment booths here in summer. Navajo Parks and Recreation collects $1.50 per visitor during the tourist season.

# EASTERN NAVAJO COUNTRY

## CANYON DE CHELLY NATIONAL MONUMENT

In Canyon de Chelly, you'll find prehistoric Anasazi cliff dwellings and traditional Navajo life preserved in spectacular canyons. The main canyons are 26-mile-long Canyon de Chelly (pronounced d'SHAY) and adjoining 35-mile-long Canyon del Muerto. Sheer sandstone walls rise up to 1,000 feet, giving the canyons a fortress-like appearance. Rim elevations range from 5,500 feet at the visitor center to 7,000 feet at the end of the scenic drives. Allow at least a full day to see some of the monument's 83,840 acres. April to October is the best time to visit. Winter brings cold weather and a chance of snow. Afternoon thunderstorms arrive almost daily in late summer. Thousands of waterfalls cascade over the rims when it rains, stopping when the skies clear.

### The First Peoples

Nomadic tribes roamed these canyons more than 2,000 years ago, collecting wild foods and hunting game. Little remains of these early visitors, who found welcome shelter from the elements in the natural rock overhangs of the canyons. The Anasazi (Alien Ancient Ones in the Navajo language), from their first appearance about A.D. 1, lived in caves during the winter and brush shelters in summer. By A.D. 500 they were cultivating permanent fields of corn, squash, and beans and were making pottery. They lived at that time in year-round pithouses, structures partly underground and roofed with sticks and mud.

Around A.D. 700 the population began to move into cliff houses of stone masonry constructed above ground. These pueblos (Spanish for "villages") also contained underground ceremonial rooms, known as kivas, used for social and religious purposes. Most of the cliff houses now visible in Canyon de Chelly date from A.D. 1100-1300, when an estimated 1,000 people occupied the many small villages. At the end of this period the Anasazi

mysteriously vanished from these canyons and from other large population centers. Archaeologists aren't sure why; possible causes may include floods, drought, overpopulation, soil erosion, and warfare.

It's likely some Anasazi moved to the Hopi mesas; Hopi religion, traditions, and farming practices are similar to those of the Ancient Ones. During the next 400 years, Hopi farmers sometimes used the canyons during the growing season, but returned to the mesas after each harvest.

### The Navajo Arrive

First entering Canyon de Chelly about A.D. 1700, the Navajo found it an ideal base for raiding nearby Indian and Spanish settlements. In 1805 the Spanish launched a punitive expedition; soldiers reported killing 115 Navajo, including 90 warriors. The Navajo identified the dead as mostly women, children, and old men. The site of the killing became known as Massacre Cave. During the Mexican era, raids were common in both directions; the Navajo sought food and livestock, while Mexicans kidnapped women and children to serve as slaves.

Contact with Americans also went badly—settlers encroached on Navajo land and soldiers proved deceitful. Conflict came to an end in the winter of 1863-64, when Colonel Kit Carson led detachments of the U.S. Cavalry into the canyons. The Army destroyed the tribe's livestock, fruit trees, and food stores and killed nearly every Indian it could find. The starving survivors had no choice but to surrender; they were then herded onto a desolate reservation in eastern New Mexico. In 1868, after four miserable years there, they were permitted to return to their beloved canyons.

Today, Navajo continue farming and grazing sheep on the canyon floors. You can see their distinctive round hogans next to the fields. More than 50 families live in the canyons, but most find it convenient to spend winters on the canyon rims, returning to their fields after the spring floods have subsided.

**Visitor Center**

Here exhibits reveal Indian history from the Archaic Period (before A.D. 1) to the present, with many displays of artifacts. You can achieve an intimate look at a Navajo hogan next to the visitor center. Rangers know about scheduled hikes, programs, and tours, and are happy to answer your questions. Books related to the region are available. It's open daily 8 a.m.-6 p.m. from May 1 to September 30, and daily 8 a.m.-5 p.m. the rest of the year; Box 588, Chinle, AZ 86503, tel. 674-5500/5501.

**Sights**

Canyons de Chelly and del Muerto each feature a paved scenic rim drive with viewpoints along the edges. Or you can travel inside the canyons by 4WD vehicle, horseback, or foot. With the exception of White House Ruin Trail, visitors must accompany an authorized Navajo guide or monument ranger when entering the canyons. This rule is definitely enforced. It protects the ruins and the privacy of families living in the canyons. All land belongs to the Navajo people; the National Park Service administers policies only within monument boundaries.

**Hiking**

**White House Ruin Trail** is the only hike possible without a guide. If you have a guide, you can hike almost anywhere. Rangers lead free half-day hikes in the lower canyon daily from late May to the end of September. The hiking pace is easy, but bring comfortable walking shoes, water, insect repellent, and hat. Some wading is usually necessary—in fact, you may insist on it. Under the hot summer sun, with red rocks all around, the cool water and shade of the trees are irresistible. Meet the ranger at the visitor center, and check departure time the day before—hikes leave promptly. Also, it's a good idea to make reservations the day before, as group size is limited.

The ranger at the visitor center can help make arrangements and issue the necessary permit. Guides charge $10 per hour for up to 15 people. Overnight trips are possible with additional charges (per group) of $10 per night for the guide and a minimum of $20 per night for the landowner.

*White House, Canyon de Chelly*

**Horseback Riding**

You'll find **Justin's Horse Rentals** near the entrance to South Rim Drive; look for the stables on the north side of the drive just past the Thunderbird Lodge/Cottonwood Campground turnoff. Rides, available all year, cost $8 per hour for each rider and $8 per hour for the guide (one per group); you can arrange trips of two hours to several days. Contact the company at Box 881, Chinle, AZ 86503; tel. 674-5678.

**Twin Trail Tours,** on the north rim of Canyon del Muerto, features two six-hour rides, each 12 miles roundtrip. Both descend into the canyon; one goes upstream to Big Cave and Mummy Cave, and the other wanders downstream to Standing Cow Ruin and Antelope House Ruin. Riders have to walk during the 700-foot descent. The starting point is 7.7 miles from the visitor center on North Rim Drive. Tours depart Mon.-Sat. at 9 a.m. from May 15 to October 15; cost is $70 per person. Two-hour, three-hour, group and overnight trips are available as well. Contact Twin Trail at Box 1706, Window Rock, AZ 86515; tel. 674-8425/5722.

You can also ride your own horse by arranging board and feed at one of the stables near the park and by hiring an authorized Navajo guide, preferably from one of the horse concessions. **Tohtsoni Ranch** offers three-hour guided horse rides down the Bat Trail in the Spider Rock area at $8/hour per person starting daily at 9 a.m.; the ranch is 1.6 miles of dirt road past the end of the South Rim Drive of Canyon de Chelly; tel. 755-6209.

### Canyon Driving Tours

Jeep tours of both canyons leave Thunderbird Lodge daily at 9 a.m. and 2 p.m. during the main season. From mid-November to early March, you should call ahead to make sure trips are scheduled; there's a minimum limit of eight passengers. The trips, very popular with visitors, occupy a half day ($32.71 adults, $24.66 children 12 and under) and a full day ($52.75 per person including lunch, summer only). You'll enjoy unobstructed views from the back of an open truck, stopping frequently for photography and to view ruins.

### Accommodations

**Thunderbird Lodge,** within the monument a half mile south of the visitor center, offers attractive landscaping with lawns and shade trees. It also features a cafeteria and large gift shop. The lodge began as a trading post for the Navajo in 1902; tourists later began arriving in sizable numbers and the lodge expanded to accommodate them. Rates from April 1 to November 15 start at $85.13 s, $89.67 d, less in winter. You can contact the lodge at Box 548, Chinle, AZ 86503; tel. 674-5841/5842. The free **Cottonwood Campground,** between the visitor center and Thunderbird Lodge, offers pleasant sites with many large cottonwood trees. It's open all year, with water available only from April to October; no showers or hookups. Reservations are accepted only for group sites. A primitive, privately owned campground has been built half a mile before the Spider Rock turnoff on the South Rim Drive, and plans were to improve the campground with full RV hookups.

Rangers present campfire programs from late May to the end of September. Cottonwoods shade a **picnic area** near the campground; water is available except in winter. Campers can usually take **showers** for $2.50 at the Chinle Chapter House, on the left 1.2 miles into Chinle from the visitor center; it's open Mon.-Fri. 8 a.m.-4 p.m.

**Holiday Inn,** at the Chinle entrance to the monument, has a pool and a restaurant; rates are $102.60 s or d; tel. 674-5000 or (800) HOLIDAY.

**Best Western Canyon de Chelly Motel,** in Chinle on Indian Route 7 about two miles west of

*jeep tours, Canyon de Chelly*

the visitor center, has a restaurant, indoor pool, and gift shop; rates April 1 to October 31 are $99.36 s, $103.68 d, less in winter. You can contact the motel at Box 295, Chinle, AZ 86503; tel. 674-5875/5288.

## Food

**Thunderbird Lodge** features a good cafeteria with low to moderate prices, open daily 6:30 a.m.-8:30 p.m. (shorter hours in winter). **Garcia's Restaurant** at Holiday Inn offers Mexican, American, and Native American cuisine daily for breakfast, lunch, and dinner. **Junction Restaurant** is open daily for breakfast, lunch, and dinner. **Tender Fried Chicken** and **Burger King** are near the **Tseyi Shopping Center,** on US 191 just north of the junction with Indian Route 7. The shopping center itself contains a supermarket, **Taco Bell,** post office, and other shops. **Church's Chicken** is several blocks east of the junction on Route 7.

## SOUTH RIM DRIVE OF CANYON DE CHELLY

All pullouts and turns are on the left. Distances include mileage between turnoffs and overlooks. Allow at least two hours for the drive. Parked vehicles should be locked and valuables removed.

**Mile 0: Visitor Center.** The nearby canyon walls stand only about 30 feet high where the Rio de Chelly enters Chinle Wash.

**Mile 2.0: Tunnel Canyon Overlook.** The canyon is about 275 feet deep here. Rangers often lead short hikes down the trail in this side canyon. Don't go hiking without a ranger or Navajo guide.

**Mile 2.3: Tsegi Overlook.** You'll see a Navajo hogan and farm below. Tsegi is the Navajo word for "rock canyon," which the Spanish pronounced "de chelle" (day SHAY-yay). American usage changed it to "de chelly" (d'SHAY).

**Mile 3.7: Junction Overlook.** Here Canyon del Muerto, across the valley, joins Canyon de Chelly. Canyon depth is about 400 feet. Look for two Anasazi cliff dwellings. First Ruin is located in the cliff at the far side of the canyon. The pueblo has 10 rooms and two kivas, and dates from the late 11th to late 13th centuries. Junction

Ruin lies straight across, where the two canyons join. It has 15 rooms and one kiva. These dwellings, like most others in the monument, were built facing south to catch the sun's warmth in winter.

**Mile 5.9: White House Overlook.** Canyon walls rise about 550 feet at this point. White House Ruin, on the far side, is one of the largest in the monument. The name comes from the original white plaster on the walls in the upper section. Parts of 60 rooms and four kivas remain in the upper and lower sections; there may have been 80 rooms before floodwaters carried away some of the lower ruin. As many as 12 Anasazi families may have lived in this village about A.D. 1060 to 1275.

From the overlook, **White House Ruin Trail** begins about 500 feet to the right. Many trails connect the rim with the canyon bottom, but few are as easy as this one. The Navajo call it Women's Trail—women often used it to move sheep. Allow two hours for the 2.5-mile roundtrip; bring water. This is the only hike in the canyon permitted without a guide; stay on the trail. You can buy a pamphlet describing the trail at the visitor center.

**Mile 12.0: Sliding House Overlook.** These ruins, perched on a narrow ledge across the canyon, are well named. The people who constructed the village on this sloping ledge tried to brace rooms with retaining walls. Natural depressions on the overlook collect water, and are still sometimes used by the Navajo.

**Mile 19.6: Face Rock Overlook.** Small cliff dwellings sit high on the rock face opposite the viewpoint. Though the rooms look impossible to reach, the Anasazi cleverly chipped hand and toeholds into the rock.

**Mile 20.6: Spider Rock Overlook.** South Rim Drive ends here, as rock walls plummet 1,000 feet from the rim to the canyon floor. Spider Rock, the highest of the twin spires, rises 800 feet from the bottom of Canyon de Chelly. Spider Woman, a Navajo deity, makes her home here. A darker side of her character, according to one legend, is her taste for naughty children. When Speaking Rock, the lower pinnacle, reports misbehaving children to Spider Woman, she catches and eats them. Look for the sun-bleached bones on top of her spire.

You can see tiny cliff dwellings in the canyon walls if you look hard enough. Monument Canyon comes in around to the right. Black Rock Butte (7,618 feet high), on the horizon, is either the weathered heart of an extinct volcano or a volcanic intrusion.

## NORTH RIM DRIVE OF CANYON DEL MUERTO

All turnoffs are on the right. Distances include mileage between turnoffs and overlooks. Allow at least two hours for the drive. Parked vehicles should be locked and valuables removed.

**Mile 0: Visitor Center.** Cross the nearby Rio de Chelly bridge and continue northeast on Indian Route 64.

**Mile 5.9: Ledge Ruin Overlook.** The ruin, set in an opening 100 feet above the canyon floor, dates from A.D. 1050 to 1275 and has 29 rooms, including two kivas in a two-story structure. Walk south a short way to another overlook; a solitary kiva is visible high in the cliff face. A hand- and toehold trail connects it with other rooms in a separate alcove to the west.

**Mile 10.0: Antelope House Overlook.** This large site had 91 rooms and a four-story building. The village layout is clear—from the overlook you gaze almost straight down on it. The round outlines are kivas. The square rooms were for living or storage. Floods have damaged some of the rooms, perhaps while the Anasazi still lived there. The site was abandoned about 1260. The site's name comes from paintings of antelope, some believed to be the work of a Navajo artist in the 1830s.

The Tomb of the Weaver sits across from Antelope House in a small alcove 50 feet above the canyon floor. Here, in the 1920s, archaeologists found the elaborate burial site of an old man. The well-preserved body had been wrapped in a blanket made from what appeared to be golden eagle feathers. A cotton blanket was enclosed; these were covered with cotton yarn topped with a spindle whorl.

Look for Navajo Fortress, the sandstone butte across the canyon, from a viewpoint a short walk east from Antelope House Overlook. When danger threatened, the Navajo climbed up the east side using log poles as ladders. They pulled in the uppermost logs and pelted attackers with a hail of rocks. Navajo used this natural fortress from the time of the Spanish until the Kit Carson campaign.

**Mile 18.7: Mummy Cave Overlook.** Archaeologists in the late 1800s named this large cliff dwelling for two mummies found in the talus slope below. Canyon del Muerto (Spanish for Canyon of the Dead) reportedly also took its name from this find. Mummy Cave Ruin sits within two separate overhangs several hundred feet above the canyon floor. The largest section is on the east (to the left), with 50 rooms and three kivas; the western cave contains 20 rooms. Between these sections is a ledge with seven rooms, including a three-story tower of unknown purpose. The tower dates from about A.D. 1284 and is thought to have been built by Anasazi from Mesa Verde in Colorado.

**Mile 20.6: Massacre Cave Overlook.** North Rim Drive ends here. In 1805, Antonio de Narbona led an expedition of Spanish soldiers and allied Indians to these canyons. A group of fleeing Navajo managed to scale the nearly 1,000 feet to this overhang. Narbona's troops, however, ascended the rim overlooking the cave and fired down. Narbona's account listed 115 Navajo killed and 33 taken captive.

From Yucca Cave Overlook nearby, you can see a cave with at least four rooms and a kiva. A small cave to the left was used for food storage; a hand- and toehold trail connected the two alcoves.

## VICINITY OF CANYON DE CHELLY NATIONAL MONUMENT

### Chinle
This small, spread-out town lies just west of Canyon de Chelly National Monument. The name Chinle is a Navajo word meaning Water Outlet—the Rio de Chelly emerges from its canyon here. A trading post opened in 1882, the first school in 1910, and the nearby monument headquarters in 1931. Chinle features a motel, several restaurants, a supermarket, shops, laundromat, and service stations. The post office is in Tseyi Shopping Center.

# NAVAJO COMMUNITY COLLEGE

## Navajo Community College
### (Tsaile Campus)

Recognizing the need for college education, the Navajo in 1957 established a scholarship fund, financed by royalties from oil. Most students had to leave the reservation to receive a college education, but the cultural gap between the Navajo and the outside world proved too great, and many students dropped out. So in 1969, the tribe created Navajo Community College. Students used temporary facilities at Many Farms, Arizona, until 1973, when campuses were completed at Tsaile and in Shiprock, New Mexico. Today a two-year program helps students prepare for university life off the reservation. They can also choose from many Navajo and Indian studies courses—crafts, language, politics, music, dance, herbology, holistic healing. The colleges offer vocational training and adult education too.

The unusual campus layout resulted from Navajo elders and healers working together with conventional architects. It was decided that because all important Navajo activities take place

within a circle, the campus grounds would be laid out in that shape. If you know your way around a hogan, you'll find it easy getting around campus: the library is tucked in where the medicine bundle is kept during a ceremony, the cooking area (dining hall) lies in the center, sleeping (dormitories) is centered in the west, the teaching area (classrooms) occupies the south, and the recreation area (student union and gym) is in the north. The central campus entrance, marked by the glass-walled Ned A. Hatathli Center, faces east to the rising sun.

The **Hatathli Museum** claims to be the "first *true* Indian museum." Managed entirely by Indians, the collection occupies the third and fourth floors of the hogan-shaped Hatathli Center. Exhibits interpret the cultures of prehistoric peoples as well as Navajo and other modern tribes. The museum and adjacent sales gallery are open Mon.-Fri. 8:30 a.m.-4:30 p.m.; tel. 724-6650. A donation is requested. Ned Hatathli was the first Navajo manager of the tribal Arts and Crafts guild, and a member of the Tribal Council.

**Navajo Community College Press** publishes and sells books on the Navajo and related topics on the first floor of the Hatathli Center; it's open Mon.-Fri. 8 a.m.-5 p.m. The college library and dining hall are also open to visitors. The Tsaile campus lies 23 miles east of the Canyon de Chelly Visitor Center and 54 miles north of Window Rock.

### Wheatfields Lake

This large mountain lake lies in a ponderosa forest east of Canyon de Chelly National Monument. Visitors enjoy camping and trout fishing at this pretty spot. You'll need Navajo fishing and boat permits, as on all tribal waters. Campground charges run $2 per person for ages six and over. **Lakeside Store** (when open) sells groceries, fishing supplies, and permits. Wheatfields Lake is 10 miles south of Tsaile and 44 miles north of Window Rock on Indian Route 12.

## WINDOW ROCK

In the early 1930s, "The Rock With a Hole in It" so impressed Commissioner of Indian Affairs John Collier that he chose the site for a Navajo administration center. An octagonal Navajo Council House went up, and Window Rock became the capital of the Navajo Nation. The structure represents a great ceremonial hogan; murals on interior walls depict Navajo history. Tribal Council delegates meet here to decide on reservation policies and regulations.

Window Rock is a small (area pop. about 8,000) but growing town at an elevation of 6,750 feet. Besides the Council Chambers and offices, the town contains a museum, small zoo, two parks, a motel, and a shopping center. Window Rock's downtown is the shopping center at the junction of AZ 264 and Indian Route 12. Get ready for a traffic light at the corner, a rarity in Navajoland. Window Rock hosts the world's largest American Indian fair, held on the first weekend in September. The five-day festival offers a mixture of traditional and modern attractions, including singing and dancing, a parade, agricultural shows, food, crafts, concerts, rodeo, and the crowning of Miss Navajo. Write for a free brochure from the Navajo Nation Fair Office, Drawer U, Window Rock, AZ 86515; tel. 871-6478/6282.

*Window Rock*

### Navajo Nation Museum

Exhibits introduce you to the land and early cultures of the region, and then summarize the history of the Navajo people. Examples of Navajo weaving and silversmithing show the development of varied, distinctive styles. The museum features a good selection of Navajo and regional books for sale. A large arts and crafts shop in the same building sells Navajo paintings, rugs, jewelry, jewelry-making supplies, and crafts by other Southwest tribes. It's open Mon.-Fri. 8 a.m.-5 p.m. and also Saturday 8 a.m.-5 p.m. from early June to late September; tel. 871-6673. It's on AZ 264 on the west side of the Navajo Nation Inn; admission is free. The museum and library will eventually move to a new building one block east of the Navajo Nation Inn.

### Navajo Nation Zoological and Botanical Park

Set beneath towering sandstone pinnacles known as The Haystacks, the zoo offers a close look at animals of the Southwest. Once past the rattlesnakes near the entrance, you'll wander by golden eagles, hawks, elk, wolves, bobcats, mountain lions, coyotes, black bears, and other creatures. Domestic breeds include the Navajo Churro sheep, an animal with double fleece and often four horns introduced to the Southwest by the Spanish. Prairie dogs, free of restricting cages, run almost everywhere. Native crops grow near the forked-stick and crib-log hogans in summer. Visit daily 8 a.m.-5 p.m.; free; tel. 871-6573/6574. It's north of AZ 264 a half mile east of Window Rock Shopping Center.

### Tse Bonito Tribal Park

This open area northeast of the new museum and library building includes a couple of shaded picnic tables, but no water. A spring, now dry, gave the place its Navajo name, meaning Water Between the Rocks. The Navajo camped here in 1864 on the Long Walk to eastern New Mexico.

### Window Rock Tribal Park

This is a beautiful spot shaded by juniper trees at the foot of Window Rock. The "window" is a great hole, averaging 47 feet across, in a sandstone ridge. Loose stones just below the hole mark the site of a prehistoric Indian pueblo. You're not allowed to climb up to the hole, though a trail around to the left passes through wonderfully sculptured hills. The park has picnic tables, water, and restrooms; day-use only. The park is being re-landscaped and a monument to veterans will be added. Turn east off Indian Route 12 about a half mile north of AZ 264, then head a half mile in, passing the Council Chambers on your left just before the park.

### Accommodations and Campgrounds

**Navajo Nation Inn** has a dining room and swimming pool. Rooms cost $61.56 s or d; Box 2340, Window Rock, AZ 86515; tel. 871-4108 or (800) 662-6189. The inn is on AZ 264, just east of the shopping center. Window Rock lacks RV parks or developed campgrounds, but there's plenty of room in **Tse Bonito Tribal Park,** mentioned earlier; a $2-per-person camping fee is sometimes collected.

### Food

The **Navajo Nation Inn** dining room is open daily for breakfast, lunch, and dinner. **Window Rock Shopping Center,** at the highway inter-

section, offers **King of China Restaurant. Basha's,** just west on AZ 264, has a supermarket and deli; **McDonald's** and **Church's Chicken** lie nearby. A trio of fast-food places, **Kentucky Fried Chicken, Blakes,** and **Dunkin' Donuts,** are east one mile across into New Mexico. **Tuller Cafe,** 2.4 miles west in St. Michaels, is open Mon.-Sat. for breakfast, lunch, and dinner, Mon.-Fri. in winter.

### Services

Visit the **Window Rock Shopping Center** for the post office, bank, auto repairs, movie theater, and other stores. **Two Story Trading Post** is an old-style establishment several miles west on AZ 264.

### Information

The **Navajo Nation Tourism Department** office has literature and information for visitors to the Navajo Indian Reservation; it's open Mon.-Fri. 8 a.m.-5 p.m. in the Economic Development Bldg., 2.5 miles west of Window Rock on AZ 264; Box 663, Window Rock, AZ 86515; tel. 871-6436, fax 871-7381. Fishing and hunting on the Navajo Indian Reservation require tribal permits from **Navajo Fish and Wildlife,** behind the Motor Pool; Box 1480, Window Rock, AZ 86515; tel. 871-6451/6452. Arizona Game and Fish has no jurisdiction over the reservation; you need only tribal permits. For hiking and camping information and permits on Navajo lands, contact the **Navajo Parks and Recreation Department,** next door to the Zoological and Botanical Park; Box 9000, Window Rock, AZ 86515; tel. 871-6647/6635/6636.

### Transport

**Navajo Transit System** connects Window Rock with many communities on the Navajo and Hopi reservations; see "Getting Around" at the beginning of this chapter."

## VICINITY OF WINDOW ROCK

### Fort Defiance

Permanent springs in a nearby canyon attracted the Navajo, who named the area Tsehotsoi, "Meadow between the Rocks". Colonel Edwin Vose Sumner had another name in mind in September 1851, when, in defiance of the Navajo, he established a fort on an overlooking hillside. Though the Navajo nearly overran Fort Defiance in 1860, the Army successfully repelled a series of attacks. The fort was abandoned during the Civil War. In 1863-64, Colonel Kit Carson headquartered at the fort while killing, rounding up, and moving the Navajo. After the Navajo returned, destitute, in 1868, the first Navajo Agency offices issued them sheep and supplies here. The first school on the reservation opened in 1869, the first regular medical service arrived in 1880. The old fort is gone now, but the town remains an administrative center with a hospital, schools, and Bureau of Indian Affairs offices.

### Navajo, New Mexico

Trees from the extensive woodlands that surround the town of Navajo supply the town's large sawmill. **Navajo Pine Shopping Center** includes a supermarket, general store, and laundromat. Nearby **Red Lake,** named for the color of its aquatic vegetation, has fishing and primitive camping ($2 per person ages six and over). Navajo is 17 miles north of Window Rock on Route 12, on the way to Wheatfields Lake, Tsaile, and Canyon de Chelly. This scenic, high-country road crosses pastures and forests in the foothills of the Chuska Mountains.

### St. Michael's Mission

In 1898, Franciscan friars opened a mission to serve the Navajo. The large stone church dates from 1937, when it replaced an earlier adobe structure. St. Michael's School, opened by the Sisters of the Blessed Sacrament in 1902, lies a short distance away. A small historical museum occupies the original mission building. Step inside to see displays of Indian culture and information on the life of the early missionaries. The museum sells regional books, cards, and posters; admission is free. It's open daily 9 a.m.-5 p.m. from Memorial Day to Labor Day; other times by appointment; tel. 871-4171. St. Michael's Mission is 2.9 miles west of Window Rock Shopping Center on AZ 264, then 0.2 mile south at the sign.

### Summit Campground

Escape the summer heat by picnicking or camping among the cool ponderosa pines. Head nine miles west of Window Rock on AZ 264 (19 miles east of Ganado) to where the road climbs over a 7,750-foot pass. The turnoffs, on both sides of the highway, are signed Rest Area. Picnic tables are provided but there's no water; a camping charge of $2 per person ages six and over may be collected.

## GANADO

The Spanish called this place Pueblo Colorado ("Colored House") after a nearby Anasazi ruin. The name later changed to Ganado, honoring one of the great Navajo chiefs, Ganado Mucho, or Big Water Clansman, a signer of the treaty of June 1868 that returned the Navajo lands. A Presbyterian mission founded here in 1901 provided the Navajo with a school and hospital. The school, now converted into a hospital, grew into the two-year College of Ganado, where students learned forestry, business administration, and general subjects.

Visit the nearby Hubbell Trading Post, Arizona's most famous such post, to experience a genuine part of the Old West. Ganado is on AZ 264, 30 miles west of Window Rock, 44 miles east of Keams Canyon, and 36 miles south of Chinle. There are no accommodations in the area, but you can find American and Mexican food at **Ramon's Restaurant,** open daily except Sunday for breakfast, lunch, and dinner; turn north one block on the street opposite the junction of AZ 264 and US 191. The **Sage Cafe** offers bargain-priced meals on the old college campus. It's open Mon.-Fri. for breakfast, lunch, and dinner; turn north into the hospital and follow the signs. The last sign will seem to require one last turn but actually points at the cafe which is a two-story building at the north end of an open park; the playground is next to the cafe. You can also have lunch at the **Ganado Chapter House** on weekdays.

## HUBBELL TRADING POST NATIONAL HISTORIC SITE

John Lorenzo Hubbell began trading in 1876, a difficult time for the Navajo, who were still recovering from their traumatic internment at Fort Sumner. Born in New Mexico, Hubbell had already learned some Navajo culture and language by the time he set up shop. Money rarely exchanged hands during a transaction; an Indian would bring in blankets or jewelry and receive credit. S/he would then point out desired items: coffee, flour, sugar, cloth, harnesses. If after buying the desired items the Indian still enjoyed unspent credit, s/he usually preferred silver or turquoise to money. Tribespeople bringing wool or sheep to the trading post usually received cash, however.

Hubbell distinguished himself by his honesty and appreciation of the Navajo. His insistence on excellence in weaving and silverwork led to better prices for Indian craftspeople. The trading post helped bridge the Anglo and Indian cultures: Navajo often called on Hubbell to explain government programs and to write letters to officials explaining Indian concerns.

### Visitor Center, Hubbell's House, and Trading Post

National Park Service exhibits and programs explain not only Hubbell's work, but how trading posts once linked the Navajo with the outside world. Weavers (usually women) and silversmiths (usually men) often demonstrate their skills in the visitor center. Books about Indian art and culture are available. You can take a scheduled guided tour of Hubbell's house or a self-guided tour of the grounds; both are free. The house contains superb rugs, paintings, baskets, and other crafts collected by Hubbell before his death in 1930, and by the Hubbell family thereafter.

The trading post still operates much as it always has. You can buy high-quality crafts or

*weaving Navajo, Hubbell Trading Post*

most anything else. Canned and yard goods jam the shelves, glass cases display pocket knives and other small items, horse collars and harnesses still hang from the ceiling, and Navajo still drop in with items for trade. A tree-shaded picnic area is next to the visitor center. It's open daily 8 a.m.-6 p.m. from June to September, 8 a.m.-5 p.m. the rest of the year, and closed Thanksgiving, Christmas, and New Year's Day. It's one mile west of Ganado.

# HOPI COUNTRY

For centuries the Hopi people have made their homes in villages atop three narrow mesas, fingerlike extensions running south from Black Mesa. Early European visitors dubbed these extensions First Mesa, Second Mesa, and Third Mesa. Arizona 264 skirts First Mesa and crosses over Second and Third mesas on the way from Window Rock to Tuba City.

The mesas have provided the Hopi with water from reliable springs as well as protection from enemies, the 600-foot cliffs discouraging assailants. Hardworking farmers, the Hopi are usually peaceable and independent. They keep in close touch with nature and have developed a rich ceremonial life, seeking to maintain balance and harmony with their surroundings and one another. Villages remain largely autonomous even today. The Hopi Tribal Council, which the federal government forced upon the Hopi, serves mainly as a liaison between villages and agencies of the federal and state governments.

### Visiting Hopi Villages

The Hopi tend to be very private people, though they do welcome visitors to their lands. Policies vary from village to village, and are often posted.

All villages prohibit such disturbing activities as photography, sketching, and recording. To give residents their privacy, try to visit only between 8 a.m. and 5 p.m. Walpi, Shipaulovi, and other villages may ask that visitors enter only with an authorized Hopi guide.

The best time to visit a village is during a ceremony open to the public. Recently, some ceremonies have been placed off limits because of lack of respect from visitors. Please remember these are religious ceremonies and you are a guest. Check with each village to make sure that visitors are welcome. If so, inhabitants will expect visitors and you'll be allowed to experience Hopi culture. Dances take place in plazas in one or more villages on many weekends; a good source for information is the Hopi Tribe Office of the Chairman, tel. 734-2441, ext. 102. Also try Second Mesa Cultural Center, tel. 734-2401/2421.

## KEAMS CANYON

This, the easternmost community on the Hopi Reservation, is not a Hopi village, but an administrative town with a hospital and various U.S. government agencies. The settlement lies

*Walpi, "Sky Village"*

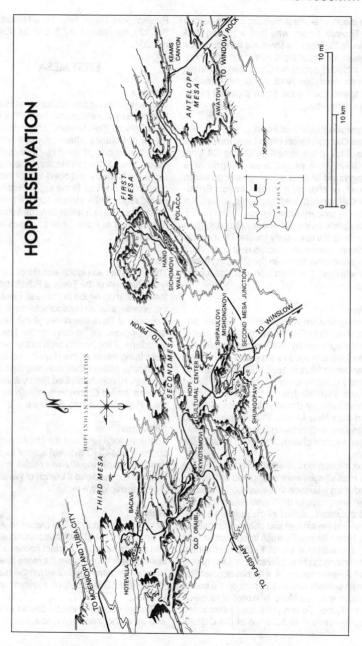

HOPI RESERVATION

HOPI INDIAN RESERVATION

ARIZONA

KEAMS CANYON

ANTELOPE MESA

AWA'TOVI

TO WINDOW ROCK

FIRST MESA

POLACCA

HANO

SICHOMOVI

WALPI

SHIPAULOVI

MISHONGNOVI

SECOND MESA JUNCTION

TO WINSLOW

TO PIÑON

SECOND MESA

HOPI CULTURAL CENTER

KYKOTSMOVI

SHUNGOPAVI

OLD ORAIBI

BACAVI

HOTEVILLA

THIRD MESA

TO MOENKOPI AND TUBA CITY

TO FLAGSTAFF

10 mi

10 km

at the mouth of a scenic wooded canyon named after Thomas Keam, who built a trading post here in 1875. From the town, the canyon winds northeast for about eight miles; the first three miles includes a road. Kit Carson engraved his name on Inscription Rock, about two miles beyond town. You'll pass some pleasant picnic spots on the way.

### Accommodations and Food
**Keams Canyon Motel** offers basic rooms ($42 s or d, $45) at the turnoff for Keams Canyon; tel. 738-2297. A **picnic area** and **primitive campground** lie across the highway: no water, facilities, or charge. **Keams Canyon Shopping Center** features McGee's Indian Art Gallery, a grocery store, an ice cream parlor, and a cafe serving American, Mexican, and Indian food; it's open daily for breakfast, lunch, and dinner. A service station is next door. You'll find a laundromat between the shopping center and the motel. The town also includes a **post office.**

### Awatovi
Beginning as a small village in the 12th century, Awatovi (ah-WAHT-o-vee) had become an important Hopi town by 1540, when Spanish explorers from Coronado's expedition arrived.

Franciscan friars in 1629 built a large church and friary using Indian labor. The mission lasted 51 years. In 1680, fearing their culture would be destroyed by Christianity, Hopi villagers joined their New Mexico Pueblo neighbors in successfully overthrowing Spanish rule, wrecking the Awatovi church and killing most of the priests.

The mission was re-established in 1700, but other Hopi villages were so angered by this continued alien influence that they too banded together and promptly destroyed Awatovi. Of the 800 inhabitants, almost all the men were massacred and the women and children removed to other Hopi villages. Spanish troops retaliated a year later with little effect. Further missionary efforts among the Hopi proved futile. Only ghosts live at Awatovi today—it was never resettled. The ruin sprawls across 23 acres on the southwest tip of Antelope Mesa, with piles of rubble as high as 30 feet. To visit you'll need a permit and a Hopi guide; ask in advance at the Cultural

Preservations Office, Hopi Tribal Headquarters, Box 123, Kykotsmovi, AZ 86039; tel. 734-2441, ext. 201.

## FIRST MESA

### Polacca
With an increasing population, some Hopi have built houses in settlements below the mesas, as at Polacca (po-LAH-kah). Still, if you ask residents of Polacca where they're from, they'll likely name one of the three villages on the mesa above. Polacca stretches for about a mile along the highway, but offers little of interest. A bigger thrill is a visit to the top of First Mesa. A paved road climbs steeply for one mile to the crest. If you have a trailer or large vehicle, you must park it in Polacca or at a parking area halfway up.

### Hano
The first village you reach *looks* Hopi, but is really a settlement of the Tewa, a Pueblo tribe from the Rio Grande region to the east. Fleeing from the Spanish after an unsuccessful revolt in 1696, a number of Tewa sought refuge with Hopi. Hopi leaders agreed, on the condition the Tewa act as guardians of the access path to the mesa. Despite living close to the Hopi for so long, the Tewa have retained their own language and ceremonies. Hano's fascinating history is detailed in *A Tewa Indian Community in Arizona* by Edward P. Dozier (see the Booklist).

### Sichomovi
To the visitor, Hano and the Hopi village of Sichomovi (see-CHO-mo-vee) appear as one, but residents know exactly where the line is. Sichomovi is considered a branch of Walpi, the village at the tip of the mesa.

### Walpi
One of the most inspiring places in Arizona, Walpi (WAHL-pee) stands surrounded by sky and distant horizons. Ancient houses of yellow stone appear to grow from the mesa itself. Coming from Sichomovi, you'll watch the mesa narrow to just 15 feet before widening again at Walpi.

Visitors may enter this traditional village only with an authorized Hopi guide; Walpi is small (pop. about 30) and its occupants sensitive. Free tours to Walpi leave either from Ponsi Hall, in Sichomovi, or from the tourist booth at Walpi Parking Lot. The 40-minute walking tours leave daily from 9:30 a.m.-4:15 p.m.; tel. 737-2262 (Ponsi Hall) or 737-2670 (Community Development office).

Unlike other Hopi villages, Walpi lacks electricity and running water. Residents have to walk back toward Sichomovi to obtain water or wash. Look for bowl-shaped depressions used to collect rainwater. Precipitous foot trails and ruins of old defenses and buildings cling to the mesa slopes far below. Inhabited since the 13th century, Walpi is well known for its ceremonial dances and crafts. Kachina dolls carved by the men and pottery created by the women are sold in the village; signs indicate which houses sell crafts. With sweeping panoramas at every turn and a determined hold on traditions, Walpi is probably the most rewarding of all the Hopi villages.

## SECOND MESA

### Second Mesa (Junction)

Highways AZ 264 and AZ 87 meet at the foot of Second Mesa, seven miles west of Polacca and 60 miles north of Winslow. Here you'll find **Secakuku Trading Post,** a supermarket, open daily; **Second Mesa Nova-ki,** a cafe with American, Mexican, and a few Hopi dishes, open daily for breakfast, lunch, and dinner; and a **post office. Honani Crafts Gallery** and a service station lie a half mile west at the turnoff for Shipaulovi and Mishongnovi villages.

### Shipaulovi and Mishongnovi

These villages are close neighbors on a projection of Second Mesa. Dances often take place; ask at the Cultural Center for dates. Shipaulovi offers village tours; call the community center for times and cost, tel. 737-2570. You reach Shipaulovi (shih-PAW-lo-vee) and Mishongnovi (mih-SHONG-no-vee) by a short paved road that climbs steeply from AZ 264, a half mile west of the intersection with AZ 87, or by a mesa-top road (also paved) 0.2 mile east of the Cultural Center. Mishongnovi is the easternmost village, at the end of the mesa.

### Shungopavi

Shungopavi (shong-O-po-vee or shih-MO-pah-vee) is the largest (pop. 742) of the three Second Mesa villages. Dances performed include the Butterfly Dance (a social dance) and the Snake Dance (late August in even-numbered years). Buy crafts from the villagers or at **Dawa's Art and Crafts** on the road into the village. Shungopavi lies 0.8 mile south off AZ 264, midway between the junction with AZ 87 and the Cultural Center.

## HOPI CULTURAL CENTER

Proclaiming itself "At the Center of the Universe," this excellent pueblo-style museum/motel/restaurant/gift shop complex is popular with both visitors and local Hopi. The Hopi Cultural Center is situated on the west side of Second Mesa just before the road plunges down on the way to Third Mesa. For a shortcut to Chinle and Canyon de Chelly, turn north off AZ 264 beside the Cultural Center to Pinon Trading Post, 26 miles (mostly rough and only partly paved), then east 42 miles on paved roads.

The museum displays good exhibits of Hopi customs, ceremonies, crafts, and history; it's open all year Mon.-Fri. 8 a.m.-5 p.m. and Sat.-Sun. 9 a.m.-3 p.m., usually closed Saturday and Sunday in winter. Costs: $3 adults, $1 children 13 and under; tel. 734-6650. The Hopi consider some ceremonial religious objects secret; they won't be displayed. To learn more of Hopi mythology and customs, dig into off-reservation sources such as the NAU Special Collections or Museum of Northern Arizona libraries, both in Flagstaff.

The modern motel's nonsmoking rooms run $75 s, $80 d, $5 each additional person; $20 less in winter. Reservations are recommended; Box 67, Second Mesa, AZ 86043; tel. 734-2401/2421. You'll find free camping and picnic grounds next door, between the Cultural Center and the Hopi Arts and Crafts shop. No water or hookups, but you can use the restrooms in the Cultural Center.

The restaurant serves good American and Hopi dishes. This is your big chance to try baduf-su-ki (pinto bean and hominy soup), or maybe some nok-qui-vi (traditional stew of Hopi corn and lamb), or a breakfast of blue pancakes made of Hopi corn. It's open daily for breakfast, lunch, and dinner.

**Hopi Arts and Crafts** (Silvercrafts Cooperative Guild), a short walk across the camping area, houses a big selection. You can often see Hopi silversmiths at work here.

## THIRD MESA

### Kykotsmovi

The name means Mound of Ruined Houses. Hopi from Old Oraibi (o-RYE-bee) founded this settlement near a spring at the base of Third Mesa. Peach trees add greenery to the town. Kykotsmovi (kee-KEUTS-mo-vee), also known as New Oraibi, is headquarters for the Hopi Tribal Council.

The **Office of the Chairman** provides information for visitors and is near the Tribal Council building one mile south of AZ 264; Box 123,

Kykotsmovi, AZ 86039, tel. 734-2441, ext. 102. The **Kykotsmovi Village Store** in town sells groceries; **Hopikiva Arts & Crafts** is a good source of souvenirs. You can stop for a **picnic** at Oraibi Wash, 0.8 mile east of the Kykotsmovi turnoff, or the Pumpkin Seed Hill overlook 1.2 miles west on the climb to Old Oraibi. Indian Route 2 leading south to Leupp (pronounced "loop") is paved and is the shortest way to Flagstaff.

### Old Oraibi

This dusty pueblo perched on the edge of Third Mesa dates from A.D. 1150 and is probably the oldest continuously inhabited community in the United States.

The 20th century has been difficult for this ancient village. In 1900 it ranked as one of the largest Hopi settlements, with a population of more than 800, but dissension caused many to leave. The first major dispute occurred in 1906 between two chiefs, You-ke-oma and Tawa-

*Hopi family, early 1900s*

quap-tewa. Instead of letting fly with bullets and arrows, the leaders staged a strange "push-of-war" contest. A line was cut into the mesa and the two groups stood on either side. They pushed against each other as hard as they could until one group lost. You-ke-oma, the loser, left with his faction to establish Hotevilla four miles away. This event was recorded a quarter mile north of Oraibi with the line and inscription: "Well, it have to be done this way now, that when you pass this LINE it will be DONE, Sept. 8, 1906." A bear paw cut in the rock is the symbol of Tawa-quap-tewa and his Bear Clan, while a skull represents You-ke-oma and his Skeleton Clan. Other residents split off to join New Oraibi at the foot of the mesa.

A ruin near Old Oraibi on the south end of the mesa is all that remains of a church built in 1901 by the Mennonite minister, H.R. Voth. Most villagers disliked having this "thing" so close to their homes, and were no doubt relieved when lightning destroyed the church in 1942.

Old Oraibi lies two miles west of Kykotsmovi. Avoid driving through the village and stirring up dust; park outside—or next to the Old Oraibi Crafts shop—and walk. Hopi arts and crafts are available at the **Calnimptewa Gallery** east of the turnoff for Old Oraibi, **Monongya Gallery** west of the Old Oraibi turnoff, and **Old Oraibi Crafts** in the village.

## Hotevilla

Hotevilla (HOAT-vih-lah) is known for its dances, basketry, and other crafts.

Founded in 1906 after the split from Old Oraibi, Hotevilla got off to a shaky start. Federal officials demanded that the group move back to Old Oraibi so their children could attend school there. Twenty-five men agreed to return with their families, despite continued bad feelings; about 53 others refused to leave Hotevilla. The recalcitrant men were jailed for 90 days while their children were forcibly removed to a Keams Canyon boarding school. That winter the women and infants fended for themselves, with little food and inadequate shelter. In the following year the men returned, building better houses and planting crops. Exasperated authorities continued to haul You-ke-oma off to jail for his lack of cooperation and refusal to

*the Mad Hatter's Teapot rock formation in the Hopi Reservation*

ROBERT BLAKE

send village children to school. In 1912, government officials invited the chief to Washington for a meeting with President Taft, but the meeting didn't soften You-ke-oma's stance.

The turnoff for Hotevilla is 3.7 miles northwest of Old Oraibi and 46 miles southeast of Tuba City.

## Bacavi

The You-ke-oma loyalists who returned to Old Oraibi under federal pressure continued to clash with the people of Tawa-quap-tewa. At one point, when two of the returning women died in quick succession, cries of witchcraft went up. Finally, in November 1909, tensions became unbearable. Members of the unwelcome group packed their bags once more and settled at a new site called Bacavi (BAH-kah-vee) Spring. The name means Jointed Reed, taken from a plant found at the spring. Bacavi lies on the opposite side of the highway from Hotevilla.

# HOPI KACHINAS AND CALENDAR

Kachinas appear to the Hopi from the winter solstice on December 21 until mid-July. They dance and sing in unison, symbolizing the harmony of good thought and deed, harmony required for rain to fall and for a balanced life. The rest of the year the kachinas remain in their home in the San Francisco Peaks.

A kachina can take three forms: a powerful unseen spirit, a dancer filled with the spirit, or a wooden figure representing the spirit. Dancers are always male, even when the kachina spirit is female. The Hopi believe men are more in touch than women with the divine. Gifts of kachina figures are presented by the men to women and children during the dances. Each village has its own style of ceremony.

## HOPI CALENDAR

**Wuwuchim and Soyala (November to December)**
These months symbolize the time of creation of the world. The villages tend to be quiet, as Hopi spend time in silence, prayer, and meditation.

Wuwuchim, a tribal initiation ceremony, marks the start of the ceremonial calendar year. Young men are initiated into adulthood, joining one of four ceremonial societies. The society a man joins depends on his sponsor. Upon acceptance, the initiate receives instruction in Hopi creation beliefs. He's presented with a new name, and his childhood name is never used again.

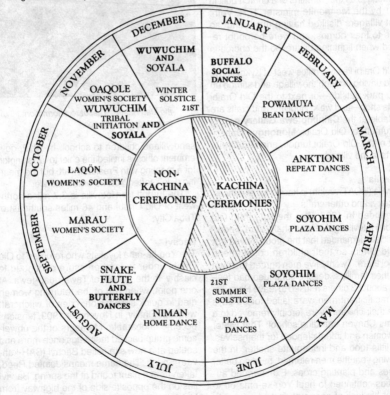

Currently only the Shungopavi village performs the entire Wuwuchim ceremony and then not every year. Other villages engage in parts of the Wuwuchim.

The Soyala Kachina appears from the west in the winter solstice ceremony, marking the beginning of the kachina season. As the days get longer, the Hopi begin planning the upcoming planting season; fertility is a major concern in the ceremony.

**Buffalo Dances (January)**
Men, women, and children perform these social dances in the plazas. They deal with fertility, especially the need for winter moisture in the form of snow.

**Powamuya, The Bean Dance (February)**
Bean sprouts are grown in a kiva as part of a 16-day ceremony. On the final day, kachina dancers snake in a long parade through the village. Children of 13 and 14 years are initiated into kachina societies during the Powamuya. This is the time when ogre kachinas appear on First and Second mesas.

**Kiva Dances (March)**
A second set of nighttime kiva dances consists of Anktioni or "repeat dances."

**Plaza Dances (April, May, and June)**
The kachina dancers perform in all-day ceremonies lasting from sunrise to sunset, with breaks between dances. The group, and the people watching, concentrate in a community prayer calling on the spirits to bring rain for the growing crops.

**Niman, The "Home Dance" (July)**
At the summer solstice on June 21, the plaza dances end and preparations begin for the Going Home Ceremony. In a 16-day rite, the last of the season, kachina dancers present the first green corn ears, then dance for rain to hasten growth of the remaining crops. Their spiritual work done, the kachinas return to their mountain home.

**Snake, Flute, and Butterfly Dances (August)**
The Snake and Flute ceremonies, held in alternate years, represent the clan groups, who perform them in the interests of a good harvest and prosperity. The Snake Dance, usually closed to non-Hopi, takes place in even-numbered years at Shungopavi and in odd-numbered years at Mishongnovi. The snakes, often poisonous rattlers, act as messengers to the spirits.

The Flute Ceremony takes place in odd-numbered years at Shungopavi and Walpi.

The Butterfly Dance, a social dance performed mainly by children, takes place in all villages. It also celebrates the harvest.

**Women's Society Dances
(September, October, and Early November)**
Held in the plazas, these ceremonies celebrate the harvest with wishes for health and prosperity. Chaos reigns during the Basket Dances; women dancers throw out baskets and other valuables to the audience, who engage in a mad free-for-all to grab the prizes. End of the ceremonial year.

**Coal Mine Canyon**
This is a scenic little canyon 31 miles northwest of Bacavi (15 miles southeast of Tuba City) on AZ 264. Look for a windmill and the Coal Mine Mesa Rodeo Ground on the north side of the highway (no signs), and turn in across the cattleguard. Hopi have long obtained coal from the seam just below the rim.

**Moenkopi**
This Hopi village lies two miles southeast of Tuba City. Prehistoric Pueblo Indians built villages in the area but abandoned them by A.D. 1300. Chief Tuba of Oraibi, 48 miles southeast, founded Moenkopi ("The Place of Running Water") in the 1870s. Mormons constructed a woolen mill in 1879 with plans to use Indian labor, but the Hopi disliked working with machinery and the project failed. Moenkopi has two sections—only the upper village participates in the Hopi Tribal Council; the more conservative lower village does not. Water from springs irrigates fields, an advantage not enjoyed by other Hopi villages.

# NORTH-CENTRAL ARIZONA

The high country of north-central Arizona offers dramatic and varied scenery. Cool forests, which cover much of the region, provide a delightful respite from the desert. The remarkably diverse landscapes of the region entice many visitors, whatever their style of travel. Highways wind through a number of scenic and historic areas, yet backcountry travelers can explore all day on trails or forest roads without ever crossing a paved road. Anglers can choose among many lakes on the Colorado Plateau and the streams below it. In winter, skiers come to enjoy the downhill runs on the San Francisco Peaks near Flagstaff and the shorter runs on Bill Williams Mountain near Williams. Cross-country skiers can strike out on their own or glide along groomed trails near the San Francisco Peaks or at Mormon Lake.

## THE LAND

Most of northern Arizona lies atop the Colorado Plateau, a giant uplifted landmass extending into adjacent Utah, Colorado, and New Mexico. As the land rose, vigorous rivers cut deeply through the rock layers, revealing beautiful forms and the many colors of countless canyons.

While rivers cut down, volcanoes shot up. For millions of years, large and small volcanoes sprouted in the San Francisco Volcanic Field around Flagstaff. The most striking include the San Francisco Peaks; Humphrey's Peak at 12,633 feet is Arizona's tallest mountain. Sunset Crater, the state's most beautiful volcano, is the youngster of the bunch, last erupting about 700 years ago—just yesterday, geologically speaking.

A crater of a different sort lies east of Flagstaff. Meteor Crater was formed about 49,000 years ago when a speeding mass of rock smashed into the earth, displacing an estimated 300 million tons of earth.

North-central Arizona's elevations drop more than 9,000 feet from the heights of Humphrey's Peak to the lower Verde and Agua Fria river valleys to the south. Most of the region lies between 4,000 and 8,000 feet. Sheer cliffs of the

Mogollon (MUGGY-own) Rim mark the southern edge of the Colorado Plateau.

## Climate

Expect a cool, invigorating mountain climate in most of north-central Arizona. Spring, summer, and fall temperatures are ideal in the higher country, where temperatures peak in the 70s and 80s F. Lower valleys often bake in the heat, but you can always reach the mountains in less than an hour. From early July into September, thunderstorm clouds billow into the air, dropping scattered downpours. Winter is a battle between snow and sun. Cold-season temperatures vary greatly—from the bitter cold of storms to the warmth of bright Arizona sunshine. In Flagstaff (elev. 7,000 feet), average winter lows reach the teens, warming to highs in the lower 40s. Still, the winter visitor should be prepared for anything from sub-zero freezing weather to warm, spring-like temperatures. Skiers enjoy the snow, though not many people brave the higher elevations for camping or backpacking. The lower country experiences milder winters, with only occasional snowfalls. Annual precipitation, arriving mostly in summer and winter, varies between 10 and 30 inches, depending on elevation and rain shadows.

## Flora and Fauna

The great range in elevation, together with a varied topography, provide many different habitats for wildlife. Tiny alpine plants hug the ground against strong winds and extreme cold on the highest slopes of the San Francisco Peaks, where no trees can survive. At lower elevations, dense groves of aspen, fir, and pine thrive on the mountainsides and in protected canyons.

Squirrels busy themselves storing away food for the long winters here, where larger animals just visit for the summer.

Vast forests of ponderosa pine and Gambel oak cover much of the Colorado Plateau. Elk, mule deer, a few black bear, coyote, and smaller animals make these forests their home. Some of the many birds you'll likely see include the ubiquitous common raven, noisy Steller's jay, and feisty hummingbird. Drier parts of north-central Arizona support forests of juniper, piñon pine, oak, and Arizona cypress. In other semiarid zones, dense shrubs and stunted trees of the chaparral separate the ponderosa forests above from the desert below. Common plants of the chaparral include manzanita, silk-tassel bush, shrub live oak, catclaw acacia, and buckbrush. Streams flowing from the Mogollon Rim attract animals from both the plateau and the desert, often supporting beaver. The Arizona Game and Fish Department stocks nonnative rainbow trout in lakes and permanent streams.

In drier country grow the grasses, yuccas, agave, cacti, catclaw acacia, and other plants of the desert. Wildlife at home here include coyote, gray fox, spotted skunk, black-tailed jackrabbit, desert cottontail, deer mouse, side-blotched lizard, gopher snake, and western rattlesnake. Herds of pronghorn, a graceful, antelope-like creature, roam the arid grasslands north of the San Francisco Volcanic Field. Birds such as the golden eagle, red-tailed hawk, and common raven scavenge in the desert, but usually nest elsewhere. Gambel's quail, roadrunner, horned lark, and black-throated sparrow use bushes for cover and nesting sites.

Canyons create strange variations in climate: a north-facing slope may feature dense growths

*greater roadrunner* (Geococcyx californianus)

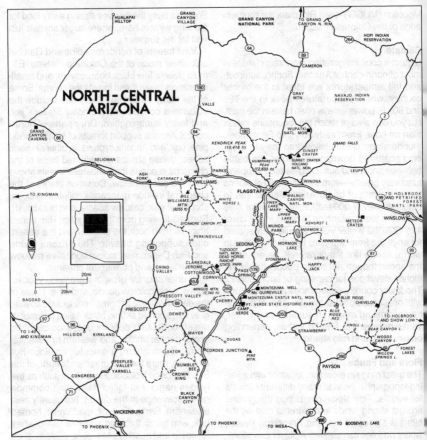

NORTH-CENTRAL ARIZONA

of fir and pine while only yuccas, grasses, and sparse stunted trees grow on the opposite slope. Or you could see juniper trees growing near the top of a canyon and Douglas firs below, a reversal of the normal order of climate zones.

## HISTORY

### Native Americans

Archaeologists have dated prehistoric Indian sites along the Little Colorado River as far back as 15,000 B.C., when now-extinct species of bison, camel, antelope, and horse roamed the land. Although some Indian groups engaged in

agriculture between 2,000 and 500 B.C., they maintained a seasonal migration pattern of hunting and gathering. These nomadic groups planted corn, squash, and beans in the spring, continued their travels, then returned to harvest the fields in autumn.

From about A.D. 200 to 500, as the Indians devoted more time to farming, they built clusters of pithouses near the fields. Regional cultures then began to form: the Anasazi of the Colorado Plateau, the Mogollon of the eastern Arizona uplands, and the Hohokam of the desert to the south. A fourth culture evolved near present-day Flagstaff between A.D. 900 and 1000 as a blend of the three earlier cultures. These people are known as Sinagua (Spanish for "Without Water") in honor of the area's porous volcanic soil which quickly absorbs rains and snowmelt.

As these societies developed further, the people started to build pueblos above ground. Villages, usually situated on hilltops or in cliff overhangs, were widely scattered over north-central Arizona. By about A.D. 1100 the population reached its peak. Inhabitants then mysteriously began to abandon villages and even whole areas. Archaeologists attempt to explain these departures with theories of drought, soil erosion, disease, and raids by the newly arrived Apache. By the 1500s, when Spanish explorers arrived in northern Arizona, the Pueblo Indians had retreated to northeast Arizona and adjacent New Mexico. Thousands of empty villages remain in north-central Arizona, some protected in the four national monuments of Wupatki, Walnut Canyon, Tuzigoot, and Montezuma Castle-Montezuma Well. You might also discover ruins while hiking in the backcountry.

Sometime after A.D. 1400, bands of Yavapai and Apache moved into the Verde Valley and Mogollon Rim areas. They did some farming, but obtained most of their food by hunting and collecting wild plants.

### The Search for Gold and Silver

Antonio de Espejo, the first of several Spanish explorers, visited north-central Arizona in 1583 seeking precious metals. Later expeditions staked claims near present-day Prescott, but the Spaniards never developed them. When American prospectors rediscovered these deposits in the early 1860s, they had to work the mines while fending off attacks from the Apache. Fort Whipple, built by the Army in 1863, provided some protection.

### Americans Settle In

In 1864, surveyors marked out a town along Granite Creek near Fort Whipple. Carved out of the wilderness, the carefully planned community became Arizona's territorial capital. Arizona had just been separated from New Mexico, and President Lincoln wanted the capital a comfortable distance from the southern settlements of Tucson and Tubac, home to too many Texans and other Confederate sympathizers. The town's settlers didn't forget Arizona's Spanish-American heritage; they christened the settlement Prescott after William Hickling Prescott, author of *The History of the Conquest of Mexico*.

Development farther north took longer. Captain Lorenzo Sitgreaves brought a surveying expedition across northern Arizona in 1851, leading to the building of rough wagon roads by Lieutenant Edward Beale and others, but hostile Indians and poor farming land discouraged settlement. The coming of the railroad in 1882, thriving lumber mills, and success in sheep and cattle ranching opened up the region and led to the growth of railroad towns such as Flagstaff and Williams.

## TRANSPORT

You really need your own vehicle to visit the national monuments and most of the scenic and recreation areas. Tours make brief stops at highlights of the region but tend to be rushed; see "Transport" in the Flagstaff section. Greyhound provides frequent bus service across northern Arizona via Flagstaff and between Flagstaff and Phoenix. Nava-Hopi buses connect Flagstaff with the Grand Canyon to the north. Amtrak runs daily trains across northern Arizona in each direction between Los Angeles and Albuquerque and beyond. Regional airlines serve Flagstaff, Sedona, Prescott, and the Grand Canyon.

# FLAGSTAFF

Surrounded by pine forest in the center of northern Arizona, Flagstaff (pop. 54,280) has long served as an important stop for ranchers, Indians, and travelers. The older, downtown part of Flagstaff still offers a bit of that frontier feeling, expressed by its many historic buildings. But what most visitors first see of this small city is a seemingly endless line of flashing signs advertising a profusion of motels, restaurants, bars, and service stations.

Fortunately, there's far more to see here in Flagstaff than auto row. To visit the distant past, when the land was lifting, volcanoes erupting, and the early Indians arriving, just drop by the Museum of Northern Arizona. To learn about the pioneers of 100 years ago, head over to the Pioneer Historical Museum. See work by local artists in the Art Barn, Coconino Center for the Arts, and University Art Galleries. For a trip out of this world, visit the Lowell Observatory, where astronomers discovered Pluto, or the U.S. Geological Survey, where astrogeologists map celestial bodies.

For the great outdoors, head for the hills—Arizona's highest mountains begin at the northern outskirts of town. In summer, the mountains, hills, and meadows offer pleasant forest walks and challenging climbs. Winter snows transform the countryside into some of the state's best downhill and cross-country skiing areas. As a local guidebook, *Coconino County, the Wonderland of America,* put it in 1916, Flagstaff "offers you the advantages of any city of twice its size; it has, free for the taking, the healthiest and most invigorating of climates; its surrounding scenic beauties will fill one season, from May to November, full to overflowing with enjoyment the life of any tourist, vacationist, camper or out doors man or woman who will but come to commune with nature."

## History

Indian groups had settled near the site of present-day Flagstaff, but their villages were long abandoned when the first white people arrived. Many ruins of old pueblos lie near town. Walnut Canyon National Monument, just east of Flagstaff, contains well-preserved cliff dwellings of the Sinagua people.

Spanish explorers and missionaries knew of the Flagstaff area, but they had little interest in a place with no valuable minerals to mine or souls to save. Beginning in the 1820s, mountain men such as Antoine Leroux became expert trappers and guides in this little-known region between Santa Fe and California. Early travelers sent out glowing reports of the climate, water, and scenery of the region, but hostile Apache, Navajo, Yavapai, and Paiute discouraged settlement.

Samuel Cozzens, a former Tucson judge, traveled east to stir up prospective settlers with a large, well-illustrated book titled *The Marvellous Country; or, Three Years in Arizona and New Mexico, the Apache's Home.* The subtitle expanded upon this theme: *Comprising a Description of this Wonderful Country, Its Immense Mineral Wealth, Its Magnificent Mountain Scenery, the Ruins of Ancient Towns and Cities Found Therein, With a Complete History of the Apache Tribe, and a Description of the Author's Guide Cochise, the Great Apache War Chief, the Whole Interspersed with Strange Events and Adventures.* Cozzens's book sold well in New England and he stayed busy giving talks to eager audiences. With each retelling, his descriptions of Arizona's climate, forests, water, and mineral wealth grew and improved. By 1875, the Arizona Colonization Company, with Cozzens as president, was established in Boston. In February 1876, a group of about 50 men, each with 300 pounds of tools and clothing, set off for Arizona under the auspices of the company. In May a second group embarked for the "marvellous country."

After 90 days of arduous travel, the first group arrived only to find the land already claimed by Mormons. The group continued west to the San Francisco Peaks and started to build a settlement, dubbed Agassiz. But finding no land suitable for farming or mining, they gave up and left for Prescott and California, even before the second group arrived. The second group gave up too, but not before erecting a flagpole to celebrate July 4th.

## FLAGSTAFF~WHAT'S IN A NAME?

It's obvious that Flagstaff was named for a flag-pole. The question is, which flagpole?

The first group of settlers to arrive from Boston claimed to have erected a flagpole in April or May of 1876, before the July 4th celebration held by the second Boston group later that year. Both parties claimed to have sunk the pole that served as the town's namesake.

Other early settlers regarded a tall tree, trimmed of all branches, at the foot of McMillan Mesa as *the* flagstaff. Still others disputed this, claiming Lieutenant Edward Beale delimbed the tree in the 1850s; others said it was the work of a later railroad-surveying party. And no record actually exists of a flag ever flying from the tree. Another flagpole, standing near Antelope Spring, *did* fly a flag.

At any rate, citizens gathered in the spring of 1881 and chose the name "Flagstaff" for the settlement.

Thomas Forsythe McMillan, who arrived from California with a herd of sheep in 1876, became Flagstaff's first permanent settler. Other ranchers soon moved into the area, bringing the total population to 67 in 1880. On August 1, 1882, the rails reached Flagstaff. Construction of the railroad brought new opportunities, new stores, restaurants, saloons, banks, and Flagstaff's first physician.

## SIGHTS

### Pioneer Historical Museum

This venerable stone building dates from 1907-08. For 30 years it served as the Coconino County Hospital for the Indigent. Townspeople also knew it as the "poor farm"—because stronger patients grew vegetables in the yard.

Today the building serves as a museum for the Northern Division of the Arizona Historical Society. Old photos, branding irons, saddles, logging tools, and other artifacts illustrate life in Flagstaff's pioneering days. A giant stuffed bear greets visitors on the second floor; slip by the beast to see more exhibits. One room displays camera gear and photos of Emery Kolb, who

came to the Grand Canyon in 1902, set up a photo studio there with brother Ellsworth, and continued making movies and stills until 1976. Another room features memorabilia of Percival Lowell and his observatory.

More exhibits can be seen, when staffing permits, outside on the grounds. The restored Ben Doney Cabin (1880s) has been moved here from a site east of town. Antique cars, buggies, and other large items are housed in the annex behind the museum. Old farm machinery lies on the lawn nearby. An antique steam locomotive sits in front of the museum. The Pioneer Historical Museum is open Mon.-Sat. 9 a.m.-5 p.m.; donation requested; tel. 774-6272. From downtown, the museum lies on the right about two miles northwest on US 180.

### Coconino Center for the Arts

Unique to the region, The Coconino Center for the Arts is an award-winning, multidisciplinary, nonprofit arts organization that provides year-round visual arts, performances, and literary and educational programs for residents and visitors. The center features a spacious, 4,000-square-foot gallery, an intimate 200-seat amphitheater, and the elegant Gallery Shop specializing in handmade arts and crafts by northern Arizona artists.

The gift shop offers a fine selection of artwork, Indian jewelry and other crafts, ceramics, posters, and books. The center is open Tues.-Sun. 10 a.m.-5 p.m. all year. Admission is free to the center's gallery; there are modest admission fees for performances and workshops; tel. 779-6921. Drive two miles northwest on US 180, turn in at the sign beside the Pioneer Historical Museum, and proceed one block.

### The Art Barn

Regional artists and art patrons have banded together to operate this large sales gallery. Here you'll find a good selection of works by both Native American and Anglo artisans, including paintings, prints, sketches, photography, ceramics, Indian jewelry, kachina dolls, and Navajo rugs. Prices are right too, since there's no distributor markup or big advertising budget. The Art Barn is open daily 9 a.m.-5 p.m. except in winter, when hours are reduced to 10 a.m.-5 p.m. It's conveniently located next to the Coconino Center for the Arts; tel. 774-0822

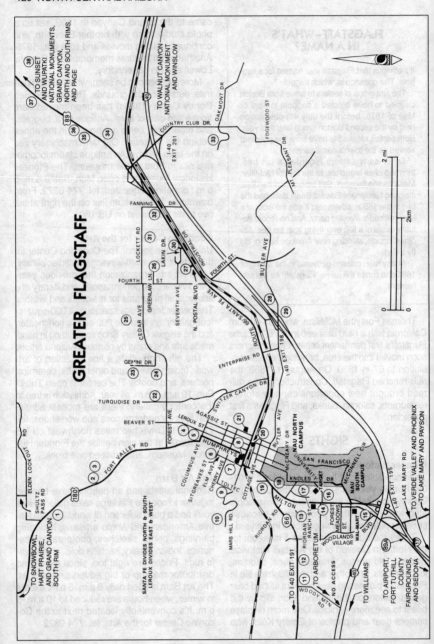

# GREATER FLAGSTAFF

TO SNOWBOWL, HART PRAIRIE, AND GRAND CANYON SOUTH RIM

TO SUNSET AND WUPATKI NATIONAL MONUMENTS, GRAND CANYON, NORTH AND SOUTH RIMS, AND PAGE

TO WALNUT CANYON NATIONAL MONUMENT AND WINSLOW

2 mi

2 km

SANTA FE DIVIDES NORTH & SOUTH
LEROUX DIVIDES EAST & WEST

SHULTZ PASS RD

ELDEN LOOKOUT RD

FORT VALLEY RD

COUNTRY CLUB DR.

OAKMONT DR

EDGEWOOD ST

MT PLEASANT DR

FANNING DR

BUTLER AVE

LOCKETT RD

FOURTH ST

FOURTH

LAKIN DR.

GREENLAW LN.

INDUSTRIAL DR

N. POSTAL BLVD.

SEVENTH AVE

CEDAR AVE

GEMINI DR.

TURQUOISE DR

BEAVER ST

LEROUX ST

FOREST AVE.

AGASSIZ ST

SWITZER CANYON DR

ENTERPRISE RD

SANTA FE AVE

ROUTE 66

HUMPHREYS

ELM AVE.

CHERRY AVE

TOLTEC

COTTAGE AVE

SITGREAVES ST

COLUMBUS AVE

MARS HILL RD

RIORDAN RD

MILTON

MCCREARY DR

KNOLES DR

MCCONNELL CIR

NAU NORTH CAMPUS

SAN FRANCISCO

NAU SOUTH CAMPUS

TARGET

FOREST MEADOWS ST.

WAL-MART

WOODLANDS VILLAGE

RIORDAN RANCH ST

BLVD.

LAKE MARY RD

I-40 EXIT 201

I-40 EXIT 198

I-40 EXIT 195

I-40 EXIT 191

TO I-40 EXIT 191

TO ARBORETUM

NO ACCESS

WOODY MTN

TO WILLIAMS

TO AIRPORT, FORT TUTHILL COUNTY FAIRGROUNDS, AND SEDONA

TO VERDE VALLEY AND PHOENIX TO LAKE MARY AND PAYSON

# GREATER FLAGSTAFF

1. Museum of Northern Arizona
2. Pioneer Historical Museum
3. Coconino Center for the Arts; Art Barn
4. Flagstaff Medical Center (both sides of Beaver St.)
5. Fort Valley Shopping Center
6. Flagstaff High School
7. public library
8. City Hall
9. Thorpe Park; Adult Center
10. Lowell Observatory
11. Woody Mountain Campground
12. Kit Carson RV Park
13. University Plaza Shopping Center
14. Sherwood Forest Shopping Center
15. Woodlands Village Plaza
16. Green Tree Village Shopping Center
17. Riordan State Historic Park
18. Northern Arizona University Campus
19. Greyhound Bus
20. Amtrak/Flagstaff Visitor Center
21. post office (downtown branch)
22. J. Lively Ice Rink
23. Buffalo Park
24. Flagstaff Field Center of U.S.G.S.
25. Cedar Plaza Shopping Center
26. U.S. Forest Service (supervisor's Office)
27. post office (main)
28. Black Bart's Steak House & RV Park
29. Little America
30. Kachina Square Shopping Center
31. Bushmaster Park
32. Park Santa Fe Shopping Center
33. Elden Hills Golf Course; Continental Country Club Restaurant
34. Flagstaff Mall (indoors)
35. U.S. Forest Service (Peaks Ranger Station)
36. Elden Trailhead
37. KOA Campground
38. Big Tree Campground/Swap Meet

## Museum of Northern Arizona

This active museum features excellent displays of the archaeology, anthropology, geology, cultures, and fine art of the Colorado Plateau. Contemporary Native American exhibits illustrate the culture of northern Arizona tribes and their basketry, pottery, weaving, kachina dolls, and ceremonies.

This area of the museum contains a full-size Hopi kiva. An art gallery features changing exhibits of Indian and Southwestern art.

Popular museum-sponsored Hopi, Navajo, and Zuni shows take place May-Sept., exhibiting the best arts and crafts of each tribe. The museum shop sells Native American crafts, including Navajo blankets, Navajo, Hopi, and Zuni jewelry, Hopi kachina dolls, and pottery by various tribes. A bookstore stocks a large selection of books and posters related to the region. You can use the library—one of the most extensive on the Southwest—across the highway in the Research Center; it's open Mon.-Fri. 9 a.m.-5 p.m.

A visit to the Museum of Northern Arizona is highly recommended for anyone planning to buy Indian crafts or visit the reservations of northern Arizona, or to better understand the area surrounding the Grand Canyon.

Set beside a little canyon in a pine forest, the museum has a nature trail and courtyard where you'll find native plants and animals. The museum is open daily 9 a.m.-5 p.m.; $5 adults, $2 ages 7-17, $3 students with I.D., $4 seniors; tel. 774-5213. From downtown Flagstaff, head three miles northwest on US 180; the museum is on the left.

## Lowell Observatory

Lowell Observatory was founded in 1894 by Percival Lowell—one of the wealthy Boston Lowells—who used his personal fortune to fund a search for signs of intelligent life on Mars. The observatory's contributions to astronomy include spectroscopic photographs by V.M. Slipher that resulted in the discovery of the expanding universe, and the discovery of Pluto in 1930 by Clyde Tombaugh. The visitor center is open daily 9 a.m.-5 p.m. April-Nov. and noon-5 p.m. the rest of the year; $2.50 adults, $1 ages 5-17. Visitor center exhibits include the spectroscope used in the discovery of the expanding universe and the Pluto discovery plates—you can see the same view Tombaugh enjoyed at the instant he discovered Pluto. There are also many interactive exhibits, a lecture hall, and a bookstore.

In summer, daily one-hour tours begin at 10 a.m., 1 p.m., and 3 p.m. Tours start with a slide show illustrating the history and work of the observatory, then visit the 1896 24-inch Clark refractor telescope. On Monday, Tuesday, Wednesday, Friday, and Saturday nights during the

FLAGSTAFF CHAMBER OF COMMERCE

*Lowell Observatory*

summer (weather permitting), the observatory presents a planetary slide show and allows visitors to gaze through a telescope at the same fees as a daytime visit; open 8-10 p.m.; call for times the rest of the year; tel. 774-2096.

The observatory is one mile from downtown; drive or walk west on Santa Fe Ave. to the signed road up Mars Hill. In winter this steep road can require caution and even snow chains.

### Northern Arizona University (NAU) Observatory

Built by the U.S. Air Force as an atmospheric research observatory in the early 1950s, the NAU observatory is still used today for research but primarily serves as an educational tool for university students and the general public. Recently, a roll-off-roof observatory was built in front of the domed observatory for use by students. Open house is generally held Friday night at 7:30 with special open nights for astronomical events such as eclipses and occultations. It's off S. San Francisco St. just north of a high-rise dormitory and practice field; tel. 523-7170/7096. Admission is free, but donations are request-

ed. Tour operators are volunteers, mostly astronomy club members.

### Astrogeology

Many of the scientists at the Flagstaff Field Center of the U.S. Geological Survey study and map Earth's moon, the planets, and other bodies of our solar system. They also investigate Earth landforms such as volcanoes and sand dunes, thought to be formed by the same processes as those working on extraterrestrial objects. The Apollo astronauts learned their lunar geology here, and were later guided on the moon by scientists from this center.

Though there's no visitor center or regular tours, you're welcome to peruse the exhibits in the hallways. Giant maps and spectacular color photos taken by spacecraft cover the walls. Photos include shots of Jupiter and Saturn and their moons, remote-sensing products showing the Earth's features, and views sent back by crafts landing on Mars and Venus. The geology of the Moon and most solid-surfaced planets and their satellites have been mapped in surprising detail. Even cloud-covered Venus is mapped using radar images with computer-gen-

# PLANET X

The ancients recorded five bright starlike wandering bodies. Later generations accepted that Earth was also a planet. William Herschel, who was conducting star surveys, discovered a seventh planet in 1781. The planet, now known as Uranus, had been plotted on sky charts at least two dozen times as a star. Astronomers used these positions to plot the planet's orbit, but Uranus was not moving according to Newton's mechanics. In the early 1820s, it was moving too slow but by the end of that decade it was moving too fast.

British astronomer John Couch Adams and French astronomer Urbain Leverrier, working independently, performed laborious calculations based on the assumption that the gravitational pull of an undiscovered eighth planet was affecting movement of Uranus in much the same way that the draft of a passing commercial truck forces a small car to swerve. Both men's predicted positions for the new planet were very close and a short telescopic search soon revealed the "new" planet, which was named Neptune.

Neptune had also been plotted as a star on several charts before its 1846 discovery. Again, the planet did not seem to be following a perfect orbit. Several astronomers started calculations to find a ninth planet, which they dubbed "Planet X." Percival Lowell spent years calculating a position for Planet X but did not have suitable telescopes to search the sky for it. Since his main interest lay in finding signs of life on Mars, his instruments were powerful, did not show wide-angle views, and were so slow photographically that some exposures required guidance hour after hour, in some cases night after night—for a single photograph.

Lowell died before a suitable telescope could be built, and the sky search for Planet X did not begin for more than a decade. But Harvard president A. Lawrence Lowell (Percival's brother) donated money to build a small but wide-angled, photographically fast telescope. This instrument exposed plates 14 inches by 17 inches covering a field 12 by 14 degrees and required less than an hour of guided exposure.

Each plate showed between 40,000 and one million stars. Since the distant planet was too far away to be recognizable as one in any telescope, only its motion against the background of stars as it circled the sun would reveal it as a planet. Thus, each plate would be duplicated several days later and then each star image would be compared from plate to plate until one of the "stars" was found to have moved a distance appropriate for a planet that far from the sun.

Taking the photographs was the easy part. Next, astronomy student and Kansas farm boy Clyde Tombaugh used a blink comparator to conduct the search. It would flash a view of part of one plate through a microscope eyepiece, and then flash a view of the same part of the corresponding plate. If an object had moved it would appear in the eyepiece as if it were jumping back and forth. That sounds easy but Tombaugh examined hundreds of thousands of star images before finding one that moved an appropriate distance. He also discovered a number of asteroids and variable stars in the process.

Although Tombaugh discovered Pluto on Feb. 18, 1930, using plates made Jan. 23rd and Jan. 29th, Lowell Observatory cautiously waited several weeks to announce the new planet, studying its motion in the meantime to verify that it was truly the long-sought Planet X.

Many people wanted to name the new planet for Percival Lowell; others favored Clyde Tombaugh. An English schoolgirl sent in the winning suggestion "Pluto" in honor of the Greek god of the underworld, brother of Jupiter and Neptune. The planet's astronomical symbol became "P" with an "L" bottom stem. This abbreviation for Pluto was also Percival Lowell's initials and honored his contribution.

erated color. Building 1 (Astrogeology) features most of the exhibits, as well as a specialized library open to the public. More maps and photos line the hallways of Buildings 3 and 4.

You may visit Mon.-Fri. 8 a.m.-4:30 p.m. Remember that the people working here are normally too busy to show visitors around. Also, don't enter offices or labs unless invited. Tours for scientific or educational groups can be arranged; call or write in advance to the Planetary Data Facility, 2255 N. Gemini Dr., Flagstaff, AZ 86001; tel. 556-7264. The U.S. Geological Survey is atop McMillan Mesa off Cedar Ave., 1.5 miles northeast of downtown.

## Riordan State Historic Park

The Riordan brothers, Timothy and Michael, arrived in Flagstaff during the mid-1880s and eventually took over the Arizona Lumber & Timber Company. Both became involved with the social, business, and political life of early Flagstaff. In 1904, they built a grand mansion just south of downtown. A "Rendezvous Room" connected the wing occupied by each brother's family. The architect Charles Whittlesey, who also designed El Tovar Hotel on the rim of the Grand Canyon, used a similar rustic style of logs and stonework for the mansion exterior. The brothers christened their joint home Kinlichi, Navajo for Red House.

Tours of the house reveal how the wealthy lived in Flagstaff during the early 1900s. Guides offer history and comment on architectural features. It's open daily 8 a.m.-5 p.m. from early May to late September and daily 11 a.m.-5 p.m. the rest of the year; $3 adults, $2 ages 12-17. It's best to phone in advance for reservations, as you may enter only in a group and tour times may change. You'll find this bit of historic Flagstaff at 1300 Riordan Ranch St. (behind Carl's Jr.) between S. Milton Rd. and Northern Arizona University, about a half mile south of downtown; there is also an entrance from the university; tel. 779-4395.

## Northern Arizona University (NAU)

Flagstaff's character and population owe much to this school, just south of downtown. The university began in 1899 as Northern Arizona Normal School, housed in a vacant reformatory building. Four young women received their diplomas and teaching certificates two years later.

In 1925 the school began offering a four-year Bachelor of Education degree, taking the name Northern Arizona State Teachers College. The program broadened over the years to include other degrees, a program in forestry, and graduate studies. In 1966 the institution became a university.

The sprawling campus now covers 686 acres, supplemented by the School of Forestry's 4,000-acre laboratory forest. Be ready for almost anything in the **Marguerite Hettel Weiss Museum and Gallery,** in the historic 1893 Old Main/Ashurst Building (first and second floors) and another gallery in Room 231 of the Creative Arts Building;

*Flagstaff and the San Francisco Peaks; Northern Arizona University is in the foreground.*

call 523-3471 to find what's going on and when.

Visitors are welcome in the university's art galleries, food service facilities, libraries, and indoor swimming pool, and at theater and sporting events. To learn about NAU services and events, call or visit the University Union Information Desk, tel. 523-4636, or call the switchboard, tel. 523-9011. A free shuttle bus makes a loop around the northern and southern parts of the main campus. Ask someone the location of the stop nearest you. The service runs about every 15 minutes Mon.-Thurs. 7:35 a.m.-10 p.m. and Friday 7:35 a.m.-4 p.m. during the main school terms. To park on campus, pick up a free visitor's permit from the **Parking Services/Visitor Information** building at the southwestern corner of Butler Ave. and S. Beaver Street.

## The Arboretum

Plant enthusiasts at the Arboretum research native and nonnative flora that thrive in the cool climate of the Flagstaff area. More than 700 species of plants and trees grow on the 200-

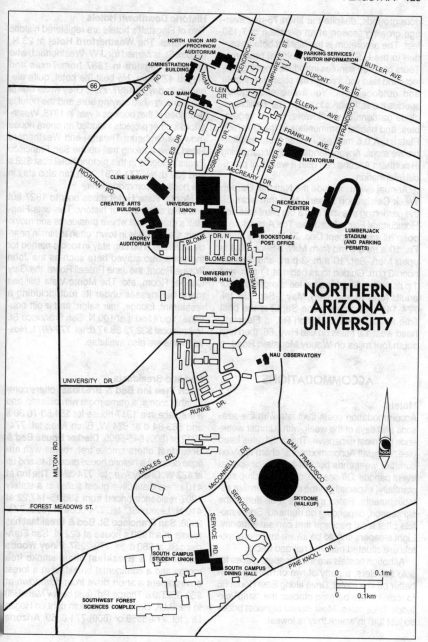

NORTH UNION AND
PROCHNOW
AUDITORIUM

PARKING SERVICES /
VISITOR INFORMATION

ADMINISTRATION
BUILDING

OLD MAIN

MCMULLEN
CIR.

66

MILTON RD.

KENDRICK ST.

HUMPHREYS ST.

DUPONT AVE. ST.

BUTLER AVE.

ELLERY AVE.

FRANKLIN AVE.

SAN FRANCISCO ST.

OSBORNE DR.

BEAVER ST.

CLINE LIBRARY

RIORDAN RD.

KNOLES DR.

McCREARY DR.

NATATORIUM

CREATIVE ARTS
BUILDING

UNIVERSITY
UNION

ARDREY
AUDITORIUM

BLOME DR. N

BOOKSTORE /
POST OFFICE

RECREATION
CENTER

LUMBERJACK
STADIUM
(AND PARKING
PERMITS)

BLOME DR. S

UNIVERSITY
DINING HALL

UNIVERSITY DR.

NORTHERN
ARIZONA
UNIVERSITY

NAU OBSERVATORY

RUNKE DR.

MOON

UNIVERSITY DR.

KNOLES RD.

MILTON RD.

McCONNELL DR.

SERVICE RD.

SAN FRANCISCO ST.

SKYDOME
(WALKUP)

FOREST MEADOWS ST.

SERVICE RD.

SOUTH CAMPUS
STUDENT UNION

SOUTH CAMPUS
DINING HALL

PINE KNOLL DR.

SOUTHWEST FOREST
SCIENCES COMPLEX

0        0.1mi

0        0.1km

acre grounds, despite the short 75-day average growing season at an elevation of 7,150 feet. The arboretum is the highest botanic garden in the U.S. doing horticultural research. Tours of 45-60 minutes introduce ongoing projects and take you through the solar greenhouse and outdoor plots. You'll see endangered species the staff works to propagate. Exhibits include gardens of wildflowers, herbs, vegetables, and habitat communities of the Colorado Plateau. A 0.6-mile nature trail features interpretive stops. Anyone landscaping or gardening in northern Arizona can gain a wealth of practical information.

Annual events include the National Garden Week Celebration in early May that kicks off the gardening season, and a big plant sale and Horticultural Fair in late June. The Arboretum is open all year (except Dec. 24-Mar. 14) Mon.-Fri. 10 a.m.-3 p.m.; from May 1-Sept. 30 it is open Mon.-Sat. 10 a.m.-3 p.m. and Sunday noon-3 p.m. Guided tours begin at 11 a.m. and 1 p.m., with a $3 admission fee charged only for adults (age 18 and over), May 1-Sept. 30; tel. 774-1441. Summer (June-Sept.) is the best time to visit. From S. Milton Rd. in Flagstaff, head west 1.9 miles on Old Hwy. 66, then turn south four miles on Woody Mountain Road.

## ACCOMMODATIONS

### Motels

Accommodation costs fluctuate with the seasons and days of the week, with summer weekends the most expensive. The motel rates listed (see "Flagstaff Accommodations" chart) apply on summer weekends but not holiday or special event periods. Off-season, prices can drop substantially, especially at the more expensive establishments. Rates may rise a bit during the ski season, depending on demand. Some motels offer a ski package that can save money. Light sleepers should be aware that many motels are situated near the railroad tracks.

Although hostels are the cheapest places for solo travelers, a party of two or more is often better off in a motel. Drive along East Route 66 to look for the bargain places; the "strip" extends three miles. Most motels signpost prices so just turn in where they're lowest.

### Historic Downtown Hotels

Two of Flagstaff's hotels are registered historic landmarks. The **Weatherford Hotel** at 23 N. Leroux St. is named for J.W. Weatherford, who came to Flagstaff in 1887 from Texas and stayed 47 years. He built the hotel, quite elegant in its day, in 1897. Zane Grey wrote *Call of the Canyon* while staying here and the hotel is described in that book as it was in 1918. Weatherford's other projects included an opera house (now the Orpheum Theatre) and Weatherford Road (now a hiking trail up the San Francisco Peaks). Rooms in this historic hotel cost $28 s and $32 d; tel. 774-2731. You can also stay in the hostel accommodations.

**Monte Vista Hotel** dates only to 1927 but has also seen a lot of history. This was Flagstaff's grand hotel where presidents and movie stars stayed while in town, often to film in nearby locations. You can stay in rooms named for the stars who stayed here such as the John Wayne Room, the Jane Russell Room, the Gary Cooper Room, etc. The Monte Vista still has many businesses under its roof including a restaurant, lounge, hair salon, and a gift boutique. You'll find it at 100 N. San Francisco St. Rooms cost $32.72-38.17 d; tel. 779-6971. Hostel rooms are also available.

### Bed and Breakfasts

**Birch Tree Inn Bed & Breakfast** offers comfortable rooms, a game room with billiards, and a fireplace in a 1917 house for $54.50-76.30 s and $63-84 d at 824 W. Birch Ave.; tel. 774-1042 or (800) 645-5805. **Dierker House Bed & Breakfast** offers smoke free rooms with antique decor in a historic house priced $45 and up at 423 W. Cherry Ave.; tel. 774-3249. **The Inn at 410** offers distinctive guest suites in a stately 1907 residence priced from $98.15-147.22 at 410 N. Leroux St.; tel. 774-0088 or (800) 774-2008. **San Francisco St. Bed & Breakfast** has rooms in a 1930's house at 622 N. San Francisco St. at $80 d; tel. 779-2257. **Piney Woods Lodge Bed & Breakfast** offers smoke free rooms and a continental breakfast in a forest environment a short drive from downtown at $60-95. Take Thorpe Rd. (just below Mars Hill) to the B.I.A. Dorm drive and turn right on Hogan Dr.; tel. 774-8859 or (800) 774-8859. **Arizona**

# FLAGSTAFF ACCOMMODATIONS
(summer weekend rates for basic room)

Add 9.05% tax to all rates.

## SOUTH AND WEST OF DOWNTOWN

**Townhouse Motel;** 122 W. Rt. 66; $75-88 s, $82-92 d; 774-5081 or 779-5082; some waterbeds, close to downtown

**Family Inn;** 121 S. Sitgreaves St.; $50 s, $78 d; 774-8821

**University TraveLodge;** 801 W. Rt. 66; $56 s, $58 d; 774-3381 or (800) 578-7878; spas, sauna

**Saga Budget Host;** 820 W. Rt. 66; $50 s, $55 d; 779-3631 or (800) BUD-HOST; pool

**Hidden Village;** 822 W. Rt. 66; $45-55 s or d; 774-1443; indoor heated pool

**Days Inn;** 1000 W. Rt. 66; $78-82 s or d; 774-5221 or (800) 329-7466; pool, cafeteria-style restaurant

**Woodlands Plaza Hotel (Best Western);** 1175 W. Rt. 66; $99 s, $109 d; 773-8888 or (800) 528-1234; exercise room, pool, spas, sauna

**Highland Country Inn;** 223 S. Milton; $36-56 s or d; 774-5041 or (800) 642-4186; pool, kitchenettes

**Economy Inn;** 224 S. Mikes Pike; $59 s or d; 774-8888

**Starlite Motel;** 500 S. Milton Rd.; $70 s, $80 d; 774-7301 or (800) 843-5644; room phones

**Knight's Inn Suites;** 602 W. Rt. 66; $90-95 s or d; 774-4581 or (800) 654-4667; pool, spas

**Embassy Suites Hotel;** 706 S. Milton Rd.; $129 s, $139 d; 774-4333 or (800) EMBASSY; free breakfast

**Arizonan Motel;** 910 S. Milton Rd.; $98 d; 774-7171; kitchenettes

**Rodeway Inn West;** 913 S. Milton Rd.; $99 d; 774-5038 or (800) 228-2000; pool, spa

**Comfort Inn;** 914 S. Milton Rd.; $81 d; 774-7326 or (800) 221-2222; pool

**Autolodge;** 1313 S. Milton Rd.; $40-42 s or d; 774-6621

**Quality Inn;** 2000 S. Milton Rd.; $96 s, $105 d; 774-8771 or (800) 228-5151; pool

**Fairfield Inn by Marriot;** 2005 S. Milton Rd.; $80 s, $82 d; 773-1300 or (800) 228-2800; pool, continental breakfast

**Econo Lodge West;** 2355 Beulah Blvd.; $85 s, $90 d; 774-2225 or (800) 553-2666; pool, spas

**AmeriSuites;** 2455 Beulah Blvd.; $99 s, $109 d; 774-8042 or (800) 833-1516; microwave, refrigerator, jacuzzi

**Motel 6 Flagstaff West;** 2745 S. Woodlands Village Blvd.; $39 s, $45 d; 779-3757; pool

**Ramada Ltd. Suites;** 2755 S. Woodlands Village Blvd.; $85 s, $95 d; 773-1111 or (800) 2-RAMADA; continental breakfast, pool, exercise room

## EAST OF DOWNTOWN

**Snowbowl Motel;** 618 E. Rt. 66; $26 s, $42 d; 774-4877

**Whispering Winds Motel;** 922 E. Rt. 66; $35 s, $40 d; 774-7391; kitchenettes

**Inn Suites;** 1008 E. Rt. 66; $95-119 s or d; 774-7356; kitchenettes, pool

**Red Carpet Motel;** 1500 E. Rt. 66; $53 s, $70 d; 779-4469

**Red Roof Inn;** 1526 E. Rt. 66; $42 s or d; 774-2791

**King's House Motel (Best Western);** 1560 E. Rt. 66; $60-65 s, $70-85 d; 774-7186 or (800) 528-1234; pool, continental breakfast

*(continues on next page)*

# FLAGSTAFF ACCOMMODATIONS
*(continued)*

**Western Hills Motel;** 1580 E. Rt. 66; $30 s, $35 d; 774-6633; kitchenettes, pool, DaraThai Restaurant

**Chalet Lodge;** 1900 E. Rt. 66; $60-65 s or d; 774-2779; waterbed available

**Wonderland Motel;** 2000 E. Rt. 66; $48 s, $58 d; 779-6119

**Twilite Motel;** 2010 E. Rt. 66; $35 s, $40; 774-3364; kitchenettes

**Timberline Motel;** 2040 E. Rt. 66; $50 s, 65 d; 774-7481; kitchenettes

**66 Motel;** 2100 E. Rt. 66; $21 s, $28 d; 774-6403; kitchenettes

**Royal Inn;** 2138 E. Rt. 66; $49-89 d; 774-7308

**Flagstaff Motel;** 2204 E. Rt. 66; $30 s, $35 d; 774-0280

**Alpine Motel;** 2226 E. Rt. 66; $35 s, $45 d; 779-3136 or (800) JET-PINE, fax 774-0891; kitchenettes

**Master Hosts/Mason Five Flag Inns;** 2610 E. Rt. 66; $59-66 s or d; 526-1399 or (800) 535-2466; pool, Mason Jar Restaurant

**Pine Crest Motel;** 2818 E. Rt. 66; $25-75 s or d; 526-1950; kitchenettes

**Carousel Inn Motel;** 2918 E. Rt. 66; $45-75 d; 526-3595

**Pony Soldier Motel (Best Western);** 3030 E. Rt. 66; $62-75 d; 526-2388 or (800) 356-4143; indoor pool, spa, restaurant

**Geronimo Motel;** 3100 E. Rt. 66; $45 s, $49 d; 526-2091

**HoJo Inn;** 3300 E. Rt. 66; $64 s or d; 526-1826 or (800) 437-7137; Crown Restaurant open 24 hours

**Hampton Inn;** 3501 E. Lockett Rd.; $89 s or d; 526-1885 or (800) HAMPTON; cont. breakfast, pool

**Econo Lodge Lockett Road;** 3601 E. Lockett Rd.; $55-99 d; 527-1477 or (800) 446-6900; spa

**Super 8 Motel;** 3725 Kaspar Ave.; $49 s, $55 d; 526-0818 or (800) 800-8000; jacuzzi, spa

**Residence Inn by Marriott;** 3440 N. Country Club Rd.; $159 s or d; 526-5555 or (800) 331-3131; pool, spa, airport shuttle

## BUTLER AVENUE AREA (I-40 EXIT 198)

**Motel 6 Butler Avenue;** 2010 E. Butler Ave.; $37 s, $43 d; 774-1801; pool

**Howard Johnson Hotel;** 2200 E. Butler Ave.; $99-119 s or d; 779-6944 or (800) 446-4656; suites, pool, game room

**Flagstaff Inn;** 2285 E. Butler Ave.; $69 s or d; 774-1821 or (800) 533-8992; pool, sauna

**Little America;** 2515 E. Butler Ave.; $119 s or d; 779-2741 or (800) 352-4386; suites, pool, 24-hour restaurant

**Holiday Inn;** 2320 E. Lucky Ln.; $99 d; 526-1150 or (800) 465-4329; suites, pool, spa

**Budget Inn;** 2350 E. Lucky Ln.; $68 s, $78 d; 779-3614; pool

**Econo Lodge Lucky Lane;** 2480 E. Lucky Ln.; $68 s, $78 d; 774-7701 or (800) 446-6900; pool

**Motel 6;** 2440 E. Lucky Ln.; $34 s, $40 d; 774-8756; pool

**Motel 6;** 2500 E. Lucky Ln.; $34 s, $40 d; 779-6184; pool

**Grand Canyon TraveLodge;** 2520 E. Lucky Ln. at I-40; $54 s, $59 d; 779-5121 or (800) 255-3050; spa, pool

*(continues on next page)*

**Mountain Inn** has some B&B rooms at $98.10-119.90 plus both non-breakfast rooms ($87.20-109) and rustic cabins ($81.75-114.45) about three miles from downtown at 685 Lake Mary Rd.; tel. 774-8959.

## Hostels

The historic **Weatherford Hotel** in downtown Flagstaff offers bunk beds in shared rooms for $12 to members year-round. Check in 7-10 a.m. or 5-10 p.m. It's centrally located at the corner of 23 N. Leroux St. and Aspen Ave.; tel. 774-2731. Regular hotel rooms are available too, $28 s and $32 d. Hostelers can use the kitchen or dine downstairs at **Charly's,** the hotel's restaurant and pub. Hostelers get a small discount. Musicians often perform foot-tapping bluegrass, country, or folk in the evenings.

**Monte Vista Hotel** offers hostel rooms in a grand old hotel at 100 N. San Francisco St. for $12 with no membership required; tel. 779-2731.

**Downtowner Grand Canyon International Hostel** offers dorm beds at $9 and beds in double rooms at $11; no hostel card needed. Guests can use the kitchen, bicycles, and common room and receive discounts at local businesses, including car rental agencies. It's downtown at 19 S. San Francisco and Phoenix Ave.; tel. 779-9421.

The **Du Beau International Hostel,** also an independent hostel (no hostel card needed), rents rooms for $12. Motel rooms cost $22 s, $25 d. Both hostel and motel guests receive free breakfasts and can use bicycles, a kitchen, and a common room. It's downtown at 19 W. Phoenix Ave.; tel. 774-6731.

## Campgrounds

Your only camping option close to downtown and its bus and train connections lies in the courtyard of the **Du Beau Motel.** The tent-only camping costs $6 per night including shower and breakfast. Otherwise, you really need your own vehicle to camp.

For developed campgrounds, all with showers except as noted, try: **Fort Tuthill County Campground,** open May 1-Sept. 30, $9 for tent or RV. Water and sewer hookups cost $4 each and are available at 11 sites. The campground is five miles south of downtown off I-17 Exit 337; tel. 774-3464.

**Black Bart's RV Park** is open all year, $13.02 tent and $19.53 RV w/hookups with lower rates in winter; it's two miles east of downtown near I-40 Butler Ave. Exit 198; tel. 774-1912. **Flagstaff KOA** is open all year, $23.99 tent or RV with water and electricity ($25.08 full hookups) and $31.62 for a kamping kabin; it's five miles northeast of downtown on Route 66/US 89, one mile north from I-40 Exit 201; tel. 526-9926. **Big Tree Campground,** also open all year, is a half mile farther north on US 89; $14.35 tent, $15.95 RV w/hookups; tel. 526-2583. **Greer's Pine Shadows** is an adult RV park for self-contained rigs (no restrooms or showers). It's across the highway from Big Tree Campground; open mid-April to Nov. 1; $15.91 w/hookups; tel. 526-4977.

**J&H RV Park** has sites for RVs only at 7901 N. Hwy. 89, three miles north of I-40 Exit 201; open March 1-Nov. 15; $19.86 w/hookups; tel. 526-1829. **Kit Carson RV Park** is open year-round, $20 RV w/hookups; you'll find it two miles west of downtown on W. Old Hwy. 66 (I-40 Exits 191 or 195); tel. 774-6993. **Woody Mountain Campground** is a half mile farther west and open early May-Oct.; rates are $16.36 tents or RVs without hookups, $21.81 w/hookups; tel. 774-7727. **Munds Park RV Campground** offers sites 17 miles south of Flagstaff, near I-17 Exit 322; it's open April 1-Oct. 31; $18.92 w/hookups; tel. 286-1309.

Most established campgrounds on U.S. Forest Service land lie 14 or more miles outside Flagstaff: southeast off Lake Mary Rd., south in Oak Creek Canyon, and north near Sunset Crater National Monument. There's a camping area about five miles out on Lake Mary Road, just after a cattleguard at the Flagstaff city limits; no facilities beyond a campground host and dumpster, but groceries, supplies, and well water are available at **Lake Mary Country Store** a mile down the road, just before the lake; tel. 774-1742. Both the campground and store are open seasonally. The closest National Forest campground to Flagstaff is Little Elden Springs Horse Camp, five miles northeast of Flagstaff off Hwy. 89. Take FR 556 two miles west then turn north on FR 556A and drive a short distance to the campground. Facilities include pull-through campsites, picnic tables, restrooms, water, dumpsters, and hitching posts; it's open late

## DOWNTOWN FLAGSTAFF

LOWELL OBSERVATORY

1. Flagstaff Medical Center
2. Fort Valley Shopping Center
3. Expeditions, Inc.
4. Humphrey Summit Ski (downhill and cross-country)
5. Chez Marc Bistro
6. Flagstaff High School
7. Thorpe Park; Adult Center
8. public library
9. Andy's Sporting Goods (fishing and hunting); proposed parking garage
10. Four Winds Traders (Indian crafts); Nava-Hopi Tours

11. Orpheum Theatre
12. Peace Surplus (camping gear)
13. Alpine Pizza
14. Weatherford Hotel (youth hostel)
15. Downtown Diner
16. Hong Kong Cafe
17. Amtrak/Flagstaff Visitor Center
18. Kathy's Cafe
19. Pasto
20. Monte Vista Hotel
21. McGaugh's Newsstand
22. Cafe Espress; Martan's Burrito Palace

23. Grand Canyon Cafe
24. post office (downtown branch)
25. Greyhound Bus
26. Cottage Place Restaurant
27. NiMarco's Pizza
28. Macy's European Coffee House & Bakery; La Bellavia Sandwich Shoppe
29. Du Beau Motel (hostel, tent camping)
30. Downtowner Grand Canyon International Hostel
31. Morning Glory Cafe; Cosmic Cycles
32. El Charro Cafe

© MOON PUBLICATIONS INC

May-mid Oct.; the fee is $6. For more information or reservations contact the Peaks Ranger Station, 5075 N. Hwy. 89, Flagstaff, AZ 86004; tel. 526-0866.

Consider dispersed camping on Forest Service lands surrounding town. The ponderosa pine forests offer lots of room but no facilities—just be sure you're not on private or state land. The Coconino National Forest map outlines Forest Service land and traces the routes of back roads. Carry water and be *very* careful

with fire; in dry weather the Forest Service often prohibits all fires in the woods and may even close some areas.

## FOOD

Flagstaff, for its size, offers an amazing number of places to eat. But then, it has a lot of hungry tourists and students to serve. Most restaurants cater to the eat-and-run crowd. You'll find the well-known chains and fast-food places on the main highways, but with a little effort you can discover some unique restaurants and cafes. Come downtown for local atmosphere—old-fashioned home-style eateries abound.

## Downtown (North of the Tracks)

**Chez Marc Bistro** offers fine French cuisine in a historic 1911 residence; it's open daily for lunch (11:30 a.m.) and dinner (5:30 p.m.) at 503 N. Humphreys St.; tel. 774-1343. **Charly's Pub and Restaurant,** in the old Weatherford Hotel, serves good American food; it's open weekends for breakfast and daily for lunch and dinner at 23 N. Leroux St.; tel. 779-1919. **Downtown Diner** dishes out bargain-priced breakfasts and lunches daily except Sunday, but don't expect much in the way of decor; 7 E. Aspen Ave.; tel. 774-3492. **Pasto** serves Italian food, including vegetarian and wheat-free options, indoors or in a courtyard. It's at 19 E. Aspen; tel. 779-1937. The historic Monte Vista Hotel offers a **coffee shop,** open daily for breakfast, lunch, and dinner at 100 N. San Francisco St.; tel. 556-3077.

**Café Espress** serves homemade natural foods, including many vegetarian items, plus fancy coffees from the espresso bar and baked goodies from the oven; it's open daily for breakfast, lunch, and dinner at 16 N. San Francisco St.; tel. 774-0541. **Kathy's** is a cozy little cafe with American standbys and a few exotic items such as Aussie burgers and Navajo tacos; it's open daily for breakfast and lunch at 7 N. San Francisco St.; tel. 774-1951. **Alpine Pizza** is open daily at 7 N. Leroux St.; tel. 779-4109.

If you're looking for inexpensive Chinese-American food and don't care about the decor, try the **Grand Canyon Cafe** at 110 E. Rt. 66, tel. 774-2252 or the **Hong Kong Cafe** at 6 E. Rt. 66, tel. 774-9801; both are open Mon.-Sat. for breakfast, lunch, and dinner. You'll find good Mexican food, at bargain rates, at **Martan's Burrito Palace,** open Tues.-Sat. at 10 N. San Francisco St.; tel. 773-4701. **Kachina Downtown** serves Mexican food in a fancier setting Mon.-Sat. for breakfast and lunch and Sunday for dinner at 522 E. Rt. 66; tel. 779-1944.

## Downtown (South of the Tracks)

**Macy's European Coffee House and Bakery** offers a big selection of fresh-roasted coffee and a menu of pasta dishes, sandwiches, soups, salads, quiches, and home-baked goodies; open daily for breakfast, lunch, and dinner at 14 S. Beaver St.; tel. 774-2243. **La Bellavia Sandwich Shoppe** is a cozy little cafe for breakfast and lunch; open daily at 18 S. Beaver St.; tel. 774-8301. **NiMarco's Pizza** is open daily at 101 S. Beaver St.; tel. 779-2691. **Beaver Street Brewery/Whistle Stop Cafe** serves award winning woodfired pizza and gourmet cuisine daily for lunch and dinner at 11 S. Beaver St.; tel. 779-0079. **Cottage Place** serves American and continental specialties in an elegant setting; open Tues.-Sun. for dinner at 126 Cottage Ave.; tel. 774-8431.

**Main Street Bar & Grill** offers fajitas, burgers, salads, homemade pot pies, soups, and desserts daily for lunch and dinner plus live entertainment Thurs.-Sat. nights at 14 S. San Francisco; tel. 774-1519. **Morning Glory Cafe** offers breakfast, plus blue corn tamales, other Mexican items, and a variety of salads and soups for lunch, all vegetarian. It's open Mon.-Sat. 8 a.m.-4 p.m. at 115 S. San Francisco St.; tel. 774-3705. **Cafe Ole** at 119 S. San Francisco St. specializes in homemade Mexican dishes; it's open Mon.-Fri. for lunch and dinner; tel. 774-8272. **Hassib's** serves tasty Middle Eastern, Greek, and Indian specialties (deli and takeout too); it's open Mon.-Sat. for lunch and dinner at 211 S. San Francisco St.; tel. 774-1037.

**El Charro** is a popular Mexican cafe; open Mon.-Sat. at 409 S. San Francisco St.; tel. 779-0552. **Gretel's Blackforesthouse** features German food; open Tues.-Fri. for lunch and dinner and Saturday for dinner only at 605 Riordan Ranch Rd.; tel. 773-1551. **Delhi Palace** offers fine Indian cuisine daily for lunch (buffet available) and dinner at 2700 S. Woodland Village Blvd., near Wal-Mart; tel. 556-0019.

## Northern Arizona University

**North Union** has a cafeteria and the Timber Inn (try the barbecued beef). In the **University Union** you'll find the **Atrium,** a restaurant with a garden atmosphere serving lunches of specialty sandwiches, salads, and soups; **Pizzano's,** with pizza and pasta; **Mt. Jack's** fast food; **The Eatery,** offering deli sandwiches, soups, salads, a bakery, and fast food; and the **Yogurt Stop.** In the center of campus, the **University Dining Hall** features a large cafeteria. More cafeteria fare is available at the **South Campus Dining**

Hall; the **South Campus Student Union** offers **The Peaks,** serving food ready to go.

## Other Areas
The large Mexican-American population of Flagstaff provides the town with some tasty food. In addition to those Mexican eateries listed above, try **Ramona's Cantina** at the corner of Woodlands Village Blvd. and Hwy. 89A, tel. 774-3397, or **El Chilito,** 1551 S. Milton Rd., tel. 774-4666. **Woodlands Cafe** serves American food in a Southwestern atmosphere at Woodlands Plaza Hotel, 1175 W. Rt. 66; tel. 773-9118. **Sakura Restaurant,** also in the Woodlands Plaza Hotel, prepares Japanese teppanyaki and sushi; tel. 773-9118.

Mama Luisa's has excellent Italian cuisine— dinner is served nightly and reservations are advised—at Kachina Square, corner of E. Rt. 66 and Steve's Blvd.; tel. 526-6809. **The Pasta Works** dishes out generous servings of Italian food in an informal atmosphere; 2700 S. Woodlands Village Blvd. near Wal-Mart; tel. 774-6775. More Italian food is available at **Dan's Italian Dining,** open for lunch and dinner Mon.-Sat. at 1850 N. Fort Valley Rd., on the route to the Grand Canyon; tel. 779-9349.

Dine Chinese at **Szechuan,** 1451 S. Milton Rd., tel. 774-8039; **Hunan West,** closed Monday, is in University Plaza off S. Milton Rd., tel. 779-2229; and **Hunan East,** 2028 N. Fourth St., tel. 526-1009. Or, try **Golden Dragon Bowl,** 2730 Lakin Dr. across from Kachina Square, tel. 527-3238; and **Mandarin Gardens,** Park Santa Fe Shopping Center, 3518 E. Rt. 66, tel. 526-5033.

Popular American food joints include the two **Sizzlers,** 2105 S. Milton Rd., tel. 779-3267, and 3540 E. Rt. 66, tel. 526-3391; **Buster's,** 1800 S. Milton Rd. in Green Tree Village, tel. 774-5155; and **Furr's Cafeteria,** 1200 S. Milton Rd., tel. 779-4104. Enjoy economically priced, standard American cafe fare at **Mike and Ronda's,** 21 S. Milton Rd., tel. 774-7008; or at Park Santa Fe Shopping Center, 3518 E. Rt. 66, tel. 526-8138. The **Adobe Grill** serves good Mexican and American food daily for dinner at 914 E. Rt. 66; tel. 774-4802. Thai food devotees can try the **Dara Thai Restaurant,** 1580 E. Rt. 66 in the Western Hills Motel; tel. 774-0047. The **Little America** dining room and coffee shop at 2515 E. Butler Ave. serves a buffet

lunch Mon.-Fri. and a big brunch on Sunday; tel. 779-7950. **Country Club Restaurant** serves good American food in the Continental Country Club, 2580 N. Oakmont Dr.; tel. 527-7998. **Christmas Tree Restaurant** is another American favorite; 5200 E. Cortland Blvd., off Country Club Dr.; tel. 526-0776.

**Black Bart's Steak House** serves up steak, seafood, and other American fare; it's open daily for dinner with singing waiters and waitresses to entertain you. Bart's is at 2760 E. Butler Ave., near I-40 Exit 198; tel. 779-3142. Many locals say you'll find the best steaks in town at **Bob Lupo's Horsemen Lodge,** which serves trout and other specialties as well; it's open for dinner except Sunday; located on US 89, just over three miles from I-40 Exit 201; tel. 526-2655.

## Natural Foods
**New Frontiers** sells natural foods and offers deli dining and take out at 1000 S. Milton Rd.; tel. 774-5747. You'll find supermarkets in most of the shopping centers.

# ENTERTAINMENT

## Movies
Catch movies downtown in the **Orpheum Theatre,** 15 W. Aspen Ave., tel. 774-7823. To find out what's being shown on the NAU campus, call 523-6904. The **University Plaza Theatres** in University Plaza off S. Milton Rd., tel. 774-4433, and **Green Tree Village Theatre,** 1800 S. Milton Rd., tel. 779-3202, both lie south of downtown. East of downtown, you can watch movies at **Flag-East Theatre,** 2009 N. Fourth St., tel. 774-6992, and at **Flagstaff Mall Cinema,** 4650 N. US 89, tel. 526-4555.

## Musical Revue
During summer, performers ham it up with song, dance, and real family entertainment with no extra charge at **Black Bart's Steak House,** 2760 E. Butler Ave. near I-40 Exit 198; tel. 779-3142.

## Theater
Enjoy live stage productions at **Theatrikos Community Theater.** Four mainstage plays are presented per year, each running just over two

dusted

weeks. Tuesday at 7 p.m. an improv group called **Improvikos** puts on musicals, dinner theater, showcase pieces, plus experimental, original, and controversial pieces. The newest production at Theatrikos is **Murder Mystery Dinner Theater** in which the audience participates. All performances are at the **Flagstaff Playhouse** at the corner of Beaver and Cherry Streets, three blocks north of Rt. 66; Saturday matinee admission is $7 with all other performances at $10; tel. 774-1662.

## NAU Culture and Sports

Northern Arizona University presents theater, opera, dance, concerts, and a variety of sports events. For information and tickets, contact NAU Central Ticket Office in the University Union; tel. 523-5661. In late July and early August the **Arizona Cardinals** show up for summer training camp. For best times to watch the Cardinals in action call 523-CARDS.

## Events

Folks from Flagstaff put on a variety of festivals, fairs, shows, and concerts during the year. The Flagstaff visitor center will tell you what's happening; tel. 774-9541 or (800) 842-7293. Major annual events include the **Luminarios** at Northern Arizona University in early-mid-December, and Flagstaff **Winter Festival** in

February, featuring skiing, sled-dog races, clinics, workshops, games, and entertainment. In May residents celebrate **Cinco de Mayo** with a parade, coronation, dance, and barbecue. June brings the **Rt. 66 Festival, Horse Show, Gem and Mineral Show, Pine Country Rodeo and Parade,** and the **Festival of Native American Arts,** featuring Indian art and craft exhibitions, demonstrations, and dance performances. In July comes the **Festival of the Arts,** with concerts, musicals, and plays, July 4th fireworks, and horse racing. The Festival of the Arts continues in August, as does the Festival of Native American Arts. August also sees **Festival in the Pines**—arts and crafts with musical performances—and the **Coconino County Fair.**

# RECREATION

Impress your friends by saying you went skiing and swimming on the same day in Flagstaff. Try the **indoor pools** at the university's Natatorium, tel. 523-4508, or at East Flagstaff Junior High School, corner of N. Fourth St. and Cedar Ave., tel. 779-7690. The indoor pool at Flagstaff High School is open in summer at 400 W. Elm Ave.; tel. 779-7690.

Play **tennis** at the courts in Thorpe Park, off Toltec St. in west Flagstaff; or Bushmaster Park, off Lockett Rd. in east Flagstaff. Both parks also offer picnic tables and playgrounds. Joggers and strollers alike enjoy **Buffalo Park,** off Cedar Avenue. **Ice-skate** from mid-October to mid-April, **roller-skate** the rest of the year at J. Lively Memorial Ice Rink, 1850 N. Turquoise Dr.; tel. 774-1051. Play **golf** at Elden Hills 18-hole course, 2380 N. Oakmont Drive. Take I-40 Exit 201, go south 0.8 mile on Country Club Rd., then turn right on Oakmont Dr.; it's closed in winter; tel. 527-7997.

## Horseback Riding

The Flagstaff area has some great horse country. If you don't have your own steed, local riding stables can provide one; advance reservations are advisable. In winter, stables usually close; their horses often head south to join the snowbirds on the desert.

**The Flying Heart Barn** offers rides year-round on and near the San Francisco Peaks; hourly rates are $21.60, and all-day and overnight trips can be arranged. Head 3.5 miles north on US 89 from I-40 Exit 201; tel. 526-2788. **Hitchin' Post Stables** offers trail rides, hayrides, sleigh rides, cowboy breakfasts, and steak dinner rides 4.5 miles south of town on S. Lake Mary Rd., tel. 774-1719/7131, and trail rides (only) from the stables at Continental Country Club, tel. 774-1719—ask for stables; it's $20 for one hour or $35 for two. **Old West Adventures** at the Mormon Lake Lodge offers riding at $13 for one hour, $25 for two hours, $50 half day, and $85 all day plus pack trips at $150 per day and hay rides at $150 per party; tel. 354-2492.

## Downhill Skiing

**Arizona Snowbowl,** on the San Francisco Peaks, has some of Arizona's best downhill action. Four chair lifts and a tow rope service 30 trails ranging from novice to expert. It's 2,300 feet down from the top of Agassiz Chair Lift; some runs exceed two miles. With sufficient snow, the season begins by mid-December and lasts through Easter. It's open for skiing daily 9 a.m.-4 p.m. Lift tickets cost $31 ($25 half day on weekends and holidays; $19 half day on weekdays) for adults; $17 ($12 half day) for ages 8-12; $11 seniors 65-70; and free for kids (seven and younger) and seniors (over 70).

There's also a ski school for all levels with a bargain beginner package. Equipment rentals are available on the mountain at the Hart Prairie Day Lodge. To reach the Snowbowl, drive northwest seven miles from downtown on US 180 to the turnoff, then either take the shuttle bus ($4 roundtrip) or drive the remaining seven miles—paved, but sometimes requiring chains and/or 4WD. Call 779-1951 for weather and road conditions, and info about lifts, rentals, and instruction. Call (800) 828-7285 for information about motels that offer ski packages.

**Ski Lift Lodge,** across Hwy. 180 from Snow Bowl Road, includes a restaurant. It's not affiliated with the Snowbowl and does not offer a ski package; tel. 774-0729.

## Cross-Country Skiing

**Flagstaff Nordic Center** offers 40 km of snowcat-groomed trails ranging from beginner to advanced near Hart Prairie and the San Francisco Peaks. A five-km marked trail leads to the Hochderrfer Hills (maximum elevation 9,200 feet). The center features ski lessons, with beginner packages, a snowshoe-only trail, equipment rentals and sales, and a snack bar. Races, clinics, and moonlight tours highlight the center's entertainment calendar. It's open daily from about mid-November until mid-April, weather permitting. Trail passes, for people 13-64, are $12; ages 8-12 and 65-69 are $7.50. Younger than 8 and older than 69 ski free. Call 779-1951. Take 180 north 16 miles to near Milepost 232. During the summer the ski routes are used for mountain bike trails and the Nordic Center rents mountain bikes and equipment.

Cross-country skiers also head to Hart Prairie and Wing Mountain, two undeveloped skiing areas near the San Francisco Peaks. The rolling meadow and forest country is ideal for ski touring. Reach Hart Prairie by driving 9.5 miles northwest of town on US 180, then turning right on the south end of Forest Route 151 and continuing as far as the road is clear. Parking on US 180 is prohibited. For Wing Mountain, continue on US 180 just past Hart Prairie Rd., then turn left onto Forest Route 222B. For road and skiing conditions near the Peaks, call the Forest Service (Peaks Ranger Station) at 526-0866.

The groomed trails of Mormon Lake also attract cross-country skiers. **Mormon Lake Ski**

**Center,** in the village of Mormon Lake, has 20 km of groomed diagonal and skating trails ranging from easy to challenging. It's open daily in season with maintained trails ($5 adult, $15 family), rental waxless ski sets ($11), and instruction (starts at $15 for 1.5 hours in a small group); tel. 354-2240 (toll call from Flagstaff). Drive 20 miles southeast on Lake Mary Rd., then turn right and travel eight miles on Mormon Lake Loop Road. **Mormon Lake Lodge** has ten motel rooms and some cabins; tel. 774-0462 (Flagstaff) or 354-2227 (local). For Mormon Lake road and ski conditions, call the Forest Service (Mormon Lake Ranger Station) at 556-7474.

## SHOPPING

### Art Galleries and Indian Crafts
Shops in downtown Flagstaff display a wealth of regional arts and crafts. Native American artists produce especially distinctive work; you'll see paintings, jewelry, Navajo rugs, Hopi kachina dolls, pottery, and baskets. **Four Winds Traders** at 118 W. Rt. 66, is one of the largest and best Indian galleries in the state—Indians themselves also shop here for stones and jewelry-making supplies; it's closed Sunday and Monday. Look for other shops and galleries nearby on Rt. 66, N. Leroux St., N. San Francisco St., and Aspen Avenue. The gift shops at the **Museum of Northern Arizona, Coconino Center for the Arts,** and the **Art Barn,** all northeast of town on US 180, feature excellent selections of Indian arts and crafts.

### Camping Supplies
Outdoor supplies, books, maps, and information, as well as climbing gear, are available from **The Edge,** 12 E. Aspen Ave., tel. 774-4775; **Aspen Sports,** 15 N. San Francisco St., tel. 779-1935; **Mountain Sports,** 1800 S. Milton Rd., tel. 779-5156; **Peace Surplus,** 14 W. Rt. 66, tel. 779-4521; and **Popular Outfitters,** 901 S. Milton Rd., tel. 774-0598. **Andy's Sporting Goods** specializes in hunting and fishing gear; 107 W. Aspen, tel. 774-4401. **Expeditions, Inc.** carries river-running equipment, including kayaks, rafts, wet and dry suits, and river books; it also organizes Grand Canyon raft trips; 625 N. Beaver St., tel. 779-3769.

### Photo Equipment and Supplies
Discount and grocery stores can meet common film needs. For refrigerated professional film and medium and large format film, try **Photo Outfitters** one block off Rt. 66 at 25 N. San Francisco; tel. 779-5181. Camera repair services are offered at **P.R. Camera Repair,** 111 E. Aspen; tel. 779-5263.

### Ski Rentals and Supplies
Cross-country and downhill rentals are available from **Agassiz Ski Haus,** 801 N. Humphrey' St., tel. 774-7671; **Humphrey Summit Ski,** 505 N. Beaver St., tel. 779-1308; and at the Snowbowl turnoff, tel. 774-7852; **Peace Surplus,** 14 W. Rt. 66, tel. 779-4521; and **Mountain Sports,** 1800 S. Milton Rd., tel. 779-5156. Cross-country ski equipment is also available at **The Edge,** 12 E. Aspen Ave., tel. 774-4775; **Inner Basin,** 113A S. San Francisco St., tel. 773-1291; and **Aspen Sports,** 15 N. San Francisco St., tel. 779-1935, as well as **Flagstaff Nordic Center** and **Mormon Lake Ski Center.**

## SERVICES

The main **post office** is at 2400 N. Postal Blvd., just north of E. Rt. 66; tel. 527-2440. There's a downtown branch at 104 N. Agassiz St., and another in the university bookstore basement. Bookman's at 1520 Riordan Ranch St., also provides some postal services.

If you need medical attention, it's cheaper to go directly to a doctor's office than to the hospital. You'll find many offices along N. Beaver Street. **Flagstaff Medical Center,** the local hospital, is at 1200 N. Beaver St.; tel. 779-3366. In **emergencies**—police, fire, and medical—dial 911.

You can find summer jobs in Flagstaff, but pay tends to be rock bottom; for **job information** contact the Department of Economic Security, 397 Malpais Ln.; tel. 779-4513.

The **Adult Center** hosts several clubs and offers classes in yoga, martial arts, dancing, and much more. You're sure to find something of interest if staying in town awhile. Organizations meeting here include the Flagstaff Hiking Club, Northern Arizona Paddlers Club, and Street Masters Car Club. The Adult Center is on the west edge of downtown next to Thorpe Park at 245 N. Thorpe Rd.; tel. 774-1068.

Flagstaff's historic railroad depot is now also a visitor information center.

## INFORMATION

The very helpful **Flagstaff Chamber of Commerce's Visitor Center** staff can answer your questions and tell you what's going on. The office, south of central downtown in the Amtrak depot (1 E. Rt. 66, Flagstaff, AZ 86001), is open daily 8 a.m.-7 p.m. (until 5 p.m. on Sunday and holidays); tel. 774-9541 or (800) 842-7293.

The **U.S. Forest Service** provides information and maps about camping, hiking, and road conditions in the Coconino National Forest surrounding Flagstaff. The **supervisor's office** is at 2323 E. Greenlaw Ln. (Flagstaff, AZ 86004) behind Knoles Village Shopping Center; it's open Mon.-Fri. 7:30 a.m.-4:30 p.m.; tel. 527-3600. You can buy any of the National Forest maps for Arizona here for $3. The Coconino Forest map is also available at the chamber of commerce and sporting goods stores.

For more detailed information on the Mt. Elden, Humphrey's Peak, and O'Leary Peak areas, contact the **Peaks Ranger Station** at 5075 N. Hwy. 89 (Flagstaff, AZ 86004); it's open Mon.-Fri. 7:30 a.m.-4:30 p.m. (and Saturday from early June to early September); tel. 526-0866. For the lake and forest country south of Flagstaff, contact the **Mormon Lake Ranger District** office at 4825 S. Lake Mary Rd. (Flagstaff, AZ 86001); it's open Mon.-Fri. 7:30 a.m.-4:30 p.m.; tel. 556-7474.

**Arizona Game and Fish Department** offers fishing and hunting licenses and information at 3500 S. Lake Mary Rd. (Flagstaff, AZ 86001); it's open Mon.-Fri. 8 a.m.-5 p.m.; tel. 774-5045.

### Libraries
Looking for a good place to keep dry on a rainy day, pass the time during a long bus wait, or just want to read up on Arizona? Check out the **Flagstaff City Library:** its attractive ski-lodge architecture makes it an especially enjoyable place. You'll find it downtown at the corner of 300 W. Aspen Ave. and Sitgreaves St., open Mon.-Thurs. 10 a.m.-9 p.m., Friday and Saturday 10 a.m.-6 p.m., and Sunday 1-4 p.m.; tel. 774-4000 (recorded information), 779-7670 (reference desk). Many good regional books complement the Arizona Collection. Art exhibitions change monthly—expect work by local artists and photographers, mostly showing local scenery.

NAU's **Cline Library** carries many books and periodicals and a large map collection; hikers can plan trips and copy maps here. Cline Library is open (regular sessions, not student holidays) Mon.-Thurs. 7:30 a.m.-11:30 p.m., Friday 7:30 a.m.-6 p.m., Saturday 9 a.m.-6 p.m., and Sunday noon-11 p.m.; tel. 523-2171. The Cline Library's **Special Collections and Archives Department** contains an outstanding array of Arizona-related publications and photos; it's open Mon.-Fri. 8 a.m.-5 p.m.; tel. 523-5551. The **Museum of Northern Arizona** has an excellent regional library in the Research Center across the highway from the museum; it's open Mon.-Fri. 9 a.m.-5 p.m.; tel. 774-5211.

## Bookstores

**McGaugh's Newsstand** downtown features a good selection of newspapers, magazines, Arizona books, and general reading at 24 N. San Francisco Street. The **NAU Bookstore** also offers many regional and general publications. The **Museum of Northern Arizona** sells excellent books on Southwestern Native American cultures, archaeology, and natural history. For new and used books, including many regional titles, drop by **Bookman's Used Books** at 1520 S. Riordan Ranch St., featuring 250,000 new and used books as well as music, videos, and games. A few doors south, **Hastings** sells discounted books, music, and videos. At the corner of S. San Francisco and Butler Ave., **Dragon's Plunder** has over 65,000 used books available for trade or purchase. **Starlight Books** at 15 N. Leroux St. has a smaller selection but is conveniently located downtown. **Waldenbooks** in the Flagstaff Mall stocks good regional and general reading selections.

# TRANSPORT

## Tours

**Nava-Hopi Tours** (The Gray Line) operates regional bus tours and scheduled Grand Canyon bus service. The tours tend to cover a lot in a short period of time. Nava-Hopi offers day-trips to the Flagstaff area (Museum of Northern Arizona, Sunset Crater, and Wupatki, for $34), the Grand Canyon ($38), Oak Creek Canyon-Sedona-Montezuma Castle-Jerome ($36), the Hopi Indian Reservation ($62), Petrified Forest-Painted Desert-Meteor Crater ($58), and Monument Valley ($74). Nava-Hopi requires at least 24 hours' advance notice; children 5-15 ride at half price. Some tours don't operate in winter. Buses leave from the 114 W. Rt. 66. station; tel. 774-5003 or (800) 892-8687.

**Seven Wonders Scenic Tours** runs van excursions to scenic and cultural areas of northern Arizona; tel. 526-2501. **Frontier Tours Sightseeing** offers a variety of tours with free pickup from area motels at 8:30 a.m. and departure at 9 a.m. The Grand Canyon tour lasts over eight hours and costs $37 per person. A tour of Sedona, Jerome, and Montezuma Castle lasts eight hours and costs $35 per person. A tour of Sunset Crater and Walnut Canyon national monuments plus Lowell Observatory lasts over six hours and costs $33 per person. A tour of historic Route 66 includes Meteor Crater, the Painted Desert, and La Posada (an historic Harvey House) lasts nine hours and costs $57 per person. Frontier Tours is located at 2700 Woodlands Village Blvd.; tel. 774-4920.

For an aerial perspective, go with **Flagstaff Safe Fliers,** taking off from the Flagstaff airport to Meteor Crater, San Francisco Peaks, Sunset Crater, Monument Valley, Grand Canyon, Oak Creek Canyon, Sedona, and other scenic spots; tel. 774-7858 or (800) 4-FUNFLY. **Windwalker Air** also offers air tours from Flagstaff with a 30 minute Sedona flight ($45 adult, $30 child) and a variety of Grand Canyon flights; tel. 556-9972.

## Car Rental and Taxi

A rental car allows more extensive sightseeing than public transport and costs less if several people get together. Rates fluctuate with supply and demand, competition, and the mood of the operators; call around for the best deals. See the Yellow Pages for agencies; you'll find offces in town and at the airport. For a taxi, call **Alpine Taxi Cab,** tel. 526-4123; **My Chauffeur Taxi and Tours,** tel. 526-1442; or **A Friendly Cab,** tel. 774-4444.

## Local Bus

**Pine Country Transit** serves most of the city with three routes Mon.-Fri. and one route on Saturday; tel. 779-6624 or 779-6635 (TDD). Pick up a schedule at the Flagstaff Visitor Center.

## Long-Distance Bus

**Greyhound** offers daily departures to Phoenix (four times daily, $20), Holbrook (two times daily, $15), Gallup (four times daily, $37), Kingman (three times daily, $26), Los Angeles (six times daily, $59), Las Vegas (three times daily, $45), and San Francisco (five times daily, $105). The station lies a half mile south of central downtown at 399 S. Malpais Ln.; it's open 4 a.m.-11 p.m.; tel. 774-4573.

**Nava-Hopi** buses head north to the Grand Canyon at least once daily ($12.50 each way) and south to Glendale/Phoenix/Sky Harbor Airport once nightly ($21.50 each way); 114 W. Rt. 66.; tel. 774-5003 or (800) 892-8687.

### Train

**Amtrak** trains leave every evening for Los Angeles ($87 one-way), and every morning for Albuquerque ($82 one-way) and on to New Orleans or Chicago. Amtrak often offers substantial discounts on roundtrip tickets. The station is downtown at 1 E. Rt. 66; tel. (800) 872-7245 for reservations or 774-8679 for the station.

### Air

**America West** flies about nine times daily to Phoenix ($99-139 one-way); tel. (800) 235-9292. Pulliam Field, Flagstaff's airport, lies five miles south of town; take I-17 Exit 337.

### Airport Shuttle

Many travelers have found it more economical to reach connections at Sky Harbor Airport in Phoenix by ground shuttle than by flying. **Eagle Shuttle Inc.** offers a one way ride for $35; tel. 527-1400 or (800) 440-6001. **Nava-Hopi Tours** offers a one-way ride at $21.50; tel. 774-5003 or (800) 892-8687.

# EAST OF FLAGSTAFF

## WALNUT CANYON NATIONAL MONUMENT

The Sinagua tribe called this pretty canyon home more than 800 years ago. Ledges eroded out of the limestone cliffs provided shelter from rain and snow—the Sinagua merely had to build walls under the ready-made roofs. Good farmland, wild plant foods, and forests filled with game lay close by. The clear waters of Walnut Creek flowed in the canyon bottom.

The Sinagua occupied this site from A.D. 1120 to 1250, then, for unknown reasons, left. Perhaps some of their descendants now live among the modern Pueblo tribes. More than 300 Sinagua cliff dwellings remain; some can be seen and entered along a loop trail constructed by the National Park Service.

### Visitor Center

A small museum displays pottery and other artifacts of the Sinagua. Exhibits show how the Indians farmed and how they used wild plants for baskets, sandals, mats, soap, food, and medicine. A map illustrates trading routes to other indigenous cultures. Rangers will answer questions about the archaeology and natural history of Walnut Canyon. During the summer, they give talks several times a day. A wide selection of books, maps, and videos related to the monument and region are for sale.

The self-guided one-mile **Island Trail** begins behind the visitor center and winds past 25 cliff dwellings. Take some time and get a feeling of what it was like to live here as a Sinagua. The paved path descends 185 feet, which you'll have to climb on the way out. Allow 45-60 minutes for the Island Trail. Because of the high elevation (6,690 feet), the trail isn't recommended for people with mobility, respiratory, or cardiovascular problems. The easier **Rim Trail** visits two scenic viewpoints and two stabilized surface dwellings; signs describe the varied plants and wildlife found here. Allow 20-30 minutes for the half-mile loop. Vegetation changes dramatically, from the piñon and juniper forests near the rim to the tall Douglas firs clinging to the canyon ledges. Black walnut and several other kinds of deciduous trees grow at the bottom.

Walnut Canyon National Monument remains open all year (except Christmas), though snows can close the trails for short periods. The visitor center is open daily 8 a.m.-5 p.m. with extended hours in summer. Island Trail closes one hour before the visitor center does. The entrance fee is $4 per family. You'll find picnic areas near the visitor center and on the drive in. From Flagstaff, head east seven miles on I-40 to Walnut Canyon Exit 204, then go south three

# SUDDEN IMPACT

A huge, speeding mass of meteoric iron smashed into the earth's crust east of where Flagstaff is today about 49,500 years ago. The humongous chunk of extraterrestrial rock, weighing many millions of tons, struck the earth with such force that fragments of the meteor were buried hundreds of feet deep. Most of the rock exploded into a gaseous cloud that spread out for tremendous distances, flattened trees, and killed every living thing in its path.

Though larger impact craters exist on our planet, none are so well preserved. The giant pit measures 570 feet deep and 4,100 feet across—enough room for 20 football fields.

When westerners first discovered the crater in 1871, they believed the pit to be of volcanic origin. Philadelphia mining engineer Daniel Barringer devoted the last 25 years of his life to proving the crater was of meteoric origin. The scientific community finally came around in 1929, the year of Barringer's death.

miles on a paved road; tel. 526-3367. Half a mile before the national monument entrance you will see a sign at forest road 303 pointing to the **Arizona Trail** 1.7 miles to the west along a well graded dirt road. Monument rangers can provide information about this section of the trail.

## METEOR CRATER

Apollo astronauts learned about crater geology here, practicing travel on the lunarlike surface. A visitor center perched on the edge of Meteor Crater offers exhibits on meteorites and the Apollo program. You can look closely at a hefty 1,406-pound meteorite found nearby, and hear a recorded lecture on the crater's origin and history. Apollo exhibits include a test capsule, spacesuit, Astronaut Hall of Fame, and short films.

Staff at the privately owned Meteor Crater won't let you descend the hazardous trail into the crater, but will give guided tours along the 3.5-mile rim trail around the crater at no extra charge. Tours leave on the hour 10 a.m.-2 p.m., weather permitting. The visitor center offers lapidary, gift, and coffee shops.

Meteor Crater is open daily 6 a.m.-6 p.m. in summer, mid-May to mid-September, 8 a.m.-5 p.m. in winter, mid-September to mid-May; tel. 289-2362 (local) or (800) 289-5895. Admission is $7 adults, $6 ages 60 and over, $2 children 6-17, and $1 children 6-12.

Meteor Crater is 40 miles east of Flagstaff and 20 miles west of Winslow; take I-40 Meteor Crater Exit 233, then head south six miles on a paved road.

**Meteor Crater RV Park** offers year-round camping for tents ($12.66) and RVs ($16.97, no tents); it's near the I-40 exit for Meteor Crater; tel. 289-4002 or (800) 478-4002.

## GRAND FALLS OF
## THE LITTLE COLORADO RIVER

In the spring, this thundering torrent of muddy brown water plunges 185 feet into the canyon of the Little Colorado River about 30 miles northeast of Flagstaff. The best time to see the spectacle is during March and April; in other months the river may dry up and yield nothing but an unimpressive trickle.

A lava flow from Merriam Crater, the large cinder cone 10 miles southwest, created the falls about 100,000 years ago. The tongue of lava filled the canyon, forcing the river out of its gorge, around the dam, and back over the rim into the original channel.

Grand Falls is on the southwest corner of the Navajo Indian Reservation. From Flagstaff, take US 89 north 1.8 miles past Flagstaff Mall, turn right and travel eight miles on the Camp Townsend-Winona Rd., then turn left onto Leupp Road. Follow Leupp Rd. northeast 13 miles to the sign "Grand Falls 10 Miles" and turn left. The Grand Falls road is dirt but acceptable for passenger vehicles. Notice the hues of the Painted Desert as the road descends to the river. Other approaches: I-40 Winona Exit 211 (seven miles east of Flagstaff)—drive two miles on the Townsend-Winona Rd., then right on Leupp Rd. to the Grand Falls turnoff; I-40 Exit 245 (46 miles east of Flagstaff)—take AZ 99 to Leupp, then Leupp Rd. to the Grand Falls turnoff. From Kykotsmovi, on the Hopi Indian Reservation, take paved Indian Route 2 southwest 49 miles to Leupp, then Leupp Rd. to the Grand Falls turnoff.

Admission is free, though the Navajo Tribe asks you to help keep the area clean and leash your dogs so they won't disturb livestock.

# NORTH OF FLAGSTAFF:
# THE SAN FRANCISCO VOLCANIC FIELD

Volcanic peaks, cinder cones, and lava flows cover about 3,000 square miles around Flagstaff. The majestic San Francisco Peaks, highest of all Arizona mountains, soar 5,000 feet above the surrounding plateau.

Eruptions beginning about 10 million years ago formed a giant volcano. During Pleistocene ice ages, glaciers then carved deep valleys on its slopes. Hundreds of small cinder cones, of which Sunset Crater is the youngest, surround the Peaks. There's no reason to assume the San Francisco Volcanic Field is finished, either. The area has experienced volcanic activity, with periods of calm, all during its long history. Peaceful today, the volcanic field presents some impressive landscapes and geology.

In 1984 the federal government set aside 18,200 acres of this venerable volcano for the Kachina Peaks Wilderness. Many of the peaks and hills make good day-hike destinations. Foresters at the **Peaks Ranger Station** offer maps and hiking information for this region; 5075 N. Hwy. 89, Flagstaff, AZ 86004, tel. 526-0866.

Indians of northern Arizona regard the San Francisco Peaks as a sacred place. The Hopi believe the Peaks are the winter home of their kachina spirits, and the source of clouds that bring rain for crops. The Peaks also occupy a prominent place in Navajo legends and ceremonies, representing one of the cardinal directions.

## SUNSET CRATER
## VOLCANO NATIONAL MONUMENT

Sunset Crater Volcano, a beautiful black cinder cone tinged with yellows and oranges, rises 1,000 feet above jagged lava flows about 15 miles northeast of Flagstaff. Although more than 700 years have passed since the last eruptions, the landscape still presents a lunarlike appearance, with trees and plants struggling to grow.

Visitor center exhibits illustrate the forces deep within the earth and their fury during volcanic eruptions. A seismograph tracks the earth's movements. Film clips of Hawaiian volcanic eruptions show how Sunset Crater may have looked during its periods of activity. Rangers

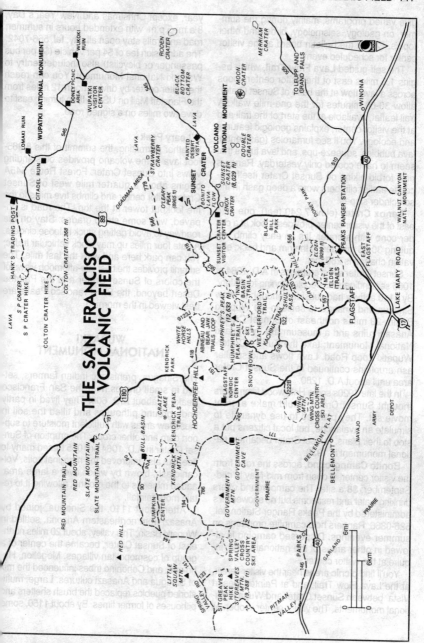

THE SAN FRANCISCO VOLCANIC FIELD

give varied programs, mainly during the summer, on geology, seismology, birds, and other topics. Check the bulletin board at the visitor center for scheduled events.

The self-guided **Lava Flow Trail,** which begins 1.5 miles east of the visitor center, loops across a lava flow at the base of Sunset Crater; allow 30-60 minutes for the one-mile walk. A trail leaflet, available at the start of the trail and at the visitor center, explains geologic features and ecology. You'll see fumaroles (gas vents), lava bubbles, squeeze-ups, and lava tubes that seem to have cooled only yesterday. Rangers now forbid hiking on Sunset Crater itself, because earlier climbers wore a deep gash in the soft cinder slopes.

**Lenox Crater** (elev. 7,240 feet), one mile east of the visitor center, provides a look at a cinder cone with a crater. It's an easy climb, requiring 30-45 minutes to the rim and back; elevation change is 280 feet.

Sunset Crater's first eruptions in A.D. 1064 or 1065 sent indigenous people running for safety. By 1110 activity had subsided enough to allow Sinagua and Anasazi to settle in the Wupatki Basin, 20 miles northeast of Sunset Crater. Anasazi ruins and a museum are in Wupatki National Monument; take the Sunset Crater-Wupatki Loop Road. Lava flows and smaller ash eruptions continued in the Sunset Crater area until about A.D. 1280.

In the late 1920s some Hollywood filmmakers thought Sunset Crater would make a great movie set. They planned to use dynamite to simulate an avalanche, but local citizens put a stop to their plans. Sunset Crater became a national monument in 1930.

**Bonito Campground,** across the road from the visitor center, is open from mid-May to mid-September; $8 a site. The campground offers drinking water and restrooms but no showers; it's administered by the Peaks Ranger Station; tel. 526-0866. Rangers hold campfire programs on summer evenings. Dispersed camping is allowed in other areas of the national forest; inquire at the visitor center.

You'll find **picnic areas** near the visitor center, at the Lava Flow Trail, and at Painted Desert Vista, between Sunset Crater and Wupatki national monuments. The visitor center is open all year, except Christmas and New Year's Day, 8 a.m.-5 p.m. with extended hours in summer; road and trails stay open all day; tel. 556-7042. The admission fee of $4 per vehicle ($1 per bus passenger or bicyclist) also includes entry to Wupatki National Monument. You can reach the visitor center by driving north 12 miles from the Flagstaff Mall on US 89, then turning east to drive two miles on a signed road.

## O'Leary Peak
Weather permitting, the summit of this 8,965-foot lava-dome volcano provides outstanding views into Sunset Crater. Forest Route 545A begins about a quarter mile west of Sunset Crater visitor center and climbs five miles to the fire lookout tower at the top. The road is unpaved, with some steep grades. Stay on the roadway to avoid getting stuck in loose cinders. A gate four miles up may block vehicular traffic; you can park here and walk the last mile. The summit provides the best late-afternoon views of the colors of Sunset Crater and the Painted Desert beyond; the San Francisco Peaks are best viewed in the morning.

# WUPATKI NATIONAL MONUMENT

The Sinagua, prehistoric Indian farmers, settled in small groups near the San Francisco Peaks in about A.D. 600. They lived in partly underground pithouses and tilled the soil in those few areas with sufficient moisture to support corn and other crops. The eruption of Sunset Crater in A.D. 1064 or 1065 forced many to flee, but also improved the marginal soils. Volcanic ash, blown by winds over a large area, added minerals to the ground, allowing it to retain more rainfall.

After about 1110, the Sinagua, joined by Anasazi from northeastern Arizona, settled in Wupatki Basin. This valley, about 20 miles northeast of Sunset Crater, became the center of a group of cosmopolitan villages. Mogollon, Hohokam, and Cohonino tribes influenced the mix of Sinagua and Anasazi cultures. Large, multistoried pueblos replaced the brush shelters and pithouses of former times. By about 1150, some villages had consolidated inside walls, possibly indicating the strain of population pressure. No evidence of conflict has been found, though.

During the 1200s, people began to leave the area, perhaps because of drier conditions and declining soil fertility. By 1300 only ruins remained. Archaeologists think the inhabitants retreated southward to the Verde Valley and northeastward to the Hopi mesas. Hopi legends trace the modern Parrot and Snake clans to the Wupatki area. An estimated 2,700 archaeological sites lie scattered within the monument. Some of the best feature road and trail access, but most of the monument remains closed to visitors. You need a permit to hike beyond open sites. Overnight camping is forbidden.

## Wupatki Visitor Center

You'll see pottery, tools, jewelry, and other artifacts of early cultures on exhibit here. A Wupatki room reconstruction shows how the interior of a typical living chamber might have looked. You'll also learn a little about the present-day Navajo and Hopi tribes who live near the monument. Insect and flowering-plant collections illustrate the flora and fauna of this high-desert country. You can buy books, posters, maps, and videos related to the region. Rangers offer 15-minute orientation talks and provide cultural demonstrations of prehistoric and modern crafts and activities at Wupatki Ruin; most programs take place in summer, but groups can schedule them at other times.

Wupatki visitor center is open daily 8 a.m.-5 p.m. with extended hours in summer; closed Christmas; tel. 556-7040. The visitor center lies 14 miles east of the US 89 turnoff between Flagstaff and Cameron, and 20 miles north of Sunset Crater National Monument. **Doney Picnic Area** sits between cinder cones about three miles northwest on the loop road. **Doney Mountain Trail** climbs gradually for a half mile from the picnic area up a cinder cone to provide a panorama of the Painted Desert and San Francisco Peaks; interpretive signs explain area ecology, the exploits of prospector Ben Doney, and two Indian ruins passed on the way. The nearest accommodations and supplies are in Flagstaff and Gray Mountain. Closest camping is at Sunset Crater and Flagstaff.

## Wupatki Ruin

At its peak, Wupatki (Hopi for "Tall House") contained nearly 100 rooms and towered three stories. A self-guided trail, beginning behind the visitor center, explains many of the features of Wupatki; pick up a trail brochure at the start.

The ball court at one end of the village resembles those used in Mexico for games; these likely had a religious function. The court is one of several found in northern Arizona, probably introduced by the Hohokam of the southern deserts. Archaeologists reconstructed the court from a wall remnant; the rest of Wupatki Ruin is stabilized.

An open-air amphitheater lies to one side of Wupatki; perhaps village meetings and ceremonies took place here. A blowhole, 100 feet east of the ball court, may have had religious importance. A system of underground cracks connects this natural feature with other blowholes in the area; air blows out, rushes in, or does nothing at all, depending on weather conditions. Cavers once tried to enter the system but couldn't get through the narrow passageways.

## Wukoki Ruin

Wukoki is Hopi for "Big and Wide House". Indians lived in this small pueblo for three generations; you can step inside the rooms for a closer look. From the Wupatki visitor center, drive a quarter mile toward Sunset Crater, then turn left and drive 2.6 miles on a paved road.

## Citadel Ruin

This fortress-like pueblo, perched atop a small volcanic butte, stood one or two stories high and contained about 50 rooms. From the top, look for some of the more than 10 other ruins nearby. On the path to the Citadel, you'll pass the pueblo of **Nalakihu,** Hopi for "House Standing Outside the Village". Nalakihu consisted of two stories with 13 or 14 rooms. You can visit both sites on a short, self-guided trail. From Wupatki visitor center, drive nine miles northwest on the loop road.

## Lomaki Ruin

Lomaki, Hopi for "Beautiful House", is one of the best-preserved ruins in the monument. Tree-ring dating of roof timbers indicates the occupants lived here from about A.D. 1190 to 1240.

Wukoki

The small, two-story pueblo contained at least nine rooms. A quarter-mile trail from the parking area also passes small ruins beside Box Canyon. The turnoff for Lomaki lies nine miles northwest of Wupatki visitor center, 0.3 mile beyond Citadel Ruin on the opposite side of the road.

**Crack-in-Rock Ruin**

Rangers lead overnight backpack trips to this dramatic ruin during April and October. Crack-in-Rock sits atop an easily defended mesa with sweeping views of the Little Colorado River and distant hills. Check out the petroglyphs carved around the base of the mesa and on two nearby mesas. You'll also see many other pueblo sites. The 14-mile roundtrip ranger-guided hike is moderately difficult, and costs $25. Call or write for information at least two months in advance; Wupatki National Monument, HC 33, Box 444A, Flagstaff, AZ 86004, tel. 556-7040.

## STRAWBERRY CRATER WILDERNESS

Extrusions of slow-moving basaltic andesite formed this crater 50,000 to 100,000 years ago. Strawberry Crater's jagged features contrast with the much younger cinder cones nearby. Because the San Francisco Peaks form a rain shadow over this area, the crater receives only about seven inches of annual precipitation. Sparse vegetation of juniper, piñon pine, cliffrose,

and a few ponderosa pines cover the gently rolling terrain of cinders and lava. The 10,140-acre wilderness offers good cross-country hiking and a challenging climb to the crater summit. Indian ruins lie in the area as well.

Strawberry Crater is northeast of Flagstaff between Sunset Crater and Wupatki national monuments. The wilderness boundary lies just north of the Painted Desert Vista area on the road between the monuments, but a long hike is required to reach the crater. The best way to the crater involves driving about 16 miles north from the Flagstaff Mall on US 89 to the bottom of a long grade, turning east and traveling 3.4 miles on Forest Route 546, then continuing 1.1 miles east on Forest Route 779 to a set of power lines. An unmarked trail contours left around the crater to the inner basin; this is the best route to the summit. Help preserve Strawberry Crater by not hiking on the steeper slopes; they're fragile and easily damaged.

## MOUNT ELDEN TRAIL SYSTEM

To reach the summit of Mt. Elden, a 9,299-foot peak on the north edge of Flagstaff, you can hike any of several good trails or drive up a rough road. Wildflowers, various types of forests, and panoramic views reward those who ascend even partway up. A fire-lookout tower marks the summit. Climb the tower, if it's open, for the best views. On a clear day you'll see much of north-central Arizona: Oak Creek Canyon and Mormon Lake to the south; the Painted Desert to the east; Humphrey's Peak, Sunset Crater, and other volcanoes to the north; and Bill Williams Mountain to the west. Flagstaff lies directly below.

The hiking season runs from May to October, a bit longer for the drier eastern slope. Carry water. To avoid the hair-raising experience of afternoon thunderstorms, set out early when hiking during July and August, the peak storm

months. Allow at least a half day for a hike to the summit and back. Mount Elden elevations range from 6,900 to 9,299 feet. Hikers, horseback riders, and mountain bicyclists all use the trail system. Contact the Peaks Ranger Station for current trail information; tel. 526-0866.

### Elden Lookout Trail

This three-mile trail at first seems easy, then begins a steep climb up the rocky east slope of Mt. Elden to the lookout tower. Elevation gain is

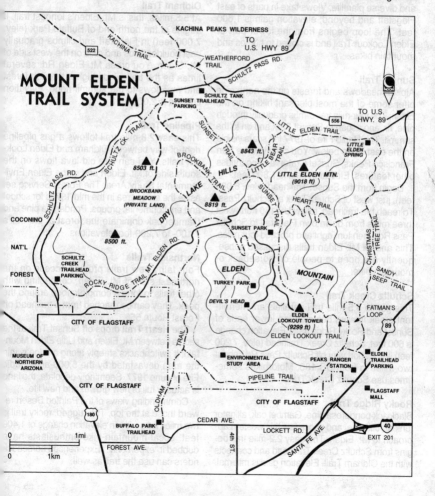

2,400 feet. Begin from the Elden Trailhead (elev. 6,900 feet) on US 89, just north past the Peaks Ranger Station. From Flagstaff, head east through town on Santa Fe Ave. or take I-40 Exit 201 toward Page. The grades and loose surface of this trail make it too hazardous for horse travel or mountain bikes; neither is allowed.

## Fatman's Loop Trail

An easy two-mile walk, except for a few short steep sections, past volcanic rock formations and diverse plantlife. Views take in parts of east Flagstaff and beyond; elevation gain is 1,600 feet. The loop begins from the lower part of Elden Lookout Trail and is closed to horses and mountain bikes.

## Sunset Trail

Alpine meadows and forests on the north side offer some of the most pleasant hiking on Mt. Elden. The four-mile trail climbs gradually through pine, fir, and aspen to Sunset Park and on to the summit. The Radio Fire of 1977 left scars visible on the east slope below. You can view the San Francisco Peaks, Sunset Crater, and countless other features. Elevation gain is 1,300 feet.

Begin from the Sunset Trailhead (elev. 8,000 feet), just west of Schultz Tank at Schultz Pass. To reach the trailhead, follow US 180 northwest three miles from downtown Flagstaff to Schultz Pass Rd., then turn right and proceed four miles. This and all Mt. Elden trails discussed subsequently are open to people on horseback or mountain bike.

## Schultz Creek Trail

This gentle 3.5-mile trail parallels an intermittent creek flowing between the lower ends of Sunset and Rocky Ridge trails. Elevation change is 600 feet. Schultz Creek Trailhead (elev. 7,200 feet) lies a short way off Schultz Pass Rd., about two miles in from US 180. Motorbikes sometimes use Schultz Creek Trail.

## Rocky Ridge Trail

Blackjack ponderosa pine, Gambel oak, alligator juniper, cliffrose, and yucca line this western approach to Mt. Elden. The easy 2.2-mile trail begins from Schultz Creek Trailhead and connects with the Oldham Trail. Elevation gain is minimal.

## Brookbank Trail

This easy 2.5-mile trail climbs through a forested drainage to the edge of Brookbank Meadow, owned by the Navajo Tribe, then continues to eventually meet Sunset Trail at a low saddle. Elevation gain is 1,000 feet. The trailhead (elev. 7,800 feet) can be reached by hiking the Oldham Trail or by driving a half mile in on Schultz Pass Rd. from US 180, then going 2.5 miles up Mt. Elden Road.

## Oldham Trail

At 5.5 miles, this is Mt. Elden's longest trail. It begins at the north end of Buffalo Park (elev. 7,000 feet) in Flagstaff and climbs gradually past boulder fields and cliffs on the west side of Mt. Elden. You cross Mt. Elden Rd. several times as the trail winds higher through forest and meadows to the summit ridge. Elevation change is 2,000 feet.

## Pipeline Trail

This easy 2.8-mile trail follows a gas pipeline right-of-way between Oldham and Elden Lookout trails. You can see old lava flows on the south side of Mt. Elden and in the Elden Environmental Study Area. The Forest Service set aside the study area in the mid-1970s for school and environmental groups. Ponderosa pine and Gambel oak dominate the forest at the trail's 7,100- to 7,200-foot elevations.

## Northside Trails

Four fairly new trails provide access on the northeast side of Mt. Elden, connecting with other trails to form a complete loop around the peak. They can be reached from a trailhead off Forest Route 556.

The **Heart Trail** drops off Sunset Trail at the saddle between Mt. Elden and Little Elden Mountain; it switchbacks steeply along a ridge within the area devastated by the 5,000-acre Radio Fire of June 1977. Seemingly desolate, the land is actually full of new growth and new life.

Commanding views of the Painted Desert reward those at the top. The rugged, rocky trail is two miles long with an elevation change of 1,400 feet. Local mountain-bike enthusiasts have dubbed it "expert only." Experienced horseback riders can use the trail as well.

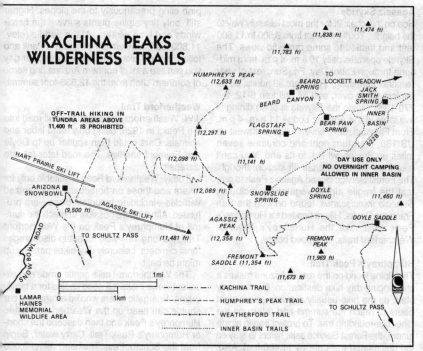

# KACHINA PEAKS WILDERNESS TRAILS

OFF-TRAIL HIKING IN TUNDRA AREAS ABOVE 11,400 ft IS PROHIBITED

HUMPHREY'S PEAK (12,633 ft)

(12,297 ft)

(12,098 ft)

(12,089 ft)

(11,783 ft)

(11,838 ft)

(11,474 ft)

TO LOCKETT MEADOW

BEARD SPRING

BEARD CANYON

JACK SMITH SPRING

FLAGSTAFF SPRING

BEAR PAW SPRING

INNER BASIN

5228

(11,141 ft)

DAY USE ONLY
NO OVERNIGHT CAMPING
ALLOWED IN INNER BASIN

SNOWSLIDE SPRING

DOYLE SPRING

(11,460 ft)

AGASSIZ PEAK (12,356 ft)

AGASSIZ SKI LIFT

HART PRAIRIE SKI LIFT

ARIZONA SNOWBOWL

(9,500 ft)

TO SCHULTZ PASS

AGASSIZ SKI LIFT

(11,481 ft)

FREMONT SADDLE (11,354 ft)

FREMONT PEAK (11,969 ft)

DOYLE SADDLE

SNOW BOWL ROAD

LAMAR HAINES MEMORIAL WILDLIFE AREA

(11,673 ft)

TO SCHULTZ PASS

0     1mi
0     1km

KACHINA TRAIL
HUMPHREY'S PEAK TRAIL
WEATHERFORD TRAIL
INNER BASIN TRAILS

The other three trails—**Christmas Tree Trail, Sandy Seep Trail,** and **Little Elden Spring Trail**—connect the northern end of Fatman's Loop with Little Elden Spring (three miles) and continue on to Schultz Pass (about another 2.5 miles). These easy trails offer a variety of views and terrain—from the dry ponderosa pine and Gambel oak of the east flank of Mt. Elden, past the four Robinson Hills and lower reaches of the Radio Fire, around the buttress of Little Elden Mountain, and into the cooler fir/pine forest of the north slope. **Little Bear Trail** is planned as a three-mile-long connector from the Little Elden Spring Trail, starting just over halfway from Schultz Tank to Little Elden Spring. It climbs—steeply, in places—with switchbacks to reach a 1,000-foot rise to join the Sunset Trail close to the Brookbank-Sunset Trail junction.

## SAN FRANCISCO PEAKS

**Kachina Peaks Wilderness** protects 18,960 acres on the Peaks. The name was selected because of the religious importance of the area to the Hopi Tribe. The Forest Service maintains a network of trails in the wilderness, some of which are described below. For current hiking conditions, maps, and other trails, contact the Peaks Ranger Station at 526-0866.

### Lamar Haines Memorial Wildlife Area
A small pond fed by two springs attracts birds and other wildlife. Ludwig Veit, for whom the springs are named, homesteaded here in 1892. Petroglyphs decorate nearby volcanic rocks. From the parking area, near Milepost 4.5 on paved Snowbowl Rd., walk through the gate and turn right 0.7 mile on an abandoned road. Lamar Haines (1927-86) was active in education and conservation in the Flagstaff area.

## Agassiz Skyride

Hop on this chair lift for the most leisurely way to the heights. You'll be swept from 9,500 to 11,600 feet and treated to some fantastic views. The Skyride operates daily 10 a.m.-4 p.m. from mid-June through Labor Day, Fri.-Sun. rest of year (weather permitting). Rates are $9 adults, $6.50 seniors 65 or over, and $5 children 6-12; tel. 779-1951. While the Skyride is open dining is available at the Agassiz Lodge 11 a.m.-4 p.m. From Flagstaff, drive seven miles northwest on US 180, then turn right and continue seven miles up Snowbowl Rd. to its end. You can't hike from the upper chair lift station, though. The Forest Service closed Agassiz Peak to protect the fragile alpine vegetation, including *Senecio franciscanus,* found only on the San Francisco Peaks. Hikers headed for Humphrey's Peak must take the Humphrey's Peak or Weatherford trails, described below.

## Humphrey's Peak Trail

The alpine world on the roof of Arizona makes a challenging day-hike destination. Get an early start, as the hike usually requires about eight hours to reach the summit and return on the nine-mile-roundtrip trail. To protect fragile alpine tundra, the Forest Service asks hikers to stay on the designated trails above 11,400 feet. Also, don't build campfires or set up camps.

Snow blocks the way much of the year, so the hiking season usually runs only from late June to September. Come prepared for bad weather with good rain- and windgear; getting caught in a storm near the top with just a T-shirt and shorts could be deadly. Lightning frequently zaps the Peaks, especially during July and August; stay away if storms threaten. In winter, winds and sub-zero cold can be extremely dangerous—only the most experienced groups should attempt a climb then. Carry plenty of water; you'll use more when hiking at these high elevations.

A climb to the summit is strenuous, but many hikers enjoy shorter walks on the trail. The trail begins from the Snowbowl area (elev. 9,300 feet), contours under the Hart Prairie chair-lift, then switchbacks up the mountain. You'll hike through dense forests of Engelmann spruce, corkbark fir, and quaking aspen. Near 11,400 feet, stunted Engelmann spruce and bristlecone

pine cling precariously to the slopes. Higher still, only tiny alpine plants survive the fierce winds and long winters. At the saddle (elev 11,800 feet), turn left for Humphrey's Peak and follow the trail along the ridge. On a clear day you can see a lot of northern Arizona and some of southern Utah from the 12,633-foot summit.

## Weatherford Trail

J.W. Weatherford completed this toll road into the Peaks in 1926, using only hand labor and animals. Cars could then sputter up to Doyle and Fremont saddles. The road later fell into disrepair.

Today, Weatherford Road is suitable only for hikers and those on horseback; mechanized vehicles—including mountain bikes—are prohibited. Although it's possible to reach the summit of Humphrey's Peak on the Weatherford Trail, the long 19.4-mile roundtrip discourages most climbers. Leisurely day-hikes partway up might be best.

The Weatherford Trail's gentle grade and excellent views make it a good choice for a family outing. Energetic hikers who've arranged a car shuttle can head up the Weatherford Trail to Humphrey's Peak and then descend the shorter Humphrey's Peak Trail. Carry water. Begin from the Schultz Pass Trailhead (elev. 8,000 feet), just west of Schultz Tank. To reach the trailhead, follow US 180 northwest three miles from downtown Flagstaff to Schultz Pass Rd. and turn right four miles.

## Kachina Trail

This new trail on the southern slopes of Humphrey's Peak is 6.5 miles long one-way. From the upper trailhead, on the south end of the lower Snowbowl parking lot (elev. 9,300 feet), the Kachina winds east through spruce, fir, aspen, and ponderosa pine to the Sunset Trailhead at Schultz Pass (elev. 8,000 feet). Carry water.

## Inner Basin Hiking

The San Francisco Peaks form a giant U-shaped valley known as the Inner Basin. Aspen, fir, and spruce thrive here. You can reach Lockett Meadow, at the Inner Basin entrance, by car from the northeast. Park here and continue on foot. Other roads and trails extend as far as 3.5

miles up the Inner Basin; all offer wonderful hiking. Elevations range from 8,600 feet at Lockett Meadow to about 11,000 feet at Snowslide Spring. No one should hike above Snowslide because of the danger to tundra vegetation. The many springs in the Inner Basin supply some of Flagstaff's water, but most are covered and locked; it's safest to carry your own water. Aspen put on a magnificent golden show in late September and early October. You can camp near Lockett Meadow, but not in the Inner Basin just beyond.

From the Flagstaff Mall, drive north 12.5 miles on US 89 and turn left on Forest Route 552. The turnoff lacks signs; look for a dirt road beside a large black cinder pit between Mileposts 431 and 432; the turnoff is 0.7 mile past the Sunset Crater junction. Follow Forest Route 552 past the cinder pit for 1.3 miles, then turn right just before a gravel pit; Lockett Meadow is 3.5 miles farther. Low-slung cars and large vehicles may experience difficulty on this road.

### Abineau and Bear Jaw Trails

These two trails climb about halfway up the

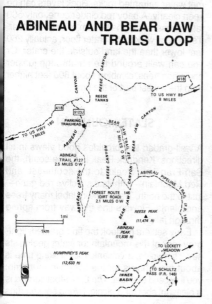

north side of the San Francisco Peaks. On either path you'll enjoy cool forests of pine, fir, and aspen. Wildflowers grow in rocky alpine meadows near the top of Abineau Trail. Both trails start near Reese Tanks. Abineau Pipeline Trail, a dirt road closed to vehicles, connects the upper ends. With this road, Abineau and Bear Jaw make a good 6.5-mile hiking loop. Abineau is probably the prettier of the two, a good choice if you don't want to do the whole loop.

The trailhead lies on the opposite side of the Peaks from Flagstaff. Either take US 180, Forest Route 151 (second turnoff), and Forest Route 418 around the west side of the Peaks, or follow US 89 and Forest Route 418 around the east slopes; consult the Coconino Forest map. Beginning at Flagstaff, each drive is about 26 miles long. A sign on Forest Route 418 marks the turnoff for the trailhead, about a half mile in on Forest Route 9123J. Park and walk up the trail to a T-intersection: Abineau Trail goes to the right, Bear Jaw to the left. Signs and tree blazes mark both trails. Abineau Trail soon enters Abineau Canyon—actually more of a valley—and stays in it all the way to Abineau Pipeline Trail, 2.5 miles away. You can retrace your steps or turn left 2.1 miles on the pipeline trail to the upper trailhead for Bear Jaw Trail, marked by stone cairns, tree blazes, and a wide spot in the road.

Bear Jaw Trail, two miles one-way, doesn't follow a valley at all—you have to be very careful to look for signs and tree blazes. Take special care near the bottom when following a road, because the trail later turns left away from the road; this turn is easy to miss. Allow four to five hours for the complete loop. You'll begin at 8,500 feet at the trailhead and reach 10,500 feet at the upper end of Abineau Trail. Carry water and raingear.

## SP CRATER AND COLTON CRATER

These two volcanic craters, about 14 miles due north of the San Francisco Peaks, offer interesting geology and good hiking. SP Crater's graceful shape and the black tongue of lava flowing from its base resemble the contours of Sunset Crater. SP even features some reddish lava on its rim. Although Sunset Crater is closed to climbing, you can still hike up SP Crater. The near-perfect symmetry of this cinder cone has earned it photos in many geology textbooks.

Actually "SP" isn't the real name of this little volcano. Most likely prudish mapmakers were redfaced when they heard what local cowboys called it. These earthy men of the West saw the black spatter on the rim of the bowl-shaped crater and the leaking lava flow below, and determined the thing "looks just like a shit pot." The name stuck.

### Climbing SP Crater

The climb is moderately difficult; you ascend 800 feet to the rim. Any time of the year is alright for a hike as long as the weather is good. The Coconino Forest map or the 15-minute SP MTN topo map help in navigating the dirt roads, none of which are signed. From Flagstaff, drive 27 miles north on US 89 to Hank's Trading Post (Milepost 446). Or, from the Wupatki National Monument turnoff, go north 1.2 miles to the trading post. Turn left (west) on the unsigned dirt road just south of the trading post. You can pick out SP, straight ahead, among the other volcanoes by its height and symmetry. Keep left where the road forks and drive a half mile. When SP Crater is on your right, six miles in from the highway, you'll pass a large, black water tank on the left, then come to another road fork. Keep right at the fork, then look for a vehicle track on the right 100 yards farther. Take this track for a half mile and park. People four-wheeling beyond this point have made deep ruts on the slope.

Follow the track on foot to the grassy ridgetop—SP Crater adjoins it on the right—then start up the black-cinder slope of SP itself. There's no real trail—it's one step up and two steps back on the loose sliding cinders. Perseverance will get you onto the rim for a close look at lava formations and a panoramic view of the San Francisco Volcanic Field. Walking around the rim is rewarding, but descending into the 360-foot-deep crater is hazardous. The thick, blocky lava flow from SP's base extends 4.3 miles north, and is about 70,000 years old.

### Climbing Colton Crater

If you'd like to see another volcano or desire an easier hike, visit nearby Colton Crater. Colton lies two miles due south of SP; on the roads in

view of SP Crater from Colton Crater

take the other fork near the black water tank, then go south two miles to an intersection with a road from the right. Park near here and head up the gentle slope to the rim, ascending about 300 feet. A gigantic explosion blew out the center of this volcano when hot basaltic magma met water-saturated rocks. Rock layers can be seen clearly. A baby red cinder cone, only 500 feet across, sits at the bottom of Colton Crater. It's an easy walk to the crater floor, actually 260 feet lower than the land outside the crater. Or you can walk around the rim through juniper and piñon trees, climbing about 600 feet higher than the lowest part of the rim.

## SLATE MOUNTAIN

A well-graded trail provides good views in all directions. Kendrick Peak is to the south, the San Francisco Peaks to the southeast, and Red Mountain—with its distinctive red gash—just to the north. Trail markers label many trees and plants. Flowers line the way from spring through fall.

Early settlers mistook the fine-grained, light-gray rock of this mountain for slate; geologists say it's rhyolite, a volcanic rock. Hiking time is about three hours for the five-mile roundtrip; you'll ascend 900 feet. The 8,215-foot summit is a pleasant spot for a picnic. Hiking season runs from May to October; carry water. To reach the trailhead, drive northwest 27 miles from Flagstaff on US 180, then turn west two miles on Forest Route 191, between Mileposts 242 and 243 on US 180. A sign marks the trailhead.

## RED MOUNTAIN

Ever wanted to walk into the heart of a volcano? Then try Red Mountain, 33 miles northwest of Flagstaff. Unusual erosion has dissected the cinder cone from the summit straight down to its base. Walk through a little canyon between towers of black cinders to enter the volcano. A six-foot-high stone wall here is the only real climb. Ranchers built the wall for a stock pond, but cinders filled it in. Either clamber over this former dam or take the trail up the cinder slope to the right.

Beyond the dam you'll enter a magical land of towering pinnacles and narrow canyons. This is a great place to explore; children will love it. Trees offer shade for a picnic. Most of Red Mountain is soft volcanic tuff. Look for the rocks and minerals extruding from it: blocks and bombs of lava; small crystals of plagioclase

feldspar, transparent, with striations; black, glassy pyroxene and hornblende; and volcanic dust, cinders, and lapilli (large cinders). A lava flow covers part of Red Mountain's southwest side about 100 feet below the summit. To reach the top (elev. 7,965 feet), take the trail back out of the crater and climb the gentle cinder slopes on the southeast side. You'll ascend about 1,000 feet.

Red Mountain is easy to reach; drive 33 miles northwest from Flagstaff on US 180—or 42 miles southeast from Grand Canyon National Park—to Milepost 247, then turn west on the dirt road. Red Mountain lies 1.5 miles in, but vehicles can proceed only a half mile. You can't miss the red cinders of the volcano. A less-used road forks off to the left and climbs most of the way to the summit.

## KENDRICK PEAK WILDERNESS

Although the San Francisco Peaks are higher, Kendrick Peak might well provide the better view—you get not only a splendid panorama of northern Arizona, but a view of the Peaks themselves. The Painted Desert, Hopi mesas, and

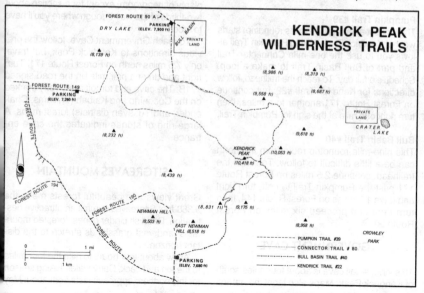

FOREST ROUTE 90 A
DRY LAKE
PARKING (ELEV. 7,900 ft)
BULL BASIN
PRIVATE LAND

### KENDRICK PEAK WILDERNESS TRAILS

(8,139 ft)
(8,986 ft)
(8,319 ft)
FOREST ROUTE 149
PARKING (ELEV. 7,260 ft)
(9,558 ft)
(8,687 ft)
PRIVATE LAND
(8,232 ft)
CRATER LAKE
(9,618 ft)
KENDRICK PEAK (10,418 ft)
(10,053 ft)
(8,439 ft)
FOREST ROUTE 194
FOREST ROUTE 190
NEWMAN HILL (8,503 ft)
(8,831 ft)
(9,175 ft)
EAST NEWMAN HILL (8,518 ft)
(8,958 ft)
FOREST ROUTE 171
CROWLEY PARK
PARKING (ELEV. 7,680 ft)

0    1 mi
0    1 km

PUMPKIN TRAIL #39
CONNECTOR TRAIL # 80
BULL BASIN TRAIL #40
KENDRICK TRAIL #22

far-distant Navajo Mountain lie to the northeast; the north rim of the Grand Canyon juts up to the north; Sitgreaves and Bill Williams mountains poke up to the west; Oak Creek Canyon and the Mazatzals lie to the south; and the magnificent San Francisco Peaks, surrounded by many smaller volcanoes, rise directly to the east. Three trails, ranging in length 8-11 miles roundtrip, lead to Kendrick's 10,418-foot summit and fire-lookout tower. Hiking season lasts from late June to September; longer on the southern Kendrick Trail. Carry water.

## Kendrick Trail #22

This shortest trail, eight miles roundtrip, is the one most used. Because it climbs the sunny southern slopes, it's the best choice early or late in the season. A lookout cabin, equipped with a wood stove and three bare bunk beds, sits on the ridge a quarter mile below the summit. Hikers may use this little cabin, which has withstood the elements since 1912. To reach the trailhead, take I-40 Bellemont Exit 185 (10 miles west of Flagstaff), follow the frontage road one mile west, drive 12.5 miles north on Forest Route 171, then turn right one mile on a road signed Kendrick Trail.

## Pumpkin Trail #39

The longest approach (11 miles roundtrip) starts west of Kendrick Peak. Hiking Pumpkin Trail allows you to use the one-mile Connector Trail and part of Bull Basin Trail to make a loop. Schedule a full day. To reach the trailhead, follow directions for Kendrick Trail #22, but continue on Forest Route 171 another four miles, then turn right one mile at the sign for Pumpkin Trail.

## Bull Basin Trail #40

This nine-mile-roundtrip route from the north can be a little difficult to follow. To reach the trailhead, continue 2.5 miles on Forest Route 171 past the Pumpkin Trail turnoff, turn right and drive 1.5 miles on Forest Route 144, then turn right and proceed six miles on Forest Route 90.

## GOVERNMENT CAVE

This long, small cave is about four miles south of Kendrick Peak. Maps also label the natural underground tunnel Lava River Cave. Red-hot lava broke through the ground near the San Francisco Peaks about 100,000 years ago, then moved westward across Hart and Government prairies, reaching a thickness of more than 100 feet in places. As the outer layers of the smoking mass cooled, some of the fiery-hot interior burst through a weak spot in the surface, partly draining the lava flow. This underground river of fire eventually cooled, too.

A collapsed ceiling today reveals the passageway. No one knows the total length of this lava-tube cave, but about 0.7 mile is easily explored. The interior remains cool year-round, so a jacket or sweater is recommended. Bring at least two flashlights to explore the cave; it's no fun trying to feel your way out because your one and only light died.

The walls and ceiling form an amazingly symmetrical tunnel. The former lava river on the floor still displays all the ripple marks, cracks, and squeeze-ups of its last days. There's only one main passageway, though a small loop branches off to the right about one-third of the way through and then rejoins the main channel. The main channel is large, with plenty of headroom, except for a section about two-thirds of the way through where you'll have to stoop.

To reach Government Cave, follow the previous directions to Kendrick Peak, but travel only 7.5 miles north on Forest Route 171. Turn right and drive a half mile on the road signed 171B. The cave and turnoff are clearly marked on the Coconino and Kaibab (Williams, Chalender, and Tusayan districts) forest maps. A large ring of stones indicates the cave entrance.

## SITGREAVES MOUNTAIN

Great views and beautiful forests make the 9,388-foot Sitgreaves summit an attractive destination. Reddish cinder cones, forested mountains, and vast grasslands stretch to the distant horizon.

Allow about four hours to hike the four miles to the top and back. Carry water. Hiking season for this northern approach lasts from about May to October. The route follows a valley from the trailhead to the summit ridge, then turns right up the ridge to the highest point. No established trails or signs exist on Sitgreaves but none are needed—just stay in the valley until you reach the ridge. Be sure to descend via the same valley, unless you want a much longer hike. Walking is a bit easier if you keep to the right when going up—not so many fallen trees. Beautiful groves of aspen find this cool, moist, sheltered area to their liking.

Sitgreaves Mountain lies about seven miles north of I-40, about two-thirds of the way from Flagstaff to Williams. To find the trailhead you'll need either the Coconino or Kaibab (Williams, Chalender, and Tusayan districts) forest map. Take I-40 Pittman Valley Exit 171, go north seven miles on Forest Route 74 to its end, turn right and drive three miles on Forest Route 141 (Spring Valley Rd.), then look *real hard* on the right for a small road. The turnoff is very easy to miss and probably won't be signed. Map designations for the turnoff are T.23N., R.3E., sec. 13. You can drive your car in about one mile. When the road gives out, continue walking in the same direction up the valley.

# WEST OF FLAGSTAFF

## WILLIAMS

Small and friendly Williams proudly proclaims itself "Gateway to the Grand Canyon." The town (pop. 2,600) nestles among pine-forested hills and expansive meadows at an elevation of 6,780 feet. Downtown Williams may lack charm, but it does offer less expensive accommodations and food than Grand Canyon Village to the north. Arizona 64, on the west edge of town, is the shortest route—58 miles—between I-40 and the famous park. Most travelers, in a hurry to get someplace else, miss the pretty country surrounding Williams—splendid Sycamore Canyon, small fishing lakes, high volcanoes, forest drives, and hiking trails.

### History
Charles Rodgers, the first white settler here, started a cattle operation in 1878. The railroad and lumber town founded several years later took its name from Bill Williams Mountain just to the south. The mountain in turn honored mountain man Bill Williams, who roamed the West from 1825 until his death at the hands of Ute Indians in 1849. He earned a reputation as a skilled marksman, trapper, trader, and guide—he was also an accomplished horse thief, preacher of profane sermons, and prodigious drinker.

Today the Bill Williams Mountain Men perpetuate his adventurous spirit. The group dresses in buckskin clothing and fur hats, stages an annual 180-mile horseback ride from Williams to Phoenix, and works to keep the history of the mountain men alive. The Buckskinners, a family-oriented group, put on frontier-era garb and engage in black-powder shoots.

A more recent period of Western history came to an end at Williams in October 1984, when I-40 bypassed the last section of old US Route 66. A sentimental ceremony, complete with songwriter Bobby Troup of "Route 66" fame, marked the transition. The famous highway from Chicago to Los Angeles carried many families to a new life in Arizona and California. Its replacement, I-40, now travels an unbroken 2,400-mile path from Durham, North Carolina, to Barstow, California.

### The Train
Passenger trains first steamed out of Williams to view the Grand Canyon's scenic splendor in 1901. Railroad service ended in 1968, but started anew after a 21-year hiatus. **Grand Canyon Railway** steam trains (diesel in winter) now provide service from downtown Williams to the historic log depot in Grand Canyon Village. Before the ride starts you can enjoy the free museum (open daily 7:30 a.m.-10 a.m. except Dec. 24th and 25th) and a wild west show. Weather permitting, passengers enjoy a staged horseback chase and train robbery. Trains are scheduled daily except Dec. 24th and 25th. Roundtrip fare is $57.17 adults and $20.62 children ages 3-16 ($4 more for park admission fee ages 17-61); packages are available including lodging; tel. (800) THE-TRAIN.

## Accommodations

Business Route I-40 divides downtown, becoming Bill Williams Ave. (eastbound) and Railroad Ave. (westbound). Most of the town's 30 motels (more are on the way) lie along Bill Williams Avenue.

**Fray Marcos Hotel** is in the Grand Canyon Railway's historic Williams Depot complex and offers rooms decorated in classic southwestern style plus **Spenser's Restaurant** where breakfast, lunch, and dinner are served daily; tel. (800) 843-8724. **Quality Inn Mountain Ranch** is out in the country six miles east of town near I-40 Exit 171; horseback riding is offered in summer; tel. 635-2693. **Railside RV Ranch,** is the closest camping facility to downtown and the railroad depot, just off the tracks one mile to the northeast with shuttle service available; rates are $16.25 tents, $17.62 RV w/hookups; tel. 635-4077. **Red Lake Campground and Hostel,** 10 miles north on AZ 64 from I-40 Exit 165, is open all year with coin-operated showers; $10.51 tents, $12.61 RV (no hookups), $16.82 RV w/hookups; tel. 635-4753. The hostel facilities are available at $11 per person or $33 for a private room. Two KOA campgrounds lie a short distance from Williams: **Circle Pines KOA** is three miles east at I-40 Exit 167; $19.03 tents, $21.10 RV w/hookups, $30.06 kamping kabins with volleyball, badminton, basketball courts, game room, indoor pool, and summer horseback riding ($11.88 half hour, $18.36 full hour); open year-round; tel. 635-4545. **Grand Canyon KOA,** five miles north of Williams on AZ 64 (I-40 Exit 165) on the way to the Grand Canyon, offers tents ($17.40), RV sites with no hookups ($21.10-23.21), RV spots w/hookups ($30.60-33.76), amenities include indoor pool and showers. It's open March 1 to December 1; tel. 635-2307.

The Forest Service maintains four campgrounds, all on small fishing lakes, with drinking water but no showers. They're open from early May to about mid-October for $6-10 a night. Elevations range from 6,600 to 7,100 feet. Boaters can use motors up to eight h.p. on Cataract and Kaibab lakes, but only electric motors are allowed on the other lakes. **Cataract Campground** lies two miles northwest of town; head west on Railroad Ave. across I-40 to Country Club Dr. (or take I-40 Exit 161 and go north),

then turn right one mile immediately after going under railroad tracks and look for the entrance on the left; it's closed mid-October to early May. **Kaibab Campground** is four miles northeast of town; drive east on Bill Williams Ave. across I-40 (or turn north from I-40 Exit 165), go north two miles on AZ 64, then left one mile at the sign.

**Dogtown Campground** and several trails lie 7.5 miles southeast of town; drive 3.5 miles south on Fourth St. (a.k.a. Perkinsville Road), turn left and drive three miles on Forest Route 140, then make a left at the sign. **White Horse Lake Campground** lies 19 miles southeast, near Sycamore Canyon; go eight miles south on Fourth St., turn left on Forest Route 110, and follow signs. **White Horse Lake Resort** offers similar camping facilities. Anglers catch trout and catfish in White Horse Lake. Winter visitors enjoy ice fishing, cross-country skiing, and snowmobiling.

## Food

**Rod's Steak House** is a Western-style restaurant serving good steak, seafood, and sandwiches; it's open daily for lunch and dinner at 301 E. Bill Williams Ave.; tel. 635-2671. The **Dining Car Restaurant** features new American gourmet cuisine, it's open daily for dinner in the summer, at 642 E. Bill Williams Ave.; tel. 635-4184. **Fireside Italian Restaurant** offers pasta meals as well as chicken and veal specialties; open daily for lunch and dinner at 106 S. Ninth St. and Bill Williams Ave.; tel. 635-4130. **Cowboy's Kitchen** offers homestyle cooking daily for breakfast, lunch, and dinner at 117 E. Bill Williams Ave.; tel. 635-2708. **Old Smoky's Restaurant** is a good place to head for breakfast; it also serves sandwiches and burgers for lunch; it's open daily at 624 W. Bill Williams Ave.; tel. 635-2091.

**Parker House Restaurant,** 525 W. Bill Williams Ave., tel. 635-4590, and the nearby **Hoffman House,** 425 W. Bill Williams Ave., tel. 635-9955, serve breakfast, lunch, and dinner daily. **Becky's El Sombrero Cafe** proffers Mexican food at 126 W. Railroad Ave.; it's open Mon.-Sat. for lunch and dinner; tel. 635-2209. **Pancho McGillicuddy's Mexican Cantina** serves both Mexican and American food daily 3-10 p.m. at 141 W. Railroad Ave.; tel. 635-4150.

**The Great Wall** is a Chinese cafe open Mon.-Fri. for lunch and Mon.-Sat. for dinner at 412 N. Grand Canyon Blvd.; tel. 635-2045. **Pronto Pizza** fixes pizza and sandwiches Mon.-Sat. for lunch and daily for dinner at 106 S. Third St.; tel. 635-4157.

**Tiffany's Restaurant,** a popular local hangout, dispenses beer and pizza daily at 233 W. Bill Williams Ave.; tel. 635-2445. Health food is available from **Winter Wheat Natural Foods** at 106 S. 2nd St.; tel. 635-1414.

## Events

The Buckskinners and Mountain Men ride into town for the **Bill Williams Rendezvous** on Memorial Day weekend. Powder shoots, canoeing, roping, and cow-chip-throwing contests are held along with an arts-and-crafts show and barbecue. Townsfolk celebrate **July 4th** with fireworks, roping events, an ice-cream social, and a barbecue. The **Christmas Period Ball** in early to mid December features celebrants in 19th century costume.

## Services and Recreation

The **post office** is on First St., just south of Bill Williams Avenue. **Williams Emergency Center** provides medical treatment at 301 S. Seventh St.; tel. 635-4441. **Buckskinner Park,** on Sixth St. one mile south of Bill Williams Ave., is a pleasant spot for a picnic. Play golf at the nine-hole (soon to be expanded to 18 holes) **Elephant Rocks Golf Course;** go west on Railroad Ave. across I-40 (or take I-40 Exit 161 and head north) and drive one mile; tel. 635-4936.

Downhill-ski in winter at the small **Williams Ski Area,** four miles south of town on Bill Williams Mountain. Facilities include a 2,000-foot poma lift (600 vertical feet), 700-foot rope tow for the beginners' slope ($20 adult all day weekend lift tickets, $15 for children and seniors, lower rates for weekdays and halfday tickets), snack bar, rental shop, and ski shop. Cross-country skiers can rent gear and ski on marked trails. Season lasts from about mid-December to the end of March; turn south 2.2 miles on Fourth St., then right at the sign; tel. 635-9330.

The Forest Service maintains **cross-country ski trail loops** near Spring Valley; go 14.5 miles east on I-40 to Parks Exit 178, then head north six miles on Forest Route 141; pick up a ski trail map at the Forest Service office, 501 W. Bill Williams Avenue. Undeveloped cross-country ski areas include the White Horse Lake area and Sevier Flat and Barney Flat, on the way to Williams Ski Area. **Benham Snow Play Area** is on the right, four miles south of town on Fourth Street. **Oak Hill Snow Play Area** is reached by driving eight miles east of town on I-40 to the Pittman Valley Rd./Deer Farm Exit then turning north under I-40, then east onto Rt. 66 for two miles to the ski play area.

## Information

The **Williams-Grand Canyon Chamber of Commerce** serves so many travelers headed for the Grand Canyon it stocks maps and brochures for that area too. The office and historical museum are open all year daily 8 a.m.-5 p.m.; it's near the center of town at 200 W. Railroad Ave. (Williams, AZ 86046); tel. 635-4061.

To inquire about hiking, camping, fishing, and road conditions in the Kaibab National Forest, visit the **Chalender Ranger District** office downtown at 501 W. Bill Williams Ave. (Williams, AZ 86046); open Mon.-Fri. 7:30 a.m.-4 p.m.; tel. 635-2676. The **Williams Ranger District** office of the Kaibab National Forest lies 1.5 miles west of downtown on the I-40 frontage road (Rt. 1, Box 142, Williams, AZ 86046); tel. 635-2633. You can try either office for recreation information and forest maps, though the Chalender office specializes in areas east and north of town, while the Williams office concentrates on the Bill Williams Mountain area.

The **public library** is at 113 S. First St., just south of Bill Williams Ave.; tel. 635-2263.

## Transport

**Greyhound** offers several east- and west-bound departures daily. No station in town—buses stop at the corner of Bill Williams Ave. and Third Street.

# VICINITY OF WILLIAMS

## Grand Canyon Deer Farm

This well-run petting zoo for children allows folks to hand-feed deer, llamas, miniature donkeys, and other tame animals, while peacocks strut across the grounds. The Deer Farm is open daily in summer 8 a.m.-dusk, daily in spring and autumn 9 a.m.-dusk, daily in November and December 10 a.m.-dusk; call for days and hours in January and February; Rates are $5 adults, $2.75 children 3-13, and $4 seniors 62 and over; tel. (800) 926-DEER. The zoo is eight miles east of Williams, just off I-40 at the Pittman Valley/Deer Farm Exit 171.

## Bill Williams Mountain

You can reach the summit of this 9,255-foot peak by any of three hiking trails or by road. Pine, oak, and juniper trees cover the lower mountain slopes, and dense forests of aspen, fir, and spruce grow in protected valleys and at higher elevations. On a clear day, you'll enjoy views of the Grand Canyon to the north, San Francisco Peaks and many smaller volcanoes to the east, Sycamore Canyon and parts of the Verde Valley to the west, and vast rangelands to the west. If it's open, climb up the Forest Service lookout tower at the top for the best views. Hiking season lasts from about June to September. Carry water on either trail.

With a car shuttle, you can link both trails together, or hike a trail just one-way. The seven-mile roundtrip **Bill Williams Mountain Trail** climbs the north face of the mountain. You'll reach the road about a half mile from the summit; either continue on the trail across the road or turn up the road itself. Bill Williams Mountain Trailhead (elev. 7,000 feet) is near the Williams Ranger Station, 1.5 miles west of town; from I-40, take Exit 171 toward Williams, then turn right (west) 0.7 mile on the frontage road. The nine-mile roundtrip **Benham Trail** climbs the south and east slopes, crossing the road to the lookout tower several times. To reach the Benham Trailhead (elev. 7,265 feet) from Williams, go south 3.5 miles on Fourth St., then turn right and travel about 0.3 mile on Benham Ranch Road. The gentler grade of this trail makes it good for horseback riders as well as hikers. The **Bixler Saddle Trail** starts at Bixler Saddle on the west side of Bill Williams Mountain, passing majestic rock formations. It joins the Bill Williams Mountain Trail fairly close to the top. This trail is two miles long and will consume two hours or more. The road to the saddle is reached by taking I-40 west from Williams to Devil Dog Rd. exit, heading south on Forest Rd. 108 about a

mile to Forest Rd. 45/Bixler Saddle Rd. and then driving to the end. The last bit requires a high clearance vehicle.

You can also drive up (high-clearance vehicles recommended); from Williams head 4.7 miles south on Fourth St., then turn right and drive seven miles on Forest Route 111. The road closes in winter.

## Keyhole Sink Trail

For a pleasant one hour stroll try this trail that leads to a pleasant and scenic box canyon where prehistoric inhabitants left images pecked into the surface of dark basaltic rock using only another rock as a tool. Archaeologists estimate the age of the petroglyphs at about 1,000 years. To reach the trailhead, drive east on I-40 from Williams to the Pittman Valley exit and head north under the highway then head east (right) on Historic Rt. 66 for two miles to the parking area for Oak Hill Snow Play Area. The trailhead is north, across the road.

## Dogtown Trails

Dogtown Lake offers a campground and good hiking. **Dogtown Nature Trail** is an easy, level, quarter-mile loop in Dogtown Wash; interpretive signs tell of the forest environment. The trailhead (elev. 7,100 feet) lies at the east end of the lake. **Dogtown Lake Trail** offers a pleasant 1.8-mile stroll around the lake. **Davenport Hill Trail** begins at the east end of Dogtown Nature Trail, follows Dogtown Wash 0.3 mile, climbs to a flat, follows an old logging road, then turns north to the 7,805-foot summit. You'll pass through ponderosa pine, Douglas fir, white fir, and aspen. The trail is five miles roundtrip and has an elevation gain of 700 feet.

## Sycamore Canyon Point

Sycamore Canyon remains wild and rugged, without any roads or facilities. Elk, deer, black bear, and other animals find food and shelter on the canyon's rim and within its depths. Hikers and horseback riders can use a network of trails (see "Sycamore Canyon Wilderness" in the Sedona section). Sycamore Canyon Point, 23 miles southeast of Williams, offers a breathtaking panorama. From town, drive eight miles south on Fourth St./Perkinsville Rd., then turn left on Forest Route 110 and travel to its end, approximately 15 miles farther. The last five miles are single lane and may be signed Not For Low-Clearance Vehicles, but careful drivers may make it. No trails enter the canyon from this side, though you can spot a path coming down the opposite side.

## Sycamore Rim Trail

This 11-mile loop overlooks parts of upper Sycamore Canyon and travels past seasonal waterfalls, lumber mill and railroad sites, lily ponds (good swimming), and pretty forest country. Stone cairns mark the trail, shown on both the Kaibab and Coconino forest maps. Trailheads lie southeast of Williams near the junction of Forest Routes 13 and 56, at the end of Forest Route 56, at Pomeroy Tanks off Forest Route 109, and at Sycamore Falls off Forest Route 109; see the Kaibab or Coconino forest maps. If you're in the mood for only a short hike, walk 0.3 mile south from the end of Forest Route 56 to an overlook of Sycamore Canyon. The Forest Service office in downtown Williams proffers a map and trail description for Sycamore Rim Trail.

## Sycamore Falls

You can easily reach two waterfalls near White Horse Lake. The spectacle, however, occurs only during spring runoff and after heavy rains. From the store at White Horse Lake, cross the cattleguard in front and turn right two miles (north) on Forest Route 109 to the Sycamore Falls Trailhead, about two miles south of the junction with Forest Route 13. A small waterfall is visible in a canyon just to the right, but walk ahead and a bit to the left to see a larger falls, 80-100 feet high.

## Perkinsville Road

Beginning as Fourth St. in downtown Williams, Perkinsville Rd. heads south through the pine forests of the Mogollon Rim, drops down to the high-desert lands of the Verde Valley, crosses the Verde River at historic Perkinsville Ranch, then climbs rugged hills to the old mining town of Jerome. The first 25 miles are paved, followed by 27 miles of dirt. Though dusty and bumpy in spots, the route is usually okay in dry weather. No vehicle should attempt the unpaved section after winter snowstorms or heavy summer rains. Allow three hours for a one-way drive, more if you'd like to stop to admire the views. Stock up

on gas and water before heading down this lonely road. The Prescott National Forest map covers the entire route.

# ASH FORK

Declaring itself the "Flagstone Capital of the USA," Ash Fork occupies high-desert grasslands, 19 miles west of Williams and 50 miles north of Prescott. Its location at the junction of I-40 and AZ 89 makes this small community a handy stopping place for travelers. The town grew up around a railroad siding built near Ash Creek in 1882; passengers and freight transferred to stagecoaches or wagons for Prescott and Phoenix. Ash Fork (pop. 650) now serves as a highway stop and center for livestock raising and sandstone quarrying.

## Accommodations

As in Williams, most of the motels and other businesses lie along two parallel one-way streets—Lewis Ave. for westbound traffic and Park Ave. for eastbound. Take I-40 Exits 144 or 146. Places to stay include **Stagecoach Motel,** 823 Park Ave., tel. 637-2551; **Copper State Motel,** 101 E. Lewis Ave., tel. 637-2335; and **Ashfork Inn,** west of downtown near I-40 Exit 144, tel. 637-2514.

**Ash Fork KOA** features a swimming pool and showers; $13.26 tents or RVs without hookups, $16.44 w/hookups and rustic cabins at $24.39; turn in on Eighth St. beside the Stagecoach Motel; tel. 637-2521. **Cauthen's Hillside RV Park** is on the south frontage road near I-40 Exit 144; $5.30 tents or RVs without hookups, $12.72 w/hookups; showers an extra $1; tel. 637-2300. Both campgrounds stay open all year. They're also close to the noise of I-40.

## Food

**Bull Pen Restaurant,** on the east side of town, caters mainly to truckers; it's open 24 hours.

# SELIGMAN

Another old railroad town, Seligman (pop. 900) now relies more on ranching and tourists. The first residents arrived in 1886 and called the place

Prescott Junction, because a rail line branched south to Prescott. Though the Prescott line was later abandoned, the town survived. The present name of "Seligman" honors brothers who owned the Hash Knife Cattle Company. Modern travelers on I-40 can take Exits 121 or 123 for the motels and restaurants in town or head off on old Route 66. This former transcontinental highway is a longer route to Kingman than I-40, but offers a change of pace and a glimpse of America's motoring past. Also take the old highway west to reach the Havasupai and Hualapai Indian reservations (see "The Grand Canyon and The Arizona Strip"). There are two motels in Truxton, one at the Pearce Ferry turnoff, six miles west of Hackberry. If approaching Seligman from the east, you can take a shortcut on Route 66; turn off I-40 at Crookton Rd., Exit 139.

## Accommodations

Nearly all businesses lie along Chino Avenue. Places to stay include **Bil-Mar-Den Motel,** just east of town, tel. 422-3470; **Motel Deluxe,** 203 E. Chino Ave., tel. 422-3244; **Canyon Shadows Motel,** 114 E. Chino, tel. 422-3255; **Romney Motel,** 122 W. Chino, tel. 422-3294; **Supai Motel,** 134 W. Chino, tel. 422-3663; and **Historic Rt. 66 Motel** on west edge of town, tel. 422-3204.

**Seligman KOA,** just east of town, has a swimming pool and showers; $14.25 tent, $17.75-19.75 RV w/hookups; tel. 422-3358. **Historic Route 66 General Store and Campground,** on the west end of town, charges $10.55 for tents or RVs without hookups and $12.66-14.77 w/hookups; tel. 422-3549.

## Food

**Chat & Chew,** on the east edge of town, is a cafe open daily for breakfast, lunch, and dinner. The **Copper Cart Restaurant** downtown offers a varied American menu; it's open daily for breakfast, lunch, and dinner. Get your malts, sodas, and fast food at **Delgadillo's Snow Cap. Mr. J's Coffee Shop** is a cafe offering American breakfasts, lunches, and dinners on the west edge of town.

# GRAND CANYON CAVERNS

Large underground chambers and pretty limestone formations attract travelers on old Route 66. The caverns lie 25 miles northwest of Seligman, then one mile off the highway. A giant dinosaur stands guard in front. On 45-minute guided tours, you descend 21 stories by elevator to the caverns and walk about a quarter mile. Tours operate daily 8 a.m.-6 p.m. in summer and 10 a.m.-5 p.m. in winter (closed December 25); $7.50 adults, $4.75 children 4-12. A gift shop at the entrance features a small museum of mining and ranching artifacts. **Grand Canyon Caverns Inn** offers year-round accommodations ($39.28 s, $45.65 d, lower rates in winter). A nearby campground (for self contained RVs only) offers drinking water but no showers or hookups; $5. The cavern restaurant is open about the same hours as the tours. For information on cave tours, tours of the area around the western Grand Canyon, or motel reservations, call 422-3223.

# SOUTH OF FLAGSTAFF: LAKE AND RIM COUNTRY

More than a dozen mountain lakes dot the pine-forested plateau country southeast of Flagstaff. Anglers, picnickers, hikers, and campers enjoy the quiet waters, rolling hills, and scenic canyons of the region. Animal life flourishes—you might spot elk, deer, turkey, maybe even bear. Abert's squirrels with long, tufted ears scamper through the trees. The best times to see wildlife are early and late in the day. Rim-country temperatures remain comfortably cool even in midsummer, and showers fall almost daily on July and August afternoons.

Campgrounds often fill up during the peak summer months; you'll find less crowded conditions early and late in the season, or at any time away from developed sites. Nearly all campgrounds are run by the U.S. Forest Service; most feature drinking water, though none offer showers or hookups. Campgrounds usually stay open from about May to September. Dispersed camping is available almost anywhere in any season within the national forests, though you're asked to avoid camping on meadows, or within a quarter mile of springs, streams, stock tanks, or lakes. Only fee campgrounds offer trash collection; everywhere else you need to pack it out. Boats are limited to those with electric motors on the smaller lakes and eighth-h.p. gas motors on the larger ones; no restrictions apply on Upper Lake Mary.

## MORMON LAKE RANGER DISTRICT

For information about recreation and road conditions, stop at the **Mormon Lake Ranger District** office at 4373 S. Lake Mary Rd. (Flagstaff, AZ 86001). The office is about one mile from US 89A; books and forest and topo maps sold; open Mon.-Fri. 7:30 a.m.-4:30 p.m.; tel. 774-1182.

### Lower and Upper Lake Mary

Beginning just eight miles from Flagstaff, these long, narrow reservoirs offer fishing, boating, and birdwatching. Walnut Creek, dammed to form these lakes, once continued downstream through Walnut Canyon past the many Sinagua Indian ruins there. The Riordan brothers, who built the first reservoir early in this century to supply water to their sawmill, named the lake for one of their daughters.

Lower Lake Mary now varies greatly in size, depending on rainfall and water needs. Lower Lake Mary Boating and Picnicking Area, near the dam, offers tables, grills, ramadas, and a place to hand-launch boats. Anglers mostly catch northern pike.

Waterskiers zip across Upper Lake Mary in summer—it's one of the few lakes in this part of Arizona long and deep enough for the sport. Anglers pull catfish, northern pike, walleye, sunfish, and bluegill from the waters. Lake Mary Boat Landing features picnic tables, grills, ramadas, and a paved boat ramp; on Lake Mary Rd. 0.8 mile upstream from the dam. The Narrows Picnic Area, on Lake Mary Rd. 1.5 miles farther uplake, features a fishing area with wheelchair access, tables, grills, ramadas, and a paved boat ramp.

Lakeview Campground provides the closest camping to the lakes; some sites are too small for trailers. The campground lies across the road from the Narrows of Upper Lake Mary (14 miles southeast of Flagstaff); drinking water is included in the $7 site fee. Lake Mary Rd. (Forest Hwy. 3) parallels the shores of both lakes.

From downtown Flagstaff, head south on Milton Rd., turn right on Forest Meadows St. before the I-40 junction, turn left on Beulah Blvd. (US 89A), then follow signs for Lake Mary Road. I-40 travelers should take Exit 195B for Flagstaff, make the first right (Exit 341), turn left on McConnell Dr. under Milton Rd., left on Beulah Blvd. (US 89A), and follow signs. If driving north on I-17, take Exit 339 just before the I-40 junction.

### Sandys Canyon Trail

This is an easy two-mile roundtrip trail with canyon, forest, and mountain views. The cliffs, visible from the first few hundred feet of the trail, are a local favorite with rock climbers. The path follows the rim of Walnut Canyon a short way, drops down Sandys Canyon, then follows the floor of Walnut Canyon to a junction with the **Arizona Trail.** Here you can continue southeast about four miles to Marshall Lake or north one mile to Fisher Point. The trailhead lies six miles down Lake Mary Rd.; turn left (north) just past the second cattleguard. During winter you can park off the road near the locked gate and walk to the trailhead.

### Marshall Lake

This small trout lake, complete with a primitive boat ramp, lies north of Upper Lake Mary. Head nine miles down Lake Mary Rd. to the signed Marshall Lake turnoff, between Upper and Lower Lake Mary; turn in and drive three miles to the lake.

### Ashurst Lake

Anglers pursue rainbow trout while windsurfers slice through the water on this small lake. Two campgrounds, both with water for a $7 fee, sit beside the lake—**Ashurst Campground** on the west shore and **Forked Pine** on the east. On the way in you'll pass the **Ashurst Dispersed Camping Area,** which offers a campground host and dumpsters but no water, toilets, or fee. There's a boat ramp near the entrance to Ashurst Campground. From Flagstaff, travel 18 miles southeast on Lake Mary Rd., then turn left and drive four miles on paved Forest Route 82E. **Coconino Reservoir,** one mile south on a dirt road, also has a good reputation for rainbow trout.

### Pine Grove Campground

Entrance to this large campground lies opposite the turnoff for Ashurst Lake, 18 miles southeast of Flagstaff; turn west and drive 0.8 mile on Forest Route 651 from Lake Mary Road. The camping area features drinking water, paved roads, and an $8 fee. Although not on a lake, Pine Grove is within a few miles of Upper Lake Mary and Ashurst and Mormon lakes.

### Mormon Lake

Mormon settlers arrived on the shores of this lake in 1878 and started a dairy farm. Although

Mormon is the largest natural lake in Arizona, the average depth is only 10 feet. The water level fluctuates; when it's low the lake is not much more than a marsh. Occasionally it dries up completely. Still, anglers reel in sizable bullhead catfish and northern pike. Boats must be hand-carried to the water.

Lake Mary Rd. parallels the east shore; Mormon Lake Loop Rd. (Forest Route 90) circles around the west side. **Dairy Springs** and **Double Springs** campgrounds on this loop road both have drinking water and a $7 fee; sites can be reserved by calling (800) 280-CAMP. From Flagstaff, head 20 miles southeast on Lake Mary Rd., then turn right and drive four miles on Mormon Lake Loop Rd. to Dairy Springs, or go two miles farther to Double Springs.

**Lakeview Trail** (two miles roundtrip) climbs a small hill from Double Springs Campground. For a longer trip, start near Dairy Springs Campground and hike 1,500 feet above Mormon Lake on the six-mile-roundtrip **Mormon Mountain Trail;** it's pretty forest country, though trees block views at the top. Learn more about the plants and animals of the area on the half-mile interpretive **Dairy Springs Trail,** also beginning from Dairy Springs Campground. **Ledge Trail,** an easy 1.5-mile-roundtrip hike from Dairy Springs Campground, runs out to a ledge overlooking the lake.

**Montezuma Lodge,** tucked in the woods a quarter mile beyond Dairy Springs Campground, has cabins from early May to the end of October; tel. 354-2220. **Mormon Lake Lodge,** on the loop road at the south end of the lake, serves as a recreational center for many visitors. The lodge offers a variety of rooms and cabins ($63-84 s or d with ski packages available), cafe serving breakfast and lunch, Western-style steak house serving dinner daily, saloon, grocery store with fishing and hunting supplies, and gas station; tel. 774-0462 (Flagstaff) or 354-2227 (local). **The Stables at Mormon Lake,** next to the lodge, offer trail, wagon, and stagecoach rides May 1-Oct. 15. Across the road, **Mormon Lake Ski Touring Center** offers trails, rentals, and lessons for cross-country skiers. Snowmobiles can be rented through the lodge. **Munds Park,** 11 miles west of the Mormon Lake Loop Rd. via unpaved Forest Route 240, has a motel, an

RV campground, restaurants, and a service station. Munds Park is at I-17 Exit 322, 18 miles south of Flagstaff.

### Kinnikinick Lake
You're likely to catch rainbow and brown trout, with the occasional catfish, at this lake. Because it lies off the paved roads, you're more likely to find solitude here. Kinnikinick Lake has a free campground and boat ramp but there's no drinking water. From Flagstaff, go southeast 25 miles on Lake Mary Rd. to just past Mormon Lake, then turn left and travel four miles on Forest Route 125, then right and travel four miles on Forest Route 82.

## LONG VALLEY RANGER DISTRICT

Workers at the **Happy Jack Ranger Station,** 13 miles south of Mormon Lake on Lake Mary Rd., can advise you on camping, hiking, and back-road conditions in the Long Valley Ranger District; it's open Mon.-Fri. 7:30 a.m.-4 p.m.; HC 31, Box 68, Happy Jack, AZ 86024; tel. 354-2216.

### Stoneman Lake
An unusual lake set in a circular depression. Geologists have not decided whether this is an old volcanic crater or a sinkhole. Anglers agree that its waters are a hot spot for yellow perch; record catches have been landed here. Pike and sunfish also thrive here. There's a picnic area and boat ramp but no campground on the lake. To reach Stoneman, either take the I-17 Stoneman Lake Exit 306 (34 miles south of Flagstaff) and go east nine miles on mostly unpaved Forest Route 213, or head south on Lake Mary Rd. eight miles past Mormon Lake, then turn west and drive seven miles on Forest Route 213.

### West Clear Creek Wilderness
The transparent waters of this year-round creek wind below pretty canyon walls on the way to Verde River. Of the many canyons in the Mogollon Rim, west Clear Creek is the longest—40 miles. Cross-bed patterns of ancient sand dunes in Coconino Sandstone show up clearly on the sheer cliffs. The creek offers excellent hiking, swimming, and fishing, though it may be difficult to entice the trout onto a hook.

Several trails into the canyon provide a choice of day-hikes or overnight trips. Adventurous hikers could spend a week traveling downstream to Bull Pen Ranch or Clear Creek Campground. Or, you can day-hike to the upper reaches of West Clear Creek and along the tributaries of Willow and Clover creeks; **Maxwell Trail** provides the easiest access to this area.

The warmer months are best for a visit to this canyon. There isn't much of a trail, so you'll be wading and swimming much of the time. In spring, snowmelt can raise the stream level too high for hiking, as can very heavy rains any season. Water is always available from the creek; purify first. Hikers should remember that trails out can be difficult to spot. Exceptions include the **Tramway Trail,** marked by a steel cable across the creek, and a trail near the power lines—two sets of high-tension lines shown on the Coconino Forest map.

A hike between these points makes a good overnight backpacking trip, but you'll have to cross a deep pool about 150 feet long hemmed in by cliffs. Try a small inflatable boat. The pool is about 0.7 mile upstream of the power lines. Many more deep pools, including one a quarter mile long, must be crossed if you're going downstream from the powerlines.

To reach the Tramway trailhead (Forest Trail 32), go eight miles south of Happy Jack on the Lake Mary Rd., then eight miles in on dirt Forest Routes 81 and 81E; keep straight past the turnoff for Maxwell Trail, go about 1.5 miles, then turn left at the fork. Tramway descends steeply less than a mile into the canyon. At the power lines downstream, a rough trail connects the creek with Forest Route 142A on the south rim. This trailhead is about 18 miles southwest of Clints Well via AZ 87 and Forest Routes 142 and 142A. Roads to the trailheads may be too rough for cars after heavy rains.

### Clints Well
Natural springs here, a rarity in the region, have long been a stopping place for travelers. These were named for Clint Wingfield, an early pioneer. Lake Mary Rd. (Forest Hwy. 3) meets AZ

87 at Clints Well; turn left for Winslow, right for Payson and Mesa. A small Forest Service campground near the end of Lake Mary Rd. is free but lacks water. **Long Valley Cafe,** grocery store, and service station are a half mile south on AZ 87.

### Kehl Springs

This small campground near the Mogollon Rim doesn't charge a fee but lacks drinking water. Aspen and oak trees put on a colorful display in autumn. The Mogollon Rim and great views lie just a short walk away. From Clints Well, go southwest 3.3 miles on AZ 87, then left on Forest Route 147 to the Rim Rd. (see Coconino Forest Map). These roads tend to be rough and dusty, but should be okay for passenger vehicles in good weather.

### Cinch Hook Snow Recreation Area

Winter storms on the Mogollon Rim transform a large gravel pit into a snowy playground. Families bring their inner tubes and inflatables—no sleds or other hard objects allowed—to slide the slopes of this three-sided bowl. The grades, relatively smooth and free of trees and large rocks, range from very gentle for the toddler set to steep for thrillseekers.

The Forest Service clears an area in the center for parking and provides outhouses. Caretakers limit the number of visitors on weekends and holidays if the slopes or parking area are full; no parking permitted on the highway. The recreation area lies just east of the junction of AZ 87 and AZ 260 (General Crook Trail), 11 miles south of Clints Well. Chains or snow tires are strongly recommended.

## BLUE RIDGE
## RANGER DISTRICT

For camping, fishing, hiking, and back-road information in the Blue Ridge Reservoir area, contact the **Blue Ridge Ranger Station** Mon.-Fri. 7:30 a.m.-noon and 1-4 p.m., and sometimes daily in summer; HC 31, Box 300, Happy Jack, AZ 86024; tel. 477-2255. From Clints Well, go northeast 10 miles on AZ 87 to the office on the right. From Winslow, go 43 miles southwest on AZ 87.

### Blue Ridge Reservoir

Hemmed in by the canyon walls of East Clear Creek, this skinny lake offers good trout fishing—best in spring and autumn—and great scenery. Steep terrain makes road access difficult; you can launch small boats. Trails lead to the water's edge, but fishing is easier from a boat. **Rock Crossing Campground** nearby offers good views and ranks as one of the most popular camping spots on the Mogollon Rim. Season runs Memorial Day to Labor Day; drinking water is supplied and there's a $5 fee. From Clints Well, go northeast five miles on AZ 87 and turn right three miles on Forest Route 751 to the campground, then another three miles to the dam.

The smaller **Blue Ridge Campground** is open during the same season for the same fee; trailers are limited to 16 feet. From Clints Well, go northeast nine miles on AZ 87, then turn right and drive one mile on Forest Route 138. Anglers use Blue Ridge Campground as a base for Blue Ridge Reservoir, East Clear Creek, and Long Lake. You can also camp at Long Lake (no facilities). Catfish and northern pike are the most popular fish pulled from Long Lake, but the waters offer trout, bass, walleye, and panfish as well.

### East Clear Creek Hiking

This canyon may be less spectacular than other places on the Mogollon Rim, but the trailheads are easily reached. Deep, clear pools invite swimming or solitary fishing. Beavers live and work along the stream, though you'll be lucky to see one of these shy, nocturnal animals. Watch out for snakes; most are harmless, rattlesnakes are not. A rough trail follows the canyon, crossing the creek in many places. Crossings shouldn't be more than knee deep, though spring snowmelt or heavy rains can raise the creek too high for hiking. Long pants will protect your legs from bramble patches. Water is always available; purify first. This creek is not related to West Clear Creek; East Clear Creek flows northeast, in the opposite direction, and joins the Little Colorado River near Winslow.

Of all the trailheads, Macks Crossing, only two miles from AZ 87, is the easiest to reach. From Clints Well, go 15 miles northeast (4.5 miles past Blue Ridge Ranger Station) and turn right on Enchanted Ln. (shown as Forest Route 137 on the Coconino Forest map). After a short distance, turn right on Green Ridge Rd. and go 0.7 mile. Then turn right again on Juniper, which leads to Forest Route 137. The narrow, rocky road descends one mile across a cliff face—no guardrails—to the creek. Park at the top or at several places on the way down. Near the creek and on the other side, the road is too rough for cars. From Macks Crossing, a good overnight loop hike (15 miles) involves going upstream on East Clear Creek to Kinder Crossing Trail, taking this trail to Forest Route 137, and following the forest road back to Macks Crossing. The section of road requires only two to three hours of easy walking—at least three times as fast as hiking in the creek.

Kinder Crossing Trail also features a west trailhead on Forest Route 95, about 4.5 miles south of Blue Ridge Ranger Station. The trail (#19) is marked by tree blazes down to the creek, then by stone cairns and tree blazes for a half mile downstream along the creek before climbing the other side of the canyon to Forest Route 137. Both the topo and Coconino Forest maps may incorrectly show the trail as simply crossing the creek and climbing the opposite side, instead of following the creek a half mile.

Horse Crossing Trail #20 (see Coconino Forest map) also descends into the canyon from both sides. Kinder Crossing and Horse Crossing trailheads should be distinct and signed. Horse Crossing Trail can be very difficult to spot while walking along the creek; pay careful attention to a topo map and tree blazes.

### Other Hikes

The unfinished **Arizona Trail** crosses the district on its journey between Mexico and Utah. **Cabin Loop Trail** connects three historic guard stations—Pinchot, General Springs, and Buck Springs—in a 28-mile trail network.

### Knoll Lake

A rocky island in the middle gives this lake its name. Knoll Lake is in Leonard Canyon, several miles north of the Mogollon Rim. There's a campground on a hill near the lake; the fee is $5. Camping season lasts from Memorial Day to Labor Day; drinking water is available. A road and a hiking trail lead down to the boat ramp. Anglers come mostly to seek out rainbow trout. Getting here involves about 28 miles of dirt road from either AZ 87 or Woods Canyon Lake off AZ 260.

## CHEVELON RANGER DISTRICT

Foresters at the Chevelon Ranger District of the Apache-Sitgreaves National Forest provide information and maps on recreation in the Mogollon Rim country from Winslow to the Woods Canyon Lake area; it's open daily except Sunday in summer 8 a.m.-4:30 p.m., then Mon.-Fri. 7:30 a.m.-4 p.m. the rest of the year. The office is 42 miles south of Winslow on AZ 99 (HC 62, Box 600, Winslow, AZ 86047); tel. 289-2471. To accommodate the throngs of summer visitors, the district maintains its regular campgrounds and designated dispersed sites; the latter consist of marked areas along sections of Forest Routes 300, 169, 195, 9350, and 9354; no water, facilities, or fee.

### Chevelon Crossing

This small campground overlooks Chevelon Creek many miles downstream from Woods Canyon Lake. The sites remain open most of the year (elev. 6,200 feet) with no water or fee. Parking is tight; small vehicles will fit best. Try fishing in the large pools upstream that harbor rainbow trout. There are three routes to this remote campground: Forest Route 504 is the usual way in; turn off AZ 260 one mile west of Heber. Or take AZ 99 south from Winslow and turn left on Forest Route 504. Or you can take Forest Route 169 by turning north from Forest Route 300 (the Rim Rd.) west of Woods Canyon Lake.

### Chevelon Canyon Lake

This long, skinny reservoir lies 12 miles upstream from Chevelon Crossing via Forest Routes 169 and 169B. See the Apache-Sitgreaves Forest map for other ways of getting here. The lake offers trophy fishing for rainbow and brown trout; anglers must use artificial lures and observe size and catch limits. With 208 surface acres, this is one of the larger lakes on the Mogollon Rim. There's a primitive campground (elev. 6,400 feet, no water or fee) near the north shore.

**Bear Canyon Lake**

Anglers enjoy fishing with artificial lures or bait on this trout lake. The shore is steep and tree-covered, so it's easier to use boats for fishing, though you'll have to lug them to the water. There's a campground (no water or fee) near the north end. From Woods Canyon Lake, travel west 10 miles on Forest Route 300 (the Rim Rd.), then turn north and drive 2.5 miles on Forest Route 89.

**Woods Canyon Lake**

This popular lake was one of the first of seven created on the Rim. Camp at either Aspen Campground ($10) or Spillway Campground ($10) near the lakeshore; both have drinking water. Call (800) 280-CAMP to reserve a site; season runs May to mid-September. A store, which stays open into the fall, has groceries, boat rentals, and motors (only electrics are permitted here). **Rocky Point Picnic Area** is on the south side of the lake; it's free but open for day-use only. From AZ 260, near the edge of the Mogollon Rim, turn northwest and drive five miles on paved Forest Routes 300 and 105.

**Rim Lakes Vista Trail**

This easy trail follows the Rim for three miles with some fine views between Rim and Mogollon campgrounds, both off Forest Route 300. **Military Sinkhole Trail** drops west and south 2.25 miles from Rim Lakes Vista Trail to Two-Sixty Trailhead and the Highline National Recreation Trail; you'll find the upper trailhead 1.9 miles in on Forest Route 300 from AZ 260, and the Two-Sixty Trailhead 27 miles east of Payson just off AZ 260.

# HEBER RANGER DISTRICT

See foresters at the **Heber Ranger Station** (Hwy. 260, Milepost 307.5, two miles east of downtown Herber) for recreation information on the Rim Country southwest of Heber. Books and forest and topo maps are also sold here. The office is open Mon.-Sat. 8 a.m.-4:30 p.m. For more information, write Box 968, Overgaard, AZ 85933; tel. 535-4481. A **Visitor Information Center** is open during the warmer months at Al Fulton Point, across from the AZ 260 and Forest Route 300 junction. The district also has **designated dispersed sites** along Forest Route 171 east of Al Fulton Point; no water, facilities, or fee. Mountain bicyclists enjoy **Willow Springs Loop,** a 7.8-mile series of forest roads signed for nonmotorized use; from AZ 260, go a half mile north on Forest Route 237 to the junction with 236.

**Willow Springs Lake**

Anglers catch mostly rainbow trout in this U-shaped lake. There's a boat ramp but no campground. You can camp in designated dispersed areas nearby or at Sinkhole Campground; there's water available and a $6 fee from mid-May to late October. Turn in a half mile on Forest Route 149 from AZ 260; Willow Springs Lake is 3.5 miles farther in. Forest Route 149 turns off AZ 260 about one mile east of the Rim Rd. junction and four miles west of Canyon Point Campground. **Rim, Crook,** and **Mogollon campgrounds** lie along Forest Route 300, beginning 0.8 mile in from AZ 260; all are open mid-May to late October with water and a $6 fee.

**Canyon Point Campground**

This large, easily accessible campground has drinking water and showers and is open mid-May to late September. Sites cost $10 with no hookups; Loop A has hookups at $12. **Sinkhole Trail** begins from Loop B and leads to a sinkhole (one mile roundtrip). Canyon Point Campground lies just off AZ 260, five miles east of the Woods Canyon Lake turnoff.

**Forest Lakes Touring Center**

In winter, cross-country skiers come here to use approximately 30 miles of marked and groomed trails and skating lanes atop the Mogollon Rim. Trail passes cost $6. The center also offers rentals, lessons, and tours (all cost $10 per person). Summer visitors can rent canoes and fishing boats with trolling motors for $28 per day; rentals ($15 per day) include paddles and life jackets. For ski or canoe information and winter road conditions, call 535-4047.

Stay in cabins year-round at the **Forest Lakes Touring Center;** $55-68 d Fri.-Sat. and holidays, $43-50 d Sun.-Thurs.; tel. 535-4047. **Forest Lakes Lodge** has motel rooms open all year at $57.27 s, $62.57 d Fri.-Sat. and holidays; $41.36 s, $51.97 d Sun.-Thurs.; tel. 535-4727. Forest

Lakes Touring Center is in the village of Forest Lakes on AZ 260 6.5 miles east of the Woods Canyon Lake turnoff or 36 miles east of Payson. Forest Lakes also offers the Wagon Wheel Steak House, stores, and RV parks. Heber, 15 miles east, has a few motels and cafes.

### Black Canyon Lake
This small trout lake doesn't have a campground, but **Black Canyon Rim** and **Gentry** campgrounds are within a few miles. Black Canyon Rim has water and a $6 fee from mid-May to late September; Gentry has no water or fee. They stay open all year, when not blocked by snow. From Canyon Point Campground, go east 4.5 miles on AZ 260, turn right and proceed 2.5 miles on Forest Route 300, then turn left and drive three miles on Forest Route 86 to Black Canyon Lake.

# SEDONA AND THE RED ROCK COUNTRY

Drifting clouds, towering pinnacles, and sheer canyon walls create a magical setting for the Red Rock Country of Sedona. Monoliths of vivid red sandstone stand as if cast adrift from the Mogollon Rim. Oak Creek, which carved this landscape, glides gracefully through Sedona. A ribbon of green along the creek contrasts sharply with the surrounding desert.

### Early History
The prehistoric Hohokam and Sinagua Indians tilled the soil along Oak Creek for corn, beans, and squash long before white people came.

American settlers first arrived in the late 1800s to farm and run cattle in the valley. The town dates from 1902, when Theodore Schnebly opened a post office, naming it "Sedona" for his wife. In the same year, Schnebly also built a wagon road up the rim to haul vegetables and fruit to Flagstaff and lumber back to Sedona; the journey took about 11 hours each way.

### Modern Times
From a tiny agricultural community of just 25 years ago, Sedona has developed into a major art center, resort, and spiritual retreat. The present area population of more than 14,000 includes many retired people, artists, and nature lovers.

Sunny skies and pleasant temperatures prevail here. At an elevation of 4,500 feet, Sedona avoids the extremes of both low desert and high mountains. The community lies 28 miles south of Flagstaff, sprawling haphazardly around the junction of AZ 89A and AZ 179. Residents refer to this junction as the "Y" when giving directions.

### Vortexes
New age people believe strong spiritual energies concentrate here in vortexes, or psychic-energy points. In the early 1980s, Page Bryant and her otherworldly guide, Albion, identified seven vortexes in the Sedona area. Prominent among them are Bell Rock and Airport Mesa, emanating "electric energy" to invigorate and inspire visitors, and Cathedral Rock, bearer of calming "magnetic energy." You'll often see altars or medicine wheels made of rocks at the sites.

If you'd like to learn more about these energy fields, drop by some of the many spiritual and New Age bookstores and gift shops (see "Information" below). Sedona believers also offer Vortex Tours to the sacred sites. Ask around—each company offers a different perspective (see "Tours" below).

## SIGHTS

**Slide Rock State Park,** 5.5 miles north of Sedona in Oak Creek Canyon, attracts many swimmers; the fun involves sliding through a natural chute. Wear jeans, as this ride is hard on the seat, and try to avoid summer weekends, when the spot is most crowded. Other attractions in the 55-acre park include a half-mile trail along the creek, picnic spots, and a working apple orchard. A snack bar sells apples, apple juice, and sandwiches (may close in winter). Slide Rock State Park is open all year for day-use only; $5 per vehicle; tel. 282-3034. **Grasshopper Point** is a natural swimming hole two miles north of town. The gated access is open 9 a.m.-8 p.m. and a $2 parking fee is charged; parking is limited but you may park nearby and walk in.

*slidin' off the rock*

**Red Rock State Park** preserves a beautiful section of Oak Creek southwest of Sedona. Visitors come for picnics and to enjoy nature. Birdwatching is good, with 150 species identified; ask for a list. Short hiking trails wind through the valley and nearby hills. Smoke Trail, a 0.4-mile loop from the visitor center, follows the shore of Oak Creek. Eagles Nest Trail crosses the creek to a scenic overlook, 1.8 miles roundtrip. Rangers offer tours of the distinctive **House of Apache Fire** across the valley, 1.6 miles roundtrip. Ask for times as the tours are irregularly scheduled. Drop into the visitor center to see exhibits and attend special programs. To protect the fragile riparian area, no swimming or pets are allowed; some areas may be closed to protect wildlife.

The park is open all year for day use only; $5 per vehicle, $1 per person on foot, bicycle, or horseback; tel. 282-6907. From Sedona, head southwest on AZ 89A, turn left (east) and travel three miles on Lower Red Rock Loop Rd., then turn right into the park. The visitor center sits at the end of the park road, 0.8 mile farther. You can also drive via Upper Red Rock Loop Rd., two miles of pavement followed by 1.25 miles of bumpy dirt road. On this route you will see a turnoff to the famous **Red Rock Crossing,** site of many scenes in old western movies.

The gates are open to Red Rock Crossing 9 a.m.-8 p.m. and parking costs $2/vehicle. Some locals are pushing for a highway across this landmark area to relieve downtown traffic congestion while others are fighting for its preservation.

In addition to the surrounding scenery, Sedona's attractions include outstanding art galleries, elegant restaurants, and luxurious resorts. The showiest place in town is **Tlaquepaque** (t'lah-kay-PAH-kay), a re-created village reminiscent of a suburb of Guadalajara, Mexico. Among the tiled courtyards and fountains are restaurants and a great variety of art galleries and crafts shops.

Many of Sedona's cultural activities center on the **Sedona Arts Center,** on the north edge of town at N. Hwy. 89A and Art Barn Road. Art exhibits are open to the public daily 10 a.m.-4 p.m. free of admission. A gift shop sells work by local artists. Sedona Arts Center often schedules concerts, plays, and other evening events; tel. 282-3865.

South of town, the **Chapel of the Holy Cross** presents a striking sight atop a sandstone ridge and welcomes visitors daily 9 a.m.-6 p.m.; drive three miles south on AZ 179 to Chapel Rd. and turn left one mile. Meet and feed trout at the **Page Springs Hatchery,** open daily 7 a.m.-

3:30 p.m.; tel. 634-4805. From the Y, head southeast 10 miles on AZ 89A, then turn left and drive 3.2 miles on Page Springs Road.

Probably the prettiest sights are offered by nature itself. **Oak Creek Canyon,** just upstream from Sedona, is the best-known spot and is easily reached. A 16-mile drive north on AZ 89A toward Flagstaff takes you through this canyon, past dramatic rock formations and dense forests. In autumn (mid-October to mid-November), multicolored leaves add to the rich hues of the sculptured canyon walls.

Some of the best views in the Sedona area lie along **Schnebly Hill Road.** Take the signed turnoff from AZ 179, a half mile south of the AZ 89A junction; you'll soon leave the pavement and wind high up the cliffs of the Mogollon Rim, reaching Exit 320 of I-17 11.5 miles farther. Schnebly Hill Rd. also offers the most spectacular approach to Sedona. Cautious drivers can usually complete this trip in good weather; call the National Forest office in Sedona for road conditions. The road is closed in winter; tel. 282-4119.

Hikers heading into the wilderness can explore the West Fork of Oak Creek, Wilson Mountain, Munds Mountain, Pumphouse Wash, and hundreds of other areas. Consult the U.S. Forest Service office in Sedona and see "Hiking in the Sedona Area."

## ACCOMMODATIONS

Confirm your reservations if coming to Sedona for the weekend—the popular places fill up fast during the March-Nov. peak season. Prices in Sedona climb then, dropping 10% or so in winter. Rates listed here apply to peak season, though prices can go higher on holidays. Campers headed for Oak Creek Canyon on a summer weekend should plan to arrive Friday morning. All campgrounds close in winter. The Camp Verde and Cottonwood areas to the south offer less expensive motels and year-round camping.

Sedona-Oak Creek Chamber of Commerce, tel. 282-7722, can supply up-to-date information about local housing. Call Sedona Central Reservations at 282-1518 or (800) 445-4128, or Outwest Reservation Center at 282-5112 or (800) OUT-WEST.

### Resorts
Take advantage of the fitness center, spa, pools, and tennis courts at the **Enchantment Resort,** 525 Boynton Canyon Rd. (take Dry Creek Rd.); rates are $188.46-543.83; tel. 282-2900 or (800) 826-4180. **L'Auberge de Sedona,** a French country inn at 301 L'Auberge Ln. (off Hwy. 89A), has a pool; rooms are $144.37-2669.72; tel. 282-1661 or (800) 272-

*Chapel of the Holy Cross*

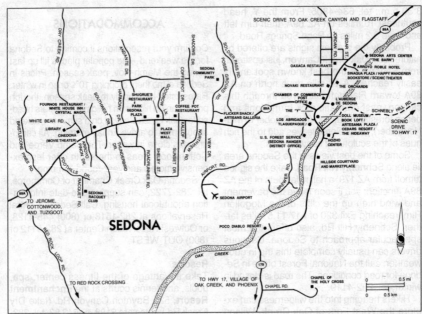

6777. **Los Abrigados,** 160 Portal Ln. (next to Tlaquepaque), offers tennis courts and a restaurant; rates are $233.21-438.65; tel. 282-1777 or (800) 521-3131. Play golf, tennis, or racquetball at **Poco Diablo Resort** ("Little Devil"), Hwy. 179 (two miles south of Hwy. 89A). You can also swim in the pools, soak in the jacuzzi, get a massage, or drop by the restaurant for a bite to eat. Rooms are $149.92-205.44 d, with suites from $266.52; tel. 282-7333, (800) 528-4275, or (800) 352-5710.

Head north of town, along Oak Creek, to find more places to stay. **Red Rock Lodge** offers fireplaces and a spa to weary travelers; rooms are $54.44-194.44 d; tel. 282-3591. **Briar Patch Inn,** 2.7 miles north on Hwy. 89A, has cabins and serves breakfast; rates are $143.17-206.80 d; tel. 282-2342. **Oak Creek Terrace Resort,** 4 miles north on Hwy. 89A, features kitchenettes, fireplaces, and a jacuzzi; rooms are $72.87-168.98 d; tel. 282-3562 or (800) 224-2229. Cozy up by the fireplaces at **Slide Rock Lodge and Cabins,** six miles north on Hwy. 89A; rooms are $84.84-111.35 d, and the cabin is $132; tel. 282-3531. **Garland's Oak Creek Lodge** is 7.5

miles north on Hwy. 89A, closed mid-Nov. to March. Rates are $161.20-182.41 d, including breakfast and dinner; tel. 282-3343. **Junipine Resort,** eight miles north on Hwy. 89A, features a restaurant, kitchens, and fireplaces for $190.89-281.03 d; tel. 282-3375 or (800) 742-7463. **Forest Houses Resort,** 8.9 miles north on Hwy. 89A, requires a four-day minimum stay in summer, and is closed January 1 to mid-March.; rooms are $68.64-95.05 d; tel. 282-2999. For rustic or modern cabins, try **Don Hoel's Cabins,** 10 miles north on Hwy. 89A; rates are $63.37-95.05 d; tel. 282-3560.

### Bed and Breakfasts

**A Touch of Sedona Bed and Breakfast** offers rooms with fireplaces or a suite at 595 Jordan Rd. for $109-159; tel. 282-6462. **Canyon Villa Bed and Breakfast** has rooms with fireplaces plus a pool at 125 Canyon Circle Dr. for $125-205; tel. 284-1226 or (800) 453-1116. **Casa Sedona** has rooms with fireplaces plus a pool and jacuzzi at 55 Hozoni Dr. for $105-150; tel. 282-2938 or (800) 525-3756. **Cathedral Rock Lodge Bed and Breakfast** offers rooms

# SEDONA ACCOMMODATIONS

**Bell Rock Inn;** 6246 Hwy. 179 (Village of Oak Creek); $68.93-132.56 s, $83.78-148.47 d; 282-4161; pool, spa

**Best Western Arroyo Roble Hotel;** 400 N. Hwy. 89A; $122.16 s, $138.18 d; 282-4001 or (800) 528-1234; pool, spa, sauna

**Best Western Inn of Sedona;** 1200 W. Hwy. 89A; $94.39-133.26 s or d; 282-3072 or (800) 292-6344; pool, jacuzzi

**Canyon Portal Motel;** 280 N. Hwy. 89A; $54.41-93.28 s or d, $122.16 house; 282-7125 or (800) 542-8484; pool, fireplace

**Cedars Resort;** 20 N. Hwy. 89A; $44.42-77.73 s or d; 282-7010; spa

**Cimarron Inn;** 2991 W. Hwy. 89A; $64.41-66.63 s or d; 282-9166; pool

**Comfort Inn;** half mile south on Hwy. 179 from Hwy. 89A; $111.05 s or d; 282-3132 or (800) 221-2222; pool, jacuzzi

**Desert Quail Inn;** 6626 Hwy. 179 (Oak Creek Village); $52-137.80 s or d; 284-1433 or (800) 385-0927; kitchens, fireplaces, pool, suites

**Holiday Inn Express;** 6175 Hwy. 179 (Village of Oak Creek); $85.31 s or d; 284-0711 or (800) 465-4329; breakfast bar, pool, spa

**La Vista Motel;** 500 N. Hwy. 89A; $43.14-94.02 d; 282-7301 or (800) 896-7301; kitchens, fireplaces

**Lo Lo Mai Lodge;** 50 Willow Way (off Hwy. 89A); $61.08-66.63 s or d; 282-2835 or 282-9416; kitchenettes, spa

**Matterhorn Motor Lodge;** 230 Apple Ave. off N. Hwy. 89A; $82.18-93.28 d; 282-7176; pool, spa

**New Earth Lodge;** 665 Sunset Dr.; $150.50 s or d; 282-2644; vacation apartments

**Quality Inn/King's Ransom;** half mile south on Hwy. 179 from Hwy. 89A; $91.06-133.26 d; (800) 221-2222; pool, spa, restaurant

**Red Rock Inn at Sedona;** 2545 W. Hwy. 89A; $73.29 s or d; 282-1533 or (800) 858-7245; restaurant, pool, railroad excursions

**Rose Tree Inn;** 376 Cedar St.; $76.62-108.83 s, $94.39-127.21 d; 282-2065; some kitchens, spa, VCR's

**Sedona Motel;** Hwy. 179; one block south of AZ 89A; $76.62-105.50; 282-7187

**Sky Ranch Lodge;** Airport Rd.; $49.73 s, $66.63-161.02 d; 282-6400; kitchenettes, pool, fireplaces, two cottages

**Southwest Inn at Sedona;** 3250 W. Hwy. 89A; $116.60-194.34 s or d; 282-3344 or (800) 483-7422; fireplaces, jacuzzi

**Star Motel;** 295 Jordan Rd. (off N. Hwy. 89A); $43.14 s, $94.02 d; 282-3641or (800) 896-7301

**Sugar Loaf Lodge;** 1870 W. Hwy. 89A; $61.08 s or d; 282-9451

**A Touch of the Southwest Motel & Suites;** 410 Jordan Rd.; one bedroom $88.84-116.60, two bedrooms $138.18-227.65; 282-4747, kitchens

**White House Inn;** 2986 W. Hwy. 89A; $46.64-83.29 d; 282-6680; some kitchenettes and a romantic cabin outside town on Red Rock Loop at $74.24-116.65; tel. 282-7608. **The Graham Bed & Breakfast Inn** offers rooms with fireplaces and free bicycle use in the Village of Oak Creek at $99.69-216.34 s or $115.59-232.25 d; tel. 284-1425 or (800) 228-1425. **The Inn at Oak Creek** offers rooms with fireplaces and whirlpool tubs (some have private observation decks overlooking Oak Creek) at 556 Hwy. 179, almost a mile from the Y junction. Rates are $144.37 s and $249.86 d; tel. 282-7896 or (800) 499-7896. **Lantern Light Inn Bed & Breakfast** offers rooms with an elegant country French decor at 3085 W. Hwy. 89A from $83.29-105.50 s and $88.84-122.16 d; tel. 282-3419. **Territorial House, an Old West Bed and Breakfast** offers rooms and suites with an exercise room at 65 Piki Dr. priced from $80-140 s and $90-95 d; tel. 204-2737 or (800) 801-2737. There are also many charming smaller bed and breakfasts in the Sedona area. Contact the chamber of commerce for a full listing.

### Campgrounds

You'll find the prettiest places in Oak Creek Canyon. The U.S. Forest Service maintains five campgrounds here, all on Hwy. 89A: **Manzanita**, six miles north of Sedona; **Banjo Bill**, eight miles north; **Bootlegger**, 8.8 miles north; **Cave Spring**, 11.5 miles north; and **Pine Flat**, 12.5 miles north. All but Bootlegger have drinking water; none offer hookups or showers. Showers are available for $2 at **Hawkeye Red Rock RV Park** in Sedona.

Reserve one of Cave Spring's 11 sites by calling (800) 280-2267. Trailers and large RVs (up to 30 feet) are accepted only in Cave Spring and Pine Flat campgrounds. The campgrounds, all $10 per night, begin to open in early March and start to close in late October; some may stay open for longer seasons, call to check. Manzanita Campground stays open all year.

**Chavez Group Campground** lies at the south edge of town off 179, just beyond Poco Diablo Resort. Sites are available by reservation only; tel. (800) 280-2267. Groups consist of 10-130 people and sites run $30-70. Dispersed camping is forbidden in Oak Creek Canyon, but you can easily find spots elsewhere in the national forests. The Sedona Ranger Station dis-

penses information on camping and hiking in the area; tel. 282-4119.

**Rancho Sedona RV Park** offers shaded sites along Oak Creek all year for RVs only ($27.88-33.45 w/hookups). It's centrally located a half mile south on Hwy. 179 from Hwy. 89A, then left and a quarter mile on Schnebly Hill Rd., tel. 282-7255, and has on-site showers and laundry. **Hawkeye Red Rock RV Park** offers shaded sites year-round along Oak Creek for tents and RVs at $19-30.66; showers ($2 for nonguests) and laundry; on the north edge of uptown Sedona at 40 Art Barn Rd.; tel. 282-2222. **Oak Creek Mobilodge** lies one mile south on Hwy. 179 from Hwy. 89A; $20 RV w/hookups (no tents); tel. 282-7701. **Sedona RV Resort** is six miles west of the Y at 6701 W. Hwy. 89A and offers RV spaces for $23.86-25.98. Amenities include a pool, restaurant, and miniature golf; tel. 282-6640 or (800) 547-8727.

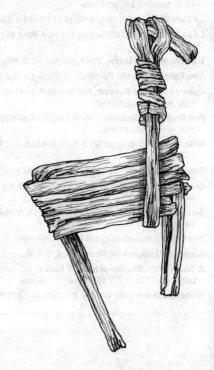

# FOOD

## American and Continental

You can enjoy some of Arizona's finest dining in Sedona. Reservations are recommended at the more expensive places. Restaurants are marked: $: Inexpensive (to $8); $$: Moderate ($8-15); $$$: Expensive (over $15). Ratings refer to price ranges for dinners (per person).

**$$ Rene at Tlaquepaque:** Serves outstanding American and continental cuisine in a French Provincial atmosphere; it's open for lunch and dinner daily in Tlaquepaque, 0.3 mile south on Hwy. 179 from Hwy. 89A; tel. 282-9225.

**$$$ L'Auberge de Sedona:** An elegant French restaurant open daily for breakfast, lunch, and dinner at 301 L'Auberge Ln. (off N. Hwy. 89A one block north of Hwy. 179); tel. 282-1667.

**$$-$$$** Los Abrigados Resort's **Celebrity Room:** Serves signature dishes including flaming deserts daily for dinner at 160 Portal Lane (0.2 mile south on Hwy. 179 from Hwy. 89A); tel. 204-7849.

**$$-$$$** Poco Diablo Resort's **Willows dining room:** Offers an extensive menu of Southwestern and continental dishes daily for breakfast, lunch, and dinner; there's a daily buffet, and the Sunday brunch buffet offers overwhelming choices 10:30 a.m.-2:30 p.m. It's two miles south on Hwy. 179 from Hwy. 89A; tel. 282-7333, ext. 235.

**$$$ The Enchantment** resort: Serves fine continental cuisine and has beautiful canyon views; it's open daily for breakfast, lunch, and dinner at 525 Boynton Canyon, off Dry Creek Rd.; tel. 282-2900.

**$$-$$$ Shugrue's:** Features steak and seafood among other specialties; it's open daily for breakfast (except Monday), lunch, and dinner at 2250 W. Hwy. 89A; tel. 282-2943. **Shugrue's Hillside Grill** offers a similar menu daily for lunch and dinner in Hillside Courtyard at 671 Hwy. 179; tel. 282-5300.

**$$-$$$ Fournos:** Offers a varied continental and seafood menu with some Greek dishes; it's usually open Sunday for brunch and Thurs.-Sat. for dinner at 3000 W. Hwy. 89A; tel. 282-3331.

**$$ The Orchards:** Specializes in unusual regional American fare; it's open daily for breakfast, lunch, and dinner at 254 N. Hwy. 89A; tel. 282-7200.

**$$ Sedona Swiss Restaurant and Cafe:** Serves breakfast, light lunches (salads, soups, and sandwiches), and Italian and Swiss cuisine for dinner, as well as Swiss chocolate and pastries at 350 Jordan Rd. off Hwy. 89A; tel. 282-7959.

**$$-$$$ La Mediterranee Restaurant:** Serves Italian, French, and eastern Mediterranean food with a dozen vegetarian selections available daily for breakfast, lunch, and dinner at 771 Hwy. 89A; tel. 282-7006.

## American Cafes

**$ Coffee Pot Restaurant:** Cooks up 101 omelettes and serves breakfasts all day; it's open daily for breakfast, lunch, and dinner at 2050 W. Hwy. 89A; tel. 282-6626.

**$$-$$$ Heartline Cafe:** Serves standard American fare and new cuisine for lunch and dinner Mon.-Sat. and dinner only Sunday at 1610 W. Hwy. 89A; tel. 282-0785.

**$-$$ The Sedona Airport Restaurant:** Offers hearty eating as well as good views atop Airport Mesa; it's open daily for breakfast, lunch, and dinner; take Airport Rd. off Hwy. 89A; tel. 282-3576.

**$-$$ Hitching Post Restaurant:** Open daily for breakfast, lunch, and dinner in the Uptown Mall, 269 N. Hwy. 89A; tel. 282-7761.

**$$ Rainbow's End Steakhouse:** Serves steak, ribs, prime rib, and chicken, and features country music bands Friday and Saturday nights; it's open daily for lunch and dinner at 3235 W. Hwy. 89A; tel. 282-1593.

**$$ Steak & Sticks:** Features steaks, chops, and grilled seafood as well as Sedona's only billiard club; it's open daily for breakfast and dinner at Los Abrigados, 160 Portal Lane; tel. 204-STIX.

## Mexican

**$-$$ El Rincon Restaurante Mexicano:** This Tlaquepaque restaurant serves excellent Mexican/Navajo-inspired food; it's open Tues.-Sat. for lunch and dinner, and Sunday for lunch; tel. 282-4648.

**$-$$ The Oaxaca Restaurante:** Offers Mexican and American food and is open daily for breakfast, lunch, and dinner at 231 N. Hwy. 89A; tel. 282-4179.

**$-$$ Pepe Muldoon:** Sedona's newest Mexican restaurant has flamboyant decor and is open daily for lunch and dinner at 2620 Hwy. 89A; tel. 282-4849.

## Italian

**$$ Dahl and DiLuca Ristorante Italiano:** Its chef from Rome offers traditional Italian cuisine, and seafood, chicken, and steaks daily for lunch and dinner at 2321 W. Hwy. 89A; tel. 282-5219.

**$ The Hideaway:** Overlooking Oak Creek, serves good Italian food—spaghetti, fettucine, manicotti, pizza; it's open daily for lunch and dinner in the Country Square shopping center on Hwy. 179, 0.2 mile south of Hwy. 89A; tel. 282-4204.

**$$ Joey Bistro:** Offers Southern Italian specialties including fresh pasta, seafood, and veal served daily for dinner plus a Sunday bocce ball brunch at Los Abrigados, 160 Portal Lane; tel. 204-JOEY.

## Asian

**$-$$ Lotus Garden:** Serves Chinese cuisine daily for lunch and dinner at 164 H Coffee Pot Rd.; tel. 282-3118.

**$-$$ Thai Spices Natural:** Prepares flavorful fresh Thai food daily for lunch (except Sunday) and dinner at 2986 W. Hwy. 89A; tel. 282-0599.

**$$ Takashi Japanese Restaurant** serves Japanese cuisine for lunch and dinner Tues.-Sun. at 465 Jordan Rd.; tel. 282-2334.

## Vegetarian

**$-$$ The Sage** serves an excellent value in a vegetarian lunch buffet ($8.60) daily at 2611 W. Hwy. 89A; tel. 204-2079. It hopes to add breakfasts and dinner.

## Dining out of Town

A number of Oak Creek Canyon resorts offer fine dining to the public; be sure to make reservations before venturing out.

**$$$ Garland's Oak Creek Lodge:** Serves memorable meals for breakfast and dinner during the April to mid-November season; it's 7.6 miles north of Sedona on Hwy. 89A; tel. 282-3343.

**$$-$$$ Junipine Cafe and Grill:** Located at the Junipine Resort, Junipine Cafe serves Southwestern and continental fare; it's 7.9 miles north of Sedona on Hwy. 89A; tel. 282-7406.

The Village of Oak Creek, on Hwy. 179 about midway between Sedona and I-17, features several good places to eat.

**$-$$ Bell Rock Inn:** Serves American food daily for breakfast, lunch, and dinner at 6246 Hwy. 179; tel. 282-4161.

**$-$$ Wild Toucan:** Offers American and Mexican food daily for lunch and dinner at 6376 N. Hwy. 179; tel. 284-1604.

**$ Irene's:** Home-style cafe serving standard American fare as well as vegetarian selections and Mexican items; open daily for breakfast, lunch, and dinner at Castle Rock Plaza, 6446 Hwy. 179; tel. 284-2240.

**$$ Mexicalli Rose:** Also in Castle Rock Plaza, it's open daily for lunch and dinner; tel. 284-4693.

**$ Desert Flour Breadery and Bistro:** You can buy breads, pastries, and enjoy specialty lunches in Castle Rock Plaza; tel. 284-4633.

**$-$$ Mandarin House:** Serves good Chinese food; it's open daily for lunch (buffet available) and dinner in Castle Rock Plaza; tel. 284-9088.

**$$ Sasaki Japanese Restaurant:** Offers the largest menu of Japanese cuisine in the U.S.A. daily (except Mon. for lunch) for lunch and dinner at 65 Bell Rock Blvd.; tel. 284-1757.

**$-$$ Page Springs Restaurant:** Western-style restaurant overlooks Oak Creek downstream from Sedona; steak, seafood, and chicken dominate the menu; it's open daily for lunch and dinner; go southwest 10 miles on Hwy. 89A from the Y, then turn left 2.5 miles on Page Springs Rd.; tel. 634-9954. During the day (7 a.m.-4 p.m.) you can visit the trout at **Page Springs Hatchery** down the road.

## OTHER PRACTICALITIES

### Entertainment

See the latest flicks at the **Flicker Shack** in a shopping center on W. Hwy. 89A, 1.5 miles west of the Y; tel. 282-3777. One of Sedona's newest cinemas is the **Cinedona** at 3190 W. Hwy. 89A; tel. 282-0707. **Harkins** six-theater cinema shows films at 2081 W. Hwy. 89A; tel. 282-0222 (business office 282-2221).You might catch a concert or play at the **Sedona Arts Center** in "The Barn," N. Hwy. 89A and Art Barn Rd. on the north edge of town; tel. 282-3809. To get the latest on Sedona's music, events, and nightlife, check the weekly *Red Rock News* newspapers.

### Events

Sedona goes Irish every March for a **St. Patrick's Day Parade,** said to be the largest in the West. Clowns, bands, and floats roll through town in a noisy celebration. The Queen of the Green receives her crown in a gala coronation ball before the big day.

**Hopi Days,** in May, brings Hopi Indians to town for dances, food, arts, and crafts. Fireworks light the sky on **July 4th.** Other annual Sedona events celebrate music and the arts: the **Chamber Music Festival** in June; **Pops Concert in the Park** in September; **Jazz on the Rocks** festival, also in September; **Fiesta del Tlaquepaque** mariachi bands, Mexican dances, food, arts,

and crafts) on the first weekend in October; and the **Sedona Arts Festival** (entertainment, arts and crafts, and food) in October. More than 5,000 candle-lit luminarias brighten Tlaquepaque during the **Festival of Lights** in December; usually held on the second Saturday before Christmas. From about the third week in December through the first week in January enjoy the **Red Rock Fantasy of Light** at Los Abrigados.

### Recreation

**The Posse Ground** has picnic tables, a playground, and ball fields on Posse Ground Rd., 0.3 mile north of Hwy. 89A. The **Sedona Racquet Club** offers tennis courts, year-round pool, jacuzzi, weight room, and snack bar on Racquet Rd.; go 3.8 miles west on Hwy. 89A from the Y, head south on Foothills Dr., then right on Racquet Rd.; tel. 282-4197.

**Poco Diablo Resort** features tennis courts (call and ask for the tennis shop to make reservations) and a nine-hole golf course; the resort

ROBERT BLAKE

*You'll see many beautiful waterfalls near Sedona—after it rains.*

is two miles south of town on Hwy. 179; tel. 282-7333. **Village of Oak Creek Country Club** has an 18-hole golf course; go 6.5 miles south of the Y on Hwy. 179, then right on Bell Rock Rd.; tel. 284-1660. **Sedona Golf Resort** also has an 18-hole course open to the public at 7260 Hwy. 179; tel. 284-9355, 258-1443 in Phoenix. **Canyon Mesa Country Club** offers a nine-hole course at 500 Jacks Canyon Rd. in the Village of Oak Creek; tel. 284-0036.

Anglers can pull rainbow trout from Oak Creek. The **Rainbow Trout Farm** offers easier fishing but charges a fee; equipment is supplied and no license is needed. The farm is three miles north of Sedona in Oak Creek Canyon; it's open daily; tel. 282-5799.

**Kachina Riding Stables** offers trail rides year-round in the Red Rock Country around Sedona; the stables are five miles southwest of town off lower Red Rock Loop Rd.; rates are $26.38 one hour, $39.03 two hours, $103.39 all day; breakfast, steak, and pack trips are available too; call 282-7252 for directions and reservations. **El Rojo Grande Ranch** offers stagecoach excursions and private horseback trail rides seven miles west of the Y just past Milepost 368; tel. 282-1898. **Legends of Sedona Ranch,** not far from the base of Doe Mountain, offers group cookouts; it also rents horses for $36.26 one hour, $48.38 two hours; call for directions at tel. 282-3300 or (800) 848-7728.

### Services
The **post office** is conveniently on Hwy. 89A just west of the Y; tel. 282-3511. The brand new **Sedona Medical Center** is at the edge of town at 3700 W. Hwy. 89A; tel. 204-3000. The nearest hospital is the **Marcus Lawrence Hospital** at 202 S. Willard in Cottonwood, 19 miles southwest of Sedona; tel. 282-1831 or 634-2251. For **emergencies** (fire, police, ambulance) call 911.

### Shopping
As an art center, what Sedona lacks in size, it makes up for in quality. Its 40 art galleries display an impressive range of original art. Southwestern themes run through much of the work, in colors, forms, Indian motifs, and cowboy legends.

Most of the art galleries lie along the first half mile of Hwy. 179 south of the Y, and in Old Town, along the first half mile of Hwy. 89A north

of the Y. **Tlaquepaque,** 0.3 mile south on Hwy. 179 from Hwy. 89A, makes a good starting point for a trip into Sedona's art world. Fountains, sycamore-shaded courtyards, and Spanish-colonial architecture create a delightful atmosphere. Even nonshoppers will enjoy exploring the many shops and galleries here. **Hillside Courtyard & Marketplace** offers prestigious galleries, designer clothing shops, custom jewelry, fossils, gems, upscale dining, special events such as concerts, and much more in an attractive shopping area decorated with sculpture; it's less than half a mile from the Y on Hwy. 179; tel. 282-4500. **Artisans Galleria** offers more than 300 booth spaces where artists sell their goods directly; 1420 Hwy. 89A; tel. 282-2300. **Sinagua Plaza,** in uptown Sedona, offers arts and crafts, dining, and a bookstore.

**Sedona Sports** sells outdoor sports gear and rents mountain bikes at 245 N. Hwy. 89A; tel. 282-1317. **Mountain Bike Heaven** sells and rents mountain bikes and offers parts and repairs at 1695 W. Hwy. 89A, tel. 282-1312. **Canyon Outfitters** also has a large selection of outdoor gear available at 2701 W. Hwy. 89A; tel. 282-5293. **Oak Creek Factory Stores** features brand-name bargains at 6600 Hwy. 179 in the Village of Oak Creek; tel. 284-2150.

### Information
**Sedona-Oak Creek Canyon Chamber of Commerce** has a good supply of literature and information on sights, services, and upcoming events. It's open Mon.-Sat. 8:30 a.m.-5 p.m. and Sunday 9 a.m.-3 p.m. March to October. The rest of the year it's open Mon.-Sat. 9 a.m.-5 p.m., Sunday 9 a.m.-3 p.m. Closed Thanksgiving, Christmas, and New Year's Day. It's at the corner of N. Hwy. 89A and Forest Rd., just north of the Y (Box 478, Sedona, AZ 86339); tel. 282-7722. The **Sedona Ranger District** office of the U.S. Forest Service dispenses information on Indian ruins, camping, hiking, and road conditions in the National Forests surrounding Sedona, in addition to trail descriptions, forest maps, and books. It's open Mon.-Fri. and sometimes Saturday in summer 7:30 a.m.-4:30 p.m. Visit the office at 250 Brewer Rd. (take the street opposite the post office on W. Hwy. 89A) or write to Box 300, Sedona, AZ 86339; tel. 282-4119.

*Tlaquepaque art*

**Sedona Public Library** is open Mon.-Sat. (call for hours); located at the end of White Bear Rd., one block up Dry Creek Rd. off Hwy. 89A; tel. 282-7714. The latest on dining, nightlife, art exhibits, events, and local news is listed in the weekly *Sedona Times* and *Red Rock News*.

**The Worm Books & Music** carries an excellent selection of regional, new age, general reading, plus topo maps and audio tapes at 207 N. Hwy. 89A; tel. 282-3471. **The Loft** sells both new and used books at 175 Hwy. 179; tel. 282-5173. **The Happy Wanderer** bookstore specializes in travel, hiking, nature, and maps with many Southwest titles in stock; 320 N. Hwy. 89A; tel. 282-4690 or (800) 282-4714.

New age bookstores and gift shops include **The Eye of the Vortex,** 1405 W. Hwy. 89A, tel. 282-5614; **Crystal Magic,** 2978 W. Hwy. 89A, tel. 282-1622; **The Hub of New Age,** 1575 W. Hwy. 89A, tel. 282-3856; and **Golden Word Book Centre,** 3150 W. Hwy. 89A, tel. 282-2688. **The Center for the New Age** serves residents and visitors interested in metaphysics with information on events and services; open daily at 341 Hwy. 179, tel. 282-2085.

**Tours**

Many companies offer jeep trips into the rugged backcountry. The first five listed here offer relatively gentle rides, while the final two feature some serious four-wheeling on very difficult roads. **Pink Jeep Ancient Expeditions** specializes in trips to prehistoric Indian ruins; its vortex tours approach the subject from a scientific background. A 2.5-hour tour to a well-preserved cliff dwelling costs $59.13 per person; other trips can be arranged as well. Pink Jeep Ancient Expeditions is located at 276 N. Hwy. 89A; tel. 282-2137 or (800) 999-2137. **Sedona Adventures** offers 4WD touring with a mix of backcountry rides and hiking; the cost is $27-38 for two-hour trips. Vortex "self-discovery" tours and "pampered camping" overnight trips are offered too. You'll find Sedona Adventures at 273 N. Hwy. 89A; tel. 282-3500 or (800) 888-9494. **Roadrunner Tours** offers a long distance sight seeing trip including Oak Creek Canyon, Williams, Sycamore Canyon Viewpoint, a pioneer homestead, a frontier cattle ranch, and the historic mining town of Jerome in a Humvee (HUMMER) at $110 per person for an all day tour, $50 half day, and $30 for a two hour Sedona tour; tel. 282-4696.

**Earth Wisdom Tours** concentrates on Indian legends and philosophies in a three-hour $48 vortex tour; other trips explore ecology, native plants, and rock art in the Sedona area, and on the Navajo and Hopi Indian reservations. Earth Wisdom is centered at 293 N. Hwy. 89A; tel. 282-4714 or (800) 282-4714. **Kiva Serenity Tours** introduces facts on geology, flora and fauna, anthropology, and archaeology on three-hour custom tours for $53.50; 135 Kiva Dr.; tel. 282-5696. **Sedona Photo Tours** covers many great shutterbug locations near Sedona. Rates are $18 for one hour and $35 for two hours; tel. 282-4320. You can also choose from a variety of scenic, historic, and vortex trips at similar prices with **Pink Jeep Tours,** 204 N. Hwy. 89A, tel. 282-5000 or 800-8-SEDONA, and **Sedona Red Rock Jeep Tours,** 260 N. Hwy. 89A, tel. 282-6826 or 800-848-7728.

Tours of the Hopi and Navajo Indian reservations, Sedona, and the Grand Canyon are offered by **Dorian Tours,** tel. 282-4562, and **Sedona Touring Company,** tel. 282-2800 or 800-658-5825.

For aerial views, fly with **Scenic Airlines.** Flights take in the Grand Canyon for $145 per person (minimum two people), or the Grand Canyon, Meteor Crater, Canyon de Chelly, Monument Valley, and Lake Powell at $230 per person (minimum two people). Other destinations can be arranged as well; tel. 282-7935 or (800) 535-4448. **Sedona Air Tours** start as low as $20 per person for a 15 minute tour of the Sedona area with 30 minute tours at $40 per person; tel. 282-3485. **Arizona Helicopter Adventures** offers six tours of the Sedona area and northern Arizona lasting 10 minutes to 2.5 hours at rates of $32-495 (two-person minimum). The company is based at Sedona Airport; tel. 282-0904 or (800) 282-5141. **Skydance Helicopters** offers five tours ranging 10-40 minutes at $33-133. The office is at 221 N. Hwy. 89A and flights depart from the Sedona Airport; tel. 282-1651 or (800) 882-1651. Fly high in a balloon with **Inflated Ego,** tel. 284-9483, **Northern Light Balloon Expeditions,** tel. 282-2274 or (800) 230-6222, **Sky High Balloon Adventures,** 204-1395 or (800) 551-7597, or **Red Rock Balloon Adventures,** tel. 284-0040 or (800) 258-3754.

*Oak Creek*

**Transport**

For a taxi, call **Bob's Taxi Service** at tel. 282-1234. You can rent a car at the airport or in town; consult the Yellow Pages.

The **Sedona-Phoenix Shuttle** travels three times daily south to Camp Verde, Cottonwood, Phoenix, and Sky Harbor Airport ($30 one-way, $55 roundtrip). The shuttle leaves from Bell Rock Inn in the Village of Oak Creek and from Railroad Inn on Hwy. 89A; tel. 282-2066 or (800) 448-7988 (Arizona only).

**Scenic Airlines Sedona** offers tours and charters; tel. 282-7935 or (800) 634-6801. The Sedona airport sits atop a mesa southwest of town; take Airport Rd. from W. Hwy. 89A.

## HIKING IN THE SEDONA AREA

Rugged canyons, delicate natural arches, and solitude await those who venture into the backcountry. Much of this land remains unchanged from prehistoric times. Hiking possibilities are virtually limitless—you can venture out on easy day-hikes or chart a weeklong trek across the wilderness. Spring and autumn offer the most pleasant temperatures, but hiking is possible all year. Summer visitors can avoid 100°-plus desert temperatures by starting early for the high country; winter hikers keep to the desert and canyon areas when snow blocks trails in the ponderosa pine forests above.

The best source of information for backcountry travel is the U.S Forest Service office in Sedona at 250 Brewer Rd., tel. 282-4119. Its Coconino Forest map ($3) shows back roads and many trails. Also, consult *Sedona Hike and Mountain Bike Rides* by Richard and Sherry Mangum.

The following seven hikes will acquaint you with this colorful land. The first five lie within the **Red Rock/Secret Mountain Wilderness** where no mechanized vehicles or mountain bikes are allowed.

### Devil's Bridge Trail #120

From the trailhead (elev. 4,600 feet), a well-graded path climbs steadily through juniper, piñon pine, Arizona cypress, and manzanita to the base of a long natural arch. You can't see

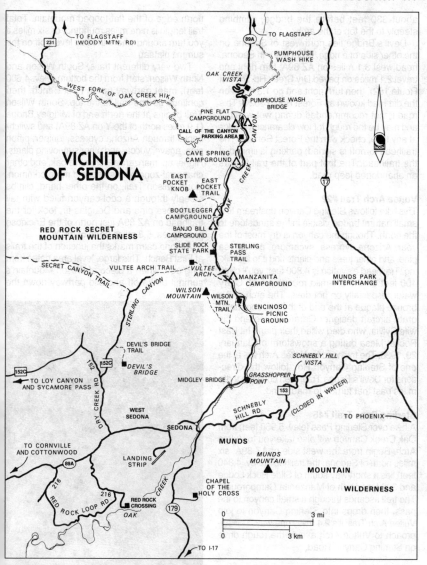

# VICINITY OF SEDONA

TO FLAGSTAFF (WOODY MTN. RD)

TO FLAGSTAFF

231

89A

PUMPHOUSE WASH HIKE

OAK CREEK VISTA

WEST FORK OF OAK CREEK HIKE

PUMPHOUSE WASH BRIDGE

PINE FLAT CAMPGROUND

CALL OF THE CANYON PARKING AREA

CAVE SPRING CAMPGROUND

EAST POCKET KNOB

EAST POCKET TRAIL

17

OAK CREEK CANYON

BOOTLEGGER CAMPGROUND

RED ROCK SECRET MOUNTAIN WILDERNESS

BANJO BILL CAMPGROUND

SLIDE ROCK STATE PARK

STERLING PASS TRAIL

OAK CREEK

SECRET CANYON TRAIL

VULTEE ARCH TRAIL

VULTEE ARCH

MANZANITA CAMPGROUND

MUNDS PARK INTERCHANGE

STERLING CANYON

WILSON MOUNTAIN

WILSON MTN. TRAIL

ENCINOSO PICNIC GROUND

DEVIL'S BRIDGE TRAIL

SCHNEBLY HILL VISTA

152C

152C

DEVIL'S BRIDGE

MIDGLEY BRIDGE

GRASSHOPPER POINT

DRY CREEK RD

152

TO LOY CANYON AND SYCAMORE PASS

WEST SEDONA

153

(CLOSED IN WINTER)

TO CORNVILLE AND COTTONWOOD

89A

SEDONA

SCHNEBLY HILL RD

TO PHOENIX

MUNDS

216

LANDING STRIP

MUNDS MOUNTAIN

MOUNTAIN WILDERNESS

216

RED ROCK LOOP RD

OAK CREEK

RED ROCK CROSSING

CHAPEL OF THE HOLY CROSS

179

0        3 mi

0        3 km

TO I-17

MOON

---

the bridge until you're almost there, but when you arrive, the majestic sweep of the arch and fine views of distant canyons and mountains reward your effort. To reach the top of the arch, continue toward the base of the cliff to the left of where the trail passes under the overhanging cliff. The 1.8-mile roundtrip hike gains 400 feet in elevation. A smaller trail forks off to the right about 330 feet before the bridge, climbing steeply to the top of the arch.

Devil's Bridge lies northwest of Sedona on the other side of a ridge. From the Y in Sedona, head west 3.1 miles on AZ 89A, turn right and travel 2.1 miles on paved Dry Creek Rd. (Forest Route 152), then turn right and go 1.3 miles on the dirt road known as Forest Route 152C. This road is not recommended during wet weather and may be too rough for low clearance vehicles at any time; check with the Forest Service. The trailhead turnoff is signed; parking is limited at the trailhead. The first part of the trail follows an abandoned jeep road.

**Vultee Arch Trail #22**

This hike follows Sterling Canyon upstream to a small natural bridge visible in the sandstone to the north. Though the canyon is dry most of the year, Arizona cypress, sycamore, ponderosa pine, and other trees and plants find it to their liking. Trailhead elevation is 4,800 feet; you'll climb 400 feet on the 3.4-mile roundtrip trail. Carry water, especially on hot days. The arch and a bronze plaque at the end of the trail commemorate aircraft designer Gerard Vultee and his wife Sylvia, who died when their plane hit East Pocket Mesa during a snowstorm on January 29, 1938. The trailhead for Vultee Arch lies at the end of Sterling Canyon Rd.; follow the directions for Devil's Bridge Trail, then continue three miles past that turnoff to road's end.

**Sterling Pass Trail #46**

A hike over Sterling Pass (elev. 5,960 feet) from Oak Creek Canyon will also take you to Vultee Arch. Begin from the west side of AZ 89A, six miles north of Sedona; the trailhead (elev. 4,840 feet) lies a short way south of Slide Rock Lodge and 300 feet north of Manzanita Campground. The trail ascends through a small canyon to the pass, then drops into Sterling Canyon to join Vultee Arch Trail; it's 2.4 miles one-way. This approach to Vultee Arch avoids the rough drive on Sterling Canyon Road.

**Wilson Mountain Trail #10**

Energetic hikers will enjoy this climb from the bottom of Oak Creek Canyon to the top of Wilson Mountain. A stiff 2,300-foot ascent is followed by a long, level stretch extending to the north edge of the flat-topped mountain. Total trail length is nine miles roundtrip, or six miles if you turn around where the trail levels off on the summit plateau.

Two very different trails, South Wilson and North Wilson, start from the bottom (elev. 4,600 feet), meet partway up on First Bench, then continue as one trail to the top. South Wilson Trail begins at the north end of Midgley Bridge (1.9 miles north of the Y on AZ 89A) and switchbacks through Arizona cypress, piñon pine, agave, yucca, and other sun-loving plants. Higher up, manzanita, scrub live oak, and other chaparral-zone plants become more common. North Wilson Trail, on the other hand, climbs steeply through a cool canyon filled with tall ponderosa pine and Douglas fir; look for the trailhead on AZ 89A just north of the Encinoso picnic area, 5.3 miles north of the Y.

A stone cairn marks the junction of the trails at First Bench. This large, level area dates from long ago, when a piece of Wilson Mountain's summit broke off and slid partway down the

*Hikers are dwarfed by the scale of the red rocks of Sedona.*

mountain. More climbing takes you to the rim of Wilson Mountain; keep right where the trail forks and follow the path north to some spectacular viewpoints. From the northernmost overlook, you can see tiny Vultee Arch far below across Sterling Canyon. Beyond, on the horizon, stand the San Francisco Peaks. Small meadows and forests of ponderosa pine and Gambel oak cover the large expanse of Wilson's summit. Carry two to three quarts of water on this hike. Ignore old trail descriptions of South Wilson Trail heading up Wilson Canyon; the new route leaves the canyon directly from the trailhead near Midgley Bridge.

Wilson Canyon and Mountain get their names from Richard Wilson, a bear hunter who lost a battle with a grizzly in June 1885. Wilson's bear gun was undergoing repairs on the day he spotted grizzly tracks in Oak Creek Canyon, but he set out after the bear anyway, toting a smaller rifle. Nine days later, horsemen found Wilson's badly mauled body up what's now Wilson Canyon.

### East Pocket (A.B. Young) Trail #100

This well-graded but strenuous trail climbs out of Oak Creek Canyon to East Pocket Mesa, north of Wilson Mountain. The trail makes more than 30 switchbacks to reach the ponderosa pine-forested rim, a 1,600-foot climb and 3.2-mile roundtrip. From the rim, the trail climbs gently to East Pocket Knob Lookout Tower, another 0.8 mile and 400 feet higher. You can enjoy excellent views of Oak Creek Canyon on the way up, from the rim, and atop the lookout tower (open during the fire season in summer). The trailhead (elev. 5,200 feet) lies across Oak Creek from Bootlegger Campground, just north of Milepost 383 on AZ 89A, 8.8 miles north of Sedona. Wade or hop stones across the creek—though don't cross if it's flooded—to a dirt road paralleling the bank, then look for a well-used trail climbing the slope.

After leaving the woodlands along Oak Creek, the trail ascends through chaparral. Allow three to four hours and carry one to two quarts of water. Cattle ranchers built this trail in the 1880s to bring herds to pasture. The Civilian Conservation Corps under A.B. Young improved it in the 1930s.

### West Fork Trail #108

An easy, almost level trail extends about 2.5 miles upstream through the narrow canyon of West Fork, a major tributary of Oak Creek. Sheer canyon walls, luxuriant vegetation, and a beautiful, clear stream make this an idyllic spot. Because of the number and diversity of plant and animal species here, the lower six miles of the canyon have been designated a Research Natural Area. The stream, which you'll cross many times, usually only flows ankle deep. Carry water and plenty of film. Don't camp or build fires in the Natural Area.

**Call of the Canyon Picnic Area**—between Mileposts 384 and 385, 10 miles north of Sedona—offers parking ($2, open 9 a.m.-8 p.m.) and a trail that leads to the West Fork trailhead. Although most visitors come for a leisurely day-hike, strong hikers can travel the entire 14-mile length of West Fork canyon in one day. It helps to get an early start and arrange a car shuttle. Those making the 14-mile trip should start at the upstream trailhead, where Forest Route 231, or Woody Mountain Rd., crosses West Fork. Woody Mountain Rd. begins as a turnoff from Old Hwy. 66, about two miles west of Flagstaff.

Only the lower end of the canyon features a trail; in other areas you must walk in the streambed or clamber over boulders. The first six miles from the upper trailhead are usually dry, but this stretch is followed by a series of deep pools that may require swimming. Avoid hiking in the canyon after heavy rains; floods are possible. The rough terrain and deep pools make backpacking difficult, so most people make the trip as a long day-hike. From the picnic area you can follow a trail to another traillhead—**Thomas Point Trail #142.** This trail rises about 900 feet in one mile of hiking to the rim on the east side of the canyon and offers great scenery but should be considered strenuous.

## SYCAMORE CANYON WILDERNESS

Imagine Oak Creek Canyon without the highway, resorts, campgrounds, and Sedona. That's Sycamore Canyon, a twisting slash in the earth 21 miles long and up to seven miles wide. As the crow flies, Sycamore Canyon lies about 15 miles west of Oak Creek Canyon. A wilderness designation protects the canyon; only hikers and horseback riders may descend to its depths. Several trails wind down to Sycamore Creek, mostly from the east side, but not a single road. Motorists may enjoy only the sweeping view from Sycamore Point on the west rim, approached from Williams.

Sycamore Canyon Wilderness is under the confusing jurisdiction of three different national forests: Coconino, Kaibab, and Prescott. The ranger station in Sedona (Coconino National Forest) is your best source of information for trail conditions, trailhead access, and water sources; 250 Brewer Rd.; tel. 282-4119.

# ALONG THE VERDE RIVER

Below the cream- and red-colored cliffs of the Mogollon Rim, the Verde (Spanish for green) River brings life to a broad desert valley. The waters come from narrow canyons of Oak Creek, Wet and Dry Beaver creeks, West Clear Creek, Sycamore Creek, and other streams.

Prehistoric Indians made camp in the area, finding a great variety of wild plant food and game between the 3,000-foot elevation of the lower valley and the Rim country 4,000 feet higher. From about A.D. 600-700, Native American groups began cultivating the Verde Valley, taking advantage of the fine climate, fertile land, and abundant water. Trade and contacts with the Hohokam culture to the south also aided development of the region. Hohokam people probably migrated into the Verde Valley too, though archaeologists can't determine whether early farming communities were actually Hohokam or simply influenced by Hohokam culture. Verde inhabitants learned to grow cotton, weave cloth, make pottery, and build ball courts.

The Sinagua people from the Flagstaff area arrived between A.D. 1125 and 1200, gradually absorbing the cultures already there. Villages then started to consolidate. Large, multistoried pueblos replaced the small pithouses of earlier times. Two of these pueblos, Montezuma Castle and Tuzigoot, are now national monuments. Archaeologists don't know why, but the Verde Valley population departed by 1425. The elaborate Hohokam culture, based in the Gila and Salt river valleys to the south, also disappeared about this time. Perhaps some of the Sinagua migrated north, eventually arriving at the Hopi and Zuni pueblos.

Early Spanish explorers, arriving a century and a half later, found small bands of nomadic Tonto Apache and Yavapai Indians roaming the valley. In language and culture, the Tonto Apache were related to the Apache and Navajo tribes to the east, while the Yavapai shared cultural traits with the Hualapai and Havasupai to the northwest.

Anglos and Mexicans poured into the valley during a gold rush at the Hassayampa River and Lynx Creek in 1863. Farmers and ranchers followed, taking for themselves the best agricultural land along the Verde. The displaced Indians attacked the settlements but failed to drive off the newcomers. Soon the Army arrived, building Camp Lincoln (later christened Fort Verde). General George Crook eventually subdued local tribes through clever campaigning and the enlistment of Apache scouts.

The Tonto Apache and Yavapai Indians were herded onto the Rio Verde Reservation in 1873, but the federal government took it away two years later, ordering the displaced Indians to proceed to the San Carlos Reservation, 150 miles away. In the cold February of 1875, the Indians started the two-week journey on foot; of the 1,451 who began the trek, at least 90 died from exposure, were killed by infighting, or escaped.

Early in this century some Apache and Yavapai received permission to return to their Verde River homelands. What were once thousands of Indians occupying millions of acres now number less than 1,000 people on a few remnants of their former lands on the Camp Verde, Prescott, and Fort McDowell reservations.

Meanwhile, Anglo farmers in the Verde Valley prospered. Cottonwood, founded in 1879, became the valley's main trading center. Copper mining succeeded on a large scale at Jerome, which sprang to life high on a mountainside in 1882. Mine company officials built a giant smelter below Jerome in 1910 and laid out the town of Clarkdale. Ore bodies were depleted in the early

1. the San Francisco Peaks from atop Sunset Crater (climbing Sunset Crater is no longer permitted); 2. Lockett Meadow and the Inner Basin of the San Francisco Peaks; 3. Inner Basin of the San Francisco Peaks; 4. Hart Prairie and the San Francisco Peaks; 5. inside Tonto Natural Bridge, near Payson (all photos by B. Weir)

**1.** Mary Lou Gulley, owner and guide at Mystery Castle near Phoenix; **2.** shopping on the Navajo Indian Reservation; **3.** DeGrazia Studio, Tucson; **4.** Tony Rose on the Beamer Trail, Grand Canyon National Park; **5.** Melanie Bertram showing off Onyx Bridge in Petrified Forest National Park; **6.** Carlos Villanueva coming down the lower Paria Canyon (all photos by B. Weir)

1950s, however, forcing many residents of Jerome and Clarkdale to seek jobs elsewhere. Today the Verde Valley prospers from industry, farming, and popularity with tourists and retirees.

## CAMP VERDE

Early in 1865, 19 men set out from Prescott aiming to start a farming settlement in the Verde Valley. They knew the mining camps around Arizona's new capital would pay well for fresh food. The eager farmers chose land where West Clear Creek joins the Verde, about five miles downstream from the modern town of Camp Verde. After the farmers planted fields, dug an irrigation system, and built a fort, Indians arrived to destroy much of the crops and livestock. Army troops marched in and built Camp Lincoln, one mile north of the present townsite. As too many place-names then commemorated the former president, the Army later changed the post's name to Camp Verde.

Indians kept the cavalry and infantry busy during the late 1860s and early 1870s. The infantry built a road, later known as the General Crook Trail, west to Fort Whipple (near Prescott) and east along the Mogollon Rim to Fort Apache. In 1871 the post moved one mile south to its current location, where more than 20 buildings were neatly laid out around a parade field. An 1882 battle at Big Dry Wash marked the last large engagement between soldiers and Indians in Arizona. Having served its purpose, Fort Verde closed in 1891.

Today exhibits and the four surviving fort buildings at Fort Verde State Historic Park give a feeling of what life was like for the enlisted men, officers, and women who lived here. Other attractions near town include the multistoried cliff dwelling of Montezuma Castle, the unusual springs at Montezuma Well, camp sites, hiking trails, and the Verde River.

## SIGHTS

### Fort Verde State Historic Park

Like most posts of the period, Fort Verde never had a protective wall around it, nor did Indians ever attack it. Army patrols used Fort Verde as

*Dr. Edgar A. Mearns, post surgeon at Fort Verde 1884-88, spent much of his time excavating prehistoric Indian sites in the Verde Valley.*

MEARNS COLLECTION, LIBRARY OF CONGRESS

a supply post and staging area. The 12-acre park preserves the administration building, commanding officer's house, bachelors' quarters, doctor's quarters, and old parade ground.

Begin your visit at the adobe administration building, used by General George Crook during the winter campaign of 1872-73 that largely ended Indian raids in the region. Exhibits recall the soldiers and their families, Apache Army scouts, settlers, and prospectors who came through here more than 100 years ago. You'll see old photos, maps, letters, rifles, uniforms, pack saddles, and Indian crafts. The three adobe buildings of Officers' Row have been restored and are now furnished as they were in the 1880s. Cavalry, infantry, and Indian scout reenactments take place several times a year.

Fort Verde State Historic Park is open daily 8 a.m.-5 p.m.; $2 adults, $1 ages 12-17; tel. 567-3275. From Main St. in Camp Verde (two miles east of I-17 Exit 287), turn north and travel one block on Hollamon Street.

## Montezuma Castle National Monument

This towering cliff dwelling so impressed early visitors they believed the famous Aztec ruler of Mexico had built it. Actually, of course, this pueblo was neither a castle nor part of Montezuma's empire. Sinagua Indians built it in the 12th and 13th centuries, toward the end of their stay in the Verde Valley. The five-story stone and mortar structure contains 20 rooms tucked back under a cliff 100 feet above Beaver Creek. The overhang shielded the village from rain, snow, and the hot summer sun but allowed the sun's low winter rays to warm the dwellings. The well-preserved ruins, once occupied by about 50 people, are too fragile to enter; you must view them from below. An even larger pueblo once stood against the base of the cliff; Castle A had six stories and about 45 rooms, but little of it remains today. Military re-enactments in period costume are held at the park during Armed Forces Day in May and during Fort Verde Days the second weekend in October. A level, one-third-mile trail loops below Montezuma Castle to the foundations of this second ruin.

*Montezuma Castle*

The visitor center displays Sinagua artifacts and offers exhibits depicting the people's everyday life, as well as the plants, animals, and geology of the Verde Valley. Related books, videos, and maps are sold. Giant Arizona sycamore trees shade a picnic area beside the river. Montezuma Castle National Monument is open daily 8 a.m.-5 p.m. in winter, extended to 8 a.m.-6 p.m. in spring and autumn and 8 a.m.-7 p.m. in summer (Memorial Day-Labor Day); $2 per person (free under 17 or 62 and over); tel. 567-3322. Take I-17 Exit 289 and follow signs two miles; from Camp Verde, drive north three miles on Montezuma Castle Rd., then turn right and travel two miles at the sign.

## Montezuma Well

This natural sinkhole and small lake, 11 miles northeast of Montezuma Castle, is worth visiting both for its scenic beauty as a desert oasis and for its Indian ruins. A one-third-mile, self-guiding loop trail climbs to the rim. Other trails wind down to the lake and to an outlet where water enters an ancient irrigation ditch. The sinkhole measures 470 feet across and is only partly filled by a 55-foot-deep lake. The lake's clear water attracts ducks, coots, and other birds.

The Sinagua built pueblos here between A.D. 1125 and 1400, using lake water to irrigate their crops. Parts of their villages and irrigation canals can still be seen. Modern farmers continue to use the water, which flows at 1,100 gallons per minute. Look for the Hohokam pithouse exhibit beside the road on the left a quarter mile before Montezuma Well. Timbers that once held up the walls and roof have long since rotted away, but distinct outlines remain of the supporting poles, walls, entrance, and fire pit.

You'll find a tree-shaded picnic area a half mile before Montezuma Well. The Well is part of Montezuma Castle National Monument and is open during the same hours (no admission charge). From Camp Verde or Montezuma Castle, take I-17 north to Exit 293 and follow signs five miles; another approach involves taking I-17 Sedona Exit 298 and heading south 4.5 miles on a gravel road.

# ON THE ROAD IN CAMP VERDE

## Accommodations

In Camp Verde, you can stay at the **Fort Verde Motel** ($40 d, tel. 567-3486). **Super 8 Motel** offers a pool and spa; $55.61 s, $62.31 d; at 1550 W. Hwy. 260, just east of I-17 Exit 287; tel. 567-2622 or (800) 800-8000. **Comfort Inn** is building an 88 unit motel at I-17 Exit 287 with a pool and spa; $58-75.82 s, $64.67-82.51 d; tel. (800) 221-2222. **Cliff Castle Lodge and Casino (Best Western)** offers luxury accommodations, a casino, restaurant, pool, and spa; $88.15 s, $94.60 d; three miles outside town on Middle Verde Rd. near the turnoff for Montezuma Castle, or take I-17 Exit 289; tel. 567-6611 or (800) 622-7853. **Beaver Creek Golf Resort** lies north in the planned community of Lake Montezuma, near Montezuma Well; rates are $56.21 s or d. Take I-17 Exit 293 and follow signs three miles; tel. 567-4475.

## Campgrounds

**Yavapai-Apache RV Park** lies three miles north of town at the junction of I-17 Exit 289 and Middle Verde Rd. (Montezuma Castle Exit) and is open all year. Rates are $9 tent, $13.50 RV w/hookups, and showers are available; check in at the Star Mart; tel. 567-4019.

**Verde River Resort** offers year-round sites for tents ($15) and RVs ($20 w/hookups) near the river; amenities include showers, pool, jacuzzi, tennis, miniature golf, fishing, scheduled activities, and store. Take Finnie Flats Rd. (AZ 260) or I-17 Exit 287, go northwest two miles past I-17, then turn right and drive 1.1 miles on Horseshoe Bend Dr.; tel. 567-5262.

The Forest Service maintains **Clear Creek Campground** (six miles southeast on Main St./AZ 260) and **Beaver Creek Campground** (take I-17 north to Sedona Exit 298, then turn south and drive 2.3 miles on Forest Route 618). Sites have drinking water all year and a $7 fee.

## Food

At **Bo's Valley View Ranch Restaurant** you can choose from seafood, steak, chicken, veal, and pork dishes, as well as a long list of sandwiches, while enjoying views of the Verde Valley; it's open daily for breakfast, lunch, and dinner; located on the north edge of downtown; tel. 567-3592. The **Steak House** is a cafe open daily for breakfast, lunch, and dinner on Main St.; tel. 567-3497.

The **Branding Iron Restaurant** is open daily for breakfast and lunch in the Fort Verde Shopping Center; tel. 567-3136. **Verde Cafe** serves breakfast, lunch, and dinner daily on Main St.; tel. 567-6521. **Custard's Last Stand** is a family restaurant and candy store; it's open daily for breakfast, lunch, and dinner on Main St.; tel. 567-9900. **Sister's and Co. Cafe,** in the Outpost Mall on Finnie Flats Rd., tel. 567-0351, serves standard American fare Mon.-Fri. for breakfast, lunch, and dinner and weekends for breakfast and lunch only.

**Cliff Castle Lodge** offers dining 24 hours daily; three miles north of town on Montezuma Castle Hwy.; tel. 567-6611. **Rio Verde Restaurant** is open daily for lunch and dinner with Mexican and American food on the south edge of town (South Access Rd.); tel. 567-9966. **La Fonda Mexican Restaurant** lies about four miles outside town on Finnie Flats Rd. (AZ 260) toward Cottonwood; go two miles past I-17, then turn right and drive 0.1 mile on Horseshoe Bend Drive. It's open Tues.-Thurs. for dinner and Fri.-Sun. for lunch and dinner; tel. 567-3500.

**Ming House** serves Chinese food in Fort Verde Plaza; it's open daily except Monday for lunch and dinner and offers a lunch buffet.; tel. 567-9488. Stop for pizza at **Babe's Round Up** on Montezuma Castle Rd. at the north edge of town; tel. 567-6969. Eat the same at **Crusty's Pizza** in the Outpost Mall on Finnie Flats Rd.; tel. 567-6444. **The Ranch House,** beside Beaver Creek Golf Course at Lake Montezuma (near Montezuma Well), offers a wide range of food; dinner specialties include steak, prime rib, and seafood plus country favorites such as mesquite cooked barbecue. It's open daily for breakfast, lunch, and dinner; tel. 567-4492. Buy groceries at **Basha's** in the Outpost Mall on Finnie Flats Road.

## Events, Services, Recreation, and Shopping

Anglers try their luck in the **Catfish Contest** on Memorial Day weekend. The **Garlic Festival** features a "Chefs' Row," arts and crafts, games, and entertainment on the last weekend in June.

During **Fort Verde Days,** on the second weekend in October, the community brings back the old days with cavalry parades and drills, a barbecue, roping events, arts and crafts shows, games, and a dance.

The **post office** lies just west of downtown on Finnie Flats Road. Play **golf** at Beaver Creek's 18-hole course at Lake Montezuma (near Montezuma Well); tel. 567-4487. **San Dominique Winery** welcomes visitors daily 10 a.m.-5 p.m. all year; the winery specializes in production of high-quality varietal wines plus offers specialty items in the deli, and is located nine miles south of Camp Verde off the I-17 Cherry Rd. East Exit; tel. 945-8583 (Scottsdale office). **Cliff Castle Lodge and Casino** offers 370 slot machines plus video poker and keno at I-17 Exit 287; tel. (800) 524-6343. **Blazing Trails, Inc.,** also at Cliff Castle Lodge and Casino, offers horseback riding priced at $20.77 one hour, $34 two hours, and $46.86 for three hours as well as custom horseback rides; tel. 567-6611.

**White Hills Indian Arts** and **Suttler's Trading Co.** on Main St. offer a good selection of jewelry and other work by the Indians of Arizona and New Mexico.

### Information

The **Camp Verde Chamber of Commerce** can help you with area sights and services; it's open Mon.-Fri. 9 a.m.-4 p.m. and sometimes on Saturday in summer. It's downtown at Main and First in a 1911 schoolhouse (Box 1665, Camp Verde, AZ 86322); tel. 567-9294.

The **Verde Ranger District** office of the Prescott National Forest provides information on running the Verde River, camping, hiking, and road conditions for the lands south and west of town, and sells books and maps; it's open weekdays 8 a.m.-4:30 p.m. Head southeast one mile from downtown on Main St./AZ 260 (Box 670, Camp Verde, AZ 86322); tel. 567-4121.

Folks at the **Beaver Creek Ranger District** office of the Coconino National Forest will help you explore the Mogollon Rim country north and east of Camp Verde; open Mon.-Fri. 7:30 a.m.-4:30 p.m.; it's north of Camp Verde near Beaver Creek Campground. Take I-17 north to Sedona Exit 298, then turn south and drive two miles on Forest Route 618 (HC 64, Box 240, Rimrock, AZ 86335); tel. 567-4501.

## VICINITY OF CAMP VERDE (BEAVER CREEK RANGER DISTRICT)

### Wet Beaver Wilderness

Sycamore, cottonwood, ash, alder, Arizona walnut, and wildflowers grow along this pretty creek. Yet, a short way from the water, the prickly pear cactus, agave, Utah juniper, and piñon pine of the high desert take over. You might see mule or

*General George Crook on his mule "Apache"; Indian scout Chief Alchesay stands on right, late 1870s.*

white-tailed deer, ringtail cat, coyote, javelina, Gambel's quail, red-tailed hawk, bald eagle, and great blue heron. Keep an eye out for rattlesnakes and poison ivy. Verde trout, some brown and rainbow, and suckers live in the creek, though most people find fishing conditions poor. Hikers enjoy trails along the lower creek, climbs to the Mogollon Rim, and difficult routes through the upper canyons. The many swimming holes in Wet Beaver Creek are at their best in summer, though the lower canyon offers pleasant hiking year-round.

To reach these 6,700 acres of rugged wilderness, take I-17 Sedona Exit 298, turn southeast and drive two miles on Forest Route 618, then left for a quarter mile at the sign to **Bell Trail #13** (elev. 3,820 feet). The **Beaver Creek Ranger District** office, a short drive beyond the trailhead turnoff, has maps and trail descriptions; see "Information" under "On the Road in Camp Verde."

The first two miles of trail follow an old jeep road into the canyon, where the way narrows to a footpath. **Apache Maid Trail #15** begins at this point, climbing steeply out of the canyon to the north, then continuing at a moderate grade to Forest Route 620 near Apache Maid Mountain. This route is 9.5 miles one-way and involves a 2,380-foot elevation gain. The Bell Trail continues upstream another mile past pretty pools to Bell Crossing, where it crosses the creek and climbs out to the west to Forest Route 214 near Five Mile Pass; you'll cover 10.8 miles one-way and gain 2,450 feet in elevation.

The Crack, a deep pool 150 feet upstream from Bell Crossing, makes a good turnaround point for a leisurely day-hike. Please don't camp here, as the area gets heavy use.

Adventurous hikers can continue upstream if they're willing to swim through many deep pools of cold, clear water; bring some flotation devices, especially if toting a camera or pack. Experienced hikers can also enter the upper canyon via Waldroup, Jacks, or Brady canyons. These routes involve some brush, and descents on small cliff faces. Contact foresters at the Beaver Creek Ranger Station for advice on exploring the area. Beaver Creek and unpalatable stock tanks are the only sources of water, so it's best to bring your own. Topo maps are a must for off-trail travel or the sometimes-faint trails on the Mogollon Rim.

## West Clear Creek Wilderness (Western End)

This 13,600-acre wilderness offers some of the most awe-inspiring canyon country of the Mogollon Rim. Deep pools in the middle section and few access points anywhere make most of the wilderness difficult to visit. The lower end of the canyon, however, can easily be explored on **West Clear Creek Trail #17.**

From I-17, take any of the Camp Verde exits and drive through town, continue east five miles on the General Crook Trail (AZ 260), turn left (north) and travel two miles on Forest Route 618, then right (east) four miles to the east end of Bull Pen dispersed camping area (elev. 3,700 feet). The first six miles are an easy walk along the creek, past fishing spots and swimming holes. You'll have to cross the creek several times, which can be difficult or impossible during high water. After six miles, the trail turns northwest and climbs steeply two miles to Forest Route 214A (elev. 5,780 feet).

**Blodgett Basin Trail #31** can be combined with the Clear Creek Trail and 2.5 miles of forest roads (214A and 214) to make a 12.7-mile loop. The trailhead is a bit easier to reach than the one for Clear Creek Trail. From the General Crook Trail, turn north and head four miles on Forest Route 618, then east 4.3 miles on Forest Route 214 to the trailhead (elev. 5,280 feet). Blodgett Basin Trail drops steadily in 2.5 miles to West Clear Creek Trail, about a half mile in from Bull Pen. To make the loop, turn up West Clear Creek Trail to its end at Forest Route 214A, follow the road 1.2 miles to Forest Route 214, then turn left and drive 1.3 miles to the Blodgett Basin Trailhead.

## Fossil Springs Wilderness

Springs gush forth millions of gallons of heavily mineralized water per hour northwest of Strawberry. The water, a constant 72° where it emerges, supports a lush riparian environment. This 11,550-acre wilderness protects the scenic beauty and abundant wildlife of Fossil Creek and some of its tributaries. Few trails enter the canyons, so much hiking is cross-country. Several trails provide access to the wilderness from the north and south sides. Flume Road, between the springs and Irving Power Plant, is open for hikers and bicyclists and closed to motor vehicles. The power plant has produced electricity at this remote location since 1916. Contact the Beaver Creek Ranger District office for trailhead locations and hiking conditions.

## General Crook National Recreation Trail

This historic trail dates back to 1871, when the Army needed a trail to supply its forts and secure the region from hostile Apache. In that year, General George Crook led a small group of cavalry to survey the route from Fort Apache in eastern Arizona to the territorial capital in Prescott. Work began in 1872, and two years later the first wagon trains covered the 200-mile distance.

The route had long been abandoned when groups of Boy Scouts cleared and marked the old path for a bicentennial project. About 138 miles are now open to hikers and horseback riders. From Camp Verde, the western section stretches 21 miles through Copper Canyon to Cherry Road. The long eastern section climbs from Camp Verde to the pine-forested Mogollon Rim, then follows the Rim 114 miles to a point west of Show Low. Much of the route appears today as the old Army cavalry knew it. Some mileposts, carved on boulders or trees, can still be seen.

Spring and autumn are the best times to hike; cross-country skiers can tour the higher elevations in winter. For trail information, obtain *A Guide to the General Crook Trail* by Eldon Bowman, published by the Museum of Northern Arizona and the Boy Scouts of America in 1978, or contact the U.S. Forest Service. The July 1982 issue of *Arizona Highways* includes excellent photos and historical articles on the General Crook Trail.

## VICINITY OF CAMP VERDE (VERDE RANGER DISTRICT)

### River-Running on the Verde

Experienced boaters in kayaks or rafts can venture downriver from Camp Verde to Sheep Bridge near Horseshoe Reservoir, 59 miles away. People are just beginning to discover this wild and scenic stretch of river. You're likely to see well-preserved Indian ruins and wildlife along the way. An area of shoreline is closed Dec.-April to protect a bald eagle nesting site. The main river-running season lasts from Jan-

uary to early April during spring runoff, but inflatable kayaks can sometimes negotiate the shallow waters off-season. The ice-cold water in winter and spring necessitates use of full or partial wetsuits. With time for rest stops and scouting rapids, rafts typically average two miles per hour.

The wildest water flows between Beasley Flats and Childs. Canoeists often experience trouble negotiating the rapids here, winding up with smashed boats. Unless you really know what you're doing, it's best to avoid the potentially dangerous conditions below Beasley Flats.

The Forest Service offers a *River Runners Guide to the Verde River;* contact the Verde or Beaver Creek ranger districts or the Tonto National Forest office at 2324 E. McDowell Rd. in Phoenix; tel. 225-5200. From about February to May, you can join commercial trips down the Verde led by **Desert Voyagers** (Box 9053, Scottsdale, AZ 85252, tel. 602-998-RAFT or 800-222-RAFT) or **Sun Country Rafting** (Box 9429, Phoenix, AZ 85068; tel. 800-2PADDLE).

### Pine Mountain Wilderness

Pine Mountain (6,814 feet) crowns the Verde Rim south of Camp Verde. The wilderness is small—about 20,000 acres—but offers solitude and natural beauty far from towns and highways. Majestic ponderosa pine forests, chaparral, and juniper and piñon woodlands cover the rough terrain. You might see mule or white-tailed deer, javelina, bear, or mountain lion.

To reach the trailhead, take I-17 Exit 268 (Dugas Rd.)—18 miles south of Camp Verde and six miles north of Cordes Junction—then head east 22 miles on dirt Forest Route 68 to the Salt Grounds, a quarter mile before Nelson Place. This road is best attempted in passenger vehicles only in good weather.

From the parking area there's a one-mile walk to the wilderness boundary. An eight-mile roundtrip loop to the top of Pine Mountain uses Forest Trails 159, 14, 161, and 12. Allow six hours for the trip, and carry water. Elevation gain is about 1,600 feet. Consult the Prescott, Tonto, or Coconino forest maps and the Tule Mesa (7.5 minute) topo map. The Verde Ranger District office in Camp Verde can provide road and trail conditions.

# COTTONWOOD

Named for the trees along the Verde River, Cottonwood provides a handy base for visiting the old mining town of Jerome, the prehistoric Tuzigoot ruins, and the other attractions of the Verde Valley. The town is 14 miles northwest of Camp Verde, 17 miles southwest of Sedona, and 41 miles northeast across Mingus Mountain from Prescott.

Cottonwood features two downtowns—a new section along AZ 89A and the original "Old Town," now bypassed by the highway. Clarkdale, just two miles northwest of Cottonwood, offers many old houses and businesses dating from its years as a smelter town. Although many

residents lost their jobs when the smelter shut down in 1952, others were glad to be rid of its heavy black smoke. A newer industry, the Phoenix Cement Company, supplied the cement used in building Glen Canyon Dam on the Colorado River.

## Tuzigoot National Monument

Sinagua Indians built and lived in this hilltop pueblo from A.D. 1125 to 1425. Tuzigoot (TOO-zee-goot) stood two stories and contained about 97 rooms. At its peak, the pueblo housed 250 people. It's believed the large size of the ruin is the result of a drought in the 1200s, which forced many dry-land farmers to resettle at Tuzigoot and other villages near the Verde River.

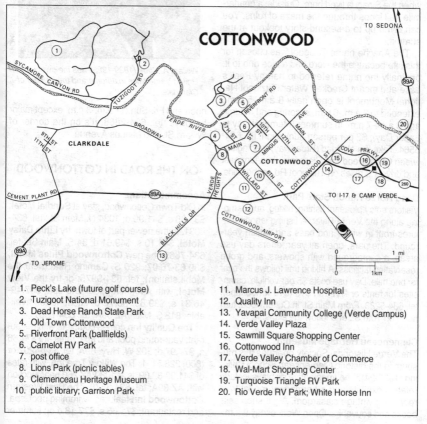

1. Peck's Lake (future golf course)
2. Tuzigoot National Monument
3. Dead Horse Ranch State Park
4. Old Town Cottonwood
5. Riverfront Park (ballfields)
6. Camelot RV Park
7. post office
8. Lions Park (picnic tables)
9. Clemenceau Heritage Museum
10. public library; Garrison Park
11. Marcus J. Lawrence Hospital
12. Quality Inn
13. Yavapai Community College (Verde Campus)
14. Verde Valley Plaza
15. Sawmill Square Shopping Center
16. Cottonwood Inn
17. Verde Valley Chamber of Commerce
18. Wal-Mart Shopping Center
19. Turquoise Triangle RV Park
20. Rio Verde RV Park; White Horse Inn

Most rooms lacked doorways—a ladder through a hatchway in the roof permitted entry. The original roofs, now gone, were pine and sycamore beams covered by willow branches and sealed with mud. While excavating the site in 1933-34, University of Arizona researchers found a wide variety of artifacts, including grave offerings for 408 burials.

A visitor center next to the ruins displays some of the archaeological finds, including stone axes and tools, projectile points, pottery, turquoise and shell jewelry, and religious objects. Other exhibits illustrate what's known about Sinagua agriculture, weaving, building techniques, and burials. A reconstruction shows how one of Tuzigoot's rooms might have looked when the Sinagua lived here. Outside, a quarter-mile trail loops through the maze of ruins. You can climb up to a second-story lookout at the summit.

The Apache name Tuzigoot was chosen for this site because the word has a nice ring to it; originally the name referred to nearby Peck's Lake and meant Crooked Water. Tuzigoot National Monument is open daily 8 a.m.-5 p.m., extended to 8 a.m.-6 p.m. in spring and autumn and 8 a.m.-7 p.m. in summer (Memorial Day to Labor Day); $2 per person admission; tel. 634-5564. Take the old road (Broadway) running between Cottonwood and Clarkdale, then turn east and drive 1.3 miles on Tuzigoot Rd. to the ruins.

### Dead Horse Ranch State Park

Visitors enjoy pleasant fishing, hiking, and camping along the Verde River. A fishing lagoon features trout in winter and bass and catfish year-round. The park, open all year, offers day-use areas, a campground with showers, and group reservation facilities. A hiking trail follows the river for one mile. Day use costs $5 per vehicle, campsites for tents or RVs run $10 ($15 w/hookups); tel. 634-5283. From Main St. in Cottonwood, turn north on 10th St. and follow the signs.

### Clemenceau Heritage Museum

The Verde Historical Society operates this museum in the historic Clemenceau School Building (1923-24). The imaginative displays include rotating exhibits and a permanent model train room and vintage classroom. A gift shop sells books and souvenirs. Open Wednesday 9 a.m.-

JEROME STATE HISTORIC PARK

*William A. Clark (1839-1925) was the owner of United Verde Mine in Jerome and the founder of Clarkdale.*

noon and Fri.-Sun. 11 a.m.-3 p.m. except major holidays; tel. 634-2868. It's on the corner of Willard St. and Mingus Avenue.

## ON THE ROAD IN COTTONWOOD

### Accommodations

In Old Town Cottonwood, stay at **Sundial Motel;** $33.08 s, $41.90 d; 1034 N. Main St.; tel. 634-8031. In the newer part of town, try **Little Daisy Motel,** $44.10 s, $49.61 d; 34 S. Main St.; tel. 634-7865; the new **Cottonwood Pines Motel,** $39.63-76.07; 920 S. Camino Real (near the Mobil station); tel. 634-9975; or try the **View Motel,** with swimming pool and spa; $37.49-46.31 s, $39.69.-50.72 d, kitchenettes available; 818 S. Main/AZ 89A; tel. 634-7581.

The **Quality Inn** comes complete with restaurant, year-round pool, and spa; rates are $71.66 s, $74.97 d; 302 W. Hwy. 89A; tel. 634-4207 or (800) 228-5151. The **Willow Tree Inn,** with rates of $41.90-82.69, is at 1089 AZ 260 near junction with AZ 89A; tel. 634-3678. The Best Western **Cottonwood Inn** features swimming pool, spa, and restaurant; $71.66 s, $77.18 d on summer weekends, reduced rates other times; 993 S. Main St. at the corner of AZ 89A and AZ 260; tel. 634-5575 or tel. (800) 528-1234.

### Campgrounds

Besides Dead Horse Ranch State Park, you can stay at **Turquoise Triangle RV Park,** open for RV use all year with showers; $11.36-18.59 w/hookups; tel. 634-5294. The park is on AZ 89A, 1.5 blocks east of the junction with AZ 260. **Rio Verde RV Park** has showers and is open all year; rates are $9.36 tents or RVs ($18.56 w/hookups); go east on AZ 89A one mile from the junction with AZ 260; tel. 634-5990. **Camelot RV Park** is in town at 858 E. Main St.; open year-round with showers; $16.16 RV w/hookups (no tents); tel. 634-3011.

### Food

**Country Kitchen Restaurant** offers a varied menu and pleasant atmosphere; it's open daily for breakfast, lunch, and dinner at Cottonwood Inn, 991 S. Main St. at the junction of AZ 89A and AZ 260; tel. 634-3696. **Sizzler,** across the street at 1041 Hwy. 260, has steak, seafood, and a

*Dr. James S. "Rawhide Jimmy" Douglas (1867-1949) bought the Little Daisy Mine in 1912, and then built the mansion now known as Jerome State Historic Park.*

big salad bar; open daily for lunch and dinner plus a weekend breakfast buffet; tel. 634-3605. **Gratella's Ristorante** offers authentic home-made Italian cuisine daily for dinner at 1075 Hwy. 260; tel. 634-0880. **Chanelle's Fine Dining** offers American and continental cuisine in an atmosphere of Old World ambience daily for lunch and dinner plus Sunday brunch at 2181 E. Hwy. 89 A; tel. 634-0505. **White Horse Inn** features steak, seafood, prime rib, and a good salad bar; open weekdays for lunch and dinner; go east on AZ 89A one mile from the junction with AZ 260; tel. 634-2271.

**Rosalie's Bluewaters Inn** serves breakfast, lunch, and dinner Tues.-Sun. at 517 N. 12th St. in Cottonwood; tel. 634-8702. **Hobo Joe's** serves American food for breakfast and lunch daily at 660 E. Mingus; tel. 634-2651. **Georgie's Cafe** specializes in breakfast; it's open daily for breakfast and lunch and Friday for dinner; Verde Valley Plaza (junction of AZ 89A and Cotton-wood St.); tel. 639-0751. **Golden Dragon** features Mandarin and Szechwan cuisine in the Sawmill Square Shopping Center; open daily except Monday for lunch and dinner; tel. 634-0588. **Blazin' M Ranch** offers not only chuck-wagon suppers but also a Western stage show, a shooting gallery, a petting zoo, and a sarsa-parilla bar plus much more; take 10th St. to Dead Horse Ranch State Park and follow the signs past the park entrance; tel. 634-0334.

**Guero's,** in the Sawmill Square Shopping Center, serves Mexican and American food; open Mon.-Sat. for lunch and dinner; tel. 634-6470. Also try **Oliva's,** which serves Mexican food, open for lunch and dinner daily; 302 W. Hwy. 89A next to Quality Inn; tel. 634-3244; or **Diego's,** which serves lunch and dinner Tues.-Sun.; 747 S. Main; tel. 634-8370. **Su Casa** is another south-of-the-border cafe, open daily for lunch and dinner in Clarkdale at 1000 S. Main St.; tel. 634-2771. **JR's Black Hills Restaurant** has steak, seafood, barbecued ribs, and other items; it's open Tues.-Sat. for lunch and dinner; 910 Main St. in Clarkdale; tel. 634-9792.

You can buy groceries at **Smith's** in the Wal-Mart Shopping Center, at **Safeway** in the Sawmill Square Shopping Center, or at **Basha's** in Verde Valley Plaza. **Mount Hope Natural Foods** is on the west edge of Old Town Cottonwood at 104 Main Street.

## Entertainment and Events

Catch movies at the **Old Town Palace,** 914 N. Main St. in Old Town Cottonwood, tel. 634-7167, or at **Movieola Big Screen Cinema** at 1389 E. Hwy. 89A, tel. 634-9041. Major annual events include the **Verde Valley Gem and Mineral Show** in March, **Verde Valley Fair** in April, **Verde River Days** (environmental programs) on the last Saturday in September, and a **Christmas Parade** in December.

## Services

The **post office** is at 700 E. Mingus Avenue. Medical services are provided by the **Marcus J. Lawrence Hospital,** 202 S. Willard St.; tel. 634-2251. A **swimming pool** open in summer, tel. 634-7468, and **tennis courts** are at Garrison Park, near the corner of E. Mingus Ave. and Sixth Street.

## Information

People at the **Cottonwood/Verde Valley Chamber of Commerce** will tell you about the sights, events, and facilities in the area; it's open daily except holidays 9 a.m.-5 p.m.; tel. 634-7593. The office is in an adobe-style building conveniently located at the intersection of AZ 89A and AZ 260 (1010 S. Main St., Cottonwood, AZ 86326). You'll find Cottonwood's excellent new **public library** at 100 S. Sixth St.; tel. 634-7559. **Jesse's Books-Music-Video** sells regional books, topo maps, and many other offerings, in the Wal-Mart Shopping Center; tel. 634-2576 or (800) 293-7245.

## Tours and Transport

Ride the rails through the Verde River Canyon on the **Verde River Railroad.** The trips begin in Clarkdale and head upcanyon, taking about four hours. You have a choice of a basic excursion ($34.95 adults, $19.95 children under 12, $30.95 seniors over 65) or first-class ($52.95) service. Trains run year-round; check schedules and make reservations at 300 N. Broadway St., Clarkdale, AZ 86324; tel. 639-0010.

The **Sedona-Phoenix Shuttle** operates six times daily between Sedona and Phoenix with stops at Cottonwood and Camp Verde; area tours can be arranged as well; tel. 282-2066 or (800) 448-7988.

# JEROME

Jerome, clinging to the slopes of Cleopatra Hill above the Verde Valley, might be Arizona's most unusual town, in both its layout and history. For more than 70 years the town's booming mines produced copper, gold, and silver. Most residents departed after 1953 when the mines closed, but Jerome itself survived. Museums, art galleries, antique shops, and restaurants brought the hillside town back to life. Old-fashioned buildings—some restored, others abandoned but still standing—add to the atmosphere.

Walking Jerome's winding streets is like touring a museum of early 20th-century American architecture. From almost any point in town, you can enjoy expansive views across the Verde Valley to Sedona red rock country, Sycamore Canyon, Mogollon Rim, and the pointed San Francisco Peaks. Three very different museums will introduce you to the people and mining history of the area.

## History

Prehistoric Indians came long ago to dig brilliant blue azurite and other copper minerals for use as paint and jewelry. Spanish explorers, shown the diggings by Indian guides, failed to see any worth in the place. In 1876, several American prospectors staked claims to the rich copper deposits, but lacked the resources to develop them. Eugene Jerome, a wealthy lawyer and financier, smelled a profit and offered financial backing to those who would mine the ore. A surveyor laying out the townsite named it in honor of the Jerome family, though Eugene himself never visited the area.

From the time the United Verde Copper Company began operating in 1882, the town's economy went on a wild roller-coaster ride dependent on copper prices. Mines closed for brief periods, then reopened. So many saloons, gambling dens, and brothels thrived in Jerome that a New York newspaper called it the "wickedest town in the West." Fires roared through the frame houses and businesses three times between 1897 and 1899, yet Jerome rose again and again, eventually becoming Arizona's fifth-largest city. Floods and underground blasting shook the earth so much that buildings keeled

JEROME STATE HISTORIC PARK

*the blast furnace of Jerome's first smelter*

over; banks refused to take the average Jerome house or business as collateral. The town's famous sliding jail one day took off across the street and down the hillside, where it still lies today.

The community enjoyed its greatest prosperity during the Roaring '20s, when the population hit 15,000. The stock market crash and ensuing Depression spelled disaster for the copper industry; mines and smelter shut down and the population plummeted to less than 5,000. World War II brought Jerome's last period of prosperity before the mines shut down for good in 1953. Many people thought Jerome would become a ghost town when the population shrank to only 50 souls. But, beginning in the late 1960s, artists, shop owners, tourists, retirees, and others rediscovered Jerome's unique character and setting.

## SIGHTS

### Jerome State Historic Park

The Douglas Mansion, built in 1917 by James "Rawhide Jimmy" Douglas, tops a hill overlooking the Little Daisy Mine. Today, the old mansion brims with Jerome mining lore. Outside sits a giant stamp mill and the more primitive *arrastre* (drag-stone mill) and Chilean wheels once used to pulverize ore. Signs at viewpoints identify some of Jerome's historic buildings.

Inside, a video presentation illustrates the many changes that have wracked Jerome. An assay office, the Douglas library, old photos, mining tools, smelter models, and mineral displays show different aspects of the effort expended to extract metals from the earth. Upstairs, a neat three-dimensional model illustrates Jerome's mine shafts, underground work areas, and geologic features. Jerome State Historic Park is open daily 8 a.m.-5 p.m.; $2 adults, $1 ages 12-17; tel. 634-5381. A small picnic area beside the mansion offers expansive views of the Verde Valley. Turn off AZ 89A at Milepost 345 at the lower end of Jerome (eight miles west of Cottonwood), then follow the paved road one mile.

### Jerome Historical Society Mine Museum

Look for the two large half-wheels at the corner of Main St. (AZ 89A) and Jerome Avenue. Paintings, photos, stock certificates, mining tools, and ore samples illustrate Jerome's development. The museum is open daily 9 a.m.-4:30 p.m.; admission is 50 cents adults, free for children under 12; tel. 634-5477.

### Gold King Mine Museum

If you're fascinated by old machinery, or if you've ever wanted to poke around a ghost town, this collection might satisfy your curiosity. Among the hoists, pumps, engines, and ore cars, look for the replica of a mine shaft, a blacksmith shop, a 1930s gas station, and an assay office. You can watch an antique sawmill in operation daily. A small petting zoo attracts the kids.

Enter through the gift shop, which sells mining memorabilia and other souvenirs. The museum is open daily 9 a.m.-5 p.m.; admission is $3 adults, $2 children 6-12, $2.50 seniors 65 and over; tel. 634-0053. From the upper switchback on AZ 89A in Jerome, turn northwest and drive one mile on Perkinsville Road. On the way you'll pass a large open-pit mine on the left, where Jerome's smelter was at the turn of the century.

## ON THE ROAD IN JEROME

### Accommodations

Modern motels have yet to hit town; if that's what you're looking for, stay in Cottonwood, eight miles south. Jerome does offer at least one hotel, old-fashioned by today's standards but well kept. Reservations should be made for weekends. The **Inn at Jerome,** 309 Main St., features Victorian-style rooms—one with private bath—at $60.23-93.08 d including breakfast; tel. 634-5094. The **Connor Hotel** at 168 Main St. is undergoing restoration but may not offer rooms. **Cottage Inn** occupies a house built in 1904; rates are $60 d; Box 823, Jerome, AZ 86331; tel. 634-0701. **Ghost City Inn** occupies an 1898 Victorian house filled with antiques; rates are $82.13-104.03 d; 541 N. Main St., Box 382, Jerome, AZ 86331; tel. 63-GHOST.

### Campgrounds

Stay at **Dead Horse Ranch State Park** or the RV parks in Cottonwood below town, or at the cool **Potato Patch** or **Mingus Mountain campgrounds** in the hills above. Both campgrounds are accessible via a seven-mile drive southwest

Century plants bloom near the ghost town of Jerome.

of Jerome; head right a half mile for Potato Patch or left six miles on Forest Route 104 for the Mingus campground. Both are closed by winter snow; no water or fee.

### Food and Entertainment

The **House of Joy** certainly enjoys a colorful reputation. In the old days, painted ladies did a lively business in this house. Present owners have kept the red lights and other brothel decor while eschewing sexual services in favor of excellent continental cuisine at moderate prices. This popular dining spot is open for dinner only on Saturday and Sunday; make reservations well in advance by calling after 9 a.m.; tel. 634-5339. The House of Joy is on the right side of Hull St., at the beginning of the uphill one-way section of AZ 89A.

**Flatiron Cafe,** at the fork in the road in the Flat Iron District, serves sandwiches, baked goods, fancy coffees, eclectic salads, and other refreshments; it's open daily in the morning and afternoon, tel. 634-2733. Next door, the **Wedge on the Edge,** serves pizza, salad, and baked goods for lunch and dinner Tues.-Sun.; tel. 634-

5554. The **Jerome Grill,** 309 Main St., serves breakfast, lunch, and dinner daily; tel. 634-5094. **Marcy's,** 363 Main St., offers sandwiches, salads, and ice cream. **Jerome Market and Coffee House,** offers gourmet sandwiches and pastries at 515 Main Street. **English Kitchen,** 119 Jerome Ave., is the oldest restaurant in Arizona, in business since 1899. It serves breakfast and lunch daily except Monday; tel. 634-2132.

For entertainment, locals hang out in the Spirit Room of the **Connor Hotel** and at **Paul & Jerry's Saloon,** both on upper Main Street.

### Events
On the third weekend of May the **Jerome Home Tour** visits historic houses and buildings not normally open to the public. A varied program of folk, Western, and rhythm and blues is the highlight of the **Music Festival,** held in autumn.

### Shopping, Services, and Information
Shops up and down Main St. display a wide variety of artwork, crafts, antiques, jewelry, and clothing. The **Old Mingus Art Center** houses galleries in a former school building at the lower end of town. The **post office** is at 134 Main Street. Obtain free maps and brochures from the **chamber of commerce** in Blue Heron Gifts on Main St., next to the post office; Box K, Jerome, AZ 86331; tel. 634-2900. The **Jerome Public Library** at 109 Jerome Ave. is open variable days and hours; tel. 639-0574.

# PRESCOTT AND VICINITY

That's *Prescutt,* pardner. Unlike most Western towns, which haphazardly boomed into existence, Prescott is a city carefully laid out.

The mile-high town rests in a mountain basin ringed by the pine-forested Bradshaws, towering Thumb Butte, the jumbled mass of Granite Mountain, boulder-strewn Granite Dells, and the vast grasslands of Chino and Lonesome valleys. Downtown, the Doric-columned courthouse sits in a spacious, grassy plaza surrounded by tall elm trees. The equestrian statue in front of the courthouse commemorates the spirit of William "Buckey" O'Neill, newspaperman, sheriff, mayor, adventurer, and Spanish-American War hero. O'Neill led a company of Theodore Roosevelt's Rough Riders in Cuba, where an enemy bullet cut him down.

The Palace Bar, on Montezuma St. opposite the courthouse, carries on the tradition of "Whiskey Row," where more than 20 saloons roared full-blast day and night at the turn of the century. The Sharlot Hall Museum, two blocks west, preserves Prescott's past with early buildings and excellent historical collections. On the other side of town, the Smoki (SMOKE-eye) Museum displays a wealth of artifacts from American Indian cultures. About 100 Yavapai Indians live in the Prescott area, mostly on a 1,400-acre reservation just north of town.

Though Prescott is small (pop. 30,000), it contains several art galleries, an active artists' community, two colleges, and an aeronautical university. Just outside town the visitor will discover the area's beautiful forests, fishing lakes, mountains, and ghost towns.

### History
Soon after Congress carved the territory of Arizona from New Mexico in 1863, Governor John Goodwin and a party of appointed officials set off from Washington on a tour of their territory. Their arduous three-month journey took them to the rich mineral districts of central Arizona, a promising new land relatively free of the Confederate sympathizers who occupied the southern towns of Tucson and Tubac.

Goodwin and his party first set up a temporary capital at Fort Whipple in Chino Valley. Then, to be closer to mining activities and timbered land, both the government and the fort moved 17 miles south to a site along Granite Creek. Fort Whipple served as the center for campaigns against Tonto Apache and Yavapai Indians during the 1860s and 1870s. Sentries were constantly alert for Indian attacks as workers felled trees to build the Capitol and Governor's Mansion.

Early citizens named the settlement after William Hickling Prescott, a historian noted for his work on Mexico. Unlike the towns to the south, with their adobe buildings and strong Spanish-Mexican flavor, Prescott derived its

*Cortez Street bicycle race, ca. 1900*

character from the settlers of New England and the Midwest. Vast forests provided timber for log cabins and, later, frame buildings.

In 1867 the Legislature had a change of heart and moved the capital down to Tucson. Prescott's future looked bleak, as Apache attacks and high transportation costs threatened further mining and agricultural development. Improved mining techniques and the gold strikes of the 1870s brought the region back to life. Even the Legislature returned, in 1877, before moving to Phoenix for good in 1889. By then Prescott was a thriving city that no longer needed the politicians or their business. Mining, ranching, and trade prospered.

Even a disastrous fire in 1900, which wiped out Prescott's entire business district—including Whiskey Row—couldn't destroy community spirit. Undaunted, the saloonkeepers moved their salvaged stock across the street, continuing to serve libations as the fires blazed. Within days the townsfolk began rebuilding, creating the downtown the visitor sees today. Agriculture and a bit of mining continue in the Prescott area, but it's the ambience of the place that charms most people. It's found in the many historic buildings lining Prescott's tree-shaded streets; the

clean, pine-scented air; and the agreeable four-season climate.

## SIGHTS

### Sharlot Hall Museum

A dozen buildings make up this excellent historical museum; start anywhere you like. It's open Mon.-Sat. 10 a.m.-5 p.m. (4 p.m. in winter) and Sunday 1-5 p.m.; closed winter Mondays. Admission is free, but the suggested $2 adult donation is welcomed. The complex is centered at 415 W. Gurley St., two blocks west of the plaza. Offices, research library, conservation laboratory, and rotating exhibits fill the modern, solar-heated **Museum Center;** tel. 445-3122.

Sharlot Hall founded the museum in 1928, displaying her personal belongings in the Governor's Mansion. Herself a pioneer, Hall arrived in Arizona in 1882 by wagon at the tender age of 12. She developed a keen interest in the land and people of Arizona and shared her impressions in stories and poems. From 1909 to 1911 Hall served as the territory's first historian, traveling Arizona's primitive roads to collect information and stories firsthand.

The two-story **Governor's Mansion,** built from logs on this site in 1864, might today seem too primitive to qualify as a "mansion," but not when one recalls that in those days most people lived in tents or lean-tos. This place was a castle by comparison. In the beginning, Governor John Goodwin and Territorial Secretary Richard McCormick occupied opposite ends of the building. The territorial Legislature met here, among other places, for its session, awaiting completion of the Capitol. The mansion has been restored and furnished as it existed during the early years.

The **Sharlot Hall Building,** completed in 1934, houses most of the Indian and pioneer displays. Excellent exhibits re-create military life at Fort Whipple, and recall early ranches, frontier saloons and stores, and Prescott heroes. A Native American room displays many fine examples of Indian pottery, basketry, jewelry, and other crafts from both prehistoric and modern tribes of the Southwest.

The **Fremont House,** built in 1875, moved to this site in 1972. It contains furnishings typical of a well-to-do family of the late 1870s. John C. Fremont, Arizona's fifth territorial governor, rented the house from 1878 to 1881. Fremont had earned fame as an explorer of the West, but he failed miserably in Arizona politics. Fremont didn't care for Prescott's climate and spent long periods back East or in Tucson. Public pressure forced his resignation after three years in office. The **Bashford House,** built in 1877 and moved to its present location in 1974, contains a gift shop offering books on Arizona history and baskets by Tohono O'odham Indians. William Bashford bought the house and remodeled it during the 1880s in an ornate late-Victorian style.

The museum complex also includes the **Ranch House,** a little log cabin with branding irons, saddles, harnesses, and other cowboy gear, and **Fort Misery,** one of Prescott's earliest buildings, a general store dating from 1864. There Judge John Howard, according to legend, dispensed "misery" to lawbreakers. The cabin appears as it did when he lived in it.

The **schoolhouse** is a replica of the territory's first public school, built near Granite Creek in 1864. A **blacksmith shop** is used in restoration projects. The **transportation building** exhibits a Star auto used by Sharlot Hall, a stage-coach, wagons, sleighs, and bicycles. Each of the more than 350 flowers in the **rose garden** commemorates an outstanding Arizona woman.

## Smoki Museum

From a split-twig figure of 4,000 years ago to the baskets and pottery of modern tribes, this collection preserves a wide variety of Southwest Indian artifacts. A kiva floor plan duplicates a Hopi dwelling at Oraibi. A Zuni Shalako (spirit of the rain clouds) towers 10 feet high. Some of the pottery and stone tools come from prehistoric pithouses excavated in nearby Chino Valley. It's open daily 10 a.m.-4 p.m. except 1-4 p.m. Sunday from May 1 to September 30, closed Wednesday. Groups can also visit by appointment; tel. 445-1230. Admission is $2 adults, free for children under 12. The pueblo-style museum building is at 126 N. Arizona St., one block north of E. Gurley Street.

Originally, white members of the community organized the Smoki "tribe" in 1921 to raise funds for the annual Frontier Days Rodeo by performing Indian dances. Later the group took a more serious interest in Native American rituals, dance, and artifacts. Members of the organization are identified by a four-dot tattoo on the side of the left hand. Today the Smoki Native American Festival, on the first or second weekend in August, features Indian dancers, crafts, and demonstrations.

## The Bead Museum

A bead museum? Yes, this collection contains beads and other personal adornments from the far corners of the earth. It's open Mon.-Sat. 9:30 a.m.-4:30 p.m., and admission is free. Beads are also for sale. Enter through Liese Interiors and Artifacts on Whiskey Row, 140 S. Montezuma St.; tel. 445-2431.

## Phippen Museum of Western Art

Paintings, sketches, and the occasional bronze by outstanding artists celebrate Western heritage and art. Promising new artists receive attention as well. The museum honors George Phippen, a well-known Western artist who founded Cowboy Artists of America, serving as its first president. A gift shop sells cards, jewelry, crafts, and artwork. It's open daily except Tuesday 1-4 p.m.; admission is $2 adults, $1.50

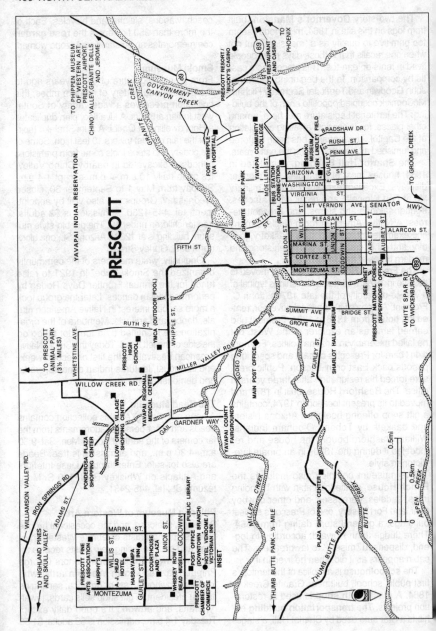

PRESCOTT

TO PHIPPEN MUSEUM OF WESTERN ART, PRESCOTT AIRPORT, CHINO VALLEY GRANITE DELLS AND JEROME

GOVERNMENT CANYON CREEK

GRANITE CREEK

PRESCOTT RESORT / BUCKY'S CASINO

MARIO'S RESTAURANT AND CASINO

TO PHOENIX

69

89

FORT WHIPPLE (VA HOSPITAL)

YAVAPAI COMMUNITY COLLEGE

YAVAPAI INDIAN RESERVATION

BRADSHAW DR.

SMOKI MUSEUM

KEN LINDLEY FIELD

RUSH ST.

PENN AVE.

MOELLER ST.

BUS STATION (RURAL CONNECTION)

ARIZONA ST.

E. GURLEY ST.

WASHINGTON ST.

VIRGINIA ST.

TO GROOM CREEK

GRANITE CREEK PARK

MT VERNON AVE.

SENATOR HWY

SIXTH ST

WILLIS ST.

PLEASANT ST.

CARLETON ST.

ALARCON ST.

AUBREY ST.

SHELDON ST.

UNION ST.

GOODWIN ST.

FIFTH ST

MARINA ST.

CORTEZ ST.

MONTEZUMA ST.

SEE INSET

PRESCOTT NATIONAL FOREST (SUPERVISOR'S OFFICE)

89

WHITE SPAR RD. TO WICKENBURG

WHETSTINE AVE.

RUTH ST. (OUTDOOR POOL)

WHIPPLE ST.

SUMMIT AVE.

GROVE AVE.

BRIDGE ST.

SHARLOT HALL MUSEUM

TO PRESCOTT ANIMAL PARK (3½ MILES)

PRESCOTT HIGH SCHOOL

YMCA

MILLER VALLEY RD.

RODEO DR.

W GURLEY ST.

MAIN POST OFFICE

WILLOW CREEK RD.

YAVAPAI REGIONAL MEDICAL CENTER

GAIL GARDNER WAY

YAVAPAI COUNTY FAIRGROUNDS

MILLER CREEK

WILLOW CREEK VILLAGE SHOPPING CENTER

0.5mi

0.5km

ASPEN CREEK

PONDEROSA PLAZA SHOPPING CENTER

IRON SPRINGS RD.

WILLIAMSON VALLEY RD.

ADAMS ST.

PLAZA SHOPPING CENTER

THUMB BUTTE RD.

BUTTE CREEK

TO HIGHLAND PINES AND SKULL VALLEY

THUMB BUTTE PARK – ½ MILE

## INSET

MARINA ST.

WILLIS ST.

GOODWIN ST.

PRESCOTT FINE ARTS ASSOCIATION

MURPHY'S

A. J. HEAD HOTEL

HASSAYAMPA

UNION ST.

PUBLIC LIBRARY

POST OFFICE (DOWNTOWN BRANCH)

HOTEL VENDOME / VICTORIAN INN

COURTHOUSE AND PLAZA

GURLEY ST.

WHISKEY ROW

BEAD MUSEUM

PRESCOTT CHAMBER OF COMMERCE

MONTEZUMA

seniors 60 and over, $1 children and students, free for children under 12; tel. 778-1385. The museum is in a ranch-style building six miles north of Prescott at 4701 N. Hwy. 89, one mile north of the AZ 89A turnoff.

**Prescott Animal Park**
Meet denizens of the Southwest, exotic creatures, and farm animals at this small but growing zoo. A reptile region houses our many scaled friends. Open Sun.- Thurs. 10 a.m.-5 p.m. and Fri.-Sat. 10 a.m.-7 p.m. in summer, then Mon.-Fri. 11 a.m.-4 p.m. and Sat.-Sun. 10 a.m.-5 p.m. in winter; admission is $4 adults, $3.50 seniors 65 and over, $1.50 children 2-12; tel. 778-4242. It's about six miles north of town on Heritage Park Rd., just off Willow Creek Road.

**Fort Whipple**
This historic Army fort dates from 1863. It honors Brigadier General Amiel Weeks Whipple, who served with the Army Corps of Topographical Engineers until his death in the Civil War. The post played a major role during the Indian wars and was maintained until 1912. Ten years later it became a Veterans Administration hospital. Many of the military buildings, including the barracks and officers' quarters, date from the turn of the century. You're welcome to visit the hospital grounds, though there's no museum or visitor center. Fort Whipple lies on the northeast edge of town off AZ 89.

# ACCOMMODATIONS

Prescott offers a fine selection of places to stay. Try to secure reservations for weekends during the warmer months. Rates tend to go up on summer weekends, dropping a bit in winter. Regular summer rates are quoted here. Book far in advance for Frontier Days, held around July 4th, and expect to pay more.

**Historic**
Prescott's old hotels, dating from the early 1900s, offer an experience flavored with history. The **Hassayampa Inn** ranked as the town's premier grand hotel in 1927 and is still number one today, thanks to recent renovations. The plush lobby features a painted ceiling, old piano,

and other antiques. All rooms have private baths and a/c; rates are $97.05-190.83 d. The hotel's Peacock Room offers elegant dining; 122 E. Gurley St.; tel. 778-9434 or (800) 322-1927. The **Hotel Vendome,** built in 1917, also offers attractively restored rooms with private baths for $92.69-136.31 d; 230 S. Cortez St.; tel. 776-0900.

The **A.J. Head Hotel** (built 1898-1903) has been restored on a more modest scale. Rooms, some with private bath, cost $33.80-59.97 d, while weekly rates run from $113.41 s, $190.84 d; a restaurant serves dinner some evenings; 129 N. Cortez St.; tel. 778-1776. The **Highland Hotel,** built in 1903, was once a brothel where women scouted potential customers from the bay windows. The hotel has not been restored much, but then neither have the prices. Rooms, with the communal bath down the hall, cost $35 s or d; weekly and monthly rates are available; it's on Whiskey Row at 154 S. Montezuma St.; tel. 445-9059. The **Hotel St. Michael** began life in 1900 as the Hotel Burke; rooms, all with private baths, go for $39.25-45.80 s, $45.80-52.34 d, $67.61-78.51 suite. A San Francisco-style coffeehouse serves refreshments at the corner of 205 W. Gurley and Montezuma streets; tel. 776-1999.

**Bed and Breakfasts**
**Prescott Pines Inn Bed and Breakfast** offers "country Victorian" rooms for $64.34-103.60 d ($5 extra for breakfast) on the south edge of town at 901 White Spar Rd. (S. AZ 89); tel. 445-7270 or (800) 541-5374. The nearby **Prescott Country Inn Bed and Breakfast** offers rooms, suites, and cottages with country decor for $103.60-162.48 d; 503 S. Montezuma; tel. 445-7991. **Marks House Inn Bed and Breakfast** is an 1894 Victorian house with antique decor and feather beds; rates are $81.78-136.31 d; 203 E. Union; tel. 778-4632 or (800) THE-UNION. **Mt. Vernon Inn** offers bed and breakfast at 204 N. Mt. Vernon Ave.; $98.55-120.45 d; tel. 778-0886.

**Victorian Inn of Prescott Bed and Breakfast** occupies an 1893 house at 246 S. Cortez St.; rates are $98.15-147.22 d on weekends; tel. 778-2642 or (800) 704-2642. **Pleasant Street Inn** offers bed and breakfast with a variety of rooms and suites at 142 S. Pleasant and Goodwin streets; $87.24-130.86 d; tel. 445-4774. **Lynx Creek Farm Bed and Breakfast** features an organic orchard and garden and farm animals in the hills five miles east of town; rates are $84.84-111.35 d; tel. 778-9573.

## Motels

These include the **Wheel Inn Motel**, $42.71-49.28 s $64.61 d, close to downtown at 333 S. Montezuma St., tel. 778-7346; **Clarion Carriage House Inn**, $82.13-109.50 s, $109.50-164.25 d at 230 S. Cortez St.; tel. 776-0900 or (800) 221-2222; **Sierra Inn**, $53.66-82.13 d, $104.03 w/kitchen at 809 White Spar Rd., tel. 445-1250; **Comfort Inn**, $66.80-84.32 s and $69-84.32 d, 1290 White Spar Rd., tel. 778-5770; **Motel 6**, $42.71 s and $49.28 d, 1111 E. Sheldon St., tel. 776-0160; **Super 8 Motel**, $55.48-60.94 s and $60.94-66.39 d, 1105 E. Sheldon St.; tel. 776-1282 or (800) 800-8000; **Senator Inn**, $86.15 s and $97.05 d, 1117 E. Gurley St., tel. 445-1440; and **Apache Lodge Motel**, $64.61-86.51 d, 1130 E. Gurley St., tel. 445-1422.

Also try the **Colony Inn**, $76.65 s or d, 1225 E. Gurley St., tel. 445-7057; **Best Western Prescottonian Motel**, $86.51-94.17 d, 1317 E. Gurley St., tel. 445-3096 or (800) 528-1234; and **Prescott Resort**, $149.87 s or d, 1500 Hwy. 69, then up the hill, tel. 776-1666 or (800) 967-4637. **Antelope Hills Inn-Suites** is near the airport and Antelope Hills Golf Course at the junction of AZ 89 and Willow Creek Rd.; $60.23-70.08; tel. 778-6000.

**Forest Villas Hotel**, is a new luxury hotel at 3645 Lee Circle (four miles east of downtown, off Hwy. 69), $107.96-151.58 s or d; tel. 717-1200 or (800) 223-2449.

You'll find other new accommodations in **Prescott Valley**, a fast-growing suburb of Prescott 10 minutes' drive east on Hwy. 69. These include **Days Inn**, $68.23 s, $75.93 d; 7875 E. Hwy. 69, tel. 772-9412 or (800) DAYSINN, and **Prescott Valley Motel**, $54.03-64.83 s or d, 8390 E. Hwy. 69, tel. 772-9412.

## Campgrounds

**White Spar Campground**, 2.5 miles south of downtown on AZ 89, has drinking water year-round but no showers or hookups; $6. One loop stays open in winter; obtain water from a

*Granite Basin Lake*

faucet near the campground entrance. **Indian Creek Campground** lies four miles south on AZ 89, then left 0.7 mile on Forest Route 97; it's open mid-May to the end of September (no water or fee).

**Lynx Lake** and nearby **Hilltop** campgrounds sit above a pretty lake containing trout and catfish. Lynx sites are open April 1 -Nov. 15 while Hilltop is open May 15-Sept. 30; both have drinking water but no showers or hookups, $8. Picnickers may use tables at a vista point on the north end of the lake and near the boat ramp at the south end free of charge. You can reserve some sites at White Spar and Lynx Lake campgrounds by calling (800) 280-CAMP. To reach Lynx Lake, head east three miles on AZ 69 (from N. AZ 89), then turn south and drive 2.5 miles on Walker

Rd.; Hilltop Campground is one mile farther. A store and boat rentals occupy the north end of Lynx Lake.

**Granite Basin Campground** lies near a small lake at the base of Granite Mountain, northwest of town; it's open all year; no water or fee. From W. Gurley St., turn northwest and drive 4.3 miles on Grove Ave./Miller Valley Rd./Iron Springs Rd., then turn north and proceed 3.5 miles on Forest Route 374. **Lower Wolf Creek Campground** south of town is open mid-May to mid-November; no drinking water or fee. Take Senator Hwy. (Forest Route 52) south 7.5 miles, then turn west and drive one mile on Forest Route 97. Or from AZ 89, four miles south of Prescott, turn east and travel five miles on Forest Route 97. Groups can reserve **Upper Wolf Creek Campground** and an area of Granite Basin Campground; tel. (800) 280-CAMP.

You and your horse can stay at **Groom Creek Horsecamp;** individual ($8) and group reservation sites are available; it's open year-round (with water) near the start of Forest Trail 307; go 6.5 miles south on Senator Hwy. (Forest Route 52) from town.

**Watson Lake Park,** beside Granite Dells, is open all year and has showers; $8 tents or RVs, $1.50 for day use; it's four miles north of town on AZ 89; tel. 778-4338 or 445-9978. **Point of Rocks RV Campground,** just north of Watson Lake Park, is open all year with RV sites for $16.17 w/hookups (no tents); tel. 445-9018. **Willow Lake RV and Camping Resort** features a swimming pool, fishing, store, and showers for $14.18 tent or RV (no hookups), $18-20 RV w/hookups; it's five miles north of town off Willow Creek Rd.; tel. 445-6311.

**Powell Springs Campground,** in ponderosa pines near the village of Cherry, stays open all year and has spring water (no charge). From the turnoff on AZ 169 (25 miles east of Prescott and 5.5 miles west of I-17 Exit 278), turn north 4.5 miles on Forest Route 372 (Cherry Rd.); see a highway or forest map. Forest Route 372 is a winding, gravel road with good scenery. You can also drive in from the Verde Valley; take I-17 Exit 287, go northwest 2.8 miles, then turn left (south) and drive 12.6 miles on Cherry Rd. to Powell Springs Campground.

# FOOD

Restaurants are marked: $: Inexpensive (to $8); $$: Moderate ($8-15); $$$: Expensive (over $15). Ratings refer to price ranges for dinners (per person).

## American and Continental Cuisine

**$$ Murphy's:** Serves sandwiches, steak, prime rib, seafood, and other dishes in an old mercantile building dating from 1890. Dim lighting, antiques, and greenery add to the romantic setting. It's open daily for lunch and dinner at 201 N. Cortez St.; tel. 445-4044.

**$$ Peacock Room:** Located in the Hassayampa Inn, Peacock Room offers an old-fashioned atmosphere for its varied menu of American and continental specialties; it's open daily for breakfast, lunch, and dinner at 122 E. Gurley St.; tel. 778-9434.

**$$ NOLAZ Restaurant & Lounge:** Serves Louisiana Bayou cuisine from jambalaya and etouffee to alligator; it's open Mon.-Fri. for lunch and Mon.-Sat. for dinner at 216-220 W. Gurley St.; tel. 445-3765.

**$-$$ Clancy's Pub:** Features northern New Mexican cuisine, sandwiches, and burgers with a selection of soups, stews, and salads. It's open Mon.-Sat. for lunch and dinner at 129 N. Montezuma St.; tel. 445-1904.

**$-$$ Panzulla's:** Features northern Italian cuisine. It's open daily for lunch and dinner at 1350 Iron Springs Rd.; tel. 776-7062.

**$$ Marshal John's Restaurant:** Features ribs, Santa Fe chicken, buffalo burgers, steak, and a monthly Greekfest; it's open daily for lunch and dinner at 415 White Spar Rd.; tel. 778-3663.

**$$ Pine Cone Inn:** Menu lists steak, seafood, and other American cuisine; it's open daily for breakfast, lunch, and dinner, with live dinner music Tues.-Sun. at 1245 White Spar Rd.; tel. 445-2970.

**$-$$ Dry Gulch Steak House:** Another good place for steak and seafood; it's open Tues.-Fri. for lunch and Tues.-Sun. for dinner at 1630 Adams St., two blocks west of Ponderosa Plaza off Iron Springs Rd.; tel. 778-9693.

**$$ Thumb Butte Room:** Offers fine dining for Sunday brunch and is open daily for breakfast, lunch, and dinner at the Sheraton Resort, 1500 Hwy. 69; tel. 776-1666.

**$-$$ Mario's:** Serves Italian dinners, pizza, and sandwiches daily for lunch and dinner; it's east of downtown at 1505 E. Gurley/AZ 69; tel. 445-1122.

**$-$$ Roman Italian Restaurant and Deli:** Features pasta dishes, veal, and seafood; it's open Tues.-Sat. for lunch and dinner at 627 Miller Valley Rd.; tel. 778-0740.

**$$ Gurley Street Grille:** Serves upscale burgers, pasta, pizza, and sandwiches; it's open daily for lunch and dinner at 230 W. Gurley; tel. 445-3388.

**Other Cuisines**
**$ Los Amigos Casita:** Serves Mexican food Tues.-Sat. for lunch and dinner on Whiskey Row at 150 S. Montezuma St.; tel. 445-3683.

**$ El Charro:** Another Mexican cafe, open daily for lunch and dinner at 120 N. Montezuma St.; tel. 445-7130.

**$-$$ Canton Cafe:** Offers Chinese dining daily (except Sunday) for lunch and dinner at 1102 Willow Creek Rd.; tel. 445-0070.

**$-$$ China Jade Restaurant:** Specializes in Mandarin-style cuisine; it's open Tues.-Sun. for lunch and dinner at 1781 E. Hwy. 69 (Wal-Mart Shopping Center); tel. 445-4072.

**Inexpensive American**
**Greens & Things** offers omelettes, Belgian waffles, bagels, sandwiches, and fruit drinks; it's open daily for breakfast and lunch at 106 W. Gurley St.; tel. 445-3234.

**Maude's** serves breakfast and lunch Mon.-Sat. and breakfast Sunday at 146 S. Montezuma St. on Whiskey Row; tel. 778-3080.

**Berry's Soup and Sandwich Express** is open daily for lunch and dinner at 1106 E. Gurley St.; tel. 778-6330.

**Denny's** offers 24-hour service for breakfast, lunch, and dinner at 1316 Iron Springs Rd.; tel. 778-1230.

The **Dog House** dishes out different hot dogs and other sandwiches; it's open daily except Sunday for lunch at 126 S. Montezuma St.; tel. 445-7962.

**Juniper House** is a family restaurant open daily for breakfast, lunch, and dinner at 810 White Spar Rd. (S. AZ 89); tel. 445-3250.

**Super Carrot Natural Foods** offers health foods and a lunch counter; it's open daily (lunch counter open weekdays only) at 236 S. Montezuma St.; tel. 776-0365.

**New Frontiers** offers health food and a deli (take out or eat in) open daily at 1112 Iron Springs Rd.; tel. 445-7370.

## ENTERTAINMENT

The **Prescott Fine Arts Association** maintains an art gallery, gallery gift shop, and theater at 208 N. Marina St. (presenting plays, musicals, concerts, and family theater); it's open Wed.-Sat. 11 a.m.-4 p.m. and Sunday noon-4 p.m.; tel. 445-3286 or 778-7888. There's something happening every summer night on the **Courthouse Plaza**—could be a concert, dance, or speech. **Yavapai Community College** sponsors a variety of performances and other events; call the switchboard for specifics at 445-7300. Catch movies at the **Marina Theatres,** 205 N. Marina and Willis streets, tel. 445-1010, or **Plaza West Cinemas,** Fry's Shopping Center at 1509 W. Gurley St., tel. 778-0207.

You'll find two casinos on the east edge of town off Hwy. 69, a few hundred feet past the Hwy. 89 turnoff. Both offer slot machines, keno, bingo, and off-track betting. **Bucky's Casino** is at the Prescott Resort, 1500 Hwy. 69; tel. 776-1666 or (800) SLOTS-44. The Yavapai Casino and Gaming Center is behind Mario's Restaurant at 1505 Hwy. 69; tel. 445-1122 or (800) SLOTS-44.

The bars along Whiskey Row (Montezuma St.) sometimes have live bands. The **Pine Cone**

Inn offers more sedate live dinner music at 1245 White Spar Rd.; tel. 445-2970. **Softball** fans can catch a game in season—Prescott bills itself as the Softball Capital of the World. Local newspapers the *Prescott Sun* and the *Prescott Courier* list what's going on in town.

## EVENTS

Prescott's major annual events include the **Prescott Off Street Festival** in May. Prescott Downs thoroughbred and quarter horse race season also begins in May, held at the county fairgrounds most weekends and holidays from Memorial Day to Labor Day.

In June the **Sharlot Hall Folk Art Fair** celebrates pioneer skills with costumed participants demonstrating blacksmithing, horseshoeing, woodworking, spinning, weaving, churning, and cowboy cooking. **Territorial Prescott Days** in June features games, art shows, music, and dancing.

**Frontier Days Rodeo and Parade,** held during the July 4th holiday, draws spectators from all over Arizona and beyond for the "world's oldest rodeo," a Western art show, entertainment, dances, and fireworks. Downhome musicians pick and holler during July's **Bluegrass Festival.**

In August Prescott hosts the **Antique Auto Show** and the **Smoki Native American Festival,** the latter featuring Indian dancers, crafts, and demonstrations. **The Faire on the Square** is a juried arts and crafts show held on Labor Day weekend on the Courthouse Plaza.

Enjoy seasonal celebrations at the **Fallfest in the Park** and the **Folk Music Festival,** both held the first weekend of October. In December comes the **Courthouse Christmas Lighting** and **Christmas Parade.**

## SHOPPING AND SERVICES

The **Yavapai Community College Art Gallery**'s monthly shows represent college, community, and state artists; open Mon.- Sat. 10 a.m.-3 p.m.; it's on the left as you drive onto campus; tel. 776-2033. Antique shopping enthusiasts will find a bonanza of antique shops and antique malls in the two blocks of N. Cortez

St. north of Courthouse Plaza. **The Basecamp** maintains a good stock of topo maps and outdoor supplies, including hiking, backpacking, and cross-country ski gear, at 142 N. Cortez St.; tel. 445-8310. **Granite Mountain Outfitters** offers outdoor equipment and supplies at 320 W. Gurley St.; tel. 776-4949. **Popular Outfitters** offers outdoor supplies at 1841 E. Hwy. 69 in the Target Center; tel. 445-2430.

The main **post office** is at 442 Miller Valley Rd.; tel. 778-1890. The downtown **post office** sits on the corner of Goodwin and Cortez, across from the Courthouse Plaza; tel. 778-7411. **Yavapai Regional Medical Center** provides hospital services at 1003 Willow Creek Rd.; tel. 445-2700.

Go swimming at the **YMCA outdoor pool** in summer, 750 Whipple St.; tel. 445-7221. Or swim year-round at the indoor **Yavapai College pool**—turn north onto the campus from 1100 E. Sheldon Street. The swimming pool is in the main cluster of buildings at the end of the drive, on the left; tel. 776-2175. For a swimming pool with a small water slide only ten minutes' drive east of town, try Prescott Valley's **Mountain Valley Splash** at 8600 E. Nace; tel. 775-3165.

Play **tennis** at Yavapai College, at Prescott High School (on Ruth St.), or next to Ken Lindley Field (E. Gurley and Arizona streets). **Granite Mountain Stables** offers hourly and overnight rides year-round; it's north of town off Williamson Valley Rd.; tel. 771-9551. **Double D Ranch and Wagon Train** offers horseback riding, covered wagon excursions, black powder shooting, and more 25 miles north of Prescott in Paulden; tel. 636-0418. Play **golf** on 36-hole courses at **Antelope Hills Golf Course,** next to the airport, seven miles north of town on AZ 89; tel. 445-0583, or for reservations tel. 776-PUTT. Or try the 18 holes at **Prescott Country Club,** 14 miles east on AZ 69; tel. 772-8984.

## INFORMATION

The **Prescott Chamber of Commerce** can help you find what you're looking for. It's open Mon.-Sat. 9 a.m.-5 p.m. (and Sunday 10 a.m.-4 p.m.); tel. 445-2000 or (800) 266-7534. At other times call the chamber for a telephone recording of local sights and events. Chamber of commerce-sponsored walking tours are given Monday and Friday at 10 a.m. June 5th-Sept. 1. Call for information. The office is at 117 W. Goodwin St. opposite the plaza (Box 1147, Prescott, AZ 86302).

**U.S. Forest Service** offices stock maps and brochures on hiking, camping, and the back roads of Prescott National Forest. The **supervisor's office** has general information and books at 344 S. Cortez St.; it's open Mon.-Fri. 8 a.m.-4:30 p.m.; tel. 445-1762. You'll get the best firsthand information on the Prescott area from rangers at the **Bradshaw Mountain District** office at 2230 E. Hwy. 69 (Prescott, AZ 86301), one mile east of town; it's open Mon.-Sat. 8 a.m.-4:30 p.m.; tel. 445-7253.

Prescott's excellent **public library** includes a Southwest collection; it's open daily except Sunday at 215 E. Goodwin St.; tel. 445-8110. **Yavapai Community College** also has a fine library, open daily during school terms; turn north onto the campus from 1100 E. Sheldon St.; tel. 776-2265. The **Worm** bookstore stocks topo maps and books about Arizona; 128 S. Montezuma St.; tel. 445-0361. The selection of regional and general reading at the **Satisfied Mind** is bound to please; 113 W. Goodwin St.; tel. 776-9766. **Prescott Newsstand** has a fine selection of periodicals and regional books at 123 N. Cortez St.; tel. 778-0072. The **Book Nook,** at 324 W. Gurley St., buys and sells used books; tel. 778-2130.

## TOURS AND TRANSPORT

On **Prescott Historical Tours,** Melissa Ruffner dresses in a turn-of-the-century costume to lead visitors around the original Prescott town site; tel. 445-4567. **Bradshaw Mountain Backcountry Tours** takes you into the mountains, desert, and ghost towns near Prescott on two-hour, half-day, and full-day jeep trips. Sunset tours, hiking trips, and cowboy cookouts are offered as well; tel. 445-3032.

**Rural Connection** routes a daily bus to Camp Verde, where you can connect with Greyhound to Phoenix or Flagstaff; 820 E. Sheldon St.; tel. 445-5470. **Shuttle "U"** will take you to the Sky Harbor Airport in Phoenix at $29 one-

way. Call for times; tel. 772-6114 or (800) 304-6114. For a taxi, call **Ace** at 445-5510. You can rent cars at the airport and in town; consult the Yellow Pages.

## VICINITY OF PRESCOTT

### Granite Dells

With giant boulders that have weathered into delicately balanced forms and fanciful shapes, the scenic Dells are a good place for a picnic or hike. Rock climbers like to tackle the challenging granite formations. Unearthed ruins and artifacts indicate that Indians used to hide out here. From the 1920s to the '50s, Granite Dells Resort attracted crowds of vacationers; a large dance pavilion of that era still stands. Watson Lake Park (camping and free day use) lies at the south edge of the Dells, four miles north of town on AZ 89.

### Thumb Butte Trail

This popular loop hike begins just west of town and climbs Thumb Butte Saddle (elev. 6,300 feet) for good views of Prescott and the surrounding countryside. The trail winds through a valley of dense ponderosa pine, then crosses windswept ridges where piñon, juniper, oak, and prickly pear grow. Two short spur trails lead to vista points where you can see the city, Granite Dells, Chino Valley, and countless mountains, including the distant San Francisco Peaks.

Reaching the fractured granite summit of Thumb Butte takes some effort and skill; the last 200-foot ascent is best left to rock climbers. The trail itself is a moderately easy outing, 1.7 miles roundtrip with an elevation gain of 600 feet; allow 2.5 hours. Signs identify many of the plants along the way. Hiking season runs year-round, except after winter snowstorms.

From downtown, head west 3.5 miles on Gurley St./Thumb Butte Rd. to Thumb Butte Park; the trailhead is on the left side of the road. Picnic tables are nearby.

### Granite Mountain Wilderness

On a day-trip, hikers can explore the rugged Granite Mountain Wilderness and enjoy fine views from an overlook (elev. 7,125 feet). Rock climbers come to challenge the granite cliffs, which offer a nearly complete range of difficulties. Five trails allow many hiking combinations, but only **Granite Mountain Trail #261** climbs to the top. This trail ascends gently 1.3 miles to a trail junction at Blair Pass, then turns right and switchbacks another 1.3 miles to a saddle on Granite Mountain; from here the trail turns southeast, climbing another mile to a viewpoint. Ponderosa pines grow at the trailhead and on top of Granite Mountain, though much of the trail passes through manzanita, mountain mahogany, piñon, agave, and other plants of the chaparral.

Average hiking time for the 7.5-mile roundtrip hike is six hours. It's a moderately difficult trip with an elevation gain of 1,500 feet; carry water. It's open all year when not blocked by snow. The Iron Springs and Jerome Canyon 7.5-minute topo maps cover this area. From W. Gurley St. in Prescott, drive northwest 4.3 miles on Grove Ave./Miller Valley Rd./Iron Springs Rd., then turn right and travel five miles on Forest Route 374 past the campground and lake turnoffs.

### Other Hikes

Dozens of trails wind through the rugged Bradshaw and Mingus mountains near Prescott. See Forest Service staff for trail descriptions, maps, and back-road information; the Bradshaw District office is at 2230 E. Hwy. 69, one mile east of town; tel. 445-7253.

Probably the most unusual trail is the 1,200-foot **Groom Creek School Nature Trail,** built by the Sunrise Lions Club of Prescott especially for blind people. Trail pamphlets—obtain from the Bradshaw office—in both Braille and print explain natural features and processes. The trail lies just past the village of Groom Creek, six miles south of town on Senator Highway.

### Crown King and Vicinity

Old mines, ghost towns, and wilderness surround this rustic village 55 miles southeast of Prescott. Prospectors discovered gold at the Crown King Mine in the 1870s, but mine owners had to wait until the late 1880s before the ore could be processed profitably. A branch line of the Prescott and Eastern Railroad reached the site in 1904. Legal battles closed mine operations in the early 1900s, and today the mining camp attracts retired people and serves as an

escape from summer heat. The Crown King Saloon goes way back to 1898, when it was built at Oro Belle camp, five miles southwest. Pack mules later hauled the structure piece by piece to Crown King.

Rough roads discourage the average tourist, but the region can be explored with maps, determination, and a high-clearance vehicle. The easiest way in is from Cleator on Forest Route 259, reached from the I-17 Bumble Bee or Cordes exits. You'll follow the twisting path of the old railroad on the drive up; cautiously driven passenger vehicles can make it okay. Rougher roads approach Crown King from Prescott and Mayer. The Prescott National Forest map, $3 from Forest Service offices, shows back roads and most trails.

In Crown King, you can eat at the saloon or at a restaurant, or buy food from the general store. No motels or RV parks here, but you can camp in the Forest Service campgrounds at **Horsethief Basin Recreation Site,** seven miles to the southeast. The usual season for Kentuck Springs and Hazlett Hollow campgrounds (elev. 6,000 feet) is May 1-Nov. 30; neither charges a fee, but Hazlett Hollow has water.

**Turney Gulch Campground** is a group area with water; make the required reservations by calling (800) 280-CAMP. **Castle Creek Wilderness,** east of the campgrounds, offers very steep and rocky terrain; vegetation ranges from chaparral to ponderosa pine. The staff at Crown King Work Center, up the hill from town, can tell you about trails and roads; they're mostly local people who know the area well. *Arizona's Best Ghost Towns* by Phillip Varney contains good information on this historic and very scenic part of Arizona.

### Bloody Basin Road

Drivers with high-clearance vehicles can leave the crowds behind on this 60-mile scenic back road through the Tonto National Forest, connecting I-17 Bloody Basin/Crown King Exit 259 with Carefree and Cave Creek north of Phoenix. You'll enjoy views of the Mazatzals, rugged high-desert hill country, and wooded canyons. In Bloody Basin, 26 miles from I-17, a side road goes southeast 12 miles to the Verde River and Sheep Bridge, where hikers can head into the Mazatzal Wilderness. Primitive camping is possible almost anywhere in Tonto National Forest, or you can stop at Seven Springs, CCC, or Cave Creek campgrounds near the southern end of Bloody Basin Road.

# ARCOSANTI

The otherworldly creation of visionary Italian architect Paolo Soleri is constantly on view in the high-desert country between Flagstaff and Phoenix. Here Soleri and his *compañeros* seek to treat many of the world's ills through the theory and practice of benign building. Soleri has dubbed his joining of architecture and ecology "arcology." His city of Arcosanti, designed to make the best use of energy and land while providing a stress-free environment for its residents, is growing vertically, using pedestrian walkways and elevators instead of freeways. Arcosanti's strangely shaped buildings make efficient use of the sun's energy.

Construction began in 1970, and progresses slowly, as funds come in. Forty to 65 souls dwell here; Soleri himself lives in Scottsdale. When finished, this city will house 5,000 people. In his dreams, Soleri envisions vast megalopolises triple the size of the Empire State Building, housing millions of happy, contented, productive citizens.

The public is welcome to visit this project, the first of its kind, open daily 9 a.m.-5 p.m. all year. Tours, lasting about one hour, take visitors through some of the buildings; guides explain Soleri's methods and goals. Cost: $5 adults, under 12 free. The visitor center features a model of Arcosanti, architectural exhibits, and books by and about Soleri. His famous Cosanti bronze and clay windbells make attractive gifts and help finance the project. A cafe and bakery (open daily) serve good lunches. Arcosanti regularly schedules concerts, usually preceded by dinner and often followed by Pictograph 2000, a light and sound show projected onto the mesa opposite Arcosanti. Seminars and workshops allow interested people to participate in construction of the city.

For information on seminars, workshops, Elderhostel, silt workshops (the method used in constructing Arcosanti), and other events, write Arcosanti, HC 74, Box 4136, Mayer, AZ 86333, or call 632-7135. Hotel accommodations are $15-20 s, $20-25 d (reservations suggested); the cafe is open for breakfast and dinner for overnight guests. Arcosanti lies 34 miles southeast of Prescott and 65 miles north of Phoenix. It's easy to reach from I-17; take Cordes Junction Exit 262A, then follow signs 2.5 miles on a dirt road. You'll find a motel, cafes, RV park, and gas stations near the interchange.

# WESTERN ARIZONA

Few landlocked states can boast more than 1,000 miles of shoreline, but Arizona can. The Colorado River, after its wild run through the Grand Canyon, begins a new life in the western part of the state. Tamed by massive dams and irrigation projects, the Colorado here flows placidly toward the Gulf of California. The deep blue waters of the river and the lakes it makes form Arizona's western boundary, separating the state from California and Nevada. Boaters and anglers enjoy this watery paradise, breezing along on waterskis or seeking quiet backwaters for fishing.

But once you step away from the life-giving waters, you're in desert country, the real desert, where legends abound—of Indian tribes, hardy prospectors, determined pioneer families, even a U.S. Army camel corps.

## THE LAND

Numerous small ranges of rocky hills break up the monotonous desert plains of western Arizona; much of the region lies at elevations under 2,000 feet. The valley of the Colorado River, home to most of the human inhabitants of western Arizona, drops from about 1,220 feet at the west boundary of the Grand Canyon to just 70 feet at the Mexican border.

A few mountain ranges in the north rise high enough to support forests of manzanita, oak, piñon, and ponderosa pine, and even some fir and aspen. Highest and most notable of these "biological islands" are the Hualapai Mountains, easily reached by road from Kingman. Hualapai Peak (8,417 feet) crowns the range. Old mines and ghost towns dot the mineral-rich Cerbat and Black mountains, also in the north. The Kofa and Castle Dome mountains in the south make up the Kofa National Wildlife Refuge, home of desert bighorn sheep, mule deer, desert tortoise, Gambel's quail, and rare native palm trees.

Along the Colorado River, the three national wildlife refuges of Havasu, Cibola, and Imperial protect migratory and native birds, plants, and animals.

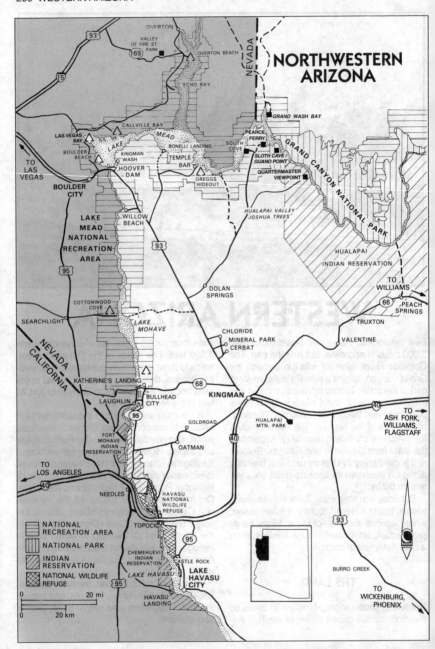

NORTHWESTERN ARIZONA

OVERTON
VALLEY OF FIRE ST. PARK
OVERTON BEACH
ECHO BAY
GRAND WASH BAY
CALLVILLE BAY
PEARCE FERRY
LAS VEGAS BAY
KINGMAN WASH
BONELLI LANDING
TEMPLE BAR
SOUTH COVE
SLOTH CAVE
GUANO POINT
QUARTERMASTER VIEWPOINT
BOULDER BEACH
HOOVER DAM
GREGGS HIDEOUT
BOULDER CITY
GRAND CANYON NATIONAL PARK
HUALAPAI VALLEY JOSHUA TREES
LAKE MEAD NATIONAL RECREATION AREA
WILLOW BEACH
HUALAPAI INDIAN RESERVATION
TO LAS VEGAS
TO WILLIAMS
DOLAN SPRINGS
COTTONWOOD COVE
LAKE MOHAVE
PEACH SPRINGS
SEARCHLIGHT
CHLORIDE
MINERAL PARK
CERBAT
TRUXTON
VALENTINE
NEVADA
CALIFORNIA
KATHERINE'S LANDING
KINGMAN
TO ASH FORK, WILLIAMS, FLAGSTAFF
LAUGHLIN
BULLHEAD CITY
GOLDROAD
HUALAPAI MTN. PARK
FORT MOHAVE INDIAN RESERVATION
OATMAN
TO LOS ANGELES
NEEDLES
HAVASU NATIONAL WILDLIFE REFUGE
TOPOCK
CHEMEHUEVI INDIAN RESERVATION
CASTLE ROCK
LAKE HAVASU
LAKE HAVASU CITY
HAVASU LANDING
BURRO CREEK
TO WICKENBURG, PHOENIX

NATIONAL RECREATION AREA
NATIONAL PARK
INDIAN RESERVATION
NATIONAL WILDLIFE REFUGE

0        20 mi
0        20 km

## Climate

The sun shines down from the azure skies nearly every day; perhaps no place in the United States receives more sunshine than western Arizona. In winter, thousands of snowbirds descend on the desert from northern climes to enjoy the sun and fresh air. Winter nights can be frosty, but daytime temperatures usually warm to the 60s or 70s F. Spring and autumn often offer perfect weather—wildflowers, too, in the early spring.

By May the snowbirds are gone, and Arizona towns along the Colorado River often make the news as the hottest spots in the country. Parker holds the Arizona record—127° F on one day in 1905. Yet despite average highs that exceed 100° F from June to September, many visitors do come in summer to play in the water, cooling off by boating, waterskiing, swimming, and tubing.

So western Arizona actually has two seasons: a winter that attracts many retirees and others who enjoy fishing, exploring ghost towns, prospecting, and hiking in the desert; and a summer of active water sports. Annual rainfall ranges from about 10 inches in the high country to less than three inches in the south near Yuma.

## Flora and Fauna

For most of the year, plant and animal life in the desert appears very sparse. Actually it's there—a great variety of plants, reptiles, amphibians, mammals, and birds—just awaiting the right conditions to emerge. With good winter or summer rains, dormant seeds spring to life, quickly bloom, and produce new seeds; seemingly dead sticks sprout leaves and flowers. Cactus and other succulents rapidly absorb precious rain for the long dry spells ahead.

Most animals, large and small, hide out during the day in caves, burrows, or bushes. The small pocket mice and kangaroo rats do not even require drinking water; they feed mainly on seeds and manufacture their own water. Larger animals include western spotted skunk, kit and gray fox, badger, ringtail cat, bobcat, mountain lion, mule deer, and desert bighorn sheep. Your best chance of seeing desert critters is in early morning and evening; binoculars are handy.

Birds flock to the wetlands along the Colorado River in great numbers, especially in spring and autumn. Canada geese and many species of ducks winter here. Nesters include the great blue heron, great egret, green heron, least bittern, white-winged dove, and Yuma clapper rail.

# HISTORY

## Native Americans

Indians lived along the shores of the lower Colorado River long before the first white people arrived. Frequent wars between the tribes, lasting into the mid-19th century, forced the Maricopa Indians to migrate up the Gila River to what is now south-central Arizona. The victorious Mohave, Quechan, and Cocopa tribes were joined in the early 1800s by a nomadic Paiute group, the Chemehuevi. They all lived simply in brush-and-mud shelters and farmed, hunted, and gathered wild plant foods from the desert. In 1865 the Colorado River Reservation was established.

A number of Hopi and Navajo from northeast Arizona also live on the reservation. Their voluntary resettlement, begun in 1945, was possible because the reservation was established to serve "Indians of said river and its tributaries" and because the Colorado River Tribal Council gave the go-ahead.

## Spanish Explorations

Spanish explorers made their first tentative forays up the Colorado River in 1540, but they didn't stay. A tireless Jesuit priest, Eusebio Francisco Kino, explored the lower Colorado in 1700-02, collecting information for the mapmakers of the day.

During the 1760s, fear of Russian expansion down the coast of California caused the Spanish to build coastal settlements there, opening a land route from Mexico. In 1780, Spanish troops and missionaries built two missions on the Colorado River, La Purísima Concepción (opposite today's Yuma) and nearby San Pedro y San Pablo de Bicuner. Abuses by these foreigners infuriated local Quechan Indians, who revolted the following year. Father Francisco Garcés and most of the male Spaniards were killed; women and children were taken captive. Spanish troops ransomed the captives, then made no more attempts to settle along the Colorado River.

## Americans Arrive

Rugged mountain men such as James Ohio Pattie, who later wrote an account of his travels (see "Booklist"), explored the Colorado River area in search of beaver and adventure during the early 1800s. The Army established Camp Yuma (later Fort Yuma) in 1851 at the river crossing of the Southern Overland Trail (Cooke's Road) to assist Americans headed west for the California goldfields. Ten years later, troops built Fort Mohave upstream on the Colorado River to protect travelers trekking along the Beale Wagon Road across northern Arizona.

Government surveyors explored much of the lower Colorado during the 1850s, but maps still labeled the northwest corner of the territory "unexplored." It wasn't until 1869 that John Wesley Powell filled the last big gap on his epic boat voyage down the Colorado from Green River, Wyoming, to Callville, Nevada (now under Lake Mead).

Although Spanish miners worked gold deposits in western Arizona before Mexican independence in 1821, large-scale mining in the region didn't begin until the 1860s. Gold discovered in 1858 at Gila City, 20 miles upstream from Yuma, attracted 1,200 miners by 1861. Three years later the gold played out, a traveler reporting that "the promising metropolis of Arizona consisted of three chimneys and a coyote." Prospectors later found many other gold and silver deposits up and down western Arizona, hastening development of the region. Lead-zinc and copper mines opened too. Most of the old workings lie abandoned now, marked by piles of tailings, foundations, and decaying walls.

Steamboats plied the Colorado River after 1852, providing faster and safer transport than wagon trains. For more than 50 years they served the forts and mining camps along the river. Some of the giant riverboats stood three decks high and were more than 140 feet long, yet drew only two feet of water. These giant sternwheelers took on cargo from ocean ships at Port Isabel on the Gulf of California, then headed upstream as much as 600 miles. Boat traffic declined when the Southern Pacific Railroad went through Yuma in 1877, and it virtually ended in 1909 with the construction of Laguna Dam.

*Mohave chief*

Land speculators in southern California had long eyed Colorado River water, and in 1901 they began diverting it to fields around the Salton Sink. Four years later, however, a flood destroyed controlling gates and the entire Colorado River roared down the canal, flooding the Imperial Valley. Frantic rock-filling by Southern Pacific finally returned the river to its normal seaward course in 1907, but it left a new body of water behind—the 35-mile-long Salton Sea. More canals and dams have since been built on the Colorado.

## INDIAN TRIBES

Six tribes now live along the lower Colorado between the west end of the Grand Canyon and the Gulf of California. The three Yuman-speaking tribes, Mohave, Quechan, and Cocopa, have occupied this land since prehistoric times. Later they were joined by Uto-Aztecan-speaking Chemehuevi, followed by some Hopi and Navajo of northeastern Arizona.

## Mohave

Northernmost of the Yuman tribes, the Mohave formerly lived in loosely organized bands, uniting only for warfare or defense. They farmed the bottomlands, hunted, and gathered wild foods. Crafts included finely made baskets, pottery, and beadwork. Ceremonial dances and long funeral wakes played important roles in Mohave social life. Even today, the Mohave and Quechan cremate their dead—a rare practice among American Indian tribes.

Mohave live on the Fort Mohave Reservation near Needles, California, and in a larger group on the Colorado River Reservation near Parker, Arizona. You can learn more about the tribe and view Mohave crafts at the tribal museum just south of Parker.

## Chemehuevi

This group of Paiute Indians once roamed the eastern Mohave Desert as hunting and gathering nomads. They settled in the Chemehuevi Valley of the Colorado River in the early 1800s, taking up the agricultural practices of their Mohave neighbors. The U.S. government granted the Chemehuevi a reservation in 1907, but Lake Havasu inundated much of their farmland in 1938. The tribe now lives on the Chemehuevi Reservation opposite Lake Havasu City and on the Colorado River Reservation.

## Quechan

Formerly known as the Yuma, the tribe now prefers the name Quechan. In the 19th century, Quechan territory included much of the lower Colorado and about 25 miles of the Gila River valley. Federal government action trimmed their land considerably during the late 19th and early 20th centuries. Today the tribe lives in California

on the Fort Yuma Indian Reservation opposite Yuma, Arizona. It has a museum in a historic building that was once part of Camp Yuma.

## Cocopa

Before the arrival of white people, the Cocopa lived downstream from the Quechan in the Colorado River delta, once one of the most fertile areas of the Southwest. Like other Colorado River tribes, though, it suffered greatly from European-introduced diseases. Today the Cocopa live on two tiny reservations south of Yuma and in the Mexican states of Sonora and Baja California.

# TRANSPORT

Regional airports in Yuma, Blythe (California), Lake Havasu City, and Bullhead City offer connections to Phoenix, southern California, and Las Vegas.

Greyhound buses and Amtrak trains serve Kingman on routes across northern Arizona, and Yuma on southern Arizona routes. K-T Services stops at Laughlin/Bullhead City, Needles (California), Lake Havasu City, and Parker on its route between Las Vegas and Phoenix. Greyhound connects Kingman and Laughlin/Bullhead City with Las Vegas and Phoenix on a more direct route, bypassing the Colorado River towns.

Boat cruises and raft trips show visitors some of the scenery in Lake Mead National Recreation Area; other boat tours float through the scenic Topock Gorge between Lake Havasu City and Laughlin, Nevada. Your own car (or boat) allows you to explore the quiet and scenic backcountry of western Arizona.

# THE NORTHWEST CORNER

## KINGMAN

Kingman sits in high desert country (elev. 3,325 feet) surrounded by the Cerbat, Hualapai, and Black mountain ranges. Lewis Kingman came through the area in 1880 while surveying a right-of-way for the Atlantic and Pacific Railroad between Albuquerque, New Mexico, and Needles, California. The railroad camp that later bore his name grew into a major mining, ranching, and transportation center for northwestern Arizona. A county election in 1866 required the county seat to move from Mineral Park to Kingman, but residents of Mineral Park balked at turning over county records. Kingmanites, according to one story, then sneaked over to Mineral Park in the dead of night to snatch the records and bring them to Kingman, where they've stayed ever since.

Kingman (area population 35,000) serves many motorists on their way across the country on I-40. The vicinity of Kingman contains the longest stretch of continuous Rt. 66, so locals proclaim Kingman the "Heart of Historic Rt. 66." Kingman boosters proclaim the town's nearly 2,000 rooms and 50 restaurants "fit for a king." Attractions include Hoover Dam and Lake Mead National Recreation Area, ghost towns and old town sites such as Oatman and Chloride, the cool forests of Hualapai Mountain Park, London Bridge in Lake Havasu City, and the glittering casinos of Laughlin and Las Vegas.

### Mohave Museum of History and Arts

This museum's varied collection is a good introduction to the history of northwestern Arizona. Dioramas, murals, and many artifacts show development from prehistoric times to the present. The Hualapai Indian Room contains a full-size wickiup brush shelter, pottery, baskets, cradle board, and other crafts. You can try your hand at grinding mesquite beans with the Indian mano and metate.

Other sights include paintings, sculpture, and crafts in the art gallery, photos showing construction of Hoover Dam, carved turquoise mined in the Kingman area, portraits of U.S. presidents with their first ladies, memorabilia of local-boy-turned-movie-star Andy Devine, and outdoor mining exhibits plus a 1923 railroad caboose. The museum even features a pipe organ, used in concerts here. History buffs can dig into the museum's library. A gift shop sells regional books and Indian crafts. The museum is open Mon.-Fri. 9 a.m.-5 p.m., Saturday and Sunday 1-5 p.m., closed major holidays; admission is $2 ages 13 and up, free for children 12 and under with adult; tel. 753-3195. You'll find it at 400 W. Beale St.; take I-40 Exit 48 and go east 0.3 mile on Beale Street.

### Wagon Tracks

Wagons creaking down the hill into Kingman from the 1870s to the early 1900s carved deep ruts in the soft volcanic bedrock. Another road bypassed this spot in 1912, leaving the old road in its original condition.

Evenly spaced holes beside the road have stirred up debate. Some people think that wagon masters jammed long poles in the holes for braking; others say the local board of supervisors planned to dynamite the road.

The site lies near a pretty canyon just a short drive from town. From the museum, take Grandview Ave. north 0.4 mile from Beale St., then turn right and drive 0.6 mile on Lead Street. Look for a wooden footbridge on the right; follow the path across to the old wagon road.

### Bonelli House

This historic house of native tufa stone reflects the lifestyle and taste of a prominent Kingman family early in this century. The Bonellis built their home in 1915 using both American and European designs. Thick walls insulate the interior from the temperature extremes of Kingman's desert climate. The Bonelli family lived here until 1973, when the city of Kingman bought the home for restoration as a bicentennial project. The house, 430 E. Spring and N. Fifth Streets, is open Thurs.-Mon. 1-4 p.m. except major holidays; donation requested; tel. 753-1413.

*wagon tracks, with mysterious holes*

## Accommodations and Campgrounds

Most of Kingman's motels and restaurants line E. Andy Devine Ave. (AZ 66/US 93) between I-40 Exits 44 and 53, or W. Beale St. (US 93) off I-40 Exit 48. Prices are pretty competitive, making it worth driving a bit to choose a suitable rate, quality, and location. Rooms often fill up on summer weekends, when reservations are recommended.

The **Kingman KOA** is open year-round with pool, showers, game room, store, and miniature golf; $17.47 tent or RV no hookups, $21.85 RV w/hookups, $27.32 kamping kabin; take I-40 Exit 53 (Andy Devine) and go northeast one mile on AZ 66, turn left on Airway and drive one mile, turn right on Roosevelt to the campground; tel. 757-4397. **Zuni Village RV Park** is open all year with pool, hot tub, store, laundromat, and showers; $5.48 tent, $16.26 RV w/hookups; tel. 692-6202. **Circle S Campground** has RV spaces year-round ($17.50 w/hookups) and a store at 2360 Airway; tel. 757-3235. Hualapai Mountain Park, 14 miles southeast of town, offers tent and RV sites in cool pine forests.

## Food

You'll find all the popular chain and fast-food places among the motels on Andy Devine. For local atmosphere, try **City Cafe,** 1929 E. Andy Devine, tel. 753-3550; **Mr. D'z Rt. 66 Diner,** 105 E. Andy Devine, tel. 718-0066; **Oldtown Coffeehouse,** 616 E. Beale St., tel. 753-2244; and **Dambar Steakhouse,** 1960 E. Andy Devine, tel. 753-3523.

For 24-hour restaurants, drop into **Kingman 76 Auto-Truck Plaza,** 946 W. Beale at I-40 Exit 48, tel. 753-7600; **Flying J Travel Plaza,** 3300 E. Andy Devine at I-40 Exit 53, tel. 757-7300; or **Denny's,** 3255 Andy Devine, tel. 757-2028.

Get pizza and Italian food at **Vito's Pizza,** 2775 Northern, tel. 757-7279; or **Pizza Hut,** 3395 E. Andy Devine, tel. 757-3292, or 2911 Stockton Hill Rd., tel. 753-7788.

For Mexican food try **La Poblanita** at 1921 Club Ave., off Stockton Hill Rd., tel. 753-5087; or **El Palacio,** at 401 E. Andy Devine, tel. 718-0018.

Dine Chinese at **House of Chan,** 960 W. Beale, tel. 753-3232, closed Sunday; **Hing's Restaurant,** 3370 Stockton Hill, tel. 757-3207;

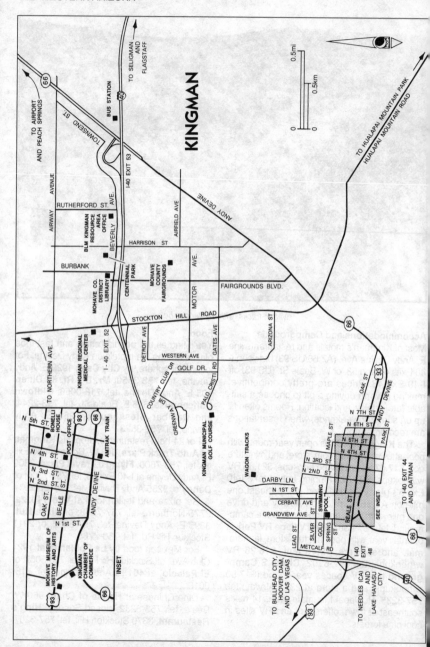

KINGMAN

**1.** a Navajo and his sheep (Arizona Office of Tourism); **2.** trekking through Paria Canyon (B. Weir);
**3.** Pine Country Rodeo, Flagstaff (B. Weir); **4.** rafting in the Grand Canyon (Arizona Office of
Tourism); **5.** the Narrows of Paria Canyon (B. Weir)

1. Keet Seel Ruin, Navajo National Monument; 2. prehistoric pottery fragments; 3. Box Canyon Ruin, Wupatki National Monument; 4. Wupatki Ruin, Wupatki National Monument; 5. Betatakin Ruin, Navajo National Monument (all photos by B. Weir)

*Kingman at the turn of the century*

and **Golden China Restaurant,** 4135 Stockton Hill, tel. 757-5265.

## Entertainment and Events

Catch movies at **The Movies,** 4055 Stockton Hill; tel. 757-7985. The Kingman Chamber of Commerce provides information on local happenings.

Classic and antique cars highlight the **Route 66 Fun Run Road Rally** in late April. Artists and craftspeople display their work at the **Festival of the Arts** on Mothers' Day weekend in May.

Take in the exhibits and entertainment of the **Mohave County Fair** in September. Kingmanites and visitors celebrate **Andy Devine Days** with a parade, the PRCA rodeo, and other festivities in late September or early October. See handmade crafts in the **American Cancer Society Arts and Crafts Fair,** second weekend in November.

## Services

The main **post office** is at 1901 Johnson, tel. 753-2480, though the downtown branch on N. Fourth St. can be more convenient. **Kingman Regional Medical Center** is at 3269 Stockton Hill Rd. just north from I-40 Exit 52; tel. 757-2101.

You'll find **swimming pools** downtown at the corner of Grandview Ave. and Gold St., tel. 753-8155, and in Centennial Park at 3333 N. Harrison, tel. 757-7910. **Centennial Park** also features tennis and racquetball courts, ball fields, and picnicking. The **Cerbat Hills Golf Course** offers 18 holes at 1001 E. Gates, west off Stockton Hill Rd.; tel. 753-6593. **Valle Vista** offers an 18-hole course at 9686 Concho Dr., 14 miles northeast on AZ 66; tel. 757-8744.

## Information

The **Kingman Chamber of Commerce** can help you explore this corner of Arizona. It's open Mon.-Fri. 8 a.m.-5 p.m., Saturday and Sunday 10 a.m.-4 p.m., downtown at 333 W. Andy Devine (Box 1150, Kingman, AZ 86402); tel. 753-6106. Find out about recreation areas and the backcountry near Kingman at the **BLM Kingman Resource Area** office; it's open Mon.-Fri. 7:30 a.m.-4:30 p.m. at 2475 Beverly Ave. (Kingman, AZ 86401); tel. 757-3161. You'll find the **public library** at 3269 Burbank St. near I-40 Exit 52; tel. 692-2665. Regional books are available at **Hastings Books,** 3153 Stockton Hill Rd.; tel. 753-1010.

## Transport

Buses run by **Greyhound** and **K-T Services** stop at the tiny station behind McDonald's at 3264 Andy Devine, near I-40 Exit 53; open daily; tel. 757-8400. **Amtrak** has daily passenger train service west to Los Angeles and east to Flagstaff, Albuquerque, and beyond; tel. (800) 872-7245 for info and reservations. The terminal is downtown at the corner of Fourth St. and Andy Devine. See the Yellow Pages for car rental agencies. For a taxi call **Kingman Cab;** tel. 753-3624.

# VICINITY OF KINGMAN

## Hualapai Mountain Park

The Hualapai Indians, whose name means Pine Tree Folk, lived in these mountains until the military relocated the tribe northward in the 1870s. Now a county park, the mountains are easily reached on a 14-mile paved road that runs southeast from Kingman.

The park offers dense forests, scenic views, hiking trails, picnicking, camping, and rustic cabins. Elevations range from 5,000 to 8,417 feet, attracting animals and birds rarely seen elsewhere in northwestern Arizona. The forested slopes support groves of manzanita, scrub and Gambel oak, piñon and ponderosa pine, white fir, and aspen. Such animals as mule deer, elk, mountain lion, fox, and raccoon roam the forests. The park office maintains checklists of plants, animals, and birds found here. Hiking trails wind through the mountains, visiting overlooks and winding up Aspen and Hayden peaks.

Campsites feature drinking water (except in winter) but no showers, $6. A small RV area offers hookups for $12. Cabins, built for a Civilian Conservation Corps camp in the 1930s, offer kitchens and bathrooms; $25-55. You can visit the park any time of year, though winter snows sometimes require chains or 4WD. For information and reservations at the cabins, visit or call the Mohave County Parks Department; open Mon.-Fri. 8 a.m.-5 p.m. at 3675 E. Andy Devine (Box 7000, Kingman, AZ 86402); tel. 757-0915. The Hualapai Ranger Station is near the park entrance; tel. 757-3859.

The nearby **Hualapai Mountain Lodge** offers a motel, RV park, restaurant, and store. Some of the well-preserved buildings here once belonged to the Civilian Conservation Corps camp. The motel ($52.70 d) and restaurant are open Tues.-Sun. year-round; the restaurant serves breakfast (Saturday and Sunday), lunch, and dinner; tel. 757-3545. Self-contained RVs can park overnight; no hookups. From Kingman, drive to the county park, then continue on the paved road three quarters of a mile past the ranger station.

*played out—the Golden Gem Mill in Cerbat*

The Bureau of Land Management's **Wild Cow Springs Campground** ($4, no water) sits in a ponderosa pine and oak forest at an elevation of 6,200 feet. From Hualapai Mountain Park, continue south five miles on unpaved BLM Rd. 2123.

### Burro Creek Campground

A perennial stream flows through this scenic canyon area (elev. 2,200 feet). Visitors enjoy picnicking, birdwatching, swimming, hiking, jeeping, and rockhounding for agates. The BLM campground has drinking water but no showers; $6 per night. Head southeast 70 miles from Kingman on US 93, or northwest 60 miles from Wickenburg.

### Cerbat

Gold and silver deposits in the Cerbat Mountains, north of present-day Kingman, attracted miners in the late 1860s. They founded the town of Cerbat and worked such mines as the Esmeralda, Golden Gem, and Vanderbilt. Cerbat became the Mohave County seat in 1871 but lost the honor two years later to nearby Mineral Park. By 1912 the Cerbat post office had closed. The Golden Gem mill and headframe still stand, structures that rarely survive in other ghost towns. You'll also see stone foundations and several buildings.

The turnoff for Cerbat lies nine miles northwest of Kingman on US 93, near Milepost 62; head east 0.8 mile on a good dirt road, turn left and drive a half mile, then turn right and travel another two miles to the site. Keep left when passing a group of modern buildings just outside old Cerbat.

### Mineral Park

During most of the 1870s and 1880s, Mineral Park reigned as the county seat and most important town in the area, losing those distinctions in 1887 to Kingman. By 1912 Mineral Park had even lost its post office. Very little remains today but the modern Duval copper mine, which shut down in 1981. The turnoff for Mineral Park lies 14 miles northwest of Kingman on US 93, between Mileposts 58 and 59. Turn east and drive five miles on a paved road to the site.

### Chloride

After discovering silver chloride ore here in the early 1860s, prospectors founded this town—the oldest mining camp in northwestern Arizona. Hualapai Indians made life precarious during Chloride's first years until Army troops subdued the tribe. Several buildings survive from the town's lengthy mining period, which lasted into the 1940s. A few hundred people, including many retirees, now live here.

An old miner's shack and other buildings occupy the historical grounds. The Silver Bells, a group of women dedicated to preserving Chloride history, run a playhouse and make and sell antique-style clothing at Shep's Store.

Artist Roy Purcell painted giant, brightly colored murals in 1966 and 1975 on cliffs two miles southeast of town. He titled his work "The Journey—Images from an Inward Search for Self." There are also Indian petroglyphs in the area. From Chloride, take Tennessee Ave. (the main road into town) past the post office and

*Chloride art*

Tennessee Mine, then follow signs; the road may be too rough for low-slung cars.

**Sheps Store** offers apartment rentals (month or longer), RV park, Mining Camp (closed Monday), dance hall (country-western music Saturday evenings), artist gallery (including a saddlemaker, leatherworker, etc.), antique store, and secondhand store. Country and western musicians play on the boardwalk in front of Shep's Store summer evenings. The store is on Second St., 1.5 blocks south of the post office; tel. 565-3643. The **Tennessee Saloon and Cafe** and other food and drink establishments occupy Tennessee and Second Streets. **"Mellerdramas"** and a **swap meet** take place year-round on the first and third Saturday of each month. Townspeople dress up in old-fashioned clothing on **Old Miners' Day,** the first Saturday in May, for a parade, barbecue, games, burro and mule packing contest, and shootouts. A town potluck barbecue and fireworks show are held to celebrate **July 4th.**

Chloride lies 20 miles northwest of Kingman on US 93, then east three miles on a paved road at Grasshopper Junction. The BLM runs two campgrounds in the vicinity. From the Chloride turnoff, drive two miles farther north to the Chloride/Big Wash turnoff and go east nine miles for **Packsaddle Recreation Site** or two additional miles for **Windy Point Recreation Site;** both sites have picnic tables and vault toilets but no water or fee.

### Oatman

The weathered old gold-mining town of Oatman sits on the western foothills of the Black Mountains, 28 miles southwest of Kingman. Elephant's Tooth, the gleaming white quartz pinnacle east of town, beckoned prospectors, who knew that gold and silver often run with quartz. Gold mining began in 1904, attracting hordes of miners and businesspeople. These folks named the community for the Oatman family, victims of an 1851 Apache attack.

Oatman prospered, attracting many new businesses, seven hotels, 20 saloons, and even a stock exchange. Area mines produced nearly two million ounces of gold before panning out in the 1930s. The town, which once boasted more than 12,000 citizens, began to fade away, and might have disappeared altogether had it not become a travelers' stop on Rt. 66. Oatman lost its highway traffic in 1952, when engineers rerouted the road to the south. A few hundred citizens hang on today, relying largely on the growing tourist business.

Many old buildings survive, some now used as gift shops and cafes. The **Oatman Hotel,** a two-story adobe structure built in 1902, features upstairs exhibits on life in the boom days. In March 1939, newly wedded Clark Gable and Carole Lombard spent part of their honeymoon in the hotel. Oatman was one of Gable's favorite areas, a place where he could get away from the hectic pace of Hollywood and enjoy poker with the miners. The hotel is planning a renovation so it can again rent rooms; $35 s or d, standard rooms; $45 s or d honeymoon suite. Small rock shops and gift shops, cafes, the public library, and the post office lie along Main Street. An antique book shop is planned about a mile southwest of town. Pick up a self-guiding tour sheet at one of the local shops to learn more about Oatman history. The town plans to build a visitor information facility. You're almost sure to meet the town's wild burros, which wander the streets looking for handouts. Buy feed from one of the shops.

Oatman celebrates **Gold Camp Days** on Labor Day weekend with shootouts, a costume parade, and dancing. **Shootouts,** usually just for fun, also take place every Saturday, Sunday, and holiday on Main Street.

The **Oatman Mining Company, Mission Inn Coffee Shop,** and **Cactus Joe's** serve food and usually feature live bands on weekend afternoons. RVs can park at **Blackstone RV Park** about 12 miles west of town; tel. 768-3303.

# BULLHEAD CITY

This growing community (population more than 26,000) lines AZ 95 and the Colorado River for about 10 miles. Gamblers, anglers, and boaters enjoy this desert oasis. The empty and remote site lay deserted until the 1940s, when construction workers arrived to build Davis Dam upstream. With completion of the dam in 1953, everyone thought the construction camp called Bullhead City would disappear. Instead it became a center for outdoor recreation.

In addition to the Colorado River at the town's doorstep, 240 square miles of deep blue water beckon six miles north in Lake Mohave. The "bullhead" rock formation that gave the place its name did disappear, under the waters of the lake.

Bullhead City lies 35 miles west of Kingman via AZ 68, and 25 miles north of Needles, California, on AZ 95. The bright lights of gambling casinos in sister city Laughlin glitter from across the river in Nevada.

## Colorado River Historical Society Museum

See artifacts commemorating the local Indians, steamboating on the Colorado River, mining activities, ranching, and dam construction. Photographs and maps show the growth of the Bullhead City/Laughlin area from early beginnings to modern times. It's open Tues.-Sat. 9:30 a.m.-2:30 p.m. Sept.-May with free admission just north of the Laughlin Bridge turnoff; tel. 754-3399.

## Accommodations and Campgrounds

You have a choice of about 25 motels and 14 RV parks in Bullhead City, or you can stay across the river at the casinos in Laughlin. Try to make reservations for motels, casinos, and RV parks, especially if you're arriving on a weekend. You can save money at many places by visiting Sunday through Thursday. Casino rates are very competitive, and it is not unusual to see Sun.-Thurs. rates under $15; weekend rates are higher.

Campgrounds and RV parks stay open year-round. Most RV parks prefer that guests stay a week or longer. **Davis Camp Park,** maintained by Mohave County, offers beach sites for tents and RVs ($8 no hookups, $11-15 w/hookups), a picnic area and boat ramps ($3 day use), and showers (available to noncampers for $3). The park is just off AZ 95 north of town; tel. 754-4606.

Many RVers just park for the night in the vast casino parking lots in Laughlin. You'll also find a motel, RV park, and campground six miles north of Bullhead City at **Katherine Landing.**

## Food

For dining in Bullhead City, try **D'Angelo's** for homemade Italian dinners, pizza, calzone, and hot and cold sandwiches; it's open daily at 2141 Clearwater; tel. 758-0085. Enjoy Chinese cuisine at **China Szechuan,** 1890 Hwy. 95, tel. 763-2610; or **China Panda,** 2164 Hwy. 95, tel. 763-8899. Mexican cuisine is available at **Casa Serrano,** 5230 Hwy. 95, tel. 768-1881; **Casa Garcia,** 967 Hancock Rd., tel. 758-8777; **El Encanto,** 125 Long Ave., tel. 754-5100; or **El Palacio,** 1864 Hwy. 95, tel. 763-2494. Some of your best eating deals are on the Nevada side; most casinos feature restaurants and buffets that entice you with breakfasts under $3, lunches under $4, dinners under $5, and seafood feasts under $10.

## Events

Lake Mohave Resort sponsors a **U.S. Bass Fishing Team Tournament** in April. Also in April is the **Chili Cookoff.** In May, Nevadans celebrate **Laughlin River Days** with a parade, games, and food. Also in May, you can enjoy food and games—but no burro—at the **Burro Barbecue** in Bullhead Community Park. **Fireworks** light the skies on July 4th. Boats at Lake Mohave Resort (Katherine Landing) stage a **Parade of Lights** in December.

## Services and Recreation

**Bullhead Community Park,** just north of the chamber of commerce, is a pleasant spot for a picnic. The **post office** is downtown at 990 Hwy. 95; tel. 754-3717. It also has a branch at 1882 Lakeside Dr.; tel. 758-5711. **Bullhead Community Hospital** is at 2735 Silver Creek Rd.; tel. 763-2273.

One of the best fishing areas along the Colorado River is right in front of Bullhead City. The cold and swift waters from Davis Dam harbor large rainbow trout, channel catfish, and, during late spring and early summer, giant striped bass weighing 20 pounds and more.

Golfers can play on the nine-hole **Chaparral Country Club** course, 1260 E. Mohave Dr., five miles south of town, tel. 758-6330; the nine-hole **Riverview RV Resort Golf Course,** 2000 E. Ramar, three miles south on AZ 95, then 1.5 miles east on Ramar, tel. 763-1818; or the 18-hole **Desert Lakes Golf Course,** 10 miles south on AZ 95, then east on Joy Ln., tel. 768-1000.

## Information

The **Bullhead Area Chamber of Commerce** staff will tell you about area sights and services;

it's open all year Mon.-Fri. 9 a.m.-5 p.m. and Saturday 10 a.m.-2 p.m. When the office is closed, you can pick up literature from the rack outside. The office is on the south side of Bullhead Community Park at 1251 Hwy. 95, Bullhead City, AZ 86429; tel. (520) 754-4121.

The **Laughlin Chamber of Commerce** will answer questions about casinos and events on the Nevada side; it's open Mon.-Fri. 8 a.m.-4:30 p.m. across from the Flamingo Hilton at 1725 Casino Dr.; Box 2280, Laughlin, NV 89029; tel. (702) 298-2214 or (800) 227-5245. The **Visitors Bureau** can also help with local or statewide information at 1555 Casino Dr., at the corner of Casino Dr. and Laughlin Civic Dr., Box 502, Laughlin, NV 89029; tel. (702) 298-3321. There's a **public library** in the south part of Bullhead City at 1170 E. Hancock Rd.; tel. (520) 758-0714. Books of regional interest are available at **Hastings Books,** 1985 Hwy. 95; tel. (520) 763-0025.

## Transport

**Greyhound** and **K-T Services** run more than a dozen buses daily; the station is at the southeastern corner of Riverside Casino at the north edge of the lineup of casinos in Laughlin; tel. (702) 763-7070. **USAir Express** flies to Phoenix and southern California; tel. (800) 428-4322. **Air Grand Canyon** offers three tours to the Grand Canyon: Western Canyon Highlights (two hours, $119.95 per person); The Eagle's Eye View (2.5-3 hours, $189.95 per person); and The Ultimate Eagle (3.5 hours, $229.95 per person). You can have special ground tours added to Grand Canyon flight tours at $19.95 (one hour), $39.95 (two hours), $54.95 (three hours), and $65.95 (four hours). Trips are scheduled year-round with a two-person minimum; tel.

(520) 754-2240 or (800) 860-6007. The airport is just north of Bullhead City at 600 Hwy. 95. See the Yellow Pages for auto rental agencies.

## Laughlin, Nevada

The casinos on the Nevada side of the river will happily accept your money. Low-cost bus tours from Arizona and southern California cities bring people by the thousands. Laughlin's casinos have a more casual—some say more friendly—atmosphere than the bigger gambling centers of Las Vegas and Reno. Besides the games of chance, you can check out the movies, live shows, hotel rooms, swimming pools, and dining bargains offered by many casinos.

Visit either the Bullhead City or Laughlin chambers of commerce for information guides and pamphlets listing casino attractions and services.

**Laughlin River Tours** runs hour-and-a-quarter river cruises on the Colorado from the Edgewater Casino and Harrah's del Rio Casino docks; fares are $10 adult, $6 child, tel. (702) 298-1047 or (800) 228-9825 out of state. **Blue River Safari** offers a variety of cruise and bus tours. Trips include a narrated bus tour to the ghost town of Oatman; $15. Trips depart from the Colorado Belle Hotel and Casino; tel. (702) 298-0910 or (800) 345-8990. The **USS *Riverside*** departs from Riverside Casino for a visit to Davis Dam; fares are $10 adult, $6 children; tel. (702) 298-2535, ext. 5770, or (800) 227-3849, ext. 5770.

From Bullhead City you can drive across the Colorado River bridge just north of town or take the eight-mile route via Davis Dam farther north. Some casinos offer passenger ferries that leave from the shore north of downtown Bullhead City. Shuttle buses connect the casinos.

# LAKE MEAD NATIONAL RECREATION AREA

The Colorado River forms two long lakes as it winds more than 144 miles through Lake Mead National Recreation Area. From Grand Canyon National Park, the blue waters flow around the extreme northwest corner of Arizona past black volcanic rocks, stark hillsides, and white, sandy beaches. Striking desert scenery and inviting waters make the area a paradise for boaters, anglers, waterskiers, swimmers, and scuba divers. Visitors often sight bighorn sheep on the canyon cliffs and wild burros in the more level areas. Adventurous hikers can explore the hills and canyons of this wild, solitary country; the land rarely hosts human visitors.

To get the most from a visit to Lake Mohave and Lake Mead, you really need a boat; roads approach the waterline only at a few scattered points. If you don't own your own, marinas offer rentals, from humble fishing craft to luxurious houseboats. Boat tours take in some of the scenery of Lake Mead from Boulder Beach. You can also glide through Black Canyon below Hoover Dam on raft tours. The National Park Service provides free boat ramps, campgrounds ($8-9 per night, no showers or hookups), and ranger stations at most developed areas. Park Service people also staff the Alan Bible Visitor Center at the turnoff for Boulder Beach, four miles west of Hoover Dam.

Though the boating and camping season lasts all year at the lakes, spring and autumn are the ideal times to visit. Most people come in summer, and though it's hot, swimmers and waterskiers best appreciate the water then. In winter, you wouldn't want to hop in without a wetsuit, though topside temperatures are usually pleasant during the day.

## Fishing

Both Lake Mohave and Lake Mead offer excellent fishing year-round. In either lake you'll find trout, largemouth and striped bass, channel catfish, crappie, and bluegill. Lake Mohave's upper reaches are especially good for rainbow trout, while Lake Mead offers hot fishing for striped bass; some specimens top 50 pounds. Most marinas sell licenses and tackle. Marinas and ranger stations can advise you on the fishing

Hoover Dam under construction

regulations and the best spots to fish. Shore anglers need a license only from the state they're in. If you fish from a boat, you'll need a license from one state and a special-use stamp from the other.

## LAKE MOHAVE

Heading upstream from Bullhead City, you first arrive at Lake Mohave. Squeezed between hills and canyon walls, the lake seems like a calmer version of the Colorado River. Though 67 miles long, Mohave spans but four miles at its widest point. **Davis Dam,** which holds back the lake, is open daily 7:30 a.m.-3:30 p.m. for free self-guided tours; tel. 754-3628.

**Katherine Landing,** known as Katy's Gulch to some folks, lies six miles north of Bullhead City. An **information center** near the entrance is open daily 8 a.m.-4 p.m. all year. Katherine Landing offers a public swimming beach, boat ramp, campground ($8), marina with boat rentals (fishing, ski, patio, and houseboat), RV park ($19), motel ($63.30-87.57 d, rates lower in winter), restaurant, and store. Showers and laundry are available too. For motel, RV park, and boat reservations, contact **Lake Mohave Resort,** Bullhead City, AZ 86430; tel. 754-3245 or (800) 752-9669.

**Cottonwood Cove** is about halfway upstream on the main body of water on the Nevada side. If driving, turn off US 95 at Searchlight and go east 14 miles on NV 164. Cottonwood Cove has a motel ($95.40-100.70 d, less in winter), RV park ($18.02), campground ($8), restaurant, marina with rentals (including houseboats) and a launch ramp, and a public swimming beach; contact **Cottonwood Cove Marina,** Box 1000, Cottonwood Cove, NV 89046; tel. (702) 297-1464, (800) 255-5561 for houseboats.

Northward, the lake narrows at **Eldorado Canyon,** becoming a river again. Trout and trout anglers occupy the cold river currents upstream. A road (NV 165) approaches Eldorado Canyon from the Nevada side; no campground or resort.

About a dozen river miles before Hoover Dam you'll reach **Willow Beach** on the Arizona shore —only a four-mile paved detour from US 93. Officials determined that the old resort here was built on a floodplain and closed it. The resort cafe is still open and can offer limited services such as food, fishing boat rentals, and fuel until the new resort is built on safer ground; tel. (520) 767-4747. The "Wall of Fame" in the resort cafe and store features photos of anglers and their trophy trout catches. After a concessionaire has been selected, the new resort will be built over five years, so it would be wise to call ahead to see what is open. A ranger station can also give information about the current resort status; tel. (520) 767-4000.

**Willow Beach National Fish Hatchery,** a half mile upstream by road, raises large numbers of rainbow trout for stocking the Colorado and Lake Mohave. Hatchery staff also study and propagate the endangered native species Colorado River squawfish and bonytail chub. You're welcome to visit inside displays and the raceways outside during daylight hours; it's open daily 8 a.m.-4 p.m. all year; tel. (520) 767-3456.

A popular **float trip** for canoes, kayaks, and rafts begins below Hoover Dam, following the swift Colorado beneath the sheer 1,500-foot cliffs of Black Canyon to Willow Beach (11 miles) or Eldorado Canyon (25 miles). Hot springs at the base of the cliffs make an enjoyable stop.

Boats can also continue across Lake Mohave to Cottonwood Cove (50 miles) or Katherine Landing (72 miles); this section below Eldorado Canyon isn't recommended for nonmotorized boats from April through October because of the prevailing southerly winds. Obtain permission to launch your boat below Hoover Dam at least three weeks in advance from the Bureau of Reclamation, Attn.: LCD-130, Box 60400, Boulder City, NV 89006-0400; tel. (702) 293-8204. Call Mon.-Fri. 8 a.m.-4 p.m. Nevada time. The launch charge is $5 for a single craft, with substantial savings on multiple craft launches. You must follow regulations carefully; write for equipment requirements, trip description, maps, and a list of boat rental companies. **Black Canyon Raft Tours** runs this trip daily February 1 to November 30 for $65 adults and $35 children under 12; it includes three hours on the river, lunch, and transport from the tour office at 1297 Nevada Hwy. (Hwy. 93) in Boulder City; tel. (702) 293-3776 or (800) 696-RAFT (7238).

### Arizona Hot Springs Hike

This six-mile-roundtrip hike follows a canyon through layers of volcanic rock to hot springs near the Colorado River, downstream from Hoover Dam. The highly mineralized spring water surfaces in a side canyon at temperatures ranging from 113° to 142° F.

Allow five hours for the hike down and back, plus more time to soak in the hot springs. You'll descend 800 feet to the river. Rangers warn that bathers can contract a dangerous amoebic infection here; avoid it by keeping your head out of the water. Hiking isn't recommended in summer, when temperatures can reach hazardous heights. As for any desert hike of this length, bring water (one gallon per person) and wear a sun hat; also be alert for rattlesnakes and flash floods. Don't hike if thunderstorms threaten. Check trail conditions with a ranger before departing—the route may be difficult to follow in spots.

From Hoover Dam, drive 4.2 miles southeast on US 93 to a dirt parking area on the right, at the head of White Rock Canyon. Follow the canyon on foot down to the Colorado River, then walk a quarter mile downstream along the river to the side canyon with the hot springs. Climb a 20-foot ladder to reach the best springs.

## HOOVER DAM

When completed in 1935, this immense concrete structure was one of the world's greatest engineering feats. It remains almost as impressive today, especially when you contemplate the mind-numbing statistics: the dam contains 3,250,000 cubic yards of concrete, rises 726 feet above the bedrock, and produces more than four billion kilowatt-hours of energy per year.

With all these numbers coming at you, it's easy to miss the beauty of the dam. Look for the graceful curves, the sculptures of the Winged Figures of the Republic, the art deco embellishments, and terrazzo floor designs.

The new visitor center offers a parking area that can accommodate cars and motor homes. Guided tours (wheelchair accessible) last 35 minutes and leave frequently every day 8:30 a.m.-5:40 p.m. except Thanksgiving and Christmas; cost is $5 adults, $2.50 seniors 62 and up and children 10-16, free for ages nine and under; tel. (702) 294-3523. Three theaters show 12-minute presentations covering the importance of water to life, events leading to the construction of the dam, and construction and operation of the dam. An exhibit gallery houses static and interactive displays about the dam and the area. Across the road is an exhibit room with a relief map of the Colorado River, a model of a generating unit, and memorabilia from construction of the dam. Nearby, a cafeteria offers dining and gift shopping.

## LAKE MEAD

Lake Mead, held back by Hoover Dam, is the largest artificial lake in the United States. The reservoir holds the equivalent of two years' flow of the Colorado River. Its shape is a rough "Y"; one arm of Lake Mead reaches north up the Virgin River, while the longer, east arm stretch-

*Winged Figure of the Republic, Hoover Dam*

es up the Colorado River into the Grand Canyon. Boaters enjoy lots of room on the 110-mile-long lake. Countless little beaches and coves provide hideaways for camping and swimming. Largemouth black bass, striped bass, trout, channel catfish, bluegill, and crappie swim in the waters.

## Alan Bible Visitor Center
Park Service exhibits introduce Lake Mead Area fishing, boating, wildlife, and desert recreation. A 15-minute movie, *Some People Just Call It the Lake,* is screened every half-hour. A botanical garden displays and identifies local flora. Books on lake history, geology, plants, and wildlife are for sale. Nautical and topo maps are sold as well. Rangers provide handouts and information on backcountry camping, roads, and trails. Drop in for evening programs on weekends from April to October. The visitor center is open daily 8:30 a.m.-4:30 p.m. (to 5 p.m. in summer); 601 Nevada Hwy., Boulder City, NV 89005-2426; tel. (702) 293-8990. It's on US 93 at the NV 166 turnoff for Boulder Beach, four miles west of Hoover Dam.

## Boulder Basin
Above Hoover Dam, the lake opens into the broad Boulder Basin. You'll find campgrounds and marinas at Boulder Beach, Las Vegas Bay, and Callville Bay. The first facilities you'll reach are a boat ramp and campground ($9) at Hemenway Harbor just a mile from the Alan Bible Visitor Center. **Boulder Beach,** two miles by car from Alan Bible Visitor Center, offers good swimming with picnic sites. The campground lies on the south side of the beach. RVers can stay just south of Boulder Beach in **Lakeshore Trailer Village** ($14.84 w/hookups and showers, no tents), 268 Lakeshore Rd., Boulder City, NV 89005; tel. (702) 293-2540.

**Lake Mead Lodge** on the north side of Boulder Beach features lake views ($53 s, $68.90 d, may drop mid-winter) and a restaurant at 322 Lakeshore Rd., Boulder City, NV 89005; tel. (702) 293-2074 or (800) 752-9669. **Lake Mead Resort Marina,** one mile farther north, has boat rentals and a store; tel. (702) 293-2074 or (800) 752-9669. The *Desert Princess*, a triple-decked sternwheeler, leaves from a new dock half a mile down the road four to six times a day for a

scenic 90-minute trip on the lake to Hoover Dam; $14.50 tour only, $21 breakfast cruise, $29 dinner cruise, and $43 dinner/dance cruise; children 3-12 travel at reduced rates; tel. (702) 293-6180.

You're welcome to drop in at the **Lake Mead Fish Hatchery** to see the trout and exhibits; open daily 8 a.m.-4 p.m. The Nevada Department of Wildlife raises trout and sends most of them to Lake Mohave; others go to Lake Mead and scattered locations around southern Nevada. The hatchery is just off Lakeshore Scenic Dr. between Boulder Beach and Las Vegas Bay.

**Las Vegas Bay** has a primitive campground ($9), restaurant, store, and marina (fishing, ski, and patio boat rentals), Box 91150, Henderson, NV 89009; tel. (702) 565-9111. **Callville Bay Resort & Marina** offers an RV park ($18.02 w/hookups and showers), coffee shop, and boat rentals (including houseboats); write HCR 30, Box 100, Las Vegas, NV 89124; tel. (702) 565-8958 or (800) 255-5561 for houseboat reservations. **Kingman Wash,** on the Arizona shore near Hoover Dam, offers only primitive camping.

## Virgin Basin
Upstream from Boulder Basin you pass through a six-mile-long section called the Narrows before emerging into Virgin Basin, the largest and most dramatic part of Lake Mead. Rock formations with names such as Napoleon's Tomb, the Haystacks, and the Temple are scenic landmarks. Many narrow coves snake far back into the mountains.

Two resorts lie along the giant Overton Arm, which branches north into the Virgin River. **Echo Bay Resort** features a motel ($73.14-89.04 d all year), RV park ($19.08 w/hookups and showers), restaurant, and boat rentals (including houseboats); Overton, NV 89040, tel. (702) 394-4000 or (800) 752-9669.

**Overton Beach Resort,** farther north, offers an RV park ($16 w/hookups, showers extra, open to the public), snack bar, store, and marina with patioboat rentals; Overton, NV 89040, tel. (702) 394-4040. The Echo Bay area features a Park Service campground ($9) as well.

**Valley of Fire State Park,** about five miles west of Overton Beach, is noted for its impressive rock formations of 150-million-year-old red Jurassic sandstone. Open all year; $3/vehicle,

$1/pedestrian or bicyclist; the park includes visitor center exhibits (open daily 8:30 a.m.-4:30 p.m.), two campgrounds ($7), picnic areas, and hiking trails; tel. (702) 397-2088.

See Indian artifacts from Pueblo Grande de Nevada in the **Lost City Museum;** open daily 8:30 a.m.-4:30 p.m. on a hill at the south edge of Overton, 11 miles north of Overton Beach; $2 ages 18 and over; tel. (702) 397-2193. Built on an actual Virgin Anasazi site, the museum includes a reconstructed pithouse and pueblo, pottery, jewelry, lithic tools and other artifacts and historic exhibits; Civilian Conservation Corps workers in the 1930s excavated artifacts from numerous prehistoric sites, some now lost beneath Lake Mead. This adobe museum was built to house them.

**Temple Bar Resort,** Arizona's only development on Lake Mead, has fishing cabins ($45.37-93.90), a motel ($72.80 d), kitchenettes (93.90), RV park ($18.99), restaurant, and marina with boat rentals (fishing, ski, and patio). Proceed to Temple Bar, AZ 86443; tel. (520) 767-3211 or (800) 752-9669 for reservations. There's also a Park Service campground here ($8). From Hoover Dam, go southeast 19 miles on US 93, then turn left and drive 28 miles on a paved road.

Take the dirt road off the route to Temple Bar to reach **Bonelli Landing,** a primitive campground/parking area on the Arizona shore.

### South Cove

Upstream, the lake narrows in Virgin Canyon before opening into Gregg's Basin, the uppermost large open-water area of Lake Mead. There's a boat ramp at South Cove on the Arizona side and a new picnic area but no campground or resort. By car, you reach South Cove on a paved 45-mile road branching off US 93 between Hoover Dam and Kingman. You'll pass through **Dolan Springs**—small motel, RV parks, restaurants, and stores—and an area with Joshua trees up to 25 feet tall. The tree looks like a strange cactus but really belongs to the lily family.

**Pearce Ferry,** accessible by dirt road off the road to South Cove, offers primitive boat ramps and campsites at the upper end of Lake Mead. Grand Canyon National Park begins just upstream.

**Grand Wash Bay** extends north into Nevada above Iceberg Canyon; no facilities. You'll need a high-clearance, 4WD vehicle and a good map to reach this lonely spot, as much of the way follows sandy washes. Check road conditions and weather forecasts before attempting this route.

# WEST-CENTRAL ARIZONA

## LAKE HAVASU CITY

In 1964, upon spotting Lake Havasu from the air, the late Robert McCulloch decided to build a town along its shores. The planned community came to life on the east shore of Lake Havasu, 19 miles south of I-40 and 73 miles north of I-10, both major cross-country routes. Factories provided employment for the town's residents. Still, Lake Havasu City might have become just another ho-hum town if not for a brainstorm by McCulloch and town planner C.V. Wood. They decided to buy London Bridge.

Back in England, the 136-year-old bridge was slowly sinking into the Thames. No longer able to handle busy city traffic, the famous London landmark was put up for sale in 1967. Mc-

Culloch snapped it up for $2,460,000, then spent more than twice that amount to have 10,276 granite blocks shipped to Long Beach, California, trucked to Lake Havasu City, and painstakingly reassembled. After three years of construction, the bridge was up and ready in its new home. The Lord Mayor of London graciously came over in October 1971 to preside at the bridge dedication. London Bridge may be one of the stranger sights on the Arizona desert, but it certainly put Lake Havasu City on the map.

More has been added since—an English Village complete with shops and galleries, a double-deck bus, and even a bright-red British telephone booth. Nearby London Bridge Resort adds more English atmosphere.

At first, the bridge spanned only dry land. Workers later dug a water channel underneath,

ARIZONA OFFICE OF TOURISM

*London Bridge*

cutting off Pittsburgh Point. Now you walk or drive across London Bridge to reach the campgrounds, RV parks, beaches, marina, and other facilities on the new island, still known as Pittsburgh Point.

As in other Colorado River towns, fun on the water draws many visitors. Lake Havasu, 45 miles long and three miles wide, offers great boating, waterskiing, and sailing. Boat rentals, boat tours, swimming beaches, tennis, and golf courses are readily available as well. The present population of Lake Havasu City is more than 25,000.

## Accommodations

The visitor can choose from about two dozen motels and resorts. Rates go up on Friday and Saturday at many locales. **London Bridge Resort,** close to London Bridge and the water, features an 18-hole golf course, tennis, swimming pools, and elegant decor; rooms run $65.20-98.35 d, suites run $197.80-264.10 d overlooking the water. It's worth stepping inside the plush lobby to see the world's only replica of the ornate Gold State Coach. The original, built in 1762, has carried all British monarchs since George III to coronation ceremonies at Westminster Abbey. Look for London Bridge Resort at 1477 Queen's Bay Rd.; tel. 855-0888 or (800) 624-7939.

**Nautical Inn,** on the water across London Bridge, offers restaurants, an 18-hole golf course, tennis, swimming pool, and spas; rooms cost $64.99-76.25 d March 13-Oct. 31 and $98.35-120.45 d Nov. 1-March 12; 1000 McCulloch Blvd.; tel. 855-2141 or (800) 892-2141. **Island Inn** offers deluxe accommodations with restaurant, pool, and spa; $71.83-121.55 d March-Nov. and $49.73-71.83 d Nov.-Feb.; 1300 McCulloch Blvd., just one block before State Beach; tel. 680-0606 or (800) 243-9955. **Sands Vacation Resort** features suites with kitchens, tennis, and pool; rooms go for $55.26-121.56 d year-round; 2040 Mesquite Ave.; tel. 855-1388 or (800) 521-0360.

Less expensive places include **Bridgeview Motel,** 101 London Bridge Rd., tel. 855-5559; **Holiday Inn,** 245 London Bridge Rd., tel. 855-4071 or (800) HOLIDAY; **Super 8 Motel,** 305 London Bridge Rd., tel. 855-8844 or (800) 843-1991; **Howard Johnson Lodge and Suites,** 335 London Bridge Rd., tel. 453-4656 or (800) 446-4656; **Lakeview Motel,** 440 London Bridge Rd., tel. 855-3605; **Windsor Inn,** 451 London Bridge Rd., tel. 855-4135 or (800) 245-4135; **TraveLodge,** 480 London Bridge Rd., tel. 680-9202 or (800) 578-7878; **Inn at Tamarisk,** 3101 London Bridge Rd., tel. 764-3033; **Pioneer Hotel,** 271 S. Lake Havasu Ave., tel. 855-1111 or

(800) 528-5169; **Sandman Inn,** 1700 McCulloch Blvd., tel. 855-7841; **Best Western/Lake Place Inn,** 31 Wings Loop, tel. 855-2146 or (800) 258-8558; **Shakespeare Inn,** 2190 McCulloch Blvd., tel. 855-4157; **E-Z 8 Motel,** 41 S. Acoma Blvd., tel. 855-4023; **Acoma Inn,** 89 N. Acoma Blvd., tel. 855-2084; and **Havasu Motel** (all kitchenette units), 2035 W. Acoma Blvd., tel. 855-2311. See the tourist office in English Village (beside London Bridge) for other places to stay.

## Campgrounds

**Lake Havasu State Park** features 45 miles of shoreline, covering most of the Arizona side of the lake. Besides the state and concession-run campgrounds, boaters can choose among 225 primitive camping sites accessible by water only. **Windsor Beach** has tent and RV camping ($10 with showers but no hookups), picnic areas, swimming beaches, and two boat ramps; it's 1.5 miles north of London Bridge

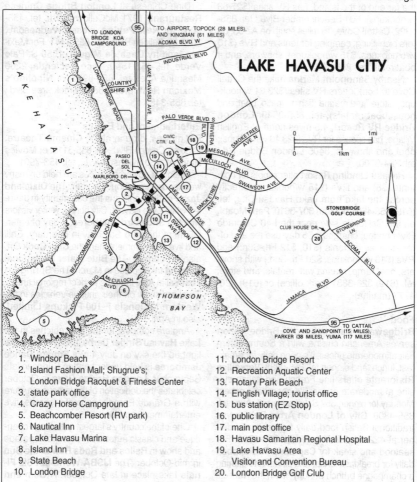

**LAKE HAVASU CITY**

TO LONDON BRIDGE KOA CAMPGROUND

TO AIRPORT, TOPOCK (28 MILES), AND KINGMAN (61 MILES)

ACOMA BLVD. W

INDUSTRIAL BLVD.

COUNTRY SHIRE AVE.

LONDON BRIDGE ROAD

LAKE HAVASU AVE. N

PALO VERDE BLVD. N

CIVIC CTR. LN.

PASEO DEL SOL

RIVIERA BLVD.

CAPRI BLVD.

SMOKETREE AVE. N

MESQUITE AVE.

McCULLOCH BLVD.

MARLBORO DR.

LAKE HAVASU AVE. S

SMOKETREE AVE. S

SWANSON AVE.

MULBERRY AVE.

STONEBRIDGE GOLF COURSE

CLUB HOUSE DR.

STONEBRIDGE LN.

SWANSON AVE.

BEACHCOMBER BLVD.

McCULLOCH BLVD.

THOMPSON BAY

ACOMA BLVD. S

JAMAICA BLVD. S

COVE AND SANDPOINT (15 MILES), PARKER (38 MILES), YUMA (117 MILES) TO CATTAIL

0 — 1mi
0 — 1km

1. Windsor Beach
2. Island Fashion Mall; Shugrue's; London Bridge Racquet & Fitness Center
3. state park office
4. Crazy Horse Campground
5. Beachcomber Resort (RV park)
6. Nautical Inn
7. Lake Havasu Marina
8. Island Inn
9. State Beach
10. London Bridge
11. London Bridge Resort
12. Recreation Aquatic Center
13. Rotary Park Beach
14. English Village; tourist office
15. bus station (EZ Stop)
16. public library
17. main post office
18. Havasu Samaritan Regional Hospital
19. Lake Havasu Area Visitor and Convention Bureau
20. London Bridge Golf Club

off London Bridge Rd.; tel. 855-2784. **Crazy Horse Campground,** a half mile across London Bridge on the island, offers primitive tent camping ($22) and RV sites ($22 w/hookups); it has showers and a store; 1534 Beachcomber Blvd.; tel. 855-2127.

**Islander RV Resort** provides sites for $26.52 ($24.31 November to April); 751 Beachcomber Blvd., just past Nautical Inn; tel. 855-5005. **Beachcomber Resort,** two miles southwest at the far end of the island, has RV sites ($27.63 w/hookups); 601 Beachcomber Blvd.; tel. 855-2322. **Cattail Cove,** 15 miles south on AZ 95, offers picnicking, camping for tents and RVs ($10 w/o hookups, $15 w/hookups), showers, and a boat ramp; tel. 855-1223.

Nearby **Sandpoint Marina** (take the Cattail Cove turnoff), offers RV sites ($23.21 w/hookups), store, and marina (fishing, patio, boat, and houseboat rentals); tel. 855-0549. **London Bridge RV Resort,** 4.5 miles north of English Village, has spaces for RVs ($23.10 w/hookups); pool and showers; 3405 London Bridge Rd.; tel. 764-3700.

**Havasu Landing Resort** offers spots for both tents ($8) and RVs ($15 w/hookups), directly across the lake from Lake Havasu City; tel. (619) 858-4606 or (800) 307-3610. **Park Moabi,** on the California side near the I-40 Colorado River bridge, charges a $6 day-use fee and offers spaces for tents ($10, $12 Fri.-Sun.) and RVs ($18 w/hookups, $20 Fri.-Sun.) with showers, boat ramp, marina with rentals, and store; tel. (619) 326-3831 (park office) or (619) 326-4777 (marina).

### Food

**Bridgewater Cafe** in London Bridge Resort serves American cuisine with a Southwestern flair at moderate prices; it's open daily for breakfast, lunch, and dinner; tel. 855-0888. **Versailles Ristorante** offers fine French and Italian cuisine at moderate prices; it's open daily except Monday for dinner; 357 S. Lake Havasu Ave.; tel. 855-4800. **City of London Arms Pub** serves traditional British food daily for lunch and dinner at 422 English Village; tel. 855-8782. For seafood and steak try **Captain's Table,** open daily for breakfast, lunch, and dinner and offering a champagne brunch Sunday; it's in the Nautical Inn, 1000 McCulloch Blvd.; tel. 855-2141.

**Shugrue's** is open daily for lunch and dinner in Island Fashion Mall, just across London Bridge; tel. 453-1400. Or try **Krystal's Fine Dining,** 460 El Camino Way; tel. 453-2999.

For pizza and other Italian dishes, you can choose from **Papa Leone's Pizza,** 304 English Village, tel. 453-5200; **Nicolino's Italian Restaurant and Bakery,** 86 S. Smoketree Blvd., tel. 855-3484; and **Pizza Hut,** 1543 Marlboro Dr., tel. 855-6071.

Dine Chinese at **London Bridge Chinese Restaurant,** 1971 McCulloch Blvd., tel. 453-5002; or **New Peking,** closed Wednesday, 2010 McCulloch Blvd., tel. 855-4441. For Mexican food try **Casa de Miguel,** 1550 S. Palo Verde, tel. 453-1550; **Taco Hacienda,** 2200 Mesquite Ave., tel. 855-8932; or **Nicolino's Mexican Restaurant,** 86 S. Smoketree Blvd., tel. 855-3484.

### Entertainment and Events

For movies, drop in at the **Cinema Theatre,** 2130 McCulloch Blvd., tel. 855-3111, or **Movies Havasu,** 180 Swanson Ave., tel. 453-7901.

Sailing or powerboat races are held on many weekends throughout the year. The **Dixieland Jazz Festival** enlivens the community in January while Lake Havasu City honors winter visitors with the **Snowbird Jamboree,** a day of entertainment the third Saturday in February. Chili and live entertainment mark the **Chili Cook Off,** also in February. The **Blue Water Invitational Regatta** takes place in March. The **Spring Art Festival** in April features work of regional artists. Truckers show off their antique vehicles in the **Western Nationals F-100 Pickups Limited,** also in April.

Anglers compete for the best catches in the **Lake Havasu Striper Derby** in May. **Fireworks** light up the sky on July 4th; a **Square Dance Jamboree** is held under London Bridge in late September. **London Bridge Days** in October celebrates the dedication of the famous structure with a Grande Parade, contests, games, live entertainment, and food.

One of the country's largest gatherings of antique and classic autos converges for a parade and show in **Relics and Rods Run to the Sun** in mid-October. The **IJSBA World Jet Ski Finals** take place in late October. A **Gem and Mineral Show** is held in November; radio-controlled model airplanes take off in the **London Bridge Seaplane Classic** in November. A **Christmas Boat Parade of Lights** brightens early December.

Check with the visitor bureau for dates and details.

### Recreation

For swimming, head a half mile across London Bridge to **State Beach;** free. The **Recreation Aquatic Center** at 100 Park Ave. (on Hwy. 95 just southeast of Swanson Ave.) features an indoor wave pool, a 253-foot water slide, a hot tub and spa, a children's pool, and an adjacent gymnasium; tel. 453-8686 or 453-2687. **Rotary Park Beach,** south of the English Village area, offers beaches, picnic tables, and ball fields. **Windsor Beach,** another park with beach areas, picnic areas, and boat ramps, lies 1.5 miles north of London Bridge on the mainland; $3 day use, $10 camping; tel. 855-2784.

The **London Bridge Racquet & Fitness Center** has tennis and racquetball courts at 1425 McCulloch Blvd. in Island Fashion Mall, on the right just after crossing the bridge toward

the island; tel. 855-6274. **London Bridge Golf Club** features two 18-hole courses; 2400 Club House Dr. off S. Acoma Blvd.; tel. 855-2719. A third 18-hole course is available at **Nautical Inn,** 1000 McCulloch Blvd., one mile across London Bridge; tel. 855-2131. **Queen's Bay Golf Course and Country Club** has a nine-hole course adjacent to London Bridge Resort; tel. 855-4777.

Many places in town rent water sports equipment; ask the tourist office for a Recreation Guide. **Fun Center,** on the water next to English Village, rents pedal boats and other craft; tel. 453-4386. The Nautical Inn **Water Sport Center,** on the island, offers wave runner and jet ski rentals, waterski and parasail rides, and scuba gear; tel. 855-2141.

**Lake Havasu Marina,** 1100 McCulloch Blvd., rents fishing, pontoon, and ski boats; tel. 855-2159. **Sandpoint Marina,** 14 miles south on the Arizona side (take the Cattail Cove turnoff), offers fishing boat, patio boat, and houseboat rentals; tel. 855-0549. **Park Moabi,** in California near the I-40 Colorado River bridge, also has a boat ramp and marina with rentals; tel. (619) 326-4777.

*The City of London Arms*

Anglers discovered this lake long before any developer. Fishing was good—and still is—for largemouth bass, crappie, and channel catfish. Saltwater striped bass, introduced in the early '60s, have thrived. Weighing up to 60 pounds, this landlocked fish is now the hottest thing in the lake. The stripers feed in spring and summer below Davis Dam, eating threadfin shad and other fish churned up by water flowing from the turbines. During fall and winter the bass return to the lake and are sought out by thousands of eager anglers. Pick up a local fishing booklet for tips on striper techniques.

### Services
The main **post office** is on the corner of 1750 McCulloch and Capri Boulevards; tel. 855-2361. **Havasu Samaritan Regional Hospital** is at 101 Civic Center Ln.; tel. 855-8185.

### Information
The **Lake Havasu Area Visitor and Convention Bureau** maintains two offices, both stocked with literature. The one in the English Village is easier to find; it's open daily 9 a.m.-5 p.m.; tel. 855-5655. The main office, 1930 Mesquite Ave. #3 and Riviera Blvd., Lake Havasu City, AZ 86403, is open Mon.-Fri. 9 a.m.-5 p.m.; tel. 855-4115 or (800) 242-8278.

**Lake Havasu State Park** rangers will impart information about state recreational areas; the office lies on the island just across London Bridge on the right; tel. 855-7851. The **BLM Havasu Resource Area** office administers recreational areas along the Colorado River between Davis Dam and sites 10 miles north of Quartzsite; it's open Mon.-Fri. 8 a.m.-4:30 p.m.; at the south end of town on AZ 95 (1801 Hwy. 95, Lake Havasu City, AZ 86406); tel. 855-8017.

The **public library** is at 1787 McCulloch Blvd.; tel. 453-0718. **Book Nook** sells a variety of books, periodicals, and topo maps at 1640 McCulloch Blvd.; tel. 855-8825. **Hastings Books** offers books and periodicals at 1775 McCulloch Blvd.; tel. 680-7272.

### Tours
Several boat tours leave from the shore at English Village. You can take narrated 45-minute tours of the area with **Dixie Belle Cruises** ($12 adults, $5 children 6-12; tel. 453-6776). **Lake**

**Havasu Boat Tours** leaves from the shore of Island Fashion Mall ($10 adults, free children under 12; tel. 855-7979). **Bluewater Charters** offers three-hour trips upstream into the spectacular Topock Gorge; $19.80 adults, $10.71 children; a passenger minimum applies on all tours. The office lies at the north end of the seawall in English Village; tel. 855-7171.

**Adler's Sailing Center** offers sailboat tours, rentals, and lessons at London Bridge; tel. 855-1555. **Outback Off-Road Adventures** features educational 4WD transportation. Half-day tours cover Mojave Chief Gold Mine, Lost Dutchman Mine, and Bill Williams River for $69.55 each. Or spend a full day at Swansea, a ghost town, for $139.10. The Outback office is at 1350 McCulloch Blvd.; tel. 680-6151. The gambling casinos in Laughlin offer free bus rides, free food, and other inducements to attract you and your money; check the brochures in the tourist office.

### Transport
**K-T Services** buses run daily to Las Vegas ($32) via Needles, California ($10), and Laughlin/Bullhead City ($15); and to Phoenix ($30) via Parker ($10) and Wickenburg ($17); they leave from EZ Stop, 54 N. Lake Havasu Ave. at Mesquite; tel. 453-6633. **America West Express** serves cities in Arizona, New Mexico, and Colorado; tel. (800) 235-9292. The airport lies off AZ 95 about seven miles north of town.

## VICINITY OF LAKE HAVASU CITY

### Topock Gorge by Canoe
This is a perfect one-day outing on the cool waters of the Colorado River above Lake Havasu. The usual put-in point is Park Moabi, California, or Topock, Arizona, where I-40 crosses the river. Swift currents speed canoeists down the river without rapids or serious turbulence. Take-out is at Castle Rock on the upper end of Lake Havasu, about seven hours and 17 river miles later. Topock Gorge is part of the Havasu National Wildlife Refuge, where you can spot hundreds of bird species. Look for the mud nests of swallows clinging to the cliffs; herons, ducks, geese, long-billed prospectors, and red-winged blackbirds also visit the canyon. If you're lucky,

you may spot a desert bighorn sheep on the steep slopes.

Indian petroglyphs cover Picture Rock, a huge, dark mass about halfway between Devil's Elbow and Blankenship Bend. The sandy beaches are ideal for a walk or picnic, but no fires or camping are permitted.

Summer temperatures can get uncomfortable, but a hop in the river will cool you off. Bring a hat and sunscreen to protect yourself from the Arizona sun. Other kinds of boats besides canoes can make the trip. Rafts require more time, and powerboat skippers should watch for sandbars. Topo maps (1:24,000 scale) for the area include Topock, Ariz.-Calif.; and Castle Rock, Calif.-Arizona.

**Jerkwater Canoe Co.** offers rentals, shuttle service, meals, and bed and breakfast in Topock; tel. 768-7753 or (800) 421-7803. **Bob's Canoe Trips** offers rentals and canoe transport in Lake Havasu City; tel. 855-4406. **WACKO** rents canoes and kayaks and provides transportation in Lake Havasu City; tel. 855-6414. Many other canoe trips are possible; for example, you can start at Needles for a two-day trip or at Bullhead City for a three- or four-day canoe excursion.

### Havasu National Wildlife Refuge

The marshes, open water, and adjacent desert of the refuge support many types of birds and animals. The main part of the refuge includes Topock Marsh near Needles, California, extending southward to just north of Lake Havasu City. Most of the more than 44,371 acres lie in Arizona. **Bill Williams River Wildlife Refuge** protects the lower 12 miles (6,000 acres) of Bill Williams River south of Lake Havasu City. In winter, the two refuge areas are home for the snow goose, Canada goose, and other waterfowl.

Boating, fishing, and other water sports are permitted except where signed. No camping is allowed in Mesquite Bay, Topock Gorge, or Topock Marsh. You can boat camp on the Arizona shore below the south entrance to Topock Gorge, except in Mesquite Bay. For a map, bird list, and regulations, visit the Havasu National Wildlife Refuge office, open Mon.-Fri. 8 a.m.-4 p.m. at 331 Mesquite Ave., across from the highway patrol office; or write Box 3009, Needles, CA 92363, tel. (619) 326-3853. Or visit

the Bill Williams River Wildlife Refuge office, open Mon.-Fri. 8 a.m.-4 p.m. one mile south of the Bill Williams River across from Milepost 161; or write 60911 Hwy. 95, Parker, AZ 85344, tel. (520) 667-4144.

**Five Mile Landing** is a private campground ($7.35 dry camping for tent or RV, $14.95 w/hookups) and marina (boat rentals, slips, and ramp) on the east side of Topock Marsh off AZ 95, five miles north of I-40 and 35 miles south of Bullhead City; tel. 768-2350. RV spaces tend to be filled.

## PARKER AND THE PARKER STRIP

From 1871 to 1908, Parker was nothing but a post office on the Colorado River Indian Reservation. When the railroad came through, the town began to expand, becoming a trading center for the reservation and nearby mining operations. Mining later declined, but agriculture and tourism thrived with the construction of two dams upstream.

The Headgate Rock Dam, finished in 1941, forms Lake Moovalya, which provides water for the irrigation of reservation farmlands. In 1938 workers completed Parker Dam, which created Lake Havasu, supplying water and electrical power to southern California. Resorts and parks line Lake Moovalya and both shores of the river, drawing visitors year-round. Better known as the Parker Strip, this 11-mile stretch of scenic waterway begins several miles north of Parker and extends north to Parker Dam. Despite hot summer temperatures—among the nation's highest—many people enjoy the excellent boating and waterskiing from Easter through Labor Day. In September the scene calms and the temperature cools. Winter visitors, many retired, enjoy fishing, hunting, hiking, rockhounding, and exploring ghost towns.

### Accommodations

You can stay in town or upstream along the Parker Strip. The six or so motels in town are easy to find along Parker's two major streets, California Ave. and Agency Rd./Riverside Drive. About five miles north on AZ 95, you'll see a long line of RV parks, resorts, restaurants, and marinas. Places to stay include **Arizona Shores Resort Motel**, 5.5 miles north of Parker, tel. 667-2685; **Branson's Resort**, 7.5 miles north of Parker, tel. 667-3346; **Casa del Rio Resort**, 15 miles north of Parker, tel. 667-2727; and **Havasu Springs Resort**, 16 miles north of Parker, tel. 667-3361.

You'll also find places on the California shore opposite the Parker Strip: **River Shore Resort**, seven miles from Parker, tel. (619) 665-2572; **Big River Inn**, eight miles from Parker, tel. (619) 665-9440; **Windmill Resort**, 9.5 miles from Parker, tel. (619) 663-3717; **Big Bend Resort**, 12 miles from Parker, tel. (619) 663-3755; **River Lodge**, 14 miles from Parker, tel. (619) 663-3891; and **Black Meadow Landing** on Lake Havasu, 25 miles from Parker, tel. (619) 663-4901.

## Campgrounds

RVs are welcome in Parker at **Lazy D Mobile Park**, 16th and Arizona, $14 RV w/hookups; tel. 669-8797. More than three dozen trailer parks and campgrounds line the water along the Parker Strip and the California shore. The Parker Chamber of Commerce will provide a list and map.

**La Paz County Park** covers a long section of riverbank about eight miles north of Parker, offering picnicking, tent and RV camping, hookups, showers, tennis, the 18-hole Emerald Canyon Golf Course, swimming beach, and boat ramp. Fees run $2 per person ages 12 and over for day use, $8 per car (two people) dry camping, $12 (two people) RV w/hookups; tel. 667-2069.

**Buckskin Mountain State Park**, 11 miles north of Parker, sits on a secluded section of grassy shoreline backed by low cliffs; a concession runs a snack bar, marina, inner-tube rental outfit, boat ramp, and store; tel. 667-3210. A short hiking trail begins opposite the highway turnoff; you'll find picnic sites and a campground (hookups and showers) near the water; $5 day use, $15 camping (all sites with hookups), $20 beach cabana site; tel. 667-3231.

A second section of Buckskin Mountain State Park lies two miles farther upstream; this smaller **River Island Unit** offers picnicking, camping (showers but no hookups), swimming beach, and boat ramp; $5 day use, $10 camping; tel. 667-3386.

The Bureau of Land Management's **Empire Landing**, eight miles from Parker on the California side, offers a beach, picnicking, and camping (cold showers and hookups); free day use, camping costs $8 per vehicle; tel. (602) 855-8017.

## Food

**County Seat Restaurant** features steak, seafood, and ribs at 1005 Arizona; it's open daily for lunch and dinner, weekends for breakfast; tel. 669-9474. Look for American fare at **Coffee Ern's**, open 24 hours, 1720 California Ave., tel. 669-8145; and **T-Bob's** daily for breakfast, lunch, and dinner, 1000 Hopi Ave., tel. 669-9396. The **Early Bird Cafe**, 904 California Ave., tel. 669-5355, and **Hole in the Wall**, 612 California Ave., tel. 669-9755, serve breakfast, lunch, and dinner daily.

**Los Arcos** serves Mexican food; it's closed Sunday; 1200 California Ave.; tel. 669-9904. **Jalapeño's** offers Mexican lunches and dinners daily except Monday; 621 Riverside Dr.; tel. 669-2309. For pizza try **La Piazza**, closed Wednesday, 801 11th St., tel. 669-2441; or **Toby's Pizza**, open Mon.-Fri. for lunch and dinner, Saturday dinner only, 1317 Joshua Ave., tel. 669-9388. A variety of other restaurants lie along the Parker Strip north of town.

## Entertainment and Events

Annual events include the **Parker Score 400** off-road vehicle rally on the last full weekend in January; **International Water Ski Race** in February or March; **Balloonfest** in February or March; **La Paz County Fair** in March; and **Parker Enduro Classic** races in late March.

The **River Run** car and boat show occurs on the first weekend in May. There's an **Inner-tube Race** in June; **fireworks** on July 4th; **Indian Day Celebration** in September; **Parker Rodeo and Parade** in mid-October; **Parker Mini-Boat Enduro** in November; **Christmas Lighted Boat Parade** in late November/early December; and **All Indian Rodeo** in December.

**Blue Waters Casino** offers slot machines, video poker, a bingo parlor, and a card room at 119 W. Riverside Dr., in the Movalya Plaza shopping center; tel. 669-7777 or (800) 747-8777. Look for the new **Bluewater Resort Hotel and Casino** to be built between Hwy. 95 and the

Blue Water Strip on the Colorado River. Facilities will include a hotel with 504 rooms and suites, an RV park, cafe, specialty restaurant, and a golf course and country club.

### Recreation

Other free BLM recreation sites on the California side of the river include **Rock House Boating Facility** (boat launch and day-use area just south of Empire Landing); **Crossroads** (camping and day-use area on the river one mile south of Empire Landing, no water); **Bullfrog** (day-use beach and picnic area two miles north of Empire Landing); and **Quail Hollow** (day-use picnic and wildlife interpretive area, four miles north of Empire Landing and just north of Big Bend Resort). On the Arizona shore, the BLM's **Patria Flats** offers picnicking 6.7 miles north of Parker; free, day-use only.

Cool off in Parker's public **swimming pool,** 1317 Ninth St.; tel. 669-5678. Play golf at the 18-hole **Emerald Canyon Golf Course,** across the road from La Paz County Park, eight miles north of Parker (tel. 667-3366), or **Havasu Spring**'s nine-hole course, 16 miles north of Parker (tel. 667-3361).

No one offers boat tours in the area, but rentals are readily available from marinas along the Parker Strip. Anglers head for the river below Headgate Rock Dam for largemouth and smallmouth bass, striped bass, catfish, crappie, and bluegill. Boaters and waterskiers keep some anglers from Lake Moovalya, but the fish are there. You need reservation fishing permits for lower Lake Moovalya and the Colorado River downstream. Tubers enjoy leisurely trips downriver; a popular ride is the seven-mile, three-hour float from Parker to Big River Park on the California side.

### Services

The main **post office** is at the corner of Joshua Ave. and 14th Street; tel. 669-8179. **Parker Community Hospital** is at 1200 Mohave Rd.; tel. 669-9201.

### Information

The **Parker Chamber of Commerce** staff will help you find the resort you're looking for. The office is open Mon.-Fri. 9 a.m.-5 p.m. at 1217 California Ave. (Box 627, Parker, AZ 85344);

tel. 669-2174. The **public library** is at the corner of 1001 Navajo Ave. and Agency Rd.; tel. 669-2622.

## VICINITY OF PARKER

### Colorado River Indian Reservation

Established in 1865, this 268,691-acre reservation lies mostly in Arizona. Inhabitants include Mohave, Chemehuevi, Hopi, and Navajo people. Don't expect any picturesque Indian villages: the 6,000-plus inhabitants live in modern houses and work at farms and jobs like everyone else along the Colorado River.

To learn about the tribes and others who've passed this way, visit the **Colorado River Indian Tribes (CRIT) Museum** two miles southwest of Parker. There you'll see artifacts from the prehistoric Anasazi, Hohokam, and Patayan cultures; models showing traditional shelters of the modern tribes; and a large collection of baskets and other crafts. Old photos and artifacts illustrate early reservation life. A library houses an extensive collection of books, manuscripts, photographs, and tapes relating to various tribes. Baskets, beadwork, and other Indian crafts are sold in the gift shop. The museum is open Mon.-Fri. 8 a.m.-noon and 1-5 p.m. and Saturday 10 a.m.-2 p.m.; donations are accepted; tel. 669-9211, ext. 335. From downtown Parker, head southwest two miles on either Agency or Mohave Road. The museum is 300 feet north on Mohave from Second Avenue.

### Parker Dam

The world's deepest dam lies about 15 miles upriver from its namesake, the town of Parker. During construction, workers had to dig down 235 feet through the sand and gravel of the riverbed before hitting the bedrock needed to secure the foundation. Today, only the top third of the dam is visible. Lake Havasu, the reservoir behind the dam, has a storage capacity of 211 billion gallons. Pumps transfer one billion gallons a day into the Colorado River Aqueduct for southern California destinations. You can take a free, self-guided tour of the dam and power plant, open daily 7:30 a.m.-4:30 p.m. Arizona time.

## Quartzsite

Like swallows returning to Capistrano, thousands of snowbirds flock to this tiny desert town every winter. From an estimated 2,000 to 3,000 summer residents, the population jumps to about one million during the gem and mineral shows from mid-January to mid-February.

Charles Tyson settled here in 1856, building a fort to fend off Indian attacks. Tyson's Wells soon became an important stage stop on the run from Ehrenburg to Prescott. Later the place was renamed Quartzite, after the rock, but the post office added an "s" for a name of Quartzsite.

The venerable Hadji Ali lies under a pyramid-shaped marker in the local cemetery. Ali was one of several camel drivers imported by the U.S. Army from the Middle East with about 80 camels in 1856-57. The Army hoped the large, hardy beasts would improve transportation and communication in the Southwest deserts. Although the camels showed promise, the Army abandoned the experiment during the Civil War. Most of the camels were turned loose on the desert, terrorizing stock and wild animals for many years. While the other camel drivers, homesick for their native lands, sailed home, Hadji Ali, whose name soldiers changed to "Hi Jolly," stayed in Arizona and took up prospecting.

Quartzsite lies 35 miles south of Parker and

20 miles east of Blythe, California, at the junction of I-10 and AZ 95. A good collection of motels, RV parks, and restaurants serve passing motorists and the winter community. Even more facilities are available in nearby Salome. Most RVers, however, prefer the open freedom of the desert and head for **La Posa Long-term Visitor Area** just south of town. La Posa is divided into four sections, with vault toilets and a dump station. Visitors pay a $50 fee for long-term use Sept. 15-April 15; for shorter visits a $10 seven-day permit is available. You can camp free (14-day limit) off-season at La Posa and year-round in undeveloped areas such as **Mile Markers 99 and 112** on US 95. The Bureau of Land Management Yuma District office can advise you on these recreation areas; tel. 726-6300.

The giant **Quartzsite gem and mineral shows and swap meets** take place from November to mid-February. People attend this giant flea market to buy and sell rocks, minerals, gems, lapidary supplies, crafts, antiques, and other treasures. A smaller swap meet takes place the rest of the winter, from October to March.

The **Quartzsite Chamber of Commerce** provides visitor information Mon.-Fri. 9 a.m.-5 p.m. at 9 Palm Plaza, a quarter mile north on AZ 95 from Business I-10. Or write Box 85, Quartzsite, AZ 85346; tel. 927-5600.

*Hi Jolly monument in Quartzsite*

## Alamo Lake State Park

This Alamo lies far from the one where Davy Crockett and his friends fought it out with the Mexicans. The lake, at an elevation of 1,200 feet, lies on the Bill Williams River. When Alamo Lake began to fill in the mid-'60s, cottonwood, mesquite, and palo verde trees were flooded, becoming homes for small fish. Hungry large-mouth bass and channel catfish fed on the small bluegill, sunfish, and tilapia. Anglers then moved in to feed on the bass and catfish.

A marina provides groceries, fishing supplies, and rental boats. The state park features picnic tables, campgrounds with showers and hookups, and a boat ramp; $3 day use, $8 w/o hookups, $13 w/hookups; tel. 669-2088. Spring and autumn are the most popular times for a visit to this remote desert lake. To get there, drive to Wenden (60 miles southeast of Parker or 108 miles northwest of Phoenix), then go 35 miles north on a paved road.

## Swansea

Of the ghost towns near Parker, Swansea is the best preserved, with ruins of a large brick smelter, mine, and more than a dozen buildings. The Clara Consolidated Gold and Copper Mining Co. built the smelter in the early 1900s to process its ore locally, instead of sending the stuff to such faraway places as Swansea, Wales. Clara Consolidated closed the smelter in 1912, but other companies continued mining until 1924.

You should use a high-clearance vehicle to navigate the dirt roads to the site. From Bouse, 27 miles southeast of Parker, take the road north across the railroad tracks and go 13 miles to Midway (keep left at a fork three miles from Bouse). Take the left fork at Midway, crossing under power lines after 0.4 mile, and go northwest 5.7 miles to a road junction, then turn right and drive 7.2 miles to Swansea. In this last section you'll cross a pipeline twice and pass through very scenic desert hills and a natural arch. Another approach involves roads east from Parker. Obtain local advice and good maps such as the Swansea 15-minute topo map.

# THE SOUTHWEST CORNER

## YUMA

Yuma's rich historical background and sunny, subtropical climate make it an attractive destination. In winter, an estimated 60,000 snowbirds double the town's normal population, filling the many trailer parks in town, along the river, and out on the desert. Boaters and anglers can explore countless lakes and quiet backwaters on the Colorado River. Date palms, citrus trees, and vegetables grow on irrigated farmlands around Yuma. The Mexican city of San Luis offers shopping just 25 miles south.

## Yuma's Beginnings

The long recorded history of Yuma begins in 1540, nearly 70 years before the founding of Jamestown, Virginia. Captain Hernando de Alarcón, the first white person to visit the area, led a Spanish naval expedition along the west coast of Mexico and then a short way up the Colorado River. He hoped to meet and resupply Francisco Vásquez de Coronado's expedition to the fabled Seven Cities of Cíbola farther east, but the two groups never met.

While searching for a land route between Mexico and California, Spanish explorers discovered the best crossing on the lower Colorado River lay just below the mouth of the Gila River. Soldiers and missionaries built a fort and missions here, across from present-day Yuma. Angry Quechan destroyed the settlements during a violent uprising in 1781, ending Spanish domination of Yuma Crossing.

Although small bands of American mountain men started drifting through in the early 1800s, little attention was paid to the area until the Mexican War. Kit Carson passed this way in 1829 with a group of trappers, returning in 1846 to guide Colonel Stephen Kearny and 100 soldiers seeking to secure former Mexican lands between Santa Fe and San Diego. Captain Philip Cooke followed with the Mormon Battalion and supply wagons, blazing the first transcontinental road across the Southwest. Crowds of '49ers, seeking gold in the Sierra Nevada of

California, pushed westward along Cooke's Road a few years later.

In 1851 the Army built Camp Yuma atop a hill on the California side to protect Yuma Crossing from Indian attacks. Nearby mining successes, the coming of steamboats, and road improvements encouraged the founding of Colorado City in 1854. Residents changed the name to Arizona City in 1858, then rebuilt on higher ground after a disastrous 1862 flood. The present name of Yuma was adopted in 1873.

Yuma Territorial Prison, the town's first major construction project, went up in 1876. Laguna Dam ended the riverboat era in 1909, guaranteeing water for the fertile desert valleys.

## Modern Yuma

Today Yuma is one of Arizona's most important cities, the center of a rich agricultural area. The military is here in some force too. You'll probably see aircraft speeding overhead from the Marine Corps Air Station on the southeast edge of town. The Army checks out combat vehicles, weapon systems, and other gear at the Yuma Proving Grounds, 26 miles north.

You can explore downtown Yuma on foot. The Yuma County Chamber of Commerce is a good starting point for a visit to shops and galleries on Main St.; follow the row of small shops signed 224 Main Street west and across Madison Ave. to reach the Century House Museum. Continue west and north several blocks to visit the Yuma Quartermaster Depot.

# SIGHTS

## Yuma Territorial Prison

The old Yuma Territorial Prison, the "Hellhole of Arizona," is now a state park. Photos show the faces of men and women once imprisoned here; stories tell of inmates, guards, riots, and escape attempts. A gift shop sells souvenirs. Outside, you can explore the cellblocks, climb the main watchtower, and visit the prison graveyard. Picnic tables are available on the grounds and in a small park off Prison Hill Road.

Yuma Territorial Prison is open daily 8 a.m.-5 p.m.; admission is $3 adults, $2 ages 12-17; tel. 783-4771. Take Prison Hill Rd. off Giss Parkway. **Yuma Crossing Park** will offer historic exhibits along the river between the prison and the Yuma Quartermaster Depot.

For additional information about the history of the prison, consult *The History of Yuma and the Territorial Prison* by Robert Woznicki.

## Yuma Quartermaster Depot

Another good place to get a feel for Yuma's history is the Yuma Quartermaster Depot. The Army used the depot from 1864 to 1883, supplying military posts in the Southwest during the Indian wars. Ships carried cargo to Port Isabel, near the mouth of the Colorado River, where dockworkers transferred goods to river steamers for the trip to Yuma. Later the Customs Service took over the depot. The Signal Corps, Weather Bureau, and Bureau of Reclamation have all been based here too. Except for the stone-block reservoir, all structures were built of adobe; that was all early builders had.

Stop first at the visitor center and then begin your tour of the other buildings on the grounds. View the award-winning video and listen as costumed tour guides tell you about more than 500 years of history at the Yuma Crossing. You can visit the Commanding Officer's Quarters, built in the late 1850s and possibly the oldest Anglo house in Arizona, as well as the cookhouse, reservoir, two surviving warehouses, and the spartan quarters of the corral house. Period rooms, old photos, guns, swords, steamboat relics, and letters tell the story of these historic buildings. Many have been restored to their 1876 appearance, when the depot was at its peak. In the years after, the railroad arrived and greatly reduced waterfront business. A Southern Pacific steam locomotive and a freight wagon sit outside. You can also visit the Emigrant's Encampment and meet with people of the year 1850, dressed in period costume, as they prepare to cross the Colorado River on their way to the California goldfields.

The depot is open daily (except Thanksgiving and Christmas) 10 a.m.-5 p.m.; admission is $3 adults, $2 ages 6-17, $2.50 seniors 55 and over, $8 family pass; tel. 329-0404 or (800) 829-YUMA. It's on Fourth Ave. just south of the Colorado River. The Quartermaster Depot is operated by the Yuma Crossing

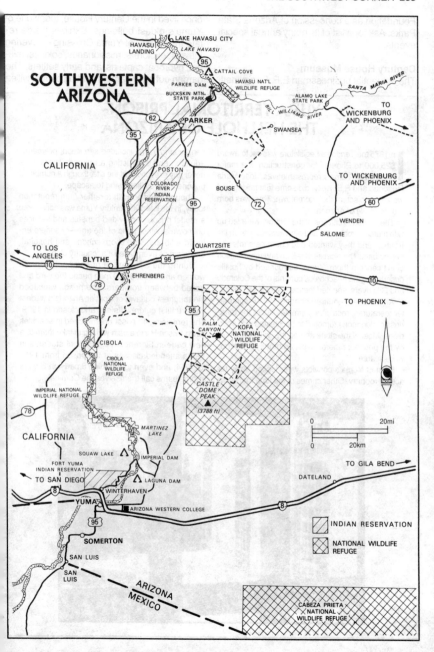

Foundation as a concession of Arizona State Parks. Ask for a list of its many annual special events.

**Century House Museum**

The influential businessman E.F. Sanguinetti once lived in the Century House, today one of Yuma's oldest buildings. Exhibits inside relate the history of Yuma Crossing—covering Indians, explorers, missionaries, soldiers, miners, riverboat captains, and early settlers. The garden out back harbors flaming bougainvillea

# YUMA TERRITORIAL PRISON~ THE HELLHOLE OF ARIZONA

In 1875 the Territorial Legislature was set to award $25,000 to Phoenix for construction of a major prison. But Yuma's representatives, Jose Maria Redondo and R.B. Kelly, did some fast talking and won the project for their hometown. Thus was born the "Hellhole of Arizona."

The righteous citizens of the territory were fed up with murders, robberies, and other lawless acts on the frontier, and they wanted bad characters interred behind bars. The niceties of reform and rehabilitation didn't concern them. Yuma, surrounded by hostile deserts and the treacherous currents of the Colorado and Gila rivers, seemed the ideal spot for a prison.

All prisoners endured searing 120° F summer temperatures; recalcitrant inmates faced the darkness of dungeons rumored to be infested with scorpions. Most of the stone and adobe walls were built by the prisoners themselves, as money and labor were scarce.

Most of Yuma's convicts were locked away for acts of robbery. Other crimes of the time that could

send you to Yuma included seduction, polygamy, adultery, and obstructing a railroad. There were never any executions at the site, though a number of prisoners were killed trying to escape.

Though saddled with a rather grim reputation today, in the late 19th century Yuma was considered a model prison. It provided benefits and services unknown at other pens of the age—prisoners enjoyed a library, workshop, school, and hospital. Some critics even called it a "country club."

During the 33 years of prison operation, 29 women and about 3,000 men paced the yard and gazed between iron bars. The prison withstood the toughest outlaws of frontier Arizona's wildest years until it outgrew its site and closed in 1909. The remaining 40 prisoners marched in shackles down Prison Hill to a train waiting to take them to a new cage in Florence. High school students in Yuma attended classes at the prison from 1910 to 1914, and even today the Yuma High School sports teams call themselves the Criminals.

and chattering parakeets, colorful parrots, and peacocks.

It's open Tues.-Sat. 10 a.m.-4 p.m. all year; free admission; tel. 782-1841. Century House is in the north part of town at 240 S. Madison Avenue. **Adobe Annex,** next to Century House, sells local crafts and offers an excellent selection of books on regional history, Indians, and gold mining. The **Garden Cafe** serves breakfast and lunch on a patio adjacent to the museum gardens.

## Quechan Indian Museum (Fort Yuma)

On the hill just across the Colorado River from Yuma, the museum building dates from 1855 and the days of Camp Yuma. Renamed Fort Yuma in 1861, the site now belongs to the Quechan Indians, who established a museum and tribal offices here. Museum exhibits illustrate the arrival of the Spanish missionary Father Francisco Garcés, the Quechan Revolt, history of Fort Yuma, and Quechan Indian life. Artifacts include clay figurines, flutes, gourd rattles, headdresses, bows and arrows, and war clubs. It's open Mon.-Fri. 8 a.m.-noon and 1-5 p.m. and Sat. 10 a.m.-4 p.m.; admission is $1, free for children under 12; tel. (619) 572-0661. The nearby St. Thomas Mission occupies the site of Concepción Mission, where Indians murdered Father Garcés in 1781. Take Indian Hill Rd. off Picacho Road.

## Yuma Fine Arts Association

The Yuma Art Center burned down and has not yet been permanently relocated. However, the Yuma Fine Arts Association has reopened with displays at 301 Main St., where you'll see contemporary work by many Arizonans including Anglo, Indian, and Hispanic artists who reflect their cultures and feelings in their paintings, prints, sculptures, and crafts. Some works are for sale. The gallery is open Tues.-Sat. 10 a.m.-5 p.m.; admission is $1 adult, 50 cents children 12 and under; tel. 783-2314.

## Arizona Western College

This community college has teamed up with Northern Arizona University to offer vocational, undergraduate, and graduate classes. Points of interest on the campus, seven miles east of town, include **Gallery Milepost Nine,** with changing art exhibits in the Fine Arts Center, open Mon.-Thurs. 9 a.m.-8 p.m., closed in summer, tel. 344-7598; and the library's **special collection** of regional books; tel. 344-7660. The college mailing address is Box 929, Yuma, AZ 85366; tel. 726-1000. From Yuma, take I-8 east to Exit 7, go north 0.4 mile, turn right, and proceed 1.7 miles.

## Saihati Camel Farm

Enjoy a close encounter with animals native to the Arabian Desert at Saihati Camel Farm. Tours feature encounters with fourteen species, including one of America's largest herds of Arabian camels, horses, oryx, African pygmy goats, Asian water buffalo, Watusi cattle, and more. Tours run at 10 a.m. and 2 p.m. Mon.-Sat. and 2 p.m. Sunday Oct.-May and 10 a.m. Mon.-Sat. June-Sept.; admission is $3 (free age three and under); from I-8, exit at 3E and go south eight miles to 16 St., then west two miles to Ave. 1E, then 500 feet north; tel. 627-2553.

# ON THE ROAD IN YUMA

## Accommodations

Yuma, midway between Phoenix and San Diego, is a convenient travelers' stop. Most of the two dozen or so motels in town lie along Business I-8 (old US 80) on 32nd St. and Fourth Avenue. Daily rates rise by as much as $10 during the popular winter and spring seasons, though the less-expensive places experience little or no seasonal increase.

Deluxe motels include **TraveLodge,** 711 E. 32nd St., tel. 726-4721 or (800) 835-1132; **Best Western Chilton Inn,** 300 E. 32nd St., tel. 344-1050 or (800) 528-1234; **Best Western Coronado,** 233 N. Fourth Ave., tel. 783-4453 or (800) 528-1234; **Best Western Innsuites Yuma,** 1450 Castle Dome Ave., off I-8 16th St. exit, tel. 783-8341 or (800) 922-2034; **Radisson Suites,** 2600 S. Fourth Ave., tel. 726-4830 or (800) 333-3333; and **Desert Grove Motel,** 3500 S. Fourth Ave., tel. 726-1400. Try also **La Fuente TraveLodge,** 1513 E. 16th St., tel. 329-1814; **Holiday Inn Express,** 3181 S. Fourth Ave., tel. 344-1420 or (800) HOLIDAY; **Rega**

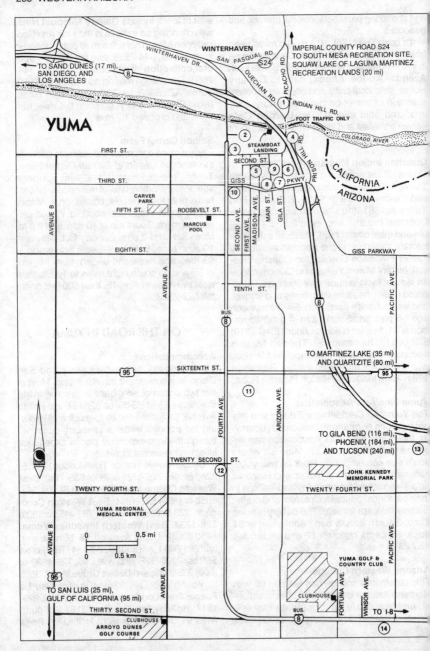

WINTERHAVEN

WINTERHAVEN DR.

SAN PASQUAL RD.

IMPERIAL COUNTY ROAD S24
TO SOUTH MESA RECREATION SITE,
SQUAW LAKE OF LAGUNA MARTINEZ
RECREATION LANDS (20 mi)

← TO SAND DUNES (17 mi),
SAN DIEGO, AND
LOS ANGELES

8

PICACHO RD.

QUECHAN RD.

S24

INDIAN HILL RD.

FOOT TRAFFIC ONLY

COLORADO RIVER

YUMA

PRISON RD.

CALIFORNIA

ARIZONA

FIRST ST.

1

2

4

STEAMBOAT
LANDING

3

SECOND ST.

GISS

5    9    6

8    7    PKWY.

THIRD ST.

CARVER PARK

FIFTH ST.

ROOSEVELT ST.

10

AVENUE B

MARCUS POOL

EIGHTH ST.

SECOND AVE.

FIRST AVE.

MADISON AVE.

MAIN ST.

GILA ST.

GISS PARKWAY

AVENUE A

TENTH ST.

BUS.
8

PACIFIC AVE.

TO MARTINEZ LAKE (35 mi)
AND QUARTZITE (80 mi)

95

SIXTEENTH ST.

95

8

MOON

11

ARIZONA AVE.

FOURTH AVE.

TO GILA BEND (116 mi),
PHOENIX (184 mi),
AND TUCSON (240 mi)

13

TWENTY SECOND ST.

12

TWENTY FOURTH ST.

TWENTY FOURTH ST.

JOHN KENNEDY
MEMORIAL PARK

YUMA REGIONAL
MEDICAL CENTER

AVENUE B

0        0.5 mi

0        0.5 km

AVENUE A

PACIFIC AVE.

YUMA GOLF &
COUNTRY CLUB

FORTUNA AVE.

CLUBHOUSE

WINSOR AVE.

TO I-8

95

TO SAN LUIS (25 mi),
GULF OF CALIFORNIA (95 mi)

THIRTY SECOND ST.

CLUBHOUSE

ARROYO DUNES
GOLF COURSE

BUS.
8

14

## YUMA

1. Quechan Indian Museum; St. Thomas Mission
2. Yuma Quartermaster Depot
3. Kofa National Wildlife Refuge office (U.S. Fish and Wildlife Service)
4. Yuma Territorial Prison
5. Century House Museum
6. Amtrak train
7. Yuma County Chamber of Commerce
8. post office branch
9. Yuma Fine Arts Association
10. public library
11. bus station
12. main post office
13. Bureau of Land Management
14. airport

**Lodge Motel,** 344 S. Fourth Ave., tel. 782-4571 or (800) 777-4571; **Royal Motor Inn,** 2941 S. Fourth Ave., tel. 344-0550 or (800) 729-0550; **Shilo Inn,** 1550 Castle Dome Ave., off I-8 16th St. exit, tel. 782-9511 or (800) 222-2244; **Trave-Lodge Fourth Avenue,** 2050 S. Fourth Ave., tel. 782-3831 or (800) 255-3050; and **Yuma Cabana,** 2151 S. Fourth Ave., tel. 783-8311 or (800) 874-0811.

For low-budget accommodations ($25-35), try **El Cortez Motel,** 124 S. First Ave., tel. 783-4456; **El Rancho Motel,** 2201 S. Fourth Ave., tel. 783-4481; **Hacienda Motel,** 2150 S. Fourth Ave., tel. 782-4316; **Motel 6,** 1640 S. Arizona Ave., tel. 782-6561, and 1445 E. 16th St., tel. 782-9521; and **Palms Inn,** 2655 S. Fourth Ave., tel. 344-0082.

### Campgrounds

The more than five dozen RV parks in and around Yuma cater mostly to retired people. Only a few parks welcome families with children, and usually only in the slow season (summer and autumn). Very few parks will consider renting tent spaces and then only off season. Ask the Yuma County Chamber of Commerce for the latest listing of RV parks.

All the following have showers. **Windhaven RV park** has tent spaces ($13.61) and RV w/hookups ($20.15) and allows extra people per space at $2 each; 6580 E. Hwy. 80; tel.

726-0284. **Lucky Park del Sur** has family spaces—when they're available—at 5790 W. Eighth St., $9.50 tent or RV w/hookups; tel. 783-7201. Those RV parks that prefer adults include **Azure Sky,** 5510 E. Hwy. 80, $19.62 RV w/hookups, tel. 726-0160; **Bonita Mesa,** 9400 N. Frontage Rd., I-8 Exit 12, $22.16 RV w/hookups, tel. 342-2999; **First Street Trailer Park,** 1850 W. First St., $13 RV w/hookups, tel. 782-0090; **Hidden Cove Trailer Park and Marina,** 2450 W. Water St., $15 RV w/hookups, tel. 783-3534; **Shangri-la,** 10498 N. Frontage Rd., I-8 Exit 12, $15.91 RV w/hookups, tel. 342-9123; and **Windhaven RV Park,** 6620 E. Hwy. 80, $20.15 RV w/hookups, tel. 726-0284.

**Dateland,** 65 miles east on I-8 (Exit 67), offers tent ($5) and RV ($12 w/hookups) camping (families welcome) and an American-Mexican cafe famed for its date milkshakes; you can buy dates, too; tel. 454-2772.

Some of the best camping lies upstream on the Colorado River. **Laguna Martinez National Recreation Area,** 20 miles north on the California side, is perfect for families and anyone seeking to enjoy desert walks, fishing, or boating. Cross the river to Winterhaven, California, then turn north on Imperial County Rd. S-24 and follow signs. The **Imperial Dam Long-term Visitor Area** includes the sites of Quail Hill, Kripple Kreek, Skunk Hollow, Beehive Mesa, and Coyote Ridge, serving self-contained vehicles only (the sites lack improvements). A $50 season pass or a $10 seven-day pass is required for any stay within the Sept. 15-April 15 season; at other times, camping is free but limited to stays of 14 days.

**South Mesa Recreation Site,** also within the Imperial Dam visitor area, offers water, restrooms, and outside showers; the same season and fee apply. **Squaw Lake Campground,** at the end of the road, offers water, restrooms, outside showers, paved parking, and two boat ramps; $8 per night year-round. An easy two-mile nature trail winds through river vegetation and desert hills from the north end of the parking lot. Contact the Bureau of Land Management Yuma District office for information on these and other recreation areas; tel. 726-6300. **Hidden Shores RV** is nearby on the Arizona side, close to Imperial Dam; tent or RV dry camping or w/hookups costs $12.73; showers available (to visitors as well), store, restaurant, and boat ramps; tel. 783-1448.

**Martinez Lake** is on the Arizona side farther upstream, about 35 miles north of Yuma; go north 24 miles on US 95, then turn left and drive 11 miles on Martinez Lake Road. **Fisher's Landing** has tent ($3 per person) and RV ($12 w/hookups) camping, a restaurant, store, and marina; tel. 783-6513. Nearby **Martinez Lake Resort** offers motel rooms (from $36.16 d), RV park ($15.50 w/hookups), restaurant, and marina with boat rentals; tel. 783-9589.

## Food

For American food, try **Brownie's Restaurant,** 1145 S. Fourth Ave., tel. 783-7911; **Chester's Chuckwagon,** 2256 S. Fourth Ave., tel. 782-4152; **Golden Corral Steak House,** 2401 S. Fourth Ave., tel. 726-4428; **Hungry Hunter Restaurant,** 2355 S. Fourth Ave., tel. 782-3637; **Shoney's,** 575 E. 16th St., tel. 329-0000; **Home Town Buffet,** 2195 S. Fourth Ave., tel. 317-1303; or **Tom Tate's Country Buffets,** 2550 S. Fourth Ave., tel. 344-2968. **Bella Vita** serves Italian cuisine at 2755 S. Fourth Ave.; tel. 344-3989.

Good places for Mexican dining include **Beto's Mexican Food,** 812 E. 21st St., tel. 782-6551; **Chretin's,** 485 S. 15th Ave., tel. 782-1291; and **El Charro,** 601 W. Eighth St., tel. 783-9790.

Dine Chinese at **Gene's,** 771 S. Fourth Ave., tel. 783-0080; **Lee's Golden Dragon,** 1314 S. Fourth Ave., tel. 783-1408; **Mandarin Palace,** 350 E. 32nd St., tel. 344-2805; or **The Panda,** 711 E. 32nd St., tel. 341-0323.

Places for pizza include **Domino's,** 741 S. Fourth Ave., tel. 782-7561, and 710 E. 32nd St., tel. 344-0555, and 1701 S. Ave. B, tel. 783-3030; **Rocky's New York Style Pizzeria,** 2601 S. Fourth Ave., tel. 344-4260; and **Village Inn Pizza Parlor,** E. 16th St., tel. 783-8353. You'll find supermarkets and many other restaurants along S. Fourth Ave. and E. 32nd St. (Business I-8).

## Entertainment

Catch movies at **Plaza Theatres,** 1560 S. Fourth Ave., tel. 782-9292; or at **Mandarin Cinemas,** 3142 S. Arizona Ave., tel. 782-7409. Enjoy live theater at **Yuma Community Theater,** 2265 E. 16 St., where four productions are given per year

—the 48 performances include 16 Sunday matinees; tel. 783-1780. For local color visit **Lute's Casino** for dominoes, pinball, and pool; a snack bar serves burgers and tacos; 221 S. Main St.; tel. 782-2192. For the latest info on dining, night spots, concerts, plays, art exhibits, sports, and other local events, see *Que Pasa,* a magazine supplement to the Thursday *Yuma Daily Sun.* Or call the Cultural Council of Yuma to learn what's happening in theater, ballet, etc.; tel. 783-2423.

## Events

Yuma offers the following annual events.

**January:** Gem and Mineral Show, All States Picnic (a big snowbird jamboree), Hospice Roping and Barbecue, and Fiddlers' Contest.

**February:** Yuma Crossing Day (pioneer crafts demonstrations, Indian dances, art exhibits, and a big-name band), Quartzsite Pow Wow, Silver Spur Rodeo and Parade, and Golden Knights Army Parachute Team.

**March:** Old Town Festival Arts and Crafts Show and Sale on Main Street Plaza, and Square and Round Dance Festival.

**April:** Yuma County Fair.

**May:** Military Appreciation Days (air show and static displays at the U.S. Marine Corps base) and Cinco de Mayo Fiesta on Main Street Plaza.

**July:** July 4th Celebration.

**October:** Kiwanis Technology Show.

**November:** Arizona City Days (celebration of Yuma's pioneer days with music, art, and special museum exhibits), horse racing (third and fourth weekends), Colorado River Balloon Festival, and Gold Rock Ranch Roundup.

**December:** AKC All Breed Dog Show, Nutcracker Ballet.

## Recreation

Jump in one of the public **swimming pools** (tel. 343-8686): **Carver,** corner Fifth St. and 13th Ave.; **Kennedy,** corner 24th St. and Kennedy Ln.; and **Marcus,** corner Fifth St. and Fifth Avenue. Play **tennis** at **Desert Sun Courts** near the Convention Center, 35th St. and Ave. A, tel. 344-3800; or **golf** on the 18-hole courses at **Arroyo Dunes,** 32nd St. and Ave. A, tel. 726-8350, **Desert Hills Municipal,** 1245 Desert Hills Dr., tel. 344-0644, and **Mesa del Sol,** 10583 Camino del Sol, tel. 342-1283.

Anglers on the Colorado River and nearby lakes catch largemouth black bass, striped bass, channel catfish, tilapia, bluegill, and crappie. Check fishing regulations with **Arizona Game and Fish,** tel. 342-0091; or **Quechan Indian Fish and Game** in California, tel. (619) 572-0544. The chamber of commerce offers fishing information.

## Services

The main **post office** is at 2222 S. Fourth Ave., tel. 783-2124. A downtown branch, 370 S. Main St., is across from the chamber of commerce. The **Yuma Regional Medical Center** occupies 2400 S. Ave. A, tel. 344-2000. **Sanborn's** offers auto insurance and information for drives into Mexico at Schuman Insurance Agency, 670 E. 32nd St. #11, tel. 726-0300. **Farm Bureau Insurance** sells policies at 1000 16th St., tel. 782-1638. **Popular Outfitters** features hiking and camping gear at 1111 S. Fourth Ave., tel. 783-8509.

## Information

The **Yuma County Chamber of Commerce** is open Mon.-Fri. 9 a.m.-5 p.m., Saturday 9 a.m.-5 p.m. and Sun. 10 a.m.-1 p.m. October-April; Box 10831, Yuma, AZ 85366-0831; tel. 782-0071/2567. The office is downtown at the corner of Giss Parkway and Main St.; take I-8 Exit 1.

The **Kofa National Wildlife Refuge** office of the U.S. Fish and Wildlife Service has information about the Kofa backcountry; it's open Mon.-Fri. 8 a.m.-noon and 1-5 p.m.; downtown near the river at 356 W. First Street (Box 6290, Yuma, AZ 85366); tel. 783-7861. Staff at the **Bureau of Land Management**'s Yuma District office can advise on camping in various areas of the region; it's open Mon.-Fri. 7:45 a.m.-4:30 p.m.; 2555 E. Gila Ridge Rd., Yuma, AZ 85365; tel. 726-6300. This is a new address, and this phone number is subject to change.

**Arizona Game and Fish** offers information, licenses, and watercraft registration at 9140 E. County $10^{1}/_{2}$ St. (Yuma, AZ 85365); it's open Mon.-Fri. 8 a.m.-5 p.m.; tel. 342-0091. The large and attractive **Yuma Library** is at 350 S. Third Ave.; open Mon.-Thurs. 9 a.m.-9 p.m., Friday and Saturday 9 a.m.-5 p.m.; tel. 782-1871 or 782-5697. Books of regional interest are available at **Hastings,** 2838 S. Fourth Ave.; tel. 344-4614.

## Tours

Hop on the **Yuma Valley Railway** for a short excursion along a levee beside the Colorado River. From October to May, a 1941 diesel locomotive pulls a 1922 Pullman coach. The two-hour roundtrip covers 22 miles; tickets cost $9 adults, $8 ages 55 and over, and $5 ages 4-16. Steak dinner and picnic rides are sometimes offered; call for information; tel. 783-3456. To reach the starting point, head west six miles on Eighth St. from Fourth Avenue.

Skim across the Colorado River by jetboat with **Yuma River Tours,** which offers three-hour tours ($25 including lunch or dinner) or full-day cruises ($49 including lunch, half price children 12 and under). Jeep tours may be available. You can combine canoe rides with jetboat tours. Jetboat trips are scheduled year-round. The office is in the Durashield Building at 1920 Arizona Ave., between 18th and 19th Streets; tel. 783-4400.

The **Yuma County Chamber of Commerce** organizes tours to local points of interest during the winter; participants provide their own transportation. Chamber staff can also advise on tour operators in the area; tel. 782-2567.

## Transport

For a taxi call **Yellow Taxi,** tel. 783-4444, or **Yuma City Cab,** tel. 782-0111. Rent cars from **Avis,** airport, tel. 726-5737; **Budget,** airport, tel. 344-1822; **Hertz,** airport, tel. 726-5160; or **Ugly Duckling,** 1701 S. First Ave., tel. 783-7874.

**Greyhound** travels three times a day to Phoenix ($30 one-way), Tucson ($45), Los Angeles ($33), and San Diego ($29). The bus station is open weekdays 9 a.m.-6:30 p.m. and weekends 9 a.m.-2 p.m. and 5-5:30 p.m.; tel. 783-4403; at 170 E. 17th Place, off 16th St. behind Staples, two blocks east of Fourth Avenue.

**Amtrak** trains run three times a week to Phoenix ($44 one-way), Los Angeles ($61), and New Orleans ($222) with roundtrip discounts available. The depot is at 281 Gila St.; tel. (800) 872-7245.

**Yuma International Airport** is conveniently located on the south side of town, off 32nd Street. The airport includes a travel agency, restaurant, and car rentals. **SkyWest,** tel. (800) 453-9417, and **America West,** tel. (800) 247-

5692, offer frequent service every day to Phoenix and Los Angeles with onward connections. Fares vary widely depending on seat availability and competition.

## VICINITY OF YUMA

### San Luis (Mexico)

San Luis shopping attracts many visitors, who simply park on the Arizona side and walk across the border. More than a dozen shops lie within a few blocks of the crossing. Many local craftspeople work with leather; you can see them turning out belts, bags, and saddles in some shops. Other crafts come from all over Mexico—including clothing, blankets, pottery, carved onyx chess sets, glassware, and musical instruments.

San Luis Rio Colorado was founded by farmers in 1906. The current population of about 150,000 makes it the largest city along the Arizona-Mexico border. A spacious park with welcome greenery and flowers marks the downtown area.

The nearby bus station, corner of Av. Juárez and Calle Quinta, serves three bus lines running to places such as Tijuana, Mexicali, Ensenada, San Felipe, Santa Rosalía, Hermosillo, Mazatlán, Guadalajara, and Mexico City. White sandy beaches, fishing, and swimming on the Gulf of California draw sun lovers. El Golfo de Santa Clara, a small fishing village 70 miles south, and the larger town of San Felipe 125 miles southwest, are both approached by paved roads.

U.S. citizens may visit San Luis, El Golfo, San Felipe, and Mexicali without formalities for as long as 72 hours. You need a tourist card for longer stays or more distant destinations; obtain cards at the border or from a Mexican consulate or Mexican tourist office. Cards are free, but you need to show proof of citizenship—passport, birth or naturalization certificate, voting registration card, or notarized affidavit of citizenship. You need a permit for your vehicle unless you're headed for border areas or Baja California; obtain at the border by showing proof of ownership. You must also buy Mexican insurance beforehand.

Visitors from countries who need a U.S. visa can usually make a border-town visit without formalities, but check first with U.S. Immigration. For a longer visit, a multiple-entry or new visa will likely be required to return to the United States. Hermosillo and other major Mexican cities have U.S. consulates.

### Sand Dunes

Though not typical of the Sonoran Desert, barren sand dunes lie about 17 miles west of Yuma on I-8. Movie producers have used this "Great American Sahara" for films ranging from *Beau Geste* to *Star Wars*. People at the Yuma Chamber of Commerce can tell you about recent or current filming.

Dune-buggy drivers like to play here too. A rest area off I-8 in the middle of the dunes provides a place to stop and park. From 1915 to

*Palm Canyon*

1926, motorists crossed the dunes on a road made of wooden planks. Remnants of this road are still visible.

## Cabeza Prieta National Wildlife Refuge

These 860,000 acres of desert valleys and small rocky ranges remain as wild as ever. There are no paved roads, so 4WD vehicles are required. Here, there's just the desert: very hot in summer, wildflower-beautiful in spring. Endangered Sonoran pronghorn, desert mule deer, and desert bighorn live here. Because the military sometimes uses the skies for gunnery and missile tests, be sure to get a permit before entering. Obtain permits and information from the Refuge Visitor Center in Ajo.

## Imperial National Wildlife Refuge

Plants and animals of the Colorado River receive protection within this long, narrow refuge. Birds are quite conspicuous, especially in spring and autumn. The refuge includes the river, backwater lakes, ponds, marshland, river-bottom land, and desert. Fishing, canoeing, and birding are popular activities, though some areas are signed against entry. No camping is permitted in the refuge, but waterskiers can use part of it. Martinez Lake Resort and Fisher's Landing offer camping, a motel, restaurants, and marinas just downstream. For a bird list and more info on Imperial, visit the refuge headquarters on the north side of Martinez Lake or write Box 72217, Martinez Lake, AZ 85365; tel. 783-3371. The refuge is about 40 miles north of Yuma; head north on US 95, then turn left and drive 15 miles on Martinez Lake Road.

## Cibola National Wildlife Refuge

Cibola lies along the Colorado River just upstream from Imperial Refuge. Habitats and wildlife are similar to those of Imperial. Canada geese and sandhill cranes winter here. You're welcome to hike, boat, or fish, but camping is prohibited. For map and info, write Box AP, Blythe, CA 92225; tel. (602) 857-3253. Access to Cibola is best accomplished from the California side, off CA 78. You can reach the refuge headquarters in Arizona by taking the I-10 Neighbours Blvd. Exit (two miles west of Blythe, Cali-fornia), then proceeding south 14 miles on Neighbours Blvd. to Farmers Bridge over the Colorado River. It's 3.5 miles farther to the headquarters.

## Kofa National Wildlife Refuge

Desert critters such as coyote, cottontail, bobcat, fox, desert mule deer, and desert bighorn sheep live in the dry, rugged Castle Dome and Kofa mountain ranges. Gambel's quail scurry into the brush, while falcons and golden eagles soar above. Rare stands of native palm grow in Palm Canyon.

Gold, discovered in 1896, led to development of the King of Arizona Mine, from which the Kofa Mountains took their name. Some mining claims remain today; some may be signed against trespassers. Several roads penetrate the scenic mountains and canyons, but these routes tend to be rough, suited best to 4WD vehicles.

Hikers can explore this rugged country more extensively. The refuge covers 665,400 acres of wilderness, of which 82% is officially designated as wilderness. The place is totally lacking in visitor facilities; you must carry water and all supplies. A short hike up **Palm Canyon** reveals tall California fan palms *(Washingtonia filifera)* tucked into tiny side canyons.

To reach the trailhead, go north 62 miles on US 95 from Yuma (or south 18 miles from Quartzsite) and turn east onto Palm Canyon Rd. between Mileposts 85 and 86. The road is dirt but passable. At road's end, nine miles farther on, follow the trail into Palm Canyon for about a half mile. Use the trail that passes by the wooden brochure dispenser. You'll see towering palms in clefts on the north side of the main canyon. Take care if climbing up to the palms; you'll cross sheer cliffs and contend with loose rock.

The trail pretty much ends here, though it's possible to rock-scramble another half mile up the main canyon to a large palmless natural amphitheater. Allow one hour from the trailhead to the palms and back, or three hours to go all the way to the amphitheater and back. Other areas of the Kofas are better for long hikes; ask a refuge employee for suggestions. For info on the Kofa Refuge, visit the Kofa National Wildlife Refuge office in Yuma at 356 W. First St. or write Box 6290, Yuma, AZ 85366; tel. 783-7861.

# SOUTH-CENTRAL ARIZONA

Nowhere else in Arizona do you find such a contrast between city and wilderness as in the south-central part of the state. More than half the state's population lives in the urban sprawl surrounding Phoenix in the Valley of the Sun. Yet just beyond its borders you'll find craggy mountains, vast woodlands, and seemingly endless desert. People tend to keep close to the rivers, which provide water to nourish crops and cities. It was a different kind of thirst—for gold and silver—that lured many pioneers into the rugged mountains of south-central Arizona. Most of the towns they founded have faded into memory; only those communities with copper, tourists, or other resources survive.

### The Land
None of the mountains in this region achieve great height; most summit elevations range from 3,000 to 8,000 feet. What they lack in size they possess in challenging terrain—off-trail travel can be very difficult. The major ranges, all with good hiking and a chance to experience wilderness, lie north and east of Phoenix. These in-

clude the Bradshaw, Mazatzal, Sierra Ancha, Superstition, and Pinal Mountains. South and west from Phoenix you'll find a very different sort of country—the often harsh desert most people associate with Arizona, plains of rock and sand with small craggy ranges breaking through here and there. Springs and streams are nearly nonexistent; only hardy desert plants and wildlife survive.

### Climate
Because most of south-central Arizona is under 4,500 feet, temperatures stay on the warm side. This is great in winter—you'll enjoy springlike weather while people in the north are digging out from snowstorms. Spring and autumn here warm up just enough; the high country is very pleasant then, and it's a good time to be outdoors. In summer, though, the sun turns the desert valleys into a giant oven—highs over 100° F are common. Drink plenty of liquids and wear a hat when venturing out into the summer heat.

Annual rainfall varies from about five inches in the lowest desert to more than 20 inches in the highest mountains. Most moisture arrives in two seasons—as gentle rain between December and March, and as spectacular thunderstorms during July and August. The summer storms kick up huge clouds of dust, cause flash floods, and start lightning-ignited brush fires.

## Flora and Fauna

Cacti feel right at home across much of the region. Most common are prickly pear, cholla, barrel cactus, and giant saguaro. Small plants and low trees also thrive. Rainfall prompts spectacular floral displays in early spring and sometimes in summer. Learn more about desert flora at the Desert Botanical Garden in Phoenix and the Boyce Thompson Southwestern Arboretum near Superior.

Most animals hole up during the day, though lizards seem to enjoy sitting on hot rocks. In the larger mountain ranges you might meet mountain lion, black bear, bighorn sheep, javelina,

pronghorn, or deer. Always watch where you put hands and feet in the desert so you don't disturb rattlesnakes, Gila monsters, scorpions, or poisonous spiders.

## Getting There and Around

The Phoenix Sky Harbor Airport has by far the best connections in Arizona. You also have a good choice of rental cars and long-distance bus connections from the city. Amtrak offers train service across southern Arizona, stopping at Yuma, Phoenix, Casa Grande, Tucson, and Benson, three times a week in each direction.

# INDIANS

## Hohokam

Nomadic groups roamed across Arizona in seasonal cycles for thousands of years before learning to cultivate the land. Around 200-300 B.C.,

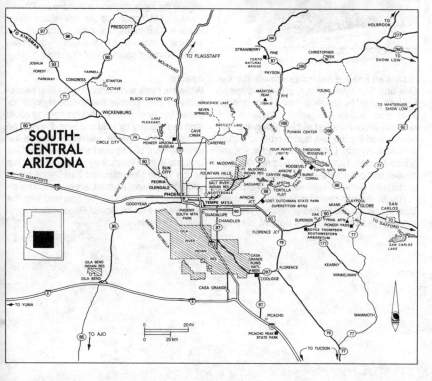

CARTER COLLECTION, NATIONAL ARCHIVES

*Pima woman, late 1800s*

Indians we know as the Hohokam settled in the Gila and Salt river valleys, growing crops in fields irrigated by canals or runoff from storms. They also continued to gather wild plants and hunt for game. For most of their history the Hohokam lived in pithouses built of brush and mud over shallow pits. Later, some lived in square adobe houses. Larger towns had hundreds of houses and ball courts—large walled fields likely made for games played with rubber balls.

Hardy, drought-resistant corn was the main food, supplemented by beans, squash, and wild foods. The Hohokam made pottery, clay fig-urines, stone bowls, shell jewelry, paint palettes, and cotton cloth. Industrious agriculturalists, the Hohokam dug more than 300 miles of irrigation canals in the Salt River Valley alone. The larger canals were more than 15 feet wide and 10 feet deep. Where the Hohokam came from and where they went remain mysteries; they disappeared around A.D. 1450.

## Pima and Maricopa

The Pima Indians followed the Hohokam, with whom they had much in common; the two groups may have been related. Living along the valleys of the Gila and Salt rivers, the Pima used the farming methods of their predecessors but suffered greatly when white people built dams upstream early in this century. Today the Pima farm, raise cattle, work in small industries, and create traditional handicrafts.

Maricopa Indians, who originally lived along the Colorado River, migrated up the Gila River to escape the more aggressive Mohave and Yuma. Pima and Maricopa Indians now share reservations. The tribes maintain a museum, gift shop, and restaurant on the Gila River Reservation 30 miles southeast of Phoenix.

## Apache

While the Pima and Maricopa got along peacefully with white people, the Apache strongly opposed the newcomers. Though nothing could stop men hungry for gold and land, the Apache certainly tried. Apache resistance slowed the development of Arizona towns and industries until late in the 19th century. Today Apache live on the White Mountain and San Carlos reservations in eastern Arizona, several small reservations in north-central Arizona, and with the Mohave on Fort McDowell Reservation northeast of Phoenix.

# PHOENIX

Hub of the sprawling Valley of the Sun, Phoenix has a larger population, bigger businesses, and greater clout than any other city in Arizona. Here state laws are made and big corporate deals signed. The Phoenix area is also a cultural and sports center. A Western sense of informality and leisure keeps the pace slow, and the relaxed style is quickly picked up by newcomers. And there have been a lot of them—Phoenix is the eighth-largest city in the country and one of the fastest growing. The city's population is more than a million, with more than two million when the surrounding cities are added. Many retired people live in the Valley of the Sun, and whole towns are planned around them.

Though you'll frequently hear people call the Phoenix area the Valley of the Sun, you'll rarely see the name on a map. Still, it accurately reflects the Valley's pleasant winters and the 300 days of sunshine per average year.

You'll find dozens of museums in the Valley: historical, archaeological, religious, art, and unusual. Foreign visitors are amused to discover that Arizonans regard early 20th-century buildings as very old. The Heard Museum ranks as the best local museum; it's a good choice if you have time to see only one Phoenix museum. Because the area is so large, you'll need a city map to find your way around; buy one from a convenience store or service station.

## The Mountains

Desert mountains form the skyline of the Valley. Some, like Squaw Peak, poke up in the middle of Phoenix, rewarding hikers with a panorama of the city. Camelback Mountain is a Phoenix landmark northeast of downtown. The bulky South Mountains offer nearly 15,000 acres of hiking, horseback riding, and picnicking—the world's largest city park. More remote are the Sierra Estrellas to the southwest and the White Tank Mountains to the west. The highest peaks in the area lie northeast in the Mazatzals, crowned by 7,894-foot Mazatzal Peak.

The most famous range of all has to be the Superstitions to the east. Stories of Jacob Waltz's lost gold mine, which may exist somewhere in these jagged mountains, still excite the imagination.

## Climate

Phoenix lies at an elevation of roughly 1,100 feet in the desert, where you can expect average summer highs to go over 100° F, dropping to the 70s or 80s at night. The Valley comes into its own from October to May, when flocks of snowbirds migrate from the northern states and provinces. Even in midwinter, daytime temperatures range in the 60s or low 70s. You won't need a snow shovel. Average rainfall is only 7.45 inches a year.

# HISTORY

## Why Phoenix?

It's the water. Hohokam Indians tamed the Salt River as early as 300 B.C., channeling its waters through intricate networks of canals to fields of beans, corn, squash, and cotton. At their peak, around A.D. 1100, the Hohokam settlements contained a population of between 50,000 and 100,000. The Hohokam culture may have been the most sophisticated ever developed north of Mexico. Hohokam cities featured multistory adobe buildings and ball courts; the people introduced cotton and weaving to the Southwest. For at least 1,700 years the Hohokam tilled the soil until their mysterious disappearance about A.D. 1450. You can see some of their ruins, canals, and artifacts at Pueblo Grande Museum.

The Pima Indians, who later settled here, referred to their predecessors as Hohokam, meaning "all used up" or "departed." American pioneers discovered the canal system in the 1860s and soon put it back to work irrigating their farms.

## Americans Arrive

Spanish and early American explorers overlooked the area. It wasn't until after the Civil War that stories of gold in Prescott and other areas of central Arizona attracted streams of fortune hunters into this wild land. Pinal and Tonto Apache continued to discourage outsiders, but in September 1865 the Army arrived to build Camp McDowell. Ranching and businesses soon followed.

It was Jack Swilling, a former Confederate soldier-turned-prospector, who first took advantage of the Valley's farming potential. In 1867 he formed a company with $400, eight mules, and 16 unemployed miners to dig out the Hohokam canals. By the summer of 1868 he harvested his first crops of wheat and barley. Swilling's success attracted 30 more farmers the following year; soon rose the beginnings of a town.

Darrel Duppa, one of the early settlers, predicted a new city would rise from the ruins of the Hohokam civilization, just as the mythical phoenix rose from its own ashes. Surveyors laid out the new town in 1870, marking off lots selling for $20-140 apiece. Wood was scarce in early Phoenix, so adobe was used for building. The results looked, according to some accounts, much like an ancient Hohokam village.

## Phoenix Comes of Age

With increasing prosperity and a nearby railroad line, residents built ornate Victorian houses, planted trees, put in sidewalks, and opened an icehouse. Soon Phoenix resembled a town transplanted from the Midwest.

By 1889 Phoenix had enough energy and political muscle to wrest the state capital from Prescott. Not even 20 years old, Phoenix had established itself as the business, political, and agricultural center of the territory. Roosevelt Dam, dedicated by Theodore Roosevelt in 1911, ensured water for continued growth. Easterners sought out the glamorous West, now that it was safe, flocking to dude ranches. There they could dress like cowboys, ride the range, and eat mesquite-grilled steaks.

World War II brought new industry and an increased military presence. Growth has been frantic ever since, helped by the development of air-conditioning, which makes the desert summer bearable. Though major manufacturing and service industries now dominate the Phoenix economy, agriculture is still important. Area farmers raise crops of citrus, cotton, melons, sugar beets, and vegetables.

## GETTING AROUND

Downtown Phoenix is the heart of the Valley. Here you'll find the State Capitol, Phoenix Civic Center, Heritage Square, and many offices. Streets are named for U.S. presidents—Van Buren, Monroe, Adams, Washington, Jefferson. A newer downtown, or "midtown," lies one mile north on Central Avenue. Along this strip you'll find the main library, Art Museum, Little Theatre, Heard Museum, and still more office buildings. Central Avenue, which runs north-south, connects and neatly divides both downtown and midtown. North-south roads west of Central are called Avenues, those east are Streets.

**Phoenix Transit** (tel. 253-5000) will get you around the Valley with an extensive and low-cost bus service. **Downtown Area Shuttle (DASH)** (also at 253-5000) will get you around downtown for pennies. It's best, however, if you're not in much of a hurry. A little planning and phone-checking will save a lot of time, as distances can be great and traffic slow. Despite some new freeways, traffic gets very thick during rush hour; there's certainly no "rush" about it. Smoke from industry and the many cars has created a serious air pollution problem, something not historically associated with the blue skies of Arizona.

## DOWNTOWN PHOENIX

### Arizona State Capitol

The old state capitol, with its shiny copper dome, was completed in 1900, some 12 years before statehood. The Arizona Legislature outgrew this structure in 1960, moving into new quarters just behind it. The old capitol is now a museum, carefully restored to look as it did in 1912, when Arizona became a state. You'll see a lifelike statue of then-governor George W.P. Hunt sitting behind his desk. The Senate and House chambers and other rooms are full of Arizona historical photos, tales of frontier days, a silver service set from the battleship USS *Arizona*, a scale model of the same ship, and other memorabilia.

Guided tours leave at 10 a.m. and 2 p.m., or

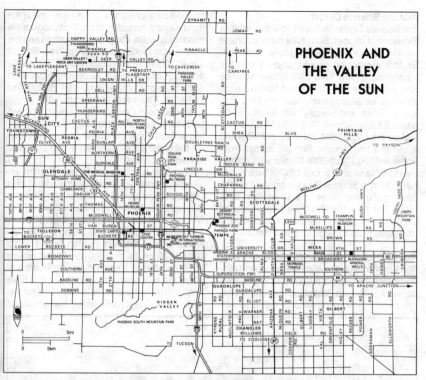

## PHOENIX AND THE VALLEY OF THE SUN

you can take a self-guided tour. Groups of 12 or more must schedule tours in advance. To dig deeper into the state's past, drop into the research library, Room 300. A gift shop is on the first floor. The Capitol is open Mon.-Fri. 8 a.m.-5 p.m.; free; tel. 542-4675. It's at 1700 W. Washington, with free parking across the street in front in Wesley Bolin Memorial Plaza; turn in from Adams Street.

### Arizona Hall of Fame

Historic exhibits in a classic-eclectic-style building honor those who've made outstanding contributions to the state. It opened as Phoenix's Carnegie Public Library in 1908. Hours are Mon.-Fri. 8 a.m.-5 p.m.; free; tel. 255-2110. It's downtown at 1101 W. Washington.

### Phoenix Museum of History

This museum features early Arizona history.

Displayed articles represent important milestones in the development of early Phoenix. They include surveying equipment, the first local printing press, an ostrich egg from the old ostrich farm near Phoenix, tools used to build the old state capitol, a collection of firearms, a "lunger tent" used by tuberculosis patients, an 1883 steam engine that powered one of the first high-wheeled motorcycles, a steam locomotive from early mining operations, an early general store exhibit, and a reconstruction of an 1890s seamstress' home. Visitors can also enjoy interactive displays.

The museum and gift shop are open Mon.-Sat. 10 a.m.-5 p.m. and Sunday noon-5 p.m.; admission is $5 adults, $3.50 seniors (65 and older), $2.50 ages 6-12, and free for children ages six and younger. The museum is in Heritage and Science Park at 105 N. 5th St.; tel. 253-2734.

## Arizona Science Center

The Science Center features interactive exhibits for people of all ages. Build giant bubbles, create weather phenomena, touch a snake, and more. Explore exhibits on energy, physics, and the human body and take part in live science demonstrations. The Center also features a gift shop and ice cream parlor. Hours are Mon.-Sat. 9 a.m.- 5 p.m. and Sunday noon-5 p.m.; $4.50 adults, $3.50 children 4-12, and $3.50 seniors 65 and over; tel. 256-9388. It's at the corner of 147 E. Adams and Second Streets, across from Phoenix Civic Plaza. The Center was scheduled to close in early to mid-1997 (it's moving to Heritage and Science Park) to prepare for the opening of a new state-of-the-art facility in early 1997. The new 120,000-square-foot Science Center will contain hundreds of new exhibits, a planetarium, and a large screen theater.

## Rosson House/Heritage and Science Park

The Victorian-style Rosson House, built in 1895, dominates the block of historic buildings known as Heritage Square. Meticulous restoration has returned the Rosson House to its original turn-of-

the-century appearance, when it was one of the most elegant houses in town. You can tour the interior and learn about its construction and the people who lived here; it's open Wed.-Sat. 10 a.m.-3:30 p.m. and Sunday noon-3:30 p.m.; $3 adults, $1 children 6-12, $2 seniors. Buy tickets at the Burgess Carriage House; tel. 262-5070 or 262-5071. Tours start at the front gate.

The Burgess Carriage House next door was built in a colonial Williamsburg style rarely seen this far west. Originally built at Second and Taylor, this home is the first of two structures moved to Heritage Square.

The other buildings on Heritage Square are also representative of early Phoenix. The Duplex (1923) is now used for offices; the Stevens House (1901) displays the Arizona Doll and Toy Museum (separate admission charge: $2 adult, $1 child; tel. 253-9337); the Stevens-Haustgen House (1901) displays exhibits from Pueblo Grande Museum; the Bouvier-Teeter House (1899) is now the Teeter House Tea Room and offers tea and lunch (tel. 252-4682); the Silva House (1900) displays Salt River Project exhibits; and a second Carriage House (about

*downtown Phoenix*

1900) now houses Carriage House Bakery and Deli, offering sandwiches, soups, salads, and pastries daily. The Lath Pavilion dates from 1980 but is typical of early Phoenix architecture. New buildings are being added to the collection including Thomas House and Baird Machine Shop, both from the early 1900s.

Heritage Square is open Tues.-Sat. 10 a.m.-4 p.m. and Sunday noon-4 p.m. (call for summer hours); closed August. The square is at Sixth and Monroe Streets, one block east of Civic Plaza.

### Arizona Mining and Mineral Museum

Many Arizona pioneers came in search of gold, silver, or copper. In this museum you'll see examples of these and many other minerals. Most eye-catching are the beautiful specimens of copper ore—azurite, malachite, chrysocolla, cuprite, chalcanthite, and turquoise. Old mining tools, lamps, assay kits, photos, and models reveal how miners worked. Lapidary exhibits display the art of gem cutting and polishing.

The museum staff can tell you of upcoming rock and mineral shows—most held during the winter—and put you in touch with local rock shops and clubs. A gift shop sells specimens, gold pans, handcrafted jewelry, and books. Hours are Mon.-Fri. 8 a.m.-5 p.m. and Saturday 1-5 p.m.; closed state holidays; free; tel. 255-3791. The museum sits on the northwest corner of 1502 W. Washington St. and 15th Ave.; look for parking on the north side.

# CENTRAL AVENUE CORRIDOR

### Phoenix Art Museum

A varied collection of more than 13,000 works of art spans the Renaissance to the Contemporary period. Particularly strong are the exhibits of 18th-century French painting and the Asian, Contemporary, Latin American, and Western Art collections. The famous Thorne Miniature Rooms document historic interiors of Europe and America.

The museum schedules half-hour gallery talks at 12:15 p.m. Tours of the permanent collection take place Tues.-Sun. at 1 p.m. and special exhibition tours take place Tues.-Sun. at 2 p.m. and Wednesday at 6 p.m. There is an exten-sive on-site reference library; you'll find art souvenirs just inside the entrance to the museum store. Hours are Tues.-Sat. 10 a.m.-5 p.m. (till 9 p.m. on Wednesday) and Sunday noon-5 p.m.; $4 adults, $1.50 students six and over, $3 seniors 65 and up; tel. 257-1222 (recorded information) or 257-1880. It's at 1625 N. Central Ave. at McDowell.

### Heard Museum

The Heard features the best exhibits on Southwest Indians you're likely to see anywhere. The collection is large enough to provide a good overview of regional Indian cultures but small enough so it won't overwhelm you. Native Americans talk about their culture in *Our Voices Our Land,* an audiovisual program with beautiful photography and native music. See exhibits of the Southwest's land and people from prehistoric times to the present. Clothing, tools, weapons, and even a Navajo hogan all demonstrate the resourceful nature of the tribes. Large displays feature superb Indian jewelry, mostly from Navajo, Hopi, and Zuni craftspeople. A kachina collection from the Hopi and Zuni tribes fills an entire room. The Heard Museum also features large collections of Southwest pottery, weavings, basketry, and paintings.

The Gallery of Indian Art is dedicated to the presentation of contemporary Native American artwork. Five other galleries feature changing shows. For deeper research, you can visit the extensive library. The museum's sizable shop sells authentic Indian arts and crafts and books on Native American cultures. It's open Mon.-Sat. 9:30 a.m.-5 p.m. (till 9 p.m. on Wednesday) and Sunday noon-5 p.m., closed major holidays; $5 adults, $3 ages 13-18, $4 seniors 65 and up and students, $2 ages 4-12, free Wednesday 5-9 p.m.; tel. 252-8848 (recording) or 252-8840. The museum is housed in a Spanish colonial-style building at 22 E. Monte Vista Rd., three blocks north on Central Ave. from McDowell, then a half block east on Monte Vista.

### Telephone Pioneer Museum

Interactive displays trace the development of telecommunications from the 1870s to the present; it's open 8 a.m.-5 p.m. Mon.-Fri.; free. The museum is at 20 E. Thomas Rd. and Second Street, one block east from Central; tel. 630-2060.

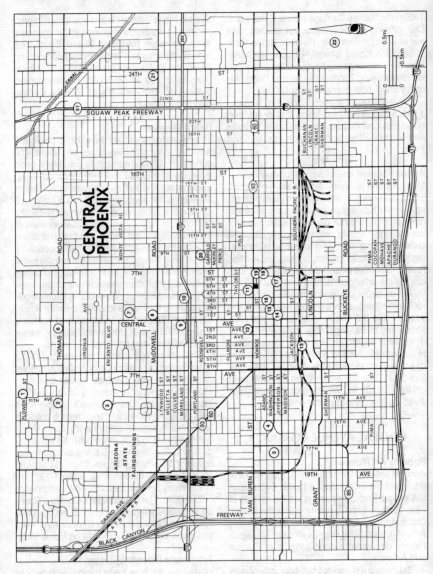

# CENTRAL PHOENIX

1. Plotkin Judaica Museum
2. Phoenix College Theatre
3. Encanto Park Bandshell
4. Arizona Mining and Mineral Museum
5. Arizona State Capitol
6. Telephone Pioneer Museum
7. Heard Museum
8. Phoenix Art Museum; Phoenix Little Theatre
9. Deck Park; main public library; Ellis-Shackelford House
10. Phoenix Performing Arts Theatre
11. Visitors Bureau (Phoenix and Valley of the Sun)
12. YMCA
13. Amtrak
14. Phoenix Transit (local bus)
15. Arizona Science Center (until 1997)
16. Symphony Hall
17. Greyhound Bus
18. Rosson House/Heritage & Science Park
19. Mercado; Museo Chicano
20. youth hostel
21. Tonto National Forest (main office)
22. Sky Harbor Airport

# NORTH PHOENIX

## Deer Valley Rock Art Center

More than 1,500 examples of Native American petroglyphs can be viewed in their original site while walking along a quarter mile paved trail. First, stop at the museum and study the interpretive displays to gain an appreciation for the art. These pictures are believed to have been carved over several periods from about 5000 B.C.-1400 A.D. Some are so old that the figures have almost been covered again with the desert varnish from which they were originally chipped. To reach the Deer Valley Rock Art Center, take the I-17 Deer Valley Rd. exit and head west. Within two miles the road ends in the 47-acre Rock Art grounds; the center is open Tues.-Fri. 9 a.m.- 2 p.m., Saturday 9 a.m.-5 p.m., and Sunday noon-5 p.m., with reduced summer hours; admission is adults $3, seniors and students (with I.D.) $2, child (ages 6-12) $1; tel. 582-8007.

## Plotkin Judaica Museum

Jewish ceremonies and religious holidays are celebrated at Temple Beth Israel's Museum, which displays many ancient artifacts from the Holy Land. Open Tues.-Thurs. 10 a.m.-3 p.m. and Sunday noon-3 p.m.; closed in summer; free; tel. 264-4428. It's at 3310 N. 10th Ave.; approach from Osborn Rd. off either Seventh or 19th Avenues.

## The Medical Museum

Displays at Phoenix Baptist Hospital and Medical Center feature antique medical and pharmaceutical artifacts from the early 1800s to more modern times including rare drug jars, doctors' medical bags, and quack medicine items. Displays are in the lobby and on each floor of the hospital. The hospital is at 6025 N. 20th Ave. at the northwest corner of Bethany Home Rd. and 19th Ave.; it's open 9 a.m.-9 p.m. daily; free; tel. 249-0212.

## Cave Creek Museum

This history collection features prehistoric Indian artifacts and mining and ranching displays. The museum is open Wed.-Sun. 1-4:30 p.m.; closed June 1 to early October and on major holidays; free; tel. 488-2764 or 488-3183. Cave Creek lies in the foothills about 30 miles north of downtown Phoenix. Drive north on Cave Creek Rd. or head east from I-17 on AZ 74 (Exit 223). Turn south on Basin Rd. to Skyline Drive.

## Pioneer Arizona Living History Museum

The frontier comes back to life here. You'll see how residents of the territory lived from the mid-1800s to statehood in 1912. Walk around to view historic exhibits and craftspeople at work. Many of the 20 or so buildings are authentic, brought here from other sites. The nearly complete little town features a school, church, sheriff's office, bank, blacksmith shop, carpenter shop, opera house, cabins, and houses—including the John Sears house, believed to be the first frame house in Phoenix.

This museum emphasizes historical accuracy, setting it apart from those "Western villages" based more on Hollywood fiction than fact. Mountain men, cavalry, gunfighters, and special exhibits enliven the community on the weekend nearest its birthday (February 14). You can usually view a melodrama or other production in the opera house; call for times. Pioneer Arizona is open Wed.-Sun. 9 a.m.-5 p.m. Oct. 1-May 31; closed in summer; $5.75 adults, $5.25 students and seniors (60 and over), $4 children 4-12; tel. 993-0212. It's set among rocky desert foothills about 30 miles north of downtown Phoenix. Take I-17 north to Pioneer Rd. (Exit 225) and follow signs.

## WEST PHOENIX

### Wildlife World Zoo

This collection of exotic wildlife began in 1974 as a breeding farm for rare and endangered species; it opened to the public 10 years later. Here you'll meet the patas monkey, fastest of all primates, which can run dog-like across the ground at 35 miles per hour. Larger animals include the scimitar-horned oryx, dama gazelle, addax (an antelope of the Sahara Desert), rhino, tapir, zebra, camel, kangaroo, and white tiger. The zoo's bird collection is quite impressive—pheasants, toucans, cockatoos, macaws, curassows, ostriches (all five of the world's species), and some birds displayed nowhere else in the country. A large, walk-in aviary contains Eyton's tree ducks of Australia, black-necked stilts of North America, and other unusual birds.

The zoo is open daily 9 a.m.-5 p.m.; $6.75 adults, $4 children 3-12; tel. 935-WILD. It lies about 18 miles west of I-17 on Northern Ave., three miles west of Litchfield Rd., just past Luke Air Force Base.

### Sun Cities Art Museum

The gallery features both local and visiting exhibitions year-round Tuesday 10 a.m.-6 p.m., Wed.-Sat. 10 a.m.-4 p.m., and Sunday 1-4 p.m.; $3 adult, $2 senior, $1 student; tel. 972-0635. You'll find it on the north side of Bell Rd. between Sun City and Sun City West at 17425 N. 115th Ave., northwest of Phoenix.

## SOUTH PHOENIX

### Mystery Castle

Boyce Luther Gulley always dreamed of building his own castle; one fine day in 1927 he followed

*Mystery Castle*

his dream, leaving his wife and daughter and disappearing into the mist. His whereabouts and his castle remained unknown until after his death in 1945. His daughter, Mary Lou Gulley, now lives in the Gulley castle, leading tours through the imaginative rooms. Everything from Stutz-Bearcat wheels to discarded bricks went into this strange mixture of American West and scrapyard. The tour is short—about 25 minutes—but anyone who's ever dreamed of owning a castle should enjoy it.

The castle is open Tues.-Sun. 11 a.m.-4 p.m. Oct.-June; $3 adults, $1.50 children 5-15; tel. 268-1581. Mystery Castle lies seven miles south of downtown Phoenix near the entrance to South Mountain Park. Drive south on Central Ave. two miles south of Baseline Rd., then east eight blocks on Mineral Road. Turn left at the sign.

## EAST PHOENIX

### Pueblo Grande Museum and Cultural Park

Exhibits explain how archaeologists dig and analyze their finds. Scientists have been able to reconstruct prehistoric Hohokam society and sur-

*Arizona Military Museum*

roundings using pollen, plant and animal remains, artifacts, and burials. They know, for example, that the average Hohokam man stood five feet four inches tall, weighed 130-140 pounds, and had a 40-year life span. You can see Hohokam crafts, stone tools, and representations of pithouses, pueblos, canals, and ball courts.

After looking at the indoor exhibits, you'll better appreciate the ruin outside. The Hohokam began construction of the Platform Mound at Pueblo Grande about A.D. 1150 on a terrace overlooking the Salt River, occupying the site for about 300 years. From the ruins you can see an oval-shaped depression thought to be a ball court. Earlier pithouse ruins nearby date from A.D. 500. Signs along a trail describe features of Pueblo Grande's construction.

The museum and cultural park are open Mon.-Sat. 9 a.m.-4:45 p.m. and Sunday 1-4:45 p.m.; $2 adult, $1.50 child 6-17 (free under age six); tel. 495-0900 (recording) or 495-0901. On the second full weekend in December, Indians present entertainment, arts and crafts, and food at the Annual Indian Market. The museum and ruins lie five miles east of downtown at 4619 E. Washington Street.

### Arizona Military Museum

This museum traces Arizona's military history from Spanish days to the present. Old maps, photos, weapons, uniforms, and other memorabilia represent each period. An outdoor exhibit features vehicles and artillery that date from WW I to Desert Storm. During WW II, the museum building served as part of a prison camp detaining German submariners.

The library is open to the public. Museum hours are Saturday and Sunday 1-4 p.m., Tuesday and Thursday 9 a.m.-2 p.m.; groups can schedule other times; free; tel. 267-2676. The museum is part of the Arizona National Guard complex at 5636 E. McDowell Rd., about seven miles east of downtown; entrance off 52nd Street.

### Desert Botanical Garden

If you're curious about all those strange cacti and other plants so abundant in the deserts of Arizona, this is the place to learn about them. A 1.5-mile trail in the gardens winds past more than 2,000 species. Signs list names and trail guides offer more. The gardens display exotic plants from other regions too, containing more than half the cactus species in the world. If you arrive in spring, you'll see many plants in bloom. A Wildflower Hotline on line during March and April tells you where to view wildflowers in Arizona; tel. 481-8134. The gift shop sells natural history books, souvenirs, and cactus specimens.

The garden is open daily 7 a.m.-10 p.m. May-Sept. and 8 a.m.-sunset Oct.-April; $6 adults, $5 ages 60 and over, and $1 children 5-12; tel. 941-1217 (recorded information) or 941-1225.

## HALL OF FLAME

In the old days the position of volunteer fire-fighter carried with it great prestige. Men eagerly joined the local fire brigade, which also served as a social club. Firefighters competed in drills and marched in parades alongside their glistening machines. Today the Phoenix Hall of Flame museum houses what may be the world's largest display of fire fighting gear. The equipment in this amazing collection comes from all over the world; many items are works of art in themselves.

The first gallery contains hand- and horse-drawn pumpers, hose carriers, and hook-and-ladder wagons from the 18th and 19th centuries. A second gallery displays antique motorized fire trucks. The third gallery features historic fire-alarm systems, including the world's first computerized dispatch system. The fourth gallery offers a fire safety exhibit. Old prints show firefighters in action.

It's open Mon.-Sat. 9 a.m.-5 p.m. and Sunday noon-4 p.m.; rates are $4 adults, $1.50 students 6-17, $3 seniors 62 and up; tel. ASK-FIRE. The Hall of Flame is opposite Papago Park at 6101 E. Van Buren Street.

The Desert Botanical Garden is off Galvin Parkway in Papago Park; exit from the 202 loop at Priest Dr., turn left on Galvin Parkway and exit at Van Buren Street.

### Phoenix Zoo

Animals and birds from both Arizona and all over the world inhabit 125 acres of rolling hills.

The zoo uses moats and steep inclines, where possible, to provide the animals with an open and natural setting. Such habitats as tropical rainforests, mountains, grasslands, temperate woodlands, and deserts are re-created for the more than 1,000 zoo residents. You'll see bighorn sheep from Arizona, oryx from the Arabian deserts, tigers from India, gorillas from Africa, and wallabies from Papua New Guinea. Children will enjoy meeting the farm animals in the Petting Zoo. If a lot of walking doesn't appeal to you, just hop aboard the Safari Train for a narrated tour of the grounds; admission is $1.50. Picnic areas and snacks are available.

The Phoenix Zoo is open daily 9 a.m.-5 p.m. (7 a.m.-4 p.m. from May 1 to Labor Day); $7 adults, $6 seniors (60 and over), $3.50 children 4-12 (with adult); tel. 273-7771 (recorded information) or 273-1341. It's off Galvin Parkway in Papago Park; enter from either 6400 E. McDowell Rd. or 5800 E. Van Buren Street.

### Salt River Project History Center

The Salt River Project displays feature Hohokam and modern canal systems, Indian artifacts, the construction of Theodore Roosevelt Dam, and the history of electric power. It's open Mon.-Fri. 9 a.m.-4 p.m.; free; tel. 236-2208. The center is at 1521 Project Dr., across from the Hall of Flame.

### Arizona Historical Society Museum

This museum features interactive exhibits on Arizona history, orientation theater, auditorium, library, restaurant, and gift shop; tel. 929-0292. It's at 1300 N. College Ave. and Curry Rd. in southeast Papago Park.

# SCOTTSDALE

Chaplain Winfield Scott, Scottsdale's first resident, fell in love with the Valley, homesteading here in the 1880s. During his frequent travels, he promoted the land as "unequaled in greater fertility or richer promise." A small, close-knit community soon formed at Brown Avenue and Main Street.

Today the little village has grown up—165,000 people now live here. Scottsdale bills itself as "The West's Most Western Town," offering innumerable porch-fronted shops selling Western clothing, Western art, and Indian crafts. Both residents and visitors enjoy the top-notch specialty shops, art galleries, cultural events, restaurants, resort hotels, and beautiful landscaping. Scottsdale, just east of Phoenix and just north of Tempe, makes an ideal base for a stay in the Valley, though it's a little more expensive than Phoenix.

## SIGHTS

### Scottsdale Historical Museum (The Little Red Schoolhouse)
Scottsdale was so small in 1909, when this schoolhouse was built, that all the town's children could fit into its two classrooms. From the 1920s into the '50s, Mexican agricultural workers used the site as a schoolhouse and community center. Today the Little Red Schoolhouse is preserved as a reminder of the town's past. Located near the center of the original Scottsdale, the schoolhouse is a good place to begin a tour of the modern city. Exhibits tell the story of the town's early days. It's open Wed.-Sat. 10 a.m.-5 p.m. and Sunday noon-4 p.m.; tel. 945-4499. The museum is at 7333 E. Scottsdale Mall in the Civic Center Complex, just east of the intersection of Brown Ave. and Main Street. The society offers a self-guided walking tour of Old Town Scottsdale; pick up a map at the schoolhouse or the chamber of commerce.

### Scottsdale Center for the Arts
Scottsdale residents have always had a keen interest in the arts. This facility contains a large gallery of contemporary art, an 800-seat performing-arts theater, a cinema, and an outdoor amphitheater. Admission to the art gallery is free, but there's a charge for performances. Call 994-ARTS to find out what's coming up.

The center is open Mon.-Sat. 10 a.m.-5 p.m. (till 8 p.m. on Thursday, except in summer) and Sunday noon-5 p.m. Part of the Civic Center Complex, the center is at Second St. and Civic Center Blvd. between the Scottsdale Historical Museum and the library. Write 7380 E. Second St., Scottsdale, AZ 85251.

### McCormick Railroad Park
Rail buffs of all ages will want to hop on the five-twelfths-scale trains for a ride around the park's grassy acres. Two old railway stations house shops with model-train supplies, railroad books, and souvenirs. Outside, a standard-gauge, Mogul-type Baldwin Steam Engine is on display. Buy snacks in a Southern Pacific caboose. On Sunday afternoons you can visit several model-railroad clubs, each running a different scale train.

McCormick Railroad Park, train rides, and a 1929 carousel are open daily. Rides cost $1 and start at 10 a.m. closing at variable hours over the seasons. Call for times. This unusual park lies at 7301 E. Indian Bend Rd. just east of Scottsdale Rd.; tel. 994-2312.

### Cosanti Foundation
Italian-born Paolo Soleri first came to Scottsdale in 1947 to study architecture with Frank Lloyd Wright. In 1956 Soleri started Cosanti, his own foundation, to design energy- and space-efficient cities. He uses the word "arcology," a combination of *architecture* and *ecology,* to describe his work.

At Cosanti Foundation you can see some of Soleri's unique structures and learn about his ideas for making the world a better place. Books, drawings, sculpture, and Soleri's famous windbells are sold in the gallery/gift shop, helping to finance the foundation. Hours are daily 9 a.m.-5 p.m. with hourly tours given 10 a.m.-4 p.m.; $1 donation; tel. 948-6145. The

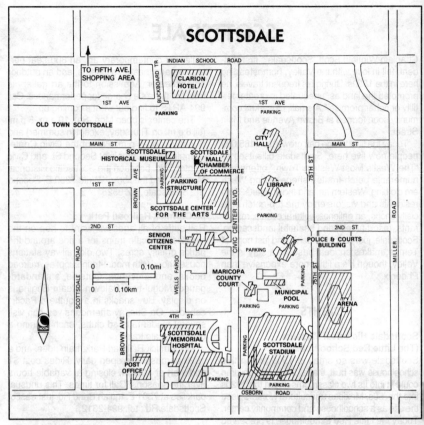

foundation is at 6433 Doubletree Ranch Rd.; from central Scottsdale go five miles north on Scottsdale Rd., then turn left and drive one mile on Doubletree Ranch Road.

**Taliesin West**

The renowned architect Frank Lloyd Wright didn't just design buildings according to plan; he let them "grow" from the inside out. His method of training student architects was similar. Apprentices needed to grow and develop far beyond facts and formulas.

Taliesin West began in 1937 as a winter home for students at Wright's Wisconsin school, opened six years earlier. Students then lived in tents and simple shelters; now, more

than 50 years later, they still do. Most stay three to five years, living and working closely with one another, the faculty, and the surrounding desert. Though Wright died in 1959, the Frank Lloyd Wright School of Architecture and Taliesin Architects carry on his high standards.

Docents or apprentices lead daily walking tours Sept. 15-May 30, 9 a.m.-4 p.m. In summer, regular tours depart 8-11 a.m.; each lasts about an hour. Call for times of special summer tours. Desert walks are conducted Nov.-April at 9 a.m. and 11:30 a.m. Mon.-Sat. at $12 per person. In-depth, behind-the-scenes tours are conducted Jan.-May on Tuesday and Thursday 9 a.m.-noon for $25 per person. On any visit, besides touring the grounds, you'll see highlights of Wright's work in models, photos, and a video presentation. Tours cost $10 adults, $8 students and seniors (65 and over), $3 children 4-12; summer rates (June-Sept.) drop to $8 adults, $6 students and seniors, $3 children 4-12; tel. 860-8810 (recorded information) or 860-2700. The visitor center has a good selection of related books and gift items.

Taliesin West is set in the western foothills of the McDowell Mountains northeast of Scottsdale. From central Scottsdale, go north 10 miles on Scottsdale Rd., turn right on Shea Blvd., continue 4.6 miles to Frank Lloyd Wright Blvd., and then turn left to Cactus Road. The entrance is on the right.

## Fleischer Museum

This museum contains a collection of American Impressionism—California School—as well as visiting exhibits. It's open daily 10 a.m.-4 p.m.; free; tel. 585-3108. You'll find it in a pink sandstone building in far north Scottsdale at 17207 N. Perimeter Dr.; go north on Pima Rd., turn left on Bell (the first street past Frank Lloyd Wright Blvd.), then right on Perimeter.

## Rawhide

Check out this replica of an 1880s Old West town with about 25 buildings containing shops, Western exhibits, a museum, saloon, Rawhide Steakhouse (steak, chicken, ribs), burro rides for the kids, and stagecoach rides. The museum displays such Western curiosities as the boots of Tom Mix, Wyatt Earp's gun, and a pair of Geronimo's moccasins. Admission is $1 adults, children under 11 free. It's open Mon.-Thurs. 5-10 p.m. and Fri.-Sun. 11 a.m.-10 p.m. (daily 5-10 p.m. June 1 to September 30). Call for info about annual events; tel. 502-1880 (recording). From central Scottsdale, go north about 13 miles to 23023 N. Scottsdale Rd., four miles north of Bell Road.

## Imax

Imax is a moving picture theater that uses a projection screen nearly seven stories tall and a projection film with 10 times the area of 35 mm film to project a fine grain, realistic image. Visitors can choose a single feature film ($6 adults and $4.50 children or seniors) or a double fea-

ture ($2.50 more). Imax is at the corner of Fifth Ave. and Civic Center Boulevard. The box office is open 11 a.m.-9 p.m.; call for show times; tel. 945-IMAX.

## Fountain Hills

The world's highest artificial fountain shoots spray 560 feet high in this community 18 miles northeast of Scottsdale. A 15-minute display takes place daily on the hour, 10 a.m.-9 p.m. The surrounding park is a fine place for a picnic or stroll. From Scottsdale, go north six miles on Scottsdale Rd., then turn right and drive 12 miles on Shea Boulevard.

## Out of Africa Wildlife Park

This unusual park features big cats from all over the world. Shows demonstrate the relationships between felines and humans. You can see the cats in both near-natural habitats and shows, where cubs are often available for viewing. A python and other scaly friends dwell in the reptile exhibit.

It's open Tues.-Sun. (except it's open Monday if it's a holiday) 9:30 a.m.-5 p.m.; hours are extended to 9:30 p.m. Saturday Memorial Day to September, when the park is closed Mon.-Tuesday. Continuous shows begin at 11 a.m.; tel. 837-7779/7677. The park features a primitive playground, patio cafe, and gift shop. Admission costs $11.95 adults, $10.95 seniors 65 and up, and $4.95 children 4-12. Out of Africa lies east of Fountain Hills, opposite the turnoff for the Fort McDowell Indian Reservation. Take the Beeline Hwy. north two miles from the intersection with Shea Blvd. and follow signs.

## Hoo-hoogam Ki Museum

Pima and Maricopa Indians on the Salt River Indian Reservation exhibit baskets, pottery, historic photos, and other artifacts just east of Scottsdale. The museum building incorporates adobe, desert plants, and stone in a traditional "sandwich" style.

It's open Mon.-Fri. 10 a.m.-4:30 p.m., closed on tribal and major American holidays; $1 adults, 50 cents children; tel. 941-7379. Take Thomas or McDowell Road east from Phoenix or Scottsdale to Longmore Rd., then turn north to 10000 E. Osborn Road.

**Buffalo Museum of America**

Experience the grandeur, grace, and power of the magnificent buffalo. Exhibits here include life-size animated animals. The museum is at 10261 N. Scottsdale Rd.; it's open Mon.-Fri. 9 a.m.-5 p.m., Sunday 1-4 p.m. by appointment only; $3 adults, $2.50 seniors (55+), $2 students; tel. 951-1022.

# TEMPE

Enterprising merchant Charles Trumbull Hayden arrived here in 1872 to set up a trading post. He chose this spot on the south bank of the Salt River as the safest place to cross his freight wagons. Hayden also found this a good location for his flour mill and ferry service.

Darrel Duppa came over from Phoenix to visit Hayden's Ferry one day, and remarked that the Salt River Valley reminded him of the Vale of Tempe between Mt. Olympus and Mt. Ossa in Thessaly, Greece. Hayden liked the name and, eventually, it stuck.

Farmers settled in Tempe (tem-PEE), raising livestock, establishing a dairy, and growing a variety of crops. In 1885 the Territorial Legislature established nearby Arizona State Teachers College, now Arizona State University; it has since grown into one of the largest schools in the country. Many of Tempe's original buildings have survived; you'll see Hayden's home, his flour mill (rebuilt in 1918 after a fire), and other old buildings along Mill Avenue. Sandwiched between Phoenix to the west and Mesa to the east, Tempe (pop. 150,000) lies just south of Scottsdale.

**Tempe Historical Museum**

This attractive new museum portrays many aspects of Tempe's history. The large main gallery features an archaeological dig, an interactive model of the Salt River and canals, shops of yesteryear, a fire station, and video programs. Changing exhibits in two smaller halls focus on other topics of historical interest. The museum also maintains a research reading room and gift shop. It's open Mon.-Thurs. and Saturday 10 a.m.-5 p.m., Sunday 1-5 p.m., closed Friday and major holidays; $2.50 adults, $2 students and seniors, $1 children 6-12; tel. 350-5100 (after-hours recording). You'll find it at the southwest corner of 809 Southern Ave. and Rural Road.

**Niels Peterson House**

Built in 1892, this Queen Anne/Victorian-style home used a clever ventilation system to keep the interior livable in summer. You can tour the inside, restored to its 1930s appearance, Tues.-Thurs. and Saturday 10 a.m.-2 p.m.; free; tel. 350-5151 or 350-5100. The house lies on the northwest corner of 1414 W. Southern Ave. and Priest Drive.

**Tempe Arts Center**

Contemporary artists display fine crafts and sculpture here. Exhibits, changing monthly, are free. Most work is for sale. The Sculpture Garden outside contains large-scale pieces. Workshops take place occasionally at the center. Hours are Tues.-Sun. noon-5 p.m.; tel. 968-0888. The center is in Tempe Beach Park along the Salt River at the corner of Mill Ave. and First Street.

## ARIZONA STATE UNIVERSITY

When the Arizona Legislature founded the school in 1885, classes met in a four-room, red-brick structure set on 20 acres of cow pasture. Today, broad lawns, stately palms, and flowering subtropical trees grace the 700-acre campus of Arizona's largest university. Growth has been spectacular in the last 30 years; the school now has more than 44,000 students and an instructional and research faculty of about 1,800. About 5,000 students attend the 300-acre ASU West campus at 4701 W. Thunderbird Rd. in Phoenix. The new ASU East campus recently opened in Mesa at the intersection of Power Rd. and Williams Field Road. Undergraduates can choose from 88 majors, while graduate students can earn a master's in 97 majors or a doctorate in 52.

Attractions on campus include the striking Gammage Auditorium, art galleries, and a variety of small museums. The well-landscaped campus is a pleasant place for a stroll. Activity slows down a bit in summer—it's *hot*—but most of the galleries and museums stay open, except as noted below.

**Tours** of campus start at the Student Services Building and last about 90 minutes; they leave Mon.-Fri. at 10:30 a.m. and 2 p.m.; tel. 965-2604. A **visitor center** lies on the northwest corner of Apache Blvd. and Scottsdale Rd.; it's open Mon.-Fri. 8 a.m.-5 p.m.; tel. 965-0100.

## Getting Around

Parking is tight, as you might expect with so many students, but you can use metered parking spaces or several pay lots on campus, or search for a spot on a side street off campus. See the accompanying map for campus parking areas. Most of the central campus is closed to motor traffic. Phoenix Transit (tel. 253-5000) connects the university with Tempe and the rest of the Valley. The open-air University Tram cruises the outlying areas of campus.

## Gammage Auditorium

You'll see this circular structure, commemorating a former ASU president, on the southwest corner of campus. Dedicated in 1964, the auditorium was the last major building designed by Frank Lloyd Wright. You can take a free half-hour tour inside, Mon.-Fri. 1-4 p.m. from Oct. 1 to mid-May; call 965-4050 for tour times or 965-3434 for concert information. The Gammage Auditorium is easy to spot, set into a curve of the Phoenix-Mesa highway (US 60/70/80/89).

## ASU Art Museum

ASU's new **Nelson Fine Arts Center** houses galleries dedicated to American, Latin American, contemporary, print, and craft art. Sculpture is displayed on several outdoor terraces. The art museum is highly recommended for its quality, size, and diversity; also worth a look is the highly unusual architecture of the building itself. The design, by architect Antoine Predock, called for a "village-like aggregation of buildings" housing the arts. Aspects of the existing campus and the Southwest can be seen in the choice of materials, forms, and colors. Light coming in from skylights reflects off surfaces a total of 10 times before illuminating the artwork, a process meant to deflect the harmful qualities of daylight.

The center includes the Galvin Playhouse and University Dance Laboratory. Museum hours are Tuesday 10 a.m.-9 p.m., Wed.-Sat. 10 a.m.-5 p.m., and Sunday 1-5 p.m.; closed major holidays; free; tel. 965-2787. The gift shop sells a variety of crafts. The Fine Arts Center is on the southeast corner of Mill Ave. and 10th St. on the west side of campus; visitor parking is available in front and to the south.

## ASU Art Museum (Matthews Center)

Head here to see a varied display of paintings, prints, sculpture, and crafts by artists from the United States, Latin America, and other parts of the world. Visiting art exhibits and an experimental gallery are also featured. It's open Wed.-Sat. 10 a.m.-5 p.m. and Sunday 1-5 p.m.; free; tel. 965-6943. The collection is on the second floor in Matthews Center.

## Harry Wood Art Gallery

See Master of Fine Arts student exhibitions of paintings, photography, or sculpture. It's open Mon.-Fri. 8 a.m.-5 p.m.; free; tel. 965-3468. The gallery is in the School of Arts building.

## Gallery of Design

Study the latest architectural techniques, illustrated by drawings and scale models. It's open Mon.-Fri. 8 a.m.-5 p.m.; free; tel. 965-3216. The Gallery of Design, along with the Howe Library of Architecture, is in the College of Architecture and Environmental Design.

## Northlight Gallery

This gallery features photographic exhibits, both historic and modern, Mon.-Thurs. 10:30 a.m.-4:30 p.m. (closed in summer); free; tel. 965-6517. It's in Matthews Hall (behind Matthews Center).

## Museum of Anthropology

Displays illustrate prehistoric Hohokam and modern Indian cultures, archaeological techniques, and concepts of anthropology. Hours are Mon.-Fri. 8 a.m.-5 p.m.; free; tel. 965-6213. In the Anthropology Building, next to Matthews Center.

## Hayden Library

The university's main library also houses the Arizona, Chicano, and East Asian special collections, along with those on the Labriola American

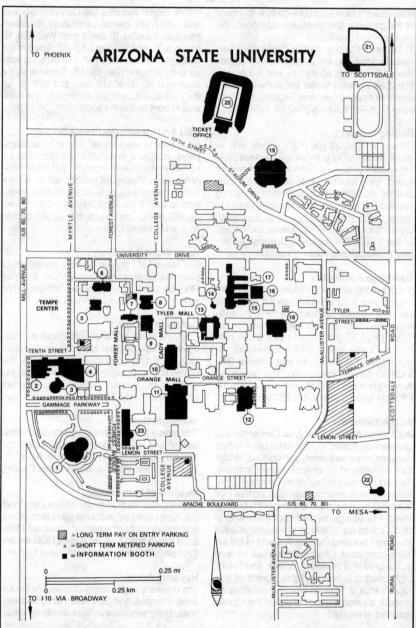

# ARIZONA STATE UNIVERSITY

TO PHOENIX

TO SCOTTSDALE

TO MESA →

TO I-10 VIA BROADWAY

TICKET OFFICE

FIFTH STREET

STADIUM DRIVE

UNIVERSITY DRIVE

MYRTLE AVENUE

FOREST AVENUE

COLLEGE AVENUE

MILL AVENUE (US 60, 70, 80)

TEMPE CENTER

TENTH STREET

GAMMAGE PARKWAY

FOREST MALL

TYLER MALL

CADY MALL

ORANGE MALL

ORANGE STREET

LEMON STREET

COLLEGE AVENUE

APACHE BOULEVARD (US 60, 70, 80)

McALLISTER AVENUE

TYLER STREET

TERRACE DRIVE

SCOTTSDALE ROAD

LEMON STREET

RURAL ROAD

McALLISTER AVENUE

= LONG TERM PAY ON ENTRY PARKING

o = SHORT TERM METERED PARKING

■ = INFORMATION BOOTH

0        0.25 mi
0        0.25 km

# ARIZONA STATE UNIVERSITY

1. Grady Gammage Auditorium
2. Nelson Fine Arts Center (art museum)
3. Music Building
4. Galvin Playhouse
5. Harry Wood Art Gallery (Art Building)
6. Gallery of Design (College of Architecture)
7. Northlight Gallery (Matthews Hall)
8. Anthropology Museum
9. University Art Museum (Matthews Center)
10. Hayden Library
11. Memorial Union
12. ASU Bookstore
13. Zoology Display (Life Sciences Center)
14. University Archives
15. Planetarium (Physical Sciences Center)
16. Geology Museum
17. Center for Meteorite Studies (Physical Sciences Center)
18. Daniel E. Noble Science Library
19. University Activity Center
20. Sun Devil Stadium
21. Packard Baseball Stadium
22. Visitor Center
23. Student Services Building

Indian Data Center and Government Documents. Hours are Mon.-Thurs. 7 a.m.-midnight, Friday 7 a.m.-7 p.m., Saturday 9 a.m.-5 p.m., and Sunday 10 a.m.-midnight; tel. 965-5902/6164. Shorter hours during summer and breaks, and for special collections.

## Memorial Union

This university social center is a good place to visit. The main floor information desk can tell you about the latest concerts, theater, art showings, and sporting events. It's open daily from early morning to late at night (shorter hours in summer and on breaks); tel. 965-5728. Near the desk you'll find a bulletin board listing apartments for rent and items for sale. Around the corner is a ride board; check it out if you're looking for a ride or someone going your way.

**Memorial Union Art Gallery,** at the north end of the building, often hosts visiting shows; it's open Mon.-Fri. 8 a.m.-8 p.m. But you might never make it that far, after encountering more

than a dozen tempting eateries along the way—deli, pizza place, grill . . . everything from Chicken Express to Cafe Olé. Stop in at The Club for regular cafeteria meals. Relax downstairs in a lounge or patio, go bowling, play a game of billiards, or see a movie.

## ASU Bookstore

A good selection of general-interest books, textbooks, supplies, and maps is sold here. Pick out a Sun Devils T-shirt or other souvenir. It's open Mon.-Thurs. 8 a.m.-6 p.m. (Friday till 5) and Saturday 10 a.m.-2 p.m.

## Life Sciences Center

Meet the university's live rattlesnakes, Gila monster, and other reptiles in hallway exhibits. Hours are Mon.-Fri. 8 a.m.-5 p.m.; free; tel. 965-6162. It's in the Life Sciences Building (east-west hallway). Plant specimens and 5,000 fossils are found in C Wing.

## Center for Meteorite Studies

See visitors from outer space in Room C-139 and the adjacent hallways of the Physical Sciences Building. This collection is reportedly one of the world's largest of its kind with more than 1,400 items. It's open Mon.-Fri. 8:30 a.m.-4 p.m.; free; tel. 965-6511.

## Geology Museum

You can check the six-story Foucault pendulum to see if the earth is still spinning, or watch the seismograph to learn if it's shaking. Exhibits illustrate geologic processes and identify rocks, minerals, and fossils. Hours are 9 a.m.-noon Mon.-Fri.; free; tel. 965-7065. Located in F Wing of the Physical Sciences Building.

## ASU Planetarium

You can attend one-hour star shows at ASU's Planetarium in the Physical Sciences Building at $2 per person. Shows are held Tuesday and Thursday at 7:30 p.m. during the school year. Call for show times during vacation; tel. 965-2266 or 727-6234.

## Daniel E. Noble Science Library

Here you'll find books used by the nearby science and engineering departments. Hikers can plan trips using the map collection and make needed photocopies. Hours for the main collection, during regular terms, are Mon.-Thurs. 7 a.m.-11:30 p.m., Friday 7 a.m.-7 p.m., Saturday 9 a.m.-5 p.m., and Sunday noon-11:30 p.m. The map collection is open Mon.-Thurs. 8 a.m.-8 p.m., Friday 8 a.m.-5 p.m. (closed weekends); tel. 965-7133 (recording), 965-7607 (information), or 965-3582 (map collection).

## Sports

ASU has fielded some top teams. Trophies, clippings, and photos are on display at the

**Sports Hall of Fame,** housed in the circular corridor of the University Activity Center; it's open Mon.-Fri. 8 a.m.-5 p.m. Football games are played in the giant, 74,000-seat Sun Devil Stadium; the 14,000-seat Activity Center serves ASU's basketball squads; the home of baseball is the 8,000-seat Packard Baseball Stadium. Buy tickets to games in front of the stadium at the Sun Devils Athletic Ticket Office; tel. 965-2381. Tours of the Sun Devil and Packard Baseball Stadiums are available; tel. 965-3933.

# MESA

In March of 1877, when a group of 84 Mormon settlers arrived, this land was desert; only thin strips of vegetation lined the Salt River. The eager families immediately began rebuilding the old Hohokam irrigation canals, hoping to make the desert green and start a prosperous new life under the warm Arizona sun. Because the land reminded them of a tabletop, they named the settlement Mesa. From the tiny adobe fort used by pioneers in the first years, Mesa has grown into Arizona's third-largest city, with a population of nearly 324,000. More people arrive in winter to enjoy the sunny climate, the lakes, and the Superstition Mountains. Mesa, next door to Tempe and 15 miles east of Phoenix, is easily reached by the Superstition Freeway.

# SIGHTS

## Mesa Southwest Museum

Re-created cave and village displays show how prehistoric Indians lived. Pioneer exhibits illustrate aspects of early Mesa life. Petroglyphs and a variety of Salado and Hohokam pottery are on display, as well as a stagecoach, an adobe schoolhouse, and life-size, animated dinosaurs. There's an authentic jail, and an opportunity to try and crack the big safe. You can work at deciphering the "secret" stone maps of the Lost Dutchman Mine, or grab a gold pan and try panning from the stream. A gift shop sells books and souvenirs. The museum is open Tues.-Sat. 10 a.m.-5 p.m. and Sunday 1-5 p.m.;

$4 ages 13-54, $2 ages 3-12, $3.50 students (with I.D.) and seniors 55 and over. It's downtown at 53 N. Macdonald near the corner of W. First St.; tel. 644-2230 (recording).

## Sirrine House

Joel Sirrine built this Queen Anne Victorian-style house in 1896 with a wraparound porch. The house is furnished with period antiques from the turn of the century including a 1906 washing machine. You can tour the house, one of the finest surviving from Mesa's early years. Hours are Saturday 10 a.m.-5 p.m. and Sunday 1-5 p.m.; free; tel. 644-2760 (Sirrine House) or 644-3416 (Mesa Southwest Museum). It's downtown at 160 N. Center Street.

## Arizona Museum for Youth

Children can participate in art programs and view art exhibits meant just for them. Related workshops are available as well. It's open Tues.-Fri. 1-5 p.m. (9 a.m.-5 p.m. in summer), Saturday 10 a.m.-5 p.m., and Sunday 1-5 p.m.; $2 ages two and up; call for exhibit schedule (changes three times a year); tel. 644-2467. You'll find it in downtown Mesa at 35 N. Robson.

## Arizona Temple

Rising from beautifully landscaped gardens, the Arizona Temple of the Mormon Church is Mesa's most notable landmark. The structure was completed in 1927 from a plan based on classical Greek architecture. Friezes at the top four corners of the exterior represent the gathering of the House of Israel from the four corners

Messerschmitt
Bf-109E3 at
Champlin Fighter
Museum

of the earth. Marriages and other sacred ceremonies take place inside.

The interior is closed to non-Mormons, but you're welcome to wander among the exotic plants in the gardens and view exhibits in the visitor center just north of the temple. Tours in the visitor center present the basic doctrines of the Mormon Church, or Church of Latter-day Saints, through a series of movies and animated dioramas. The presentation explains the importance of temples. The half-hour tours run daily 9 a.m.-9 p.m. (10 a.m.-10 p.m. in December). Garden tours point out exterior architectural details and identify some of the trees and other vegetation; it's open daily 7-9 p.m.

Special events include the Easter Pageant during the week preceding Easter and the Christmas Lights display from late November through December when 30-minute musical programs are held nightly at 7 p.m. If you'd like to know more about the Mormon religion, ask to see their other movies and videotapes. The Arizona Temple is at 525 E. Main St., just east of downtown; tel. 964-7164.

## Champlin Fighter Museum

Aircraft from WW I and WW II draw visitors to this unique collection. Here you'll also learn about the men who flew them. Autographed photos accompany stories of fighter pilots who flew in conflicts from WW I to Vietnam. Realistic

paintings show aircraft in action.

The planes themselves are housed in two giant hangars. You'll see a replica of the 1911 Mercedes-powered Rumpler Taube—the world's first combat aircraft; a Fokker Dr-1 triplane, like the one flown by Manfred von Richthofen, the "Red Baron"; a British Sopwith Camel; the extremely rare German Messerschmitt 109 and the Focke Wulf 190; the Supermarine Spitfire that helped win the Battle of Britain; the American P-51D Mustang; and dozens of other beautifully preserved planes. Famous aircraft engines include the 1941 rocket engine used in Messerschmitt 163 Komets and one of the eight engines used on Howard Hughes's *Spruce Goose*.

You can peek into the restoration area where mechanics keep these antique craft in flying condition. In a video presentation, you'll hear aces tell how they flew and fought, and see actual combat footage filmed during WW II and in Korea and Vietnam. A gift shop sells aircraft models, posters, and books. You can visit Champlin Fighter Museum's "Aircraft of the Aces" daily 10 a.m.-5 p.m.; $6 adults, $3 children 5-14; tel. 830-4540. It's at Falcon Field off McKellips Rd., on the northeast edge of Mesa about seven miles from downtown.

## Confederate Air Force-Arizona Wing

Not far from the Champlain Fighter Museum,

the Confederate Air Force displays vintage aircraft including the B-17G "Sentimental Journey," a B-25 Mitchell bomber that flew missions out of Corsica, a German Heinkel HE-111 bomber, and others, many kept in flying shape. It's at the corner of Killips Rd. and Greenfield Rd. adjacent to Falcon Field; tel. 924-1940.

## Mesa Historical Museum

The people of Mesa have put together this remarkable collection of pioneer memorabilia and antique farm equipment. Each of the many rooms has a different character, based on a particular theme. You'll see ornate saddles, harnesses, furniture, kitchens, a grist mill, and pioneer photos. Auditorium murals depict Southwest history. Tours in the museum, itself a historic school building, operate Tues.-Sat. 10 a.m.-4 p.m.; $3 adults, $2 seniors, $1 children 5-11; tel. 835-7358. It's in north Mesa at 2345 N. Horne.

On the way, you may want to stop at **Park of the Canals** to see remnants of the early Hohokam canal system, pioneer canals, and even a modern canal. The park also has picnic tables and a playground; it's at 1710 N. Horne.

## Buckhorn Mineral Wells

Travel here to experience one of the Valley's more unusual attractions. In 1939, hot underground water was discovered and developed into a health spa. You hop into your own tub (106° F) for $15 and receive a rejuvenating massage for another $25.

You can also visit a museum containing over 400 stuffed and mounted animals, most native to Arizona. Birds hang from the rafters, javelinas glare from the walls, a coyote snarls from behind a couch. Admission is $2 adults, $1 children under 12. The museum and baths are open Tues.-Sat. 9 a.m.-5 p.m.; tel. 832-1111. You can also stay here; cottages start at $45 d ($35 d in summer). Buckhorn lies seven miles east of downtown Mesa at 5900 E. Main St. and Recker Road.

## Chandler Museum

Historic exhibits in the town of Chandler, just south of Mesa, display Indian artifacts along with memorabilia of pioneer life and early agriculture. Hours are Mon.-Sat. 11 a.m.-4 p.m. from mid-September through June; tel. 786-2842. It's in downtown Chandler at 178 E. Commonwealth Ave., just east of A.J. Chandler Park. From Mesa, take the Superstition Fwy. to Country Club/AZ 87 Exit 8 and turn south. AZ 87 becomes Arizona Ave. and is the main street through Chandler. To reach the museum, go one block east on Buffalo St., one block south on Arizona Place, then one block east on Commonwealth Avenue.

## Arizona Railway Museum

Railroad enthusiasts have preserved a 1906 steam locomotive and a variety of other historic rolling stock in Chandler. Smaller exhibits are housed in the museum building, which resembles an early Southwest railroad depot. It's open Saturday and Sunday noon-4 p.m., may close in summer; free; tel. 821-1108. From Arizona Ave. downtown, turn east on Erie St. to 399 N. Delaware Street.

## Gilbert Historical Center

Exhibits in eight rooms tell the story of this small agricultural town from prehistory to the present. A lineup of antique farm machinery sits outside. It's open Tuesday and Saturday 1-4 p.m. Oct.-May, closed in summer; free; tel. 926-1577. The center is in central Gilbert, south of Mesa and east of Chandler, at 10 S. Gilbert Road.

## Arizona Theme Park

This major new theme park is to be constructed on a full square mile at the southeast corner of Pecos Rd. and Higley Rd. in Gilbert, south of Mesa. Some of the themes displayed will include a western town, based on Tombstone, a mining town, based on Jerome, a Mexican village, and Native American dwellings. Call for opening date, hours, and admission rates; tel. 979-3601.

# VALLEY OF THE SUN ACCOMMODATIONS

## Hostel

Metcalf House Hostel is a good choice for low-budget travelers. You can walk to many Phoenix sights from here or take a city bus. Facilities include kitchen, washer and dryer, and info-packed bulletin boards.

The hostel is rarely full, open on a first-come, first-served basis. Year-round cost is $10 members, $13 nonmembers. The house parents sell Hostelling International passes. A three-night stay limit may apply if the hostel is crowded. Check in is 7-10 a.m. and 5-11 p.m. It's in a residential area, one mile northeast of downtown, at 1026 N. Ninth St. between Portland and Roosevelt Streets, Phoenix, AZ 85006; tel. 254-9803. Parking is on the street. Some visitors might find the neighborhood a bit rough. From the downtown Phoenix Transit terminal at First St. and Washington, take Bus #10 and get off at the corner of Roosevelt and Ninth Streets.

## Downtown YMCA

A central, inexpensive place for both men and women at 350 N. First Ave., Phoenix, AZ 85003; tel. 253-6181. Rooms cost $20 s, $33 d; weekly rates are $73 s, $91 d. Recreation facilities include racquetball and basketball courts, running track, weight room, sauna, and spa.

## Bed and Breakfasts

These are private houses open to travelers in the European tradition. The degree of luxury varies, but the hosts offer a personal touch not found in motels. Advance reservations requested.

**Bed and Breakfast in Arizona** includes many B&Bs in the Valley; for a list contact 8900 Via Linda, Scottsdale AZ 85258; tel. 265-9511. Prices range $45-150 d.

**Mi Casa Su Casa** is Spanish for "My house [is] your house." You'll find more than 140 listings throughout the state; Box 950, Tempe, AZ 85281; tel. 990-0682 or (800) 456-0682. Prices range $40-150 d.

## HOTELS AND MOTELS

Nowhere else in Arizona will you find such a wide selection and huge price differential as in the Phoenix area. Here lies almost everything imaginable—from super-cheap dives to posh luxury resorts. The resorts, however, can be bargains in summer—prices may plummet more than 50% when the mercury soars. Seasonal savings decrease with lower-priced accommodations, but competition helps keep prices reasonable. Most all national chains are represented here—many in several locations.

A good place to search for bargain motels is along E. Van Buren St. between downtown and 40th Street. This area was once part of a major route that was bypassed when the freeways were constructed. Though some of the area may seem seedy and risky, it is convenient to Sky Harbor Airport. Other good places to search for bargain motels are along University Dr. in Tempe and along Main St. in Mesa. During peak season some budget non-chain motels raise their rates drastically; one motel owner reported charging $400 per night during Superbowl weekend despite a lack of amenities.

Check motel and resort listings in the free *Official Visitors Guide* published by the Phoenix and Valley of the Sun Convention and Visitors Bureau.

## RESORTS

The Valley of the Sun offers a huge selection of resorts from rustic cabins to truly posh world-class hotels offering so many amenities that visitors can spend weeks within the confines of a single resort without needing to venture out into the surrounding community. Resorts in the following list have been selected on the basis of offering either on-site golf courses, equestrian activities, or both.

The **Arizona Biltmore,** designed by architect William Chase McArthur, and associate of

# VALLEY OF THE SUN ACCOMMODATIONS

(winter weekend rates for basic room)

Add 10.35% tax to all rates unless otherwise noted.

## DOWNTOWN

**Best Western Executive Park Hotel;** 1100 N. Central Ave.; $99 s, $109 d; 252-2100 or (800) 528-1234; fitness center, pool

**Budget Lodge;** 402 W. Van Buren St.; $30 s, $35 d; 254-7247; near Amtrak

**E-Z 8 Motel Metrocenter;** 1820 S. 7th St.; $20.88 s, $34.88 d; 254-9787 or (800) 326-6835, ext. 67; laundromat

**Los Olivas Executive Hotel;** 202 E. McDowell Rd.; $59 s, $69 d; 258-6911 or (800) 776-5560; close to museums and library

**Omni Adams Club;** Central Ave. at Adams; $169 s, $179 d; 257-1525 or (800) 359-7253; pool, health club

**Quality Hotel;** 3600 N. 2nd Ave.; $89 s, $99 d; 248-0222 or (800) 221-2222; pool, hot tub, restaurant

**Ramada Hotel Phoenix-Downtown;** 401 N. First St.; $99-109s or d; 258-3411 or (800) 843-3300; five-star restaurant

**San Carlos Hotel-TraveLodge;** 202 N. Central Ave.; $89-159 s or d; 253-4121 or (800) 528-5446; European charm, gourmet restaurant, pool

## EAST OF DOWNTOWN/AIRPORT

**Comfort Inn;** 4120 E. Van Buren St.; $43-54 s, $48-59 d; 275-5746

**Days Inn Airport;** 3333 E. Van Buren St.; $82-88 s, $88-94 d; 244-8240 or (800) 329-7466; restaurant, pool, airport shuttle

**E-Z 8 Motel;** 1820 S. 7th St.; $30.88 s, $34.88 d; 254-9787 or (800) 326-6835, ext. 66; laundromat

**Holiday Inn Airport East;** 4300 E. Washington St.; $159 s, $169 d; 273-7778 or (800) HOLIDAY; free airport shuttle

**Howard Johnson Lodge;** 124 S. 24th St.; $74 s, $79 d; 244-8221 or (800) 446-4656; free airport shuttle

**Motel 6;** 2323 E. Van Buren St.; $25.99 s, $31.99 d; 267-7511; pool

**Nendels Valu Inn-Airport;** 3307 E. Van Buren St.; $48 s, $52 d; 275-3691; free airport shuttle

**Park View Inn;** 3547 E. Van Buren St.; $30 s, $35 d; 273-7303; laundromat, pool

**Quality Inn-Airport;** 3541 E. Van Buren St.; $65 s, $69 d; 273-7121 or (800) 221-2222; heated pool

**Rodeway Inn Airport West;** 1203 S. 24th St.; $60-85 s, $65-90 d; 985-3600 or (800) 424-4777; pool

**Sleep Inn Airport;** 2621 S. 47th Place; $39.95-49.95 s, $49.95-59.95 d; (800) 221-2222; pool

**TraveLodge;** 2900 E. Van Buren St.; $48-69 s or d; 275-7651 or (800) 578-7878; pool, free airport shuttle, continental breakfast

**TraveLodge Suites;** 3101 N. 32nd St.; $90-120 s or d; 956-6122 or (800) 578-7878; pool, airport shuttle, kitchenettes, free continental breakfast

**Wards Desert Rose;** 3037 E. Van Buren St.; $36 s, $40 d; 273-1601; pool, spa

## NORTH OF DOWNTOWN

**Best Western Bell;** 17211 N. Black Canyon Freeway; $64-70 s, $69-75 d; 993-8300 or (800) 528-1234; in-room coffee, spa

**Hampton Inn Airport East;** 8101 N. Black Canyon Freeway; $86 s, $89 d; 864-6233 or (800) HAMPTON; free continental breakfast, heated pool and whirlpool

**Hotel Westcourt;** 10220 N. Metro Parkway East; $145 s or d; 997-5900 or (800) 858-1033; pool, tennis, restaurant

**Motel 6:** 2330 W. Bell Rd.; $32.99 s, $38.99 d; 993-2353; pool

**Motel 6;** 8152 N. Black Canyon Hwy.; $29.99 s, $35.99 d; 995-7592; pool

**Premier Inns of Metro Center;** 10402 N. Black Canyon Freeway; $60.95-75.95 s or d; 943-2371 or (800) 786-6835; tennis courts, spa

**Travelers Inn;** 8130 N. Black Canyon Hwy.; $45.99 s, $52.99 d; 995-8451 or (800) 633-5900; spa

## SCOTTSDALE

**The Abode Resort Apartment Hotel;** 3635 N. 68th St.; $149-159 d; 945-3544; pool

**Best Western Thunderbird Suites;** 7515 E. Butherus Dr.; $105-140 s, $115-140 d; 951-4000 or (800) 334-1977; two-room suites

**Hospitality Suite Resort-Scottsdale;** 409 N. Scottsdale Rd.; $169 s, $199 d; 949-5115 or (800) 445-5115; free breakfast

**Inn at the Citadel;** 8700 E. Pinnacle Peak Rd.; $295 up s or d; 585-6133 or (800) 927-8367; continental breakfast

**Inn Suites at Scottsdale El Dorado Park;** 7077 E. McDowell Rd.; $109-119 s or d; 941-1202 or (800) 238-8851; pool, spa, weight room, free breakfast

**Motel 6;** 6848 E. Camelback Rd.; $33.99 s, $39.99 d; 946-2280; pool

**Ramada Hotel Valley Ho Resort;** 6850 Main St.; $135-145 s, $144-155 d; 945-6321 or (800) 321-4952; spas, pools, fitness paracourse

**Red Lion's La Posada Resort;** 4949 E. Lincoln Dr.; $219 s or d; 952-0420 or (800) 547-8010; tennis, putting green, pools

**Rodeway Inn;** 7110 E. Indian School Rd.; $90-200 s, $98-200 d; 946-3456 or (800) 424-4777; pool, continental breakfast, spa

**Safari Resort;** 4611 N. Scottsdale Rd.; $92-104 s, $102-114 d, $130 and $140 kitchenettes, suites available; 945-0721 or (800) 845-4356; whirlpool, pools

**Scottsdale 5th Ave. Inn;** 6935 E. 5th Ave.; $76 s, $87 d, $92 poolside s or d; 994-9461 or (800) 528-7396; free continental breakfast

**TEMPE** (add 9.5% tax to rates)

**Country Suites by Carlson;** 1660 W. Elliot Rd.; $75-95 d; 345-8585 or (800) 456-4000; free breakfast

**Econo Lodge of Tempe;** 2101 E. Apache Blvd.; $45-75 s, $55-89.50 d; 966-5832 or (800) 424-4777; pool

**Fiesta Inn;** 2100 E. Priest Dr.; $143 s, $153 d; 967-1441 or (800) 528-6481; spa, pool, tennis courts

**Hampton Inn Airport/Tempe;** 4234 S. 48th St.; $95 s, $105 d; 438-8688 or (800) HAMPTON; spa, pool, continental breakfast

**Holiday Inn;** 915 E. Apache Blvd.; $114 s, $124 d; 968-3451 or (800) HOLIDAY; pool, whirlpool, restaurant, airport shuttle

**Twin Palms Motel;** 225 E. Apache Blvd.; $99 s, $109 d; 967-9431 or (800) 367-0835; pool, continental breakfast

**Motel 6;** 513 W. Broadway Rd.; $29.99 s, $35.99 d; 967-8696; pool

**Ramada Plaza Hotel Sky Harbor Airport;** 1600 S. 52nd St.; $119-129 s or d; 967-6600 or (800) 272-6232; free airport shuttle, indoor and outdoor pools, spa

*(continues on next page)*

# VALLEY OF THE SUN ACCOMMODATIONS

*(continued)*

**Super 8;** 1020 E. Apache Blvd.; $73.88 s; $73.88-82.88 d; 967-8891 or (800) 800-8000, pool

**Tempe Motel;** 947 E. Apache Blvd.; $50 s, $55 d; 894-0909; pool

**Tempe/University TraveLodge;** 1005 E. Apache Blvd.; $55-85 s or d; 968-7871 or (800) 225-3050; pool, exercise room

**University Motel;** 902 S. Mill Ave.; $50 s, $55 d; 966-7221; very close to campus

**MESA** (add 7.3% tax to rates)

**Buckeroo Lodge;** 537 S. Country Club Dr.; $65 s, $70 d; tel. 969-5248, sheltered parking

**Days Inn East Mesa;** 5531 E. Main St.; $65-70 s, $75-80 d; 981-8111; continental breakfast, pool

**Hampton Inn Mesa;** 1563 S. Gilbert Rd.; $134 s or d; 926-3600 or (800) HAMPTON; pool, spa

**Hilton Pavilion Mesa;** 1011 W. Holmes Ave.; $160 s, $170 d; 833-5555 or (800) 544-5866; luxury accommodations

**Holiday Inn;** 1640 S. Country Club Rd.; $139 s, $149 d; 964-7000 or (800) HOLIDAY; sauna, spa, pool

**Mesa Oasis Inn;** 2150 W. Main St.; $45 s, $49.50 d; 962-5051; kitchenettes

**Mesa TraveLodge;** 22 S. Country Club Dr.; $50-100 s or d; 964-5694 or (800) 225-3050; pool

**Motel 6;** 630 W. Main St.; $29.99 s, $35.99 d; 969-8111; pool

**Sheraton Mesa;** 200 N. Centennial Way; $105 s, $115 d; 898-8300 or (800) 456-6372; pool, spa, exercise room

**Super 8;** 3 E. Main St.; $63.88 s, $63.88-69.88 d, 834-6060 or (800) 800-8000; pool

**Tri City Inn;** 1504 W. Main St.; $35 s, $40 d; 969-7241; mall nearby

**Quality Inn Royal-Mesa;** 951 W. Main St.; $89 s, $109 d; 833-1231 or (800) 221-2222; exercise room

---

Frank Lloyd Wright, is Phoenix's grand old resort. The architecture shows the master's influence in its stained glass, geometric designs, and the interplay of light and shadow creating a unique ambience. Featuring a gourmet restaurant, two 18-hole golf courses, a pool with a 90-foot water slide, and an athletic club, the Biltmore offers luxury normally associated with the newer Scottsdale resorts. Room rates start at $215.18 s or d May 22-June 10, $104.83 s or d June 11-Sept. 9, $303.46 Sept. 10-Dec. 31, and $348.49 s or d Jan. 1-May 8. The Biltmore is at 24th St. and Missouri, Phoenix, AZ 85016; tel. 955-6600 or (800) 950-0086.

**The Boulders** is 16 miles northeast of Scottsdale in Carefree on grounds accented by natural rock formations that give the resort its name. Amenities include two 18-hole golf courses, tennis courts, and the new Sonoran Spa. A short distance from the resort is el Pedregal, a festival style market offering shops, restaurants, and galleries. Accommodations consist of individual casitas shaped to fit in with the natural terrain and offering fully stocked mini-bars and wood-burning fireplaces. The resort is off Scottsdale Rd. at Carefree Hwy.; tel. 488-9009 or (800) 553-1717. Casitas run $486.58 s in high season, plus $138.41 for each additional person up to three. Patio homes are available from $624 during the high season. Lower rates are available during much of the year but the resort is closed in summer.

**Marriott's Camelback Inn-Resort, Golf Club & Spa** is 10 miles northeast of Sky Harbor. Accommodations are in 423 pueblo-styled casitas including 23 suites, 21 with private sundecks, seven with private pools. Amenities include six restaurants and cafes, two 18-hole golf courses, 10 tennis courts (five lighted for night use), three pools, a world-class European health spa, and much more. Camelback Inn is at 5402 E. Lincoln Drive, tel. 948-1700 or (800) 24-CAMEL. Deluxe rooms run $337.10-370.26 s or d Jan. 1-May 31, $120.47-176.84 June 1-Sept. 11, and $248.88-276.31 Sept. 12-Dec. 31. Sundeck rooms run $420 Jan. 1-May 31, $210 June 1- Sept. 11, and $303.94 Sept. 12-Dec. 31. Suites run $497.36-1713.14 Jan. 1-May 31, $221-773.68 June 1-Sept. 11, and $386-1077.62 Sept. 12-Dec. 31.

**Marriott's Mountain Shadows Resort and Golf Club** offers 336 guest rooms and suites only a dozen miles from Sky Harbor International Airport. Amenities include four restaurants (including an oyster bar and seafood restaurant), a lounge, an 18-hole golf course, eight lighted tennis courts, three pools, and a fitness center. The resort is at 5641 E. Lincoln Dr., Scottsdale, AZ 85253; tel. 948-7111 or (800) 782-2123. Rooms run $237.04 s or d most of the year with several packages available.

**Orange Tree Golf and Conference Resort** is on 56th St. off Shea Boulevard. The resort offers 160 suites on 128 acres with two restaurants, a cafe, 18 holes of golf, 16 lighted tennis courts, eight racquetball courts, a fitness center, and a sauna. One-bedroom suites run $237.04 Sept. 8-Jan. 12, $330.75 Jan. 13-Feb. 4, $264.60 Feb. 5-May 27, $137.81 May 28-Sept. 5, and $242.55 Sept. 6-Jan. 2 with an extra charge for rooms with a golf course view. The Orange Tree is at 10601 N. 56th St., Scottsdale, AZ 85254; tel. 948-6100 or (800) 228-0386.

**The Phoenician** sits on 130 acres at the base of Camelback Mountain in Scottsdale. On grounds landscaped tastefully with fountains, pools, and waterfalls are guest accommodations of 440 rooms, 107 casitas, and 33 luxury suites. For dining and recreation, The Phoenician offers four restaurants, a lounge, a tea court, a mineral water bar, poolside snacks, an ice cream parlor, an 18-hole golf course with a 19th hole snack bar and patio, a tennis garden with 10 lighted courts, a water slide, a fun club to keep the children occupied, and much more. The Phoenician is nine miles from Sky Harbor International Airport at 6000 E. Camelback Rd., Scottsdale, AZ 85251; tel. 941-8200 or (800) 888-8234. Rooms and casitas run $331.07-480.04 s or d Jan. 1-June 11, $176.57-317.94 s or d June 12-Sept. 5, and $353.14-502.12 s or d Sept. 6-Dec. 31. One-bedroom suites run $993.20-1655.33 s or d Jan.

1-June 11, $469-882.84 s or d June 12-Sept. 5, and $1103.55-1765.68 s or d Sept. 6-Dec. 31. Two-bedroom suites run $1434.62-1627.74 s or d Jan. 1-June 11, $634.54-772.49 s or d June 12-Sept. 5, $1544.98-1738.09 s or d Sept. 6-Dec. 31. Presidential suites are available.

**The Pointe Hilton on South Mountain** is just off I-10 at 48th St. and Baseline Road. Accommodations consist of suites with separate living room and bedroom, private balcony, two televisions, and a fully stocked refrigerator and wet bar. Three different levels of luxury and golf packages are available. Amenities include four restaurants, an 18-hole golf course, riding stables, six swimming pools, 10 lighted tennis courts, a fitness center, and the Kid's Club Fiesta. The Premiere Rate Plan offers a suite, breakfast, and a fitness center pass at $270.35 s or d Jan. 5-April 10, $237.25 s or d April 11-May 23, $131.32 s or d May 24-Sept. 15, and $237.25 s or d Sept. 16-Jan. 8. The Deluxe Rate Plan offers a suite and choice of breakfast or fitness center pass at $10-20 less than the above prices. The Standard Rate Plan offers a suite at $20-30 less than Premiere Rates. The resort is at 7777 S. Pointe Parkway, Phoenix, AZ 85044; tel. 438-9000 or (800) 572-7222.

**The Pointe Hilton at Tapatio Cliffs** offers two-room suites in an atmosphere of casual elegance and Spanish-Mediterranean-style architecture. Each suite features a separate living room and bedroom plus a fully stocked refrigerator. Amenities include four restaurants, an 18-hole golf course, 15 lighted tennis courts, horseback riding, 7,000 acres for hiking and mountain bike riding, seven swimming pools, and a health spa. The Deluxe Rate Plan offers a suite, buffet breakfast, plus tennis court and driving range privileges at $281.39 s or d Jan. 9-April 8, $237.25 s or d April 9-May 20, $142.35 s or d May 21-Sept. 16, and $237.25 s or d the rest of the year. The Standard Rate Plan offers the suite at $10 less than in the Deluxe Rate Plan. Tapatio Cliffs is at 1111 N. Seventh St., Phoenix, AZ 85020; tel. 866-7500 or (800) 572-7222.

**Regal McCormick Ranch** offers 125 hotel rooms and 51 two- and three-bedroom units only three miles from Scottsdale city center. Amenities include two restaurants, one lounge, two 18-hole golf courses, four lighted tennis courts, plus sailboats, paddleboats, and canoes on Camelback Lake. Rates are $121.39-204.15 s, $132.42-215.18 d May 1-June 18; $65.11-121.39 s or d June 19-Sept. 7; $121.39-204.15 s, $132.42-215.18 d Sept. 8-Jan. 4; and $186.49-274.77 s, $197.53-274.77 d Jan. 5-April 30. Suites and packages are available. Regal McCormick Ranch is at 7401 N. Scottsdale Rd., Scottsdale, AZ 85253; tel. 948-5050 or (800) 243-1332.

**Saguaro Lake Ranch Resort** is on the Salt River one mile south of Saguaro Lake and eight miles east of Mesa. Perhaps the Valley's most rustic resort, the facility is something between a guest ranch and a resort. It has a main lodge and dining rooms with fireplace, riding stables, a swimming pool, numerous hiking and riding trails, and the opportunity to float the Salt River. Bed and breakfast rates are $90.10 s, plus $10.60 per extra person. The American Plan (available Oct.-May) is $116.60 s, $201.40 d. For additional information contact Saguaro Lake Ranch Resort, 13020 Bush Hwy., Mesa, AZ 85215; tel. 984-2194.

**Scottsdale Conference Resort** is in north Scottsdale 25 minutes from Sky Harbor Airport. Accommodations include 325 guest rooms and suites housed in the three-story main building and in private casitas along the golf course. Amenities include a dining room, a cocktail lounge, two 36-hole golf courses, five lighted tennis courts, the Sports and Fitness Center, a swimming pool and an exercise pool, and horseback riding. Room rates are $341.86 s and $457.64 d. The resort is at 7700 E. McCormick Parkway, Scottsdale, AZ 85258; tel. 991-9000 or (800) 528-0293 (call for rates).

**Scottsdale Princess** is at the north end of Scottsdale just west of the Superstition Mountains. It offers 600 guest rooms and suites on 450 acres decorated with Old Stone architecture, saguaros, and cottonwood trees. Perks include four restaurants, six bars and lounges, two 18-hole golf courses, nine tennis courts, a spa and fitness center, three heated pools, and a fitness trail. Rooms rates start at $314.50 s or d Jan. 1-May 20, $137.94 s or d May 21-Sept. 16, $237.25 s or d Sept. 17-Dec 31. The Scottsdale Princess is at 7575 E. Princess Dr., Scottsdale, AZ 85255; tel. 585-4848.

The **Wigwam Resort** is in Litchfield Park, 20 minutes west of central Phoenix. Amenities offered by this resort include three restaurants, three 18-hole golf courses, nine lighted tennis courts, two swimming pools, horseback riding, trap and skeet shooting, and much, much more. Room rates start at $284.25 s, $306.11 d Jan. 8-May 25; $114.79 s, $131.19 d May 26-Sept. 4; and $229.58 s, $251.14 d Sept. 5-Jan. 6. The Wigwam is at 300 Indian School Rd., Litchfield Park, AZ 85340; tel. 935-3811 or (800) 935-3811.

# CAMPGROUNDS AND RV PARKS

Many Valley trailer parks cater to retired people; children aren't always welcome. Parks listed here accept families except where noted.

## Phoenix
**North Phoenix Campground** accepts both tents and RVs at 2550 W. Louise Dr., 17 miles north of downtown, just off I-17 Deer Valley Rd. Exit 215B; rates are $18.91 tent, $22.86 RV w/hookups; tel. 869-8189. The nearby **Desert's Edge RV Park** at 22623 N. Black Canyon Hwy. accepts adults only. Take I-17 Deer Valley Rd. Exit 215A, then go a half mile north on the east frontage road; $17.45 RV w/hookups; tel. 869-7021.

**Covered Wagon RV Park** offers sites for tents ($16.52) and RVs ($19.91) at 6540 N. Black Canyon Highway. Take the I-17 Glendale exit and go a half mile south on the west frontage road; tel. 242-2500. Closer to downtown are the **Trailer Corral** (4040 W. Van Buren St. two miles west from I-17, $15 RV w/hookups, tel. 278-6628); **Green Acres RV Park** (2605 W. Van Buren St. just west of I-17, $12.29 RV w/hookups, tel. 272-7863); and **Michigan Trailer Park** (3140 W. Osborn at Grand Ave., adults only, $18.82 RV w/hookups, tel. 269-0122).

## Tempe
**Tempe Travel Trailer Villa** lies one mile east of the ASU campus at 1831 E. Apache Blvd.; $16.64 RV w/hookups; tel. 968-1411. **Apache Palms RV Park** is nearby at 1836 E. Apache Blvd.; $20 RV w/hookups; tel. 966-7399. Or you can stay at **Green Acres III** at 1890 E. Apache Blvd.; $15 RV w/hookups; tel. 829-0106.

## Mesa

**Green Acres I** is near the Tri-City Mall at 2052 W. Main St.; $18 RV w/hookups, $19 in the adult section; tel. 964-5058. The adults-only **Goodlife RV Resort** is four miles east of downtown at 3403 E. Main St.; $30.05 RV w/hookups; tel. 832-4990. Farther out is **Mesa Regal RV Resort** (adults only) at 4700 E. Main St.; $26 RV w/hookups; tel. 830-2821.

## Apache Junction

Both tents and RVs are welcome at **Apache Trail KOA**, 1540 S. Tomahawk Rd., 1.5 miles southeast on US 60/89 from the junction with AZ 88; $15.73 tent, $16.28 RV no hookups, $20.07-23.33 RV w/hookups; tel. 982-4015. **Lost Dutchman State Park** offers simpler facilities six miles northeast on AZ 88 from US 60/89 in the foothills of the Superstition Mountains; $8 tent or RV (no showers or hookups); tel. 982-4485. **Lost Dutchman RV Resort** (adults only) is right in town at 400 N. Plaza Dr. (0.3 mile northeast on AZ 88); $29.56 RV w/hookups; tel. 982-4173. **Rock Shadows Travel Trailer Resort** (adults only) is at 600 S. Idaho Rd.; $28.76 RV w/hookups; tel. 982-0450. RVers will find the largest selection of places to stay in Apache Junction; the local chamber of commerce maintains a more complete list of RV parks.

## North of Phoenix

**Ben Avery Shooting Facility** offers sites to registered match shooters only ($4 tents, $8 RV no hookups, showers available) just west of I-17 at Exit 223, 26 miles north of Phoenix; tel. 582-8313; reservations requested. **Lake Pleasant County Park** features two new campgrounds, Roadrunner and Desert Tortoise (call for rates and amenities); primitive camping available along the lakeshore; $4 per day (24 hours) park entrance fee per vehicle plus $2 for each water craft. Take I-17 Exit 223 (26 miles north of Phoenix), go west 12 miles on AZ 74, and follow signs; tel. 566-1939.

**Seven Springs Campground** is in the Tonto National Forest just north of the Valley. Large sycamore and ash trees provide shade; sites have picnic tables and pit toilets but no drinking water. Also no fee. From the town of Cave Creek go seven miles east on Cave Creek Rd. to a junction, then keep left on Forest Route 24. The

road becomes dirt after two miles; it's another 11 miles to Seven Springs. **Cave Creek Campground,** a mile farther, is a group-fee area requiring reservations; tel. 488-3441. The Cave Creek Trail System offers about 30 miles on five major trails for hikers, horseback riders, and mountain bikers.

**Bartlett Lake** is an irrigation reservoir on the Verde River with primitive camping at Riverside Campground (vault toilets but no drinking water) or along the shore; a paved boat ramp leads anglers to bass, crappie, catfish, and bluegill. A new marina has opened and is adding amenities including snack bar, boat rental, dry storage, and bait and tackle; tel. 488-5252. The Mazatzal Mountains soar into the sky across the lake. From the town of Cave Creek go seven miles east on Cave Creek Rd., turn right and drive six miles on Forest Route 205, then continue eight miles on Forest Route 19 to the lake; call the rangers for up-to-date information; tel. 488-3441.

**Horseshoe Lake,** upstream from Bartlett, has primitive camping near the dam (vault toilets but no drinking water), a paved boat ramp, and fishing. Follow directions to Bartlett except turn left at the intersection of Forest Routes 19 and 205 and take Forest Route 205 all the way to the dam. Horseshoe has a 15 mph speed limit; no waterskiing or jet skis. Camping at both lakes is free.

For more information, contact the **Cave Creek Ranger Station** at 7171 E. Cave Creek Rd., Carefree, AZ 85377; open Mon.-Fri. 7:45 a.m.-4:30 p.m.; tel. 488-3441.

## West of Phoenix

**KOA** has a campground at 1440 N. Citrus Rd. in Goodyear 20 miles west of downtown Phoenix along I-10. Take I-10 Exit 14 then go south on Cotton Lane to Van Buren St. and turn west to Citrus Ave.; $16 tents, $15.50 RV w/o hookups, $18.50-20.50 w/hookups; tel. 853-0537.

## Other Areas

**Maricopa County** parks ring the Valley, offering camping in McDowell Mountain Regional Park to the northeast, Usery Mountain Recreation Area to the east, and White Tank Mountain Regional Park to the west. Camping areas in some of these parks close in summer.

# VALLEY OF THE SUN RESTAURANTS

The Valley has an amazing number of restaurants—enough to fill a book. And, in fact, there is such a book, titled *100 Best Restaurants in Arizona.* This book and its detailed info, revised annually, is useful for diners staying in the Phoenix area. The *Official Visitors Guide,* distributed free by the Visitors Bureau, also features restaurant listings. A third dining source is the monthly *Phoenix Magazine.*

Make reservations at the more expensive places; also check on dress regulations. The following list covers only a fraction of dining possibilities.

Restaurants are marked as $: Inexpensive (to $8), $$: Moderate ($8-15), $$$: Expensive (more than $15). Ratings refer to price ranges for dinners (per person).

## AMERICAN

**$$ The American Grill:** Offers a varied menu, from grilled seafood and chowder to steak. Open daily for lunch and dinner. In Scottsdale at Hilton Village, 6113 N. Scottsdale Rd.; tel. 948-9907. In Mesa at 1233 S. Alma School Rd.; tel. 844-1918.

**$$$ The Compass:** Glide high above the city in the Hyatt Regency's revolving restaurant. Open Mon.-Sat. for lunch and dinner, Sunday for brunch and dinner. At 122 N. Second St. in downtown Phoenix; tel. 440-3166.

**$ Furr's:** Popular cafeteria chain with a wide choice of food. Open daily for lunch and dinner. In Phoenix at 8114 N. Black Canyon Hwy.; tel. 995-1588. In Mesa at 1834 W. Main St.; tel. 962-9107. In Sun City at 10415 W. Grand Ave.; tel. 974-3639.

**$$$ Orangerie:** New American cuisine with excellent service in a newly remodeled Frank Lloyd Wright-style decor; patio dining is available. Open Mon.-Sat. for breakfast, lunch, and dinner. In Phoenix at the Arizona Biltmore Resort, Missouri Ave. and 24th St.; tel. 954-2507.

**$$ to $$$ Oscar Taylor:** Good food with Prohibition-era Chicago decor. Open daily for lunch and dinner. At Biltmore Fashion Park, 2420 E. Camelback Rd., Phoenix; tel. 956-5705.

**$ Piccadilly:** Cafeteria with varied selections. Open daily for lunch and dinner. In Phoenix at Westridge Mall, 7611 W. Thomas Rd., tel. 849-6163; and at 620 W. Osborn Rd., tel. 266-3795. In Gilbert at 1343 S. Gilbert Rd.; tel. 926-4545.

**$ Sugar Bowl:** An old-fashioned ice-cream parlor offering a myriad of tempting treats for sweet tooths. Also serves home-style meals daily for lunch and dinner. In Old Town Scottsdale at the corner of 4005 N. Scottsdale Rd. and First Ave.; tel. 946-0051.

## WESTERN

**$$ Don & Charlie's American Rib and Chop House:** Top-notch steak and barbecue. Open daily for dinner only. At 7501 E. Camelback Rd., Scottsdale; tel. 990-0900.

**$$ Mining Camp:** Great Western grub, much of it all-you-can-eat, served family style in a replica of an old mining camp's cook shanty. Great for the kids. Open daily Nov.-May for dinner with lunch available on Sunday. It's four miles northeast of Apache Junction on AZ 88 at the easternmost end of the Valley; tel. 982-3181.

**$$ Pinnacle Peak Patio:** Country music every night, hayrides on weekends. Strictly cowboy atmosphere—if you wear a tie inside, it'll be snipped off and added to the large collection hanging from the rafters. Open Sunday for lunch and daily for dinner. It's in the foothills of the McDowell Mountains about 20 miles northeast of Scottsdale, via Scottsdale and Pinnacle Peak Roads at 10426 W. Jomax and Alma School Roads; tel. 585-1599.

**$$ Rawhide Steakhouse and Saloon:** Live country-western music every night. You can choose deep-fried rattlesnake, buffalo, steak, chicken, or ribs. Open Mon.-Thurs. for lunch and daily for dinner. It's 13 miles north of central Scottsdale (four miles north of Bell Rd.) at 23023 N. Scottsdale Rd.; tel. 502-5600.

**$ Real Texas Bar-B-Que:** The decor isn't much, but the ribs are great and you can't beat the prices. Open Tues.-Sat. for lunch and dinner. At 2415 W. Bethany Home Rd., Phoenix; tel. 249-9985.

**$$ Waterin' Hole Chuckwagon 'n' Saloon:** Cowgirls serve steak, ribs, chicken, and seafood in a rustic dining room. Open daily for lunch and dinner. It's a half mile south of Pointe Hilton Resort at Tapatio Cliffs, 11111 N. Seventh St. (enter on Clinton), Phoenix; tel. 944-4451.

## MEXICAN

**$$ Aunt Chilada's:** In a century-old, former general store. Open daily for lunch and dinner. In Phoenix at Pointe Resort at Squaw Peak, 7330 N. Dreamy Draw Dr.; tel. 944-1286. In Tempe at Pointe Resort South Mountain, 2021 W. Baseline Rd.; tel. 431-6470.

**$ to $$ Garcia's:** This popular restaurant has grown into a chain spanning 11 states. All are open daily for lunch and dinner. In Phoenix, Garcia's is at 4420 E. Camelback Rd.; tel. 952-8031; and at 3301 W. Peoria Ave. near Metrocenter, tel. 866-1850. In Mesa, Garcia's is at 1940 E. University Dr.; tel. 844-0023. In Chandler, 2394 Alma School Rd., tel. 963-0067. The original Garcia's (not part of the chain) is in Phoenix at 2212 N. 35th Ave.; tel. 272-5584.

**$ La Parrilla Suiza:** Authentic Mexico City food. Open daily for lunch and dinner. At 3508 W. Peoria Ave., Phoenix; tel. 978-8334.

**$ Pancho's Mexican Buffet:** Excellent value in a buffet with initial serving cafeteria style and seconds brought to you when you raise the miniature Italian flag at your table. Open daily for lunch and dinner. In Phoenix at 1003 E. Indian School Rd., tel. 285-0899; at 8146 W. Indian School Rd., tel. 849-0995; and at Metrocenter, 10213 N. Metro Parkway, tel. 997-6221. In Mesa at S. Country Club and Southern Ave.; tel. 833-1144.

**$ Tee Pee:** Open daily with specials for lunch and dinner. At 4144 E. Indian School Rd., Phoenix; tel. 956-0178.

## SEAFOOD

**$$ Landry's Pacific Fish Company:** A good place for fresh seafood in a nautical setting. Many items broiled over mesquite charcoal. Open daily for lunch and dinner. At 4321 N. Scottsdale Rd., Scottsdale; tel. 941-0602.

**$$ to $$$ The Fish Market:** The main restaurant downstairs features mesquite-grilled fish and New England style seafood. You can also drop by the oyster bar or shop for fresh fish daily. The upstairs "Top of the Market" features gourmet dining. Open daily for lunch and dinner. Located at 1720 E. Camelback Rd., Phoenix; tel. 277-3474.

**$$$ Rusty Pelican:** The decor and food will convince you you're beside the ocean. Open daily for lunch and dinner. On the east side of I-17 across from Metrocenter at 9801-A N. Black Canyon Hwy., Phoenix; tel. 944-9646. Try the new Tempe location at 1606 W. Baseline Rd.; tel. 345-0972.

## FRENCH

**$$$ Etienne's Different Pointe of View:** Perhaps the Valley's ultimate in sophisticated dining, with a dazzling view of Phoenix. For a feast, check out the Sunday brunch. Open daily for dinner. At Pointe Resort at Tapatio Cliffs, 11111 N. Seventh St., Phoenix; tel. 863-0912.

**$$$ Bistro La Chaumiere:** Excellent food in one of Scottsdale's older houses. Open Mon.-Sat. for lunch and daily for dinner. At 6910 Main St., Scottsdale; tel. 946-5115.

**$$$ Vincent's on Camelback:** Imaginative French-classic cuisine with a Southwestern touch and first-rate service. Open weekdays for lunch and daily for dinner; closed Sunday in summer. At 3930 E. Camelback Rd., Phoenix; tel. 224-0225.

**$$$ Voltaire:** Superb food and friendly atmosphere. Open Mon.-Sat. for dinner only; closed June 1-Sept. 30. At 8340 E. McDonald Dr., Scottsdale; tel. 948-1005.

## ITALIAN

**$$$ Avanti:** Italian cuisine dominates the varied menu. Open daily for dinner. At 2728 E. Thomas Rd.; tel.956-0900. In Scottsdale at 3102 N. Scottsdale Rd.; tel. 949-8333.

**$$$ Mancuso's:** Outstanding northern Italian and continental cuisine prepared from family recipes. Open daily for dinner only. At the Borgata Shopping Center, 6166 N. Scottsdale Rd., Scottsdale; tel. 948-9988.

**$$ Prego Ristorante:** Fine cuisine from both northern and southern Italy. Open Mon.-Fri. for lunch and dinner, Saturday and Sunday for dinner only. At 5816 N. 16th St., Phoenix; tel. 241-0288.

**$$$ Pronto Ristorante:** Features regional Italian cuisine in a wood paneled dining area decorated with antique clocks and musical instruments. Open Mon.-Fri. for lunch and dinner, Saturday for dinner only. At 3950 E. Campbell Ave., Phoenix; tel. 956-4049.

**$$ Tomaso's:** Northern Italian dining. Open Mon.-Fri. for lunch and dinner, Saturday and Sunday for dinner only. At 3225 E. Camelback Rd., Phoenix; tel. 956-0836.

**$$ Tony's New Yorker Restaurant:** Great pasta in an informal, neighborhood restaurant. Open daily for dinner. At 107 E. Broadway, Tempe; tel. 967-3073.

## GERMAN

**$$ Felsen Haus:** Authentic food and beer with lively polka music. Open daily for lunch and dinner. At 1008 E. Camelback Rd., Phoenix; tel. 277-1119.

## GREEK

**$$ Greekfest:** Tasty food at family prices. Open Mon.-Sat. for lunch and dinner and Sunday for dinner. At 1940 E. Camelback Rd., Phoenix; tel. 265-2990.

## INDIAN

**$$ Delhi Palace:** Vegetarian and nonvegetarian food in tandoori and other styles. Open daily for lunch and dinner; the lunch buffet is a good value. In Phoenix at 16842 N. Seventh St.; tel. 942-4224. In Tempe at 933 E. University Ave.; tel. 921-2200.

**$$ Jewel of the Crown:** Both vegetarian and carnivore dishes are offered in tandoori and other styles. Open daily for lunch and dinner. At 4141 N. Scottsdale Rd., Scottsdale; tel. 840-2412.

## MIDDLE EASTERN

**$ Haji-Baba:** Excellent inexpensive meals. Also Middle Eastern groceries, magazines, records, and musical instruments. Open Mon.-Sat. for lunch and dinner (closes Saturday at 6 p.m.). At 1513 E. Apache Blvd., Tempe; tel. 894-1905.

**$ Mediterranean House:** The cafe's owner has an Israeli and Yemeni background. Open Mon.-Fri. for lunch and Mon.-Sat. for dinner. At 1588 E. Bethany Home Rd., Phoenix; tel. 248-8460.

## CHINESE

**$$ China Doll:** Very large selection of Cantonese specialties, including dim sum. The shrimp in garlic sauce is a special favorite. Open daily for lunch and dinner. At 3336 N. Seventh Ave. at Osborn Rd., Phoenix; tel. 264-0538.

**$ China Gate:** A Valley favorite with the best in Mandarin, Szechuan, and Hunan cuisines.

Open Mon.-Sat. for lunch and daily for dinner. At Metrocenter in north Phoenix, 3033 W. Peoria Ave.; tel. 944-1982. In Scottsdale at 7820 E. McDowell Rd.; tel. 946-0720. And in Mesa at 2050 W. Guadalupe Rd.; tel. 897-0607.

**$$ Golden Phoenix:** Mandarin cuisine. Open Sun.-Fri. for lunch and daily for dinner. In Phoenix at 6048 N. 16th St., tel. 263-8049; and at 1534 W. Camelback Rd., tel. 279-4447. In Scottsdale at 7910 E. Chaparral Rd.; tel. 941-9355.

**$$ Sesame Inn:** Top Szechuan, Mandarin, and Hunan cuisine. Open Mon.-Fri. for lunch and Mon.-Sat. for dinner in Phoenix at 541 E. Van Buren St. in the Mercado; tel. 252-0111. Other Phoenix locations open daily for lunch and dinner are at 2900 N. Central Ave., tel. 230-7500; and at 3912 E. Camelback Rd., tel. 957-3993. In Scottsdale at 13600 N. Scottsdale Rd.; tel. 483-9696. And in Chandler at 3002 N. Arizona Ave.; tel. 926-7171.

**$$ Szechuan Inn:** Szechuan and Mandarin dining. Open daily for lunch and dinner, Saturday and Sunday for dinner only. At 1617 E. Thomas Rd., Phoenix; tel. 274-7051.

## THAI

**$ to $$ Char's:** Authentic and fiery cuisine in the restaurant that introduced Thai food to the Valley. Open daily for lunch and dinner. In Tempe at 927 E. University Dr.; tel. 967-6013.

**$ to $$ Daa's Thai Room:** Great food with pleasant surroundings. Don't ask for hot spices unless you can take it *very* hot. Open Tues.-Fri. for lunch and dinner, Saturday and Sunday for dinner only. In Scottsdale at 7419 E. Indian Plaza (near Camelback Rd. and 74th St.); tel. 941-9015.

**$ to $$ Mallee's on Main:** Many tempting dishes of gourmet Thai food. Open Mon.-Sat. for lunch and daily for dinner. In Old Town Scottsdale at 7131 E. Main St.; tel. 947-6042.

**$ to $$ Royal Barge:** Great selection of tasty Thai food. Open Mon.-Fri. for lunch and daily for dinner. In Scottsdale at El Pueblo Shopping Plaza, 8140 N. Hayden Rd.; tel. 443-1953.

**$ Thai Rama:** Inexpensive Thai food on a varied menu. Open Mon.-Sat. for lunch and daily for dinner. In Phoenix at 1702 W. Camelback Rd.; tel. 285-1123.

## VIETNAMESE

**$ to $$ To Do:** Try another spicy Asian cuisine. Open daily for lunch and dinner. In Phoenix at 7828 N. 19th Ave., just south of Northern Ave.; tel. 864-6759.

## JAPANESE

**$$ to $$$ Ayako of Tokyo:** Chefs offer teppanyaki table-top cooking, tempura, and a sushi bar. Open Mon.-Fri. for lunch and dinner, Saturday and Sunday for dinner only. At Biltmore Fashion Park, 2564 E. Camelback Rd., Phoenix; tel. 955-7007.

**$$ Shogun:** You can choose from meat and seafood entrees or one of the many items at the sushi-sashimi bar. Open Mon.-Sat. for lunch and daily for dinner. At 12615 N. Tatum Blvd., Paradise Valley; tel. 953-3264.

**$ Tokyo Express:** Inexpensive but good food. Open daily for lunch and dinner. In Phoenix at 3517 E. Thomas Rd., tel. 955-1051; at 5130 N. 19th Ave., tel. 433-1311; at 914 E. Camelback Rd., tel. 277-4666; at 4105 N. 51st Ave., tel. 245-1166; and at 13637 N. Tatum Blvd., tel. 996-0101. In Mesa at 1120 S. Dobson Rd.; tel. 898-3090.

**$$ Yamakasa:** A popular place for sushi, tempura, sukiyaki, shabu shabu, and other styles. Open Mon.-Sat. for lunch and dinner. At 9301 E. Shea Blvd. in Scottsdale; tel. 860-5605.

## KOREAN

**$$ Korean Restaurant:** Flavorful bulkogi (barbecued beef) and other specialties; try the tangy kimchee (marinated vegetables) too. Open Tues.-Sun. for lunch and daily for dinner. At 1414 N. Scottsdale Rd. in Scottsdale; tel. 994-5995.

**$$ Korean Garden:** offers authentic Korean home-cooked food in a pleasant environment. Open Mon.-Sat. for lunch and daily for dinner in Tempe (near ASU) at 1324 S. Rural Rd.; tel. 967-1133.

## SOUL FOOD

**$ Golden Rule Cafe:** Good cookin' by Mrs. White. Open Mon.-Fri. for lunch, and dinner. At 808 E. Jefferson St., Phoenix; tel. 262-9256.

## PIZZA

**$ Pizzafarro's:** One of the Valley's best. Open daily except Monday for dinner only. In Phoenix at 4730 E. Indian School Rd.; tel. 840-7990. In Scottsdale at 7120 E. Mercer Ln.; tel. 991-0331. In Carefree at 36889 N. Tom Darlington Dr.; tel. 488-0703.

**$ Tommy's Pizza:** Open daily for lunch and dinner. In Phoenix at 518 E. Dunlap Ave.; tel. 997-7578.

## DELIS

**$ Gentle Strength Co-op & Deli:** Tasty and healthy vegetarian food. Open Mon.-Sat. for lunch and Mon.-Fri. for a light dinner; Saturday for a pizza lunch and dinner; Sunday for brunch. At 234 W. University Dr., near ASU in Tempe; tel. 968-4831.

**$ Katz:** Open daily for breakfast and lunch, Tues.-Fri. for dinner. At 5144 N. Central Ave., Phoenix; tel. 277-8814.

**$ Miracle Mile:** A kosher-style cafeteria with good portions of excellent food. Open Mon.-Sat. for breakfast, lunch, and dinner and Sunday for dinner. In Phoenix at 9 Park Central Mall; tel. 277-4783. In West Phoenix at Christ-Town Mall, 1733 W. Bethany Home Rd.; tel. 249-2904.

## SPECIALTY FOOD STORES

**Italian:** DeFalco's Italian Grocery, 2724 N. 68th St., Scottsdale; tel. 990-8660.

**Kosher:** Segal's Kosher Foods, 4818 N. Seventh St., Phoenix; tel. 285-1515.

**Middle East:** Ararat Foods, 4119 N. 19th Ave., Phoenix; tel. 277-3517. **Middle Eastern Bakery and Deli, Inc.,** 3052 N. 16th St., Phoenix; tel. 277-4927.

**Natural:** Gentle Strength Cooperative, 234 W. University Dr., Tempe; tel. 968-4831.

**Asian:** Win Fong, 3838 N. 19th Ave., Phoenix; tel. 277-7717. **Loiphat,** 1702 W. Camelback Rd., Phoenix; tel. 242-6119.

# VALLEY OF THE SUN ENTERTAINMENT

## EVENTS

Concerts, festivals, shows, and other special events happen nearly every day in the Valley; the Visitors Bureau will keep you apprised. Pick up a *Calendar of Events* brochure or the *Official Visitors Guide,* or call the **Visitors Hotline,** tel. 252-5588.

Following are some of the best-known annual happenings.

**January**
The **Fiesta Bowl** kicks off the year on January 1 at Arizona State University's Sun Devil Stadium. Competitors put their best stock forward during the **Arizona National Livestock Show.** Top PGA golfers compete in the **Phoenix Open. Parada del Sol** in Scottsdale features the world's longest horse-drawn parade and a big rodeo.

**February**
The horsey set enjoys Scottsdale's **All-Arabian Horse Show and Sale.** Native Americans host the **O'odham Tash Indian Pow Wow** near the city of Casa Grande, 45 miles south of Phoenix, with a parade, rodeo, dances, and crowning of the O'odham queen. Fountain Hills hosts the **Great Fair,** featuring a hot-air balloon race, 5K and 10K runs, and the Southwest Arts and Crafts Show. **Lost Dutchman Days** presents a parade, rodeo, and bluegrass festival in Apache Junction. Step back to the 16th century for **The Arizona Renaissance Festival,** when King's Equestrian Area, a vast site southeast of Apache Junction, is transformed into a medieval playground of tournament jousting, theater, crafts, food, and costumed performers.

**March**
The **Renaissance Festival** continues from February. **Maricopa County Fair** features entertainment, rides, and agricultural exhibits at the Arizona State Fairgrounds. The **Heard Museum Guild Indian Fair** presents Southwestern Indi-

an food, dances, art, and crafts. **Spring Festival of the Arts** features work by some of the Southwest's best artists and craftspeople, along with food treats and live performances; action takes place along Mill Ave. at Fourth, Fifth, and Sixth Streets in Old Town Tempe. Chandler hosts the annual **Ostrich Festival** with ostrich races and arts and crafts booths. Williams Gateway Airport in Mesa hosts the **Phoenix 500 Air Races and Fly In** with aerobic performances by a military jet demonstration team.

**April**
The **Phoenix Jazz Festival** draws top performers to the city. **Yaqui Indian Easter Celebration** begins on Ash Wednesday and continues every Friday until Holy Week, then Wednesday to Easter Sunday. Dancers wear special masks and costumes in a reenactment of the crucifixion. The ceremonies, believed to be nearly 300 years old, symbolize the battle between good and evil. Sponsored by the Yaqui Indian community and held at the Church Plaza between Iglesia and San Angelo roads in Guadalupe, southeast of Phoenix. **Scottsdale All-Indian Days Annual Pow Wow** brings more than 50 tribes to town for competitions in arts and crafts, music, dances, and other activities.

**May**
Mexican music, dancing, and food mark **Cinco de Mayo** (May 5), the anniversary of Mexico's 1862 expulsion of France. **Phoenix Jaycees' Rodeo of Rodeos** hosts a parade and competition for top-ranked cowboys.

**June to September**
It's too hot! Valley residents head for the nearest swimming pool or drive to the high country. Those who stay enjoy the **Summer Performing Arts** program of musicals, plays, and concerts held at the Herberger Theater Center and at Symphony Hall. **July 4th Fireworks** brighten the night skies. In September, **Fiestas Patrias** celebrates Mexican independence with fireworks, entertainment, and food.

## October

The **Arizona State Fair** in Phoenix features exhibits of the state's best in agriculture, livestock, and home crafts, along with concerts, rides, and games. The Phoenix Art Museum puts on a **Cowboy Artists of America Exhibition.** Scottsdale's **Rodeo Showdown** pits some of the best Canadian riders and teams against Americans.

## November

Bright colors fill the sky over northwest Phoenix as hot-air balloons take off for the **Thunderbird International Balloon Race,** a world-class event involving hot air balloons plus an airshow with WW II planes and modern jets.

## December

Holiday festivities include the downtown Phoenix **Fiesta of Lights,** with a festival and electric light parade and Heritage Square's Victorian Holiday. More than 100 Indian craftspeople exhibit and sell their work at the Pueblo Grande Museum **Indian Market;** tribes also perform native dances and serve traditional food. The Valley gets ready for the **Fiesta Bowl** with more than 40 events, including an impressive parade, a marathon, bicycle races, and the Pageant of Bands. Tempe's Old Town hosts the **Winter Festival of the Arts** to exhibit the work of local and visiting artists; food, music, dance, and children's entertainment add to the celebration.

## THEATER AND CONCERTS

To find out what's happening in the Valley, call the Visitor Hotline; tel. 252-5588 (recording). Newspapers, especially the weekly *New Times* (free at newsstands), review the entertainment scene.

### Phoenix

**Arizona Theatre Company** performs classic and contemporary plays and some musicals from early November to early June at Herberger Theater Center, 222 E. Monroe St.; tel. 256-6995 (AZ Theatre Company box office) or 252-8497 (Herberger Theater box office). The **Phoenix Symphony** offers a variety of concerts during the September to May season.

The music resounds at Symphony Hall in downtown Phoenix and at Scottsdale Center for the Arts; tel. 264-6363. **Ballet Arizona** productions occur from autumn to spring at Herberger Theater Center and at Symphony Hall; tel. 381-0184.

**Arizona Opera** presents productions October to March at Symphony Hall; tel. 266-7464. Symphony Hall is in the downtown Phoenix Civic Plaza at 225 E. Adams Street. **Phoenix Little Theatre,** opened in 1920, is the longest continuously running theater in the country; it's in the Phoenix Civic Center, behind the Phoenix Art Museum, near the corner of Central Ave. and McDowell Rd.; tel. 254-2151. The city of Phoenix presents free **evening concerts** featuring a variety of music April to October in Encanto Park at the south clubhouse patio; tel. 261-8991.

### Scottsdale

The **Scottsdale Center for the Arts** sponsors diverse musical and theatrical offerings at 7380 Scottsdale Mall, one block south of Indian School Rd. and two blocks east of Scottsdale Rd.; tel. 994-ARTS. **Kerr Cultural Center** offers musical ensembles and theatrical productions all year in a charming adobe recital hall at 6110 N. Scottsdale Rd.; tel. 965-5377.

### Tempe

**Gammage Center for the Performing Arts,** on the ASU campus, offers a varied program of theater, concerts, and dance in a distinctive rotund structure. The center will also inform you of other events on campus; tel. 965-3434 (box office). Free tours are available during the school year Mon.-Fri. 1-3:30 p.m; tel. 965-4050. **Red River Opry** offers performances by world-famous singing artists of country, western, gospel, blue grass, rock and roll, and nostalgia plus a Christmas show; $14.50 adults, $12.50 seniors (55 and over), $8.50 children 2-12; all seats are reserved; it's off Mill Ave. at Washington/Curry, one block north of the Mill Ave. bridge; tel. 829-OPRY or (800) 466-OPRY.

### Mesa

**Mesa Little Theatre** offers three productions per year running from October to April at the Mesa Arts Center, 155 N. Center; tel. 834-9500.

**Sun City**
**Sundome Center for the Performing Arts** frequently hosts big-name performers in a 7,000 seat facility, said to be the world's largest single level theater, at 19403 R.H. Johnson Blvd. in Sun City West; tel. 975-1900.

## SPORTING EVENTS

The **Arizona Cardinals,** a professional football team, plays home games at Arizona State University's Sun Devil Stadium in Tempe; tel. 379-0102. Major league baseball is arriving in Phoenix with the formation of the **Arizona Diamondbacks** who will call **Bank One Ballpark** home starting in 1998. The stadium is under construction at the corner of Fourth and Jefferson Streets; tel. 221-1356. The NBA **Phoenix Suns** professional basketball team's home games are held in the Arizona Veterans Memorial Coliseum, 1826 W. McDowell Rd.; tel. 379-SUNS. The **Phoenix Firebirds,** a minor league baseball team, play ball at Scottsdale Stadium, 7408 E. Osborn Rd., April to August; tel. 275-0500. The **Arizona Sandsharks** play soccer at America West Arena from late June through late September; tel. 514-KICK.

The **Phoenix Roadrunners** play hockey Oct.-April at Veterans Memorial Coliseum; tel. 340-0001. The NHL's Winnipeg Jets are coming to Phoenix as the **Phoenix Coyotes.** The **Phoenix Open** attracts big-name professional golfers each January to the Tournament Players Club in Scottsdale; tel. 870-0163.

The Arizona State University **Sun Devils** battle opponents in an active program of football, baseball, basketball, swimming, gymnastics, archery, and other sports. To find out what's going on, call Sun Devil Sports; tel. 965-2381 (ticket office) or 965-6592 (media relations). The ASU Sun Devil football stadium hosts the annual **Fiesta Bowl,** one of the country's biggest NCAA bowl games, played on New Year's Day.

Engines roar as cars strain for the finish line February to November at **Manzanita Speedway,** 35th Ave. and West Broadway; tel. 276-7575. **Phoenix International Raceway** schedules several major events each year at S. 115th Ave. and Baseline Rd.; tel. 252-3833. **Firebird International Raceway** offers both land and water racing with several courses including a professional NHRA dragstrip and a 120-acre water-sports lake just 15 miles south of Phoenix off I-10 at exit 162A; tel. 268-0200 or (800) DRAG-INFO. **American Desert Racing** is for off-road vehicles all year at various locations; tel. 274-0010. Dogs run the track at **Phoenix Greyhound Park** most nights year-round; stay cool in the air-conditioned grandstands at E.

## BATTER UP

**B**aseball teams, mostly from cold, wet parts of the country, take advantage of Arizona's sunny weather. The players warm up for the season in spring training camps here; these boys of spring call themselves the Cactus League. Visiting fans can watch players practice and see exhibition games in Valley of the Sun or Tucson Stadiums. The Colorado Rockies use Hi Corbett Field in Tucson's Randolph Park; the future Arizona Diamondbacks also plan to play here. The San Diego Padres and the Seattle Mariners use the Peoria Sports Complex at 83rd Ave. and Bell Road. The Oakland A's play in Municipal Stadium at 5999 E. Van Buren. The San Francisco Giants use Scottsdale Stadium at 7408 E. Osborn. The Chicago Cubs use HoHoKam Park at 1235 N. Center St. in Mesa. The California Angels practice in Tempe Diablo Stadium at 2525 S. 48th

Street. The Milwaukee Brewers use Compadre Stadium at 1425 W. Ocotillo Rd. in Chandler. Two Cactus League teams will share a new spring break training camp planned for Tucson. One of the teams may be new to the league. For additional information, call the Cactus League; tel. (602) 827-4700 or (800) 283-6372.

To learn when exhibition games are scheduled, consult the "Sports" section of the *Arizona Republic* or the *Tribune* newspapers or call the following numbers: Cubs, Brewers, and Oakland A's through Dillards at 678-2222 (in Arizona) or (800) 638-4253 (out of state); Padres, Mariners, and Giants through TicketMaster at 784-4444; Angels through either TicketMaster at 784-4444 or through Dillards at 678-2222; and Rockies at (800) 388-ROCK.

Washington and 40th Streets; tel. 273-7181. **Apache Greyhound Park** offers race events in Apache Junction at 2551 W. Apache Trail; tel.

982-2371. Thoroughbred and quarter horses race at **Turf Paradise** Oct.-May; 1501 W. Bell Rd. and 19th Ave.; tel. 942-1101.

# VALLEY OF THE SUN RECREATION

Valleyites take their sports seriously and the recreational facilities are limitless. You can play golf, tennis, or racquetball, go horseback riding, jump in the pool, tube the Salt River, and even go surfing. The **Phoenix Parks and Recreation Department** sponsors some excellent parks and a variety of educational and recreation programs for children, adults, and seniors; tel. 262-6861. Several large county parks ring the Valley, providing additional opportunities to escape city life; for info call the **Maricopa County Parks and Recreation Department;** tel. 506-2930. The book *Day Hikes and Trail Rides in and around Phoenix* by Roger and Ethel Freeman offers detailed trail descriptions for hikers and horseback riders.

## SPORTS

### Golf and Tennis

Both golf and tennis are extremely popular in the Valley. Enthusiasts often spend entire vacations at resorts offering top-notch facilities and professional instructors. Four Phoenix city parks feature golf courses, 32 offer tennis courts, and there are three tennis centers; tel. 262-7985. A free list of public and private golf courses is available from the Visitors Bureau.

### Swimming

Phoenix alone offers 27 public pools; see the Phoenix Yellow Pages under "Swimming Pools." If you're looking for waves and water slides, try those places listed below.

   **Kiwanis Recreation Center:** Enjoy the year-round indoor wave pool, gym, and tennis courts at 6111 S. All-America Way in the large Kiwanis Park, reached by Mill Ave. between Baseline and Guadalupe Roads in Tempe; tel. 350-5201.

   **Big Surf:** It's all here—surf, sun, and sand. Artificial waves three- to five-feet high come crashing onto the broad, sandy beach. You can

rent rafts and, for added thrills, try the water slides. Small children can play in a shallow pool. The season runs daily Memorial Day to Labor Day weekends. Big Surf is in northern Tempe at 1500 N. Hayden Rd. south of McKellips Rd.; tel. 947-SURF or 947-2477.

   **Waterworld Safari:** Water slides and a wave pool provide excitement. Ride the waves with a rented inner tube; shallow pools cater to small children. All day admissions run $12.50 adult, $10.25 child (ages 4-11), under age four free. The park is open Memorial Day to Labor Day weekends. From downtown Phoenix take I-17 north 17 miles to Pinnacle Peak Rd. (Exit 217), then go west two miles on Pinnacle Peak Rd.; tel. 581-1947.

### Tubing Down the Lower Salt River

Cool off in the summer on a leisurely float down the Salt River east of Mesa. Salt River Recreation rents inner tubes and provides shuttle bus service back to the put-in point for $8 per person (shuttle pass only, $4); tel. 984-3305. Season runs from mid-April through September. The shuttle bus serves five points along the river, with a choice of floats spanning 90 minutes to a full day.

   An extra tube will carry your cooler of cold drinks; don't bring glass containers. Weekends often bring large crowds, and the Salt becomes one big party. Wear tennis shoes to protect your feet when walking in the river. Life jackets are a good idea—a necessity with children. Don't tie your tubes together; rather, lock your feet into each other's tubes.

   Below Granite Reef Dam, the Salt is a river no more—the water is channeled into canals, leaving only a dry downstream riverbed. No camping is allowed on the lower Salt River—Stewart Mountain Dam to Granite Reef Dam—from April 1 to October 31. From the east edge of Mesa, take Bush Hwy. north to the Salt River.

### Horseback Riding

The Phoenix area offers miles of scenic trails

suitable for horses. Many of the stables can arrange lessons, breakfast rides, steak cookouts, hayrides, overnight trips, and boarding. Reservations areadvised. For rides into South Mountain Park, see **All Western Stables** (10220 S. Central Ave., tel. 276-5862), **Ponderosa Stables** (10215 S. Central Ave., tel. 268-1261), or **South Mountain Stables** (10005 S. Central Ave., tel. 276-8131). Near Papago Park, you can ride from **Papago Riding Stable,** 400 N. Scottsdale Rd. in Tempe; tel. 966-9793.

In Cave Creek, ride with **MacDonald's Ranch,** 26540 N. Scottsdale Rd.; tel. 585-0239. For guided hourly, all-day, and overnight pack trips into the wild Superstition Mountains and other desert areas, see **Superstition Riding Stables** at 2151 N. Warner Rd. (off N. Meridian Rd.) in Apache Junction, tel. 982-6353 or (800) 985-5488; or **O.K. Corral Stables,** two miles northeast of Apache Junction on AZ 88, then left at the sign, tel. 982-4040. Riding season is October to May.

## Ice-Skating

Hit the ice at **Ice Palace,** 3853 E. Thomas Rd. in Phoenix, tel. 267-0591; and **Oceanside Ice Arena,** next to Big Surf at 1520 N. Hayden Rd. in Tempe, tel. 947-2470.

## Roller Skating

Roll at **Rollero Family Roller Skating Center,** 7318 W. Indian School Rd., Phoenix; tel. 846-1510. **Skateland** has two locations: in Tempe at 1625 E. Weber Rd., tel. 968-9600; and in Mesa at 7 E. Southern Ave., tel. 833-7775. Or try **The Great Skate,** 10054 N. 43rd Ave., Glendale; tel. 842-1181.

## Casinos

Casino gambling is legal only on tribal reservations. Several tribes have turned down the opportunity to open casinos. Other tribes have casinos or have applied for casino licenses. Arizona's governor is refusing to approve new casinos and plans not to renew existing 10-year permits when they expire. This may prevent or delay two new casinos planned for Fort McDowell Reservation just east of Scottsdale.

**Fort McDowell Casino** offers 475 slot machines, high stakes bingo, $25,000 live keno, 45 poker tables, video poker and video craps; parimutuel wagering is planned for the near future. The Red Rock Cafe is open daily for breakfast, lunch, and dinner and offers a buffet. The casino is just past Shea Blvd. on the Beeline Highway. Free transportation is available throughout the Phoenix metropolitan area; tel. 837-1424 or (800) THE FORT.

**Gila River Casino** operates two facilities on the Gila River Indian Community 15 minutes south of Phoenix on I-10. The new Firebird facility opened in 1995 at I-10 exit 162A, directly across from Firebird Raceway, and offers 500 video slot machines, a 1,000 seat bingo dome, and buffet dining. A resort hotel, golf course, and an RV park and campground are planned. A mile and a half farther down Maricopa Rd. is the Lone Butte location, which offers 271 video slot machines, Keno, and video poker. Both are open 24 hours a day with full service deli dining; tel. (800) WIN-GILA.

# PARKS

## Encanto Park

A 222-acre oasis of lakes with picnic areas, a Kiddieland, an urban fishing program, two golf courses, tennis courts, volleyball, racquetball, basketball, and a swimming pool. You can check out sports equipment from the Recreation Building south of the swimming pool. Park concerts often take place in the evenings from April to October. Encanto Park lies just two miles north of downtown Phoenix at N. 15th Ave. and Encanto Blvd.; tel. 261-8991.

## Papago Park

This large area on the east edge of Phoenix was once declared a national monument, so honored because of its desert flora and Indian history. Today it's a city park, offering numerous attractions such as the Phoenix Zoo, Desert Botanical Gardens, an 18-hole golf course, and Phoenix Municipal Stadium. The park also features picnicking, hiking, a bike trail, and a small lake where children 15 and under may fish without a license. George W.P. Hunt, seven times governor of Arizona, spends eternity in the prominent pyramid tomb. Enter Papago Park from Galvin Parkway.

## Squaw Peak Park

Squaw Peak crowns a group of desert hills nine miles northeast of downtown Phoenix. This is a place for hiking and picnicking with horseback riding available nearby. Saguaro cactus, palo verde, creosote bush, and barrel and cholla cactus are among the desert plants that thrive on the hillsides.

The hike to the summit of 2,608-foot Squaw Peak is a good half-day's outing. The trail climbs steeply in places, rising 1,200 feet in 1.25 miles, but it's easy to follow. On Sunday the peak hosts a remarkable crowd of teenagers, families, joggers wearing headsets—all puffing along. In the warmer months, be sure to carry water and get an early start. For an easier hike, try the gentle trail from the end of the road.

## South Mountain Park

This is the world's largest city park, encompassing some 16,500 acres of desert mountain country. A paved road winds to the top for great views of the Valley. On the way you'll pass several picnic areas and a children's playground. Forty miles of hiking and horseback trails lead through the backcountry. Stables, just outside the park's entrance, rent horses.

Hikers will enjoy **Hidden Valley,** a half-day trip

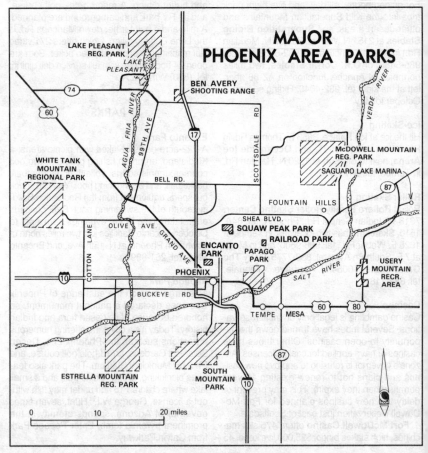

**MAJOR PHOENIX AREA PARKS**

LAKE PLEASANT REG. PARK

LAKE PLEASANT

BEN AVERY SHOOTING RANGE

74

60

17

99TH AVE.

AGUA FRIA RIVER

SCOTTSDALE RD.

VERDE RIVER

WHITE TANK MOUNTAIN REGIONAL PARK

BELL RD.

McDOWELL MOUNTAIN REG. PARK

SAGUARO LAKE MARINA

87

FOUNTAIN HILLS

SHEA BLVD.

OLIVE AVE.

COTTON LANE

GRAND AVE.

SQUAW PEAK PARK

RAILROAD PARK

ENCANTO PARK

PAPAGO PARK

SALT RIVER

USERY MOUNTAIN RECR. AREA

PHOENIX

10

BUCKEYE RD.

TEMPE   MESA

60   80

87

ESTRELLA MOUNTAIN REG. PARK

SOUTH MOUNTAIN PARK

10

0          10          20 miles

N

through a landscape of giant granite boulders and stately saguaro. To reach the trailhead, go two miles past the park entrance gate and turn left onto Summit Rd., following it for four miles; keep right past the turnoffs for two lookout points, then stay left at the next fork. Follow signs for Buena Vista Lookout. At road's end, the sign reading Hidden Valley 1.75 Miles marks the trailhead. The first quarter mile follows a ridge with good views before gently dropping into a valley. After a mile or so, some large slick rocks must be negotiated before entering wide, bowl-shaped Hidden Valley. Near the lower end of the little valley, you pass through a natural tunnel about 50 feet long. This makes a good turnaround point, or you can explore more of the valley and surrounding hills. In summer carry extra water and avoid the heat of the day.

South Mountain Park lies seven miles south of downtown Phoenix on Central Avenue.

## Saguaro Lake

Scenery, fishing, and boating attract people year-round. The 10-mile-long lake (1,100 acres) within Tonto National Forest is the last in the chain of lakes on the Salt River and the closest to Phoenix. Anglers catch largemouth and yellow bass, channel catfish, bluegill, and walleye. **Saguaro Lake Marina** features a snack bar, boating supplies, and fishing and ski boat rentals; tel. 986-0969. **Lakeshore Restaurant** serves breakfast, lunch, and dinner daily at moderate prices (reduced service in summer); tel. 984-5311. Boat tours make an 11-mile scenic loop from October to April.

The Forest Service provides day-use boat ramps and picnic areas at **Saguaro del Norte. Butcher Jones Recreation Area** offers a picnic area and a four-mile trail along the northern lakeshore; take the turnoff on the Bush Hwy. one mile north of the marina. Picnic and boating areas almost always fill up on Sunday, and sometimes Saturday, from mid-spring to mid-summer; try to arrive by early morning. Only boaters can reach **Bagley Flat Campground**— tables, pit toilets, but no water, free—about four miles from the marina. Dispersed camping is also permitted, but again, you'll need a boat.

Proceed to Saguaro Lake via the Bush Hwy., from eastern Mesa or AZ 87. The **Mesa Ranger District** office of the Tonto National Forest stocks recreation information for the Saguaro Lake, lower Salt River, Superstitions, and Four Peaks areas at 26 N. Macdonald St. in Mesa (AZ 85201). It's open Mon.-Fri. 7:45 a.m.-4:30 p.m.; tel. 379-6446.

## Ben Avery Shooting Range and Recreation Area

Shooters and archers can practice at this fine facility. Visitors also enjoy picnicking and camping; $12 w/hookups, $8 no hookups; $4 tent camping, showers available. The range operates Wed.-Sun. 7 a.m.-dark; the trap and skeet range is available for night use. It's 26 miles north of downtown Phoenix, west off I-17 Exit 223; tel. 582-8313 for rifle and pistol range, tel. 258-1901 Black Canyon Trap and Skeet Club.

## Lake Pleasant Regional Park

This large lake was augmented by completion of the Waddell Dam, which raised the lake level to about 1,700 feet during March and April; peak lake size will be 10,285 acres at high water. After drawdown for irrigation, the level will drop 100 feet or so by September or October of each year for a lake size no smaller than 3,700 acres.

An interpretive center was recently built at the Waddell Dam Overlook, along with paved boat ramps, marina, snack bar, and Roadrunner and Desert Tortoise Campgrounds with tent camping ($8), RV sites w/hookups ($12), and showers. Primitive camping is possible for boaters along the lakeshore. Small sailboats, fishing boats, and waterski boats are available for rent at the marina. The lake's open waters provide excellent conditions for sailing; races are sponsored by the Arizona Yacht Club and Lake Pleasant Sailing Club. Anglers seek out largemouth bass, white bass, catfish, bluegill, sunfish, and crappie. Jet ski races and bass fishing tournaments are annual events. If you would like to go for a cruise on the lake call **Desert Princess Cruise Ship;** tel. 230-9000.

Daily fees include $4 per vehicle, plus $2 per water craft, or $1 per cyclist; tel. 780-9875. Lake Pleasant is about 30 miles northwest of Phoenix; take I-17 north to AZ 74 (Exit 223), go west 11.5 miles on AZ 74, turn north 2.2 miles on Castle Hot Springs Rd., then turn right into the park. From Sun City go north 15 miles on 99th Ave. to AZ 74.

## McDowell Mountain Regional Park

You'll enjoy beautiful vistas from the eastern McDowells, 15 miles northeast of Scottsdale. A wide variety of desert plants grows at the 1,500- to 3,100-foot elevations. The 21,000-acre park attracts nature lovers, artists, picnickers, hikers, and horseback riders. In 1995 a fire burned off much of the vegetation on 14,000 acres.

Thirty-five miles of trails for hikers and horseback riders wind through the hills; the 1.25-mile-long Lousley Hill Trail offers good panoramas. Most trails are open to mountain bikes too. There's a campground, $12 w/hookups and showers, closed in summer; tel. 471-0173. Access is from Fountain Hills on the south side of the park via Fountain Hills Blvd. to McDowell Mountain Road.

## Usery Mountain Recreation Area

Enjoy good views of the Salt River Valley and the Superstition Mountains from the pass between Pass Mountain and Usery Mountain Range, 12 miles northeast of Mesa. Or stop for picnicking, hiking, horseback riding, and the archery range. There's a campground, $12 w/hookups and showers, closed in summer; tel. 984-0032. From Apache Blvd. (US 60/89) in Apache Junction, turn north on Ellsworth Rd., which becomes Usery Pass Road.

## Estrella Mountain Regional Park

Spanish explorers named the range Estrella

("Star") after the pattern of deeply carved canyons radiating from the summit. This 19,840-acre recreation area offers picnicking, 34 miles of trails, golf, and a rodeo arena with a $2-per-vehicle day-use charge; tel. 932-3811. A six-mile loop hike takes in Rock Nob Buggy, Pack Saddle, and Rainbow Valley trails. Hikers, horseback riders, and mountain bicyclists can all use the trail system.

**Sierra Estrella Mountain Golf Course,** in the northwest corner of the park, has 18 holes, a pro shop, and snack bar; tel. 932-3714. The rodeo arena offers trail and haywagon rides. Riding and rodeo events are held here many evenings and weekends from November to April; tel. 935-4404. From Phoenix, take I-10 about 20 miles west to the Estrella Parkway Exit, go south about five miles on Estrella Parkway to Vineyard, then turn left on Vineyard to the park entrance.

## White Tank Mountain Regional Park

Extensive trails for hikers, horseback riders, and mountain bicyclists twist through this range on the west side of the Valley. The park's 26,337 acres feature four major interconnecting trails, each three to four miles long; the one-mile Waterfall Trail is especially popular. Fifteen miles of mountain bike trails are open. The park also offers picnic and camping areas.

A $2-per-vehicle day-use fee is collected all year; campsites cost $8 with showers; tel. 935-2505. From Peoria, northwest of Phoenix, take Olive Ave. west for 15 miles.

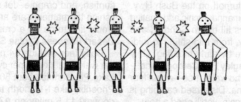

# VALLEY OF THE SUN SHOPPING AND SERVICES

## SHOPPING

The Valley features thousands of shops eager to sell you something. Glittering department stores and boutiques display the latest in fashion. Or you can visit rustic, porch-fronted shops and be outfitted in Western duds from boots to bolo ties. Western and Indian art make distinctive gifts. Anglo and Hispanic artists recall the frontier days in painting and sculpture, while Indian artists reveal their heritage in arts and crafts. Mexican import shops represent skilled craftspeople from south of the border.

### Old Town Scottsdale
Arts, crafts, clothing, and restaurants—many with an Old West theme—abound in the area centered around Brown St., just west of Scottsdale's Civic Center. More shops line Main St. west across Scottsdale Rd. to 69th Street.

### Fifth Avenue
Scottsdale's biggest shopping area lies along this curving street between Scottsdale Rd. and Indian School Road. Local businesspeople promote the huge selection of shops here as "Arizona's ultimate shopping experience."

### The Borgata
This elegant shopping center is modeled after the Italian town of San Gimignano, complete with cobblestone paths, courtyards, and medieval towers and archways. Your credit cards will take a beating in most of these stores, but window shopping is fun. The Borgata, 6166 N. Scottsdale Rd., is two miles north of Old Town Scottsdale; tel. 998-1822.

### Mercado
A Mexican marketplace with many specialty shops, restaurants, and the **Museo Chicano.** In downtown Phoenix at the southwest corner of Van Buren and Fifth Streets. The **Arizona Center,** diagonally across Van Buren, offers more

shops and restaurants as well as the Visitors Bureau, Suite 600 on the sixth floor.

### El Tianguis
An Aztec word for "marketplace," this Mexican-style *mercado* houses inexpensive Mexican cafes and shops offering high-quality crafts from Mexico and beyond. It's operated by the Mexican-American and Yaqui Indian community of Guadalupe. From I-10 near Tempe, exit east at Baseline Rd., then turn right on Avenida del Yaqui to Calle Guadalupe.

### Other Shopping Malls
**Biltmore Fashion Park,** Camelback Rd. and 24th St., Phoenix, features several restaurants

*The Borgata*

and about 70 luxury shops, including Saks Fifth Avenue, Polo/Ralph Lauren, Gucci, and Broadway; tel. 955-8400. **Chris-Town Shopping Center,** 1703 W. Bethany Home Rd., Phoenix, offers four large department stores, 27 places to eat, 11 movie theaters, a post office, and dozens of shops; tel. 242-9074.

**Los Arcos Mall,** Scottsdale and McDowell Roads in Scottsdale, contains two department stores, 10 restaurants, and 60 shops; tel. 945-6376. **Metrocenter** (exit west at Dunlap or Peoria Avenues from I-17 in north Phoenix) is *big*—four major department stores, more than 200 specialty shops, over 50 restaurants, 17 movie theaters, banks, hotels, miniature golf, and more; tel. 997-2641. **Arrowhead Town Center,** 75th Ave. and Bell Rd. in northwest Phoenix, has five department stores, 140 specialty shops, 15 eateries (three full-service restaurants), and a 14-screen cinema; tel. 979-7777. **Park Central Mall,** at Central Ave. and Osborn Rd. in Phoenix, has 50 shops and six restaurants; tel. 264-5575. **Scottsdale Fashion Mall,** 7000 E. Camelback Rd., has three major department stores, more than 160 specialty stores, seven full-service restaurants, and a seven-screen cinema; tel. 990-7800. **Superstition Springs Center,** 6555 E. Southern Ave. in Mesa, has five department stores, over 100 specialty stores, an eight-screen cinema, a 36-horse carousel, and free concerts 6-8 p.m. late April-Oct.; tel. 832-0212. **El Pedregal Festival Marketplace at the Boulders,** 34505 N. Scottsdale Rd., offers boutique shopping in a Moroccan festival style marketplace offering restaurants, fashion, books, gifts, a branch of the Heard Museum, and free concerts Thursday nights at 7 p.m. April-Sept.; tel. 488-1072.

### Outdoor Supplies

**REI Co-op** contains an excellent selection of gear for hiking, backpacking, bicycling, river-running, downhill skiing, cross-country skiing, and other sports; rentals available too. Optional lifetime memberships, available for a small fee, pay dividends of about 10% of all purchases at the end of each year. It's in Tempe at 1405 W. Southern Ave.; tel. 967-5494. **Arizona Hiking Shack** also has a fine array of outdoor gear and rentals at 11645 N. Cave Creek Rd. in north Phoenix; tel. 944-7723.

### Native American Music

**Canyon Records and Indian Arts** stocks hundreds of different Native American music titles from many American tribes, 4143 N. 16th St., Phoenix; tel. 266-4823.

## SERVICES

The Phoenix downtown **post office** is at 522 N. Central Ave. Other post offices include Scottsdale's at 7242 E. Osborn Rd.; the Tempe post office at 233 E. Southern Ave.; and Mesa's at 135 N. Center. To get the address of the post office nearest your location call 407-2028.

Exchange foreign currency at **First Interstate Bank,** 100 W. Washington St., Phoenix (or any branch office), tel. 229-4643; or at **American Exchange,** in the Biltmore Fashion Park at 2508 E. Camelback Rd.; tel. 468-1199.

Need a doctor? **Maricopa County Medical Society** will refer one to you; it's open weekdays 8 a.m.-5 p.m.; tel. 252-2844.

Down and out? **Job Service** (Arizona Department of Economic Security), 438 W. Adams St., Phoenix, offers free services; tel. 252-7771.

## INFORMATION

### Tourist Offices

**Phoenix & Valley of the Sun Convention & Visitors Bureau** has a free *Official Visitors Guide* and many brochures downtown at One Arizona Center, 400 E. Van Buren, Suite 600 (Phoenix, AZ 85004). It's open Mon.-Fri. 8 a.m.-5 p.m.; tel. 254-6500, fax 253-4415. The Visitors Bureau maintains a branch office in the nearby Hyatt Regency at the northwest corner of Adams and Second Streets; it's open Mon.-Fri. 8 a.m.-4:30 p.m.

Other helpful tourist offices in the Valley include the following: **Scottsdale Chamber of Commerce** at 7343 Scottsdale Mall (Scottsdale, AZ 85251) is open Mon.-Fri. 8:30 a.m.-5 p.m., Saturday 10 a.m.-5 p.m., and Sunday 11 a.m.-5 p.m.; tel. 945-8481 or (800) 877-1117, fax 947-4523. **Tempe Convention and Visitors Bureau** in the America West Building at Hayden Square in Old Town Tempe, off Mill Ave. (51 W. Third St., Suite 105, Tempe, AZ 85281) is open Mon.-Fri. 8:30 a.m.-5 p.m.; tel. 894-8158 or (800) 283-6734. **Mesa Con-**

## IMPORTANT VALLEY OF THE SUN TELEPHONE NUMBERS

Emergencies (police, fire, medical): 911

Police (Phoenix): 262-6151

Maricopa County sheriff: 256-1011 or (800) 352-4553

Community Information and Referral Services: 263-8856

Community Legal Services (legal aid): 258-3434

Lawyers' Referral (County Bar Association): 257-4434

Doctors' Referral (Maricopa County Medical Society): 252-2844

Phoenix Transit and Downtown Area Shuttle: 253-5000

Visitor Hotline (Valley events): 252-5588

Phoenix and Valley of the Sun Convention Visitors Bureau: 254-6500

Arizona Office of Tourism (statewide info and events): 542-8687

Herberger Theater Box Office: 252-8497

ASU Gammage Center: 965-3434

ASU Sun Devil Ticket Office: 965-2381

Sportsline (sports scores, press 9010): 271-5656

Civic Plaza Box Office: 262-7272

Forest Facts (U.S. Forest Service): 225-5296

Weather (state and local): 265-5550

Arizona Roads (ext. 7623): 861-9400

The **area code** for the metropolitan Phoenix area is 602.

vention & Visitors Bureau at 120 N. Center (Mesa, AZ 85201) is open Mon.-Fri. 8 a.m.-5 p.m.; tel. 969-1307 or (800) 283-MESA.

**Apache Junction Chamber of Commerce** in the City Hall complex at 1001 N. Idaho Rd. and Superstition Blvd./University Dr. (Box 1747, Apache Junction, AZ 85217-1747) is open Mon.-Fri. 8 a.m.-5 p.m.; tel. 982-3141 or (800) 252-3141. **Fountain Hills Chamber of Commerce** at 12635 N. Saguaro Blvd. (Box 17598, Fountain Hills, AZ 85269) is open Mon.-Sat. 10 a.m.-4 p.m., Sunday noon-4 p.m.; tel. 837-1654.

The **Arizona Office of Tourism** offers info on every region of the state at 2702 N. 3rd. St., Suite 4015 (Phoenix, AZ 85004); it's open Mon.-Fri. 8 a.m.-5 p.m.; tel. 542-8687, fax 542-4068.

## Tonto National Forest

Hike and camp in the Tonto's 2.9 million acres of forests and cactus that sprawl north and east of the Valley. The forest includes the Superstition and Mazatzal Ranges and the lakes along the Verde and Salt Rivers. The main office is at 2324 E. McDowell Rd. (Phoenix, AZ 85006); it's open Mon.-Fri. 7:45 a.m.-4:30 p.m.; tel. 225-5200 or 225-5296 (recorded info).

The **Cave Creek Ranger District** office of the Tonto National Forest knows about Bartlett and Horseshoe lakes, the Cave Creek Trail System, and other areas north of the Valley. The office, at 7171 E. Cave Creek Rd., Carefree, AZ 85377, is open Mon.-Fri. 7:45 a.m.-4:30 p.m.; tel. 488-3441.

The **Mesa Ranger District** office of Tonto National Forest stocks recreation information for the Saguaro Lake, lower Salt River, Superstitions, Four Peaks, and other areas east of the Valley. The office, at 26 N. MacDonald St., Suite 120, Mesa, AZ 85201, is open Mon.-Fri. 7:45 a.m.-4:30 p.m.; tel. 379-6446.

The **Bureau of Land Management** Phoenix District and Resource Area provides information on BLM areas in most of central and northern Arizona; 2015 W. Deer Valley Rd. (Phoenix, AZ 85027); it's open Mon.-Fri. 7:30 a.m.-4:15 p.m.; tel. 780-8090.

The offices of **Arizona State Parks** will dispense information on any of the state's parks; 1300 W. Washington (Phoenix, AZ 85007); it's open Mon.-Fri. 8 a.m.-5 p.m.; tel. 542-4174.

**Arizona Game and Fish** sells licenses for fishing and hunting; the main office is at 2222 W. Greenway Rd. (Phoenix, AZ 85023); it's open Mon.-Fri. 8 a.m.-5 p.m.; tel. 942-3000. The office for central Arizona is at 7200 E. University Dr. (Mesa, AZ 85207); tel. 981-9400.

### Libraries

The new, showplace five-floor main **Phoenix Public Library** is two blocks south of McDowell Rd. at 1221 N. Central Ave. and Willetta St.; it's open Mon.-Wed. 9 a.m.-9 p.m., Thursday and Saturday 9 a.m.-6 p.m., and Sunday 1-5 p.m.; tel. 262-4636. See the blue pages in the phone book under Phoenix libraries for information on the 11 branches scattered around town.

The **Scottsdale Public Library** at 3839 Civic Center Blvd. is open Mon.-Thurs. 10 a.m.-9 p.m.

(9 a.m.-8 p.m. in summer), Friday and Saturday 10 a.m.-6 p.m. (9 a.m.-5 p.m. in summer), and Sunday 1-5 p.m.; tel. 994-2476. Scottsdale has a branch library at 10101 N. 90th St., tel. 391-6050, and another at 12575 E. Via Linda, suite 102, tel. 391-6100.

**Tempe**'s public library occupies the southwest corner of 3500 S. Rural Rd. and Southern Ave.; it's open Mon.-Thurs. 9 a.m.-9 p.m., Friday and Saturday 9 a.m.-5:30 p.m., and Sunday (closed in summer) noon-5:30 p.m.; tel. 350-5555 (information recording) or 350-5511 (reference).

**Mesa**'s public library is downtown at 64 E. First St.; it's open Mon.-Thurs. 9:30 a.m.-9 p.m., Friday and Saturday 9:30 a.m.-5:30 p.m., and Sunday (Sept.-May) 1:30-5:30 p.m.; tel. 644-3100 (recording) or 644-2207 (reference).

The **Apache Junction Public Library** in the city hall complex at 1177 N. Idaho Rd. is open Monday, Wednesday, and Friday 9 a.m.-5 p.m., Tuesday and Thursday 9 a.m.-8 p.m., and Saturday 9 a.m.-1 p.m.; tel. 983-0204.

The **state capitol** has a research library on Arizona history at 1700 W. Washington, Room 300; other departments offer maps, state documents, federal documents, and genealogy. The library is open Mon.-Fri. 8 a.m.-5 p.m.; tel. 542-3701. You can also use libraries on the ASU campus.

## Newspapers and Magazines

The *Arizona Republic* is distributed every morning and publishes a big Sunday edition; its sister paper, the *Phoenix Gazette,* is published evenings Monday through Saturday. In the East Valley look for the various versions of the *Tribune.* For local news and entertainment, look for the weekly *New Times,* free at newsstands. *Scottsdale Life,* published weekly by the *Scottsdale Progress,* reviews the local art and entertainment scene.

*Phoenix Magazine* comes out monthly with news and useful information about the Valley. Scottsdale has its own magazines—*Scottsdale Scene* and *Scottsdale Magazine.* The monthly *Arizona Light* offers articles and resource lists for Arizona's new age community.

## Books and Maps

**The Book Store** has not only new and used books, but one of the best selections of magazines and out-of-town newspapers in the state at 4230 N. Seventh Ave.; tel. 279-3910. **Bent Cover Bookstore** offers used hardback and paperback books at 12428 N. 28th Dr. (one block west of I-17); tel. 942-3778. **Al's Family Book Store** stocks a large selection of used books at 3744 E. Indian School Rd. in Phoenix; tel. 253-6922. **Bob and Faye's Paper Book Exchange** specializes in used books in Phoenix

The U.S. Forest Service can tell you about recreation on the Salt River (pictured) and other areas of the Tonto National Forest.

at 1827 E. Indian School Rd., tel. 264-6698; and in Tempe at 2043 E. University Dr., tel. 966-2065. **Changing Hands** carries a large selection of new and used books at 414 S. Mill Ave. in Tempe; tel. 966-0203. **Old Town Books** features a small but select inventory of used books at 518 S. Mill Ave.; tel. 968-9881. **Bookman's** in Mesa boasts about a quarter million used books and tapes at 7056 S. Country Club Dr.; tel. 835-0505. Shopping malls house the popular book chains.

For maps of Arizona and the world, see **A Wide World of Maps** in Phoenix (2626 W. Indian School Rd., tel. 279-2323 or 800-279-7654) and in Mesa (1334 S. Country Club Dr., tel. 844-1134). Topo maps are also sold by **REI**, 1405 W. Southern Ave. in Tempe, tel. 967-5494; and by **Arizona Hiking Shack**, 11645 N. Cave Creek Rd. in north Phoenix, tel. 944-7723.

# TRANSPORT

## Tours

The Valley of the Sun features many tour operators—not all listed here. Drop by one of the Visitors Bureau offices for the latest brochures and *Visitors Guide* listings. The Sunday *Arizona Republic* travel section advertises special travel deals.

The **Gray Line** runs tours of the Phoenix area ($27), Sedona/Oak Creek Canyon ($55), and the Grand Canyon ($79); two-day trips visit the Grand Canyon ($139); longer trips roll to other areas of the Southwest. You'll find the Gray Line office at 1646 E. University Dr., Phoenix, AZ 85034; tel. 495-9100 or (800) 732-0327 (out of state).

To see some of Arizona's real backcountry, take a 4WD tour with **Big Red Desert Jeep Tours** (Phoenix, tel. 263-5337); **Arizona Awareness Jeep Tours** (Phoenix, tel. 947-7852); **Arizona Bound Tours** (Phoenix, tel. 994-0580); **Arrowhead Jeep Tours** (Phoenix, tel. 942-3361); **Wild West Jeep Tours** (Scottsdale, 941-8355); **Diamondback Adventures** (Scottsdale, tel. 948-8623); or **Desert/Mountain Jeep Tours** (Scottsdale, tel. 860-1777).

Raft the wild upper Salt and Verde rivers in spring and voyage year-round on the lower Salt and Verde with **Desert Voyagers**, tel. 998-RAFT or (800) 222-RAFT, or with **Sun Country Rafting**, tel. (800) 2-PADDLE.

You can catch flights to the Grand Canyon and other scenic areas of the Southwest from the Scottsdale Airport with **Scenic Airlines**, tel. 991-8252; **Sky Cab**, tel. 998-1778 or (800) 999-1778; and **Westwind Aviation**, tel. 991-5557 or (800) 765-5557. Soar in a glider with **Turf Soaring School**, Pleasant Valley Airport, tel. 439-3621; or with **Estrella Sailport Soaring School** in Maricopa, tel. 568-2318. Experience flight in an ultralight airplane with **Ultralight Flight Center** from Pleasant Valley Airport; tel. 566-8026.

Fly high over the Valley and surrounding area in a hot-air balloon during the cooler months with **Over the Rainbow**, tel. 225-5666 (BAL-LOON); **Unicorn Balloon**, tel. 991-3666 or (800) 468-2478; **Adventures Aloft**, 951-2650; **Arizona Balloonport**, tel. 953-3924 or (800) 860-6000; **Sky Climber**, tel. 483-8208; or **Cirrus Airship Company**, tel. 971-4853 or (800) 971-4853.

## Local Bus

**Phoenix Transit** will ride you around the Valley, visiting parks, shopping areas, most of the sights, and the airport—all for just $1.25. Transfers are free when requested upon boarding; tel. 253-5000. All-day passes cost $3.60; you can purchase them at the downtown terminal at First and Washington; timetables are available there as well. Most buses head for home between 6 p.m. and 10 p.m.; no service on Sunday and major holidays. On those days you can use **Dial-A-Ride**, tel. 271-4545. It operates about 6:30 a.m.-6:30 p.m.; call at least 45 minutes before you desire pickup; fares start at $2.40, and depend on distance. In the downtown area you can ride the **Downtown Area Shuttle** (DASH) for 30 cents; tel. 253-5000.

## Long-Distance Bus

The **Greyhound** bus terminal is downtown at 525 E. Washington St., tel. 271-7429. You'll find other Greyhound stations in northwest Phoenix, 2647 W. Glendale, tel. 246-4341; Tempe, 502 S. College Ave., tel. 967-4030; and Mesa, 1423 S. Country Club Dr., tel. 834-3360. There is no bus station in Youngtown, but there is a pickup point at 12006 N. 111th Ave.; call any other station in the area for times. Destinations and one-way fares include Los

Angeles, nine daily, $29; San Diego, three daily, $34; El Paso, 10 daily, $35; Tucson, 10 daily, $12; Flagstaff, four daily, $20; Globe, three daily, $15; Wickenburg, seven daily, $10; and Yuma, three daily, $30. Roundtrip fares may include a small discount. The **Nava-Hopi Express** connects Sky Harbor Airport and Phoenix with Flagstaff ($21.50 one-way) once nightly; service to the Grand Canyon and tours of northern Arizona are offered too; tel. (800) 892-8687. **White Mountain Passenger Lines** leaves daily except Sunday from several locations in the Valley to Payson and Show Low; 321 S. 24th St., Phoenix; tel. 275-4245.

## Auto Rentals

The Valley moves on wheels; if you need some, check the Yellow Pages or the Visitors Bureau's *Official Visitors Guide*. Rental companies offer many different plans; most maintain offices at the airport or make free pickups. You can rent RVs too.

## Driveaways

These are autos requiring delivery to another city. If a car's going to a place you're headed, a driveaway's like a free car rental, but you'll still have to pay for gas. You must be at least 21 years old and pay a deposit of $75-150. There are also time and mileage limits. Ask for an economy car for the lowest costs. See the Yellow Pages under "Automobile Transporters and Driveaways."

## Taxis

**Ace Taxi** (tel. 254-1999) offers lower than av-

erage rates. Other companies include **AAA Cab** (tel. 253-8294), **Checker Cab** (tel. 257-1818), **Yellow Cab** (tel. 252-5252), and **Discount Cab** (tel. 253-5500).

## Train

**Amtrak** runs three eastbound and three westbound departures each week. The terminal is downtown at 401 W. Harrison St. and Fourth Avenue. For reservations and info, call (800) 872-7245. Westbound trains depart in the evening for Yuma and other points, arriving in Los Angeles the next morning (8.5 hours, $89 one-way). Eastbound cars leave in the morning for Tucson (2.5 hours, $29 one-way), and on to either New Orleans (1.5 days, $222) or Chicago (2.5 days, $227). Amtrak offers generous discounts on some roundtrip fares.

## Air

Commercial flights to the Valley land at Sky Harbor Airport, three miles east of downtown Phoenix. See the Yellow Pages for airlines, charters, and ticket agencies. Sky Harbor offers three separate terminals, connected by a free 24-hour shuttle bus. The busy airport is well organized but you'll have to do some walking.

The **City of Phoenix** staffs information desks in Terminals 2, 3, and 4. Free telephones near the baggage claims connect many Valley hotels and motels.

Taxis waiting outside charge widely varying fares—shop around. **Phoenix Transit** buses are the cheapest way into town; they leave the airport Mon.-Sat. about every 30 minutes during the day and evening; tel. 253-5000.

# NORTHEAST OF PHOENIX

## PAYSON AND THE COUNTRY BELOW THE RIM

When the Valley bakes under the summer sun, many Phoenix-area residents drive northeast to the cool pine forests of Payson. This might be the reason why the road to Payson, AZ 87, bears the nickname "Beeline Highway." From Mesa, the Beeline Hwy. crosses the Indian reservations of Salt River and Fort McDowell, then climbs over a pass in the Mazatzal Range before winding north to Payson. In Payson, 78 miles from Mesa, you've reached an elevation of 5,000 feet and stand at almost the exact center of Arizona.

The sheer cliffs of the Mogollon Rim tower 7,000 feet high in the north. Novelist Zane Grey fell in love with this country and built a lodge at the foot of the Rim. Here he wrote many of his books, occasionally wandering off on hunting expeditions to secure both ideas for stories and trophies for his walls. Today, hunters come in season to bag elk, deer, turkey, and other game. Anglers are lured by trout-filled streams and stocked reservoirs. Hikers enjoy pleasant walks in the forest or ambitious treks in the Mazatzal and Sierra Ancha. Although Payson itself (pop. 10,000) boasts few real "sights," the town is a good base for exploring the surrounding countryside.

### History

It wasn't the cool climate and beautiful scenery that attracted Payson's first settlers, but the glitter of gold. Miners set up camp in 1881, but ranching and lumbering soon reigned as the most rewarding occupations. A fort provided protection against Apache raids in the precarious early years.

The town's name honors Senator Louis Edwin Payson, who had nothing to do with the community and never came here. Frank C. Hise, former postmaster, assigned the name to repay a political favor. See historic exhibits of northern Gila County and its forests at **Museum of the Forest,** 1001 W. Main St.; it's open noon-4 p.m. Wed.-Sun.; tel. 474-3483.

### Accommodations

You can choose between motels in town and secluded cabins in the surrounding forests, or opt for campgrounds and RV parks. Make reservations for the weekend rush, especially in summer. In town, you'll find **Payson Trave-Lodge,** Beeline Hwy. and W. Phoenix, $81.45 s, $92.31 d, tel. 474-4526 or (800) 255-3050; **Paysonglo Lodge (Best Western),** 1005 S. Beeline Hwy., $97.74-119.46, tel. 474-2382; **Trails End Motel,** 811 S. Beeline Hwy., $59.73 s, $70.59 d, tel. 474-2283; **Charleston Motor Inn,** 302 S. Beeline Hwy., $64.07-74.93, tel. 474-2201; and **Holiday Inn Express** 200 S. Beeline Hwy., $92.22 s or d and up; tel. 472-1484 or (800) HOLIDAY. **Swiss Village Lodge** is on 801 N. Beeline Hwy., $64.07-96.54 d, tel. 474-3241, (602) 255-0170 in Phoenix, or (800) 24-SWISS.

Heading east from town on AZ 260, you'll find the **Majestic Mountain Inn,** 602 E. Hwy. 260, $81.45-135.75 s or d, tel. 474-0185 or (800) 408-2442; **Payson Pueblo Inn,** 809 E. Hwy. 260, $65.07 s or d and up, tel. 474-5241 or (800) 888-9828; **Opal Ranch Inn** offers lodging for you and your horses 3.8 miles east on Hwy. 260, then 2.5 miles south on Moonlight Dr., $97.74-108.60, tel. 472-6193; **Star Valley Motel,** four miles east of Payson, $47.97 s or $53.30 d, tel. 474-5182; **Ye Ole Country Inn,** 16 miles east and north in Tonto Village, $62.89-73.55 d, tel. 478-4426.

**Kohl's Ranch Resort** features a motel, cabins, and restaurant 17 miles east of Payson, $101.27-218.53 d May 1-Sept. 30, $79.95-186.55 d Oct. 1-Apr. 30; tel. 478-4211 or (800) 331-KOHL. **Christopher Creek Lodge,** 23 miles east of Payson in the resort village of Christopher Creek, charges $47.97-90.61 d for rooms and cabins, tel. 478-4300. **Creekside Mountain Cabins** on Colcord Rd., east of Christopher Creek, rents cabins for $60-80; tel. 478-4557. Also try **Mountain Meadows Cabins,** on Colcord Rd., east of Christopher Creek, $85-117.26, tel. 478-4415; or **Grey Hackle Lodge,** Christopher Creek, $53.30-117.26 d cabins, tel. 478-4392.

## Campgrounds

The Forest Service, tel. 474-7900, maintains several campgrounds east of Payson on AZ 260, many open all year, with drinking water but no showers. The **Ponderosa,** 13 miles east of Payson, costs $11; there's also a group campground nearby. Other campgrounds include **Lower Tonto Creek,** 17 miles east of Payson,

**PAYSON**

0      0.25mi

0      0.25km

TO PINE AND STRAWBERRY

TO STAR VALLEY, KOHL'S RANCH AND CHRISTOPHER CREEK

TO MESA AND PHOENIX

1. Payson Municipal Airport
2. bus station/Pony Espresso Coffeehouse
3. Swiss Village Bakery
4. Swiss Village Lodge and Restaurant
5. Rumsey Park; rodeo grounds
6. Aunt Alice's Restaurant
7. Safeway
8. Payson Village (Basha's and Wal-Mart); Country Kitchen
9. Mario's
10. 260 Cafe
11. U.S. Forest Service (Payson Ranger District)
12. Weber's IGA
13. El Rancho Restaurant/Holiday Inn Express
14. Charleston Motor Inn
15. post office
16. Pyle Memorial Hospital
17. Payson Chamber of Commerce
18. Trails End Motel; Beeline Cafe; La Casa Pequeña
19. Paysonglo Motel
20. public library; Leaves of Autumn Books
21. Museum of the Forest/Green Valley Park
22. Payson Golf Course
23. Payson TraveLodge; Mandarin House Restaurant

$8; **Upper Tonto Creek,** 17 miles east of Payson, $8; and **Christopher Creek,** 22 miles east of Payson, $11. Several areas have been designated as dispersed camping areas and have no water or fee. The rangers can give you a map showing the location of these areas as well as the established campgrounds.

**Payson KOA** offers a pool, showers, and kamping kitchen with a choice of kamping kabins ($30.35-34.69) or sites for tents or RVs without hookups ($19.49) and RVs w/hookups ($22.76) from April 1 to October 31; it's a half mile east on AZ 260 from the Beeline Hwy.; tel. 474-8555.

For RV and trailer parks, try **Kokopelli's Retreat Adult RV Park,** open all year, 2.5 miles east on AZ 260—then follow signs, $15.50 RV w/hookups, tel. 474-931 or (800) 535-6567; **C-Bar Diamond RV Park,** four miles east on AZ 260, $13.91 RV w/hookups, tel. 474-2469; **Lamplighter Mobile & RV Park,** adults only, four miles east on AZ 260, $14.92 RV w/hookups, tel. 474-5048; **Lazy D Ranch Apts. & RV Resort,** monthly rent, four miles east on AZ 260, tel. 474-2442. Also try **Oxbow Estates RV Park,** three miles south on the Beeline Hwy., $18.92 RV w/hookups, tel. 474-2042; and **Pine Trailer Park,** 19 miles north on the Beeline Hwy. in Pine, $21.40 RV w/hookups, tel. 476-3459.

### Food
**Swiss Village Lodge** at 807 N. Beeline Hwy. includes a restaurant featuring both continental and American specialties; there's also a coffee shop; tel. 474-5800. **Swiss Village Bakery and Coffee Shoppe** turns out great pastries across from Swiss Village Lodge at 800 N. Beeline Hwy.; tel. 474-0891. **Heritage House** specializes in gourmet sandwiches, salads, and soups for lunch at 202 W. Main St.; tel. 474-5501. **Mallard's Restaurant** at 614 N. Beeline Hwy. offers standard American food daily for lunch and dinner in addition to a full seafood dinner buffet on Friday and a prime rib dinner buffet on Saturday; tel. 472-6869.

**The Oaks Restaurant** serves prime rib, steak, chicken, and veal dinners and a Sunday brunch at 302 W. Main St.; tel. 474-1929. Home cooking is featured at **Beeline Cafe,** 815 S. Beeline Hwy., tel. 474-9960; **Country Kitchen,** 210 E. Hwy. 260, tel. 474-1332; **260 Cafe,** 803 E. Hwy. 260, tel. 474-1933; and **Aunt Alice's Restaurant,** 512 N. Beeline Hwy., tel. 474-4720.

Dine Mexican at **El Rancho,** 200 S. Beeline Hwy., tel. 474-3111; **Chema's,** 430 S. Beeline Hwy., 472-6906; or **La Casa Pequeña,** 911 S. Beeline Hwy., tel. 474-6329.

**Mandarin House Restaurant** serves good Chinese food at 1200 S. Beeline Hwy. next to the Payson TraveLodge; tel. 474-1342. For Italian-American dining, try **Mario's** at 600 E. Hwy. 260, tel. 474-5429. Pick up pizza at **Mario's; Pizza Factory,** 238 E. Hwy. 260, tel. 474-1895; or **Pizza Hut,** 113 S. Beeline Hwy., tel. 474-1100.

For groceries visit **Basha's, Safeway,** or **Weber's IGA** in the shopping centers near the intersection of Hwy. 260 and Beeline Highway or the nearby **Payson Vita Health Natural Foods** across the street south of Safeway.

### Entertainment and Events
**Payson Picture Show** plays current flicks in Payson Plaza, one block east on Bonita off Beeline Hwy.; tel. 474-3918.

Major community events include a **mountain bike race** in April; the **Pro Rodeo** and **Pine/Strawberry Arts and Crafts Festival** in May; **Payson Art League Spring Arts and Crafts Show, Junior Rodeo,** and **Blue's Crafts Festival,** in June; **Pine/Strawberry Arts and Crafts Festival,** and the **Doll Show** in July; and the world's oldest **Continuous Rodeo** (since 1884), **dance,** and **Rodeo Parade** in August.

In September attend the **Pine/Strawberry Arts and Crafts Festival** and **Old-time Fiddlers' Contest.** The **Art Group Art Festival** and **Payson Art League Fall Arts and Crafts Show** occur in October; and a **Town Christmas Lighting Contest** highlights December.

### Services and Recreation
The **post office** occupies 100 W. Frontier St.; tel. 474-2972. Payson's **hospital** is at 807 S. Ponderosa St.; tel. 474-3222. You'll find a swimming pool, tennis courts, ball fields, and picnic grounds in **Rumsey Park** on N. McLane Rd.—from the junction of Beeline and Hwy. 260, go west on Overland or Longhorn roads, then right a half mile on McLane; tel. 474-2774.

Play golf on the 18-hole **Payson Golf Course,** 1504 W. Country Club; tel. 474-2273. Trail rides are offered during the warmer months at **Kohl's Ranch,** 17 miles east on AZ

260, tel. 478-4211, ext. 262 or (800) 331-KOHL; **Don Donnelly Stables** 10 miles east on Hwy. 260; tel. 982-7822; or **OK Corral Stables,** 15 miles north on Beeline Hwy. in Pine, tel. 476-4303. For camping, fishing, and hunting supplies and info, visit **Wal-Mart** at 400 E. Hwy. 260; tel. 474-0029. The new **Green Valley Park** at 1001 W. Main St. features a fishing pond, picnic areas, and the Museum of the Forest. **Mazatzal Casino** offers 300 slot machines, video poker and keno, a card room, and the **Cedar Ridge Restaurant** (serving breakfast, lunch, and dinner daily) half a mile south of Payson on the Beeline Hwy.; tel. 474-6044 or (800) 552-0938.

## Information

The **Payson Chamber of Commerce** occupies the corner of Beeline Hwy. and Main St. (Box 1380, Payson, AZ 85547); it's open Mon.-Fri. 8 a.m.-5 p.m. and Saturday and Sunday 10 a.m.-2 p.m.; tel. 474-4515 or (800) 6-PAYSON, fax 474-8812. For books, maps, and other camping, hiking, and back-road travel info, see the **Payson Ranger District** office of the U.S. Forest Service; it's open daily 7:45 a.m.-4:30 p.m. May-Oct., Mon.-Sat. in November and December, and Mon.-Fri. Jan.-April; it's one mile east of town (1009 E. Hwy. 260, Payson, AZ 85541); tel. 474-7900.

**Payson Public Library** is at 510 W. Main; tel. 474-2585. **Leaves of Autumn Books** carries a good selection of new and used books at 518 W. Main; tel. 474-3654. **Books** has 10,000 used books at 405 E South Beeline Hwy.; tel. 474-7081. **Book Book** sells used books in the Payson Village Shopping Center; tel. 472-8827.

## Transport

Buses from **White Mountain Passenger Lines** headed southwest to Phoenix and northeast to Show Low stop at the **Pony Espresso** coffeehouse at 814 N. Beeline Hwy.; tel. 474-1822.

# VICINITY OF PAYSON

## Tonto Natural Bridge State Park

Deposits left by mineral springs created the world's largest natural travertine bridge. The springs still flow as they have for many thousands of years, making the massive arch even

larger and watering lush vegetation. You might not even realize you're standing on top when you arrive—the bridge measures 400 feet in width and spans a canyon 150 feet wide. Graceful travertine formations underneath look like those inside a limestone cave. A small waterfall cascades over the top of the arch, forming jewel-like droplets of water that sparkle in the sun and create pretty rainbows.

Visitors can admire the bridge from viewpoints at the top overlooking each side of the arch and from trails in the canyon both upstream and downstream. No access is permitted under the bridge, and no pets are allowed on the trails. The park is open 8 a.m.-6 p.m. April-Oct. and 9 a.m.-5 p.m. Nov.-March, except Christmas; $5 vehicle admission; Box 1245, Payson, AZ 85547; tel. 476-4202. From Payson go 11 miles north on AZ 87, then turn left and drive three miles on a paved road to the sign. The last 1.5 miles are steep and winding; it is recommended that vehicles and trailers over 16 feet use the parking lot at the bottom of the grade.

## Strawberry

This tiny village sits just below the Mogollon Rim, 19 miles north of Payson. Wild strawberries used to grow here in abundance but nowadays they're hard to find. Turn west 1.5 miles at Strawberry Lodge to see Arizona's oldest **schoolhouse.** Pioneers built the one-room log structure in 1885. You can view the restored interior during the summer, other times by appointment; ask at Strawberry Lodge. The road continues past Fossil Creek (good hiking) to Camp Verde, though it's hard going for ordinary passenger vehicles. A better route to Camp Verde involves going north eight miles on AZ 87 up onto the Rim, then turning left on the paved General Crook Trail (AZ 260).

Rooms in **Strawberry Lodge** cost $44.77-55.43 d. The more expensive accommodations feature fireplaces and balconies. Weekend reservations should be made a couple of weeks in advance; tel. 476-3333. **Strawberry Hill Cabins** run $90.61 and $101.27 s or d; tel. 476-4252. **Strawberry Motel** rooms run $41.57 s, $52.23 d; tel. 476-3040. **Windmill Corner Inn** runs $53-63 d; tel. 476-3064.

Dine at Strawberry Lodge, open daily for breakfast, lunch, and dinner. There are a number of other places to eat in town too. The nearby town of Pine features the **High Country Inn,** $45 d; tel. 476-2150.

## Payson Zoo

Many of the more than 60 zoo residents have starred in motion pictures. Training and close contact with humans seem to make these animals more comfortable and relaxed than the creatures found in most zoos. You can meet such beasties as baboons, leopards, tigers, javelina, black bear, coyote, and ringtail cats. Pigs, chickens, and peacocks roam about as well. Open daily (weather permitting) 10 a.m.-3:30 p.m.; $4 adults, $1 children 12 and under; tel. 474-5435. From Payson, head east 6.5 miles on AZ 260 to Lion Springs Rd., then turn right.

## Zane Grey's Lodge

The canyons, great forests, and expansive views of the Rim Country inspired author Zane Grey to build a hunting cabin here in 1920. He stayed often over the next nine years, enjoying the wilderness while working on novels about the American West. A major forest fire burned the cabin in 1990. The Museum of the Forest is raising funds to build a replica of the historic cabin in Payson.

## Tonto Fish Hatchery

Rainbow, brook, and brown trout grow to mouth-watering maturity at this hatchery just east of Zane Grey's Lodge. Take an interpretive walk, learn about the life history of trout, peer into the hatchery rooms, and view fingerlings and catchable trout in outdoor raceways. Open daily 8 a.m.-4 p.m.; tel. 478-4200. Follow the same directions as to Zane Grey's Lodge, but keep straight on the paved road to its end.

## Highline National Recreation Area

Highline Trail weaves in and out for 51 miles beneath the cliffs of the Mogollon Rim. Settlers built the trail in the 1800s to link their ranches and homesteads. Today hikers, horseback riders, and mountain bicyclists use the many interconnecting trails for a wide variety of journeys.

Pine Trailhead, at the west end, lies 15 miles north of Payson just off AZ 87. Two-Sixty Trail-

head marks the eastern end, 27 miles east of Payson just off AZ 260. You can also reach the Highline from four other trailheads, from trails descending the Mogollon Rim above, and from valleys below. You can see effects of the Dude Fire of July 1990 on the central section. The Tonto National Forest *Highline Trails Guide* offers a map and brief trail descriptions; pick it up at Forest Service offices or the Payson Chamber of Commerce.

## Mazatzal Wilderness

Indians knew this vast country of desert and mountains as Mazatzal, "Land of the Deer." The name still fits, as only scattered ruins tell of the Indians, pioneers, and miners who tried to live here. The wilderness covers over 250,500 acres in a block beginning eight miles west of Payson and extending 30 miles south. Climate zones range from the Lower Sonoran Desert, with saguaro and palo verde (2,200-4,000 feet); up through the dry grasslands, oaks, piñons, and junipers of the Upper Sonoran Desert (4,000-7,000 feet); to the Transition Zone, with ponderosa pines and a few pockets of firs on the upper slopes (7,000-7,900 feet). You might meet deer, javelina, black bear, or even a mountain lion. Hikers in this big country should be self-sufficient, with maps, compass, and water; you can't rely on springs and streams in the summer.

Best times for a visit are spring and autumn; summer is okay if you're prepared for possible 100°-plus temperatures and late-season thunderstorms; winter is all right at the lower elevations, but severe snowstorms can hit the high country. No permits are needed to hike or horseback in the wilderness.

Of the 14 trailheads, the Barnhardt is the most popular. From just south of the Rye Creek bridge, 14.5 miles south of Payson on AZ 87, go west 4.8 miles on Forest Route 419 to the end of the road. You then have a choice of three trails. A popular 19-mile, two-day backpack loop encircles Mazatzal Peak via the **Barnhardt, Mazatzal Divide,** and **Y Bar Basin** (Shake Tree) trails. For detailed hiking info see the Forest Service people at Payson, tel. 474-7900, or Phoenix, tel. 225-5200. They'll provide free hiking trail literature and sell you a $4 Mazatzal Wilderness topo map.

## YOUNG

Remote and off the tourist track, Young is known as one of Arizona's last cow towns. To get here you must drive largely unpaved roads: either south 25 miles on Forest Highway 12 from the Mogollon Rim (turn off AZ 260 at Milepost 284, about 33 miles east of Payson); or north 47 miles on AZ 288 (35 miles of dirt road) from near Roosevelt Lake, off AZ 88 between Roosevelt Dam and Globe. The roads to Young are best avoided in winter and just after heavy rains, though the north road is usually okay after showers.

In the late 1800s one of Arizona's bloodiest and most savage feuds took place in Pleasant Valley, between Young and the Rim. The trouble started when the Tewksbury clan gave protection to a band of sheep brought into the area in 1887. Cattle owners led by the Graham clan couldn't stand "woollies" and attacked, killing a Navajo sheepherder and destroying or driving away the animals. The Tewksburys retaliated, and the war was on. The fighting didn't end until every Graham had been killed. All efforts by the law to restore order failed; at least 30 people died during five years of terror. History buffs can visit many of the battle sites near Young. The town cemetery features marked graves belonging to five members of the Graham clan: Harry Middleton, Al Rose, Charles Blevin, William Graham, and John Graham. Young Cemetery lies behind Young Baptist Church on the main road, a half mile east of Moon's Saloon.

Historians still debate details of the feud. Accounts of the tragedy are given in *A Little War of Our Own* by Don Dedera, *Arizona's Dark and Bloody Ground* by Earle Forrest, and *Globe, Arizona* by Clara Woody and Milton Schwartz. Zane Grey dramatized the events in his novel *To the Last Man*. Grey obtained his material during hunting trips in Pleasant Valley.

Today, a very independent breed of people inhabit Young. These folks, many retired, don't like authority or development. Even the Forest Service—Young's largest employer—represents too much government for some people.

### On the Road in Young

Young social life revolves around the **Antlers Bar and Cafe,** tel. 462-3265, and **Moon's Saloon Bar and Cafe.** Both places serve inexpensive breakfasts, lunches, and dinners daily. Antlers features a free museum, offering everything from old saddles and mining gear to an Electrolux vacuum cleaner and tuba. Dusty bears and mountain lions also stare down from the walls. The only laundromat within many miles of dirt road driving is **Emma's Wash It** next to Antlers. Limited medical services are available at **Pleasant Valley Community Medical Center;** tel. 462-3435.

**Claire's Gallery and Museum** is housed in an 87-room pueblo ruin occupied 1100-1350 A.D. by the Mogollon and Salado cultures; it's open 10 a.m.-6 p.m. Fri.-Sun. all year; tel. 462-3402. Pleasant Valley Historical Society Museum operates out of what had been Arizona's oldest continuously operating Baptist church; it serves as a center of activities during **Pleasant Valley Days,** held the third weekend in July, and will also open for groups by appointment; call Pat Murdoch, the historical society's chair-

*forever Young*

person, for hours at 462-3477 or 462-3402.

**Valley View Cabins** offers rentals with kitchens for $25 s, $30 d, plus two mobile homes at higher rates; tel. 462-3422. **Pleasant Valley Motel** is under construction. Other townspeople occasionally open cabins for rent; ask around at the Antlers Cafe or Moon's Saloon. Ten RV spaces are to be constructed at the community center. For fishing, hiking, and camping info, contact the Tonto National Forest **Pleasant Valley Ranger District** office in Young; open Mon.-Fri. 7:45-11:45 a.m. and 12:30-4:30 p.m.; also open Saturday and Sunday in summer; tel. 462-3311. To get there, turn off the main road a quarter mile east of Moon's Saloon. In the absence of a visitor or information center the rangers can offer information about the town and surrounding area. **Young Public Library** is open noon-4 p.m. Tues.-Sat.; tel. 462-3588. For road conditions call **Gila County Road Department;** tel. 462-3523. Pay phones in Young do not accept coins so all local calls are free.

# VICINITY OF YOUNG

## North of Young

The unfortunate Navajo sheepherder who fell as the first victim of the Pleasant Valley War is buried north of Young. A white cross, pile of stones, and sign mark the spot; from the main road, five miles north of Young and 21 miles south of AZ 260, turn west and drive nearly one mile on Forest Route 200.

**Valentine Ridge Campground** (no water or fee) lies 18 miles north of Young and six miles south of AZ 260, then two miles east on Forest Route 188. **Colcord Campground** (no water or fee) is just east of the main road on Forest Route 33, about three miles south of AZ 260 and 23 miles north of Young. **Canyon Creek Campground** (no water or fee) and **Canyon Creek Fish Hatchery** lie just below the Rim at an elevation of 6,600 feet; follow Forest Route 33 in five miles. The fish hatchery features a self-guided tour, open daily 8 a.m.-5 p.m. Anglers can fish in Canyon Creek for rainbow and brown trout—flies and artificial lures only—with limits of two fish per day and a minimum length of 12 inches.

**Colcord Lookout** (elev. 7,513 feet) offers a sweeping panorama of the Young area and the Mogollon Rim; turn west off the main road onto Forest Route 291 (opposite the Forest Route 33 turnoff), and drive three miles. Open mid-May through Labor Day.

## South of Young

**Workman Creek Waterfalls** plunge 200 feet in a spot south of Young; to get there, go south on SR 288 for 21 miles, turn left and drive 3.5 miles on Forest Route 487, park at the cattleguard, then walk a quarter mile to the falls. This pretty canyon supports dense stands of Douglas fir, white fir, and smaller numbers of Arizona sycamore and the relatively rare Arizona maple. There are several places to camp (no facilities) along the road to the falls. Swimmers can cool off in the **"bathtubs,"** natural pools in Workman Creek; from the Workman Creek bridge on AZ 288, follow the trail downstream 250 yards.

**Rose Creek Campground** (elev. 5,400 feet) is off the main road 23 miles south of Young; no drinking water or fee.

## Wilderness Areas near Young

The **Sierra Ancha Wilderness** contains 20,850 acres and lies 15 miles south of Young and 36 miles north of Globe. Lack of good roads and rugged terrain discourage most visitors—box canyons and sheer cliffs make travel difficult. Elevations range from 3,200 to 7,800 feet. Spring-fed creeks in the eastern portion of the wilderness have carved several short but deep box canyons, including Pueblo, Cold Springs, and Devil's Chasm. Prehistoric Salado Indians built cliff dwellings in these canyons, then departed.

Forest Route 203 (Cherry Creek Rd.) loops around the east side of the Sierra Anchas, providing views into the spectacular canyons. You need a high-clearance or 4WD vehicle for this trip; the northern part of the road is particularly rough. Allow 3.5 hours for the drive. For hiking info and a wilderness map, contact the Forest Service in Young (tel. 462-3311) or Phoenix (tel. 602-225-5200). Salome Wilderness, 15 miles southwest of Young, protects the Salome and lower Workman Creek watersheds.

**Hell's Gate Wilderness,** 13 miles northwest of Young, preserves parts of the drainages of Tonto, Haigler, Marsh, and Houston Creeks. Sheer cliffs rising above Tonto Creek form Hell's Gate; there's good fishing here, but only the most adventurous anglers make it in on the steep, difficult Forest Trail #37 (very hot in summer).

# EAST OF PHOENIX: THE APACHE TRAIL LOOP

Driving east through Phoenix, Tempe, Mesa, and Apache Junction, you might think the city will never end. But as soon as you turn onto AZ 88 in Apache Junction, the shopping centers, gas stations, and hamburger stands fade away, and you're left with just the desert, lakes, and mountains. Here begins a 200-mile loop through some of the most rugged country in the West. Allow six hours to drive this circuit around the rugged Superstition Mountains, taking AZ 88 to Globe, then returning to Apache Junction via US 60/70. The big attractions, aside from the wild scenery, are hiking and horseback riding in the Superstition Wilderness, boating on a chain of lakes within the Salt River Canyon, stepping inside prehistoric Indian cliff dwellings in Tonto National Monument, seeing copper-mining operations near Globe, Miami, and Superior, and visiting the Boyce Thompson Southwestern Arboretum—an amazing collection of plants from all over the world.

## SUPERSTITION WILDERNESS

This 159,700-acre wilderness lies south of the Salt River Canyon and Apache Trail, about 40 miles east of Phoenix. You'll find some of the Southwest's best desert hiking in the canyons and mountains of the Superstitions. Elevations range from about 2,000 feet along the west boundary to over 6,000 feet in the eastern uplands. Desert vegetation dominates, while a few pockets of ponderosa pine hang onto the highest slopes. Wildflowers put on colorful extravaganzas in early spring and following summer rains.

### Gold Fever

They say Don Miguel Peralta discovered fantastic amounts of gold somewhere in the Superstitions in 1845; he and his miners later met their deaths at the hands of Apache Indians. Peralta's Sombrero Mine remains a mystery. At least one member of Peralta's party survived the massacre and, some 30 years later, revealed the location of Peralta's Sombrero Mine to a German immigrant, Jacob Waltz. Locally known as The Dutchman, Waltz worked the mine without ever revealing its location. Those who tried to follow him into the Superstitions were either lost in the maze of canyons or found murdered. The power of the Lost Dutchman legend has intensified since the prospector's death in 1891. Although no rich gold deposits were ever found, and geologists say the Superstitions are an unlikely location for gold, the legends persist.

### Climate

Spring and autumn bring the most pleasant weather for a visit to the Superstitions. Winter is often fine at lower elevations, though snow and cold hit the higher areas. Summer, which lasts from May to October, is unbearably hot. Temperatures exceed 115° F in the shade at times, and there's precious little shade. You can venture into the Superstitions in the summer on a crack-of-dawn journey, leaving by late morning when the heat hits. Carry plenty of water, especially in summer when springs and creeks dry up.

### Hiking

Twelve trailheads and 180 miles of trail offer all kinds of possibilities. Since they're so close to Phoenix, the Superstitions get unusually heavy traffic for a wilderness area. The western half is frequented most, especially near the Peralta and First Water trailheads. You're more likely to see javelina, desert mule deer, mountain lion, black bear, and other wildlife in the

the "Narrows" of La Barge Creek in the
Superstitions

eastern half of the range. You don't need a permit to hike or camp in the Superstitions; just leave the area as you found it and limit groups to 15 people, stays to 14 days. Horses are allowed; bring feed, as grazing is prohibited. Laws protect the wilderness from prospecting involving surface disturbance; no one can file new claims. For additional information consult *Hikers Guide to the Superstition Wilderness* by Jack Carlson and Elizabeth Stewart.

**Information**

The U.S. Forest Service manages the Superstition Wilderness as part of the giant Tonto National Forest. Foresters dispense advice on travel in the Phoenix office (2324 E. McDowell Rd., Phoenix, AZ 85006, tel. 602-225-5200); Mesa (26 N. MacDonald St., Mesa, AZ 85201, tel. 602-835-1161); and Tonto Basin (Box 649, Roosevelt, AZ 85545, tel. 520-467-3200). A Superstition Wilderness topo map with background, trailhead, and trail information is also available.

## FOUR PEAKS WILDERNESS

This wilderness area covers 60,743 acres in the southern Mazatzal Mountains, north of Apache Lake opposite the Superstition Wilderness. The Four Peaks are visible over a large section of central Arizona, a major landmark since Indian times. From their deeply incised lower slopes along Canyon and Apache lakes at an elevation of 1,900 feet, the mountains top off at Brown Peak, northernmost of the four, at 7,657 feet.

Vegetation ranges from saguaro cactus at the base to ponderosa pine, Douglas fir, and aspen near the top. Javelina, deer, black bear, mountain lion, and smaller animals inhabit the slopes. Arizona's highest concentration of black bear live here; wise campers hang food out of reach at night. The Forest Service offers a pamphlet describing trails in the Four Peaks area, available from the Phoenix, Mesa, and Roosevelt offices. Trailheads can be reached from AZ 87 to the west (northeast of Mesa) and from AZ 188 to the east (northwest of Roosevelt Dam).

## THE APACHE TRAIL: APACHE JUNCTION TO ROOSEVELT DAM

Once a raiding route for Apaches, the Apache Trail is still primitive and imposing. Jagged ridges, towering cliffs, and the desert itself remind human beings of their limitations and small scale. The Apache Trail, designated a National Scenic Byway, twists and climbs as it tries to find a way through the rugged land. Watch for narrow bridges and blind curves; the road isn't recommended for large trailers.

Visible to the south is Weaver's Needle, the 4,535-foot landmark for gold seekers in the Superstition Wilderness—the Lost Dutchman Mine is said to lie in its shadow. The stories about Jacob Waltz and his Lost Dutchman Mine are probably just tall tales. Despite the efforts of thousands of gold-crazed prospectors, no major finds have ever been confirmed. Geologists studying the mountains have pronounced them remnants of volcanic calderas, an unlikely source of rich veins of precious metal. Perhaps the crafty Dutchman worked as a fence for gold

*riding in the Superstitions*

thieves employed in the Vulture Mine near Wickenburg: miners stealing nuggets wouldn't be able to sell their loot in Wickenburg, so Waltz may have run a gold-laundering operation by caching the Vulture gold in the Superstitions. If so, he still has a lot of people fooled, even after 100 years.

**Mile 0.0: AZ 88** in Apache Junction.

**Mile 2.0: O.K. Corral Stables,** two miles left on Tomahawk Rd. at the sign. The stables offer a variety of guided horseback rides in the Superstition and Goldfield mountains; "legendary hayrides" as well; overnight pack trips are available as well; tel. (602) 982-4040.

**Mile 3.5: Goldfield Ghost Town and Mine Tours** allows visitors to learn how miners worked and admire their equipment in a re-created underground mine. It's open daily 10 a.m.-5 p.m. (6 p.m. in winter); $4 adults, $2 children 6-12; tel. (602) 983-0333. Try your luck at goldpanning for $3 extra. **Mammoth Steakhouse and Saloon** serves lunch and dinner; tel. (602) 983-6402. **Superstition Mountain/Lost Dutchman Museum** displays artifacts from prehistoric Indian and Spanish/Mexican times and offers a multimedia slide presentation—check out the archival material about cowboys, miners, and prospectors, or soak up some folklore about the Lost Dutchman Mine; it's open daily 10 a.m.-4 p.m.; $3 adults, $2.50 seniors, $1 ages 6-18; tel. (602) 983-4888.

**Mile 4.2: Mining Camp Restaurant** on the right offers Western fare in a replica of an old mining camp's cook shanty. It's open daily for dinner only Nov.-May; tel. (602) 982-3181.

**Mile 4.8:** On the left you'll see **Goldfield,** a place that boomed in the 1890s with the discovery of gold but became a ghost town when mining yields dwindled in 1915. People still mine gold in this area; you'll see prominent No Trespassing signs where they do.

**Mile 5.4: Lost Dutchman State Park** on the right offers picnicking, day hiking, and camping at the base of the Superstition Mountains. A quarter-mile native plant trail near the park entrance identifies desert flora; the path is paved and handicapped-accessible. Longer trails loop onto the slopes of the adjacent Superstition Mountains. Staff lead campfire programs and guided hikes Oct.-April. Entry costs $3 per vehicle for day use or $8 per vehicle for camping (water but no hookups); tel. (602) 982-4485.

**Mile 5.7:** Following three bumpy miles, look to the right for the **First Water Trailhead,** a popular one for hikes in the Superstition Wilderness.

**Mile 7.3: Needle Vista Viewpoint** will be on the right. Weaver's Needle, the striking high pinnacle rising among the Superstitions, has often figured in lost gold mine legends. The name honors frontier scout Pauline Weaver. Local Indians had a different name for it, referring to a certain part of a stallion's anatomy.

**Mile 12.4:** There is an overlook on the right for **Canyon Lake.** The series of lakes along the Salt River provides fishing and boating for visitors and precious water for Phoenix. Canyon Lake was created by Mormon Flat Dam, completed in 1925. Past the viewpoint, the road sweeps down from the heights to the lakeshore.

**Mile 14.5: Acacia Picnic Site** is on the left, offering swimming and fishing.

**Mile 14.8:** You'll see **Palo Verde Boating Site** on the left (boat launch) and **Boulder Picnic Site** on the right (swimming and fishing).

**Mile 15.2: Canyon Lake Marina** is on the left and **Boulder Canyon Trailhead** is on the right. The marina offers boat rental and storage, fishing supplies, a restaurant, picnicking, and a campground ($9 tent or RV; no showers or hookups); tel. (602) 986-5546. Another camping area, **the Point,** is accessible only to boaters; it's on the left, three miles upstream from the marina. **Dolly's Steamboat** takes visitors on a scenic 90-minute narrated cruise and a two-hour dinner cruise; call (602) 827-9144 for times. Anglers have hooked largemouth and yellow bass, trout, catfish, bluegill, carp, walleye, and crappie. During the busy mid-spring to mid-summer season, Sunday crowds sometimes fill all available parking places in the Canyon Lake area; try to arrive early.

**Boulder Canyon Trail #103** begins across the highway, climbing up the ridge and offering spectacular views of the Superstitions and Canyon Lake area. The trail continues on through La Barge and Boulder canyons, linking with several other trails in the Superstition Wilderness.

**Mile 15.6: Laguna Boating Site** is on the left.

**Mile 17.3: Tortilla Campground** is on the left and **Tortilla Flat** (cafe, post office, country store, curio shop, and ice cream parlor—try a scoop of prickly pear) is on the right. The campground is open November to April; the water supply is questionable for drinking, and it's better to bring your own; $8 per night. Tortilla Flat (pop. six), the only town along this section of road, looks like a movie set. The tiny community is a popular traveler's stop. A hungry pioneer, who perceived the surrounding flat boulders as stacks of tortillas, reportedly gave the place its name. The cafe serves inexpensive American and Mexican meals. During winter, barbecued food is served on the patio. A large room is completely wallpapered with real dollar bills. There are lots of old mining and farming relics lying around—see if the dummy outlaw is still strung up, swinging in the breeze; tel. (602) 984-1776.

**Mile 22.9:** The pavement ends and the next 22 miles to Roosevelt Dam is graded dirt road.

**Mile 24.0: Tortilla Trailhead** for the Superstition Wilderness is on the right.

**Mile 24.4:** This begins the descent down **Fish Creek Hill** and offers spectacular views of the canyon below. Fish Creek Hill is the most exciting part of the Apache Trail, especially for the driver, who must negotiate sharp bends as the road traverses a cliff face and drops 1,500 feet in three miles. Fish Creek, near the bottom, occasionally offers a trickle of water but no fish. Hikers can head up Fish Creek Canyon.

**Mile 30.1:** On the right, Forest Route 212 travels three bumpy miles to **Reavis Trailhead. Reavis Ranch Trail #109** crosses the eastern part of the Superstition Wilderness. Elisha Reavis lived a hermit's life on his ranch from 1872 until his death in 1896.

**Mile 30.2:** From **Apache Lake Vista,** you can see the lake in the canyon below. Held back by Horse Mesa Dam, Apache Lake reaches nearly to Roosevelt Lake—a distance of 17 miles.

**Mile 32.1:** There's a turnoff on the left for **Apache Lake Recreation Area.** The **Apache Lake Marina and Resort** has a boat ramp, fishing and pontoon boat rentals, car and boat fuel, boat storage, fishing and camping supplies, restaurant, tent area (the $3 day use fee covers primitive camping), RV campground ($15.90 w/hookups and showers), and motel with kitchenettes ($51.94 d or $65.72 d kitchenette); write to Box 15627, Tortilla Flat, AZ 85290, or call (520) 467-2511. Anglers can catch smallmouth and largemouth bass, trout, yellow bass, catfish, sunfish, and walleye. Officers staff the **Maricopa County Sheriff Aid Station** at the lake on weekends and holidays; tel. (520) 467-2619.

**Mile 39.0: Burnt Corral Campground** and boat ramp are on the left, with wheelchair accessible restrooms and a picnic area; $8 single site, $12 double site, and $16 triple site, no charge for day use.

**Mile 44.3: Theodore Roosevelt Dam** lies at the end of the dirt road section. Workers built the dam with stone blocks between 1905 and 1911. An engineering feat in its day, the 280-foot-high structure is still the world's highest masonry dam. President Teddy Roosevelt motored over the Apache Trail in 1911 to dedicate the dam, which was later named in his honor. Engineers worried the original dam couldn't survive a moderate earthquake or a massive flood, so a new concrete dam was built over the old structure. An impressive new bridge now spans the lake just above the dam.

## ROOSEVELT LAKE

Roosevelt Lake, fed by Tonto Creek from the north and the Salt River from the east, stretches 23 miles and is as much as two miles wide. With approximately 17,335 surface acres, it's the largest of the four Salt River lakes. Summers at Roosevelt's 2,100-foot elevation are only slightly cooler than in the Valley, but waterskiing and boating attract many visitors. Anglers enjoy the rest of the year, when it's not so hot. Known as a good bass and crappie lake, Roosevelt also contains catfish and sunfish.

A flock of Great Basin Canada geese takes up residence during the winter at Bermuda Flat on the north arm. Part of this area is closed to the public from Nov. 15-Feb. 15, but you can view the geese from the highway. Bald eagles use the middle third of the northern shore for nesting and foraging; no camping allowed here.

### Accommodations and Food

The Forest Service maintains many recreation sites both north and south of the dam. Visitors can use the new, improved camping areas and paved boat ramps, and enjoy displays in a new visitor center for information. **Bermuda Flat Recreation Site** is to be built eight miles north of the dam and will offer a day use parking lot with portable toilets. Each year the area will be closed Nov. 15-Feb. 15 to protect the migrating Canada goose habitat. Camping is

planned here but fees are not yet determined. **Cholla Recreation Area,** about five miles north of the dam, offers paved boat ramps, a courtesy dock, playgrounds, flush toilets, and developed campsites with water and solar-heated showers; tent or RV fees run $10 per day, with oversize sites available at $16. **Windy Hill Campground,** four miles south of the dam, offers campsites, toilets, showers, a playground, concrete boat ramps, and courtesy docks; $10 single site, $16 double site. **Grapevine Group Site,** eight miles south of the dam, can accommodate groups of 15-100 people each; with showers, lake access trails, restrooms, grills, and picnic tables; reservations are required, tel. (520) 467-3200. Shoreline dispersed camping has been permitted in the past but will depend on the new lake level. **Roosevelt Marina,** two miles southeast of the dam, features a primitive campground (free), boat rentals (fishing and pontoon), wet and dry boat storage, a paved boat ramp, a snack bar, gasoline for boats and autos, and a store; the marina will be moved and expanded in 1996 or 1997; tel. (520) 467-2245. **Lakeview Trailer Park,** across the highway, has spaces with hookups ($15.99, no tents); tel. (520) 467-2203.

**Roosevelt Lake Resort** offers a motel ($37.45 d), trailer park ($12 RV w/hookups), restaurant, and boat storage facility 12 miles southeast of the dam (20 miles northwest of Globe), then east 0.6 mile; tel. (520) 467-2276. **Spring Creek Store, Roosevelt Post Office,** and a fast food restaurant lie 0.6 mile northwest of the resort turnoff; the store sells groceries, gasoline, and camping and fishing supplies. Behind Spring Creek Store you'll find **Roosevelt Lake RV Park,** where full hookups cost $15.91 per night; tel. (520) 467-2888.

**Rockhouse Store,** five miles north on the Young Hwy. (AZ 288), sells groceries and gasoline, and maintains a trailer park ($5 w/hookups); tel. (520) 467-2484. **Punkin Center,** a village 22 miles north of Roosevelt on AZ 188, offers Punkin Center Lodge ($36.24 d, $47.97 d kitchenettes); tel. (520) 479-2229. At the lodge, the Steak House, open daily except Monday for lunch and dinner, offers live entertainment on some weekends; tel. (520) 479-2234. RV parks are nearby.

## Information

Forest rangers and volunteers at the new **Roosevelt Lake Visitor Center** in Roosevelt, behind the Roosevelt Lake Marina on AZ 88, can tell you about area facilities, fishing, hiking, camping, and boating; the center also features an exhibit room, historical and educational videos, an interactive computer, and a bookstore; it's open daily 7:45 a.m.-4:30 p.m. Write to HC 02 Box 4800, Roosevelt, AZ 85545, or call (520) 467-3200 for more information.

## TONTO NATIONAL MONUMENT

Two well-preserved cliff dwellings constructed by the prehistoric Salado Indians overlook the blue waters of Roosevelt Lake. The Salado (Spanish for "salty") lived in this part of the Salt River Valley about A.D 1150-1450. Skillful farmers dug irrigation canals to water their corn, squash, beans, grain amaranth, and cotton. They also roamed the desert hills for cactus fruits, mesquite beans, deer, pronghorn, and many other wild foods. Crafts included beautiful polychrome pottery and intricately woven cotton cloth.

At first they built small, scattered pueblos along the river, but in about 1250 some of the Salado began living on more defensible ridgetops. From 1300 until their mysterious departure soon after 1400, part of the population moved into caves like those in the monument.

## Visitor Center and Ruins

Exhibits illustrate how the Salado lived and tell what we know of their history. Stone tools, pottery, cotton cloth, and other artifacts reveal their artistic talents. A self-guided trail above and behind the visitor center climbs the hillside to the Lower Ruin, which is open to the public. Originally the cave consisted of 19 rooms, with another 12 in the annex outside, but the elements have worn away those exposed. Allow one hour for the trip; you'll climb 350 feet on a paved path.

The Upper Ruin, reached by a different trail, is about twice the size of the Lower, but farther away and requiring advance planning. You must call or write ahead to check on days and times when tours are offered. Ranger-guided tours to the Upper Ruin last about three hours for the three-mile roundtrip hike; no extra charge. A nature trail near the visitor center identifies many desert plants.

The monument is open daily 8 a.m.-5 p.m. The Lower Ruin Trail closes one hour earlier; HC02 Box 4602, Roosevelt, AZ 85545; tel. (520) 467-2241. The visitor center is one mile off AZ 88, two miles southeast of Roosevelt and 28 miles northwest of Globe; $4 per vehicle. If you're driving the Apache Trail Loop, this is the halfway point; Apache Junction is three hours away.

*Lower Ruin at Tonto National Monument*

## SALT RIVER CANYON WILDERNESS

About 60 miles of lively whitewater flow upstream on the Salt River from Roosevelt Lake. Boaters typically require four days to raft or kayak through the twisting canyons. Only experienced river-runners should attempt this wild water, as several rapids. are rated Class IV and Quartzite Falls often requires portage. Quartzite Falls was dynamited by vandals, but a lawsuit may restore this section of the river—at the expense of the vandals. Don't use large rafts over 15 feet or open canoes. The Forest Service requires visitor groups of no more than 15, in suitable non-motorized craft, engaged in "no trace" camping.

Trips beginning on the White Mountain Apache Indian Reservation require a tribal permit. The Forest Service offers a detailed booklet on the Upper Salt River, available at the Globe (tel. 520-425-7189) and Phoenix (tel. 602-225-5200) offices.

Another option involves a guided trip with one of several tour companies. Commercial trips on the Upper Salt are offered by **Sun Country Rafting,** Box 9429, Phoenix, AZ 85068, tel. (602) 493-9011 or (800) 2-PADDLE; **Desert Voyagers,** Box 9053, Scottsdale, AZ 85252, tel. (602) 998-RAFT or (800) 222-RAFT; and **Far Flown Adventures,** Box 377, Terlingua, TX 79852, tel. (915) 371-2489 or (800) 359-4138.

## GLOBE

Tucked into a narrow valley between the Apache Mountains to the northeast and the Pinal Mountains to the south and west, Globe is a handy stopping place for travelers. The town's 3,500-foot elevation provides a pleasant climate most of the year. Though its years of glory as a big copper-mining center have long passed, Globe still has a lot of character. On a drive down

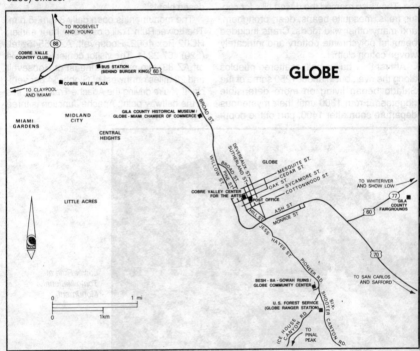

Broad St. you can visit its museum, view ruins of the Old Dominion Copper Mine, and see many buildings dating from the early 1900s. The chamber of commerce, also on Broad St., offers a *Historic Globe/Miami Downtown Walking Tour* leaflet that details the history of these old structures. You can also pick up a *Drive Yourself Mine Tour* leaflet describing six mines, historic and modern, visible from US 60 in the Globe and Miami areas; none of the mine sites are open to the public.

## History

In 1875, prospectors struck silver in the hills of the western part of San Carlos Apache Indian Reservation. Their most remarkable find, a globe-shaped silver nugget, reportedly had the rough outlines of the continents scarred on its surface. Miners converged on the area, setting up camp on the east bank of Pinal Creek. The area was officially sliced off the reservation, which didn't go over well with the Apache. They regularly menaced the camp until Geronimo's surrender in 1886.

The silver began to give out after only four years, but by then rich copper deposits had been discovered beneath the silver lodes. The Old Dominion Copper Company moved in, and during the early 1900s its copper mine ranked as one of the greatest in the world. Globe prospered too—its 50 restaurants and saloons never closed, and about 150 sporting women worked out of neat little shacks along N. Broad Street. George W.P. Hunt arrived in 1881 as a young man, and worked his way up to become a leading merchant and banker before going on to serve as Arizona's first governor. Labor troubles and declining yields began to eat into mining profits, and the Depression shut down the Old Dominion completely in 1931. Copper mining shifted to nearby Miami, leaving Globe a quiet county seat.

## SIGHTS

### Gila County Historical Museum

This small but varied collection includes Indian, pioneer, and mining artifacts. Period rooms—lady's bedroom, tack room, miner's tent, and mine superintendent's office—recall the days of pioneers. Ore cars and large machinery sit outside. It's open Mon.-Fri. (and sometimes Saturday) 10 a.m.-4 p.m.; donations are welcomed; tel. (520) 425-7385. It's opposite the Old Dominion Copper Co. Mine at 1330 N. Broad Street.

The museum building, which dates from 1914, served as the company's mine rescue station for many years.

### Cobre Valley Center for the Arts

Local artists have banded together and opened an art gallery in the old Gila County Courthouse, built 1906-07. Doing much of the restoration themselves, local volunteers have also added a theater used by the Copper Cities Community Players. You can see the art exhibits (some rotate monthly) Mon.-Sat. 9 a.m.-5 p.m. and Sunday noon-5 p.m.; free. It's downtown at the corner of Broad and Oak Streets; tel. (520) 425-0884.

### Besh-ba-gowah

Salado Indian villages lined both sides of Pinal Creek about 600 years ago. Besh-ba-gowah, exposed to both the elements and humans, is in poorer condition than the Tonto National Monument cliff dwellings, but its extensive foundations and few remaining walls testify to its original size. Archaeologists count 200 rooms at Besh-ba-gowah, built and inhabited between A.D. 1225 and 1450. An earlier village of houses in pits associated with the Hohokam stood on this site about A.D. 600-1150.

The name Besh-ba-gowah comes from an Apache word meaning "metal camp." A self-guided trail winds through the ruins, some restored, some only stabilized, some yet unexcavated. The restored rooms feature baskets, pots, ladders, and other implements, arranged as if the Salado were still living here. Pottery and other artifacts of village life and trade are on display in the adjacent museum. A scale model shows the village as it might have looked in 1325. The ethno-botanical garden contains native and cultivated plants used by prehistoric Indians.

The museum and ruins are open daily 8 a.m.-5 p.m.; $2 ages 12 and up; tel. (520) 425-0320. Besh-ba-gowah is 1.5 miles south of downtown Globe; follow S. Broad St. to its end, turn right across the bridge, curve left on Jess Hayes St./Pioneer Rd. one mile, make a sharp right to Globe Community Center, and follow signs around to the far side of the ruin. The surrounding park offers picnic tables and ball fields.

### Pinal Peak
A dirt road winds up the timber-clad slopes to the summit (elev. 7,812 feet). Weather permitting, you'll enjoy great views, hiking, picnicking, and two of the coolest campgrounds in the Tonto National Forest.

For the 18-mile drive from Globe, follow S. Broad St. to its end, turn right across the bridge, curve left on Jess Hayes St./Pioneer Rd. to the junction of Ice House Canyon and Six Shooter Canyon Roads, turn right and drive 2.5 miles on Ice House Canyon Rd., make another right and proceed three miles on Forest Route 55 (pavement ends), and then left for 12.5 miles on Forest Route 651 to the summit. In summer, you can drive all the way to the top of Signal Peak, the highest point; in other times you walk the last bit. The easy Pineline Trail System loops around the summit, connecting the campgrounds and Six Shooter, Squaw Spring, Bobtail Ridge, and Mill Creek Trails; these trails climb steeply from the valleys below. The Globe Ranger Station offers trail descriptions and maps.

## ON THE ROAD IN GLOBE

### Accommodations
You'll find Globe motels either downtown on Broad St. or along US 60 (Willow and Ash Streets) bypassing downtown.

Coming in from the north or west, you'll pass **Best Western Copper Hills Inn**, US 60 between Miami and Globe, $60.76-66.09 d, tel. (520) 425-7151 or (800) 528-1234; **Belle-Aire Motel**, 1600 N. Broad St., $28.25 s, $36.20 d, tel. (520) 425-4406; **Ember Motel**, 1105 N. Broad St., $28.38 s, $36.50 d, tel. (520) 425-5736 or (800) 253-1123; **Willow Motel**, 792 N. Willow St., $27 s, $40.51 d, tel. (520) 425-9491; and **Copper Manor Motels**, 637 E. Ash St., $49.76-56.55 s, $52.03-58.81 d, or, across the street in smaller rooms, $29.41-40.72 s or $33.93-42.98 d; tel. (520)

425-7124). A **Holiday Inn Express** is planned for Globe.

See also **El Rey Motel,** 1201 E. Ash St., $27.14 s, $35.32 d, tel. (520) 425-4427; **El Rancho Motel,** 1300 E. Ash St., $27 s, $33.76 d, tel. (520) 425-5757; and **Cloud Nine Motels,** 1699 E. Ash St., $56.30-69.80 s, $59.65-81.05 d, tel. (520) 425-5741 or (800) 432-6655.

### Campgrounds
There is overnight RV parking at **El Rey Motel,** 1201 E. Ash St., $5 no hookups, tel. (520) 425-4427; **Gila County RV Park,** 300 S. Pine St., $15 w/hookups, tel. (520) 425-4653; **Casa de Monti,** 1730 E. Ash St. near the junction of US 60 and US 70, $12 RV w/hookups, tel. (520) 425-6574; **Holiday Hills Mobile Home Park,** 6.5 miles north on AZ 88, $16 w/hookups, tel. (520) 425-8585; and **Apache Trail Mobile Park,** six miles north on AZ 88, $16 w/hookups, tel. (520) 425-7979.

Tent campers and small RVs can head south into the Pinal Mountains. The Forest Service maintains free campgrounds open April to December at **Lower Pinal** and **Upper Pinal**, elev. 7,500 feet, water from May to October, 18 miles south on Forest Route 651. There are also Forest Service sites at **Pioneer Pass,** elev. 6,000 feet, water from May to October, eight miles south on Forest Route 112. The upper site features horse corrals. **Jones Water Campground** (elev. 4,300 feet) offers sites in cottonwoods 15 miles north of town on US 60; no water or fee. See the Tonto Forest map or contact the Globe Ranger Station for camping information; tel. (520) 425-7189.

### Food
**Blue Ribbon Cafe** serves American food at 474 N. Broad St.; tel. (520) 425-4423. **Jerry's** dishes up American food next to the Copper Manor Motel; tel. (520) 425-5282. For steaks try the **Crestline Steak House** at 1901 E. Ash St., about one mile east on US 60; tel. (520) 425-6269.

Dine Mexican at **El Rey Cafe,** 999 N. Broad St., tel. (520) 425-2054; **La Casita,** 470 N. Broad St., tel. (520) 425-5029; and **Irene's Real Mexican Food,** 1601 E. Ash St., tel. (520) 425-7904. **La Luz del Dia** is a Mexican bakery and coffee shop at 304 N. Broad St.; tel. (520) 425-

8400. **Peg's Kitchen** serves Mexican and American food at 247 S. Broad St.; tel. (520) 425-4707.

**Jasmine Tea House** prepares Mandarin, Szechuan, and Hunan cuisine at 1097 N. Broad St.; tel. (520) 425-2503. Pick up pizza at **Pizza Hut,** 1497 E. Ash St.; tel. (520) 425-4401.

You'll find more restaurants, including numerous fast-food chains, on the outskirts at both ends of Globe on US 60.

### Entertainment and Events

**Globe Theatre** screens current movies at 141 N. Broad St.; tel. (520) 425-5581.

**Apache Gold Casino,** five minutes east of Globe on Hwy. 70, offers slot machines, live and video poker and keno, a deli, and a lounge and plans to build a hotel, RV park, restaurant, and show lounge; tel. (520) 425-7692.

Major Globe events include the **Gila County Gem and Mineral Show** in January or February; **Historic Home/Building Tour and Antique Show** in February; **Copper Dust Stampede Rodeo, Dance, and Parade** in April (there's a Spring Roundup Rodeo, 19 miles east in Peridot, also in April); and **Mining Country Boomtown Spree,** an arts and crafts fair in Miami, in April. There's an **Old Time Fiddlers Contest** in July; the **Gila County Fair** in September; **horse races** in October; **Apache Days** with dances, crafts, and food by Apache and other Indian groups, in October; and **Veterans Parade, Rodeo, and Pageant,** 19 miles east in San Carlos, on Veterans Day weekend in November.

### Services

The main **post office** is downtown at 101 S. Hill and Sycamore Streets; tel. (520) 425-2381. **Cobre Valley Community Hospital** is on Hospital Dr.; tel. (520) 425-3261. **Globe Community Center** has a swimming pool, picnic areas, and ball fields 1.5 miles south of downtown Globe; follow S. Broad St. to its end, turn right across the bridge, curve left on Jess Hayes St./Pioneer Rd. one mile, then make a sharp right at the sign.

**Cobre Valle Country Club** is open to the public with a nine-hole golf course and tennis and racquetball courts; it's just north on AZ 88 between Globe and Miami; tel. (520) 473-2542.

### Information

The **Globe-Miami Chamber of Commerce** is very helpful; literature includes historic walking tours of Globe and Miami and a "Drive Yourself Mine Tour"; it's open Mon.-Fri. 8 a.m.-5 p.m., also open Oct.-April on Saturday 10 a.m.-4 p.m. and Sunday 10 a.m.-4 p.m. The chamber is next to the Gila County Historical Museum on N. Broad St.; Box 2539, Globe, AZ 85502; tel. (520) 425-4495 or (800) 804-5623.

The **Globe Ranger Station** of the U.S. Forest Service stocks maps and literature for hiking trails—which tend to be steep—and camping areas; the office lies on Six-Shooter Canyon Rd., two miles southeast of downtown; it's open Mon.-Fri. 7:45-4:30 p.m.; Rt. 1, Box 33, Globe, AZ 85501; tel. (520) 425-7189. The **Globe Public Library** is at 339 S. Broad St.; tel. (520) 425-6111.

### Transport

**Greyhound** buses stop at the station behind Burger King, on US 60 about two miles northwest of downtown. Greyhound has several westbound and eastbound departures daily; tel. (520) 425-2301.

## THE APACHE TRAIL:
## GLOBE TO APACHE JUNCTION

### Miami and Claypool

The visitor is assaulted by a strange landscape on the approach to these two towns west of Globe. Many-tiered terraces of barren, buff-colored mine tailings and dark slag dumps dominate the view. Miami and Claypool stretch along Bloody Tanks Wash, named for a massacre of Apache in 1864 by a band of whites and allied Maricopa Indians. Developers arrived in 1907 to lay out a town site, named after Miami, Ohio. Giant copper-ore reduction plants built by the Miami Copper and Inspiration Companies resulted in the nickname "Concentrator City." Miami has had its ups and downs since, following the rise and fall in copper prices, but copper production continues. Miami has half a dozen historic buildings, described in a walking-tour leaflet available from the Globe Chamber of Commerce, and several restaurants.

## Miami to Superior

Highway 60 climbs over the rugged Pinal Mountains with many fine views between these two towns. Six miles west of Miami you'll see the vast workings of the open-pit Pinto Valley copper mine. The road continues climbing to a pass, then descends into Devils Canyon.

**Devils Canyon Picnic Site** is a pretty spot for lunch or overnight camping; turn and drive 0.2 mile north from just west of Devils Canyon bridge, between Mileposts 232 and 233. **Oak Flat Campground** (elev. 4,200 feet) lies in more open country nearby; turn a half mile south on Magma Mine Rd. at the sign near Milepost 231. Both areas stay open all year; no water or fee. West of Oak Flat, the highway drops through steep-walled Queen Creek Canyon to Superior.

## Superior

Opening of the rich Silver King Mine in 1875, followed by development of the Silver Queen, brought streams of fortune hunters into this mineral-laden region. As in Globe, miners found rich deposits of copper when the surface silver began to play out. Superior lies just west of scenic Queen Creek Canyon in a valley surrounded by the rugged Pinal Mountains.

North of town you'll see the high smokestack of an idle smelter and extensive tailings from the Magma Copper Mine, where shafts plunge nearly 5,000 feet underground. Rockhounds may collect "Apache tears"—a form of volcanic glass—for a fee at a site west of town; signs indicate the turnoff.

Superior offers **El Portal Motel,** $24-30 d, tel. (520) 689-2886, and several restaurants. **Apache Tear Village RV Park and Motel** offers sites with showers for tents ($10.26) and RVs ($10.26 no hookups, $13.77 w/hookups), also motel cabins ($32.67 d), in a quiet spot just west of town; tel. (520) 689-5800. **Apache Mobile Park** next door also has tent ($10.86) and RV ($13.03 w/hookups) sites and showers; tel. (520) 689-5331.

## Picket Post House

Copper-mining magnate William Boyce Thompson founded the Southwestern Arboretum in 1927 for botanical research and teaching. His 26-room mansion, Picket Post House, overlooks the grounds and can be visited on tours Mon.-Sat. 10 a.m.-5 p.m.; $5 adults, $2.50 children under 12; tel. (520) 689-5610. Entrance is 0.7 mile east of the arboretum entrance.

## Boyce Thompson Southwestern Arboretum

You can see more than 1,500 different desert plants here. Short trails lead through yuccas and agaves, a cactus garden, native desert vegetation, riparian natives, exotic plants, palms, pines, and eucalyptus. More than 174 bird and 72 animal species have been spotted. Greenhouses contain cactus and succulents that wouldn't otherwise survive winter cold.

Elevations range from 2,400 feet at the gardens to 4,400 feet atop nearby Picket Post Mountain. A heliograph station, equipped with

*Weaver's Needle from Fremont Saddle in the Superstitions*

mirrors to flash the rays of the sun, operated atop the peak during the Apache wars. The visitor center offers some exhibits and a gift shop featuring books, prints, posters, and seed packets. There's a large selection of cactus, other succulents, trees, shrubs, ground cover, and herbs for sale. The cooling tower exhibit at the visitor center creates a cool microclimate; its 30-foot tower is actually a giant evaporative cooler.

Scheduled events include an Arid Land Plant Show on the first weekend in April and a Fall Landscaping Festival. A picnic area near the parking lot is available to visitors. Today the University of Arizona, the State Parks Board, and the nonprofit Arboretum Corporation manage the arboretum. It's open daily except Christmas 8 a.m.-5 p.m.; $4 adults, $2 children 5-12; tel. (520) 689-2811 (recording). The arboretum is three miles west of Superior, 60 miles southeast of Phoenix, and 101 miles north of Tucson.

### White Canyon Wilderness Area

To reach one of Arizona's newest and smallest wilderness areas, drive 9.6 miles south on Hwy. 177, then west two miles on Battleax Rd. to an unmarked dirt road; follow it for 2.7 miles, turning right at each fork. There is no trail into the canyon—just pick your own route through the rocks . The canyon is as much as 500 feet deep with steep walls, offering a hike up to three miles long. Hikers not used to boulder hopping may find travel exhausting. For more information call the Bureau of Land Management in Phoenix; tel. (602) 780-8090.

## FLORENCE JUNCTION TO APACHE JUNCTION

### Florence Junction

Not a town at all—just a junction. If you're interested in turquoise, drop into the **Hardy Turquoise** store east of the junction; tel. (520) 463-2371. The town of Florence, which includes the excellent Pinal County Historical Museum, lies 16 miles south on US 89 (see below).

### Peralta Trailhead

One of the most popular trailheads for the Superstition Wilderness lies off US 60/89 about nine miles northwest of Florence Junction, eight miles southeast of Apache Junction. Follow the graded, dirt Forest Route 77 in for seven miles. You'll also see the Dons Camp on the left just before the trailhead. The Dons Club, an organization devoted to promoting the legends and beauty of the Southwest, hosts a big one-day event here, usually in March, when thousands of people descend on the Superstitions for hikes, demonstrations, and entertainment; tel. (602) 258-6016.

There's good hiking here, with three trails branching off into the wilderness. One of these, **Peralta Trail #102,** goes up Peralta Canyon to Fremont Saddle, where you get a great view of Weaver's Needle. It's four miles roundtrip and a 1,400-foot climb to the pass; carry water and avoid the heat of a summer day. Peralta Trail continues down the other side past the base of Weaver's Needle, connecting with other trails in the Superstitions.

# SOUTH OF PHOENIX

On the drive between Phoenix and Tucson you'll cross desert plains with views of the Superstitions, Picacho Peak, Santa Catalina Mountains, and other rugged ranges. Desert flora along the roadside blooms in blazes of bright color in spring. Several spots are worth a visit, whether you take the old Pinal Pioneer Parkway (AZ 79) or the speedier I-10.

## FLORENCE

Florence, one of the oldest white settlements in Arizona, dates back to the arrival of Levi Ruggles in 1866. Ruggles found a safe ford on the nearby Gila River and believed the valley suitable for farming. He laid out a town site that soon became a trade center and stage stop for surrounding Army camps.

Some people advocated Florence as the Arizona territorial capital, but the town had to settle for a designation as the Pinal County seat. The first county courthouse went up in 1878, constructed of adobe blocks. It survives as McFarland State Historical Park. The second county courthouse was completed in 1891; its ornate cupola is Florence's chief landmark.

Not everybody comes to Florence by choice—the Arizona State Prison sits at the edge of town. Convicts completed the prison in 1909, replacing the territorial prison at Yuma. Inmates now make up nearly half of the town's 6,800 inhabitants.

Florence has two museums and a large number of historic buildings—over 140 listed with the national register. You can pick up a visitor's guide at the tourist office or the Pinal County Historical Museum.

### Pinal County Historical Museum
There's a lot of history in this diverse collection. Indian pottery, baskets, and stone tools come from prehistoric and modern tribes of the area. An 1880 horse-drawn opera coach offers a taste of early pioneer elegance. Also displayed are early settlers' tools, mining gear, household items, and clothing. News clippings describe the tragic death of silent-screen hero Tom Mix, killed in a car accident nearby. Bullet aficionados

will find hundreds of different types on display.

The prison exhibits are sobering: used hangman's nooses framing photos of their victims, hanging board, gas-chamber chair, massive prison registers from Yuma and Florence, and the story of murderess Eva Dugan, hung and simultaneously decapitated in 1930. The museum is open Wed.-Sat. 11 a.m.-4 p.m., Sunday noon-4 p.m. Dec.-March and noon-4 p.m. April-Nov.; donations are welcomed; 715 S. Main St.; tel. (520) 868-4382.

### McFarland State Historical Park
This adobe building served as Pinal County's first courthouse, sheriff's office, and jail from 1878 to 1891, then functioned for 50 years as the county hospital. In 1883 an angry mob took two murder suspects from the jail and hung them in a corridor. Exhibits illustrate the history of Florence and the courthouse. You'll also learn about Ernest McFarland (1894-1984), who began his political career in 1925 as Pinal county attorney, then rose to serve as U.S. senator, Arizona governor, and chief justice of the State Supreme Court. Open Thurs.-Mon. 8 a.m.-5 p.m.; $2 adults, $1 ages 12-17; tel. (520) 868-5216; it's near the north end of Main St. at Ruggles Street.

### Box Canyon
This scenic canyon offers a chance to see a beautiful and photogenic canyon, enjoy a picnic, take landscape photographs, and get stuck in powder-fine sand; cars have succeeded in following this route but 4WD is much safer. From Florence drive north on Hwy. 89 for 0.3 miles then turn right after crossing the Gila River and continue 14 miles of dirt road. The Pinal County Visitor Center will give you a good map of the area.

### Tom Mix Monument
October 12, 1940, was a sad day for fans of movie hero Tom Mix. Speeding north from Tucson in his big Cord, he lost control of the car and rolled over in a ditch, subsequently renamed Tom Mix Wash. A roadside monument, topped by a riderless horse, marks the spot, 17 miles south of Florence on AZ 79.

## Poston's Butte

Charles Poston explored and mined in what is now Arizona from 1853 to 1861, but his greatest achievement was successfully lobbying in Washington, D.C., for a territorial government. Poston went on to become the first superintendent of Indian affairs in Arizona and one of the first Arizona delegates to Congress.

His congressional term finished, Poston traveled to India and became a fire worshipper. Upon returning to Arizona in 1878, he built a continuous fire—a sort of temple of the sun—atop a hill, naming it Parsee Hill. The flames died out several months later, ending a project that disbelievers mocked as "Poston's Folly." Today, Poston lies buried on the hill, renamed Poston's Butte, northwest from Florence across the Gila River.

## On the Road in Florence

Stay at **Blue Mist Motel,** junction of AZ 79 and AZ 287; $33.12-38.64 s, $44.16-49.68 d; tel.

(520) 868-5875. Or try **Taylor's Bed and Breakfast,** 321 N. Bailey St. at $54-66; tel. (520) 868-4857. Senior citizens can park their RVs at **Caliente Casa de Sol,** 2.5 miles north on AZ 79; $15 w/hookups; tel. (520) 868-5520. **Rancho Sonora RV Retreat** offers RV spaces w/hookups for $19.19, five miles south of Florence on Hwy. 79; tel. (520) 868-8000 or (800) 205-6817. You'll find several restaurants on Main Street.

For more information about the Florence area, visit the **Pinal County Visitor Center** at 912 N. Pinal St.; it's open Mon.-Fri. 9 a.m.-5 p.m., 10 a.m.-2 p.m. in summer; Box 967, Florence, AZ 85232; tel. (520) 868-4331.

## CASA GRANDE RUINS NATIONAL MONUMENT

A short turnoff from AZ 87 just north of downtown Coolidge leads to Arizona's biggest and

**CASA GRANDE ARTIFACTS**

shell finger ring

stone ax

copper bells

stone ax

most perplexing prehistoric building. The rectangular structure stands four stories high and contains 11 rooms above an earthen platform. An estimated 2,800 tons of mud went into the project, with walls ranging in thickness from 4.5 feet at the base to 1.8 feet near the top.

Archaeologists don't know the purpose of Casa Grande, but some speculate it was used for ceremonies or astronomical observations; certain holes in the walls appear to line up with the sun at the summer solstice and possibly with the moon during selected lunar events. Smaller structures and a wall surround the main building. Hohokam Indians, who had farmed the Gila Valley since about 200-300 B.C., built Casa Grande around A.D. 1350. The Casa Grande is the only structure of its type still standing.

By about 1450, after just a few generations of use, the Hohokam abandoned Casa Grande along with all their other villages. The Jesuit priest Eusebio Kino recorded the site in 1694, giving it the Spanish name for "big house."

### Visitor Center

Exhibits introduce you to the Hohokam and their irrigation canals, farming tools, jewelry, and ball courts. Various theories to account for the disappearance of the Hohokam are examined. You can take a ranger-led tour of Casa Grande or set off on a self-guided trail. Signs identify cactus and other desert plants. Books on Arizona's Indians, settlers, and natural history are sold; it's open daily 7 a.m.-6 p.m.; $2 per person, maximum $4 per vehicle; tel. (520) 723-3172.

The monument is one mile north of downtown Coolidge off AZ 87 and AZ 287 at 1100 Ruins Dr., Coolidge, AZ 85228.

These ruins shouldn't be confused with the modern town of Casa Grande, which is about 20 miles away.

### Blackwater Trading Post and Museum

This small museum offers a chance to enjoy viewing attractive Indian artifacts. Walk through the trading post and ask to see the museum, which is normally kept locked and dark. It's a little more than three miles west from the Hwy. 287/87 intersection; tel. (520) 723-5516.

## GILA RIVER ARTS AND CRAFTS CENTER

To learn about the Pima and Maricopa Indians, or just to take a break from freeway driving, stop at this cultural center on the Gila River Reservation. Museum exhibits display artifacts and interpret the history of these two tribes. Crafts in the gift shop include pottery of Maricopa and New Mexican tribes, Tohono O'odham baskets, Hopi kachina dolls, and Navajo rugs. Jewelry, paintings, and prints come from many tribes. An inexpensive restaurant offers Indian fry bread and American foods.

Outside, Heritage Park contains traditional structures of the Hohokam, Pima, Maricopa, Tohono O'odham, and Apache tribes; a booklet available at the gift shop describes each group. Gila River Arts and Crafts Center is open daily except some holidays 8 a.m.-5 p.m. (restaurant opens 8 a.m.); free admission; tel. (602) 963-3981. Indians present craft demonstrations and occasional performances on weekends. Take I-10 Exit 175, 30 miles southeast of Phoenix (90 miles northwest of Tucson), and go west a half mile on Casa Blanca Road.

**Casa Blanca RV Park,** next door to the cultural center, has sites year-round for tents and RVs; $13 w/hookups or without, showers included; tel. (520) 315-3534. Check in at the small market across the road if the manager is not available.

## CASA GRANDE

Until a few years ago, Casa Grande was just a small, sleepy agricultural town. However, Casa Grande has now been discovered by winter visitors as a convenient haven from the rat race and crime of the large cities. While Casa Grande does not offer the shopping or dining opportunities of Tucson or the Valley of the Sun, it does have its own conveniences. Located just northwest of the I-10 and I-8 intersection, with good access to each, Casa Grande is usually less than an hour's drive from downtown Phoenix and about an hour and a half from downtown Tucson.

In the 1880s Casa Grande was a mere freight depot where agricultural and mining supplies were dropped off beside the track for local shippers to handle. Originally, no town was planned. This was just a spot where the tracks stopped being laid during the summer of 1879. When the tracks continued on to Yuma, the town stayed and boomed to a population of 500 by 1882. Although downtown Casa Grande burned to the ground three times between 1884 and 1914, each time it was rebuilt. The national mining slump in the 1890s caused the town to dwindle to just a mercantile, a saloon, and two small businesses. However, agriculture allowed the town to continue. Livestock, vegetables, alfalfa, wheat, barley, citrus, and cotton contributed to the local economy. Now, the economy depends as much on the recent surge of winter visitors, which resulted in the building of one resort, several nationwide chain motels, and RV parks. Recently, Casa Grande's population passed 25,000 and the growth rate is accelerating.

**Casa Grande Valley Historical Museum**
Exhibits take you back to the days of the Indians and pioneers. Learn about area mining and view period rooms (living, bedroom, and kitchen). There's a gift shop, open 1-5 p.m. daily except Monday, Sept. 15-June 15, closed the rest of the year; tel. (520) 836-2223. The museum is at 110 W. Florence Blvd. in the town of Casa Grande, about 45 miles south of Phoenix.

**Casa Grande Art Museum**
This small but interesting museum offers visitors a chance to enjoy paintings, sculpture, photographic displays, and ceramics as well as an outdoor sculpture garden. It's open 1-4 p.m. Fri.-Sun. (evening hours are planned) late Sept.-May at 319 W. 3rd. St.; tel. (520) 836-3377.

**Accommodations**
For luxury accommodations and a chance to play 18-holes of golf, stay at the **Francisco Grande Resort and Golf Club** at 26000 Gila Bend Hwy.; tel. (520) 836-6444 or (800) 237-4238. Nationwide chain motels include **Best Western Casa Grande Suites** at 665 N. Via del Cielo, tel. (520) 836-1600 or (800) 528-1234; **Holiday Inn** at 777 N. Pinal Ave., tel. (520) 426-

3500; and **Motel 6** at 4965 Sunland Gin Rd., tel. (520) 836-3323. There are also half a dozen local motels offering off season bargain rates close to downtown and another half dozen within a short drive of Casa Grande.

**Campgrounds**
The newer RV parks in Casa Grande and surrounding area cater to long-term winter visitors and do not offer tent camping. In winter it is sometimes difficult to find an overnight site available in the trendier parks; such parks charge $25 per night. The newer parks include **Val Vista Winter Village RV Resort** at 16680 W. Val Vista Rd., tel. (520) 836-7800; **Desert Shadows RV Resort** at 195 W. Rodeo Rd., tel. (520) 421-0401; and **Fiesta Grande RV Resort** at 1500 E. Florence Blvd., tel. (520) 836-7222. In all, there are more than a dozen RV parks in the Casa Grande area.

**Recreation and Entertainment**
For movies, try **Mall Cinema 3** in the Casa Grande Mall at 1226 E. Florence Blvd. #18; tel. (520) 836-5969. For golf, try the 18-hole **Casa Grande Municipal Golf Course** at 212 N. Thornton Rd., tel. (520) 836-9216; the **Francisco Grande Resort and Golf Club** at 26000 Gila Bend Hwy., tel. (520) 426-9205; or **Tierra Grande Country Club** with its nine-hole course at 813 W. Calle Rosa, tel. (520) 793-9717. The newest Casa Grande golf course is **Vista Verde**, with 18 holes at 3290 S. Montgomery Rd.; tel. (520) 421-7121.

Casa Grande offers three mini-parks, nine neighborhood parks, four community parks, and three regional parks. In addition to playground equipment, picnic tables, grills, ramadas, volleyball and tennis courts, and horseshoe pits, some parks also offer rodeo facilities, an archery range, a public swimming pool, and much more. For park information call (520) 421-8600.

**Casa Grande Fitness and Racquet Club** offers a total fitness and recreational facility with tennis, racquetball, basketball, swimming, aerobics, weight and cardiovascular machines, and a jacuzzi and steam room at $7 daily use fee or $3 for showers; located at 2060 N. Trekell Rd.; tel. (520) 836-0613.

## Shopping and Services

Most of the larger shopping facilities in Casa Grande are found within a few blocks on E. Florence Blvd. including **Casa Grande Mall** at 1226 E. Florence Blvd., tel. (520) 421-0506; **Kmart** at 1214 E. Florence Blvd., tel. (520) 836-3466; **Wal-Mart** at 1325 E. Florence Blvd., tel. (520) 421-1200; and **JCPenney** at 1375 E. Florence Blvd., tel. (520) 421-1777. There are also two major outlet malls in the Casa Grande area. **Tanger Factory Outlet Center** has more than four dozen shops at I-10 Exit 198 on Hwy. 84; tel. (520) 836-0897 or (800) 4-TANGER (8-26437). **Factory Stores of America** has more than two dozen shops at 440 N. Camino Mercado, Ste. G, just west of I-10 Exit 194; tel. (520) 421-0112 or (800) SHOP-USA (7460-872). **Casa Grande Regional Medical Center** is at 1800 E. Florence Blvd.; tel. (520) 426-6300.

## Information

For information about Casa Grande and the surrounding area contact the **Greater Casa Grande Chamber of Commerce** at 575 N. Marshall Street. It's open 9 a.m.-5 p.m. Mon.-Fri., 10 a.m.-4 p.m. Saturday, and noon-4 p.m. Sunday; tel. (520) 836-2125 or (800) 916-1515. The **Casa Grande Public Library** is located at 405 E. 6th St.; tel. (520) 421-8690.

# PICACHO PEAK STATE PARK

Picacho Peak has served as a landmark for Indians, Spanish explorers, American frontiersmen, and modern-day motorists. Park visitors can enjoy hiking, camping, and picnicking in this scenic area. Saguaro and other plants of the Sonoran Desert thrive on the rocky hillsides. Monuments near the flagpole commemorate the Battle of Picacho Pass and the building of the road by the Mormon Battalion.

The Battle of Picacho Pass, on April 15, 1862, was the westernmost conflict of the Civil War and the only one to take place in Arizona. Confederate forces killed Lieutenant James Barrett, leader of the Union detachment, and two privates. Aware that Union reinforcements would soon arrive, the Confederates retreated back down Butterfield Road to Tucson. The battle site lies just outside the state park boundary, toward the freeway.

## Practicalities

The park features several picnic areas and a campground with showers and hookups; $3 per vehicle for day use, $8 camping, or $13 w/hookups; tel. 466-3183. Take I-10 Exit 219 (74 miles southeast of Phoenix and 40 miles northwest of Tucson) and follow signs a half mile.

## Hiking Trails

Inside the park, you can hike to the top of 3,374-foot Picacho Peak, a remnant of ancient lava flows, or try easier trails. **Hunter Trail** climbs 1,500 feet to the summit, a four-mile roundtrip requiring four to five hours. Be careful on the back side where the trail crosses some loose rock; posts and cables provide handholds in the rougher spots. **Sunset Vista Trail** traverses the back of the peak in 3.1 miles.

An easier hike, also with expansive views, follows the Hunter Trail as far as the saddle, a two-mile roundtrip of 1.5 hours. Easier still is the **Calloway Trail** to a low pass between Bugler's and Picacho peaks, 1.5 miles roundtrip, requiring an hour. Both trails begin from the large parking area near Saguaro Ramada on Barrett Loop Drive.

Gila
woodpecker
(Melanerpes
uropygialis)

Rangers offer trail maps; bring water and sun protection. A 30-minute **nature trail** loop introduces desert plants; you can begin from Memorial Plaza or the hookup campground.

## GILA BEND

The town (pop. 2,000) sits near the Gila River 68 miles southwest of Phoenix. Father Kino, who came through here in 1699, found a prosperous Maricopa Indian village with irrigated fields yielding two harvests annually. The Butterfield stagecoach first rolled through in the early 1850s; a settlement later grew around a Butterfield station.

Today the small town serves as an agricultural center and a travelers' stop. Surrounding farms raise cotton, wheat, barley, and other crops. San Lucy, a Tohono O'odham Indian village, lies just north of town. On Business Loop I-8 you'll find seven motels, three RV parks, and a variety of restaurants.

The **Gila Bend Museum and Tourist Center** is a history museum providing information about the community and surrounding area daily 8 a.m.-4 p.m.; tel. (520) 683-2002. It's on Business Loop I-8 at 644 W. Pima St.; write P.O. Drawer A, Gila Bend, AZ 85337. The **public library** is a couple of blocks off the highway at 202 N. Euclid.

# NORTHWEST OF PHOENIX

## WICKENBURG

You still get a sense of the Old West in easygoing Wickenburg. Western-style buildings line the downtown streets, and horses are a common sight. Even a bit of gold fever lingers, still drawing prospectors to mine-scarred hills. Cowboys continue to work the range, though joined now by riders from local guest ranches. The picturesque rocky hills around Wickenburg offer ideal horseback riding.

Wickenburg's cool and sunny weather lasts from November to May. Summers at the town's 2,100-foot elevation often bring very hot weather. It's 58 miles northwest of Phoenix; you can get here from Phoenix via US 60 (Grand Ave.) or the longer but less congested route past Lake Pleasant via I-17 and AZ 74.

### History

Henry Wickenburg had roamed the hills of Arizona for a year in search of gold before striking it rich at the Vulture Mine in 1863. According to one legend, he noticed the shiny nuggets when reaching down to pick up a vulture he'd shot; others claim he glimpsed the gold while picking up a rock to throw at his burro. Either way, Wickenburg set off a frenzied gold rush.

The Vulture Mine lacked water needed for processing, so miners hauled the ore 14 miles

northeast to the Hassayampa River. In just a few years, the town that grew up around the mills became Arizona's third-largest city. It missed earning the honor of territorial capital in 1866 by only two votes.

Prospectors discovered other gold deposits in the Wickenburg area until more than 80 mines operated at the height of the gold rush. Mining for gold and other minerals continues today, though on a smaller scale.

## SIGHTS

### Desert Caballeros Western Museum

This fine museum takes you back to Wickenburg's Wild West days. Dioramas illustrate the history of the Vulture Mine and the early mining community. Period rooms and a street scene indicate how Wickenburg actually looked.

An Indian Room displays a varied collection of prehistoric and modern crafts, including kachina dolls, pottery, baskets, and stone tools. Precious stones can be seen in the Mineral Room. A large art gallery features outstanding Western paintings and sculpture by Remington, Russell, and other inspired artists.

Walk over to a small park behind the museum to see *Thanks for the Rain,* a bronze sculpture by Joe Beeler.

The museum and art gallery are open Mon.-Sat. 10 a.m.-4 p.m. and Sunday 1-4 p.m.; $4

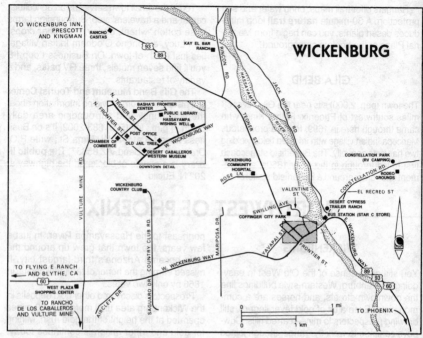

adults, $3.50 seniors 60 and over, $1 children 6-16. Located at 21 N. Frontier St., one block west of the downtown highway junction; tel. (520) 684-2272/7075.

## Old Jail Tree

The town lacked a jail in the early days, so prisoners were shackled to this old mesquite tree. The tree stands behind the Circle-K store at the highway junction downtown.

## Hassayampa River

Normally you'll see just a dry streambed through town. The river's Apache name means "river that runs upside down," because its waters flow beneath the sandy surface. A wishing well and sign at the west end of the highway bridge relate the legend that anyone drinking from the stream will never tell the truth again.

## Hassayampa River Preserve

The river pops out of the ground along a five-mile section of riverbed below town, watering lush vegetation. The Goodding willow-Fremont cottonwood forest along the banks is one of the rarest forest types in North America.

Spring-fed Palm Lake attracts many waterfowl not normally seen in the desert. Visitors have counted 230 species of birds, including zone-tailed and black hawks that fly up from Mexico to nest. The preserve, managed by the Arizona chapter of the Nature Conservancy, provides a sanctuary for these hawks and other wildlife. Visitors can enjoy quiet walks through the natural settings, reflecting on the fact that of Arizona's streamside habitats existing a century ago, only about 15% exist today.

Check in at the visitor center for trail information, or pick up regional and natural history books and literature on environmental concerns. The four-room adobe core of the visitor center, built in 1860, has served as ranch, stagecoach way station, and one of Arizona's first guest ranches. Borrow trail guides for the 1.5-mile loop **Hassayampa River Nature Trail** and the half-mile **Palm Lake Nature Trail**.

You can visit Wed.-Sun. (closed Monday and Tuesday) 8 a.m.-5 p.m. (Sept. 16-May 14) or 6 a.m.-noon (May 15-Sept. 15); a $5 suggested donation by nonmembers is appreciated. The preserve schedules guided nature walks on Saturday; call for time and reservations; tel. (520) 684-2772. Hassayampa River Preserve lies three miles southeast of Wickenburg on US 60/89 near Milepost 114.

## ON THE ROAD IN WICKENBURG

### Guest Ranches

Wickenburg takes pride in the designation "Guest Ranch Capital of the World." The degree of luxury varies, but all five guest ranches offer horseback riding and a swimming pool.

**Flying E Ranch** is open Nov. 1-April 30; rates include meals, $122.27-159.49 s, $196.70-265.81 d. It's four miles west on US 60, then one mile south, 2801 W. Wickenburg Way, Box EEE, Wickenburg, AZ 85358; tel. (520) 684-2690. **Kay El Bar Ranch** has been around so long it's on the National Register of Historic Places; open Oct. 15-April 30. Rates include meals, horseback riding, and gratuity, $145.59 s, $272.99 d. Go two miles north on AZ 89; Box 2480, Wickenburg, AZ 85358; tel. (520) 684-7593.

**Rancho Casitas,** open year-round, is three miles north off AZ 89; $927.50 one-month minimum stay, Oct. 1-April 30; Box A-3, Wickenburg, AZ 85358; tel. (520) 684-2628. **Wickenburg Inn** emphasizes tennis, with nine courts, a pro shop, and lessons; it's seven miles north off AZ 89 and open all year; rates include meals, horseback riding and service charge, $226.62-330.75 s, $336.88-453.25 d; Box P, Wickenburg, AZ 85358; tel. (520) 684-7811 or (800) 528-4227.

**Rancho de los Caballeros** is the most elegant of the group and open early Oct.-early May; guests enjoy a pool, tennis courts, and an 18-hole golf course. Rates include meals, $192-358.80 low season, $216-390 high season. Go 3.5 miles west on US 60, then south two miles to 1551 S. Vulture Mine Rd., Wickenburg, AZ 85390; tel. (520) 684-5484.

### Motels

You'll find all the motels in town along US 60, named Wickenburg Way. From east to west are

**Americinn,** 850 E. Wickenburg Way, $60 s, $66.43 d, tel. (520) 684-5461 or (800) 634-3444; **La Siesta Motel,** 486 E. Wickenburg Way, $30.04 s, $32.19 d, tel. (520) 684-2826; **Best Western Rancho Grande,** 293 E. Wickenburg Way, $52.45 s, $55.67 d, tel. (520) 5445 or (800) 528-1234.

The **Capri Motel** is at 521-A W. Wickenburg Way, tel. (520) 684-7232; **Westerner Motel** is at 680 W. Wickenburg Way, tel. (520) 684-2493. **Rincon Ranch Lodge Bed and Breakfast** is 2.5 miles northwest on N. Tegner, then 1.5 miles north on Rincon Rd., $64.30 s or d; tel. (520) 684-2328. **Sombrero Ranch Bed and Breakfast** has accommodations for horses on 48 acres at the Wickenburg city limits at 31910 W. Bralliar Rd.; from the Hwy. 60/89-93 intersection go three quarters of a mile north; $79.25 s or d; tel. (520) 684-0222.

For something different, check out the **Garden City Motel** on a hill eight miles southeast of town; the quiet spot offers good views of surrounding mountains and a chance to see wildlife. No restaurant but the cottages have kitchenettes, $42.53 per day for a room and $132.91-212.65 per week for a cottage; tel. (520) 684-2334. Look for the signs between Mileposts 118 and 119 on US 60.

### Camping

**The Desert Oasis,** 14 miles southeast on US 60, has the only full-service facilities for both tents ($9.52) and RVs ($12.70 w/hookups); tel. (602) 388-2431.

Closer in, RVs can stay at **Horspitality RV Park and Boarding Stable,** two miles southeast on US 60, $15 RV w/hookups and showers, tel. (520) 684-2519; **Aztec Mobile Home and RV Park,** 401 E. Wickenburg Way, $13.85 w/hookups and showers, tel. (520) 684-2481; **Desert Cypress Trailer Ranch,** adults only, behind McDonald's at 610 Jack Burden Rd., $17.65 w/hookups and showers, tel. (520) 684-2153; or **Constellation Park,** only $2 but no water or facilities, one mile northeast on Constellation Road.

Another possibility for both tents and RVs is camping out in the desert. Avoid washes, and be sure you're on public land.

### Food

For good American fare, try **Willows Restaurant,** 850 E. Wickenburg Way in Americinn, tel. (520) 684-5461; **Country Kitchen,** 495 E. Wickenburg Way, tel. (520) 684-3882; **Frontier Inn,** 430 E. Wickenburg Way, tel. (520) 684- 9501; **Gold Nugget Restaurant,** 222 E. Wickenburg Way, tel. (520) 684-2858; and **Rancho Bar Seven Restaurant,** 111 E. Wickenburg Way, tel. (520) 684-2492. More American food is available at the **Horseshoe Cafe,** 225 E. Center, tel. (520) 684-7377; **Coffee Break Restaurant,** 2021 W. Wickenburg Way in West Plaza Shopping Center, tel. (520) 684-2294; **Cock 'N' Bull Restaurant,** 445 N. Tegner St./AZ 89 N, tel. (520) 684-2807; or **Charley's Steak House,** 1189 W. Wickenburg Way, tel. (520) 684-2413.

You can dine Mexican at **Anita's Cocina,** 57 N. Valentine, tel. (520) 684-3777. The **Sizzling Wok** offers Chinese cuisine at 621 W. Wickenburg Way, tel. (520) 684-3977. Pick up pizza at **Sangini's,** 107 E. Wickenburg Way, tel. (520) 684-7828.

Try brunch and lunch at **The March Hare** in an historic house two blocks southwest from Tegner St. on W. Wickenburg Way; tel. (520) 684-0223. **Sandwich Saloon** has a long list of offerings at 134 N. Tegner St.; tel. (520) 684-2237. German cuisine is available at **House of Berlin** at 169 E. Wickenburg Way; tel. (520) 684-5044. For steak, seafood, and Italian cuisine try **Hagel's Prime Rib** at 683 W. Wickenburg Way; tel. (520) 684-5226.

Buffets and a la carte offerings for breakfast, lunch, and dinner are available at two guest ranches, **Rancho de los Caballeros** (tel. 520-684-5484) and **Wickenburg Inn** (tel. 520-684-7811); reservations required.

You'll find several fast-food places on E. Wickenburg Way. **West Plaza Shopping Center** on the west edge of town and **Basha's Frontier Center** on N. Tegner St. include supermarkets and other stores.

## Entertainment and Events

**Saguaro Theater** screens current films at 176 E. Wickenburg Way; tel. (520) 684-7189. **Gold Rush Days** celebrates Wickenburg's Western heritage with a shootout, parade, rodeo, concerts, "mellerdramas," gold-panning contest, and other activities on the second full weekend in February. **July 4th** brings fireworks and a watermelon feed.

The second Saturday of September **Septiembre Fiesta** celebrates Hispanic culture with dances and music mostly on Frontier St. and in the park near Desert Caballeros Western Museum. The **Wickenburg Bluegrass Festival** brings foot-tapping music and dancing to town in the fall, on the second full weekend in November. A **Cowboy Poets Gathering** presents the rich heritage of those folks who work with range beasts, held on the first weekend in December.

## Shopping and Services

Wickenburg has a good selection of shops specializing in Western apparel, Western art, or Indian arts and crafts. The **post office** is at 55 E. Yavapai St. between N. Tegner and N. Frontier; tel. (520) 684-2138. **Wickenburg Community Hospital** is at 520 Rose Ln., 0.8 mile north off Tegner St.; tel. (520) 684-5421.

**Coffinger City Park** offers picnicking, a swimming pool, tennis courts, and ball fields off N. Tegner St., just across the Sols Wash bridge. Play golf year-round at the nine-hole **Wickenburg Country Club** course (go two miles west on US 60, then north on Country Club Rd., tel. 520-684-2011) and the 18-hole course at **Rancho de los Caballeros** (three miles west on US 60, then south two miles on Vulture Mine Rd., tel. 520-684-2704). **Wickenburg Inn Stables** rents horses by the hour, half day, or full day; lessons, hayrides, and pack trips are available too; it's seven miles north off AZ 89; tel. (520) 684-7811. **Rincon Ranch Lodge** has hourly, daily, and overnight rides, steak rides, and cookouts; head 2.5 miles northwest on N. Tegner St., then 1.5 miles north on Rincon Rd.; tel. (520) 684-2328. **Wickenburg Desert Tours** offers a variety of jeep tours of the desert, a cattle company line camp, an old mine, a ghost town, and a scenic box canyon; tel. (520) 684-0438 or (800) 596-JEEP (5337).

## Information

The very helpful **Wickenburg Chamber of Commerce** is in the old railroad depot on N. Frontier St., one block west of N. Tegner St.; open Mon.-Fri. 9 a.m.-5 p.m. (year-round), Saturday 10 a.m.-3 p.m. (Oct.-May and sometimes in summer), and Sunday 1-4 p.m. (Oct.-May); Drawer CC, Wickenburg, AZ 85358; tel. (520) 684-5479. The **public library** is at 164 Apache St., one block north of Wickenburg Way and just west of the river; tel. (520) 684-2665.

**Transport**
**Greyhound** and **K-T Services** buses stop at the Star-C store, 444 E. Wickenburg Way; tel. (520) 684-2601. Greyhound runs at least twice daily east to Phoenix, northwest to Las Vegas, and west to California. K-T Services travels daily to Phoenix and Las Vegas (via Parker, Lake Havasu City, and Laughlin/Bullhead City).

## VICINITY OF WICKENBURG

**Vulture Mine**
Ruins of the Vulture Mine and the adjacent ghost town of Vulture City are remarkably well preserved. They present a rare opportunity to visit a historic mine that has been neither reconstructed nor destroyed. Mining took place at the site from the time of Henry Wickenburg's discovery in 1863 until wartime priorities shut the mine down in 1942. Gold and silver still lie in underground veins and may be mined again.

You can walk the self-guided, quarter-mile loop past the assay office, glory hole, head-frame and main shaft (more than 2,000 feet deep), blacksmith shop, ball mill, power plant, apartment houses, mess hall, and other structures. Be sure to stay on the marked trail—some areas and buildings are dangerous to enter—and wear good shoes. It's open Fri.-Mon. 8 a.m.-4 p.m.; $5 adults, $4 ages 6-12; group tours scheduled too; tel. (520) 377-0803. Goldpanning costs $4 extra, but you're sure to leave with a bit of gold.

From Wickenburg, head west three miles on Wickenburg Way, then turn south 12 miles on paved Vulture Mine Rd.; the mine is on your right.

**Robson's Arizona Mining World**
The Nella-Meda Mine is a restored ghost town with about 20 buildings, including an antique print shop, blacksmith shop, saloon, and general store. Miners dug gold ore here from the early 1900s until WW II, and there's evidence the Spanish worked the site much earlier. Call for hours (may close from mid-summer to mid-autumn); a bed and breakfast ($72.42 rooms,

*pull up a chair on the hotel porch, Stanton*

$85.06 suites) and a restaurant are open by reservation; tel. (520) 685-2609.

The mine is 30.5 miles northwest of Wickenburg on AZ 71, near Milepost 90; head west 25 miles on US 60, turn north and go four miles on AZ 71, then drive west 1.5 miles. The mailing address is Box M2, Wickenburg, AZ 85358.

## Stanton
Originally called Antelope Station, this settlement began in 1863 when prospectors found placer gold in Antelope Creek. Just five years later the population had reached 3,500. Three buildings remain from the old days: the stage stop, hotel, and opera house. A fourth building, the bathhouse, dates from 1980.

The gold began to play out by the early 1900s, and Stanton started fading away. Gold mining continues in Antelope Creek, indulged in by members of the Lost Dutchman Mining Association just for fun. Ask permission to look around the old site; no charge, though you can make a donation.

From Wickenburg follow AZ 89 north for 18 miles (two miles past Congress), then turn right on a graded dirt road signed for Stanton and Octave. You'll see old shacks, mine tailings, rusting machinery, and some new operations along the road. After entering Stanton, 6.5 miles in, turn left through the Lost Dutchman's Mining Association gate. The main road continues another mile to the site of Octave (signed No Trespassing), then becomes too rough for cars.

On Rich Hill, between Stanton and Octave, prospectors picked up gold nuggets the size of potatoes, just lying on the ground. Another road turns off at Stanton and climbs the valley to Yarnell. It's fun to search out some of the old gold mines and ghost towns surrounding Wickenburg. Caution is needed on these dirt roads; get local advice on conditions and avoid traveling after heavy rains.

## Yarnell Hill Lookout
Southbound travelers can stop at pullouts for a sweeping view of the desert and distant mountains below. The lookout lies 25 miles north of Wickenburg and a half mile south of Yarnell on AZ 89. Northbound travelers don't have access to this stop.

## Shrine of St. Joseph
A short trail leads past statues depicting the stations of the cross. Giant granite boulders weathered out of the hillside add to the beauty of the spot. Free admission. Turn west at the sign in central Yarnell. You'll find motels and restaurants in town.

## Joshua Forest
Joshua trees (Yucca brevifolia) line US 93 for 16 miles. You'll see the first ones about 22 miles northwest of Wickenburg. Large clusters of pale-green flowers appear from early February to early April.

# EASTERN ARIZONA

Eastern Arizona will surprise you. Instead of the arid desert country you might expect, you'll find 2,000 square miles of forested peaks, placid lakes, and sparkling streams in the White Mountains. The cool summer climate, abundant trout-filled waters, and winter sports are the big attractions. Mount Baldy, a peak sacred to the Apache Indians, crowns the range at 11,590 feet and is Arizona's second-highest mountain. Sunrise Ski Resort, several miles north, features some of the most challenging downhill runs in the Southwest. Cross-country skiers and summer hikers can find solitude almost anywhere in these mountains.

For a wildly scenic, high-country drive, try the Coronado Trail between Springerville and Clifton; slow and winding, the route offers almost unlimited picnicking, hiking, and camping possibilities. Over to the west, another highway presents a different surprise—you're driving along southwest of Show Low when suddenly the road begins to descend into a magnificent chasm. It's the Salt River Canyon, a smaller but equally colorful version of the Grand Canyon.

Traveling north from the White Mountains, you'll notice the scenery changing from mountain firs and pines to junipers and vast rangelands, then to the multihued, barren hills of the Painted Desert. Take a closer look at this striking desert country and its famous fossilized wood at Petrified Forest National Park.

Southward from the White Mountains, the drop in elevation is even greater—you'll move through cotton country along the Gila River. "Islands" of high mountains, such as Mt. Graham (10,717 feet) near Safford, break up the often monotonous, low-desert country. A paved road runs nearly to the top of Mt. Graham, taking you from the Lower Sonoran Zone to the Hudsonian. The Galiuro Mountains to the west are a rugged wilderness with several peaks over 7,000 feet.

## Climate

The high country provides welcome relief in summer from the searing heat of the deserts. Most eastern Arizona resort areas lie at elevations of 6,000 to 8,500 feet, where average summer temperatures are in the 60s and 70s F, and highs rarely exceed the mid-80s. Afternoon thunderstorms drench the forests almost daily from mid-July to early September, bringing about one-third of the area's 15 or so inches of annual precipitation. Early summer is the driest time of year.

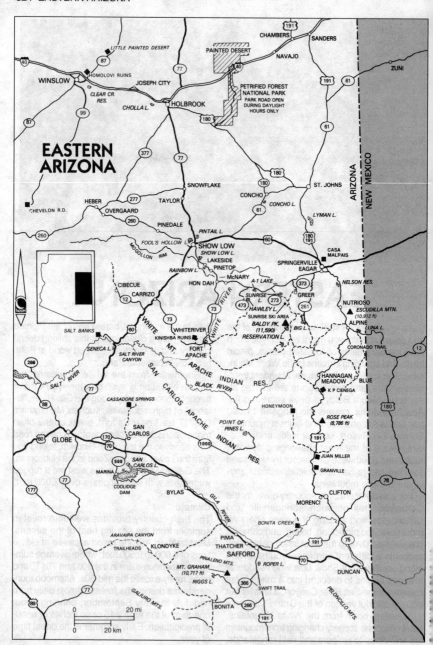

# EASTERN ARIZONA

*Apache warrior in owl-feather medicine headdress*

Camping above 6,000 feet is difficult in winter, as heavy snowfalls and lows in the teens are common. Most winter days are bright and sunny, though, and highs often reach the mid-40s F. Skiers enjoy this weather, and even some anglers are out, chopping holes in the lake ice to get at elusive lake trout. The high-desert country to the north, around Petrified Forest National Park, can be hot in summer and cold in winter, but is usually free of snow. The low desert south of the White Mountains has mild winters and rarely receives snow. As in the rest of eastern Arizona, late summer is the rainiest season.

### Getting There and Around

Eastern Arizona virtually requires private transportation. Only a few bus and train connections serve the area. White Mountain Passenger Lines maintains the most extensive bus routes, connecting Show Low and Heber in eastern Arizona with Payson and the Phoenix area. Greyhound buses stop in Winslow and Holbrook on runs across northern Arizona and at Globe and Safford on a southern route. Winslow is the only town served by Amtrak. There is no scheduled commercial air service in the area.

# THE APACHE

### Arrival

Close relatives of the Navajo, the Apache share a similar language and customs. Groups of Apache are thought to have migrated from Canada, arriving in Texas and New Mexico in the 16th century. A few moved west, forming the tribes that now live on the White Mountain and San Carlos reservations in eastern Arizona and three small reservations in central Arizona.

The early Apache lived a nomadic life—the men hunted game while the women gathered wild plant foods. They had few material possessions, and their homes were probably small conical huts covered with animal skins. Cultivation of corn, beans, and squash, learned from either the Pueblo or Navajo, later supplemented hunting and gathering.

Horses obtained from the Spanish gave the Apache great mobility, and by the mid-18th century their raiding routes stretched from the Hopi mesas in the north to central Sonora in Mexico. Their predatory habits did not endear them to their neighbors—in fact, the name Apache may have come from a Zuni Indian word for "enemy."

### Trouble with White People

The Apache vigorously defended their lands from encroaching settlers, and soon earned a reputation as the fiercest tribe in the Southwest. Attempts over the years by the Spanish, the Mexicans, and finally the Americans to exterminate the Apache caused the tribes to retaliate with a murderous vengeance. By 1870 the U.S. government finally realized that a military solution just wouldn't work.

### Reservation Life

The federal government then initiated a "Peace Policy," which placed all Indians on reservations and taught them to farm and raise livestock. The San Carlos Reservation, just south of the White Mountains, was created in 1871 as a home for various tribes—Mohave, Yavapai, Yuma, and several different groups of Apache.

Officials thought Indians would be easier to control if centralized on one reservation, but

*Tzoe, called "Peaches" by the soldiers because of his light complexion and rosy cheeks, was an Apache Indian scout under general Crook's command in central Arizona, 1880s.*

their plan may actually have extended the Apache wars. Quarrels developed between the different groups, attempts at farming fared poorly, and government agents frequently cheated the Indians. Geronimo and other war chiefs fled the reservation at times to lead raids against settlements in southern Arizona and northern Mexico. By the time Geronimo surrendered in 1886, the federal government realized the San Carlos Reservation had failed and removed all tribes except the San Carlos Apache. Meanwhile, many of the White Mountain and Cibecue Apache had succeeded in holding onto part of their own territory to the north, which became a reservation in 1897.

In 1918, a ranching program issued five head of cattle to each of 80 Apache families. Although the program nearly failed, the herds

on the Fort Apache Reservation eventually grew to 20,000 by 1931. Still, it wasn't until 1936 that white people finally removed the last of their own cattle from the reservations. Recognizing the recreational value of their lands, in the 1950s the White Mountain Apache began to build access roads, reservoirs, campgrounds, marinas, motels, and restaurants. They also own and operate a large lumber industry. The tribe has meanwhile preserved the great natural beauty of the reservation. San Carlos Apache have developed their lands for visitors as well, though on a smaller scale.

### Traditions
Driving through the Apache homeland, you might think their culture is gone—you see members of the tribe living in modern houses, frequenting the shopping centers, and working at regular jobs. But the Apache continue to use their own language and preserve the old traditions. Boys still study under medicine men to learn the prayers, rituals, and medicinal plants used in healing ceremonies. Elaborate coming-of-age ceremonies still mark young women's passage into adulthood. Known as Sunrise Dances, these rites usually take place on weekends during summer; check local papers for dates or ask at the tribal offices in Whiteriver and San Carlos.

### Crafts
Frequently on the move in pre-reservation days, the Apache created only a few utilitarian crafts. Today, some of their products—baskets, cradle boards, and beadwork—are made and sold. Look for them at trading posts on the reservations. Buckskin dresses, worn by women before the introduction of calico, are occasionally seen at Sunrise Dances. Attractive designs in beadwork decorate necklaces, bolo ties, and other adornments. Woodcarvers have recently begun fashioning realistic dolls depicting the dance movements of the Apache Spirit Dancers. Craftspeople on the San Carlos Reservation set peridot (a transparent yellow-green gemstone) in bolo ties, necklaces, earrings, and other jewelry.

# THE HIGH DESERT

## WINSLOW AND VICINITY

Founded in 1882 as a railroad terminal, the town commemorates General Edward Francis Winslow, president of the St. Louis and San Francisco Railroad, associated with the Atlantic and Pacific line that ran through town. Ranchers turned the community into a major stock-raising center and shipping point.

Today, trade and the railroad remain important to the community, though tourism, trucking, and manufacturing boost the economy too. Winslow (pop. 8,795) sits in the Little Colorado River Valley at an elevation of 4,880 feet. Travelers find this a convenient stopover: Meteor Crater is 25 miles west, the Hopi and Navajo reservations lie just to the north, Petrified Forest National Park is 50 miles east, and the Mogollon Rim forest and lake country is 40 miles south.

### Old Trails Museum

Downtown at 212 W. Kinsley, this is a small but attractive museum with displays of artifacts from everyday life in the Winslow area from Stone Age to modern times. Popular exhibits include memorabilia of the Santa Fe Railroad and Rt. 66. Of special interest is clothing worn by stage actress Norma Deane, a local girl who made it big in theater, got engaged to famed star Victor Jory, and then died on a visit home while trying to cross a flooded wash. The museum will expand to include **La Posada Harvey House,** which is being restored to its glory days, when the upper crust toured by railcar. Call for hours; tel. 289-5861.

### Brigham City

This Mormon settlement on the northeast edge of town predates Winslow by five years. The colonists' early optimism for the farming potential of bottomland along the Little Colorado soon faded as floods washed away dams and irrigation systems. Fear of Indian attacks caused residents to protect their community with walls 200 feet long and seven feet high. Although never attacked, Brigham City was abandoned in the 1880s because of continuing irrigation problems. The city of Winslow plans to open the site as a historic park.

### Homolovi Ruins State Park

Anasazi Indians lived in pithouses and later at six pueblo villages near present-day Winslow from about A.D. 600 to 1450. The inhabitants, it is believed, then migrated north to the Hopi mesas.

Legends passed down through generations of Hopi relate how ancestors emerged from a world beneath the present one, migrating in stages to their present home. Clan elders guided the migrations through revelations from dreams and meditations. The Hopi consider these ruins sacred and still leave *pahos* (prayer feathers) here for the spirits.

Serious archaeological studies have only recently begun; you're welcome to watch the archaeologists at work when they're here. The name Homolovi ("Place of the Low Hills") applies to all sites in the Winslow area; Homolovi II is the largest and forms the main section of the state park. Though badly weathered, the ruins indicate what a prehistoric site looks like before extensive excavation or reconstruction.

The visitor center and paved roads lie near Homolovi I and II; a campground offers tent camping at $8 and RV w/electrical hookups (water hookups and showers are available in summer) at $13, including park admission. Park facilities are designed for handicapped access. Take I-40 Exit 257 for AZ 87 (just east of Winslow), go north 1.3 miles to the entrance, turn and drive to the visitor center.

Nearby are a pithouse site and **Sunset Cemetery.** Lot Smith founded the first post office on the Little Colorado River at the Sunset site in 1876.

The trailhead for **Homolovi II** lies about 2.5 miles north of the visitor center on the park road. A quarter-mile-roundtrip trail, suitable for wheelchairs, leads to a mesa and along the top to the ruins. Signs interpret and describe the village. Homolovi II, occupied from 1250 to 1450, may have had a population as high as 3,000. The village comprised 700-1,200 rooms arranged around three plazas and probably stood two or three stories high.

A group of rooms in the West Plaza and a kiva in the Central Plaza have been excavated and stabilized to show the original floor plans. The village served as a major trade center and staging area for northward migrations. Waters of the Little Colorado River below attracted game and nourished crops and wild plant foods.

Archaeologists are excavating **Homolovi I,** a pueblo of 250-350 rooms near the Colorado River

and the best preserved of all the park sites. Follow the paved road and then a dirt trail to reach it.

You can visit the other sites in the park—including some rock art—as well; ask directions from park staff. **Homolovi III and IV** lie west across the Little Colorado River from Homolovi II; drive north from Winslow on North Park Dr., and then turn east on dirt roads (may not be signed). The **Cottonwood Wash** site is east of I-40 Exit 257 on a frontage road. **Chevelon Ruins** are the farthest out, about 15 miles southeast of Winslow. Dirt roads in the park become very slippery when wet.

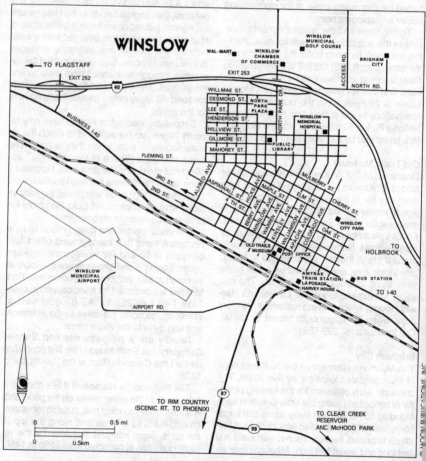

**WINSLOW**

TO FLAGSTAFF

EXIT 252

WAL-MART

WINSLOW CHAMBER OF COMMERCE

EXIT 253

WINSLOW MUNICIPAL GOLF COURSE

BRIGHAM CITY

NORTH RD.

ACCESS RD.

BUSINESS I-40

WILLMAE ST.
DESMOND ST.
LEE ST.
HENDERSON ST.
HILLVIEW ST.
GILLMORE ST.
MAHONEY ST.
FLEMING ST.

NORTH PARK PLAZA

NORTH PARK DR.

WINSLOW MEMORIAL HOSPITAL

PUBLIC LIBRARY

3RD ST.
2ND ST.

ALFRED AVE.
ASPINWALL ST.
4TH ST.
BERRY AVE.
HICKS AVE.
MAPLE ST.
WINSLOW AVE.
WARREN AVE.
KINSLEY AVE.
WILLIAMSON AVE.
APACHE AVE.
COLORADO AVE.
ELM ST.
OAK ST.
MULBERRY ST.
CHERRY ST.

WINSLOW CITY PARK

TO HOLBROOK

OLD TRAILS MUSEUM
POST OFFICE

AMTRAK TRAIN STATION/ LA POSADA HARVEY HOUSE

BUS STATION

TO I-40

WINSLOW MUNICIPAL AIRPORT

AIRPORT RD.

TO RIM COUNTRY (SCENIC RT. TO PHOENIX)

87

99

TO CLEAR CREEK RESERVOIR AND McHOOD PARK

TO CLEAR CREEK

0    0.5 mi
0    0.5km

Site visitors mustn't remove or disturb anything; federal and state laws prohibit removal of artifacts. Even the tiniest pottery shard must be left in place to preserve the sacred character of the sites. Open daily except Christmas; $3 vehicle admission; tel. 289-4106.

## Little Painted Desert County Park
Enjoy the views and beautiful sunsets from this park, 13 miles northeast of Winslow on AZ 87 (I-40 Exit 257). Facilities include a scenic rim viewpoint overlooking colorful desert hills, a hiking trail, and picnic tables.

## McHood Park
Situated on both banks of Clear Creek Reservoir, McHood features swimming, boating, fishing, picnicking, and camping. Anglers catch trout, bass, and catfish. Boaters may use the launch ramp and head 2.5 miles upstream into a scenic canyon with 200-foot cliffs; look for petroglyphs. This is also a good area for birdwatching.

Park gates are open 8 a.m.-9 p.m. April 1 to October 31 and 8 a.m.-7 p.m. the rest of the year; day use costs $3, $2 for county residents. The campground, with drinking water and showers, is open from mid-April to late October; $6 ($7 with water and electric hookups). McHood Park was closed because of flood and silt damage but is reopening; call for status before planning a visit; tel. 289-3204/5714 (city offices).

From Winslow, head south 1.2 miles on AZ 87, then left 4.3 miles on AZ 99 to the park; turn left before the reservoir bridge to reach the campground, boat ramp, and swimming area, or continue across the bridge and turn left to the picnic area and ranger residence.

## Accommodations and Food
Winslow has 24 motels and 28 restaurants, mostly along old Hwy. 66 (Bus. I-40) between I-40 Exits 252 and 257 and on North Park Dr. near I-40 Exit 253. The I-40 business route splits downtown into Third St. (westbound) and Second St. (eastbound).

## Campgrounds
**Freddie's RV Park** has RV sites ($13.44-14.50 w/hookups) at 1 Transcon Lane (I-40 Exit 255) on the east side of town; tel. 289-3201. See

also "Homolovi Ruins State Park" and "McHood Park," above.

## Events
Fireworks help celebrate **July 4th**. A **Bluegrass Festival** livens the town in mid-September. Cowboys and cowgirls show their stuff in the **West Best Rodeo** in late September. The **Christmas Parade** starts off the holiday season on the third Saturday in November.

## Shopping and Services
For Indian crafts and jewelry, check **Bruchman's Curio Store** at 113 W. Second Street. The **post office** is at 223 Williamson Ave. between Second and Third streets; tel. 289-2131. **Winslow Memorial Hospital** is on the north edge of town at 1501 Williamson Ave. (take I-40 Exit 253); tel. 289-4691.

**Winslow City Park,** at the corner of Colorado Ave. and Cherry St., has indoor and outdoor pools, tennis and racquetball courts, ball fields, weight rooms, and sports programs; tel. 289-5714 (parks and recreation), 289-4543 (indoor pool), or 289-4592 (outdoor pool). Play golf at the nine-hole **Winslow Municipal Golf Course,** off North Park Dr.; tel. 289-4915.

## Information
Staff at the **Winslow Chamber of Commerce** provides maps and info on area sights and facilities. An exhibit room introduces the land and people of northeast Arizona. The office is open Mon.-Fri. 8 a.m.-5 p.m. It's just north of I-40 Exit 253 (look for the giant Indian monument); Box 460, Winslow, AZ 86047; tel. 289-2434, fax 289-5660.

Foresters at the **Chevelon Ranger District** of the Apache-Sitgreaves National Forest dispense maps and information about recreation in the Mogollon Rim country south of Winslow; it's open daily in summer 8 a.m.-4:30 p.m., then Mon.-Fri. 7:30 a.m.-4 p.m. the rest of the year. The office is 42 miles south of town on AZ 99 (HC 62, Box 600, Winslow, AZ 86047); tel. 289-2471. The **public library** has a good collection of books on Arizona and the Southwest at 420 W. Gillmore St.; tel. 289-4982.

## Transport
**Greyhound** buses stop at the Easy 8 Motel at 1000 E. Third. St.; tel. 289-2171. **Amtrak** offers

rail service but there's no agent in town; call (800) 872-7245 for schedule and ticket information.

### Joseph City

Mormons established the farming community of Allen's Camp in 1876 under great difficulty. Attempts to dam the Little Colorado for irrigation failed repeatedly, leaving crops to wither away. Although four other Mormon settlements along the Little Colorado were abandoned, this town, renamed Joseph City, persevered. It is the oldest Anglo community in Navajo County.

## HOLBROOK

The railroad reached this site in 1881; officials named it for one of their engineers. Eastern investors recognized the surrounding rangelands as prime cattle country and wasted no time in seeking grazing rights. Within two years, the Aztec Land and Cattle Company, based near Joseph City, ran 60,000 head of cattle on the land. The Aztec, better known as the Hashknife outfit after the shape of its brand, became the

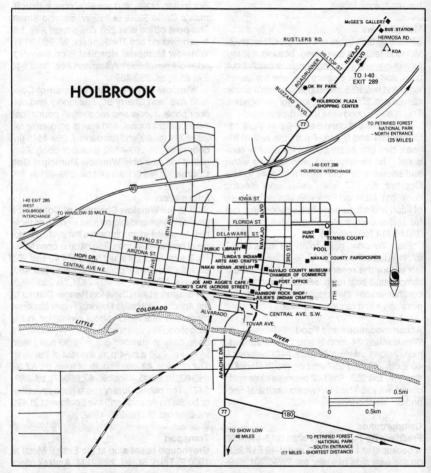

HOLBROOK

third-largest cattle empire in the United States, its cowboys working the longhorns across one million acres.

On holidays, the cowpokes, looking for a good time, rode into Holbrook with guns blazing. Rustling and poor management troubled the Hashknife operation until it shut down about 1900, but Holbrook (pop. about 5,000) remains a ranching center. Travelers often use Holbrook as a base for visiting the nearby Petrified Forest National Park and the Navajo and Hopi Indian reservations.

## Navajo County Museum

You can relive some of the area's Wild West history in this fine collection. Period rooms and artifacts trace the changes from the prehistoric Indian era to lawless frontier days to modern times. Don't miss the dungeon-like jail downstairs.

Exhibits are open in summer Mon.-Fri. 8 a.m.-5 p.m. (also 7-9 p.m. when tribal dances are performed in the evening mid-June to early August) and Saturday 8 a.m.-5 p.m., then Mon.- Fri. 8 a.m.-5 p.m. the rest of the year. The museum is in the old (1898) county courthouse, downtown at the corner of 100 E. Arizona St. and Navajo Blvd.; tel. 524-6558 or (800) 524-2459. The Holbrook Chamber of Commerce office is here too, open the same hours.

## Accommodations and Food

Holbrook's motels offer more than 1,000 rooms and twenty restaurants line Navajo Blvd. (north and south from I-40 Exit 286) and W. Hopi Dr. (east from I-40 Exit 285); the two streets meet downtown. Many of the motels post very attractive off-season rates.

## Campgrounds

**OK RV Park,** just north of I-40 Exit 286 at the corner of Roadrunner and Buzzard, is open all year with showers; $16.50 tent or RV no hookups, $19.80 w/hookups; tel. 524-3226. You'll find the **KOA** campground at 102 Hermosa, just off Navajo Blvd.; $17.56 tent, $19.75 RV no hookups, $20.85-25.26 RV w/hookups, $29.66 kamping kabins; store, pool, and showers. It's open all year; take I-40 Exit 286 or 289; tel. 524-6689.

**Cholla Lake County Park,** 10 miles west of Holbrook near a power plant, offers picnicking, camping, fishing, waterskiing, windsurfing, and swimming. Anglers pull largemouth bass, catfish, and sunfish from the 360-acre lake. The campground features showers and costs $7 per night or $10 with water and electric hookups. Day-use fee is $3, $2 for county residents; gates close at sunset. The park is open all year, though water and showers are available only from mid-March to late October; tel. 288-3717 (park) or 524-4250, ext. 344 (county office). Take I-40 Exit 277 and follow signs for one mile.

## Events

**Indian Dances** take place nightly Mon.-Fri. in summer on the lawn next to the old courthouse. The **Hashknife Pony Express** rides again every year in January or February, when riders carry the mail from Holbrook to Scottsdale. You can send a letter along too, by affixing the usual stamp and marking the lower left corner "Via Pony Express." Enclose in a second envelope and send to Postmaster, Holbrook, AZ 86025.

Local firefighters show off on **Firemen's Fun and Games Day,** the first Saturday in May, with entertainment and training games. **Old West Celebration,** in late May or early June, features Bucket of Blood bicycle and foot races, parade, arts and crafts exhibits, roping contests, cowchip-throwing contest, horseshoe tournament, and street dance. Fireworks and "the state's best barbecue" mark **July 4th. Gathering of Eagles** is a Native American art show and festival held in July.

The **Navajo County Fair** is held in September. **Navajo County Horse Races** take place the first and second weekends in September. A nighttime **Christmas Parade of Lights** brightens winter on the first Saturday in December.

## Shopping

Though forbidden to remove anything from Petrified Forest National Park, you can shop in Holbrook for samples of the strange wood-turned-to-stone. Small pieces cost just pennies; larger, polished specimens run from a few dollars into the thousands. Turquoise, geodes, and other natural treasures are available as well. Try the **Rainbow Rock Shop** at 103 Navajo Blvd. or the shops just outside the south entrance of the national park. For Indian crafts, look into **Julien's** at the corner of Hopi Dr. and Navajo Blvd., **J&J**

**Trading Post** one block south at 104 Navajo Blvd., **Nakai Indian Jewelry** at 357 Navajo Blvd., **Linda's Indian Arts & Crafts** at 405 Navajo Blvd., **Tribal Treasure** at 1601 Navajo Blvd., **McGee's Beyond Native Tradition** at 2114 Navajo Blvd., and **Lewis Traders,** four miles east of town, across from Holbrook Truck Plaza, near I-40 Exit 292. J&J is an old-style trading post patronized mostly by Navajo and Hopi Indians.

## Services and Information

Holbrook's **Hunt Park** features a picnic area, playground, outdoor swimming pool, and tennis courts; turn east on Florida St. from Navajo Blvd.; tel. 524-3331. The nine-hole **Hidden Cove Golf Course** lies about three miles west of town; take I-40 Exit 283 (Golf Course Rd.); tel. 524-3097.

The helpful **Holbrook Chamber of Commerce** offers both local and statewide literature in the old county courthouse, downtown at the corner of Navajo Blvd. and Arizona St., 100 E. Arizona St., Holbrook, AZ 86025; tel. 524-6558. The office and Navajo County Museum historical exhibits are open in summer Mon.-Fri. 8 a.m.-8 p.m. and Saturday 8 a.m.-5 p.m., then Mon.-Fri. 8 a.m.-5 p.m. the rest of the year. The **public library** is at 451 First Ave.; tel. 524-3732. The **post office** is at 216 E. Hopi Dr.; tel. 524-3311.

## Transport

**Greyhound** buses stop at Western Junk near the corner of Hermosa and Navajo Blvd.; tel. 524-3832. The shop is closed Saturday afternoons and all day Sunday, but buses still run.

# PETRIFIED FOREST NATIONAL PARK

Petrified Forest National Park, like the Grand Canyon, presents an open book to the earth's past. The park's multicolored hills, part of a widespread geologic formation called the Chinle, provide a world-famous resource of petrified wood and related fossils. The barren hills feature delicately tinted bands of reds, grays, oranges, and whites, eroded to reveal remains of life, frozen in stone, from 225 million years ago. Rivers in that period carried fallen trees from distant mountains, burying them in low-lying swamps. Before their fall, some of these giant trees had towered 200 feet high. Waterborne minerals transformed the logs to stone, replacing wood cells and filling the spaces between with brightly colored quartz and jasper crystals. This now-arid land would be unrecognizable today to its ancient inhabitants: primitive fish, massive amphibians, and fearsome reptiles.

Some of the strange animals who once crawled and swam here are preserved; you can see their fossilized remains in park exhibits. But it's the trees that have traditionally attracted the most attention. In the late 1800s, vast quantities of petrified wood were lost to collectors, who carted away logs for souvenirs or dynamited the stone trees to retrieve their crystals. The battle for preservation was won in 1906, when

President Theodore Roosevelt signed a bill establishing the Petrified Forest National Monument. A 1958 act of Congress, followed by acquisition of new lands, changed the status of the land to a national park in 1962.

## Flora and Fauna

A surprising amount of life exists today in the park, despite the meager nine-inch annual rainfall and lack of permanent water. Prickly pear and cholla cacti are widespread. Evening primrose, Indian paintbrush, mariposa lily, sunflowers, and other plants bloom when they receive sufficient moisture. Also common are buckwheat, a shrub that turns orange-brown in the fall; and saltbush, named for the tiny salt crystals formed on its leaves to conserve moisture. The most frequently seen animals in the park are birds, small mammals, and lizards. Birds include the raven, rock wren, and horned lark. You're most likely to spot prairie dogs, black-tailed jackrabbits, and desert cottontails, but pronghorn, coyotes, and bobcats live here too.

## The Three Sections

The southern section—the original national monument—contains some of the finest petrified wood specimens in the world. The central section contains the greatest number of prehistoric

Indian sites. During their stay from about A.D. 300 to 1400, the Anasazi, Sinagua, and Mogollon tribes progressed from semi-nomadic hunters and gatherers to farmers who lived in permanent pueblos, with a complex ceremonial life. Scientists trying to decode the numerous petroglyphs have discovered some were used as solar calendars.

The northern section of the park encompasses part of the Painted Desert, famed for its landscape of ever-changing colors—the effect of the sun playing on hills stained by iron, manganese, and other minerals. Colors become most vivid near sunset and sunrise, fading toward midday. Added in 1932, this northern section is the largest part of the park.

### Visiting the Park

Sightseeing in the park can be satisfactory at any time of year; just protect yourself from the sun in the warmer months. You can begin the paved 28.6-mile scenic drive through the park at either end. Coming from the west, you'll find it more convenient to use the south entrance off US 180 from Holbrook. After visiting the park, continue on I-40 from the north entrance. Coming from the east, the north entrance is more practical.

The drive is open daily in winter 8 a.m.-5 p.m.; winter snow or ice storms occasionally close the road. Start early; you can easily expend a full day enjoying all the walks, views,

and exhibits. Admission is $5 per vehicle ($3 per visitor by motorcycle, bicycle, or foot); free with a Golden Eagle, Golden Age, or Golden Access pass. For more information, contact Park Headquarters, P.O. Box 2217, Petrified Forest National Park, AZ 86028; tel. 524-6228.

Visitor centers near both entrances offer exhibits illustrating park geology, fossils, ecology, and human history. They sell books, postcards, posters, and maps. You can also talk with a ranger and obtain backcountry permits. Don't remove any petrified wood or other objects from the park. Rangers estimate that people taking one "harmless little souvenir" could result in the loss of tons of wood every year.

### Services

The park has no campgrounds or lodging; to secure accommodations you must venture west to Holbrook or travel east to the small community of Chambers. Picnic fixings come in handy, as there's but a single restaurant, near the north entrance, and a lone snack bar, across from Rainbow Forest Museum, inside the south entrance. Only the developed areas have water; you'll probably want to carry something to drink. Shops sell souvenirs at three locations: outside the park near the south entrance, inside the park at the Rainbow Forest complex, and next to the visitor center at the north entrance station.

*turned to stone*

**Backcountry Travel**

Hikers may explore the two areas designated as wilderness. The backcountry remains relatively undiscovered; only one of a thousand park visitors strays more than a short distance from the car. Hiking is usually cross-country: with plenty of landmarks and open terrain, you're free to roam. Carry water (no springs) and wear a hat for protection from the sun. Rangers can give advice and offer a hiking leaflet. They also issue the free permits required for overnight trips.

Campsites must lie within the wilderness areas, at least one mile from the road. Even if you're planning only a long day-hike, it's a good idea to divulge your plans to rangers. Horseback riding and pack animals are permitted too, with a limit of six animals per party. Carry feed and water. All backcountry users should note rules against campfires, pets (okay elsewhere in the park if on a leash), and firearms.

**Rainbow Forest Wilderness** (7,240 acres) features grasslands, badlands, abundant petrified wood, and traces of Indian inhabitants. It's in the southern half of the park; start from Flattops Trailhead.

**Painted Desert Wilderness** in the north is much larger (43,020 acres)—a colorful land of mesas, buttes, and badlands. You can visit Indian sites and petroglyphs; ask a ranger for directions. Onyx Bridge, a 50-foot-long petrified tree in the Black Forest, is another good destination; about four miles roundtrip from Kachina Point Trailhead. Pilot Rock (6,295 feet), about seven miles northwest of the trailhead, is the highest point in the park.

## SCENIC DRIVE

This description runs from south to north, but you can drive the road in either direction. Numbers in parentheses indicate distances from the north end of the drive. Mileages are applicable to the drive only and don't include side trips:

**Mile 0** (28.6): Beginning of scenic drive from US 180.

**Mile 0.1** (28.5): **Petrified Forest Museum and Trading Post** and **Crystal Forest Museum and Gift Shop** stand on opposite sides of the road just outside the park entrance. Although neither edifice is connected with the park, both exhibit dazzling collections of polished petrified wood, including giant log cross-sections and carvings. You can buy most pieces, along with unpolished petrified wood and other minerals, rocks, and fossils.

**Mile 0.2** (28.4): **Entering Petrified Forest National Park.** A ranger collects fees and gives out park brochures. If you've brought in unpolished wood or other objects, ask the ranger to mark or bag them to avoid any misunderstandings about the source. It's against the law to take *anything* from the park.

**Mile 2.4** (26.2): **Rainbow Forest Museum and visitor center.** A ferocious phytosaur *(Nicrosaurus gregorii)* skeleton cast greets you on entering the museum. This large crocodile-like reptile roamed the forests and swamps here during the Triassic period 225 million years ago. The phytosaur and other exhibits provide a look at the strange environment of cycads, ferns, fish, amphibians, reptiles, and other early life that existed then. An exhibit on the rise of dinosaurs, featuring "Gertie," found in 1984, highlights the museum. A "Conscience Wood" exhibit contains stolen petrified wood, returned with apologetic and remorseful letters.

The **Giant Logs Trail** begins behind the visitor center, winding in a half-mile loop past monster-sized logs—a rainbow of reds, yellows, grays, whites, blacks, pinks, and oranges. The base of one fallen tree stands higher than a human. **Fred Harvey's Curios and Fountain** offers souvenirs and a snack bar across the road from the visitor center.

**Mile 2.5** (26.1): **Picnic area.**

**Mile 2.6** (26.0): **Long Logs Interpretive Trail** and **Agate House** turnoff (a half mile to parking). The self-guided nature trail is an easy half-mile walk, a good opportunity to look closely at the ancient trees. The jumble of logs here is believed to be a logjam, buried in mud, sand, and volcanic ash. Many logs measure more than 100 feet long.

Agate House, on a short side trail, is a pueblo occupied about 900 years ago. Indians built the unusual structure entirely with chunks of colorful petrified wood. Two of its seven rooms have been reconstructed to show their original size.

*Agate House*

**Mile 4.7** (23.9): **Parking Area.** Hikers begin here for day and overnight backcountry trips to Puerco Ridge and other areas of the Rainbow Forest Wilderness. It is half a mile walk to the trailhead.

**Mile 8.1** (20.5): **Crystal Forest Interpretive Trail.** Some of the prettiest and most concentrated petrified wood in the park lies along this paved three-quarter-mile trail.

**Mile 9.9** (18.7): **Jasper Forest** turnoff (a half mile to parking). Great views to the west and north from the overlook. Below lie pieces of petrified wood eroded from the hillsides.

**Mile 10.1** (18.5): **Agate Bridge.** Erosion carved out a gully beneath a large log, leaving a bridge. In years past, a Hashknife cowboy rode his horse across the log on a $10 bet. Rangers won't let you do this today: it's unsafe. Because of cracking, the log was braced with a concrete beam in 1917.

**Mile 12.9** (15.7): **Blue Mesa** turnoff (three miles to parking). Blue Mesa offers several panoramic overlooks and a one-mile-loop interpretive trail. The trail provides a good introduction to the Chinle Formation and its badlands topography.

**Mile 14.5** (14.1): **The Tepees.** Symmetrical, cone-shaped hills visible from the pullout.

**Mile 16.5** (12.1): **Newspaper Rock** turnoff (0.3 mile to parking). An impressive collection of ancient petroglyphs covers a huge sandstone boulder. The drawings have not been interpreted, but seem to represent animals and spiritual figures. Bring binoculars to better examine the artwork or use the coin telescopes.

**Mile 17.4** (11.2): **Puerco Indian Ruin.** Before A.D. 1100, local Indians lived in small scattered settlements. The building of larger pueblos, such as Puerco, indicates a change to an agricultural lifestyle requiring greater pooling of efforts. The broad, meandering Puerco River provided reliable water all year and its flood plain contained rich soil for farming. The river also attracted birds, pronghorn, and other game. Indians built a one-story pueblo with about 76 rooms and at least two kivas around a rectangular plaza. You can see the foundations of these rooms and one of the kivas. Archaeologists believe this site was occupied between A.D. 1100 and 1200 and again from about 1300 to 1400. The last occupants appear to have packed up and left peaceably, perhaps over a period of years.

Help protect the ruins by remaining on the trail. Many fine petroglyphs cover the boulders below the village. Though more scattered, they're comparable to the petroglyphs at Newspaper Rock. One of the Puerco petroglyphs marks the summer solstice. About 14 sites with solar markings have been discovered in the park.

**Mile 17.7** (10.9): **Puerco River bridge.** The scene was probably far different when Indians occupied the pueblo. Records indicate cottonwood trees grew along the flood plain as late as the 19th century. Ranchers took advantage of the abundant grasslands in the late 1880s by increasing their herds, but drought in 1891-94 dried up the grass, and gross overstocking destroyed the range. Runoff carried high concentrations of salts into the river, killing less salt-resistant plants. Floods have worked their toll, scouring and widening the river and leaving loads of silt in their wake. Now the river is dry much of the year.

**Mile 18.1** (10.5): **Bridge over the railroad tracks.** The Petrified Forest first gained national attention with the completion of the Atlantic and Pacific Railroad (later the Santa Fe) across northern Arizona. Train travelers disembarked at the nearby Adamana Station, now abandoned, to visit the "trees turned to stone."

**Mile 23.6** (5.0): **Lacey Point Overlook** of the Painted Desert.

**Mile 24.1** (4.5): **Whipple Point Overlook** of the Painted Desert. One of the first white people to visit the Petrified Forest, Lieutenant A.W. Whipple arrived in 1853.

**Mile 24.3** (4.3): **Nizhoni Point Overlook** of the Painted Desert. The hillside below appears to be covered with shards of glass. These are natural pieces of selenite gypsum, a very soft mineral you can scratch with your fingernail.

**Mile 25.4** (3.2): **Pintado Point Overlook** of the Painted Desert. You're now on a volcanic lava flow, which covers the entire rim and protects the underlying, softer Chinle Formation from erosion.

**Mile 26.0** (2.6): **Chinde Point Picnic Area** turnoff (0.3 mile). Water and restrooms available in the warmer months.

**Mile 26.2** (2.4): **Painted Desert Inn** and **Kachina Point Overlook.** Herbert Lore built the original inn with Indian labor and local materials in 1924. Travelers bumping their way across Arizona on Route 66 stopped for meals and to shop for Indian crafts. The National Park Service bought the inn and surrounding land in 1936. Workers rebuilt and enlarged the inn as a park concession and information station, but its six sleeping rooms were not used after WW II. The inn closed when the Painted Desert Visitor Center opened in 1962. Plans were made for demolition of the old building, but people recognized its unique Southwestern architecture—a mixture of Spanish and Indian pueblo styles—and it was saved.

Now a national historic landmark and open to the public, Painted Desert Inn contains historical and rotating cultural exhibits; a bookstore specializes in Native American books, posters, and crafts. The trailhead for **Painted Desert Wilderness** (Onyx Bridge, Black Forest, etc.) begins near Kachina Point, behind the inn.

**Mile 26.7** (1.9): **Tawa Point Overlook** of the Painted Desert.

**Mile 27.5** (1.1): **Tiponi Point Overlook** of the Painted Desert.

**Mile 28.1** (0.5): **Painted Desert Visitor Center** and **North Entrance Station.** A 17-minute movie, shown on the hour and half-hour, illustrates the park's features and describes the formation of petrified wood. Exhibits show plant and animal fossils, and you can view a "Conscience Wood" display. A ranger will answer your questions and issue backcountry permits. **Fred Harvey Painted Desert Oasis** offers a cafeteria, curio shop, and gas station.

**Mile 28.6** (0.0): Junction with I-40.

# NORTH OF WHITE MOUNTAIN APACHE INDIAN RESERVATION

## SHOW LOW

With so many recreation opportunities in the nearby Mogollon Rim country and White Mountains, Show Low has become an important year-round resort. Attractions include excellent trout fishing, hiking, camping, horseback riding, golf, scenic drives, and big-game hunting. The town of 5,460 (more than 13,500 in summer) sits on the pine-forested Mogollon Rim at an elevation of about 6,400 feet.

Show Low took its name from a winner-take-all poker game played in 1876. Corydon Cooley, a noted Indian scout, and his partner, Marion Clark, established a 100,000-acre ranch here in 1870, but found the place wasn't big enough for both of them. Agreeing to settle their differences with a game of cards, they sat down at Cooley's kitchen table for a game of "seven-up." The two played through the night until finally Clark said, "Show low and you win." Cooley pulled out an unbeatable deuce of clubs and took the ranch.

Several years later, Mormons bought and sold the property. The town's Mormon church occupies the gaming site. Show Low's main street took its name, Deuce of Clubs, from the winning card.

## Sights

**Fool Hollow Lake** offers 140 acres stocked with trout, smallmouth and largemouth bass, catfish, and bluegill. It's just three miles northwest of Show Low; take Hwy. 260 west almost two miles, turn right on Old Linden Rd. and follow the signs two miles. Facilities include boat ramps on the east and west shores. The campground has hot showers including wheelchair facilities; $10 tents or RV with no hookups, $15 RV sites with water and electric hookups; day use $5 per vehicle, $1 pedestrian or bicyclist; tel. 537-3680.

You never know what kind of fish you'll catch at **Show Low Lake:** rainbow or brown trout, largemouth bass, walleye, or catfish. A boat ramp, store, and boat rental facility are available; boat motors are limited to eight horsepower. The Navajo County campground on the lake's west side is open year-round with water and showers (summer only) and costs $8; picnicking in the campground costs $2; a store with boat rentals is open during the warmer months; tel. 537-4126. The lake lies about five miles south of Show Low; go south about four miles on AZ 260, then turn east at the hospital onto Show Low Lake Rd. and drive 1.3 miles.

**Pintail Lake** is an unusual waterfowl area north of Show Low. Between 1977 and 1979 workers filled a natural volcanic depression with treated sewage effluent, building artificial islands to serve as nesting sites. The marshland proved an instant success with ducks and other wildlife. Go north 3.5 miles on AZ 77, then turn right on Pintail Lake Road and drive 0.4 mile. A quarter-mile trail leads to an observation platform. The trail is wheelchair accessible.

**Mogollon Rim Overlook and Nature Trail** is an easy wheelchair-accessible one-mile walk strewn with signs describing the area's forests, medicinal plants, and history. It offers good views of the forested valleys and ridges below the overlooks. The trailhead lies seven miles south of Show Low on AZ 260, between Mileposts 347 and 348.

## Accommodations

Show Low's motels lie along Deuce of Clubs. Summer rates are listed here; rates usually come down a bit in winter. From west to east are **Show Low Days Inn,** 480 W. Deuce of Clubs, $55.11 s, $63.75 d, tel. 537-4356; **Paint Pony Lodge (Best Western),** 581 W. Deuce of Clubs, $72.39 s, $77.70 d, tel. 537-5773; **Holiday Inn Express,** 151 W. Deuce of Clubs, $70.23 s, 75.64 d, tel. 537-7694; **KC Motel,** 60 W. Deuce of Clubs, $48-64 d, tel. 537-4433.

Try also **Kiva Motel,** 261 E. Deuce of Clubs, $45.38 s, $58.35 d, tel. 537-4542; **Thunderbird Motel,** 1131 E. Deuce of Clubs, $32.48 s, $41.15 d, tel. 537-4391; **Apache Pines Motel,**

1290 E. Deuce of Clubs, $65.58 s, $81.79 d, tel. 537-4328; **Snowy River Motel,** 1640 E. Deuce of Clubs, $31.33 s, $36.74 d, tel. 537-2926; and **Super 8,** 1941 E. Deuce of Clubs, $46.33 s, $51.73 d, tel. 537-7694.

## Campgrounds

Tenters and RVers can camp at Fool's Hollow Lake and Show Low Lake, described above. Or try **Camp Town,** 1221 W. McNeil, $16.20 RV w/hookups, tel. 537-2578; **K-Bar RV Resort,** 300 N. 18th Ave., $17.50-18.91 RV w/hookups, tel. 537-2886; **Country Lane Trailer Park,** Old Linden Rd. and N. Central, $5 tent or $7 RV no hookups, $9 RV w/hookups, tel. 537-5161; or **Rim Crest RV Park,** 4.4 miles south on AZ 260, $10.55 tent or RV no hookups, $17 w/hookups, tel. 537-4660.

RVers can latch onto hookups at **Pine Shadows Mobile Home Park,** 3.7 miles south on AZ 260, $18, tel. 537-2895; **Ranchero RV Mobile Home Park,** 2.9 miles south on AZ 260, $14, tel. 537-4479; **Show Low Lake RV Park,** four miles south on AZ 260, $15, tel. 537-2426; **Venture In RV Resort,** 1.3 miles west on AZ 260, $19, tel. 537-4443; and **Waltner's RV Resort,** Waltner Way, four miles south near Navapache Hospital, $19.40, tel. 537-4611.

## Food

Look for restaurants along Deuce of Clubs. You can find Western food at **Paint Pony Steakhouse,** 581 W. Deuce of Clubs, tel. 537-5773; and **Branding Iron Steak House,** 1231 E. Deuce of Clubs, tel. 537-5151. For Mexican dinners try **Guayos's,** 350 E. Deuce of Clubs, tel. 537-9503; **La Casita,** four miles south on AZ 260, tel. 537-5179; **JB's Restaurant,** 480 W. Deuce of Clubs, tel. 537-1156; or **White Mountain Restaurant,** 2101 E. Deuce of Clubs, tel. 537-9880.

Chinese food is served at **Asia Garden Restaurant,** 59 W. Deuce of Clubs, tel. 537-9333; **China Cafe,** 1201 E. Deuce of Clubs, tel. 537-5407; and **China Moon Buffet,** four miles south on AZ 260, tel. 537-8828.

Pick up pizza at **Pat's Place,** 981 E. Deuce of Clubs, tel. 537-2337; **Pizza Hut,** Pineway Center, tel. 537-5306; or **Pizza Factory,** south on AZ 260, tel. 537-7771. Along with other restaurants, the town offers the usual fast-food places.

## Events

Show Low celebrates **July 4th** with a big parade, arts and crafts fair, and fireworks. Loosen up at the **Square Dance Festival** on the second weekend in July. In December, the town hosts an **Electric Parade,** dressing up in bright lights to celebrate the holidays. Softball tournaments and other events take place throughout the year; consult the Show Low Chamber of Commerce.

## Services and Recreation

The **post office** is at 191 W. Deuce of Clubs and McNeil; tel. 537-4588. **Navapache Regional Medical Center** lies four miles south of Show Low on AZ 260, on the way to Lakeside; tel. 537-4375. The **city park** offers an indoor swimming pool, picnic areas with covered ramadas, a playground, plus tennis, basketball, softball, racquetball, and volleyball courts. Turn in opposite Northland Pioneer College. **Show Low Parks and Recreation** offers a year-round program of activities; tel. 537-2800. Enjoy movies at **Winchester Theater** one mile south of the Hwy. 60/260 intersection in town; tel. 367-8866. **Thunder Raceway** offers a variety of automotive racing including late model stock cars and mini-stocks at 4701 E. Deuce of Clubs; tel. 537-1111.

Play golf at the 18-hole **Show Low Country Club,** 860 N. 36th Dr., tel. 537-4564; or at **Silver Creek Golf Club's** 18-holes at White Mountain Lakes, seven miles north on AZ 77, then five miles east at the sign, tel. 537-2744. Obtain outdoor equipment at **Arizona Nature's Sports,** 861 E. Cooley, just off Hwy. 60; tel. 367-6200.

## Information

Folks at the **Show Low Chamber of Commerce** can help you find accommodations and other services; it's open Mon.-Fri. 9 a.m.-5 p.m. and Saturday 10 a.m.-2 p.m.; 951 W. Deuce of Clubs (Box 1083, Show Low, AZ 85901); tel. 537-2326. The **public library** is at 20 N. Sixth St. and E. McNeil; tel. 537-2447. Learn about local history at the newly opened **Show Low Historical Society Museum** at 541 E. Deuce of Clubs; call for hours; tel. 537-8181.

## Transport

**White Mountain Passenger Lines** offers bus service from Show Low to the central Arizona communities of Payson, Mesa, Tempe, and Phoenix. You'll find the main office at 1041 E. Hall St. (Box 460, Show Low, AZ 85901); tel. 537-4539.

# LAKESIDE AND PINETOP

The names well describe the lakes and pine forests surrounding these twin towns near the edge of the Mogollon Rim, some eight miles southeast of Show Low. Lakeside was originally named Fairview in 1880 by Mormon pioneers, but took its present name upon the completion of Rainbow Lake. Several smaller lakes have since been added; the town now seems to consist as much of water as of land. Soldiers undertaking the long climb up the Mogollon Rim from Fort Apache in the 1870s often stopped to rest at a place they christened Pinetop; Mormon ranchers founded a settlement there in 1878.

Today Lakeside (elev. 6,745 feet) and Pinetop (elev. 7,279 feet) are major recreational centers dotted with innumerable summer cabins and resorts. The area's year-round population of 8,000 jumps to 25,000 in summer. Though they began as separate communities, the two towns gradually expanded along the highway to become one.

## Sights
**Big Springs Environmental Study Area** offers a pleasant half-mile nature trail that winds through a variety of wildlife habitats. The trail offers interpretive signs and is quite an easy hike, though muddy after rain or snow. Turn south and drive a half mile on Woodland Rd. off AZ 260, then look for the parking area on the left.

**Rainbow Lake** is a privately owned, 80-acre reservoir in Lakeside just west of AZ 260. It's stocked with rainbow trout, brown trout, and some smallmouth bass and catfish. You can fish from the shore near the dam or rent a boat. Nearby Lakeside Campground ($8) is open mid-May to late September. Call (800) 280-CAMP for reservations.

**Scott Reservoir** is a smaller fishing lake of 70 acres about three miles northeast of Lakeside on Forest Route 45; the turnoff from AZ 260 is near the Lakeside Ranger Station. The reservoir of-

fers a boat ramp and dispersed camping; no drinking water or charge. Only electric motors are permitted.

**Woodland Reservoir** is an 18-acre, lure-only lake stocked with rainbow and brown trout and some largemouth bass, catfish, and green sunfish. Fishing is best in spring and autumn; electric boat motors only. Picnicking is allowed, but no camping. The lake lies one mile west of Pinetop on Forest Route 316.

Lakeside Ranger Station (U.S. Forest Service), across the highway from Lakeside Campground, sponsors two self-guided **auto tours** of the woodlands, wildlife, and history of the national forest; it lends cassette tapes and players free. The **Porter Mountain Tour** is 33 miles long and requires about two hours. **Lake Mountain Tour** follows a 45-mile course; allow four hours.

**Blue Ridge Trail** (Forest Trail #107) is a popular nine-mile loop for hikers and horseback riders. The trailhead lies near Lakeside off Forest Route 187, just past Springer Mountain Lookout. The Forest Service office stocks maps.

**Forest Route 300** follows the Mogollon Rim from Pinetop west nearly all the way to Camp Verde, offering many panoramic views along the way. Most of the road is dirt, best suited for high-clearance vehicles; check conditions with the Forest Service. A 113-mile hiking and horseback trail also follows the rim on the old **General Crook Trail.** Here, between 1872 and 1874, Army troops built a wagon road to move supplies and troops between Camp Verde and Fort Apache. Inquire at a Forest Service office about trail conditions and trailheads.

## Accommodations
In this, the largest resort area in the White Mountains, you have a choice between many motels, cottages, cabins, and bed and breakfasts, all nestled in cool pine forests. Rates are highest on summer weekends. The Pinetop-Lakeside Chamber of Commerce maintains a longer list of places to stay and can help you find what you're looking for.

RVers can stop at **Blue Ridge Motel,** Pinetop, $13.08, no showers, tel. 367-0758; **Elk Horn RV Park,** Lakeside, $15, tel. 368-5343; **Ponderosa Trailer Park,** Woodland Rd. in

# LAKESIDE AND PINETOP ACCOMMODATIONS

**Bartram's Bed and Breakfast;** Rt. 1, Box 1014, Lakeside, AZ 85929; $95.98 d; 367-1408 or (800) 257-0211

**Bear's Paw Motel;** Rt. 2, Box 1620, Lakeside, AZ 85929; $43.80 s, $53.50 d, plus $9 for kitchen; 368-5231; kitchenettes

**Best Western Inn of Pinetop;** Box 1006, Pinetop, AZ 85935; $63.63-74.24 s, $74.24-84.84 d; 367-6667 or (800) 528-1234; jacuzzi

**Blue Ridge Motel and Cabins;** Box 74, Pinetop, AZ 85935; $42.08 s or d, $71.64 s or d cabins; 367-0758; cabins with kitchenettes and fireplaces

**Bonanza Motel;** Box 358, Pinetop, AZ 85935; $44.51 d; 367-4440; some kitchenettes

**Buck Springs Resort;** Box 130, Pinetop, AZ 85935; $61.77-137.42 d; 369-3554; cottages w/kitchenettes, fireplaces

**Cozy Pine Cabins;** Box 212, Pinetop, AZ 85935; $55.90 d; 367-4558; kitchens, some fireplaces

**Elk Mountain Lodge;** Box 1254, Pinetop, AZ 85935; from $109; 366-0626 or (800) 238-3144; all suites

**Hilltop Motel;** Box 631, Pinetop, AZ 85935; $35 s, $51.86 d; 367-4451

**Historic Lakeview Lodge;** Box 398, Lakeside, AZ 85929; $74.86 d; 368-5253; motels or cabins

**Lake of the Woods Resort;** Box 777, Lakeside, AZ 85929; $79.12-102 d; 368-5353; cabins w/kitchenettes and fireplaces

**Lakeside Inn;** Box 1130-D, Pinetop, AZ 85935; $92-96.61 d; 368-6600 or (800) 843-4729; fireplaces, continental breakfast, jacuzzi

**Lazy Oaks Resort;** Rt. 2, Box 1215, Lakeside, AZ 85929; $55.14-72.11 d; 368-6203; kitchenettes, fireplaces, on lake, five night minimum stay in summer

Lakeside, $15, tel. 368-6989; and **Running Bear Mobile Resort,** Lakeside, $9, tel. 368-6660.

Tenters and RVers can stay at the **Lakeside Campground** in town or at **Show Low Lake** four miles north. Another possibility is to head for the woods—you can camp free almost anywhere in the Apache-Sitgreaves National Forest. People at the Lakeside Ranger Station can suggest areas.

## Food
Restaurants are surprisingly good for such small communities. For American cuisine in Lakeside, try **Piggin's Eatery,** Lakeview Lodge, tel. 368-5348, or **Christmas Tree,** tel. 367-3107.

In Pinetop, choices include American at **Farmer Dunn's Vittles,** tel. 367-3866; **Chalet Restaurant,** tel. 367-1514; and **Roundhouse Resort,** tel. 369-4848. Eat steaks at **Chuckwagon Steak House,** tel. 368-5800. Try Mexican at **La Casa Maya,** tel. 368-6444; **Casa Ter-**

**ritorial,** tel. 367-3050; and **El Rancho,** tel. 367-4557. Pinetop also features **G.J.'s Pizza,** tel. 367-3312, and a variety of fast-food places.

## Events
A family **Winterfest** takes place in February. In June, **Frontier Days** features a Western theme with a large arts and crafts show, fiddlers' contest, and chili cookoff. The **White Mountain Native American Art Festival and Indian Market** in July attracts Native Americans from all over the Southwest for dances, music, art, crafts, demonstrations, and food. August brings the **White Mountain Bluegrass Music Festival.** A colorful parade, arts and crafts show, and other presentations mark the end of summer during the **Fall Festival** in late September.

## Services and Recreation
You can go horseback riding from May to October with **Porter Mountain Stables,** Porter

**Meadows Bed and Breakfast;** Box 1110, Pinetop, AZ 85935; $106.05-185.59 d; 367-8200; Meadows Dining Room

**Meadowview Lodge;** Box 325, Pinetop, AZ 85935; $46.65 d, $52.08 w/kitchen; 367-4642; kitchenettes

**Moonridge Lodge and Cabins;** Box 1058, Pinetop, AZ 85935; motel from $41.25 d, cabins from $87.49; 367-1906; kitchenettes, fireplaces

**Mountain Hacienda Lodge;** Box 713, Pinetop, AZ 85935; $54.28 s, $59.70 d; 367-4146

**Mountain Haven Inn;** Box 309, Pinetop, AZ 85935; $65.13 -97.70; 367-2101; kitchenettes available

**Murphy's Cabins;** Box 117, Pinetop, AZ 85935; $65.13-100 d; 367-2332; kitchenettes, fireplaces

**Northwoods Resort;** Box 397, Pinetop, AZ 85935; $94.38 d; 367-2966 or (800) 813-2966; kitchenettes, fireplaces

**Pinetop Econo Lodge;** Box 1226, Pinetop, AZ 85935; $41.36-94.38 s, $51.96-94.38 d; 367-3636; jacuzzi, continental breakfast

**Pinetop Lodge;** Box 1665, Pinetop, AZ 85935; $49.36-148.09 d; 367-4367 or (800) 374-6386; some kitchenettes and fireplaces, spa

**Rainbow Lake Lodge;** Box 1140, Lakeside, AZ 85929; $81.43 d; 368-6364; kitchenettes

**Roundhouse Resort;** Box 1468, Pinetop, AZ 85935; $84.84-169.68 d; 369-4848; time-share resort (call three days ahead)

**The Place;** Rt. 3, Box 2675, Lakeside, AZ 85929; $62.57-70 d; 368-6777; cottages w/kitchenettes and fireplaces

**Timber Lodge;** Box 2959, Pinetop, AZ 85935; $59.70-65.10 d; 367-4463 or (800) 522-4463

**Whispering Pines Resort;** Box 307, Pinetop, AZ 85935; $71.64-89.01 d; 367-4386; kitchenettes, fireplaces

Mountain Rd., tel. 368-5306); and **Wilderness Ranch Stables,** off Porter Mountain Rd., tel. 368-5790. Enjoy movies at **Lakeside Cinema,** 20 E. White Mountain Blvd.; tel. 367-8866. Play golf on the 18-hole course at **Pinetop Lakes Golf & Country Club;** tel. 369-4184. Several shops along the highway sell and rent **skiing equipment** in season. A large selection of equipment for camping, hiking, skiing, and fly fishing is available at **Mountain Outfitters/The Skier's Edge** next to the Pinetop-Lakeside Chamber of Commerce; tel. 367-6200.

**Information**
Visit or write the **Pinetop-Lakeside Chamber of Commerce** to obtain the latest info. The office is centrally located in an A-frame cabin on the main highway, 592 W. White Mountain Blvd., Pinetop, AZ 85929; it's open in summer Mon.-Fri. 8:30 a.m.-5 p.m., Saturday and Sunday 9 a.m.-3 p.m., and open the rest of the year Mon.-Thurs. 9 a.m.-4 p.m., Friday 9 a.m.-5 p.m., and Saturday 9 a.m.-2 p.m.; tel. 367-4290.

Staff at the **Lakeside Ranger Station** will share information on camping, hiking, driving, and fishing in Apache-Sitgreaves National Forest. The office is across the highway from Lakeside Campground (or write Rt. 3, Box B-50, Lakeside, AZ 85929); it's open Mon.-Fri. 8 a.m.-4:30 p.m., and sometimes Saturday morning in summer; tel. 368-5111.

Fishing and hunting licenses are available from **Arizona Game and Fish** on the south edge of Pinetop; tel. 367-4281. The **public library** is in Lakeside; tel. 368-6688.

**Transport**
In nearby Show Low **White Mountain Passenger Lines** has bus connections with central Arizona (Phoenix, Tempe, Mesa, and Payson); tel. 537-4539.

# WHITE MOUNTAIN APACHE INDIAN RESERVATION

Some of Arizona's best outdoor recreation is available on the more than 1.6 million acres that belong to the White Mountain Apache. Your primary problem will be choosing among so many quality campsites, fishing streams, lakes, ski runs, and hiking trails.

Farsighted planning and development by the White Mountain Apache resulted in the high-quality recreation available today. Though tribal permits are required for almost any activity, costs are reasonable. You don't need state licenses for fishing, boating, or hunting—just the tribal permits. Some areas, such as the summit of sacred Baldy Peak, are closed or require a special use permit. All Indian ruins, except for Kinishba, are closed.

The best source of White Mountain information is the **Game and Fish Department,** Box 220, Whiteriver, AZ 85941; tel. 338-4385/4386. The office is next to the White Mountain Apache Motel in Whiteriver. You can also secure permits at Hon Dah, Hawley Lake, Sunrise Lake, and Salt River Canyon Trading Post. Off-reservation sources include Pinetop Sporting Goods in Pinetop, Woody's Exxon in Show Low, Tempe Marine in Tempe, and Bob's Bargain Barn in Tucson. Other locations sell permits seasonally; call Game and Fish for locations.

Watch for logging trucks on the reservation's many back roads. Some roads may be too rough for cars, especially after rain or snow. The Game and Fish people can advise on current conditions. Most road junctions feature signs, but it's a good idea to consult a map in finding your way around the back roads.

The Apache and the federal government disagree on the name of the reservation; government officials tend to use the term Fort Apache, while the Apache understandably prefer White Mountain Apache.

## Events
The Apache enjoy participating in and attending rodeos, which take place on many weekends through the warmer months. Major events include the **Headstart Rodeo** on Mother's Day weekend, **Cedar Creek Rodeo** on Memorial Day weekend, **Mountain Spirit Celebration** on July 4th, and **Labor Day Rodeo and Tribal Fair.** Rodeos, powwows, and other area events are listed in the local paper, the Fort Apache Scout.

## Fishing
The reservation includes 400 miles of mountain streams and more than 25 lakes. The waters are stocked with trout from fish hatcheries at Williams Creek and Alchesay Springs. If you use a boat, you'll need a boat permit—$2 per day or $10 yearly for lake use. Sunrise is the only lake where large motors are allowed; everywhere else you're limited to electrics. Anglers can go out year-round; ice fishing is popular on lakes not closed for the winter.

Fishing licenses cost $5 per day; season fees are $50 summer or $80 calendar year. Children ages 10-14 receive a 50% discount; children under 10 fish free. An agreement with the San Carlos Apache Tribe honors the fishing permits from either tribe along both banks of the Black and Salt rivers where the reservations meet; a special use permit is required.

## Hunting
Plentiful big and small game roam the reservation. The tribe has established regular hunting seasons for elk, mountain lion, javelina, and pronghorn. You'll need a guide for hunting elk, lion, bear, and pronghorn—also lots of money. The guided hunts can run more than $1000 a day, but participants report a high success rate. Smaller animals and birds are easily bagged and don't require a guide.

## Other Recreation
You'll need a $5 family permit for a picnic or sightseeing stop on the reservation unless you've already obtained a tribal permit for camping, fishing, or other recreational activity. Camping facilities are basic, usually just picnic tables,

fireplaces, and toilets; some campsites offer drinking water. Backpacking is permitted in certain areas with the proper permit. Camping fees ($6 family) must be paid in advance.

Kayakers and rafters can enjoy a section of the Salt River Canyon; best times are usually during the winter snowmelt in April and May. A special use permit is required.

Sunrise Ski Area, with its many downhill runs, is a busy place in winter; the tribe also offers cross-country ski areas near Sunrise and McNary. Snowmobiling is acceptable near Sunrise. Cross-country ski and snowmobile passes required. The tribe prohibits ATVs, horseback riding (except with authorized concessions), and swimming everywhere on the reservation.

## SALT RIVER CANYON

Father Eusebio Francisco Kino visited this colorful canyon in 1698, naming it Salado for the salt springs in the area. There are great views of the canyon from US 60 as the highway swoops down to a bridge 48 miles southwest of Show Low. You can explore further by driving on the dirt road that parallels the river. This route is highly scenic, with towering cliffs above and the river below. Take the turnoff just north of the highway bridge until you come to a fork. At the fork, you can turn left and drive under the bridge a half mile upriver to **Apache Falls,** or bear right on the road downstream to Cibecue Creek (four miles) and the Salt Banks (7.5 miles). A special use permit is required to drive past Cibecue Creek. The road is rough in spots but passable for cautious motorists.

The desert country here at 3,000 feet contrasts sharply with the White Mountains, a short drive north. Saguaro cacti grow on the slopes to the right past the ford on Cibecue Creek. Don't cross if the water is fast-flowing and muddy.

To visit the **Salt Banks,** continue three miles past Cibecue Creek, turn left at the fork, and drive a half mile to a parking area. Walk a little way downstream to the Salt Banks, a long series of salt springs that have deposited massive travertine formations. Minerals and algae color the springs orange, red, and dark green. This site has long been sacred to the Apache, who draw salt here and perform religious ceremonies.

*Salt River Canyon*

Past the Salt Banks turnoff, the road begins a steep climb, becoming too rough for cars. The White Mountain Apache have established several primitive campsites (no drinking water) along the Salt River between the highway bridge and Cibecue Creek. Salt River Canyon Trading Post, near the highway bridge, stocks supplies and permits. Anglers on the Salt River catch mostly channel catfish and some smallmouth bass and bluegill.

## CIBECUE

This small town in the western part of the reservation serves as the center for the Cibecue Apache, a group distinct from the White Mountain and San Carlos Apache. But for administration purposes, the Cibecue area is considered part of the White Mountain Reservation. Visitors can enjoy camping and good fishing for rainbow and brown trout in the upper 15 miles of nearby Cibecue Creek. The first fishing and camping spots lie five miles north of town on a dirt road paralleling the creek; you need a special use permit to drive past the town. Elevations average about 6,000 feet. Apache Traders in Cibecue offers gas and supplies. To reach Cibecue, turn northwest on Indian Route 12 from US 60, eight miles south of Carrizo.

In the winter of 1880, a Cibecue medicine man named Noch-ay-del-klinne began preaching a new religion that predicted the expulsion of all white people. Soon he enjoyed quite an enthusiastic following, worrying officers at Fort Apache. In August 1881, officers dispatched troops and 23 Apache scouts to arrest the medicine man. Fighting broke out upon their arrival at Cibecue, and Noch-ay-del-klinne was killed. The scouts then mutinied, joining the attack on the troops. Angry Apache pursued the survivors

the entire 40 miles back to the fort. Captain Hentig and six other soldiers died in what is believed to be the only revolt by Apache scouts in their 75 years with the Army.

## WHITERIVER

The administrative center of the White Mountain Apache lies in a valley at 5,000 feet, surrounded by high forested hills. It's easy to confuse the name of the town with that of the river flowing beside it, but the town is spelled as one word. Whiteriver has a trading post, motel, restaurants, shopping center, Indian Health Service Hospital, and tribal offices. The tribe owns and operates the giant Fort Apache Timber Company mill on the south edge of town.

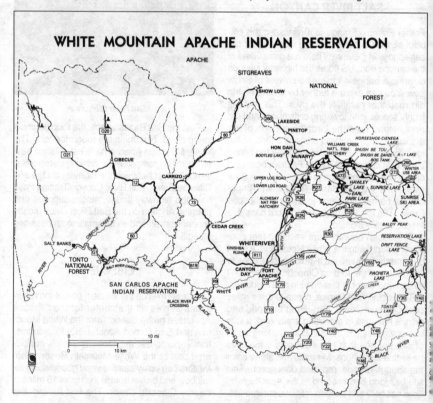

WHITE MOUNTAIN APACHE INDIAN RESERVATION

*officers' quarters,
Fort Apache*

## Practicalities

**White Mountain Apache Shopping Center,** just south of the town center, includes supermarket, stores, movie theater, and post office. **White Mountain Apache Motel,** just beyond the shopping center, features modern rooms ($50 s or d), restaurant, and gift shop; tel. 338-4927. Obtain information and permits next door at the tribal **Game and Fish Department;** it's open Mon.-Fri. 8 a.m.-noon and 1-5 p.m., extended in summer Mon.-Fri. 8 a.m.-5 p.m. and weekends 8 a.m.-5 p.m.; Box 220, Whiteriver, AZ 85941; tel. 338-4385/4386.

## VICINITY OF WHITERIVER

### Fort Apache

In 1869, Major John Green selected this site near the confluence of the north and east forks of the White River as a supply base for troops in the field. Although the White Mountain Apache proved friendly, Army officers thought it wise to keep an eye on them, meanwhile preventing white settlers from encroaching on Indian land.

Originally established as Fort Ord in 1870, the post's name was changed to Camp Mogollon, then to Camp Thomas, and finally to Camp Apache—all within one year. Troops and Apache scouts rode out to subdue rebel-lious Apache in the Tonto Basin (1872-73), and then to fight Victorio (1879) and Geronimo (1881-86).

One of the most prominent Apache scouts was Alchesay, whose name you'll see often on the reservation. Known for his honesty and dedication to both the Army and his people, Alchesay helped put down rebellions of hostile tribes and assisted General Crook in making peace with Geronimo in 1886. The last major action was the Mexican Campaign (1916-17). In 1922, the U.S. Indian Service converted the fort to a boarding school, naming it in honor of President Theodore Roosevelt. Most of the first students were Navajo, though local Apache enrolled later.

Venerable buildings still standing include the commanding officer's quarters (built of logs in 1871), adjutant's office (adobe, 1875), and officers' row (stone, 1890s). Drop into the **Apache Cultural Center** to see old photos, Apache crafts, and military artifacts and to learn about the history of the scouts and soldiers who staffed the fort.

The Apache Cultural Center is open Mon.-Fri. 8 a.m.-5 p.m. (7:30 a.m.-4:30 p.m. in summer) and sometimes on summer weekends; admission is free; tel. 338-4625. It sells a few Apache crafts. Go southwest four miles on the highway from Whiteriver and turn left across the river.

### Kinishba Ruins

Kinishba is Apache for "Brown House". Prehistoric Indians built two large pueblos and smaller buildings here between A.D. 1232 and 1320. The mixed population came from areas of the Little Colorado, central Gila, and Salt rivers. Residents abandoned the village about 1350, possibly because of insufficient water.

A University of Arizona team excavated the ruins from 1931 to 1939 and found 14 types of pottery and a great wealth of shell jewelry scattered across more than 700 rooms. Only one of the large structures has survived. Because it has not been stabilized, you may not enter, but you can view the ruins by walking around outside. You need to obtain an "Other Activities" permit. From Whiteriver, go southwest six miles on the highway, then turn right on a dirt road; the ruins are two miles in.

### Alchesay and Williams Creek National Fish Hatcheries

These hatcheries keep the streams and lakes of the reservation stocked with trout. Williams Creek receives eggs from four or five species of trout, raising the hatchlings to sportfishing size; large brood trout inhabit the raceways. Alchesay specializes in raising small native, rainbow, brown, and cutthroat trout of six to eight inches. Visitors are welcome to view exhibits and stroll along a self-guided tour on weekdays 7 a.m.-3:30 p.m. at both hatcheries; closed holidays. Alchesay also has a picnic area.

The turnoff for Alchesay Hatchery is between Mileposts 342 and 343, four miles north of Whiteriver; a signed paved road heads northeast along the White River 4.6 miles to the site. Roads to Williams Creek Hatchery lie between Mileposts 351 and 352, 13 miles north of Whiteriver, and between Mileposts 353 and 354, 15 miles north of Whiteriver or four miles south of Hon Dah. Follow signs nine miles in on gravel roads.

## FISHING AND CAMPING SPOTS EAST OF WHITERIVER

### East Fork of the White River

The stream offers rainbow and brown trout. The upper reaches are closed to fishing. From the turnoff east of Fort Apache, head east on Indian Route Y-55. Day use only.

*Kinishba Ruins*

### Upper and Lower Bonito Creek

*Bonito* is Spanish for pretty. This stream offers rainbow and brown trout; you'll need a special use permit for some sections. From the junction for Indian Route Y-70, two miles east of Fort Apache, turn in at the sign reading Tonto Lake-Pacheta Lake-Maverick-Drift Fence Lake-Hurricane Lake-Reservation Lake. The road soon turns to gravel, offering fine views of the White River Valley as you climb Seven-Mile Hill. After 11.7 miles, turn left and drive three miles on Y-70 for Upper Bonito (day use only) or continue straight three miles on Y-40 for Lower Bonito.

### Pacheta Lake

The best campsites lie on the east side of this 68-acre lake (elev. 8,170 feet). Drinking water is available. Anglers catch rainbow and brown trout. People say the name Pacheta came from two turn-of-the-century cardplaying cowboys who were caught cheating; they were dubbed the "pair-of-cheaters." The name was later contracted to Pacheta.

There are three ways to get here: follow the signs 40 miles east from Fort Apache on Indian Routes Y-70 and Y-20, take Y-55 east from Fort Apache, or drive the better roads—AZ 273, Forest Route 116, and Y20—south from AZ 260 past Sunrise and Reservation lakes. Pacheta Lake lies several miles east of the junction of Y-20 and Y-55.

## Drift Fence Lake

Cowboys gave this lake its name: During cattle roundups, stock drifted along the fence on the west side of the lake to reach lower pastures. The 16-acre lake lies close to the road between Pacheta and Reservation lakes; elevation 8,900 feet. You'll find small campsites at each end of the lake; large vehicles have more room at the north end.

## Reservation Lake

This 280-acre lake, the second largest on the reservation, offers good fishing for rainbow, brown, and brook trout. Cool forests of aspen, fir, and spruce grow at the 9,000-foot elevation. Rental boats, supplies, and permits are available from late May to early September. Several campgrounds surround the lake.

The easiest way in is from the north: from Hon Dah, take AZ 260 east 20 miles to AZ 273, head southeast on AZ 273 for 14 miles, turn south 10 miles on Forest Route 116, then turn right a half mile and cross a cattleguard to the lake. From Fort Apache, drive 46 miles east on Indian Routes Y-70 and Y-20 or take Y-55 and Y-20.

## FISHING AND CAMPING SPOTS NORTH OF WHITERIVER

### Diamond Creek

Rainbow and a few brown, brook, and native trout lurk in this creek. Special "quality fishing" regulations apply to a section of the creek; obtain a Diamond Creek fishing permit and obey additional rules. Take the turnoff for Alchesay Fish National Hatchery, four miles north of Whiteriver, then turn right onto Indian Route R-25.

### North Fork of the White River

The river is stocked with rainbow and brown trout, and you might catch a few brook and cutthroat. Take the parallel Upper Log Road to reach fishing spots along this stream. Take the Williams Creek Hatchery turnoff (Log Rd.) between Mileposts 351 and 352, 13 miles north of Whiteriver, or the turnoff between Mileposts

353 and 354, 15 miles north of Whiteriver and four miles south of Hon Dah.

## Bootleg Lake

At one time you could buy illegal booze here; today your best bet is largemouth bass, rainbow trout, channel catfish, and sunfish. Special "quality fishing" regulations apply, and you'll need a Bootleg Lake permit. Day use only. Elevation of the 10-acre lake is 6,800 feet. Turn west off AZ 73 at Milepost 355, three miles south of Hon Dah, and go in 2.2 miles.

## HON DAH

The Apache name for this traveler's stop means "Be My Guest". Nineteen miles north of Whiteriver at the intersection of AZ highways 260 and 73, the complex includes the **Hon Dah Casino** (24 hour slot machines plus video poker, keno, and blackjack), an RV park (across AZ 73, $17 w/hookups), grocery store, and service station. A motel and restaurant were to be built. Buy reservation permits and fishing gear at the Hon Dah store, Box 597, McNary, AZ 85930; tel. 369-4311/0299.

## HISTORIC, FISHING, AND CAMPING SPOTS EAST OF HON DAH

### McNary

Though there's not much to see, this old lumber town has an unusual history. Back in 1916, an energetic Flagstaff businessman named Tom Pollock chose the spot for a new lumber enterprise. Leasing the land from the Apache, he ran a railroad line in and named the place "Cooley," after Corydon E. Cooley of the famous Show Low card game.

Meanwhile, 1,000 miles east in McNary, Louisiana, the W.M. Cady Lumber Co. was quickly running out of timbered land. So in 1924 Cady bought out Pollock's Apache Lumber Co. and moved practically the whole town westward to Cooley. Renamed McNary, the town became known for its harmonious mixture of blacks, whites, Latins, and Indians. When fire destroyed the sawmill in 1979, the lumber-chewing edifice was rebuilt 40 miles east near Eagar.

### Shush Be Zahze Lake

If you can't pronounce the Apache words, just call the place "Little Bear". The 15-acre lake, at an elevation of 7,900 feet, has a small campground, and you can fish for rainbow, brown, and brook trout. Go 11 miles east of Hon Dah on AZ 260 and turn north 0.8 mile; keep left at the fork.

### Shush Be Tou Lake

The name is Apache for "Big Bear". The 18-acre lake has a campground and offers fishing similar to conditions on nearby Shush Be Zahze Lake. The directions are the same, except this time take the right fork.

### Hawley Lake

Trout swim in the waters of this 260-acre lake; in winter you can fish through the ice. Constructed in 1957, this was the first lake on the reservation designed for recreation. Facilities include a boat dock with rentals, service station/grocery store, campground ($6), trailer park ($20), cabins (from $70 s or d), and lodge rooms (from $60 s or d); tel. 335-7511. Dusty campers can use the trailer park's showers and laundromat for a small fee. Permits for fishing, camping, and other activities are available at the store. Facilities are open from about mid-May to mid-October.

From AZ 260, 11.3 miles east of Hon Dah, turn south 11 miles on AZ 473; the first nine miles are paved. Despite the 8,300-foot elevation, the road is kept open year-round.

**Earl Park Lake** (47 acres), a half mile southeast of Hawley Lake, also offers fishing.

### Horseshoe-Cienega Lake

You can fish on this 121-acre lake (elev. 8,100 feet) for rainbow, brown, and brook trout. Information, camping and fishing supplies, boat rentals, and permits are available at the boat dock and store, open from about mid-May to mid-September. The road is cleared in winter for ice anglers. Go 13.5 miles east of Hon Dah on AZ 260, turn south at the sign, and follow the road one mile across the dam to the south side of the lake.

### Little Bog Tank

This 12-acre lake (elev. 8,100 feet) is stocked with rainbow, brown, and brook trout. Day use only. Bog Tank lies 14 miles east of Hon Dah on AZ 260, then 0.3 mile north. Nearby Horseshoe-Cienega Lake has groceries and fishing supplies.

### A-1 Lake

This 24-acre lake is stocked with rainbow and brook trout; it's 18 miles east of Hon Dah on AZ 260, on the south side of the highway.

# SUNRISE PARK RESORT AND SKI AREA

### Sunrise Lake

Anglers prize this 920-acre lake (elev. 9,200 feet) for its big rainbow trout. This is the only lake on the reservation where you can use gas motors; limit 10 horsepower.

**Sunrise Park Hotel** offers restaurant, indoor pool, sauna, jacuzzi, volleyball, and seasonal horseback riding. Sky rides at the ski area are sometimes offered on holidays. The lodge closes for about six weeks at the end of the ski season in April, reopens for summer visitors from Memorial Day to mid-September, then closes again until the ski season starts. Summer rates start at $59 d; tel. 735-7669/7676 or (800) 55-HOTEL.

**Sunrise Marina** offers fishing supplies and boat rentals near the lodge. **Sunrise Sports Center,** a half mile south of the lodge, sells groceries, gas, supplies, and permits; lessons are available; tel. 735-7335. RV sites are available at $7. Visitors can rent mountain bikes in summer, snowshoes and cross-country skis in winter on 10 miles of groomed trails; snowmobile tours offered in winter.

From AZ 260, 20 miles east of Hon Dah or 18 miles west of Springerville, turn south 3.5 miles on AZ 273 to the lodge and marina. The campground is on the left just after turning onto the Sunrise Ski Area road, 0.7 mile past the lodge.

### Sunrise Ski Area

This cluster of three peaks—Sunrise, Apache, and Cyclone Circle—boasts more than 65 ski runs winding through pine and aspen forests of the White Mountains. The resort is largely geared to family skiing, with an equal division between advanced, intermediate, and beginning terrain. A combination of two quad chair lifts, three triples, two doubles, and four surface lifts keeps lines short. Snowmaking machines add to the natural snowpack for a season running from late November/early December to early April.

Lift rates are $29 per full day ($16 for ages 12 and under), $23 per half day ($11 for ages 12 and under). You can go night skiing Friday and Saturday in January and February, $15 ($10 ages 12 and under). The resort offers a variety of group and private lessons. Shops rent equipment and offer sales and repairs. Child-care services feature indoor and outdoor activities for children ages three to six and babysitting for infants up to age two.

Sunrise Ski Area offers package deals and family plans that include room and lift tickets.

Room-only rates start at $56 d, jumping to $89 d during the holiday season (mid-December to mid-January) and on Friday and Saturday during the peak ski season (January 12 until closing). For the latest accommodation and skiing info, contact Sunrise Ski Area, Box 217, McNary, AZ 85930; tel. 735-7669 (office), 735-7518 (ski school). For recorded ski conditions call (800) 772-SNOW; to make lodge reservations phone (800) 55-HOTEL.

Shuttle buses connect Sunrise Park Hotel with the ski lifts and Sunrise Day Lodge about every 15 minutes. Accommodations are tight during the ski season and many skiers stay at Greer, 15 miles to the east; Springerville, 22 miles east; or Pinetop-Lakeside, 30 miles west.

# EAST OF WHITE MOUNTAIN APACHE INDIAN RESERVATION

## GREER

This pretty valley sits high in the White Mountains at 8,500 feet. The first settlers arrived in 1879; the town was later named for Americus Vespucius Greer, a prominent Mormon pioneer.

Today the community comes to life in the summer, when visitors enjoy fishing, forest walks, and the cool mountain air. Winter is also a busy season—snow worshippers flock to the slopes of nearby Sunrise Ski Area or put on their skinny skis to glide along the miles of marked cross-country ski trails just outside town. The quietest times are mid-April to early May, when the first signs of spring appear; and autumn, when days are crisp and aspens turn gold. You can fish the waters of the three Greer Lakes, just north of town, and the Little Colorado River—all stocked with trout.

Greer lies 15 miles east of Sunrise Ski Area, 16 miles west of Springerville and 225 miles northeast of Phoenix. From AZ 260, turn south and drive five miles on AZ 373.

## Accommodations

Greer resorts offer rustic cabins, usually with kitchens and cozy fireplaces. **Snowy Mountain Inn** features rooms and cabins, along with fishing pond and jacuzzi. Its restaurant serves European cuisine. It's three miles north of town, Box 377, Greer, AZ 85927; rates are $73.17-132.56 d for rooms, $116.66-142.11 for cabins. **Greer Mountain Resort** offers RV sites in addition to rooms and cabins; it also has a restaurant. It's 2.7 miles north of town, Box 145; rates are $20 RV, $60 d w/kitchen, $85 and up cabins; tel. 735-7560. **Tripp Inn,** next to the Circle B Market, has eight rooms with TVs and VCRs for $53.03 d; write to Box 121 or call 735-7540. **White Mountain Lodge,** Box 143, features farmhouse cabins. Rates are $63.63 d w/bath, $68.93-100.75 cabins; tel. 735-7568. **Molly Butler Lodge,** Box 134, is the oldest guest lodge in Arizona (1910), open all year. Rates are $31.80-47.70 d; tel. 735-7226. **Cattle Kate's Boarding House,** Box 178, has a fishing pond. Rates are $68.93-90.14; tel. 735-7744. **The Aspens,** Box 70, has cabins. Rates are $63.60-74.55 d; tel. 735-7232.

**Big Ten Resort,** Box 124, also offers cabins; it's open all year. Rates are $79.54 d and up; tel. 735-7578. **Greer Lodge,** Box 244, features cabins and a private trout pond; it's open all year. Rates are $79.54-127.76 d; tel. 735-7515/7216. The Little Colorado River runs through the property at **Four Seasons,** Box

219; its cabins are open all year. Rates are $95.44-106.05 d; tel. 735-7333. **Greer Point Trails End,** Box 224, also offers cabins. Rates start at $63.63 d; tel. 735-7513. The restaurant at **The Peaks Resort Hotel,** Box 132, serves a free continental breakfast. Rates are $95 d, $147.41-200.43 suite, $103.93 cabin; tel. 735-7777. **Red Setter Inn Bed and Breakfast,** Box 133, offers log lodge and cabins, and serves breakfast and sack lunch. Rates are $116.66-164.38; tel. 735-7441.

**Aspen Meadow Guest Ranch** offers scenic horseback rides and good access to skiing and other winter activities. Log cabins feature three bedrooms, one bath, and kitchen; June-Sept. rates are $795 per week including meals and activities, $100.70 s or d nightly in ski season, $26.50 each additional person. To reach the guest ranch, drive one half mile west of the Greer turnoff on Hwy. 260 and go north 6.5 miles; P.O. Box 879, Eager, AZ 85925; tel. 333-2717 (ranch) or 521-0880 (cellular phone).

#### Food
The **Rendezvous** serves American food and pizza; closed in the winter. **Snowy Mountain Inn** presents international fare for dinner; tel. 735-7576, reservations requested. **Greer Mountain Resort** has breakfast and lunch daily; tel. 735-7560. **Molly Butler Lodge** offers dinners; tel. 735-7226. **Cattle Kate's Boarding House** offers country style cooking with a cowgirl theme daily for breakfast, lunch, and dinner; open all year; tel. 735-7744. **Greer Lodge** has generous family-style breakfasts, lunches in summer, and dinners; tel. 735-7515. **La Ventana at the Peaks Resort Hotel** offers southwestern and continental cuisine; tel. 735-7273.

#### Campgrounds
RV sites are available at **Mountain Aire RV Park** across from Big Ten Resort; $25; open May 1-early Oct.; tel. 735-7524. You'll pass the two national forest campgrounds of **Benny Creek** ($6) and **Rolfe C. Hoyer** ($8) on the way in to Greer. Both have water during the season, about mid-May to the end of September. Hoyer Campground is larger and offers a nature trail, $2 showers; call (800) 280-CAMP to make reservations.

#### Services and Information
**Butler Canyon Trail** is a one-mile, self-guided nature trail just north of town; turn east off AZ 373 at the sign for Montlure Camp. **Greer Lakes** are three small reservoirs offering boating (electric motors okay), trout fishing, and picnicking; turn east off AZ 373 opposite Hoyer Campground.

**Greer Stables,** opposite Molly Butler Lodge, offers guided rides, hayrides, cookouts, and mountain bike rentals. **Cross-country skiers** can enjoy a variety of loop trails in the woods northwest of town. **Pole Knoll** offers additional cross-country skiing farther west; you can reach it by skiing from Greer or by parking on the south side of AZ 260 near Milepost 383.

Local businesses have ski trail maps or you can contact the **Springerville Ranger District** office in Springerville; tel. 333-4372. Obtain groceries, fishing gear, camping supplies, and cross-country rental skis from **Circle B Market;** tel. 735-7540. Greer also has a post office and a library.

## MOUNT BALDY WILDERNESS

The pristine forests and alpine meadows of 11,590-foot Mt. Baldy present a rare opportunity to visit a subalpine vegetation zone. You'll see magnificent forests untouched by commercial logging. Engelmann and blue spruce dominate, but quaking aspen, white fir, corkbark fir, Douglas fir, southwestern white pine, and ponderosa pine also cover the slopes. You might catch a glimpse of elk, mule or white-tailed deer, black bear, beaver, wild turkey, blue grouse, or other wildlife. Mount Baldy is an extinct volcano eight or nine million years old, worn down by three periods of glaciation.

**West Fork (#94)** and **East Fork (#95)** trails follow the respective branches of the Little Colorado River on the northeast slopes of Mt. Baldy. Each trail is 6.5 miles long; they meet on the grassy summit ridge. The summit is another mile away, but the last half mile of trail crosses White Mountain Apache land, which is closed to outsiders. The Apache vigorously enforce this closure—errant hikers have been arrested, their gear confiscated—so don't try to sneak in. Apache Indians still make pilgrimages to this sacred peak.

Hiking season stretches from June to October, but plan to be off the ridges in early afternoon in July and August to avoid thunderstorms. The trailheads, about four miles apart by road, are easily reached from Sunrise, Big Lake via AZ 273, or Greer. In fact, both trails also go north to Greer, about five miles away.

The West Fork Trailhead (elev. 9,240 feet) lies just outside the wilderness boundary at the end of Forest Route 113J, a half mile in from AZ 273. The East Fork Trailhead (elev. 9,400 feet) begins near Phelps Cabin, 0.2 mile in from AZ 273. An all-day or overnight loop hike uses a 3.3-mile connecting trail that joins the lower ends of West Fork and East Fork trails. This trail, which may not appear on maps, goes from the West Fork Trail (0.3 mile up from the trailhead) to the Phelps Cabin area.

Horseback riders are welcome on the trails and may use small corrals near Phelps Cabin. Anglers catch brook, rainbow, and a few native cutthroat trout in the creeks. The Forest Service asks visitors to limit hiking and riding groups to 12 people and camping groups to six. Forest Service offices sell a topo map of Mt. Baldy Wilderness.

# BIG LAKE

Rolling mountain meadows and forested hills of spruce and fir surround this pretty lake. Top-rated for trout by many anglers, Big Lake (575 acres) boasts a marina, campgrounds, hiking trails, and a riding stable. The marina offers rental boats, motors, fishing supplies, gas, and groceries from late April/early May to mid-November. A fish-cleaning station lies across the parking lot, and a public boat ramp is a short drive away.

Nearby **Crescent Lake** (197 acres) features trout fishing and a smaller marina—boat rentals and snacks—but no campgrounds. The Forest Service operates a visitor center on the main road between the two lakes; check out the naturalist programs, displays, books, and maps.

You have a choice of four campgrounds at Big Lake—all with drinking water and fees of $10-12 per night. The campgrounds are **Rainbow, Grayling, Brookchar,** and **Cutthroat.** The roads are paved to Rainbow. Both RVers

and tenters can stay at Rainbow and Grayling, but only tents are allowed at Brookchar and Cutthroat. Camping season with water lasts mid-May to mid-September; Grayling, Brookchar, and Cutthroat stay open mid-April to Thanksgiving if weather permits. Expect cool nights at the 9,200-foot elevation even in mid-summer. Reserve campsites by calling (800) 280-CAMP.

Big Lake lies about 25 miles south of AZ 260 via AZ 261 and AZ 273; the turnoff is seven miles east of the Greer junction, or four miles west of Springerville. You might want to try your luck with rainbow trout on the way in at **Mexican Hay Lake.** Bring your own boat; no facilities.

### Vicinity of Big Lake
Mountain bikers can enjoy the marked **Indian Springs Trail #627,** a 7.5-mile loop south of Big Lake; the three-mile (one-way) **West Fork Destination Trail** branches off the loop to the West Fork of the Black River. There are many other fine rides on the forest roads as well. **Lee Valley Lake** (35 acres) contains brook trout—best early and late in the season—and great scenery. The lake (elev. 9,400 feet), near Mt. Baldy Wilderness, is off AZ 273 between Big Lake and Sunrise. **Winn Campground** lies at the end of Forest Route 554, two miles in from AZ 273. Greer, Lee Valley Lake, Sunrise Lake, Big Lake, and Crescent Lake are all bunched within a 10-mile radius. Camping season at the 8,800-foot elevation runs from mid-May to the end of September; sites, reserved by calling (800) 280-CAMP, feature drinking water and an $8 fee.

**East Fork of the Black River** offers fishing for rainbow trout. Stay at **Diamond Rock, Aspen,** or **Buffalo Crossing campgrounds;** free, with drinking water at Diamond Rock only. The season runs from early May to the end of October. The area is nine miles southeast of Big Lake and 10-14 miles southwest of Alpine.

**West Fork of the Black River** has fishing for rainbow and brown trout. **West Fork Campground** is beside the stream; free, but no drinking water. An eight-mile day or overnight hike will move you downstream from the crossing of Forest Route 116 to West Fork Campground or vice versa. The Apache-Sitgreaves National Forest map shows back roads in the area.

# SPRINGERVILLE AND EAGAR

Since Henry Springer's trading post opened in 1879, Springerville has grown into an important trade, ranching, and lumbering center. Today the town is a handy stop for travelers. Springerville and the adjacent town of Eagar lie in Round Valley beside the Little Colorado River at an elevation of 6,965 feet. Rolling grass-covered hills surround the valley.

The *Madonna of the Trail,* an 18-foot statue in the middle of town, commemorates the hardy pioneer women of yesteryear. You can't miss the giant dome of the Round Valley Ensphere in Eagar; this multipurpose building has a total floor area of 189,000 square feet, unusually large for such a small community. It is said to be the only domed high school football field in the country.

## Casa Malpais

This prehistoric Indian ruin offers some unusual features. The Mogollon people built the village, believed to be a major trade and ceremonial center, between A.D. 1265 and 1380. It sits on a series of terraces at the edge of a large lava flow, just north of present-day Springerville. Huge cracks—more than 100—under the site served as ceremonial and burial chambers, referred to as "catacombs" by some archaeologists.

The masonry pueblo at Casa Malpais ("House of the Badlands") rose two and three stories with more than 120 rooms. The impressive Great Kiva, square in the Mogollon style, measures 48 by 49 feet; archaeologists believe it once had a roof. Other features at the site include rock art, masonry stairways, and an oval wall enclosing what is believed to have been a dance plaza.

You can view excavated artifacts at a museum and visit Casa Malpais on tours sponsored by the city of Springerville. The tours, the only way to enter the ruins, last about 1.5 hours and involve a half mile of walking and a 250-foot climb; bring water and hat in summer. Ongoing excavations are often visible in spring, summer, and autumn. Because of their sacred nature, the underground chambers are closed to the public. An interpretive trail features 24 signed stations.

Meet at the museum before going to the site, 318 E. Main St. in Springerville; it's open daily 9-5 p.m., closed Monday and Tuesday in winter; tours usually leave at 9 a.m., 11 a.m., and 2:30 p.m. in good weather. Tours or general admission run $4 adults, $3 students 7-18 and seniors 55+; tel. 333-5375.

## Renee Cushman Art Collection

Renee Cushman willed her valuable collection of European art and furniture to the LDS Church in Springerville. Three display rooms house her goods, which range from Renaissance to early 20th century. Open on request; telephone numbers are posted on the museum's front door and available from the chamber of commerce; tel. 333-4514. It's at the Springerville LDS Church at 150 N. Aldrice Burk, 1.5 blocks off Main Street.

## White Mountain Historical Society Park

Historic cabins, houses, and a granary have been moved here and restored. The park is open Mon.-Fri. 1-5 p.m. from mid-May to Labor Day, by appointment at other times; donations are welcomed; tel. 333-4300. Turn south and drive three blocks on Zuni from Main.

## Accommodations, Campgrounds, and Food

Accommodations in Springerville include: **Reed's Motor Lodge** at 514 E. Main St., $28.65 s, $35.20 d, tel. 333-4323; **El Jo Motor Inn** at 435 E. Main St., $30.80 s, $37.40 d, tel. 333-4314; **Corral Motel** at 427 East Main St., $25.53 s or d, tel. 333-2264; **White Mountain Motel** at 333 E. Main St., $24 s, $28 d, tel. 333-5482; **Springerville Inn** at 242 E. Main St., $39.96 s, $44.40 d, tel. 333-4365; and **Super 8 Motel** at 123 W. Main St., $43.18 s, $45.40 d, tel. 333-2655. In Eagar stay at **Sunrise/Eagar Best Western** at 128 N. Main St., $77.31-88.52, tel. 333-2540; or **Paisley Corners Bed and Breakfast** at 287 N. Main St., tel. 333-4665. **Casa Malpais Campground** is one mile northwest on US 60; may close in winter; $11.11 tent or $17.77 RV w/hookups (showers); tel. 333-4632. Nearby Becker Lake offers trout fishing. **Jones RV Park** is at 425 E. Central Ave. in Eagar; open all year; $5.50 tent, $11.21 RV w/hookups (no showers); tel. 333-4650. Locals dine at **Mike's Place** for steak and other American cuisine, at the corner of E. Hwy. 60 at D St., tel. 333-4022; or at **Las Dos Molinas** for very spicy Mexican food at 900 E. Main St., tel. 333-4846.

### Events

The community celebrates **July 4th** with a parade, rodeo, barbecue, dance, hot-air balloons, and fireworks. **Eagar Daze,** the first weekend in August, features talent show, games, barbecue, and dance. **Valle Redondo Days** on Labor Day weekend presents Heritage Night performances, historical crafts, food, and games. A **Christmas Lights Parade and Crafts Fair** is held on the first Saturday in December.

### Shopping and Services

**Round Valley Plaza,** just south of downtown on S. Mountain Ave., features a supermarket and other stores. Pick up fishing, hunting, and camping supplies at the **Ben Franklin/Western Drug,** 106 Main St., tel. 333-4321; or at **Sport Shack,** 329 E. Main St., tel. 333-2222. **Trout Fitters** offers fishing and hunting supplies, boat rental, and guide services at 60 N. Main St. in Eagar; tel. 333-2628. **Mountain Cyclery & Ski** sells and rents mountain bicycle and ski gear at Central Ave. and Harless St. in Eagar; tel. 333-5750. The **Sweat Shop** in Eagar rents cross-country skis; tel. 333-2950.

**Springerville Park** offers shaded picnic tables and a playground next to the White Mountain Historical Society Park; turn south three blocks on Zuni from Main. **White Mountain Communities Hospital** is in downtown Springerville at 118 S. Mountain Ave.; tel. 333-4368. Eagar has the indoor **Round Valley Swimming Pool** at 116 N. Eagar St.; tel. 333-2238.

### Information

Staff at the **Round Valley Chamber of Commerce,** 148 E. Main St. in downtown Springerville, can tell you about the area and services; it's open Mon.-Sat. 9 a.m.-5 p.m. (and Sunday 10 a.m.-2 p.m. in summer); Box 31, Springerville, AZ 85938; tel. 333-2123, fax 333-5690. For maps and the latest info on recreation and road conditions in the Apache-Sitgreaves National Forest, visit either of the two **U.S. Forest Service** offices on S. Mountain Avenue.

The **Springerville Ranger District Office,** just north of Round Valley Plaza, has specific information on Big Lake, Mt. Baldy, Greer, South Fork, and other areas of the district including forest maps; it's open Mon.-Fri. 7:30 a.m.-4:30 p.m.; Box 760, Springerville, AZ 85938, tel. 333-4372. The **supervisor's office,** just south of Round Valley Plaza, has general information on Apache-Sitgreaves National Forest; it's open Mon.-Fri. 7:30 a.m.-4:30 p.m.; P.O. Box 640, Springerville, AZ 85938, tel. 333-4301. The **public library** is in Eagar Plaza behind Dairy Queen; tel. 333-4694.

## VICINITY OF SPRINGERVILLE

### Raven Site Ruin

Excavation has revealed an 800-room multistory pueblo at this prehistoric Indian site, home to both Anasazi and Mogollon. The ruins overlook the Little Colorado River about 12 miles north of Springerville. The White Mountain Archaeological Center has opened Raven Site Ruin to the public, both for tours and archaeological research. Of particular interest to the visitor is a replica of a pueblo room furnished as it would have been when the pueblo was occupied. Forty-minute tours of the ruins begin at 10 and 11 a.m. and at 1, 2, 3, and 4 p.m. daily during the early May to late September season; $3.50 adults, $2.50 seniors and ages 12-17, younger children free. Researchers serve as guides.

The participation programs are designed for anyone with a serious interest in Southwest archaeology. You can join for a day or a week in helping staff with survey work, excavation, reconstruction, and laboratory analysis. There's a charge for this participatory program, as well as for horseback and hiking tours.

Look for the signed Raven Site Ruin turnoff from US 180/191, 12 miles north of Springerville and five miles south of Lyman Lake State Park. The drive in involves a bit of dirt road. For information on tours and programs, contact the White Mountain Archaeological Center at HC 30, St. Johns, AZ 85936; tel. 333-5857.

### Lyman Lake State Park

Rain and snowmelt from the White Mountains fill this 1,500-acre lake (elev. 6,000). Though it's cold here in winter, anglers are out trying year-round. You're most likely to catch channel catfish, largemouth bass, walleye, crappie, and northern pike. Lyman Lake is large enough for sailing and waterskiing; there are no motor restrictions. Anglers enjoy a section of the west end designated as a no-wake area.

The marina stocks camping and fishing supplies and offers boat rentals. An excellent campground includes restrooms, showers, hookups, grocery store, and snack bar. Boaters can use campsites accessible only by water on the other side of the lake. Campers should prepare for strong winds on the open terrain. Charges per vehicle run $3 day use, $8 camping, or $13 with electric and water hookups.

During summer season 40-minute tours are given along a petroglyph trail across the lake. Tours depart weekends at 10 a.m. and 2 p.m. at $2 per person; limit 10 people. Call for reservations.

The park lies 17 miles north of Springerville and 12 miles south of St. Johns on US 180/191; tel. 337-4441. Look for buffalo near the entrance.

## South Fork

A national forest campground, a museum, and a resort lie near the South Fork of the Little Colorado River (elev. 7,700 feet), five miles west of Springerville. **South Fork Campground,** 2.5 miles south of AZ 260 on Forest Route 560, covers both sides of the stream. Camping season runs mid-May to the end of October; there's no water, but admission is free. From the campground you can follow the **Mexican Hay Lake Trail # 92** for six miles despite the obsolete sign that says the trail ends in three miles.

**Little House Museum** at X Diamond Ranch relates the history of the area in authentic antique log cabins, as well as in a little house. Exhibits include photos and antiques highlighted by working nickelodeons and other music machines from the past; it's open May 25-Labor Day with 90-minute tours given Thurs.-Sat. at 11 a.m. and 1:30 p.m. and Sunday and Monday at 1:30 p.m. only, closed Tuesday and Wednesday, open in winter by reservation only; admission is $4 adults, $1.50 children. It's seven miles west of Eagar on South Fork Rd.; tel. 333-2286. The X Diamond Ranch also offers fishing on private access to

the Little Colorado River (where trout range 14-20 inches) at $20 half day, $30 full day catch and release; limited to five anglers daily. The ranch also has a fishing pond where trout weighing more than two pounds can be kept at $5 per fish. Equipment is available for rent; tel. 333-2286. **South Fork Guest Ranch** offers cabins and a private pond in South Fork Canyon, 2.5 miles south of AZ 260; open all year, $36.93-137.15 d; tel. 333-4455. Next door is **MS Elle's** restaurant, open Mon.-Sat. 5-9 p.m. and Sunday (summer only) 1-9 p.m.; tel. 333-4455

## St. Johns

Spanish explorers named this spot on the Little Colorado River El Vadito (Little River Crossing). In 1871, Solomon Barth founded a settlement along the river with his brothers and some Mexican families, moving the folks six miles upstream to the present site the following year. Residents named the community San Juan after its first female resident, Señora Maria San Juan de Padilla de Baca. Postal authorities supposedly refused to accept a foreign name, so it was changed to Saint John, with an "s" added for phonetic effect. Mormon settlers arrived in 1879 from Utah.

Today, St. Johns (pop. 3,300) serves as the Apache County seat, 29 miles north of Springerville and 44 miles southeast of Petrified Forest National Park.

You can learn more about the area's history and see pioneer and Indian artifacts in the **Apache County Museum,** 180 W. Cleveland (US 180/AZ 61); it's open Mon.-Fri. 9 a.m.-5 p.m. (closed holidays); donations are welcomed; tel. 337-4737. The museum features an attractive, spacious display of artifacts from past centuries, with an early log cabin, Indian wickiup, jail, and farm equipment in the back. The **St. Johns Chamber of Commerce** is also at 180 W. Cleveland, open Mon.-Fri. 8 a.m.-5 p.m.; Box 178, St. Johns, AZ 85936; tel. 337-2000.

St. Johns has two motels and several restaurants. Events include an **S.P.R.A. rodeo** during Memorial Day weekend. The **San Juan Fiesta** in mid-June features parade, barbecue, dances, and games. A **July 4th** festival includes a barbecue, games, and fireworks; **Pioneer Day** on the weekend nearest July 24th offers a parade, rodeo, pageant, barbecue, and dances. The **Classy Chassis Car Show and Two-Day Street Fair** occurs in mid-August with games, parade, barbecue, and dance; the **Apache County Fair** takes place in September, featuring exhibits and horse races. In mid-December enjoy the living Christmas tree and 100-person community choir; the museum offers tour of historic houses not normally open to the public.

The pleasant **city park** includes covered picnic tables, playground, outdoor pool, and courts for tennis, volleyball, racquetball, and handball at Second West and Second South. From near the museum, turn south two blocks on Second West. The **public library** is at 245 West and First South; tel. 337-4405.

### Kolhuwalawa

Arizona's 23rd Indian reservation was created in 1985, returning to the Zuni (ZOO-nee) their heaven. These 1,400 acres, 14 miles north of St. Johns, are believed by the Zuni to include the place where human spirits return after death. Anthropologists believe that Zuni religious leaders have held sacred dances and ceremonies here since at least A.D. 900, when ancestors of the tribe began migrating from pueblos in Arizona to New Mexico.

The Zuni people, like the Hopi, still live in pueblos and maintain many of their old traditions. You can visit Zuni Pueblo, one of the fabled Seven Cities of Cíbola sought by Coronado in 1540. Zuni is in New Mexico, 58 miles northeast of St. Johns.

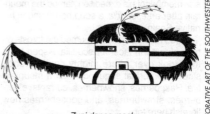

*Zuni dance mask*

DECORATIVE ART OF THE SOUTHWESTERN INDIANS

### Concho Lake

Fish for rainbow and brook trout in this 60-acre lake, located about 16 miles west of St. Johns; no boat ramp or other facilities are available at present. The adjacent **Concho Valley Country Club** has an 18-hole golf course, **Concho Valley Motel** ($31.81 s, $42.42 d), and a restaurant; tel. 337-4644.

# THE CORONADO TRAIL

Seeking treasures of the legendary Seven Cities of Cíbola in 1540, Francisco Vásquez de Coronado and his men struggled through the rugged mountains of eastern Arizona. Though the Spaniard's quest failed, the name of this scenic highway recalls his effort. You'll discover the area's real wealth on a drive over Coronado's old route—rugged mountains covered with majestic forests, rolling in blue waves towards the horizon. The blazing gold of aspen in autumn is matched only by the dazzling display of wildflowers in summer. The 123 miles of paved highway between Springerville and Clifton twist over country little changed from Coronado's time. When exploring this region, hikers, anglers, and cross-country skiers will find themselves far from the crowds.

A look at the Apache-Sitgreaves National Forest map shows many scenic backcountry loops. Allow enough time for the journey through this high country—even a nonstop highway drive requires three and a half hours. With some 460 curves between Alpine and Morenci, this route certainly isn't suitable for those in a hurry. And you'll probably want to stop often to enjoy the views, walk around, maybe have a picnic. Drivers should stock up on groceries and gas before attempting the 89 miles from Alpine to Morenci; there are no towns along this stretch.

Winter snows can close the highway from Alpine to just north of Morenci between mid-December and mid-March, though the section from Springerville to Alpine remains open. Miles of fine cross-country ski trails attract winter visitors to the forests surrounding Alpine.

### Nelson Reservoir

Rainbow, brown, and brook trout live in this 60-acre lake 10 miles south of Springerville. Picnic tables, restrooms, boat ramp, and handicapped fishing station are provided; no camping. Winter visitors can fish through the ice. Escudilla Mountain, the large rounded peak to the south, is the third highest mountain in Arizona.

## Escudilla Mountain and Wilderness

Coronado spotted the 10,912-foot summit of this ancient volcano in 1540; perhaps a homesick member of his expedition named the mountain after an *escudilla,* a soup bowl used in his native Spain.

In 1951 a disastrous fire burned the forests on the entire north face of Escudilla. Aspen trees then took over where mighty conifers once stood, the normal sequence after a mountain fire. Raspberries, snowberries, currants, elderberries, strawberries, and gooseberries now flourish here too.

The forests of spruce, fir, and pine on top escaped the fire; lower down you'll find surviving woodlands of aspen, Rocky Mountain maple, ponderosa pine, and Gambel oak. Elk, deer, black bear, and smaller animals roam the hillsides. Escudilla was once grizzly territory, but the last animal was killed by the 1930s.

Now a wilderness area of 5,200 acres, Escudilla offers excellent hiking. Outstanding views from the fire lookout—the highest in Arizona—reward those who make the climb. The actual summit (10,912 feet) lies a half mile to the north and 36 feet higher, but trees there completely block the views.

**Escudilla National Recreation Trail,** a well-graded, 3.3-mile trail from Terry Flat (elev. 9,600 feet), ascends to Escudilla Lookout through aspen, meadows, and conifers. The old Government Trail, though shown on some maps, is no longer maintained and isn't recommended; it originally began from Hulsey Lake.

From US 191 between Mileposts 420 and 421, about 21 miles south of Springerville and six miles north of Alpine, turn east and drive 4.6 miles on Forest Route 56 to Terry Flat Loop, then take the left fork 0.4 mile to the trailhead. **Terry Flat Loop** is a worthwhile destination in itself; the six-mile dirt road encircles Terry Flat Meadow with many fine views of Escudilla Mountain; cautious drivers can usually make the trip in dry weather.

# ALPINE

Mormon settlers founded this town in 1879, naming it Frisco for the nearby San Francisco River. Later, believing their mountains resembled the Alps, settlers renamed the community Alpine. The setting is pretty—a high mountain valley (elev. 8,046 feet) surrounded by extensive woodlands—but the Alps it isn't.

Alpine (pop. 600) is an excellent base for hiking, mountain biking, fishing, hunting, horseback riding, golfing, scenic drives, and—in winter—cross-country skiing, sledding, and snowmobil-

*Terry Flat and
Escudilla Mountain*

ing. If you're headed south, this is your last chance for gasoline until Morenci, 89 miles away.

## Accommodations

**Sportsman's Lodge,** on US 180, offers motel rooms for $29.68 s and $37.10 d, and kitchenettes for $47.70 d; tel. 339-4576. **Alpine Cabins,** in town next to the M&J Corral Restaurant, has a variety of kitchenettes at $47.25 d; tel. 339-4440. **Mountain Hi Lodge,** a half mile east on Main St., features rooms at $30.75 and $38.18 d and kitchenettes at $41.36-56.21 d; tel. 339-4311. **Coronado Trail Cabins** is a half mile south of town on US 191; cabins with kitchenettes are open year-round at $42.42; tel. 339-4772.

**Judd's Ranch,** a half mile north of Alpine, offers cabins with kitchenettes, horseback rides, and a fishing lake; it's open from late April to late October, $31.95 d; tel. 339-4326. **Tal-Wi-Wi Lodge,** three miles north of Alpine, features motel rooms ($52.19-94.79) and a restaurant serving breakfast, lunch, and dinner on a varied schedule; tel. 339-4319. **Sprucedale Ranch** offers accommodations at a working cattle and horse ranch at an elevation of 8,000 feet. Minimum stays are six days at $328.76 adult, reduced rate for children. From Alpine, drive 14 miles south, turn right on FR 26, after four miles take the left junction and go five miles, then right one mile on FR 24 to the ranch turnoff; P.O. Box 880, Eagar, AZ; tel. 333-4984.

## Campgrounds

**Alpine Divide Campground,** set in a forest of ponderosa pine and Gambel oak four miles north of Alpine, offers sites with drinking water, maintained from mid-May to mid-September; $5. The rest of the year camping is on a pack-in/pack-out basis, and free.

**Luna Lake Campground,** four miles east of Alpine on US 180 near the New Mexico border, lies in a ponderosa pine forest; it's open with drinking water from mid-May to mid-September; $6; reservations can be made by calling (800) 280-CAMP. Luna Lake (75 acres) has a boat launch, boat rentals, and a small store, and is open all year. Anglers go after trout in all four seasons—even through the ice in winter.

**Outpost RV & Trailer Park,** on US 180 near Luna Lake, has RV sites for $12.27 w/hookups; tel. 339-4854. **Alpine Village Trailer Park,** in

town on US 180, offers sites with showers at $3 per person tent, $14.85 RV w/hookups; tel. 339-1841. **Meadow View Trailer Park** has RV sites at $14 in town near the junction of US 191 and US 180; tel. 339-1850.

## Food

For a variety of American and Mexican food, try the **Blue Spruce Restaurant** (open daily except winter for breakfast, lunch, and dinner, tel. 339-4316) or **Bear Wallow Restaurant** (open daily for breakfast, lunch, and dinner, tel. 339-4310). The **Alpine Country Club,** five miles out of town, serves lunch (except Monday) and dinner daily (by reservation only Thursday); closed in winter; tel. 339-4944.

## Events

**Dog-Sled Races** liven up the first weekend in January. **Bush Valley Craft Fair** and **Luna Lake Trout Derby** take place in May. The **Alpine Rodeo** features a parade and rodeo in June. Shop early in the **Bush Valley Christmas Bazaar** on Labor Day weekend.

## Services

**Judd's Ranch** (tel. 339-4326) offers horseback riding. **Cross-country skiers** can roam the groomed trails northwest of town in Williams Valley or south of town at Hannagan Meadow. You can rent cross-country ski gear at the **Tackle Shop** and **Alpine Market. Alpine Hardware** and the **Tackle Shop** have outdoor supplies. **Fite's Fishery** offers private fishing (no license required) at the north edge of town; turn east on the dirt road just north of the post office and drive about three blocks to the sign; $1 admission/pole rental, $4/pound kept; open daily Memorial Day-Labor Day, then weekends only April-May and Sept.-Oct.; tel. 339-4421. See how far you can hit a golf ball through the thin mountain air at **Alpine Country Club**'s 18-hole course; rental carts and clubs and a restaurant; closed in winter. Head east three miles on US 180, then turn south and drive two miles and follow signs; tel. 339-4944.

## Information

The **Alpine Chamber of Commerce** maintains a list of accommodations and services; write Box 410, Alpine, AZ 85920; tel. 339-4330. People at the **Alpine Ranger District** office of the Apache-Sitgreaves National Forest are very helpful with information on scenic drives, fishing, hiking, mountain biking, camping, and cross-country ski trails. The district covers the north half of the Coronado Trail, including Escudilla Mountain and most of the Blue Range Primitive Area; the ranger office is open Mon.-Fri. 8 a.m.-4:30 p.m. It's in town at the junction of US 191 and 180; Box 469, Alpine, AZ 85920; tel. 339-4384. Alpine's **public library** is on US 180; tel. 339-4925.

## VICINITY OF ALPINE

The **East and West Forks of the Black River** west of town have fishing, hiking, and campgrounds; continue west for Big Lake, Crescent Lake, and other recreation areas.

### Blue River-Red Hill Scenic Loop

On this backcountry drive you'll roll by the Blue River, remote ranches, and rugged hill country. The Forest Service maintains two small campgrounds along the way—Upper Blue, with spring water, and Blue Crossing. Both lie near the Blue River at an elevation of 6,200 feet; no charge.

From Alpine, head east three miles on US 180 and turn south on Forest Route 281 (Blue Rd.). After 10 miles you'll reach the Blue River; follow it downstream nine miles to the junction with Forest Route 567 (Red Hill Rd.). A river ford here can be impassable in high water. Red Hill Rd. twists and climbs out of the valley, often following ridges with good views, to US 191, 14 miles south of Alpine. If driving the other direction, you'll find the Red Hill Rd. turnoff between Mileposts 239 and 240 on US 191. The forest roads are gravel and should be okay in dry weather for cautious drivers. See the Alpine Ranger District office for more info on this and other scenic drives in the area.

Hikers may want to try **Red Hill Trail #56;** this 7.6-mile trail follows a jeep track to the Blue Range Primitive Area, descends along ridges via Red Hill (elev. 7,714 feet), drops into Bush Creek, and follows it to Tutt Creek. **Tutt Creek Trail #105** connects the lower end of Red Hill Trail with Red Hill Rd., 0.8 mile to the east. The

upper trailhead (elev. 8,000 feet) is on Forest Route 567 one mile east of US 191; the lower trailhead (5,800 feet) is on Forest Route 567 a half mile before the Blue River.

### Mountain Bicycling

The Apache-Sitgreaves National Forest offers many good areas for mountain biking. Marked trails on the Alpine District include upper (eight miles) and lower (2.5 miles) loops near Luna Lake, Georges Lake near Alpine (4.5 miles, 7.5 miles without shuttle), Terry Flat Loop (six miles) at Escudilla Mountain, Hannagan Meadow Loop (5.5 miles) south of Alpine, and Williams Valley (five miles) northwest of Alpine. You can rent bikes in Springerville.

## BLUE RANGE PRIMITIVE AREA

This rugged wilderness country lies south of Alpine along the Arizona-New Mexico border. The south-flowing Blue River, fed by several perennial streams, neatly divides the primitive area. The Mogollon Rim, with high cliffs forming the south boundary of the Colorado Plateau, crosses the area from west to east. Geologic uplifting and downcutting have created spectacular rock formations and rough, steep canyons. Elevations range from 9,100 feet near Hannagan Meadow to 4,500 feet in the lower Blue River.

Hiking down from the rim, you'll find spruce, fir, and ponderosa pine forests giving way to piñon pine and juniper. Wildlife includes Rocky Mountain elk, Coues white-tailed deer, mule deer, black bear, mountain lion, javelina, and bobcat. You may also see such rare and endangered birds as the southern bald eagle, spotted owl, American peregrine falcon, aplomado falcon, Arizona woodpecker, black-eared bushtit, and olive warbler. The upper Blue River and some of its tributaries harbor small numbers of trout.

### Hiking

Hikers usually enjoy the best weather from April to early July and from September to late October. Violent thunderstorms lash the mountains in July and August. Snow covers much of the land from November to March. Many day-hikes and

*view near K.P. Cienega Campground*

backpacking trips are possible on Forest Service trails. You can hike from trailheads along the Coronado Trail (US 191), Forest Route 281 (Blue Rd.), and Forest Route 567 (Red Hill Rd.). Other trailheads lie to the east in New Mexico and to the south off Forest Route 475. The Forest Service office in Alpine has maps and trail descriptions.

## HANNAGAN MEADOW AND VICINITY

Splendid forests of aspen, spruce, and fir surround the tiny village of Hannagan Meadow (elev. 9,100 feet), 22 miles south of Alpine. A network of trails offers some great hiking; several trails also lead into the adjacent Blue Range Primitive Area. You'll find some of the best cross-country skiing and snowmobiling in all of Arizona, in areas relatively unknown. The road from Alpine is normally open in winter, though storms occasionally shut it down for a few days. The **Acker Lake Trail** starts at the campground between campsites #6 and #7. The trail offers access to both Acker Lake and the more remote areas of the Blue Range Primitive Area. The hike to the lake is 3.5 miles.

### Hannagan Meadow Lodge
The rustic cabins in this remote region offer comfortable year-round accommodations. Cab-

ins start at $65.75 per night; the lodge dining room is open daily in the warmer months and Thurs.-Mon. in winter. A small store stays open June to December. Information about hiking trails is available at the store. Cross-country skiers can glide along marked trails and two groomed trails during the late November to late March season and a snowmobile trail starts from the north end of the lodge area. Contact Hannagan Meadow Lodge at Box 335, Alpine, AZ 85920; tel. 339-4370.

### Hannagan Meadow Campground
This national forest campground stays open from mid-May to mid-September; no drinking water or fee; water is available from a hose in front of the store; it's 0.3 mile south of the lodge on the highway. The Acker Lake Trail begins between campsites. Other trails start across the road from the campground. Showers are available at **Black River RV Park** on FR 25 at $5 for non-guests, $18 RV sites; tel. 333-4984.

### Vicinity of Hannagan Meadow
**K.P. Cienega Campground** overlooks a large meadow (*cienega* is Spanish for meadow) and a sparkling stream. Free sites in this idyllic spot offer spring water. Turn off the Coronado Trail five miles south of Hannagan Meadow and drive 1.5 miles on a dirt road to the meadow. **K.P. Trail #70** into the Blue Range Primitive Area begins here.

**Bear Wallow Wilderness** protects 11,000 acres west of the Coronado Trail, including what's believed to be the largest stand of virgin ponderosa pine in the Southwest. **Bear Wallow Trail #63** follows Bear Wallow Creek downstream through the wilderness west to the San Carlos Indian Reservation boundary, 7.6 miles one-way; elevations range from 8,700 feet at the trailhead to 6,700 feet at the reservation boundary.

Two shorter trails drop down to the trail and creek from the north. **Reno Trail #62** (1.9 miles one-way) meets Bear Wallow Trail at Mile 2.6; **Gobbler Point Trail #59** (2.7 miles one-way) meets Bear Wallow Trail at Mile 7.1.

Reach upper trailheads from Forest Route 25, which turns off US 191 opposite the road for K.P. Cienega Campground. Foresters at the Alpine Ranger District office have more detailed trail descriptions and can advise on current conditions.

**Blue Vista Overlook and Nature Trail** sit on the very edge of the Mogollon Rim, seven miles south of Hannagan Meadow. Turn 0.3 mile southwest to paved parking, picnic tables, and wheelchair-accessible views. A gate blocks the road to the parking area in winter, but you can park outside and walk in.

In clear weather you can see countless ridges rolling away to the horizon from this 9,184-foot vantage point. Seventy miles to the south is Mt. Graham (elev. 10,717 feet), the highest peak of the Pinaleno Range. Learn more about the great variety of trees and plants on the 0.3-mile nature trail to another viewpoint and picnic table.

## BELOW THE RIM

### Strayhorse Campground
This free campground, at an elevation of 7,600 feet, offers spring water. It's four miles and 1,600 feet below Blue Vista and 64 miles north of Clifton; turnoff is near Milepost 221. **Raspberry Creek Trail #35** leads east to Blue River in the Blue Range Primitive Area. **Highline Trail #47** goes west 14.5 miles, linking with several other trails. Trails in this area, west of Strayhorse Campground, tend to be harder to follow.

### Rose Peak
At an elevation of 8,786 feet, Rose Peak offers great views. It's also a good place for bird-watching. The turnoff lies near Milepost 207, about 17 miles south of Blue Vista and 51 miles north of Clifton. You can reach the forest lookout tower on a half-mile trail or by driving up a steep, narrow, one-mile road.

### Juan Miller Campgrounds
The season runs year-round when not blocked by snow at the upper (elev. 5,800 feet) and lower (5,700 feet) campgrounds; no drinking water or fee. Head east one mile from the Coronado Trail on Forest Route 475. The turnoff is near Milepost 189, 35 miles south of Blue Vista and 33 miles north of Clifton. Forest Route 475 continues east to Blue River, another 15 miles, passing many small canyons and ridges good for day-hiking.

### Honeymoon Campground
As its name suggests, this is a secluded spot at the end of the 22-mile dirt Upper Eagle Creek Road. You can fish for trout in Eagle Creek, stocked from May to September. No drinking water or fee; carry out trash. Elevation is 5,400 feet. Turn west onto Forest Route 217 near Milepost 188 of the Coronado Trail. Many of the ranches along the way date back to the late 1800s.

### Granville Campground
This campground, and nearby **Cherry Lodge Picnic Area,** are pleasant places to stop. Sites at the 6,800-foot location have drinking water from early April to late October and are open all year; free. Campground and picnic area lie on opposite sides of the road, about 20 miles north of Clifton between Mileposts 178 and 179.

## CLIFTON

Coronado's expedition marched through this area in 1540, totally ignorant of the gold deposits and abundant copper ore lying deep within these hills. Mexican miners discovered gold in 1867 and began small-scale placer operations. As the gold played out, Eastern prospectors began salivating over the copper deposits. They

# MORENCI—THE MINE THAT ATE A TOWN

*just one section of the vast concentrator works at Morenci*

From the overlook 10 miles north of Clifton you can gaze into the Morenci Mine, one of the biggest artificial holes in the world. Giant 210-ton trucks look like toys laboring to haul copper ore out of the ever-deepening pit.

The old town of Morenci is gone; when the town got in the way of the mine, Phelps Dodge built a new community and quarried away the old one. The move, completed in 1969, was easy—Phelps Dodge owned the town as well as the mine. From the mine overlook, the road drops to modern Morenci (elev. 4,080 feet), then switchbacks down to Clifton (elev. 3,502 feet). You'll pass a giant smelter (now closed), concentrators, and a solvent extraction/electrowinning plant on the way.

Contact Phelps Dodge if you'd like to view some of its operations; free tours last about three and a half hours and take you inside the open pit mine and to the crushers, concentrators, and solvent extraction/electrowinning plant. Retired miners, who know the area and operations well, lead the tours. Visitors must sign a liability release and be at least nine years old. Tours start at 8:30 a.m. and 1:30 p.m. from the Morenci Motel; tours are popular and often booked solid weeks ahead so call for reservations; tel. 865-4521, ext. 435.

registered claims and by 1872 had staked out the town of Clifton. The nearby mining towns of Joy's Camp (later renamed Morenci) and Metcalf were also founded at this time. Miners faced great difficulties at first—the nearest railhead was in Colorado, and Apache raids were frequent.

In 1878, Arizona's first railroad connected the smelter in Clifton with the Longfellow Mine at Metcalf, nine miles north. Mules pulled the empty ore cars uphill to the mine; on the way down, the mules received a free ride. Three tiny locomotives, one on display in Clifton, later replaced the mules. Miners worked underground during the first six decades; in 1937, after a five-year Depression-era hiatus, all mining shifted to the surface, where it continues today.

Both Metcalf and old Morenci are gone now—Metcalf abandoned and destroyed, and old Morenci quarried away. The new Morenci has an attractive appearance but lacks the character of an old mining town. Clifton, the Greenlee County seat, still has its old buildings and the Copper Head locomotive, built in the 1880s. Booze joints and brothels, where desperados engaged in frequent shootouts, once lined Chase Creek Street. Today the street is quiet and the old jail empty, but Clifton remains one of Arizona's more historically distinctive towns—famed not only as the birthplace of Apache war-

Chase Creek St. in Clifton

rior Geronimo but also as the site of Arizona's first railroad, first developed mine, and first bank.

## Sights

Strolling along Chase Creek St., you can imagine how it once looked—when the boisterous miners of old came looking for a good time. The street parallels US 191 on the Morenci side of town. Drop into the **Greenlee Historical Museum** at 317 Chase Creek St. to see exhibits and artifacts of the old days; a large geologic relief map (ca. 1915) shows the ore deposits and mines of the area; the museum is open Tuesday, Thursday, and Saturday 2-4:30 p.m. or by appointment; tel. 865-3115.

Clifton's old jail, close to the old train depot/Chamber of Commerce, was built in 1881 by blasting and hacking a hole into the hillside. The jail's first occupant turned out to be the man who built it, Margarito Verala. After doing a fine job on the construction, Verala received his pay, got drunk on mescal, and proceeded to shoot up the town. You're welcome to step inside the gloomy interior. If the gate's locked, check at the city hall or police station for the key. The Copper Head locomotive of the old Coronado Railroad sits next to the jail. Tours by the Phelps Dodge Company provide a close-up look at the copper mine operations in Morenci.

A scenic drive on Forest Route 212 winds from Clifton up along the San Francisco River past ranches, old mines, and canyon scenery to Evans Point. Cars can travel at least a few miles and high-clearance 4WD vehicles farther. Head up Frisco Ave. on the west side of the river, cross the river on a concrete bridge, and continue upstream. Staff at the Clifton Ranger District office and Greenlee County Chamber of Commerce can advise you on this and other backcountry drives, such as the **Black Hills Backcountry Byway** (see special topic below), and hikes.

**Mule Creek Rd.** (AZ 78) winds into the piñon-juniper forests of the Big Lue Mountains east of town and continues into New Mexico. Begin at the "Three Way" junction 10 miles south of town. You can stay at **Black Jack Campground** (elev. 6,100 feet) about 11 miles in and at **Coal Creek Campground** (elev. 5,800 feet) five miles farther. These small campgrounds can usually be reached year-round; no water or fee.

## Accommodations and Food

**Rode Inn Motel** is at 186 S. Coronado Blvd. in south Clifton; $37.76 s, $43.17 d; tel. 865-4536. **Morenci Motel,** $40.30 s $46.66 d, six miles up the highway from Clifton, has the **Copperoom Restaurant;** tel. 865-4111. Other Morenci restaurants, including the **Kopper Kettle Kafe, Copper Willy's,** and **Dairy Queen** are located in the shopping center. A new **Super Wok** was to offer Chinese cuisine near the library. In Clifton you have a choice of **Cole's Pizza Parlor** (pizza, steak, and seafood) on

Hwy. 191, **PJ's Restaurant** (American and Mexican) at 307 S. Coronado Blvd. (US 191), or several fast-food places along the highway.

**Events**
**Horse races** take place during the spring. Drivers push their vehicles to the limit in the **Clifton Hill Climb,** a steep course in Ward's Canyon, on Labor Day weekend. The **Greenlee County Fair and Rodeo** is held during the first weekend of October.

**Shopping and Services**
Stock up on groceries at the **Phelps Dodge Mercantile** and shopping plaza, especially if headed north, as no supplies or gas are available for the next 89 miles. Limited medical care is available at Morenci's **24-hour urgent care and outpatient facility,** tel. 865-4511.

Morenci offers an outdoor **swimming pool,** tel. 865-2003; so does Clifton, tel. 865-9934. Play golf at the **Greenlee Country Club**'s nine-hole course in York Valley, 12 miles south of Clifton on AZ 75; tel. 687-1099.

**Information**
The **Greenlee County Chamber of Commerce** provides information on the history, sights, and facilities of the area. You can see old photos of Morenci, taken before it disappeared, and of Clifton in its busier days. Rockhounds can obtain directions to several agate digs. The office, at the old train depot, is open weekdays 9 a.m.-4 p.m.; Box 1237, Clifton, AZ 85533; tel. 865-3313.

For hiking and camping info on the southern half of the Coronado Trail, see the **Clifton Ranger District** office of the U.S. Forest Service at Three Way, 10 miles south of Clifton; it's open Mon.-Fri. 8 a.m.-4:30 p.m.; Box HCl-773, Duncan, AZ 85534; tel. 687-1301/1314. Clifton's **public library** is across from the county courthouse at 102 School St., tel. 865-2461; Morenci's **public library** is in the Phelps Dodge Mercantile and shopping plaza, tel. 865-2775.

# THE LOW DESERT

## SAFFORD

Surrounded by the rugged Pinaleno, Gila, and Peloncillo mountain ranges, Safford (elev. 2,900 feet) lies in the broad Gila River Valley. Hohokam, Mogollon, and Anasazi sites in the valley date from about 300 B.C. to A.D. 1200. The Apache arrived about 1700 and managed to discourage European settlers until 1874. In that year four Civil War veterans founded a town named after Anson P. Safford, territorial Arizona's third governor. Five years later Mormon settlers arrived to farm the valley, founding Smithville, later renamed Pima. Mormons also settled in Thatcher, Central, Eden, Graham, and Bryce.

The Jewish merchant Isadore Elkan Solomon arrived in a town later named for him. He opened a store and other businesses, then helped start Gila Valley Bank, which later evolved into the Valley National Bank.

Though small, Safford (pop. 8,010) serves as the Graham County seat and as the main retail and service center for a large area of southeastern Arizona. Though cotton, especially in Pima, is king, the irrigated bottomland also supports wheat, barley, alfalfa, and other crops.

Visitor highlights include the scenic drive to 10,000-foot Mt. Graham (hiking, fishing, and camping), Aravaipa and Bonita canyons (wildlife and scenery along a perennial stream), the Galiuro Wilderness (for adventurous hikers), Graham County and Pima historical museums, and Thatcher's Museum of Anthropology (archaeological exhibits).

**Discovery Park**
Safford's new science, culture, and education center is under continuous construction at the south end of town. The visitor will enjoy interactive exhibits about astronomy, mining, history, and agriculture when Discovery Park is fully developed. The Governor Aker Building is already open to the public with exhibits ranging from primitive concepts of the universe to modern-day research laboratories. The visitor can enjoy a 12-passenger spaceship simulator for a tour of the solar system, view the surrounding area through the world's largest Camera Obscura,

and observe the universe through a 20-inch astronomical telescope. A major planetarium will eventually be added. Long-term plans include additional buildings with displays on mining and agriculture. From Hwy. 70 take 20th St. south to where it curves west into 32nd Ave. at the entrance to Discovery Park. Admission rates will depend on how many of the exhibits are open; tel. 428-6260.

### Graham County Historical Museum

Period rooms show different aspects of life in the pioneer days. Exhibits of Indian artifacts illustrate the area's long prehistoric history. It's open Monday and Tuesday 1-4 p.m.; no phone.

### Cotton Gin Tours

All that cotton in Graham County fields comes to two cotton gins in the Safford area. Both offer tours during the ginning season, from early October through December and sometimes into January. Call in advance to **Safford Valley Cotton Growers Co-op,** off US 191 in Safford, tel. 428-0714; or **Glenbar Gin** just west of Pima, tel. 485-9255.

### Accommodations and Campgrounds

Safford's seven motels line US 70, also signed as Fifth St., and Thatcher Boulevard. Each motel includes air-conditioning. The more expensive locations also have swimming pools—you may want both in summer, when highs push 100 degrees.

**Roper Lake State Park,** six miles south of downtown, has pleasant campsites on the shore of a small lake. It's open all year with showers; $3 day use or $8 camping, $13 with water and electric hookups; showers; tel. 428-6760. **Coronado National Forest** has several campgrounds ($5-6) in the cool forests atop Mt. Graham.

RVers can stay at **Red Lamp Mobile Home Park,** 3341 Main St., tel. 428-3382; **Desert Hill Mobile Home Park,** 326 Eighth Ave., tel. 428-1930; **Sunrise Village Mobile Home Park,** 700 E. Hollywood, with an executive golf course, tel. 428-7676; **Safford East Mobile Home Park,** one mile east on US 70, tel. 428-4444; **Tower Mobile Park,** 1.5 miles east on US 70, tel. 428-6997; **Ivanho Mobile Home Park,** three miles east on US 70, tel. 428-3828; and **Lexington Pines Adult RV Resort,** 1535 Thatcher Blvd., tel. 428-7570.

# BLACK HILLS BACKCOUNTRY BYWAY

You can enjoy this 21-mile backcountry scenic drive in dry weather if you have a 2WD high-clearance vehicle. Start from south of Clifton or east of Safford on Hwy. 191. At each end of the drive visitors will find a National Backcountry Byway kiosk with historical information and current road conditions. Based on mileage from the Safford (southwestern) end of the drive, a BLM brochure describes history, geology, and natural resources at various points along the drive. Audiocassettes that interpret the colorful history of the byway are available from the chambers of commerce in Clifton and Safford and from the BLM in Safford. Visitors with long trailers or motorhomes should leave them at the information kiosks.

The Black Hills make up the northern end of the Peloncillo Mountains, a range of volcanic origin with alluvial sand and gravel on its flanks. Both ends of the byway are on the sand and gravel with volcanic rock in the higher, central part of the drive. Lava flows consist of dark gray and gray brown andesite, rhyolite, and dacite interlayered with multicolored ash both from windblown falls and ash flows. Ash deposits vary from red to yellow to gray.

The low sections of the drive pass through a desert scrub plant community with much creosote. Animals include diamondback rattlesnakes, whip-tailed lizards, kangaroo rats, and various species of raptors. Higher elevations include desert grasslands populated by Gambel's quail. The highest section of the drive exhibits juniper, piñon pine, and oaks. Here you may see mule deer, javelinas, black-tailed rattlesnakes, and migratory birds.

The drive offers few facilities. At 17.1 miles from the southwestern end you'll find picnic areas at both ends of the historic Old Safford Bridge, built in 1918. This area serves as a launch point for kayaks, rafts, and canoes to float on the Gila River through the Gila Box Riparian National Conservation Area to Bonita Creek, 19 miles downstream. Another picnic area lies midway through the drive at a high point overlooking the Gila River Canyon. While there are no developed campgrounds, dispersed camping is permitted.

*harvesting desert cotton*

## Food

The **Branding Iron** serves up Western-style dinners about 2.5 miles north of downtown; go north on Eighth Ave., then left on River Rd.; closed Monday; tel. 428-6252. **Golden Corral Family Steak House** is another popular place for Western food, in Gila Valley Plaza on W. US 70; tel. 428-4744.

For Italian dining try **Aria's Ristorante Italiano,** at 540 E. Hwy. 70; tel. 428-2742. For Chinese cuisine, try the **Super Wok** at 1275 Thatcher Blvd., tel. 348-9452; or **Jumbo Chinese Restaurant,** 817 W. Thatcher Blvd., tel. 428-2888. Dine Mexican at **Casa Mañana,** corner of US 70 and First Ave., tel. 428-3170; **El Charro,** 628 Main St., tel. 428-4134; **El Coronado,** 409 Main St., tel. 428-7755; **Roberto's,** 338 Main, tel. 428-1882; **Chalo's La Casa Reynoso,** 611 6th Ave.; tel. 348-9941; or **La Paloma,** five miles east in Solomon, tel. 428-2094.

You'll find supermarkets and chain restaurants in the Mt. Graham and Gila Valley shopping centers on US 70 west of downtown.

## Events

The **Old-Time Fiddlers Convention** livens up the town in the third week of February. **Sno-Bird Roundup** features dances, crafts, and food. **Horse racing** takes place at the county fairgrounds on the last weekend of March and the first weekend of April. **Bylas Rodeo and Pow Wow** in April occurs 43 miles northwest on the San Carlos Apache Indian Reservation. The **Gila Valley Rodeo** provides excitement in August.

The **Graham County Fair** features entertainment, local agricultural accomplishments, and crafts in October. The weekend after Thanksgiving you can shop at the **Cowboy Christmas Arts and Crafts Festival.** Contact the chamber of commerce for additional info; tel. 428-2511.

## Recreation

You'll find an outdoor public **swimming pool,** open from Memorial Day to Labor Day, in Firth Park behind the chamber of commerce at 1111 Thatcher Boulevard. **Tennis** players can use the lighted courts at Graham County Park, two miles south on US 191, or at the junior high school, 520 11th Street. **Graham County Park** also offers racquetball, basketball, ball fields, a jogging track, and picnicking; all but the track are lit for night use. Play golf year-round at the

18-hole **Mount Graham Golf Course,** four miles southwest of town. Turn south on 20th Ave. and follow signs; tel. 428-1260.

## Services

The **post office** occupies the corner of US 70 and Fifth Ave.; tel. 428-0220. **Mount Graham Community Hospital** lies southwest of downtown at 1600 S. 20th Ave.; tel. 348-4000. Hikers can purchase **topo maps** at Consolidated Title, 624 Main St.; tel. 428-0180.

Feeling run-down with too many aches and pains? Then take the waters at **Kachina Mineral Springs,** a hot springs spa six miles south of Safford; tel. 428-7212. Hot baths are also available at **Essence of Tranquility,** five miles south of Safford at 6074 S. Lebanon Loop Rd.; tel. 428-9312.

## Information

The **Graham County Chamber of Commerce** is very helpful and well stocked with literature and maps; it's open Mon.-Fri. 8 a.m.-5 p.m. and shorter hours on weekends. The office is on the main highway just west of downtown at 1111 Thatcher Blvd., Safford, AZ 85546; tel. 428-2511. **Safford Ranger Station** of the Coronado National Forest has travel and recreation info on Mt. Graham Scenic Drive in the Pinaleno Mountains and the Galiuro Wilderness, as well as on the lesser-known ranges of Santa Teresa and Winchester; it's open Mon.-Fri. 8 a.m.-5 p.m.; on the third floor of the post office downtown at the corner of US 70 and Fifth Ave.; or write Box 709, Safford, AZ 85548; tel. 428-4150. Plans were for this office to move to Discovery Park at 1651 32nd St., Safford, AZ 85546.

If visiting Aravaipa Canyon, you'll need a permit from the **Bureau of Land Management** (BLM) office. The office also can supply recreational information including an interactive computer guide. Rockhounds can pick up brochures about the Black Hills (between Safford and Clifton) and Round Mountain (south of Duncan) areas, home to fire agates and other gemstones. The BLM office is at 711 14th Ave., Safford, AZ 85546, across the road from the high school. It's open weekdays 7:45 a.m.-4:15 p.m.; tel. 428-4040. You can also get permits and info by mail.

The **public library** is at 808 Seventh Ave.; tel. 428-1531. The **Alumni Library** at Eastern Arizona College is both a public library and media center; on the northwest corner of Church St. and College Ave. in Thatcher; it's closed early July to mid-August; tel. 428-8304.

## Transport

**Greyhound** buses stop several times a day in each direction on a route between El Paso, Texas, and Phoenix. The station is at the corner of 404 5th St. and Hwy. 70; tel. 428-2150.

# VICINITY OF SAFFORD

## Bonita Creek

This perennial stream flows through a pretty canyon in the Gila Mountains, about 25 miles northeast of Safford. Drivers with high-clearance vehicles can drive up Bonita Creek for several miles. Summer flash floods can take out the road, which has many stream crossings, so it's a good idea to first check conditions and routes with the BLM office.

Look for prehistoric cliff dwellings—most served as granaries—in the canyon. Birding and hiking are best on weekdays. You can camp almost anywhere—just keep well above the washes to avoid being surprised by a flash flood.

From Safford cross the Gila River north on Eighth Avenue and turn right at the "Y" onto Airport Road. From there travel six more miles until you reach a Bonita Creek BLM sign and turn left onto that dirt road. Then drive five miles along the Gila River to the confluence, keeping right at a fork signed Bonita Creek. The other fork will take you to a midpoint of Bonita Creek. A restored pioneer cabin from the 1920s marks the confluence. The first two miles up the creek are relatively easy to drive. Farther upstream the route becomes rougher with the road almost nonexistent. Washout of the old road resulted in new routing, partially along the city pipeline. Stop by the BLM in town for a map of the drive. The lower 15 miles of Bonita Creek and a 23-mile section of the Gila River, including the Gila Box, receive protection as the **Gila Box Riparian National Conservation Area.**

## Safford-Morenci Trail

Pioneer ranchers and farmers built this trail in about 1874 to haul their products to the booming mines of the Morenci area. The trail fell into disuse with the advent of the automobile during the early 1900s; the Youth Conservation Corps, working with the BLM, restored and marked the route.

Hikers and horseback riders will enjoy the variety of desert and riparian environments along the way. The trail is 14 miles one-way with an elevation range of 3,700 to 6,200 feet. Bonita Creek, crossed about midway, makes a good camping spot, though the BLM recommends carrying drinking water for the whole trip. Roads to both the west and east trailheads may require 4WD vehicles in wet weather. Contact the BLM office in Safford for maps and current hiking conditions.

## Museum of Anthropology

Thatcher, just three miles northwest of Safford, is the home of Eastern Arizona College, a two-year school. The school museum features an excellent collection of old Indian pottery, axes, arrowheads, and jewelry. Visit the museum library to learn more about archaeology and anthropology. There are special displays for children including hands-on exhibits involving firemaking and corn grinding. Hours are Mon.-Fri. 9 a.m.-4 p.m. during the school year (early September to mid-May); admission is free; tel. 428-8310. The museum is near the corner of Main St. (US 70) and College Avenue.

## Eastern Arizona Museum and Historical Society (Pima)

You can learn about the Indians and pioneers of the area from this large collection. Open Wed.-Fri. 2-4 p.m. and Saturday 1-4 p.m.; visits can be arranged at other times too; admission is free; tel. 485-2288. Exhibits are sequestered in an early Pima town hall on US 70, nine miles west of Safford. Pima also features a motel and cafe.

## Cluff Ranch Wildlife Area

The Arizona Game and Fish Department maintains the 788-acre Cluff Ranch as a wildlife sanctuary and recreation area. Streams from Mt. Graham fill two ponds totaling 15 acres and support lush riparian vegetation. Anglers catch trout

*Bonita Creek*

in winter and largemouth bass, channel catfish, crappie, and bluegill year-round. Boats—oar, sail, or electric—can be used. Visitors may camp at the ponds; no facilities. Birding is good and you're almost sure to see some free-roaming deer or javelina. Orphaned or injured animals are brought here for eventual release into the wild. Strips of grain crops are planted for wildlife.

Cluff Ranch is open all year; tel. 485-9430. From US 70 in Pima, nine miles west of Safford, turn south 1.5 miles on Main St.; the road curves west and becomes Cottonwood Rd.; continue another 0.4 mile, then turn south and drive 4.5 miles.

## Roper Lake State Park

The shores of this pretty lake offer camping, picnicking, swimming, and fishing. Anglers can launch boats (electric motors okay) and try for catfish, bass, bluegill, and crappie; trout in winter. Hedonists can relax in the hot tub, fed by a natural spring. A short nature trail begins near the hot tub. Roper Lake lies six miles south of Safford off US 191.

**Dankworth Ponds** day-use area also offers good picnicking and fishing; three miles farther south on US 191. Dankworth Village, perched atop the hill above the ponds, contains replicas of Native American dwellings designed to interpret the area's cultural history. Admission fees cover both areas: $3 day use or $8 camping ($13 with water and electric hookups); showers; group sites available. Open all year; tel. 428-6760.

## Mount Graham Drive
Mount Graham (10,720 feet), in the Pinaleno Mountains, soars above Safford nearly 8,000 feet—the greatest vertical rise of any mountain in Arizona. Visitors can enjoy the views, cool breezes, hiking, picnicking, camping, and fishing.

A good road, called the Swift Trail Parkway, ascends the eastern slopes through a remarkable range of vegetation and animal life. Starting among cactus, creosote bush, and mesquite of the lower Sonoran Desert, you'll soon arrive at pygmy forests of juniper, oak, and piñon pine. Higher on the twisting road, you'll enter dense forests of ponderosa pine, Douglas fir, aspen, and white fir. Thick stands of Engelmann spruce dominate the highest ridges. The Mt. Graham red squirrel, Mt. Graham pocket gopher, white-bellied vole, and Rusby's mountain fleabane (a wild daisy) are found only in the Pinaleno Mountains.

Fire-lookout towers on two peaks offer superb views. **Heliograph Peak** (elev. 10,028 feet) offers some of the best panoramas in the region; on a clear day you can see most of southeastern Arizona. The 2.2-mile road to the lookout is gated, but feel free to walk up. The Army built a heliograph station here in 1886 to relay messages to troops using mirrors and sunlight.

**Columbine Visitor Information Station,** at mile 29 on the Swift Trail, is in an old CCC building that once housed forest workers and firefighters. The facility offers a variety of interpretive exhibits, brochures, publications, and current information about area attractions from April 15-Nov. 15, weather permitting.

**Webb Peak** (elev. 10,086 feet) offers a better view of the Gila River Valley and surrounding mountains; you can reach it by ascending a 1.7-mile gated road on foot.

Six developed campgrounds all have drinking water and are open from mid-May to late October. Fees are $5, $6 at Riggs Lake and

*Mount Graham and the Pinalenos, from Roper Lake State Park*

Columbine Corrals. Campground elevations range from 6,700 feet at Arcadia to 9,300 feet at Soldier Creek. Anglers can camp and try for trout in Riggs Lake, near the end of the Swift Trail.

To drive the 34.5-mile-long **Swift Trail Parkway,** go seven miles south from Safford on US 191, or 26 miles north from I-10, and turn west at the sign. The first 27.5 miles are paved, followed by seven miles of gravel. This last section of road is gated Nov. 15-April 15 because of snow and to protect red squirrel habitat. The drive from Safford and back takes about 4.5 hours. Stock up on gas and supplies before leaving town.

A road guide to the features of the Swift Trail and maps of the Coronado National Forest (Pinaleno Range) are available from the Safford Chamber of Commerce or the U.S. Forest Service in Safford. Hikers can choose among many trails but should be prepared for steep sections. Pick up a leaflet featuring campground and trail descriptions in the Safford Forest Service office or at the chamber of commerce.

**Emerald Peak** is the site of a series of large telescopes under construction for Mt. Graham International Observatory. Initial construction includes the Columbus Project, a 12-meter equivalent binocular telescope, a 10-meter Submillimeter Telescope, and a 1.8-meter Lennon Telescope.

Protecting red squirrel habitat is a major concern in the development of the telescope site. The side road to High Peak is closed to protect the red squirrel, so be sure to check with the Forest Service if planning a trip near the summit of Mt. Graham.

## Muleshoe Ranch
## Cooperative Management Area

Rugged and brush-covered, the Galiuro Mountains rise above the desert in two parallel ranges. Prominent peaks along the east ridge are Bassett (7,671 feet), Kennedy (7,540 feet), and Sunset (7,094 feet); along the west ridge stand Rhodes (7,116 feet), Maverick (6,990 feet), and Kielburg (6,880 feet). The terrain is so rough and steep that hikers must stick mostly to the network of trails. The 10 trails total 95 miles; you're not likely to see many other hikers in this little-known range.

The Galiuros lie southwest of Safford, on the other side of the Pinalenos. The main trailheads are on the east slopes: Ash Creek, High Creek, and Deer Creek. Deer Creek Trailhead, near the end of Forest Road 253, is popular and sometimes accessible by car.

Vegetation changes with elevation and slope orientation: the south and west slopes feature dense growths of manzanita, live oak, and other brush, with juniper, piñon, and oak trees higher up; the higher canyons and north-facing slopes are wooded with Arizona cypress, ponderosa pine, Chihuahua pine, Mexican white pine, Douglas fir, and some white fir. Sycamore, alder, aspen, and other deciduous trees grow along streambanks. Mule deer, white-tailed deer, black bear, javelina, and mountain lion roam the rugged hillsides and canyons.

The old Power's cabin (built 1910), mine shafts, and ore-milling machinery are visible in Rattlesnake Canyon. Power's Garden cabin, also in Rattlesnake Canyon, may be open to hikers.

Streams usually dry up during late spring and early summer. The more reliable springs include Power's Garden, Mud, Corral, Holdout, Cedar, Jackson, Juniper, and South Field.

The Bureau of Land Management maintains the 6,600-acre **Redfield Canyon Wilderness** adjacent to the southern end of the Galiuro Wilderness. Redfield Canyon offers scenic hiking through a narrow red-walled chasm.

The Muleshoe area, outside the wilderness at the south end of the Galiuros, has perennial streams; the Nature Conservancy operates the **Muleshoe Preserve** here. The 4WD Jackson Cabin Rd. (Forest Route 691) provides access from the south. See the Forest Service office in Safford for latest water, trail, and road conditions.

## Aravaipa Canyon Wilderness

A jewel in the desert, Aravaipa Canyon is renowned for its scenery and variety of wildlife. The waters of Aravaipa Creek flow all year, a rare occurrence in the desert, providing an oasis for birds and other animals. Giant ash, sycamore, and willow trees shade the canyon floor. Rocky hillsides, dotted with saguaro cactus and other desert plants, lie only a few steps from the lush vegetation along the creek. Birders

*Alchesay, Apache chief and U.S. Army scout*

have sighted more than 200 species in the canyon, including the bald eagle and peregrine falcon. Mule deer, javelina, and coyote frequent the area; you might even see a mountain lion or bighorn sheep. Remember to keep an eye out for any of several species of rattlesnakes.

Although there's no established trail, hiking is quite easy along the gravel creekbed. Tributary canyons invite side trips—Hell Hole Canyon is especially enchanting. Tennis shoes work well as footwear, as you'll wade frequently across the creek. Grassy terraces make inviting campsites.

To visit the 11-mile canyon—even for dayhikes—you must get a permit from the BLM office in Safford. You can make reservations up to three months in advance by phone or mail; this is especially important for the very popular spring and autumn weekends; be sure to cancel if you won't be coming or if any of your party cancels. Only 50 people per day are permitted in the canyon. The BLM has a two-night (three-day) stay limit. Horseback riders can visit on daytrips only, with not more than five animals per group. Pets are prohibited. Visitors must sign in and pay a fee of $1.50 per person per day at one of the trailheads.

Trailheads, though only 11 trail miles apart, require 160 miles of driving from one to the other. The East Trailhead is reached by Klondyke Rd. (turn off US 70 about 15 miles northwest of Safford) or Fort Grant Rd. (turn off US 191 either 19 miles south of Safford or 17 miles north of I-10's Wilcox exit). Follow signs to Aravaipa Canyon Wilderness; don't go to the settlement monikered Aravaipa. A ranger is stationed in Klondyke, 10 miles before the trailhead. The town of Klondyke was established by two veteran Yukon prospectors just after the turn of the century. Currently, the only business is the general store (not BLM affiliated) where supplies are reasonably priced considering the remoteness of the area. In addition, accommodations are available at $35-40 per person as well as hot showers for nonguests at $2; tours of the area can be arranged; tel. 828-3335. **Fourmile Campground** (drinking water; free; a $4 fee is planned in the future) is nearby; turn left just after Klondyke. You can also camp along Turkey Creek Canyon (no facilities), a pretty tributary of Aravaipa Creek near the east trailhead.

The West Trailhead is much closer to Phoenix (120 miles) and Tucson (70 miles); you can stay in Brandenburg Campsite (no facilities) along the county road three miles back from the trailhead parking area (Aravaipa permit holders only) the night before you enter the wilderness. About 11 miles south of Winkelman on AZ 77, turn east and drive 12 miles on Aravaipa Rd. to the ranger station and trailhead.

## SAN CARLOS APACHE INDIAN RESERVATION

The San Carlos Reservation offers climate and scenery for everyone: cool pine forests in the northeast, grasslands and wooded ridges in the center, cactus-studded desert in the southwest. The Black and Salt rivers form a natural boundary with the White Mountain Apache Indian Reservation to the north. Much of the land is fine cattle-grazing country and supports large tribal herds.

You can reach San Carlos Lake and Seneca Lake by paved highways, but roads to other recreation areas may be too rough for cars, especially after rains or snowmelt. You need a Recreation Access Permit ($5) to venture onto back roads or trails unless you have a fishing, camping, or special use permit.

## San Carlos

This small community is very much a government town. Neat rows of office buildings and apartments line the main street. Here you'll find most tribal offices, post office, grocery store, San Carlos Cafe, and service station.

Check the store and trading posts for Apache crafts, such as baskets, beadwork, cradle boards, and peridot jewelry. Peridot is a deep yellow-green, transparent olivine mineral; the cut stones, sold mounted or loose, resemble emeralds.

### Events

Look for Apache dances, crafts, foods, and cowboys showing off their riding skills at the **Bylas** and **San Carlos Rodeos** in April and at the **Veteran's Memorial Fair and Rodeo** on Veteran's Day weekend in November. **Traditional dances** are held during the summer; call the tribal office for dates and places; tel. 475-2361. The **Sunrise Ceremony** occurs most frequently, usually on summer weekends. It marks the coming-of-age of young women.

### San Carlos Lake

The 19,500-acre lake measures 23 miles long by two miles wide, making San Carlos the largest lake lying completely within Arizona. All this water is held back by 880-foot-high Coolidge Dam, dedicated by President Coolidge himself in 1930.

**San Carlos Lake Marina,** two miles north of the dam, provides information, permits, fishing supplies, groceries, snacks, and gasoline; tel. 475-2756. A trailer park with hookups is situated next to the marina. **Soda Canyon Point Campground** is also nearby. Other campgrounds lie on both the north and south sides of the lake.

Though famed mostly for its prolific bass population, San Carlos Lake has produced state-record specimens of flathead catfish, crappie, and bluegill. The lake and marina, at an elevation of 2,425 feet, are 13 miles south from the town of San Carlos.

### Other Recreation Areas

**Talkalai Lake:** Chief Talkalai served as an Indian scout with the Army and helped capture Geronimo. Talkalai Lake has given up some sizable largemouth bass, flathead and channel catfish, crappie, and bluegill. Gas motors up to eight h.p. are permitted. The lake and campground lie about three miles north of the town of San Carlos.

**Cassadore Springs:** This small picnic area and campground features spring water and lies about 12 miles north of the town of San Carlos.

**Point of Pines:** The 35-acre trout lake and campground (no drinking water) are in the eastern part of the reservation. From US 70, five miles east of the San Carlos turnoff, head northeast 55 miles on Indian Route 1000 to the campground; all but the last five miles or so are paved.

**Seneca Park:** Anglers catch trout, catfish, and largemouth bass in 27-acre Seneca Lake. The lake and campground are in the northwest corner of the reservation just off US 60/AZ 77, 33 miles north of Globe and five miles south of the Salt River Canyon bridge.

### Camping and Picnicking

In winter you'll probably want to stick to the low country around San Carlos Lake, then head for the hills in summer. Campsites are usually open all year. You're also generally welcome to camp outside established sites if you have the appropriate camping or special use permit. Camping and picnicking permits ($5 per day) must be bought beforehand. One day permits are good 24 hours—from midnight to midnight. Avoid camping near stock ponds. In summer, observe fire restrictions.

### Fishing, Boating, and Hunting

Fishing is the big attraction for most visitors—San Carlos Lake is known as Arizona's hottest bass spot. Farther north you can catch trout, catfish, or bass in Point of Pines Lake, Seneca Lake, the Black River, and over 100 stock ponds. Licenses cost $7 per day or $75 yearly; free if under 12 and with a permit-holding adult. Boat permits are $3 per day or $30 yearly. Water skiing permits are $10 per day or $75 yearly; free if under age 12 with a permit-holding adult. Gasoline motors can be used at San Carlos and Talkalai lakes; at other lakes you're restricted to a single electric motor.

In some areas, such as the Black and Salt rivers, you need a special use permit for fishing, hiking, camping, or river rafting—$10 per person per day. You may fish on both sides of the Black and Salt rivers with either San Carlos or White Mountain permits, but permits are otherwise not interchangeable. Hunters can pursue big and small game with the appropriate licenses. Certain areas of the reservation may be open only to tribal members. Some hunts require licensed guides.

**Permits and Information**

Permits are needed for most reservation activities. For permits and the latest regulations, fa-

cilities, fees, and road conditions, contact the **San Carlos Recreation and Wildlife Department** office at the corner of Moon Base Rd. and US 70 between Mileposts 272 and 273, 1.5 miles east of the AZ 170 junction for San Carlos; it's open Mon.-Fri. 8 a.m.-5 p.m.; Box 97, San Carlos, AZ 85550; tel. 475-2653/2343.

Other sources for permits include **Noline's Country Store,** nearby on US 70, tel. 475-2334; **Basha's,** in the town of San Carlos, tel. 475-2391; **San Carlos Lake Marina,** tel. 475-2756; **Pinky's Bait & Tackle,** Pima, tel. 428-5611; **Bob Keene's Store,** Fort Thomas, tel. 485-2261; **Tiger Mart,** Globe, tel. 425-2640; **Tempe Marine,** Mesa, tel. 844-0165; and **Dripping Springs Stop & Go,** Winkelman, tel. 356-7330.

**1.** Mission San Xavier del Bac; **2.** Pima County Courthouse, Tucson; **3.** Desert View Watchtower, Grand Canyon National Park; **4.** Ned A. Hatathli Center at Navajo Community College, Tsaile; **5.** Tumacacori National Monument, south of Tucson (all photos by B. Weir)

**THE GRAND CANYON**
**1.** from Desert View on the South Rim; **2.** on the Bright Angel Trail; **3.** view from near Grandeur Point on the South Rim; **4.** Angel's Window at Cape Royal on the North Rim; **5.** the Colorado River from Desert View (all photos by B. Weir)

# SOUTHERN ARIZONA
## INTRODUCTION

Southern Arizona is a sea of desert and grasslands, with mountains rising like islands. Giant saguaro and other hardy plants cover the Sonoran Desert from Tucson west to the Colorado River Valley. Desert grasslands fill most valleys to the east. Climate varies dramatically with elevation. Expect mild winters and very hot summers on the desert, slightly cooler and wetter weather on the grasslands. Four ranges—the Santa Catalinas, Santa Ritas, Huachucas, and Chiricahuas—have peaks over 9,000 feet where you could stand up to your neck in snow during the winter. Mount Lemmon, in the Santa Catalinas near Tucson, offers downhill ski runs. Astonishing varieties of birds, animals, and plants find niches in southern Arizona's varied topography. Some species, such as the whiskered senita cactus and the colorful trogon bird, have migrated north from Mexico and are rarely seen elsewhere in the United States.

When the Spanish entered this region about 1539, they found several groups of natives, among them the warlike, nomadic Apache and the more settled and peaceful Tohono O'odham and Pima. Most of the Spanish, Pima, and Apache have left southern Arizona, but their legacy of culture, place names, and legends remains. The Old West lives on as well, in the dozens of abandoned mining camps, on the ranches where cowboys still work vast ranges, on the streets of Tombstone where the Earps and Doc Holliday shot it out with the Clantons. Allow time to explore southern Arizona. It's a big land of big attractions.

# TUCSON

Though the Old Pueblo, as it's known locally, is modern and lively, Tucson's Old West heritage will surprise you. Tucson (TOO-sawn) has some of the finest cultural offerings in Arizona—a large university, historic sites, and a great variety of restaurants and nightlife. Yet you can actually walk this city and see most of its sights.

Set in a desert valley at an elevation of 2,400 feet, Tucson ranks as the state's second-largest city, with a metropolitan population of 735,000. Summers are warm, but not as hot as those in Phoenix or Yuma. And cool Mt. Lemmon, at 9,157 feet, is just an hour's drive away. Temperatures peak in June and July with highs generally near 98° F and lows near 70°. Even in December and January it's spring-like, with average highs in the mid-60s and lows in the upper 30s. Of the 11 or so inches of annual rainfall, over half falls in the July to September rainy season.

Desert vegetation, with palo verde, cottonwood, and mesquite trees, is surprisingly lush. Many varieties of cacti display brilliant flowers from April to late May. The mountains ringing Tucson offer skiing in the winter and great hiking almost anytime. In just minutes, hikers can get out of town west to the Tucson Mountains, northeast to the Santa Catalinas, or east to the Rincons.

## HISTORY

Hohokam Indians farmed the valley floor as far back as A.D. 100. Pima and other Indian tribes had replaced the Hohokam long before the

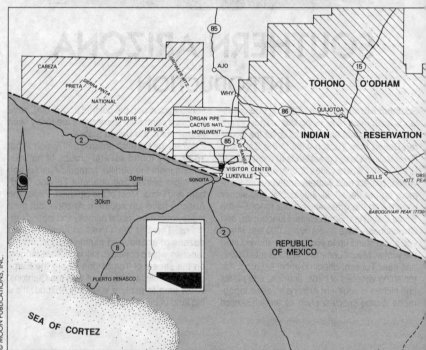

Spanish arrived in the 1500s. The first Spanish visitors found a Pima Indian village, Stjukshon (*stjuk* means "dark mountain"; *shon,* "foot of"), at the foot of Sentinel Peak, the hill with the large "A" now painted on it. The Spanish changed the name to "Tucson" when laying out the Presidio of San Agustín del Tucson in 1775.

Attacks by roving Apaches made fortifications necessary, so adobe walls 12 feet high and 750 feet long enclosed the new settlement. Mexico inherited Tucson from Spain after the 1821 revolution, but nothing much changed except the flag.

### Americans Arrive

Tucson joined the United States with the Gadsden Purchase in June 1854, but 21 months of boundary-marking and bureaucratic delays passed before the arrival of American officialdom in the form of the Army's First Dragoons. Although Apache continued to menace settlers and travelers, Americans steadily began to ar-

rive, and the Butterfield Overland Stagecoach soon opened service to Tucson.

To cope with the desert climate, Anglos adopted much of the food, building techniques, and other cultural apparatus of the Mexicans. The results of these practices, as well as of Anglo-Mexican intermarriage, are seen today in Tucson's cultural mix.

### Wars and the Wild West

Confederate cavalry under the command of Captain Sherrod Hunter captured Tucson in February 1862. Union troops led by Colonel James Carleton marched in from California two months later, clashing with the Confederates at Picacho Pass, on Butterfield Road about 42 miles northwest of Tucson. After this battle, the most westerly of the Civil War, the outnumbered Confederates retreated.

The 1860s were Tucson's Wild West years. Men rarely ventured unarmed onto the dusty streets, and shootouts occurred frequently. Still,

the town prospered, serving as the territorial capital from 1867 to 1877. By 1880, when the first train rolled in, the population had grown to over 7,000.

The Arizona Territorial University opened its doors in 1891 on land donated by a saloon-keeper and a pair of gamblers. Davis-Monthan Field brought Tucson into the aviation age and became an important training base during WW II. Many of the airmen and others passing through the city during those hectic years returned to settle here. With new postwar industries and the growth of tourism, the Old Pueblo has boomed ever since.

## HISTORIC WALKING TOUR

### Northern Section

The historic walking tour provides a look at the Spanish, Mexican, and Anglo legacies of Tucson. The **Tucson Museum of Art** is a convenient place to start. Its permanent collection is noted for Spanish colonial paintings and furnishings and for pre-Columbian artifacts from Latin America. Special exhibitions frequently appear, too. Docent tours are available; call for times. The large gift shop sells books, cards, and local crafts. Docent tours of the historic block are available through the museum from early October-Memorial Day at no charge; Wednesday and Thursday at 11 a.m. Open Mon.-Sat. 10 a.m.-4 p.m. and Sunday noon-4 p.m. (closed Monday in summer); admission is $2 adults, $1 students, $1 seniors 60 and over, free for children under 12, free admission on Tuesday; 140 N. Main; tel. 624-2333.

Walk west across the courtyard to view the **Edward Nye Fish House,** built by a rich businessman in 1868. It now houses the **Jack Goodman Pavilion of Western Art.** The building features 15-foot ceilings and solid adobe walls more than 2.5 feet thick; step inside to see the gallery's high-quality artwork, mostly from the Southwest. Next door to the Fish House is the **Stevens House,** part of which dates from 1856. Hiram Sanford Stevens was a good friend of Edward Fish, and much of Tucson's social life centered on their houses. The Stevens House is now the **Janos Restaurant.**

---

## TUCSON HISTORIC WALKING TOUR

1. Tucson Museum of Art
2. Edward Nye Fish House
3. Stevens House
4. La Casa Cordova
5. Old Town Artisans
6. Romero House
7. Corbett House/El Presidio wall plaque
8. Sam Hughes House
9. Steinfeld Mansion
10. El Charro
11. Stork's Nest
12. Governor's Corner
13. Pima County Courthouse
14. El Centro Cultural de Las Americas
15. St. Augustine Cathedral
16. *El Fronterizo*
17. Montijo House
18. Cushing Street Bar & Restaurant
19. America West Gallery
20. authentic Mexican tortilla factory
21. El Tiradito
22. Tucson Convention Center
23. Soza-Carrillo-Fremont House Museum
24. Samaniego House
25. La Placita Village
26. Garcés Footbridge
27. Allande Footbridge
28. El Presidio Park

---

Built of adobe, **La Casa Cordova** is one of the oldest houses in the area, dating from about 1848. Enter the courtyard from the back. Interior rooms have been restored to reflect life in the 1800s; Mexican exhibits are on display as well. November-March you can enjoy the *Nacimiento*—hundreds of figurines including more than 200 hand-painted terra cotta figurines that form tableaux illustrating biblical scenes as well as traditional Mexican life. La Casa Cordova is maintained by the adjacent Tucson Museum of Art and is open the same hours; free.

**Old Town Artisans** is a shop displaying arts and crafts by more than 150 artists representing Western, Indian, and Mexican styles. The sculptures, paintings, prints, and crafts are worth a look even if you're not buying. The front two rooms were built between 1862 and 1875 with

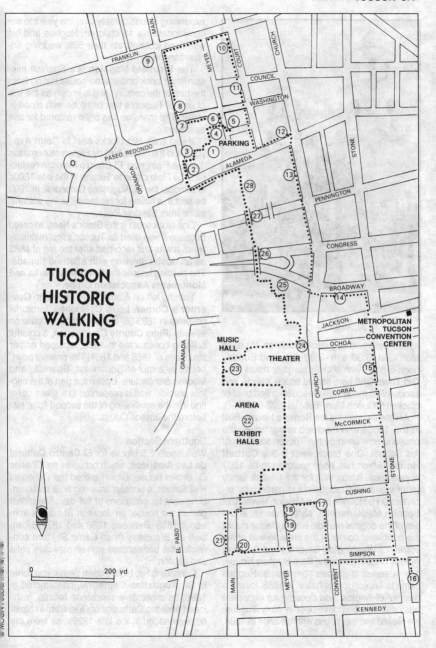

# TUCSON HISTORIC WALKING TOUR

FRANKLIN

MAIN

MEYER

COURT

CHURCH

COUNCIL

WASHINGTON

PASEO REDONDO

GRANADA

PARKING

ALAMEDA

STONE

PENNINGTON

CONGRESS

BROADWAY

METROPOLITAN TUCSON CONVENTION CENTER

JACKSON

OCHOA

MUSIC HALL

THEATER

CORRAL

McCORMICK

CHURCH

ARENA

EXHIBIT HALLS

CUSHING

STONE

GRANADA

EL PASO

MEYER

MAIN

CONVENT

SIMPSON

KENNEDY

0        200 yd

*St. Augustine Cathedral*

adobe walls and saguaro-rib ceilings. It's open Mon.-Sat. 9:30 a.m.-5:30 p.m. and Sunday noon-5 p.m., with shorter summer hours. The **Old Town Grill** here serves soups, salads, and sandwiches made with mesquite-grilled beef or chicken for lunch Mon.-Sat.; tel. 622-0351.

Across the street is the **Romero House.** Built in the 1860s and modified many times, the house is now used by the Tucson Museum of Art School. One block west is the **Corbett House,** which has been restored to its 1907 appearance. It was built for the Corbett family (after whom Hi Corbett field is named) by architect D.H. Holmes in the Mission Revival, or Spanish Mediterranean, style; it stands at the site of the original presidio wall; a plaque marks the northwest corner of the presidio wall at the corner of Washington St. and Main Avenue. Across Washington is the **Sam Hughes House,** now a series of garden apartments. Hughes came to Tucson for his health in 1858, joining a handful of Anglos, and became an important businessman and developer in early Tucson. He moved into this house with his bride in 1864,

expanding it considerably over the years to accommodate his 15 children. Hughes and his wife lived to celebrate their 50th wedding anniversary here.

The **Steinfeld Mansion** is a Spanish mission-style brick-and-stucco house dating from the turn of the century, and is known as the site of one of Tucson's first bathtubs with piped-in water. The mansion has been restored for use as offices.

If you walk two blocks east to Court Ave., you'll find the house built by French stonemason Jules le Flein, now **El Charro** Mexican restaurant. Le Flein came to Tucson in the late 1800s to remodel the St. Augustine Cathedral. In 1900 he built this house for his family, using volcanic stone from Sentinel Peak.

One block south is the **Stork's Nest,** so called because it was used as Tucson's first maternity ward. It was first recorded after the fire of 1883 as an adobe dwelling with attached ramada. The building houses the **Southwest Parks and Monuments Association Office.**

Turning left on Alameda, you come to **Governor's Corner.** Louis C. Hughes, territorial governor in 1893-96, lived in an adobe house on this site. **Pima County Courthouse,** a colorful building constructed in 1928, replaced earlier structures of 1868 and 1881. The present courthouse is a mix of Southwest, Spanish, and Moorish architecture. Upstairs, a part of the original presidio wall is preserved in a glass case; find it in the south wing of the second floor, just before the Justice Courts.

### Southern Section
Walk south 2.5 blocks for **El Centro Cultural de Las Americas,** which occupies the Charles O. Brown House. Brown owned the Congress Hall Saloon, a popular watering hole and gambling spot for politicians of the day. The oldest part of the house, on Jackson St., dates from about 1858. Between 1868 and 1877 Brown built on Broadway (then Camp St.) and connected the two sections with an attractive patio and garden.

Continuing two blocks down Stone, you come to **St. Augustine Cathedral,** constructed in 1896. Its impressive sandstone facade, fashioned after the Cathedral of Querétaro in Mexico, was added in the late 1920s, as were the stained-glass windows. A bronze statue of St. Augustine stands watch above the doorway.

The large concrete building at the corner of Stone and Cushing St., the Tucson Police Department, is not part of the historic tour, but you may wish to stop by and see the lobby display of antique police equipment and memorabilia of John Dillinger, including one of his guns.

Four more blocks down Stone is the former office of *El Fronterizo* newspaper. Carlos Y. Velasco began publishing a Spanish-language newspaper here about 1878. Around on Cushing St. is **Montijo House,** which preserves the name of the well-known Mexican ranching family that once owned it. The house was completed during the Civil War, then remodeled in the 1890s in an ornate Victorian style.

The **Cushing Street Bar and Restaurant** features attractive 1880s decor. Joseph Ferrin operated a general store and lived here about 100 years ago. Next door is **America West Gallery,** home in the 1860s to rancher Francisco Carrillo. The well-preserved house contains exotic antiques and primitive art gathered from many countries. The patio features a collection of Mexican millstones. The gallery is open Mon.-Fri. 10 a.m.-4 p.m.; tel. 623-4091. Around the corner on Main is **a traditional Mexican flour tortilla factory;** pick up fresh tortillas or just watch them being made.

**El Tiradito,** or Wishing Shrine, commemorates a tragic love triangle. The story has many versions, but one account tells of a love affair between young Juan Olivera and his mother-in-law. Juan was caught and killed by his father-in-law on this spot in 1880. Because of his sins, the dead Juan could not be laid in consecrated ground, and so was buried where he fell. The pious lit candles and prayed for his soul at the site. Later, parents came to pray for their errant daughters. The custom then developed that anyone could light a candle on the grave and make any kind of wish. If the candle burns to its base, the wish will be granted. The shrine is said to be the only one in North America dedicated to a sinner.

Follow the sidewalk around the Exhibit Hall and Arena of the Tucson Convention Center to the **Soza-Carrillo-Fremont House Museum.** Its adobe building, constructed by the Soza family in about 1880 and subsequently owned by the Carrillo family, was saved in 1969 when surrounding houses were torn down. The old structure takes its name from the fifth territorial governor, John C. Fremont, who rented it in 1881. Inside you can imagine the life of a wealthy Tucson family in the 1880s. Tour guides explain the architectural features of the house. Four different types of ceiling were used: saguaro rib, ocotillo, painted cloth, and redwood. It's open Wed.-Sat. 10 a.m.-4 p.m. and admission is free; 151 S. Granada Ave. in the Tucson Convention Center between the Music Hall and Arena; tel. 622-0956.

Staff at the Fremont House Museum lead guided tours of El Presidio Historic District on Saturday mornings, Oct.-April, lasting about two hours; $4. Call for reservations and times.

The building on the right as you leave the Fremont House is the **Tucson Convention Center Music Hall.** Walk up the steps alongside into an oasis of gardens, trees, and fountains. The small building ahead to the east is the **Leo Rich Theatre.** To the right is the giant **Arena,** featuring exhibits and sporting events. Just be-

*El Tiradito: love never dies*

yond the theater is **Samaniego House,** built in the 1840s. Mariano G. Samaniego, a stage-line owner, rancher, and local politician, purchased the place about 1880. His well-preserved house, with adobe walls and saguaro-ribbed ceilings, is now a restaurant.

Follow the map around through **La Placita Village,** a group of modern offices and shops designed to resemble a Mexican marketplace. Continue on to the **Garcés Footbridge** across Congress St., then the **Allande Footbridge** across Pennington St. to **El Presidio Park.** These modern bridges honor early Spaniards. Francisco Garcés, an explorer and Franciscan priest, was the first missionary to visit the Pima Indian village at the base of Sentinel Peak. Pedro Allande, first resident commander of the Tucson presidio, once led a spirited defense against 600 warring Apache. Despite a severe leg wound, he continued to direct his 20 presidial soldiers, eventually saving the settlement.

El Presidio Park was known as Plaza de las Armas in the original presidio. Soldiers drilled and held holiday fiestas on this spot 200 years ago. The soldiers have gone, but residents still enjoy fiestas. The park is a quiet spot to rest and enjoy the sculptures and fountains. The **Tucson Museum of Art** is just a short walk away and marks the beginning of your journey.

## SIGHTS BETWEEN DOWNTOWN AND THE UNIVERSITY OF ARIZONA

### Tucson Children's Museum

Children have fun with games and scientific experiments—using computers, learning how the human body works—in this hands-on museum. Exhibits change quarterly. A gift shop sells educational toys. It's open Wednesday 10 a.m.-6 p.m., Thurs.-Fri. 9 a.m.-1 p.m., Saturday 10 a.m.-5 p.m., and Sunday 1-5 p.m.; ticket sales end one hour before closing. It's closed Monday and holidays. Admission is $1.50 children 3-16 and seniors, $3 adults; tel. 792-9985. Located in the historic Carnegie building at 200 S. Sixth Ave. between 12th and 13th Streets.

### Arizona Historical Society Museum

If you visit only one of the dozens of historical museums in the state, make it this one. The museum offers exhibits from all the periods of Arizona's early history: Prehistoric Indian, Spanish, Mexican, Mountain Men, Territorial, and Early Statehood. Displays are well-illustrated and brimming with artifacts. Visitors of all ages enjoy the early 1900s copper mine exhibit, where you can walk through a realistic mine complete with sound effects, emerging at a giant ore stamper and other processing machinery. Period rooms and special exhibits are carefully prepared. A gift shop provides a good selection of books and crafts. The headquarters of the Arizona Historical Society is here, with a research library open to the public.

Hours are Mon.-Sat. 10 a.m.-4 p.m. and Sunday noon-4 p.m. (library closes at 1 p.m. on Saturday and all day Sunday); donations are welcome; tel. 628-5774. The museum is at 949 E. Second St. and Park Avenue.

## UNIVERSITY OF ARIZONA

In 1885, the 13th Territorial Legislature awarded Tucson $25,000 to establish Arizona's first university. Most townspeople didn't think much of the idea; they wanted the territorial capital, awarded to Prescott, or at least the territorial insane asylum, awarded to Phoenix. It was left to a handful of determined citizens to get the school built. The walls went up after land was donated by a saloonkeeper and two gamblers, but money ran out before the roof was finished. A federal loan completed the roof, and the university opened in 1891. Classrooms, library, offices, and dorms were centered in one lone university building, today known as Old Main.

Six faculty served 32 students the first year, nearly all in the Preparatory School. Like many other states, Arizona at the time suffered from a lack of secondary schools. The university has since expanded to a population capped at 35,000 students with a faculty of about 1,600. Fourteen colleges and eight schools offer 376 programs.

Visitors can enjoy theater and concert performances, the Flandrau Planetarium, sporting events, and several museums. For information,

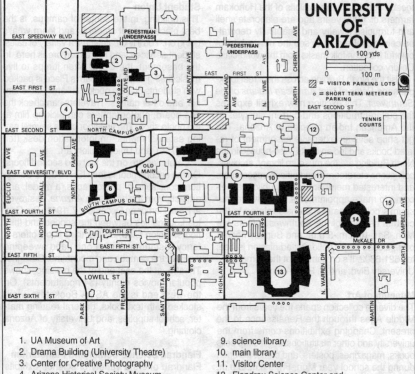

UNIVERSITY
OF
ARIZONA

0        100 yds
0        100 m

▨ = VISITOR PARKING LOTS
o = SHORT TERM METERED PARKING

1. UA Museum of Art
2. Drama Building (University Theatre)
3. Center for Creative Photography
4. Arizona Historical Society Museum
5. Arizona State Museum
6. Centennial Hall
7. Nugent Building
8. Student Union
9. science library
10. main library
11. Visitor Center
12. Flandrau Science Center and Planetarium/Mineral Museum
13. Arizona Stadium
14. McKale Memorial Center
15. pool

contact the **University Visitor Center** on the southeast corner of University and Cherry; it's open Mon.-Fri. 8 a.m.-5 p.m.; tel. 621-5130 (visitor center) or 621-2211 (switchboard). The visitor center features literature, listings of U of A events, a videotape library for public viewing, rotating exhibits, and a route map of the free campus shuttle. Visitors can park behind the visitor center; you're allowed 15 free metered minutes to dash in and ask for assistance. Free **campus tours** of the university begin Mon.-Fri. at 10 a.m. and 2 p.m. from the Nugent Building; tel. 621-3641. The campus lies about a mile east of downtown.

### Arizona State Museum

This is a good place to learn about archaeology and Arizona's American Indian peoples. Founded in 1893, the museum houses an extensive collection of artifacts from prehistoric, historic, and contemporary Native American cultures of the Southwest.

The South Building houses exhibits of prehistoric peoples of Arizona including a re-creation of an ancient cliff dwelling and artifacts of the Mogollon culture. Paleoindian artifacts include 12,000-year-old stone spear points discovered deeply imbedded in bones of the extinct woolly mammoth that roamed Arizona during the Pleistocene epoch. Among exhibits of the Hohokam farmers of 1,000 years ago are elaborate shell and turquoise jewelry and beautifully decorated ceramics. Be sure to see the new exhibit of colorful Mexican folk masks from the world-class Cordry collection.

Visit the North Building across the street to experience *Paths of Life: American Indians of the Southwest.* This exciting new exhibit explores the cultural traditions and current lifestyles of the American Indian peoples of Arizona. The gift shop sells an extensive assortment of related books and Indian crafts. Also housed in the North Building are the museum library, archives, collections storerooms, and offices; researchers and interested members of the public are welcome to make appointments to study the museum's collections of materials related to the cultural heritage of the Southwest. Hours are Mon.-Sat. 10 a.m.-5 p.m. and Sunday noon-5 p.m., closed major holidays; admission is free; tel. 621-6302. It's on campus at the corner of E. University Blvd. and N. Park Avenue.

## Museum of Art

The diverse collection spans the years from the Middle Ages through the Renaissance to the present. Changing exhibitions come from the university and other institutions. A gift shop sells books, magazines, posters, and cards. It's open during the school year Mon.-Fri. 9 a.m.-5 p.m. and Sunday noon-4 p.m.; hours in summer (May 15 to Labor Day) are Mon.-Fri. 10 a.m.-3:30 p.m. and Sunday noon-4 p.m.; admission is free; tel. 621-7567. You can park for $1/hour in the Park Avenue Garage, north of Speedway Blvd., and use the pedestrian underpass.

## Center for Creative Photography

Drop in to view traveling exhibitions of quality photographs. Examples of work by Richard Avedon, Ansel Adams, Paul Strand, Louise Dahl-Wolse, and other famous photographers can be seen by appointment. The center also stocks an extensive library of books and periodicals on photography. Staff can direct you to other photographic exhibits in town. It's open Mon.-Fri. 11 a.m.-5 p.m. and Sunday noon-5 p.m. during school terms; call for summer hours; admission is free; tel. 621-7968. The center is on Olive, just southeast of the Museum of Art.

## Student Union

This building, in the center of campus, is the best place to meet students and learn what's going on. You'll find cafeterias, a variety of cafes, student services, and recreation areas here. In the basement, the Cellar often jumps to live music during lunch hour. Sam's Place is packed with students playing pocket billiards, table tennis, and other games. Travelers can check the ride board; photographers can pick up film at the photo shop. The first floor offers several eating establishments, an information desk (tel. 621-7755), and Union Gallery art.

Cafeterias are on the first and second floors. On the second floor is the USS *Arizona* Collection, consisting of photographs, a model, and artifacts from the battleship *Arizona,* destroyed at Pearl Harbor on December 7, 1941. The Cactus Lounge lies between the second and third floors. Union Club, on the third floor, offers a fancy restaurant (lunch only) and sweeping views of the campus and mountains. Gallagher Theatre, at the east end of the building, shows popular movies nightly ($4 nonstudents). On the west end is the ASUA Bookstore, well-stocked with textbooks, general reading matter, school supplies, and University of Arizona clothing.

## Flandrau Science Center and Planetarium

Flandrau offers a variety of science exhibits designed to engage visitors of all ages. Nighttime viewing through the 16-inch telescope allows visitors to observe stars, planets, and galaxies with a professional instrument. Inside the planetarium theater, amateur stargazers can experience dynamic and entertaining programs on astronomy, Native American skylore, dinosaurs, and universal violence. The theater also presents laser light shows, with colorful laser images exploding across the dome.

Flandrau is at North Cherry Ave. and University Boulevard. Admission to nighttime telescope viewing is free. Hours are Mon.-Fri. 9 a.m.-5 p.m., Saturday and Sunday 1-5 p.m.; also open evenings Wed.-Thurs. 7-9 p.m. and Fri.-Sat. 7 p.m.-midnight. Shows cost $4.50 adults; $4 students, U of A employees, seniors 65 and over, and $3 children 3-13; no one under three admitted. Admission to just the science exhibits and basement mineral museum is $2; free with purchase of show ticket. A gift shop sells books, posters, and astronomy souvenirs. Parking, sometimes a problem in daytime, is available behind the visitor center across E. University Blvd.; turn in from N. Campbell Avenue.

## Wildcat Heritage Gallery

See photos of Wildcat teams and players dating from 1897 to the present. It's open Mon.-Fri. 8 a.m.-5 p.m., on the first and second floors of the west side of McKale Memorial Center. Purchase sports souvenirs at the Wildcatalog Store in the center.

## Pharmacy Museum

Exhibits trace the history of Arizona pharmaceuticals, with drugstore paraphernalia, old-time cure-alls, and antique medicine bottles. Look for displays near the elevators on the first, second, and third floors and off the hallway between the third-floor elevator and the Dean's Office. It's open Mon.-Fri. 8 a.m.-5 p.m.; admission is free; tel. 626-1427. Located in the College of Pharmacy Building four blocks north of the main campus at Warren Ave. and Mabel Street.

# WEST OF DOWNTOWN

## Garden of Gethsemane

While lying wounded on a WW I battlefield, Felix Lucero made a vow to dedicate his life, if he lived, to the creation of religious statues. He lived, and kept his vow; today, his life-size sculptures of the Last Supper and other subjects can be seen at the northeast corner of W. Congress St. and Bonita Ave. near I-10. Open daily 9 a.m.-4 p.m.; free admission.

## "A" Mountain

You can't miss this small peak just west of downtown. In earlier days it was a lookout point for soldiers awaiting hostile Indians, which explains its original name, Sentinel Peak. The giant "A" dates from October 23, 1915, when the local university football team beat Cal State Pomona in a 7-3 victory. Sports fans then headed out to paint the "A."

"A"-painting became a tradition, and every year freshmen whitewash the giant letter—and themselves—for all to see. To enjoy the panorama from the top of the peak, drive west on Congress St., then turn left at the sign to Sentinel Peak Road.

## Arizona-Sonora Desert Museum

This world-famous living museum contains animals and plants native to the Sonoran Desert of Arizona, the Mexican state of Sonora, and the Gulf of California region. Meet rattlesnakes, Gila monsters, scorpions, and other desert dwellers face to face. Watch frolicking otters and busy beavers through underwater panels. Try to spot the birds in the walk-in aviaries—not as easy as you'd expect, as many desert birds blend in well with their surroundings.

Mountain lion, bighorn sheep, javelina, and over 385 other types of animals as well as 1,400 species of plants dwell in nearly natural surroundings. A Life Underground exhibit lets you step below the surface to observe wildlife in their burrows. A realistic limestone cave and earth science exhibits take you even deeper underground and far back in time. You'll find desert flora well represented and labeled in the gardens.

Bring a sun hat and good walking shoes; it requires a half day to see all the exhibits. Animals are more active in the morning, which is a good time to visit. Special programs are scheduled daily to introduce visitors to some of the creatures living here. The setting is superb, with great views over the Avra Valley. Visible to the southwest are Baboquivari Peak (7,730 feet), sacred to the O'odham Indians, and the nearer Kitt Peak (6,875 feet), site of important astronomical observatories. Gift shops, a restaurant, and a snack bar are on the museum grounds. Picnic grounds are nearby in Saguaro National Monument West.

The Desert Museum is open daily 8:30 a.m.-5 p.m. Oct.-April (7:30 a.m.-6 p.m. March-Sept.); the ticket office closes one hour earlier than the museum; $8.95 adults, $1.75 ages 6-12; tel. 883-2702 (recording). No pets. The museum is in Tucson Mountain Park, 14 miles west of Tucson. Take Speedway Blvd. west across Gates Pass. Large RVs and trailer-rigs must take Ajo and Kinney Roads.

## Saguaro National Monument West

This half of the park, the Tucson Mountains District, is smaller than the eastern portion on the other side of Tucson, but it offers denser and more vigorous stands of saguaro cactus. Stop at the new **Red Hills Visitor Center** (elev. 2,561 feet) to view exhibits and obtain books, maps, and hiking information; it's open daily 8:30 a.m.-5 p.m.; tel. 733-5158. An interpretive film that gives a Tohono O'odham impression of the

Saguaro is shown every half hour 8:30 a.m.-4:30 p.m. Special programs or nature walks may be offered. Ask rangers for directions to the petroglyphs. There are five scenic picnic areas, too—four reached by road and one by trail. To get to the park from Tucson, continue two miles past the Arizona-Sonora Desert Museum. If coming from Phoenix, take the I-10 Avra Valley Rd. Exit 242 and follow signs 13 miles.

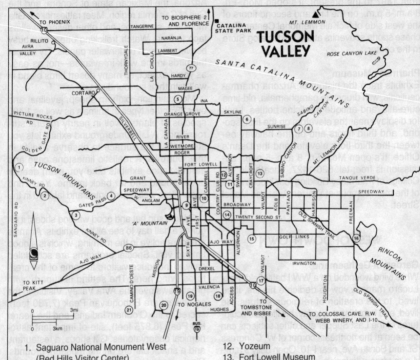

1. Saguaro National Monument West (Red Hills Visitor Center)
2. Arizona-Sonora Desert Museum
3. Old Tucson Studios
4. International Wildlife Museum
5. Tohono Chul Park
6. DeGrazia Gallery in the Sun
7. Sabino Canyon Visitor Center
8. Bear Canyon
9. downtown Tucson
10. University of Arizona
11. Tucson Botanical Gardens
12. Yozeum
13. Fort Lowell Museum
14. Reid Park Zoo
15. Davis-Monthan A.F.B. (main gate)
16. Saguaro National Monument East (Visitor Center)
17. Pima Air and Space Museum
18. Tucson International Airport
19. Desert Diamond Casino
20. Mission San Xavier del Bac
21. Casino of the Sun

© MOON PUBLICATIONS, INC.

*Old Tucson Studios*

The short, paved, and accessible **Cactus Garden Trail** beside the information center introduces the unique saguaro and other plants of the Sonoran Desert. The accessible **Desert Discovery Nature Trail** makes a half-mile loop; trailhead is 0.9 miles northwest of the center.

The six-mile **Bajada Loop Drive** takes in some of the scenic countryside; the graded dirt road begins 0.2 miles beyond the start of the one way road. **Valley View Overlook Trail** begins 0.2 miles past the start of the one-way section of the loop drive and climbs to a fine panorama; it's 1.5 miles roundtrip. Other trails wind through the scenic Sonoran Desert to Wasson Peak (4,687 feet) and other destinations. A trail map available at the center shows trails, trailheads, and distances.

### Old Tucson Studios

The West has been won many times over at this famous movie location. It began back in 1939 as the setting for the Columbia Pictures film *Arizona*. More than 250 features have been filmed here, including *Dirty Dingus McGee, Rio Lobo, Death of a Gunfighter,* and *Young Guns II.* Such well-known TV shows as "Gunsmoke" and "Little House on the Prairie" were shot here as well.

Old Tucson re-creates the Tucson of the 1860s with weathered adobe or frontier buildings, board sidewalks, and dusty streets. Stunt-

people wear period clothing and stage blazing gunfights several times a day. Visitors can participate in a trivia contest called Movie Mayhem. The Wizard of the West magic show and a musical revue are also worth a look. The Iron Door Mine, and stagecoach and train rides provide additional excitement. Children frolic in the Kid's Korral. Restaurants and picnic area are also available.

Much of Old Tucson burned down during a 1995 blaze, but plans were to rebuild and be back in operation during 1996. Open daily (tentatively) 10 a.m.-5 p.m. (call for hours); $10.95 adults, $6.95 children ages 4-11. Admission includes all activities; call 883-0100 for recorded information. It's 12 miles west of Tucson in Tucson Mountain Park. Drive west on Speedway Blvd. (not suited for large rigs) or take Ajo and Kinney Roads.

### International Wildlife Museum

This natural history museum features nearly 300 kinds of mammals and birds from all over the world. Hands-on learning is emphasized through touch exhibits, interactive computers, naturalistic habitat dioramas, and a theater with seven different full-length wildlife movies shown on the hour. Mounted specimens include both rare and extinct species such as the passenger pigeon. Wild sheep and goats cling to a 30-foot mountain. An extensive gift shop sells both

African art and ancient Egyptian replicas. A restaurant is planned.

The museum is open daily 9 a.m.-5:30 p.m.; $5 adults; $3.75 students, military, and seniors 62 and over; $1.50 children 6-12; tel. 624-4024 (recording) or 629-0100. It's at 4800 W. Gates Pass Rd.; from Tucson, head west seven miles on Speedway Blvd. from I-10.

## NORTH OF DOWNTOWN

### Tohono Chul Park

The name means Desert Corner in the Tohono O'odham language. Enjoy natural desert beauty within Tucson; nature trails wind through the grounds, with about 500 plants from northern Mexico and the Southwest arranged by genus. The Ethnobotanical Garden presents native crops and traditional cultivation methods. Javelina, desert tortoise, collared lizard, chuckwalla, ground squirrel, desert cottontail, black-tailed jackrabbit, and many species of wild birds inhabit the park. The Demonstration Garden features displays of landscaping, geology, and endangered fish. Other attractions include the Park Greenhouse (plants for sale), Exhibit House (rotating Southwestern shows), Tea Room, and two gift shops. Staff offer park and birding and wildflower tours; call for times. Picnic at one of the shaded tables scattered through the park.

Park grounds are open daily 7 a.m.-sunset; Exhibit House is open Sunday 11 a.m.-5 p.m. and Mon.-Sat. 9:30 a.m.-5 p.m.; Tea Room is open daily 8 a.m.-5 p.m.; a requested $2 donation is appreciated since the park is a nonprofit foundation; tel. 575-8468 (recording), 742-6455 (office), or 797-1711 (Tea Room). Located near the junction of Ina and Oracle Roads in northwest Tucson; the main entrance is at 7366 N. Paseo del Norte; turn north at the first stoplight on Ina west of Oracle.

### DeGrazia Gallery in the Sun

Designed to blend into the desert, this building is made of adobe and surrounded by native plants. You enter through a gate patterned after the one at Yuma Territorial Prison, then pass through a short mine shaft.

Ettore "Ted" DeGrazia, born in the Arizona mining district of Morenci, became fascinated at an early age by the desert colors and cultures of the Southwest. He became famous for his paintings, but created ceramics, sculpture, and jewelry and wrote books as well. After his death in 1982, the gallery continued as a museum. In a short movie, DeGrazia narrates the story of his life and work. Local artists display work in the Little Gallery Nov.-May.

From downtown go four miles east on E. Broadway to Swan Rd., then north six miles to 6300 N. Swan Rd. near Skyline Dr.; tel. 299-9191. It's open daily 10 a.m.-4 p.m.; admission is free; gift shop.

## SANTA CATALINA MOUNTAINS

The Santa Catalinas, crowned by 9,157-foot Mt. Lemmon, rise in ragged ridges from the north edge of Tucson. Lush woodlands cover the higher slopes. Hikers can choose among trails totaling over 150 miles in length, ranging from easy strolls to extremely difficult climbs.

**Pusch Ridge Wilderness** protects much of the range west of Mt. Lemmon Highway. This paved mountain road and Sabino Canyon Rd. offer easy access from Tucson. The Southern Arizona Hiking Club's Santa Catalina topo map shows all the main trails, distances, and trailheads. Purchase at a U.S. Forest Service office or hiking store.

### History

In 1697, the tireless Jesuit priest Eusebio Francisco Kino visited a Tohono O'odham village in what's now Tucson. He named it, and the high ranges to the north and east, Santa Catarina. Spanish prospectors found gold in Cañada del Oro; they also reportedly mined gold in the Mine with the Iron Door and silver in La Esmeralda, both lost mines lying somewhere in the range.

Raiding Apache discouraged mining until the late 1870s, when Anglo goldseekers began placer operations in Cañada del Oro, tunneling into the hillsides. Most of the mines lie in the northeastern part of the mountains.

Mount Lemmon honors botanist Sara Lemmon, who, with her husband John, discovered many species of plants on an 1881 expedition to the summit. As trails into the mountains improved, the citizens of Tucson headed to the hills more often for the cool air and scenery.

The highway to the top was completed in 1949, built largely by federal prisoners.

## Catalina State Park

This 5,500-acre park in the western foothills of the Catalinas is popular for picnicking, camping, birding, hiking, and horseback riding. Hikers can follow the **Nature Trail, Birding Trail, Romero Ruins** interpretive trail, or 2.3-mile **Canyon Loop Trail,** or climb all the way to the top of Mt. Lemmon (14 difficult miles one-way) via the **Sutherland** or **Romero Canyon trails.**

Natural swimming holes along the lower parts of the Sutherland and Romero Canyon trails make good day-hike destinations; both trails become very steep higher up. **Fifty Year Trail** is designed especially for horseback riding, though hikers enjoy it too; the six-mile (one-way) trail heads north from the Equestrian Center to connect with Sutherland Trail.

Admission is $3 for day use, $8 camping w/o electricity, $13 w/electricity; showers are available; tel. 628-5798. Your horse is welcome to stay in the Equestrian Center; you can also camp here. Catalina State Park is 14 miles north of downtown Tucson on Oracle Rd. (US 77).

## Sabino Canyon

You'll find this desert oasis in the southern foothills of the Santa Catalina Mountains. Sabino Creek begins its journey on the slopes of Mt. Lemmon, bouncing down through the canyon, supporting lush greenery and trees in which deer, javelina, coyotes, birds, and other animals find food and shelter.

In the **visitor center,** at the entrance to the canyon, you'll see exhibits on the canyon and Santa Catalina Mountains; you can buy books and maps on the area. Naturalist-led walks are scheduled; there's a self-guided nature trail behind the center, as well as a sanctuary for butterflies and hummingbirds. The visitor center is open weekdays 8 a.m.-4:30 p.m. and weekends 8:30 a.m.-4:30 p.m.; free admission; tel. 749-3223 (recorded announcements) or 749-8700 (Santa Catalina Ranger District office).

A road winds up through Sabino Canyon for 3.8 miles, crossing the creek many times. Private motor vehicles are prohibited beyond the visitor center. You can explore the canyon by hiking, horseback riding, or shuttle bus. Because Sabino and Bear canyons receive a large

METROPOLITAN TUCSON CONVENTION AND VISITORS BUREAU

number of visitors, bicycles are prohibited on Wednesday and Saturday and 9 a.m.-5 p.m. the rest of the week. No dogs, glass containers, or alcohol.

The **shuttle** leaves the visitor center daily every half hour 9 a.m.-4:30 p.m. from about mid-July through December. Shuttles depart the rest of the year every half hour on weekends and holidays and hourly—on the hour—on weekdays 9 a.m.-4 p.m. Fares are $5 adults, $2 ages 3-12; call 749-2861 (recording) to check schedules. The narrated ride lasts 45-50 minutes roundtrip; you can get on and off as often as you choose at any of the nine stops.

Hiking, birding, picnicking, and swimming are the big attractions here. The Forest Service provides picnic areas and restrooms, though you'll find drinking water only at the visitor center and the first two stops. Camping is not allowed in the canyon; to camp, backpackers must hike at least a quarter mile in from trailheads.

Hikers have a choice of many destinations at the last stop: back to the visitor center via the **Phone Line Trail** high on the east slopes of Sabino Canyon (5.5 miles one-way), to Lower Bear Canyon via Seven Falls (12 miles one-way), up the West Fork of Sabino Canyon to Hutch's Pool (eight miles roundtrip), or to Mt. Lemmon's summit (13 hard miles one-way).

Enjoy the special magic of Sabino Canyon on a **moonlight ride,** offered those evenings each month when the moon is full, April-June and Sept.-December. The Moonlight Shuttle fare is $5 adults, $2 children; reservations and prepayment required; tel. 749-2327.

Another shuttle bus leaves the visitor center for the 2.5-mile ride east to **Bear Canyon,** a picnic area and trailhead for the Catalinas. **Seven Falls,** a series of cascades 2.3 miles up Bear Canyon, is the most popular hiking destination. The best scenery doesn't begin until you leave the road, so there's no point in taking the shuttle unless you plan on hiking. The Bear Canyon shuttle leaves hourly on the hour every day 9 a.m.-4 p.m.; no narration; fare is $3 adults, $1.25 ages 3-12. Sabino Canyon lies 13 miles northeast of downtown Tucson. Take Tanque Verde Rd. to Sabino Canyon Rd., then turn north and drive 4.5 miles to the canyon entrance.

## Mount Lemmon Highway

In just an hour you can drive from the Lower Sonoran Zone desert to Canadian Zone forest. Meadows bloom with wildflowers in spring and summer. Enjoy camping, picnicking, and hiking in the warmer months, skiing in winter. The 40-mile drive from Tucson leaves the saguaro, palo verde, and cholla behind, passes through juniper and piñon, and enters pine forests at about 7,000 feet. Fir and aspen cling to the cool, north-facing slopes above 8,000 feet. *Be sure to fill up with gas before leaving Tucson, as none is available on the Mt. Lemmon Highway.*

**Molino Basin** (elev. 4,500 feet), 18 miles from Tucson, offers the closest campground. It's open only from late October to mid-April; no water, $2 day use, $5 camping. **General Hitchcock Campground,** 21 miles from Tucson, lies at 6,000 feet and is usually open all year; no water or fee. In another two miles you'll come to **Windy Point,** with sweeping panoramas of Tucson and the southern foothills. **Geology Vista,** a fraction of a mile farther, offers good views of the southeast and a sign describing the forces that created these mountains.

**Rose Canyon Lake,** 33 miles from Tucson, features trout fishing and a nearby campground but no swimming or boating; sites are open mid-April to late October; it has drinking water and a

$9 vehicle fee. You can see many mountain ranges to the east from **San Pedro Vista,** a half mile beyond Rose Canyon turnoff. A sign identifies the ranges. **Green Mountain Trail** connects San Pedro Vista with General Hitchcock Campground. Allow three hours for the four-mile (one-way) hike.

At **Palisades Ranger Station,** 36 miles from Tucson, you can hike to the top of 8,550-foot **Mt. Bigelow,** a 1.5-mile roundtrip climb of 600 feet. The ranger station is open 9 a.m.-4 p.m. daily in summer and 9 a.m.-4 p.m. Saturday and Sunday in spring and autumn. The **Butterfly Trail** also begins at this trailhead, winding through ponderosa pine, Douglas fir, and juniper-oak woodlands to Soldier Camp, 5.8 miles to the northwest; allow four to five hours between trailheads.

Primitive camping (no facilities) is possible along Bigelow Rd. and at Whitetail (restrooms), across the highway and a bit farther up. **Spencer Canyon Campground,** 38 miles from Tucson, is open mid-April to late October with drinking water and an $8 vehicle fee. **Soldier Camp** is 39 miles from Tucson and a quarter mile north of the highway. Cavalry troops from Fort Lowell camped here in the 1870s while tracking rebellious Apache. Later the soldiers used the site as a summer resort.

You'll come to a fork in the highway about 41 miles from Tucson; keep left a half mile for the tiny village of Summerhaven or keep right one mile to **Ski Valley.** Summerhaven offers two overnight lodgings convenient for skiers. The **Alpine Lodge,** a bed-and-breakfast, has six rooms at $89.25 s, $99.75 d; tel. 576-1544. The **Suite and Suite** has four cabins at $144 s or d; tel. 576-1542. A restaurant/bar and grocery outlet are nearby.

**Aspen Loop Trail,** which begins its 3.8-mile loop near Summerhaven, is a good introduction to the high country. Start at Marshall Gulch Picnic Area, one mile south of Summerhaven; a sign, Aspen Trail #93, Marshall Saddle 2.5, marks the start. A gate may block the road in winter, when you'll have to park at Summerhaven and walk in. The trail climbs through aspen, fir, and ponderosa pine and offers some good views. At Marshall Saddle, turn right down Marshall Gulch and drive 1.3 miles back to the picnic area.

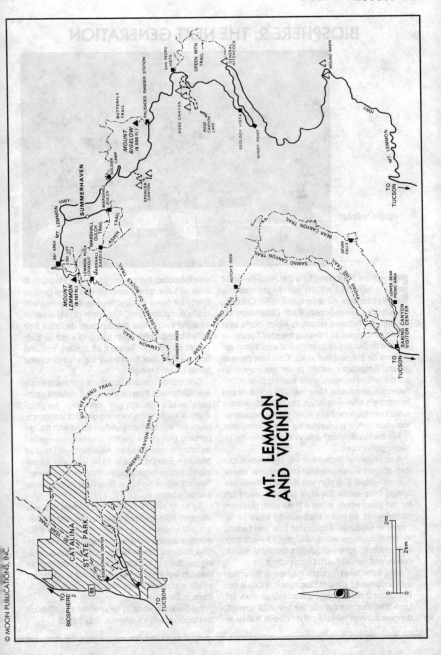

# BIOSPHERE 2: THE NEXT GENERATION

glass houses

C. ALLAN MORGAN

**B**iosphere 2 is looking for a little respect—and it just might get it, with the help of some ambitious Ivy Leaguers. As of January 1, 1996, Columbia University's Lamont-Doherty Earth Observatory will manage the battered terrarium, which looms over the Arizona desert 30 miles northeast of Tucson. In addition to directing its scientific and educational operations for the next five years, Columbia plans to expand Biosphere's visitors' center into more of an earth sciences museum, while steering clear of Disneyesque ostentation. More than 200 scientists and researchers have worked on this 200-million-dollar project with the hope that it would provide valuable information on how to preserve the earth's ecosystem.

But the future wasn't always this rosy for the gigantic greenhouse.

It all began on September 26, 1991, when four men and four women stepped into their new, space-age mini-world. The plan was this: after the airlock sealed them inside, the eight bionauts would live for two years wholly within a three-acre, glass-enclosed world. All water, food, and air would be recycled or produced within. This little world would resemble our larger world—Biosphere 1—with tropical rainforest, savannah, desert, farmland, marsh, ocean, and human-habitat ecosystems.

Well, as so often happens out here in the uncertain, uncontained world of Biosphere 1, things inside Biosphere 2 didn't proceed precisely as planned. Less than four months into the bionauts' voyage, dangerously high levels of carbon dioxide built up inside the dome, forcing project directors to pump in fresh air. Later, a crew member, who left the grounds briefly for minor medical treatment, returned with spare computer parts. And when cloudy weather inhibited their crops, the Bionauts depleted their stored-food supplies, each losing 15% of their body weight on average. To top it off, battling ants and cockroaches took time away from research and hardly boosted morale.

Critics once accused Biosphere 2 of being less a scientific project than the expensive material manifestation of a new age cult. John Allen, the philosophical leader of the founding group of visionaries, predicted that humanity—when faced with the impending peril of the Earth's environment—would be forced to colonize Mars. Allen recruited Texas oil billionaire Edward Bass in 1974, who later dipped into his fortune to back the multimillion dollar project. Bass still retains his title as Biosphere 2's sole owner and benefactor.

By early 1994, long after the original bionauts emerged from their two-year journey and another group of voyagers had settled in the dome for a 10-month stay, the Biosphere 2 experiment had almost totally succumbed to chaos. Bass was busy firing members of the board, and two of the original bionauts were first thrown off the site and later arrested, accused of participating in a raid designed to damage the dome.

But Columbia wants to forget about those fiascos and focus on serious science. Stay tuned.

At the Santa Catalina Ranger District office in the Sabino Canyon visitor center, foresters provide information on backcountry areas in other parts of the Santa Catalinas. **Peppersauce Campground** in the northeastern foothills lies among large sycamore trees at an elevation of 4,700 feet; with water; $5. If all spaces are taken seek dispersed camping along Forest Route 25 starting opposite the campground entrance. Take Forest Route 38 from Oracle (eight miles, mostly paved or well graded) or the rough Control Rd. (Forest Route 38) from the Mt. Lemmon Highway. Halfway to the campground you will see gateways to the **Arizona Trail.**

**Peppersauce Cave** is an undeveloped cavern 2.2 miles past the campground turnoff. Despite the road warning sign, you can negotiate this stretch in a street car and reach the one lane bridge, where you'll find parking. Walk a couple of dozen paces up the wash, then bear right along the well-trod path to the cave entrance. Take at least two flashlights per person. Peppersauce Cave was once well decorated but decades of souvenir collecting has trashed the cave. A 1948 *National Geographic* photograph shows cave explorers hauling out smashed-off remains of once beautiful cave formations.

**Mount Lemmon Ski Valley** is the southernmost ski area in the United States. The double-chair lift takes summer visitors and winter skiers from 8,200 to 9,150 feet. Ski season lasts from about mid-December to mid-April. Skiers have a choice of 16 runs, including a "bunny slope" for beginners. Rentals (skis, boots, and poles) cost $15; $30 per hour for private lessons or $10 for two-hour group lessons; lift tickets cost $25 per day, $10 for children 12 and under; tel. 576-1400 (recording of current ski and road conditions) or 576-1321 (business office). In summer you can take the lift up to enjoy the views and cool forests; cost is $5, $2 children 3-12.

A hiking trail also goes from the bottom of the ski lift through fir and aspen forests to the summit. It's unsigned, so ask someone to point out the start. The season runs from about May to October; allow two to three hours for the 2.2 miles roundtrip. Several more hiking trails radiate from the summit, accessible by trail or the ski lift.

The **Iron Door Restaurant** across the highway is open daily for lunch and on weekends for brunch; tel. 576-1321. The highway continues

past Ski Valley to an infrared observatory near the top of Mt. Lemmon, but both the road and observatory are likely to be closed to visitors.

## BIOSPHERE 2

Visitors are welcome to take a peek at this controversial compound, some 30 miles northeast of Tucson, and witness its strides toward scientific legitimacy. Guided and self-guided tours begin with a 15-minute multimedia show, then continue past the test module, the first sealed system built. Visitors can walk through a series of greenhouses containing the varied plant and animal environments. You can also walk around the outside of the amazing structure, peer in at the different "biomes," and perhaps see scientists working inside. An underwater viewing gallery lets you watch the tropical fish and corals of the "ocean," a one-million gallon tank of saltwater and sea creatures.

Allow at least 2.5 hours for the walking tour, which is three-quarters of a mile long. Most of the tour route is outdoors, so you'll want suitable clothing, hat, and sunscreen. A map, signs, and Biosphere staff provide details of the experiment. Still and video cameras welcome. Hours are daily 9 a.m.-3:30 p.m. (time of last tour departure); no reservations needed; $12.95 adults, $10.95 seniors 62 and over, and $6 ages 5-17; tel. 896-6200 or (800) 828-2462. To get your own "virtual tour" of Biosphere 2 without ever leaving the comforts of home, contact it via the Internet at http://www.netspace.org/biosphere2.

Gift shops sell books and videos on the project as well as souvenirs. The cafe serves breakfast, lunch, and dinner daily. Biosphere has an espresso bar and bookstore, too.

The Inn at the Biosphere offers very comfortable accommodations with great views; its popular overnight packages include room, tour, dinner, and breakfast for $89 s, $136 d Jan. 1-April 30, then $69 s, $108 d the rest of the year; room-only rates available as well; tel. 896-6200.

Biosphere 2 is a one-hour drive from Tucson or two-hour drive from Phoenix. From Tucson, head north 25 miles on Oracle Rd./AZ 79 to Oracle Junction, turn northeast and drive 5.5 miles on AZ 77, then go south 2.5 miles to the ticket booth and parking. The best route from the

Phoenix area travels via Florence and AZ 79 to Oracle Junction; or, you can take I-10 to the Ina Rd. exit, go east on Ina Rd. to Oracle Rd./AZ 79, then north to Oracle Junction.

# EAST OF DOWNTOWN

## Reid Park Zoo

Check out this small but satisfying collection of flamingos, lions, tigers, hippos, polar bears, and other exotic life. A walk-in aviary features birds from the far corners of the world. The zoo is active in breeding rare animals and participates in a species survival program. With a snack bar, gift shop, and, on the west side in Reid Park, a picnic area. It's open daily 9 a.m.-4 p.m.; $3.50 adults, $2.50 seniors 62 and over, 75 cents children 5-14; tel. 791-4022 (recording) or 791-5064. Reid Park lies 3.5 miles east of downtown. Enter from 22nd St. just east of Country Club Road. Reid Park Zoo plans to expand by the end of 1996 and may increase fees.

## Tucson Botanical Gardens

Plant lovers interested in a variety of flora, both native and exotic, will enjoy a visit here. Garden exhibits include a xeriscape-solar demonstration, native crops, roses, herbs, irises, and a tropical greenhouse. You can attend classes, workshops, tours, and a variety of special events; call for schedule at 326-9255 (recording) or 326-9686. It's open daily 8:30 a.m.-4:30 p.m.; a gift shop is open daily, with shorter hours. Garden admission is $3 adults, $2 seniors 62 and older, free for children 12 and younger. The gardens are about six miles northeast of downtown at 2150 N. Alvernon Way, just south of Grant Road.

## Yozeum

Donald F. Douglas popularized the yo-yo and gave it the modern American name. In the 1920s he saw a Filipino immigrant using such a device, shortened the Tagalog (primary Philippine dialect) word meaning "come back" to yo-yo, started mass production, and introduced it to the consumers. Now, a grandson has started this yo-yo museum, tracing development of the toy from a primitive stone age hunting device, through its first historic mention (ancient Greece), to modern times. Hundreds of yo-yos of all shapes and sizes are on display Tues.-Fri. 9 a.m.-5 p.m. and Saturday 9 a.m.-1 p.m. at Playmaxx, 2900 N. Country Club Dr.; tel. 322-0100.

## Fort Lowell Museum

U.S. Army troops chasing troublesome Apache in the 1860s needed a base. Thus, Camp Lowell, built on the outskirts of Tucson in 1866 and named in honor of an officer killed in the Civil War. The camp was moved to its present site in 1873, becoming a fort in 1879. It was a busy place during the Geronimo campaigns, which ended with the famous Apache leader's surrender in September 1886. With the Indian wars finally over, the Army abandoned the fort in 1891.

The commanding officer's quarters have been reconstructed and furnished as they were in the 1880s. Exhibits of artifacts, photos, and maps show life of the frontier soldier. Ruins of the adobe hospital and other buildings are nearby. The museum is open Wed.-Sat. 10 a.m.-4 p.m.; free admission; tel. 885-3832. The museum is in Fort Lowell Park at 2900 N. Craycroft Rd., about eight miles northeast of downtown.

## Davis-Monthan Air Force Base

Curious about what's going on at the local base? Tours are conducted by an informative Air Force guide twice weekly. Charles Lindbergh dedicated Davis-Monthan in 1927 as the country's first municipal airport. During WW II it became a training ground for crews of B-17 bombers and other aircraft. The base now trains pilots in combat aircraft.

A tenant at the base, AMARC (Aerospace Maintenance And Regeneration Center), stores a staggering number of surplus planes. The WW II and 1950s birds have all been relocated to museums, but a great variety of Vietnam-era fighters, transports, and bombers stretches for blocks.

Free bus tours (reservations needed) run on Monday and Wednesday at 9 a.m., lasting an hour to an hour and a half. Call the Public Affairs Office as far in advance as possible to make the required reservations and to check on tour times; tours often fill up as much as a month in advance; tel. 750-3358. Tours start seven miles southeast of downtown; staff give directions and parking info when you make reservations.

*at peace at the Pima Air and Space Museum*

## Pima Air and Space Museum

More than 200 historic aircraft represent the dramatic advances in aviation technology. Many famous planes from WW II through the present era are on view. A full-scale replica of the Wright Brothers' 1903 Wright Flyer, a Norden bombsight, cut-away engines, uniforms, and other memorabilia are exhibited as well. A gift shop sells aircraft models, books, and posters.

Daily hours are 9 a.m.-5 p.m.; $6 adults, $5 seniors 62 and older and active military, $3 ages 10-17, under 10 free; tel. 574-0462. The museum lies about 12 miles southeast of downtown. Take I-10 east to Valencia Rd. Exit 267, exit and turn left, then drive two miles.

## Saguaro National Monument East

This older and larger part of the park features many huge saguaro. The giant cactus matures very slowly, requiring about 25 years to grow just two feet. Youngsters need protective shade. Arms don't appear until the saguaro is about 75 years old. Old-timers live more than 200

years and may reach 50 feet. Creamy white blossoms, the state flower, appear in early May. The fruit, which matures in midsummer, resembles a flower with shiny, black seeds surrounded by a bright red shell.

Grazing cattle trampled young saguaro for many years in this area. Woodcutters took many of the "nurse plants" that shaded and sheltered the young saguaro. The cattle were removed beginning in 1958, and woodcutting is no longer allowed, but it will be a long time before the saguaro forest recovers. Today the area features mostly very old and very young specimens.

The **visitor center,** just inside the park, contains exhibits of desert geology, ecology, flora, and fauna. A 15-minute slide program shown every half-hour illustrates the biotic communities of the park. Special programs and walks may be offered as well. Books, maps, and hiking information are available. Outside, the **Cactus Garden** displays a variety of labeled desert plants.

The eight-mile **Cactus Forest Drive** winds through the foothills of the Rincon Mountains and offers many fine views. After you've driven about 2.2 miles along this route, you'll come upon the **Mica View Picnic Area** to the north; it has picnic tables and outhouses but no water. Another 0.3 mile past the turnoff, look to the left for the **Desert Ecology Trail**. On this quarter-mile accessible paved trail you can learn how plants and animals cope with the environment.

**Freeman Homestead Nature Trail** begins on the right, 200 yards down the spur road to Javelina Picnic Area. The Freeman Trail is a one-mile loop that takes you through huge saguaro and into a wash filled with mesquite. **Javelina Picnic Area** has shaded picnic tables and outhouses but no water. More than a half dozen other trails wind through the desert hills near Cactus Forest Drive. Many interconnect to allow a variety of loop hikes; ask for a trail brochure at the visitor center.

The **Tanque Verde Ridge Trail** begins near the Javelina Picnic Area and climbs into the rugged **Saguaro Wilderness** of the Rincon Mountains. Mica Mountain, at 8,666 feet the highest peak in the wilderness, lies 17.5 miles away by trail. **Douglas Spring Trail,** which begins at the east end of Speedway Blvd., crosses part of the northern park to Douglas Spring (5.9 miles one-way), then turns south to connect with Tanque Verde Ridge and other trails. Winter, spring, and autumn are the best seasons for hiking; the wilderness is especially dry and unforgiving in the heat of summer. A free permit from the visitor center is needed for backcountry camping. Carry water (one gallon per day) and topo maps.

Cactus Forest Drive is open daily 7 a.m.-sunset; $4 vehicle admission, $2 bicyclist or foot traveler. The visitor center is open daily 8:30 a.m.-5 p.m. year-round; free admission; tel. 733-5153. Saguaro National Monument East is just off Old Spanish Trail, about 16 miles east of downtown. Bicyclists particularly enjoy Cactus Forest Drive, which can be reached from Tucson on a bike path that parallels Old Spanish Trail.

## Colossal Cave

Tour guides point out the large, dusty formations in this dry, limestone cave and explain the geology, but won't reveal the location of $60,000 in hidden gold left behind by outlaws.

The tour covers a half mile and requires a great deal of stair climbing—a total of 363 steps. Tours leave about every half-hour and last 45-50 minutes. A snack bar and gift shop await outside the entrance; a free campground is nearby, gate open 9 a.m.-5 p.m.

The cave is open daily mid-September to mid-March 9 a.m.-5 p.m. (until 6 p.m. Sunday and holidays), then daily mid-March to mid-September 8 a.m.-6 p.m. (until 7 p.m. Sunday and holidays). Admission is $6.50 adults, $5 children ages 11-16, and $3.50 children ages 6-10; tel. 647-7275. The cave lies 22 miles east of downtown Tucson. Take I-10 east to Vail-Wentworth Exit 279, then go seven miles north; or take the Old Spanish Trail to Saguaro National Monument East, then go 12 miles south.

## R.W. Webb Winery

Arizona wine? Yes, and this commercial winery is the state's largest, specializing in, among others, cabernet sauvignon, petite syrah, port, and sherry. You can learn about winemaking on tours and tastings that last 30-45 minutes; $1 charge. Hours are Mon.-Sat. 10 a.m.-5 p.m. and Sunday noon-5 p.m. with tours starting one hour after opening; tel. 762-5777 (a long distance call from Tucson). It's 14 miles southeast of Tucson; take the I-10 Vail-Wentworth Exit 279, then turn east 1.5 miles on the north frontage road.

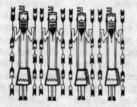

# TUCSON ACCOMMODATIONS

## HOTELS AND MOTELS

There are over 100 hotels, motels, bed and breakfasts, and resorts in Tucson—near the freeway, downtown, at the airport, near the university, and scattered around the valley. Good hunting grounds include the business route of old US 80 that parallels I-10 south of downtown, and old US 89 (AZ 79) running north-south—especially the Miracle Mile, Drachman St., Stone Ave., and Oracle Rd. sections north of downtown, near Speedway Boulevard. Though bypassed by I-10, many of these motels are well-maintained bargains both off season and during tourist season. Another good hunting area is along I-10 south and east of downtown, where bargain-priced places usually post their prices. However, many independents have been known to raise their prices drastically when special local events make motel rooms scarce.

Look for lodging listings in the *Tucson Official Visitors Guide* and *Arizona Accommodations Directory,* both distributed free at the Tucson Convention and Visitors Bureau.

The **Congress Hotel,** opened in 1919, is the last of the good old downtown hotels. Renovated rooms run $38.33 s, $42.71-49.28 d; standard rooms cost $30.66 s, $35.04-41.61 d; all rooms include bath; tel. 622-8848. **Youth hostel** spaces cost $12.05 with hostel card; guests without a card must be under 26 and pay $13.14; no reservations accepted. It's across the street from the Greyhound and Amtrak stations at 311 E. Congress Street.

## BED AND BREAKFASTS

These are private houses open to travelers in the European tradition. The degree of luxury varies, but the hosts offer a personal touch lacking in most motels. Advance reservations requested. Some B&Bs close for a month in summer. Ask the Visitors Bureau for brochures describing local establishments or check the listings in the *Tucson Official Visitors Guide.*

Three reservation services list bed and breakfasts. **Old Pueblo Homestays** (Box 13603, Tucson, AZ 85732, tel. 790-2399 or 800-333-9766) distributes a list of about 40 B&Bs in Tucson, the foothills, and other parts of southeastern Arizona; prices $45-115 d. **Bed and Breakfast in Arizona** (8900 E. Via Linda, Suite 101, Scottsdale, AZ 85258, tel. (602) 265-9511 or 800-266-7829) offers a list of many Arizona B&Bs, including some in Tucson; prices range $45-120 d. **Mi Casa Su Casa** (Box 950, Tempe, AZ 85280, tel. 990-0682 or 800-456-0682) is Spanish for "My house [is] your house"; statewide listings include a variety in the Tucson area with rates ranging $60-125 d.

A few of the bed and breakfasts close to downtown and the university include the following. **The Adobe Rose Inn** offers southwestern furnishings and a pool in a 1933 adobe at 940 N. Olsen Ave.; $105.03 d; tel. 322-9157 or (800) 328-4122. **Casa Alegre Bed and Breakfast Inn** features a pool and hot tub in a 1915 craftsman-style bungalow at 316 E. Speedway Blvd.; $94.07-105.02 d; tel. 628-1800 or (800) 628-5654. **El Presidio Bed and Breakfast Inn** operates out of a historic adobe house at 297 N. Main Ave.; $94-121 s or d; tel. 623-6151 or (800) 349-6151. **Jane Cooper House, A Bed and Breakfast Inn** provides rooms and a massage therapist at 710 N. Sixth Ave.; $71.18-82.13 d; tel. 791-9677. **La Posada del Valle** has rooms in a 1920s inn at 1640 N. Campbell Ave.; $99.55-137.87 d; tel. 795-3840. **Meyer Street House** has full-sized 1900 adobe apartments with individual patios only two blocks from the Tucson Convention Center at 562 S. Meyer St.; $94.93 d; tel. 629-0361. **Peppertrees Bed and Breakfast Inn** offers rooms in an early 1900s house at 724 E. University Blvd.; $97.36-166.25 s; tel. 622-7167 or (800) 348-5763.

## GUEST RANCHES

The Tucson area offers the world's largest concentration of guest ranches, where you can enjoy Western hospitality and activities as well as high-

# TUCSON ACCOMMODATIONS

(winter weekend rates for basic room)

Add 9.5% tax to all rates.

## DOWNTOWN/UNIVERSITY

**Arizona Inn;** 2200 E. Elm St.; $165-195 s or d; 325-1541 or (800) 933-1093; tennis, pool

**Best Western Executive Motor Hotel;** 333 Drachman St.; $85 s, $95 d; 791-7551 or (800) 528-1234; pool

**Best Western Royal Inn;** 1015 N. Stone Ave.; $89 s, $99 d; 622-8871 or (800) 528-1234; spa

**Comfort Inn;** 715 W. 22nd Ave.; $35-80 s, $40-100 d; 791-9282 or (800) 221-2222; pool, spa

**Copper Cactus Inn;** 225 W. Drachman St.; $39.99 s, $49.99 d; 622-7411; pool, kitchenettes

**Days Inn;** 222 S. Freeway (I-10 at Congress St.); $75-85 s, $81-89 d; 791-7511 or (800) DAYSINN; pool

**Discovery Inn;** 1010 S. Freeway; $59 s, $69 d; 622-5871 or (800) 622-5871; pool

**Econo Lodge;** 1165 N. Stone Ave.; $79-89 s, $89-99 d; 622-7763 or (800) 424-4777; pool

**E-Z 8 Motel;** 1007 S. Freeway; $26.88 s, $30.88 d; 624-9843 or (800) 326-6835, ext. 46; laundromat

**Frontier Motel;** 227 W. Drachman St.; $39.99 s, $49.99 d; 798-3005; pool, kitchenettes

**Hacienda Motel;** 1742 N. Oracle Rd.; $40 s, $50 d; pool, kitchenettes, gazebo

**Highland Tower Motel;** 1919 N. Oracle Rd.; $39.99 s, $49.99 d; 791-3057; pool, kitchenettes

**Holiday Inn;** 181 W. Broadway Blvd.; $89.10 s or d; 624-8711 or (800) HOLIDAY; pool

**Howard Johnson Lodge-Midtown;** 750 W. 22nd St.; $75 s or d; 624-4455 or (800) Holiday; spa, sauna, pool, continental breakfast

**La Siesta Motel;** 1602 N. Oracle Rd.; $34.99 s or d; 624-1192; pool, kitchenettes ($5 extra)

**Motel 6;** 960 S. Freeway; $29.99 s, $35.99 d; 628-1339; pool

**Park Inn Club;** 88 E. Broadway Blvd.; $69 s, $76 d; 622-4000 or (800) 622-1120; pool, sauna, whirlpool

**Plaza Hotel and Conference Center;** 1900 E. Speedway Blvd.; $58 s, $68 d; 327-7341, (800) 654-3010 (in AZ), or (800) 843-8052; pool, whirlpool

**Pueblo Inn;** 350 S. Freeway; $44.95 s or d; 622-6611 or (800) 551-1466; fitness center

**Ramada Inn University;** 1601 N. Oracle Rd.; $80-87 s, $85-92 d; 622-3000; Olympic pool, full breakfast

**Super 8;** 1248 N. Stone Ave.; $85 s, $85-90 d; 622-6446 or (800) 800-8000; pool

**TraveLodge;** 1300 N. Stone Ave.; $125-142 s or d; 770-1910 or (800) 578-7878; continental breakfast, pool, spa

**University Inn;** 950 N. Stone Ave.; $100 s, $125 d; 791-7503 or (800) 233-8466; pool, continental breakfast

## NORTH AND EAST OF DOWNTOWN

**Doubletree Inn;** 445 S. Alvernon Way; $135 s, $155 d; 881-4200 or (800) 222-TREE; pool, exercise room, breakfast

**Embassy Suites Hotel;** 5335 E. Broadway Blvd.; $129 s, $139 d; 745-2700 or (800) 362-2779; spa, pool, free breakfast

**Hotel Park Tucson;** 5151 E. Grant Rd.; $69.95 s or d; 323-6262 or (800) 882-0631; pool, spa

**La Quinta Motor Inn;** 6404 E. Broadway Blvd.; $59 s, $66 d; 747-1414 or (800) 531-5900; continental breakfast, health club

**Lodge on the Desert;** 306 N. Alvernon Way; $80-166 s, $92-178 d; 325-3366 or (800) 456-5634; hacienda atmosphere, fireplaces

**Radisson Suite Hotel;** 6555 E. Speedway Blvd.; $69-144 s or d; 721-7100 or (800) 333-3333; breakfast, golf, tennis

**Residence Inn by Marriott;** 6477 E. Speedway Blvd.; $154-184 s or d; 721-0991 or (800) 331-3131; breakfast buffet

**Smugglers Inn Motor Hotel;** 6350 E. Speedway Blvd.; $99 s, $109 d; 296-3292 or (800) 525-8852; restaurant, pool, spa

**Viscount Suite Hotel;** 4855 E. Broadway Blvd.; $115 s, $125 d; 745-6500 or (800) 527-9666; breakfast buffet

## AIRPORT VICINITY

**Clarion Hotel Airport;** 6801 S. Tucson Blvd.; $95-105 s, $115-125 d; 746-3932 or (800) 221-2222; pool, spa

**Embassy Suites Hotel and Conference Center;** 7051 S. Tucson Blvd.; $95 s or d; 573-0700 or (800) EMBASSY; exercise room, continental breakfast, all kitchenettes

**Holiday Inn Tucson Airport;** 4550 S. Palo Verde Blvd.; $98 s or d; 746-1161 or (800) HOLIDAY; free airport shuttle

**Howard Johnson Lodge-Airport;** 1025 E. Benson Hwy.; $69 s, $75 d; 623-7792 or (800) 446-4656; pool, hot tub, sauna

**The Inn at the Airport;** 7060 S. Tucson Blvd.; $99-109 s, $109-119 d; 746-0271 or (800) 772-3847; free breakfast, pool, spa

**Ramada-Palo Verde;** 5251 S. Julian Dr. (Palo Verde at I-10); $119-179 s, $129-189 d; 294-5250 or (800) 272-6232; pool, exercise room

**Redwood Lodge Motel;** 3315 E. Benson Hwy.; $29 s, $39 d; 294-3802; pool

---

quality accommodations and food. Horseback riding, hiking, birding, socializing, and relaxing are popular with most guests. Many ranches offer heated pools and tennis courts; most lie near a golf course. Meals are included with your stay and are often served family style. Advance reservations usually required. Most guest ranches close during the hot summers; a few remain open for especially hardy visitors. The following rates include service charges and tax.

**Tanque Verde Guest Ranch** lies in the foothills of the Rincon Mountains 10 miles east of Tucson at 14301 E. Speedway, Tucson, AZ 85748; tel. 296-6275 or (800) 234-DUDE (3833). The ranch dates from the 1880s and comes complete with two pools, jacuzzi and sauna, exercise room, tennis courts, horseback riding, bird banding, and nature walks. Daily rates dur-

ing the peak season of Dec. 16-April 30 are $298.90-359.90 s, $341.60-481.90 d; open the rest of the year at reduced rates.

**Lazy K Bar Guest Ranch** is an informal family ranch 16 miles northwest of Tucson at the foot of the Tucson Mountains at 8401 N. Scenic Dr., Tucson, AZ 85743; tel. 744-3050 or (800) 321-7018. Guests can enjoy horseback riding, a swimming pool, tennis courts, and hiking. Rates run $170.10 s, $139.73 d per person and up during the Feb. 1-April 30 season, less other months. Three-day minimum stay requested.

**White Stallion Ranch** sprawls over 3,000 acres some 17 miles northwest of Tucson, 9251 W. Twin Peaks Rd., Tucson, AZ 85743; tel. 297-0252 or (800) 782-5546. The ranch offers pool, spa, tennis courts, horseback riding, and varied ranch activities from early October to the end of April; rates are $144.59-171.32 s, $233.28-386.37 d.

**Rancho de la Osa Guest Ranch** dates back 250 years to a Spanish land grant; it's 66 miles southwest of Tucson near the Mexican border (Box 1, Sasabe, AZ 85633); tel. 823-4257 or (800) 872-6240. Guests can enjoy horseback riding, pool, spa, and lots of peace and quiet. It's open year-round; rates are $133.82 s, $230 d, with a two-night minimum; nonriders and summer visitors receive discounts.

## RESORTS

**Canyon Ranch Spa** is a health-and-fitness vacation resort offering an active program of exercise classes, tennis, racquetball, swimming, hiking, biking, yoga, and meditation. Chefs prepare gourmet meals from natural ingredients. The 70-acre grounds lie northeast of town near Sabino Canyon at 8600 E. Rockcliff Rd., Tucson, AZ 85750; tel. 749-9000 or (800) 742-9000. A four-night package starts at $2312.33 s or d. There's a four-night minimum stay during the high season, but off-season daily rates are sometimes available.

**Tucson National Golf & Conference Resort** features lakes, a 27-hole golf course, extensive spa services, exercise room, tennis, swimming, and fine dining on 650 acres. It's at the base of the Catalinas on the northwest side of the city at 2727 W. Club Dr., Tucson, AZ 85741; tel. 297-2271 or (800) 528-4856. In high season, spa packages (two-night minimum) cost $352.52 s, $477.12 d per night; room-only rates run $292.88-372.75.

The **Westin La Paloma** features a 27-hole golf course, tennis, racquetball, two giant pools with waterfalls, and a handful of restaurants. It's on the north edge of town next to the Catalinas at 3800 E. Sunrise Dr., Tucson, AZ 85718; tel. 742-6000 or (800) 876-3683. The high-season rate is $340.48 d.

**Sheraton Tucson El Conquistador Golf and Tennis Resort** and the nearby El Conquistador Country Club offer 45 holes of golf, 32 lighted tennis courts, 16 racquetball courts, athletic club, pools, spas, horseback riding, jeep tours, and Western, Mexican, and continental dining. It's on the northwest side of town below

the Catalinas at 10000 N. Oracle Rd., Tucson, AZ 85737; tel. 742-7000 or (800) 325-7832. High-season rates run $260.40-1302 d.

**Loews Ventana Canyon Resort,** nestled in the foothills of the Catalinas, is north of the city at 7000 North Resort Dr., Tucson, AZ 85715; tel. 299-2020 or (800) 234-5117. The 93-acre grounds enclose a natural waterfall, two 18-hole golf courses, 10 lighted tennis courts, swimming pools, spa, health club, and a selection of restaurants. High-season rates start at $314.75 s, $399.34 d; suites are $745.50-2130.

**Westward Look Resort** offers eight tennis courts (five lighted for night use), three pools, three spas, jogging trail, fitness center, aerobics, massage therapy, and continental dining in the Gold Room on 80 acres at the north edge of town at 245 E. Ina Rd.; it's seven miles east of I-10 and one mile east of Oracle Road. High season rates run $209-269 s or d; tel. 297-1151 or (800) 722-2500.

## CAMPGROUNDS AND RV PARKS

**Catalina State Park,** 12 miles north of Tucson on Oracle Rd. (US 89), offers campsites in the foothills of the Santa Catalinas; rates are $8 for non-electric sites, $13 w/electricity; showers are available; you and your horse can camp in the equestrian center; tel. 628-5798. The Coronado National Forest features several campgrounds on **Mt. Lemmon Highway;** the closest to Tucson is **Molino Basin,** 18 miles away; tel. 749-8700.

**Gilbert Ray Campground** is in Tucson Mountain Park, eight miles west of town; rates are $6 (or $9 w/hookups) for tents or RVs; no showers; tel. 883-4200. **Justin's RV Park** is an adult park (children okay in summer) eight miles west of town near Tucson Mountain Park at 3551 S. San Joaquin Rd.; $12.50 w/hookups; adjacent Justin's Water World is open in summer; tel. 883-8340. You'll find **Prince of Tucson RV Park** at 3501 N. Freeway, on the west side of I-10, four miles northwest of Tucson; take I-10 Exit 254 (Prince Rd.). Features include a swimming pool, spa, and recreation room; RV spaces are $22.30 w/hookups; tel. 887-3501.

**Tratel Tucson RV Park** also lies four miles northwest of Tucson; take I-10 Exit 254 (Prince Rd.), then go a half mile south on the west frontage road of I-10 to 2070 W. Fort Lowell Rd.; pool and recreation room; charge for RVs w/hookups is $17.91; tel. 888-5401. **Rincon Country West RV Park** is four miles south of Tucson at 4555 S. Mission Rd.; take I-19 Exit 99 (Ajo Way), go a half mile west on Ajo Way, then turn south on Mission and drive another half mile. Seniors (55+) only; spas and many organized hobby and social activities; $27.28 w/hookups (no tents); tel. 294-5608.

**Crazy Horse RV Campground** is southeast of downtown at 6660 S. Craycroft Rd.; take I-10

Exit 268, then drive a quarter mile north on Craycroft; includes heated pool, spa, recreation room, and RV repairs; $19.17 RV w/hookups; tel. 574-0157. **Cactus Country RV Resort** lies 16 miles southeast of downtown off I-10; take Exit 275, then go 0.2 mile north to 10195 S. Houghton Road. It offers a pool, spa, and organized winter activities; rates are $13.42 tent, $23.43 RV w/hookups; tel. 574-3000.

Other RV parks and trailer parks are listed in the *Tucson Official Visitors Guide* and the Yellow Pages.

# TUCSON RESTAURANTS

The Mexican food in Tucson is often as tasty as meals served in Mexico. Visitors can also choose from Chinese, Middle Eastern, Greek, Italian, German, and French. More expensive bistros may require coat and tie; ask when making reservations.

Of course Tucson also offers plenty of cowboy food—the old standbys of steak, potatoes, beans, and biscuits. The following is only a small selection of Tucson eateries; see the *Tucson Official Visitors Guide* for further listings.

Restaurants are marked **$**: Inexpensive (to $8); **$$**: Moderate ($8-15); and **$$$**: Expensive (over $15).

## AMERICAN

**$$ to $$$  Arizona Inn:** The elegant dining room is open daily for breakfast, lunch, and dinner; 2200 E. Elm St. between Campbell and Tucson Blvd., two miles northeast of downtown; tel. 325-1541.

**$$ CCC Chuckwagon Suppers:** Enjoy mass quantities of real cowboy beef, beans, and other trappings, consumed to Western instrumental music; $14 adults, $7 children. Open Tues.-Sat. for dinner from late Dec. to mid-April. Reservations required. Located near the Tucson Mountains about 12 miles from downtown at 8900 Bopp Rd.; tel. 883-2333 or (800) 446-1798.

**$$ Cafe Sweetwater:** Steak, seafood, chicken, and veal are served in a casual atmosphere.

Jazz and blues musicians perform evenings, Tuesday and Thurs.-Saturday. It's open Mon.-Fri. for lunch and Mon.-Sat. for dinner. Reservations requested. You'll find it just east of downtown at 340 E. Sixth St. and Fourth Ave.; tel. 622-6464.

**$ Egg Garden:** Eggs are in almost everything—omelettes, quiche, seafood, hamburgers, salads. Open daily for breakfast and lunch. Just east of downtown, 509 1/2 N. Fourth Ave. at Sixth St.; tel. 622-0918.

**$ Furr's Cafeterias:** Head to one of three locations for a huge selection of courses plus a buffet. All are open daily for lunch and dinner. Go six miles east of downtown to 5910 E. Broadway, tel. 747-7881; or four miles north of downtown to 4329 N. Oracle Rd., tel. 293-8550; or just north of downtown to 1095 W. St. Mary's Rd. and I-10, tel. 624-1688.

**$ Garland:** A good place for American, Mexican, Italian, and vegetarian food. Open daily for breakfast, lunch, and dinner. It's three-quarters of a mile northeast of downtown, 119 E. Speedway Blvd. at Sixth Ave.; tel. 792-4221.

**$$ Plaza Cafe:** You'll find this place, decked in Southwestern decor, in the Plaza Hotel and Conference Center. It's open daily for breakfast, lunch, and dinner less than three miles from downtown at 1900 E. Speedway Blvd.; tel. 327-7341.

**$$ Pinnacle Peak:** Don't wear a tie to this informal, family-style steakhouse; thousands of severed ties decorate the ceilings. It's open daily for dinner in Trail Dust Town, eight miles east of downtown at 6541 E. Tanque Verde Rd.; tel. 296-0911.

**$$ Sizzler:** Good value on steak or seafood dinners, with a giant salad bar. It's open daily for lunch and dinner with four locations in town: just west of downtown at 471 W. Congress, tel. 623-2888; four miles east of downtown at 4330 E. Broadway, tel. 326-5133; five miles southeast of downtown at 2048 E. Irvington Rd., tel. 889-5757; and in northwest Tucson at 3000 W. Ina Rd., tel. 742-0989.

**$$ to $$$ The Tucson Cork:** One of the best steakhouses in Tucson, it also serves chicken, seafood, and prime rib daily for dinner. Eight miles east of downtown at 6320 E. Tanque Verde Rd.; tel. 296-1631.

## SOUTHWESTERN

**$$$ Janos:** Exceptionally good and creative New Southwestern cuisine is served here in the historic Stevens House. Open Mon.-Sat. (Tues.-Sat. in summer) for dinner. It's downtown in the El Presidio district at 150 N. Main Ave.; tel. 884-9426.

## MEXICAN

**$$ Carlos Murphy's:** Feast on tasty food downtown in the historic 1890 El Paso-South-

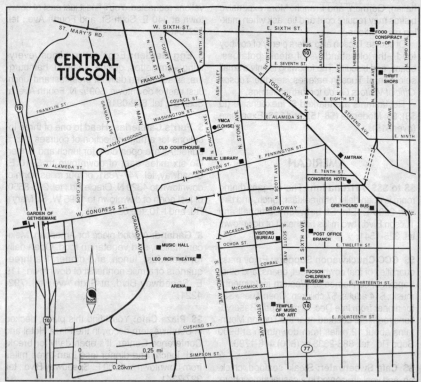

street vendor

western Depot; open daily for lunch and dinner at 419 W. Congress; tel. 628-1956.

**$ to $$ El Adobe:** Sonoran cuisine in one of Tucson's oldest Mexican restaurants; open daily except Sunday for lunch and dinner. It's at 52 W. Congress.; tel. 628-1322.

**$ to $$ El Charro:** This longtime favorite (founded 1922) is now in the historic Le Flein House downtown. Open daily for lunch and dinner, with brunch available Saturday and Sunday, at 311 N. Court Ave.; tel. 622-1922.

**$ to $$ El Parador:** The dining room features a garden atmosphere; flamenco guitar music is played several nights a week. Open daily for lunch and dinner, Sunday for brunch and dinner. It's two miles east of downtown at 2744 E. Broadway; tel. 881-2808.

**$ to $$ El Saguarito:** This healthy Mexican food alternative offers food cooked with canola oil. Open Mon.-Sat. for breakfast, lunch, and dinner. Located six miles north of downtown at 7216 N. Oracle Rd.; tel. 297-1264.

**$ El Torero:** This popular place with generous servings is open for lunch and dinner; closed Tuesday. It's in South Tucson at 231 E. 26th St., near S. Fourth Ave.; tel. 622-9534. You'll find other Mexican restaurants in the same neighborhood; South Tucson is a one-mile-square city-within-a-city just south of downtown Tucson.

**$ to $$ La Fuente Restaurant & Lounge:** Strolling mariachis serenade diners in the evenings. Lunches feature a tostada-taco bar Mon.-Thurs. and a buffet on Friday; a champagne brunch with music is offered on Sundays. It's open daily for lunch and dinner at 1749 N. Oracle Rd.; tel. 623-8659.

**$ to $$ La Parrilla Suiza:** Charcoal-grilled and other authentic Mexico City food is served daily for lunch and dinner. About seven miles northeast of downtown at 5602 E. Speedway Blvd.; tel. 747-4838. Also two miles north of downtown at 2720 N. Oracle Rd.; tel. 624-4300.

**$ Pancho's Mexican Buffet** delivers excellent value in a daily lunch and dinner buffet served cafeteria fashion. For seconds, just raise the tiny Italian flag at your table. Head eight miles east of downtown to 7701 E. Broadway Blvd.; tel. 722-3114.

## CONTINENTAL

**$$$ Charles:** This old English manor offers elegant dining Mon.-Sat. for dinner only and Sunday for brunch. Reservations required. Located eight miles east of downtown at 6400 E. El Dorado Circle; from Speedway Blvd., go north 0.2 mile on Wilmot Rd., then right on El Dorado Place and follow signs; tel. 296-7173.

**$$$ Gold Room:** Excellent food and service accompany a sweeping view of the city. Open daily for breakfast, lunch, and dinner. Reservations required. It's at the Westward Look Resort, nine miles north of downtown, 245 E. Ina Rd.; tel. 297-1151, ext. 413.

**$$ to $$$ Encore Med & Cafe Triana:** Offers continental bistro-style dining featuring cuisine of France, Spain, and Italy. The adjoining Cafe Triana serves Mediterranean fare with authentic tapas. Open for lunch and dinner daily, it's eight miles northeast of downtown at 2959 N. Swan Rd.; tel. 795-5561.

**$$$ Tack Room:** This highly rated restaurant occupies an adobe hacienda. Open daily for dinner only; may close Mondays. Reservations required. It's 10 miles northeast of downtown at 2800 N. Sabino Canyon Rd.; tel. 722-2800.

## FRENCH

**$$$ Le Rendez-Vous:** Fine French food is served in a formal setting Tues.-Fri. for lunch and Tues.-Sun. for dinner. Reservations requested. Go six miles northeast of downtown to 3844 E. Fort Lowell Rd.; tel. 323-7373.

**$$$ Penelope's:** Personal service and excellent food. It's open Tues.-Fri. for lunch and Tues.-Sun. for dinner. Reservations requested. At 3071 N. Swan Rd.; tel. 325-5080.

## ITALIAN

**$ to $$ Caruso's:** Southern Italian cooking is served in this Tucson institution dating back to the 1930s. Open Tues.-Sun. for dinner. Located just east of downtown at 434 N. Fourth Ave.; tel. 624-5765.

**$$$ Daniel's Restaurant and Trattoria:** This highly rated restaurant serves the cuisine of northern Italy daily for dinner. Located about seven miles northeast of downtown in St. Philip's Plaza at 4340 N. Campbell Ave.; tel. 742-3200.

**$$ to $$$ Scordato's:** One of the best Italian restaurants in town, it offers a wide selection of entrees and an extensive wine list. Open daily except Monday for dinner. Six miles west of downtown at 4405 W. Speedway Blvd.; tel. 624-8946, reservations requested.

## GREEK AND MIDDLE EASTERN

**$$ Athens on 4th Ave.:** Multiregion Greek cuisine cooked with many authentic, imported ingredients. Open Mon.-Fri. for lunch and Mon.-Sat. for dinner. It's half a mile from downtown at 500 N. 4th Ave. #6; tel. 624-6886.

**$ Casa Blanca:** Gyros and a variety of vegetarian specialties from the Middle East are featured here daily for lunch and dinner. Located one mile east of downtown at 974 E. University Blvd.; tel. 623-7888.

**$$ to $$$ Olive Tree:** Stop by for generous portions of Greek food and a choice of indoor or patio tables. Open Mon.-Sat. for lunch and daily for dinner. Head seven miles east of downtown to 7000 E. Tanque Verde Rd.; tel. 298-1845.

## INDIAN

**$$ Cuisine of India (New Delhi Palace):** Seafood, meats, and vegetarian food are prepared in tandoori and other styles daily for lunch (buffet and a la carte) and dinner. It's six miles

ast of downtown at 6751 E. Broadway Blvd.;
l. 296-8585.

## CHINESE

**Gee's Garden:** serves Cantonese food daily for
nch and dinner, four miles northeast of down-
wn at 1145 N. Alvernon Way; tel. 325-5353.

**$ Ki-Rin:** This popular restaurant offers a va-
ety of Chinese and Japanese cuisines daily
r lunch and dinner. It's three miles northeast of
owntown at 2511 E. Speedway; tel. 323-9886.

**$ Lotus Garden:** A long menu features Can-
nese and Szechuan specialties. Open daily
r lunch and dinner. Six miles northeast of
owntown at 5975 E. Speedway; tel. 298-3351.

## MALAYSIAN

**$ Selamat Makan:** Satay, rice curries, veg-
tarian dishes, and other flavorful food are
erved for dinner Tues.-Sunday. It's about 4.5

miles northeast of downtown in Grant Road
Plaza, 3502 E. Grant Rd.; tel. 325-6755.

## THAI

**$ to $$ China-Thai Cuisine:** Tasty Thai, Man-
darin, and Szechuan food is cooked here. Open
daily for lunch and dinner. Seven miles northeast
of downtown at 6502 E. Tanque Verde Rd.; tel.
885-6860.

**$ to $$ Mina's Thai:** Make a trip here for top-
rated Thai dining. Open Mon.-Fri. for lunch and
daily for dinner. Three miles northeast of downtown at 2744 N. Campbell Ave.; tel. 322-5040.

## VIETNAMESE

**$ to $$ Wokpan:** A large selection of spicy cui-
sine is offered daily for lunch and dinner, and an
economical buffet is served Mon.-Friday. It's
three miles east of downtown at 3250 E. Speedway Blvd.; tel. 881-4686.

# ON THE TOWN IN TUCSON

## ENTERTAINMENT

ou'll find movie, performance, and social list-
gs in the *Tucson Weekly,* free at newsstands,
nd in the entertainment sections of the *Ari-
ona Daily Star* and *Tucson Citizen.*

### heater and Concerts

he **University of Arizona** offers many fine
roductions; tel. 621-1162, Fine Arts Box Of-
ce; recorded announcement after hours. Per-
rming groups include the **University Reper-
ory Theatre,** Oct.-April in **Marroney Theatre,**
rama Building; **Studio Theatre,** inexpensive
tudent productions, call for location, Sept.-May;
nd **University of Arizona Repertory Theatre,**
ummer productions.

The **University of Arizona Artist Series**
rings prominent performers on campus to
entennial Hall, just inside the main (east)

gate on University Blvd.; tel. 621-3341 (box
office).

Many performances take place at the **Tucson
Convention Center** Music Hall, Leo Rich The-
atre, and Arena; tel. 791-4266. You can attend
performances at the Tucson Convention Center
(TCC) of the **Ballet Arizona** Nov.-April, tel. 882-
5022; the **Tucson Symphony,** Thursday and
Friday evenings Sept.-May., tel. 882-8585; the
**Arizona Opera Company,** Oct.-March, tel. 293-
4336; **Arizona Friends of Chamber Music,**
Oct.-April; tel. 298-5806; and the **Southern Ari-
zona Light Opera Company (SALOC),** Sept.-
May, tel. 323-7888.

**Pima Community College's Center for the
Arts** offers a large variety of theatrical and musical performances produced not only by the
college but by many of the area's cultural organizations. The college's facilities include
**Proscenium Theatre, Black Box Theatre,** the
**Recital Hall,** and a small art gallery within a

five minutes drive west from downtown at 2202 W. Anklam Rd.; tel. 884-6458.

**Arizona Theatre Company** presents a series of plays Oct.-May at the Temple of Music and Art, 330 S. Scott Ave.; tel. 622-2823. The experimental **Invisible Theatre** offers seven performances Sept.-June; it's one mile northeast of downtown at 1400 N. First Ave.; tel. 882-9721. For hilarious family entertainment, take in an old-fashioned melodrama at the **Gaslight Theatre,** Wed.-Sun. year-round, 7010 E. Broadway, eight miles east of downtown; tel. 886-9428. The **Tucson Jazz Society** hotline lists upcoming jazz events; tel. 743-3399.

### Sporting Events

The University of Arizona **Wildcat** teams compete in football, basketball, baseball, tennis, swimming, track and field, and other sports during the school year. For ticket info call the McKale Center; tel. 621-2411. Hi Corbett Field in Reid Park hosts the **Tucson Toros** baseball team April-Sept.-; tel. 325-2621. Greyhounds hit the track at **Tucson Greyhound Park** in South Tucson at 2601 S. Third Ave. at E. 36th St.; call for schedule, tel. 884-7576. Stock cars roar toward the finish line at **Tucson Raceway Park** March-Nov.; take the I-10 Rita Exit to 12500 S. Houghton Rd. in Vail; tel. 762-9200.

# EVENTS

Something's happening nearly every day, an the Visitors Bureau knows what it is. See the events listings in the *Tucson Official Visitors Guide.* Some of the best-known annual happenings include the following.

**January: Southern Arizona Square, Round Dance and Clogging Festival** offers dances and workshops.

**February:** The **Northern Telecom Open** draws more than 100 professional golfers. **Tucson Gem and Mineral Show** is considered the world's best. About 500 horses display their hunter-jumper skills in the **Tucson Winter Classic Horse Show.** Cowboys get together for a big four-day rodeo and a colorful parade in **La Fiesta de los Vaqueros.**

**March:** A **Pow Wow Conference** attracts Southwestern Indian groups for traditional and modern singing and dancing. Skiers celebrate the downhill in the **Mt. Lemmon Ski Carnival** with competitions and games. Top women golfers compete in the **Ping/Welch Championship.** The Easter **Tucson Festival** is a six-week extravaganza of fiestas, concerts, theater, and music celebrating the cultures and history of Tucson. Yaqui Indians of Pascua Village in Tuc-

La Fiesta
de los
Vaqueros

1. Red Rock Crossing, near Sedona; 2. Devil's Bridge, near Sedona; 3. below Havasu Falls, Havasupai Indian Reservation; 4. along the Echo Canyon Trail, Chiricahua National Monument; 5. on Desert View Trail, Organ Pipe Cactus National Monument (all photos by B. Weir)

1. desert paintbrush; 2. teddy bear cholla cactus; 3. ocotillo blossoms; 4. prickly pear cactus;
5. saguaro cactus; 6. beavertail cactus (all photos by B. Weir)

on stage the **Yaqui Easter Ceremonials,** a passion play, during the Easter season; the ceremony is a mixture of Catholic and tribal ritual concerning the forces of good overcoming those of evil. **San Xavier Pageant and Fiesta** celebrates the founding of the mission. **Simon Peter Passion Play** is a three-hour Easter pageant performed at the Tucson Convention Center.

**April:** Visit Davis-Monthan Air Force Base or **Aerospace and Arizona Days** open house and air show. During **Spring Fling,** university students stage a carnival featuring rides, games, and food. The **Fourth Avenue Street Fair** features artists, craftspeople, entertainers, and food on N. Fourth Ave. between University and Eighth St.; the fest repeats in December. The **Pima County Fair** offers a carnival, entertainment, and livestock shows at the Pima County Fairgrounds. The **Tucson International Mariachi Conference** presents a stage extravaganza, workshops, and fair.

**May:** The Hispanic community celebrates **Cinco de Mayo** on the 5th with art, music, dances, and food. Local restaurants put their best food forward at the **Taste of Tucson** fest held at the Tucson Convention Center.

**July:** Parades, picnics, and fireworks commemorate **Independence Day.**

**August:** Fiesta de San Agustín honors the birthday of Tucson's patron saint with music, dancing, and food.

**September:** The **Mexican Independence Day Celebration** is a traditional Mexican fiesta with entertainment and food.

**October:** Experience Tucson's ethnic diversity in art, music, dance, and food during **Tucson Heritage Experience Festival.** The **Tohono O'odham All-Indian Rodeo and Fair** features a parade, singing, dancing, crafts, and food—all offered by the tribe on their reservation near Sells, 58 miles southwest of Tucson.

**November:** Students compete in the **University of Arizona Rodeo.** Thousands of bicyclists challenge the clock and each other in **El Tour de Tucson** races. **Holiday in Lights** begins the Christmas season in late November/early December with lights, carriage rides, a Holiday Village, and other festivities.

**December: Fourth Avenue Street Fair** brings artists, craftspeople, entertainers, and food outdoors to N. Fourth Ave. between University and Eighth Streets. Football fans gather in Arizona Stadium at the end of the year for the NCAA **Weiser Pizza Copper Bowl.**

# RECREATION

## Reid Park

This spacious green park in the middle of Tucson features a zoo, Hi Corbett baseball field, soccer field, rose garden, lakes, and picnic areas. The park is three miles east of downtown; enter from Country Club Rd., 22nd St., or Camino Campestre. The **Tucson City Parks and Recreation** office, in the park at 900 S. Randolph Way, offers information on facilities and programs centered at Reid and other parks; tel. 791-4873.

## Swimming

Tucson Parks and Recreation maintains 19 swimming pools, most open during the summer only. Look up addresses and phone numbers in the telephone book under Tucson City Government.

You can also swim in the indoor pool at L.A. Lohse Memorial YMCA, 60 W. Alameda St., tel. 623-5200, and in the outdoor pool at University of Arizona's McKale Center, tel. 621-2599.

## Tennis

With over 200 courts in town, it's not hard to find a place to play. See "Activities and Attractions" in the Visitors Bureau's *Tucson Official Visitors Guide.* The **Randolph Recreation Complex** offers 25 lighted tennis courts, instruction, and a pro shop, as well as 10 lighted racquetball courts. It's three miles east of downtown at 50 S. Alvernon Way, just south of E. Broadway; tel. 791-4896.

## Golf

This is another sport enjoyed by many Tucson residents. About 17 courses are open to the public; see "Activities and Attractions" in the Visitors Bureau's *Tucson Official Visitors Guide.*

**Randolph Park,** just east of Reid Park, has two 18-hole courses at 602 S. Alvernon Way; tel. 791-4336 (reservations) or 325-2811 (pro shop).

The other municipal courses, all 18-hole, are **Trini Alvarez-El Rio** (tel. 791-4336 reservations, 623-6783 pro shop); **Silverbell** (tel. 791-4336 reservations, 743-7284 pro shop); and **Fred Enke** (tel. 791-4336 reservations, 296-8607 pro shop).

### Horseback Riding

Several stables will assist you in seeing the scenery from atop a horse or hay wagon; reservations suggested. **Desert High Country Stables** offers rides and cookouts in the foothills of the Tucson Mountains, about 15 miles northwest of downtown at 6501 W. Ina Rd., two miles west of I-10; tel. 744-3789. **Pusch Ridge Stables** offers many trips in the Santa Catalina foothills 14 miles north of downtown at 11220 N. Oracle Rd.; tel. 297-6908.

**El Conquistador Stables** features rides and cookouts in the Santa Catalina foothills 11 miles north of downtown, at the Sheraton Tucson El Conquistador Resort, 10000 N. Oracle Rd.; tel. 742-4200. **Redington Land and Cattle Co.** rides venture into the Rincon Mountains, east of town at 14101 E. Redington Rd.; tel. 749-5555 (office) or 749-1075 (ranch).

### Southern Arizona Hiking Club

Hikes organized by this active group range from easy to challenging. The club schedules day-hikes, backpacks, climbs, river trips, ski tours and snowshoe trips. Members also promote conservation and build trails. Visitors are welcome on hikes. Contact the club for membership information at Box 12724, Tucson, AZ 85732.

### Skiing

At **Mount Lemmon Ski Valley** in the Santa Catalina Mountains you can enjoy downhill skiing during the mid-December to mid-April season. One double chair lift and a beginner's tow take skiers up the slopes. The longest run is three-quarters of a mile, dropping from 9,150 to 8,200 feet through fir and aspen forests; tel. 576-1321. To check on snow and road conditions, call 576-1400 for a recorded message.

### Casinos

**Desert Diamond Casino** offers slot machines, video poker, Las Vegas style and video keno, video blackjack, video craps, bingo, and a card room 24 hours a day at 7350 Old Nogales Hwy., one mile south of Valencia Rd., near the Tucson International Airport; tel. 294-7777 or 889-7354. **Casino of the Sun** offers the same sort of activities in a slightly smaller place at 7406 S. Camino de Oeste; tel. 883-1700 or (800) 344-9435.

# OTHER PRACTICALITIES

## SERVICES

The **main post office** is 2.5 miles southeast of downtown at 1501 S. Cherrybell Stravanue; tel. 620-5174. The downtown branch is at 141 S. Sixth Avenue. You'll find another branch at 913 E. University Blvd., between Tyndall and Park Avenues. Exchange foreign currency at **Valley National Bank,** 2 E. Congress St. downtown, tel. 792-7317.

**Pima County Medical Society** will refer you to any sort of doctor you might need; it's open Mon.-Fri. 8:30 a.m.-4:30 p.m.; tel. 795-7985.

Down and out? **Temporary Employment** (Arizona Department of Economic Security) at 301 W. 22nd St. offers free services; tel. 628-5174.

## SHOPPING

### Fourth Avenue

The section of Fourth Ave. between Fourth and Seventh Streets features many unusual craft and antique shops and restaurants. Big street fairs take place here in late April and early December. The **Salvation Army** and **Tucson Thrift Shop** stores on Fourth Ave. at Seventh St. offer used clothing and other items. For health foods, visit the **Food Conspiracy Co-op;** it features an herb room and whole-grain flours. Open daily; nonmembers welcome; 412 N. Fourth Ave., between Sixth and Seventh Streets; tel. 624-4821.

## Shopping Centers

Tucson features four giant malls open daily, full of department stores, specialty shops, and restaurants; all but the Tucson Mall also offer movie theaters. All malls are enclosed and air-conditioned.

**El Con Mall** is three miles east of downtown at 3601 E. Broadway; tel. 795-9958. **Park Mall** is six miles east of downtown at 5870 E. Broadway and Wilmot; tel. 748-1222. **Tucson Mall** is one of the largest in the state, with more than 200 stores, 4.5 miles north of downtown at 4500 N. Oracle and Wetmore; tel. 293-7330. **Foothills Mall** has many shops, 10 miles north of downtown at 7401 N. La Cholla Blvd. and W. Ina Rd.; tel. 742-7191.

## Art Galleries

Be sure to see **DeGrazia's Gallery in the Sun** (see "North of Downtown," above). **Old Town Artisans,** in the middle of the downtown El Presidio District, offers a large selection of varied wares, including pottery, clothing, jewelry, woodcarvings, and other crafts produced by local, Indian, Mexican, and international artists. Open Mon.-Sat. 9:30 a.m.-5:30 p.m. and Sunday noon-5:30 p.m. (reduced summer hours); tel. 623-6024. On the corner of 186 N. Meyer Ave. and Telles St., near the Tucson Museum of Art.

# INFORMATION

## Tourist Office

The very helpful folks at **Metropolitan Tucson Convention & Visitors Bureau** will provide an excellent *Tucson Official Visitors Guide* and many brochures describing area sights and services; you can find them downtown at 130 S. Scott Ave., Tucson, AZ 85701; tel. 624-1817. Open Mon.-Fri. 8 a.m.-5 p.m., also Saturday and Sunday 9 a.m.-4 p.m. in winter; pick up literature outside when the office is closed.

## Coronado National Forest

The **Supervisor's Office** contains general information on all the districts in the Coronado, including many of the most scenic areas in southeastern Arizona. Open Mon.-Fri. 8 a.m.-4:30 p.m.; it's downtown in room 6A (sixth floor) of the Federal Building, 300 W. Congress St. (Tucson, AZ 85701); tel. 670-4552.

---

### IMPORTANT TUCSON TELEPHONE NUMBERS

| | |
|---|---|
| Emergencies (police, fire, medical) | 911 |
| Police (Tucson) | 791-4452 |
| Pima County sheriff | 741-4600 |
| Crisis Counseling and | |
| Suicide Prevention | 323-9373 |
| Information and Referral Services | |
| (community services) | 881-1794 |
| Weather recording (press 1020) | 296-7700 |
| Tucson Parks and Recreation | 791-4873 |
| Tucson Convention Center | |
| Box Office | 791-4266 |
| Charge Line | 791-4836 |
| University of Arizona Ticket Offices | |
| Sports Events | 621-2411 |
| Centennial Hall Box Office | 621-3341 |
| Fine Arts Box Office | 621-1162 |
| Sun Tran (city bus) | 792-9222 |

---

For specific information on the campgrounds, trails, and backcountry regions of the Santa Catalinas, contact the **Santa Catalina Ranger District** office; open Mon.-Fri. 8 a.m.-4:30 p.m. and Saturday and Sunday 8:30 a.m.-4:30 p.m.; in the Sabino Canyon Visitor Center, 5700 N. Sabino Canyon Rd. (Tucson, AZ 85715); tel. 749-8700.

For information about recreational opportunities on land administered by the Bureau of Land Management in southeastern Arizona, contact their Tucson Resource Area office Mon.-Fri. 8 a.m.-4 p.m.; 12661 E. Broadway (Tucson, AZ 85748); tel. 722-4289.

## Libraries

The main **city library** is downtown at 101 N. Stone between Pennington and Alameda; open Monday 10 a.m.-9 p.m., Tues.-Thurs. 9 a.m.-6 p.m., Friday 10 a.m.-5 p.m., Saturday 9 a.m.-5 p.m., and Sunday 1-5 p.m.; tel. 791-4114 (recording) or 791-4010 (Infoline). The library has 18 branches.

**University of Arizona libraries** are open to the public and include some outstanding collections; pick up free information pamphlets in the main library lobby. The main library is open Mon.-Thurs. 7:30 a.m.-1 a.m., Friday 7:30 a.m.-6 p.m., Saturday 10 a.m.-6 p.m., and Sunday 11 a.m.-1 a.m.; shorter hours are offered during summer and vacations; tel. 621-6441. Hikers and travelers can peruse the map collection in the basement, where topographic maps of the entire country are available for photocopying; open Mon.-Thurs. 7:30 a.m.-11 p.m., Friday 7:30 a.m.-6 p.m., Saturday 10 a.m.-6 p.m., and Sunday 11 a.m.-11 p.m. during regular semesters (late Aug. to mid-May); it's on the first floor of the main library. Other collections include Arizona, Southwest, Government Documents, Music, Oriental Studies, and the Media Center.

### Newspapers

Tucson's major dailies are the *Arizona Daily Star* in the morning and the *Tucson Citizen* in the afternoon. The *Star's* Friday "Entertainment" section reports on nightlife, concerts, theater, and dancing. Sights and special events are listed in its "Tucson Today" column (Mon.-Sat.). The "Art Calendar" in the Sunday entertainment section lists art galleries and shows.

The *Tucson Citizen* includes local happenings and movies in its "Living" section Mon.-Fri., with more detailed reports in the Thursday "Calendar" section. The *Tucson Weekly* calls itself "the city's news and arts journal"; you'll find most everything occurring in Tucson listed in its pages, along with feature articles and restaurant listings; it's free at newsstands.

### Bookstores

The **University of Arizona** bookstore sells Arizona and Southwest titles along with general reading material and textbooks. It's at the west end of the Student Union, closed on Sunday; tel. 621-2426.

Browse three excellent bookstores within three blocks. **Bookman's Used Books** claims to be Arizona's largest used-book store, with new titles and a newsstand too. It's at 1930 E. Grant Rd. at Campbell, tel. 325-5767; also at 3733 W. Ina Rd., tel. 579-0303, both open daily. **Books West Southwest,** 2452 N. Campbell Ave. (one block from Bookman's), specializes in books of the American Southwest including out of print and rare editions; tel. 326-3533. The **Book Stop** offers a large selection of used hardbound books, a fair selection of used paperback books, and some magazines at 2504 N. Campbell Ave.; tel. 326-6661.

**Audubon Nature Shop,** at 300 E. University Blvd., offers a selection of books on birdwatching as well as binoculars and other supplies; tel. 629-0510.

### Maps

For hiking, national forest, state, and Mexico maps visit **Summit Hut** (5045 E. Speedway Blvd., tel. 325-1554, and 990 E. University Blvd., tel. 792-0562) or **Tucson Maps** (3239 N. First Ave., tel. 887-4239).

# TRANSPORT

### Tours

**Tucson Tour Company** offers a city tour, shuttles out to the Arizona-Sonora Desert Museum and Old Tucson, and longer trips to Nogales and other destinations; tel. 297-2911. **Gray Line Tours** offers day-trips from mid-January to mid-April—Desert Museum/Old Tucson (Monday, $56), Nogales/Mexico (Tuesday and Saturday, $53), Desert Museum (Wednesday, $34), City Tour (Thursday, $28), Old Tucson (Friday, $34), Biosphere 2 (special request, $50), and Tombstone/Bisbee (special request, $84). Gray Line makes longer runs of two to five days to the Grand Canyon, Canyon de Chelly, and other sights of northern Arizona ($139-649), year-round; Box 1991, Tucson, AZ 85702; tel. 622-8811 or (800) 276-1528 (outside Arizona).

**Old Pueblo Tours** offers 6.5-hour tours of the Tucson area in a 14-passenger luxury minibus at $35 adult, $15 child (16 and under); departure is at 9:30 a.m.; tel. 575-1175.

Other companies offering tours at similar prices to the sights around Tucson and southeastern Arizona include **Great Western Tours,** tel. 721-0980, **Tucson Tour Company,** tel. 297-2911, and **Best of the West Detours,** tel. 749-5388.

See the rugged backcountry on jeep tours offered by **Mountain View,** tel. 622-4488 and **Sunshine Jeep Tours,** tel. 742-1943.

For hot air balloon flights in the Tucson area call **Fleur de Tucson;** rates are $110-135; tel. 529-1025 or 792-3573; or **A Southern Arizona Balloon Experience;** $115.50; tel. 624-3599 or (800) 524-3599.

**Papillon Helicopters** offers one-hour tours ver the Catalina Mountains ($160 per person, vo-person minimum), and half-hour tours over ucson, day or night ($80 per person, two-person minimum) from the Tucson International irport; tel. 573-6817.

For backcountry half day and full day mountain bike tours call **Southwestern Arizona Off Road Adventures** at 882-6567.

Tours of archaeological sites are given by a rofessional archaeologist through the Center for Desert Archaeology at 885-6283.

## axi and Auto Rentals

axis include **Allstate Cab,** tel. 798-1111, **Yellow Cab,** tel. 624-6611, and **Checker Cab,** tel. 23-1133. Tucson has over two dozen car rental gencies, with several at the airport; see the Yellow Pages.

## Auto Driveaways

These are cars awaiting delivery to another city. f the auto's destination is a place you're headed, ou can get, in effect, a free car rental. Driveaway companies do place some restrictions on ime and mileage, and you must make a deposit. For the lowest rates, ask for an economy car. See "Automobile Transporters & Driveaway Companies" in the Yellow Pages.

## Local Bus

**Sun Tran** takes you to the parks, sights, and shopping areas of the city and to the airport for only 75 cents. You must have exact change; transfers are free; ask the driver when you pay your fare. Most buses go to bed about 7 p.m., although a few routes run until 10 p.m. on weekdays. The Visitors Bureau offers free route maps. A 20-ride pass can be bought for $12.

Sun Tran also operates the **Fourth Avenue Rte. 200 Minibus** service between downtown areas and the University of Arizona Mon.-Sat.; 75 cents. For Sun Tran info call 792-9222.

## Long-Distance Bus

The **Greyhound** terminal lies downtown at 2 S. Fourth Ave. at E. Broadway; tel. (800) 231-2222 (fare and schedule) or 882-4386 (local terminal). Destinations and one-way fares include Los Angeles (six daily) $32; El Paso (seven daily) $29; Phoenix (12 daily) $12; and Flagstaff (four daily) $40.

**Bridgewater Transport** leaves the Greyhound terminal three times daily for Douglas ($19) via Sierra Vista ($14), and Bisbee ($16). **Citizen Auto Stage** departs Greyhound 14 times daily for Nogales ($6.50) with stops at communities along I-19. The station has lockers and a coffee shop.

**Arizona Shuttle Service** goes to Nogales from 844 W. Irvington Rd. ($7); tel. 795-6771.

## Train

**Amtrak** schedules three eastbound and three westbound departures every week. The terminal is downtown at 400 E. Toole Ave., two blocks north of the Greyhound station; for reservations and info call (800) 872-7245. The westbound train departs in the evening for Phoenix (three and one-quarter hours, $29 one-way), Yuma, and other locales, arriving in Los Angeles the next morning (11 hours, $110 one-way). The eastbound train leaves in the morning: one train goes to New Orleans (one and a half days, $222), the other to Chicago (two days, $227). Amtrak gives large discounts on some roundtrip fares.

## Air

The **Tucson International Airport** is 8.5 miles south of downtown. More than a dozen airlines and charters touch down here. See the Yellow Pages for airline companies and ticket agencies. To reach the airport from downtown, try a taxi, airport shuttle, or Sun Tran Bus #25. **Arizona Stagecoach** provides 24-hour shuttle service from outside the terminal to your destination. For pick-up to the airport, call 889-1000 at least four hours before your flight. **Arizona Shuttle Service** goes to Sky Harbor Airport in Phoenix from 5350 E. Speedway Blvd. and other Tucson locations ($19); tel. 795-6771.

# WEST TO ORGAN PIPE CACTUS NATIONAL MONUMENT

## TOHONO O'ODHAM INDIAN RESERVATION

Twenty-five miles west of Tucson on AZ 86 lies the main Tohono O'odham Reservation. The land appears inhospitable—dry sandy washes and plains, broken here and there by rocky hills or mountains. The first white people couldn't believe that humans lived in such wild and parched desert, yet the Tohono O'odham thrived here for centuries. Close relatives of the Pima, the Tohono O'odham once occupied a vast section of the Sonoran Desert of southern Arizona and northern Mexico. Neighboring Indians called these desert dwellers Papago, meaning Bean People, but the tribe prefers the more dignified term—Tohono O'odham, meaning Desert People Who Have Emerged from the Earth. The Tohono O'odham believe that their tribe, like the plants and animals, belongs to the earth.

Once the Tohono O'odham maintained both winter and summer villages, staying near reliable springs in the winter, then moving to fields watered by summer thunderstorms. They gathered mesquite beans, agave, cactus fruit, acorns, and other plant foods and hunted rodents, rabbits, deer, and pronghorn. They planted fields with native tepary beans, corn, and squash.

After the 1854 Gadsden Treaty split their land between Mexico and the United States, the Mexican Tohono O'odham population gradually withered away, absorbed by Mexican culture. Some families migrated into Arizona. Today only about 200 Tohono O'odham remain south of the border. In 1874, the U.S. government began setting aside land for the tribe in the 71,095-acre San Xavier Reservation. Tohono O'odham land now totals about 2,800,000 acres—roughly the size of Connecticut. The second-largest reservation in the country, it stretches across much of southern Arizona and is home to more than 8,000 people.

The old ways have largely disappeared because of contact with modern technology. Today most Tohono O'odham, like everyone else in Arizona, live in standard houses, farming, ranching, or working for wages. Still skilled basketmakers, their attractive wares are much in demand. You'll see Tohono O'odham crafts in trading posts and in the visitor center at Kitt Peak.

Early Spanish missionaries gained many converts—the Roman Catholic Church is the strongest denomination on the reservation, though there are Protestant believers as well. Almost all villages feature a small chapel.

### Visiting the Reservation

Most Tohono O'odham are friendly, but the tribe has never been much interested in tourism. Visitor facilities are sparse—gas stations few and far

senita cactus

between, campgrounds and motels nonexistent. Two attractions, in addition to the desert scenery, make a visit worthwhile: the Tohono O'odham All-Indian Rodeo and Fair and the world-famous Kitt Peak Observatory.

**Tohono O'odham All-Indian Rodeo and Fair**
Tohono O'odham cowboys show off their riding and roping skills in the tribe's big annual event, held in late January/early February. The Tohono O'odham put on a parade, exhibit crafts, serve Indian fry bread, and perform songs and dances. Obtain the dates from the tribal office in Sells, tel. 383-2221, or the Visitors Bureau in Tucson, tel. 632-6024.

## KITT PEAK

Astronomers spent three years studying 150 peaks in the Southwest before choosing this site in 1958. Large, white domes enclosing instruments that unravel the mysteries of the universe cling to the 6,900-foot summit. The 22 telescopes come in many sizes and types, including two that use radio waves. Some are owned by universities, foremost of which is the University of Arizona in Tucson.

Before Kitt Peak was built, students and women found it almost impossible to secure time at a major telescope; here they have an equal chance. Astronomers use the equipment free of charge, but there are no rain checks. People learn to be philosophical, waiting many months only to be clouded out.

Computers control the instruments; CCD (charge-coupled device) image sensors convert light into digital form and store it on computer tape for later analysis. It's rare for an observer to actually look through telescopes these days, and most instruments don't even feature an eyepiece.

Kitt Peak is funded by the National Science Foundation and managed by a consortium of 24 universities, the Association of Universities for Research in Astronomy, and by the National Optical Science Observatories.

**Visitor Center**
You're welcome to drive up and see the observatory and astronomy exhibits. Visitor center displays illustrate the nature of light and how telescopes work. A short, self-guided tour of the grounds passes some of the most impressive telescopes. These include the McMath-Pierce Solar, which doesn't look like a telescope at all; the 2.1-meter (84-inch) telescope; the Mayall four-meter (158-inch) telescope; and the new W.I.Y.N. 3.5-meter (138-inch) telescope.

Most telescopes at Kitt Peak are not designed for magnification as much as for light-gathering power—a distant star looks the same size through even the biggest scopes. An exception is the McMath-Pierce Solar Telescope, which produces a 30-inch image of the sun by using mirrors in a slanted 500-foot corridor. Three hundred of these feet run below ground. You can go inside to inspect the interior; a TV screen displays the sun's image. This telescope won an architectural award in 1962, a rare accolade for an observatory.

The 2.1-meter telescope nearby was the first large instrument on Kitt Peak for nighttime viewing; a viewing gallery and exhibits are inside. The scope is used to observe distant stars and galaxies in both the visible and infrared spectra. The Mayall four-meter, one of the world's largest telescopes, is housed in a building 19 stories high. An elevator takes you to the 10th-floor observation deck, offering panoramic views of southern Arizona and northern Sonora. Compare this facility with the size of the W.I.Y.N. building. The Mayall telescope uses an old-style mount with one axis parallel to the axis upon which the Earth rotates so that a large building is necessary to provide room for telescope movement in tracking the stars. The W.I.Y.N. instrument merely moves up and down, left and right, and a computer combines these movements to track the stars. Today, very little space is needed for telescope movement.

Kitt Peak Observatory is open daily 10 a.m.-3:30 p.m. except New Year's Day, Thanksgiving Day, and December 24 and 25. Donations are gladly accepted. A shop in the museum sells Tohono O'odham basketry at very good prices, as well as astronomy-related posters, videos, and T-shirts. Guided free, one-hour tours of the observatory are offered daily at 10:30 a.m., 1:30 p.m., and 2:30 p.m.; the one-mile walk includes climbing some steps; donations are requested.

An observatory housing a 16-inch telescope has been constructed directly above the entrance to the visitor center for future open house nights.

On the drive up, you'll pass a picnic area on the left (1.5 miles before the visitor center) with a picnic ramada, tables, drinking water, restrooms, and a soft drink vending machine; Kitt Peak has no stores or restaurants so picnickers must come prepared. The radio telescope dish towering nearby is part of the Very Long Baseline Array. Ten radio telescopes scattered about the country operate as a single unit giving great definition. As an example of its power, the array can study objects on the moon the size of a football. The air is cool up here—15-20° colder than Tucson—so a jacket or sweater is usually required. Kitt Peak lies 56 miles southwest of Tucson via AZ 86. The last 12 miles consist of a paved and well-graded mountain road. Winter storms can close the road for short periods. Check schedules, basic information, and winter road conditions by calling 318-8600.

## SELLS

Sells serves as tribal headquarters and is the largest town on the Tohono O'odham Reservation. The dependable water here has made the place a popular stop for travelers since prehistoric times. Sells was originally known as Indian Oasis, but the name was changed in 1918 to honor Indian Commissioner Cato Sells. The town lies 58 miles southwest of Tucson via AZ 86, 20 miles past the turnoff for Kitt Peak. Offices, schools, and shops are 1.5 miles south of the main highway.

**Margaret's Indian Arts and Crafts Shop** in Sells Shopping Center stocks Tohono O'odham baskets and other Indian crafts. You can buy groceries at **Basha's,** also in the shopping center. The **Papago Cafe** lies on the main highway just west of the turnoff for Sells. You'll find another trading post with Tohono O'odham crafts 22 miles west at Quijotoa.

Before camping or exploring the backcountry, check to see if you'll need a permit; you'll also need permission from districts visited (the reservation is divided into 11). Ask about road conditions if you plan to venture off the main high-

way; dirt roads can become impassable after rains. Contact **Tohono O'odham Tribe Administration,** Sells, AZ 85634; tel. 383-2221.

## ORGAN PIPE CACTUS NATIONAL MONUMENT

The Sonoran Desert is at its finest in this remote area of Arizona. Some desert plants, such as the senita cactus and elephant tree, grow only here and in Mexico. The name of Arizona's largest national monument honors the giant organ pipe cactus, which thrives in this area. In appearance it's similar to the saguaro, though the organ pipe's many branches all radiate from the base.

Animals adapt to the heat by hiding out during the hottest part of the day. They're most active morning, evening, and night. Wildlife you might see include lizards, birds, kangaroo rats, kit foxes, ringtail cats, bobcats, javelina, bighorn sheep, and pronghorn. The six species of rattlesnakes are nocturnal during hot weather—a good reason to use a flashlight at night. About 40 species of birds stay year-round, more than 230 others drop in while migrating. Quitobaquito Oasis is a prime birding spot (see "Puerto Blanco Scenic Drive," below).

If you're lucky enough to arrive in March or April after a wet winter, you'll see the desert ablaze with flowers clad in yellow, blue, red, and violet. First to bloom are annual plants, which must quickly germinate and produce seeds before the onslaught of the summer heat. Next come the smaller cacti, such as cholla and prickly pear. Last to bloom are the big saguaro and organ pipe, with blossoms peaking in May or June.

### Visitor Center
For an introduction to the highly adaptable plants and wildlife that live here, start at the visitor center, located 22 miles south of Why. A short slide program shows native animals and the effects of seasonal changes on the land. Another slide program concerns desert wildflowers. Exhibits describe plants and animals of the region and the effects of humans on the desert. Just outside, a short nature trail identifies common plants and gives more info on the desert environment.

Rangers can answer your questions and issue camping permits. Books, prints, and a topo map are sold. Naturalist programs take place during the cooler months at the visitor center, on trails, and at the campground.

Summer is the quiet season at the monument, as daytime highs commonly range from 95° to 105° F. Thunderstorms arrive in late summer, bringing about half the annual 9.5 inches or so of rain. Winters run cool to warm, with occasional gentle rains. The visitor center is open daily 8 a.m.-5 p.m.; tel. 387-6849. Monument admission is $4 per vehicle.

### Puerto Blanco Scenic Drive

Varied desert environments, Quitobaquito Oasis, and the rare desert plants of the Senita Basin are highlights of this 53-mile loop. A pamphlet explains features at numbered stops; pick one up at the visitor center or at the start of the drive, just west of the visitor center. Nearly the entire route is graded dirt, designed for slow speeds—allow at least a half day. Note that a section of the drive is one-way (counterclockwise) and that you can't turn back.

**Quitobaquito,** one mile off the loop, features a large, artificial pond surrounded by tall cottonwoods. The springs lie 100 yards north up a trail. Ducks and other waterfowl—not what you'd expect in the desert—drop in during the spring and autumn. Coots stay here year-round.

Father Kino and other early Spanish missionaries and explorers stopped here on their way to the Colorado River. The '49ers headed for the California goldfields came by too, favoring a southern route to avoid hostile Indians roaming farther north. Many goldseekers perished of thirst on the fearsome Camino del Diablo or Devil's Highway between Sonoita and the Colorado River. Quitobaquito was one of few sources of water on the route.

**Senita Basin,** four miles off the loop, is home to the senita cactus and elephant tree. Similar in appearance to organ pipe cactus, the senita is distinguished by its gray whiskers and sparse arm ribs. The elephant tree looks like the root system of an upside-down tree. Examples of both a senita and elephant tree are at stop 24.

### Ajo Mountain Drive

Heading into the more rugged country of the eastern part of the monument, this drive skirts the base of 4,808-foot Mt. Ajo. Most of the 21-mile gravel loop road is one-way; pick up a pamphlet describing the drive at the visitor center or at the start of the loop, just across the highway from the visitor center; allow at least two hours. Good views from Diablo Canyon Picnic Area and from Bull Pasture Trail.

### Hiking

Several trails begin at the campground, 1.5

*cristate growth on an organ pipe cactus*

miles from the visitor center. On the **Desert View Nature Trail,** you'll travel up a wash, then climb onto a ridge with a good panorama. **Victoria Mine Trail,** 4.5 miles roundtrip, takes you to a historic mine that produced lead, silver, and gold. Also beginning at the campground are a one-mile trail encircling the camping area and a 1.3-mile trail to the visitor center.

**Estes Canyon-Bull Pasture Trail,** off Ajo Mountain Dr., is the most spectacular established trail. The Estes Canyon section follows the canyon; the Bull Pasture part climbs a ridge. The trails meet and then continue to Bull Pasture, where ranchers once grazed cattle. The entire loop, including the spur trail to Bull Pasture, is 4.1 miles roundtrip; some sections are steep and have loose rock. Carry water. Countless other cross-country hiking trips are possible in the monument's open terrain. Rangers can help you plan. You'll need a permit for any overnight hikes.

### Accommodations, Campgrounds, and Food

The 208-site campground near the visitor center is open all year, with room for trailers to 35 feet. There's drinking water but no hookups or showers; sites cost $8 per night.

Tenters who want to leave the asphalt and flush toilets behind can camp at **Alamo Canyon Primitive Campground,** 14 miles away. This pretty spot is also a good base for day-hikes. Free (registration for monument admission required) with limited facilities and only four sites; obtain the required permit and directions beforehand. No trailers or RVs permitted.

For motels, stores, gas stations, and restaurants you must leave the monument; Lukeville (Arizona), five miles south, and Sonoita (Mexico), two miles farther, are the nearest towns.

## VICINITY OF ORGAN PIPE CACTUS NATIONAL MONUMENT

### Lukeville

Just a wide spot on the road next to the Mexican border, Lukeville was named for WW I flying ace Frank Luke. Besides the immigration and customs offices, Lukeville has a gas station, small store, and the **Gringo Pass Motel and Trailer Park;** rooms run $48.53 s, $54.86 d;

tent sites run $10.02; RV sites w/hookups run $14.77; tel. (602) 254-9284 (Phoenix).

### Sonoita

Several restaurants, motels, curio shops, and an attractive little plaza lie two miles southwest of the Mexican border in Sonoita. Beaches, fishing, and seafood lure many visitors 63 more miles to Puerto Peñasco on the Sea of Cortez. Here you'll find seaside motels, restaurants, and trailer parks. A permit is required for travel beyond Sonoita. You can buy Mexican auto insurance on both sides of the border.

### Why

Why Why? Because motorists used to call it "the Y." Why occupies the junction of AZ Highways 85 and 86 just north of Organ Pipe Cactus National Monument. For a place to stay, try **Coyote Howls Trailer Park** with coin showers but no hookups. Rates are $4.65 for a tent, van, or pickup camper, $8.24 for larger units; tel. 387-5209. Why is also home to **Las Palmas RV Park,** $10.25 tent, $14.61 (plus a metered electricity charge) RV w/hookups and showers, tel. 387-6304. **Why Not Travel Store,** with snacks and groceries, a cafe, and gas stations round out the town's practicalities. **Robert's Ranch Resort** is expected to open with RV spaces in 1996. To camp free of charge, head 1.9 miles south of Why on Hwy. 85. Just after the bridge is a dispersed camping area where contradictory signs tell you that only overnight parking is permitted (no camping), while the next sign gives a 14-day camping limit. In winter there are dozens of RVs entrenched in the area and usually a few tent campers.

## AJO

This pleasant small town appears lost in a sea of desert. It's 10 miles northwest of Why and 42 miles south of Gila Bend. The town's name (pronounced "AH-ho") may have come from the Tohono O'odham word for paint; Indians collected copper minerals here to use in painting their bodies.

Prospectors settled here as early as 1854, but Ajo didn't really get going until the dawn of this century, when suitable ore-refining techniques became available. The New Cornelia Copper Company began in 1917 and was later bought by Phelps Dodge. Squeezed between low copper prices and high costs, Phelps Dodge later shut down the mine and smelter. Formerly a town in hard times, Ajo has been discovered by retirees and winter visitors.

Graceful palms and flowering trees surround the Spanish colonial-style plaza and many public buildings downtown. Greenery and trees also decorate the miners' tiny houses.

## Sights
The **New Cornelia Open Pit Mine** just south of town is one of the world's largest, 1.5 miles across. To reach the mine lookout from downtown, turn southeast on La Mina Ave., then right on Indian Village Rd., and follow signs to a ramada with exhibits overlooking the pit. The visitor/information center is open Tues.-Sat 10 a.m.-4 p.m. The nearby **Ajo Historical Museum** houses pioneer and Indian exhibits and the extensive mineral collection of the Ajo Gem and Mineral Society in a former Catholic church. It's open daily 10 a.m.-4 p.m. but closed July 15-Aug. 15; from the mine overlook, continue to the end of Indian Village Rd. and turn left; tel. 387-7105.

## Accommodations, Campgrounds, and Food
Stay at the **Manager's House Inn** bed and breakfast, 1 Greenway Dr., $72.45-103.95 d, tel. 387-6505; **The Guest House Inn** bed and breakfast, Guest House Rd., $73.49 s or d, tel. 387-6133; **Marine Motel**, 1966 N. Hwy. 85, $52.50 s, $57.75 d, tel. 387-7626; or **La Siesta Motel**, 2561 N. Hwy. 85, $31.90 s, $40.47 d, $15 RV w/hookup, tel. 387-6569. RVers can also hook up at the **Shadow Ridge RV Resort**, 431 N. Hwy. 85, $10 tent, $16 RV w/hookups, tel. 387-5055; **Ajo RV Park**, 2000 N. Hwy. 85, $14.70 w/hookups, tel. 387-6796; **Belly Acres RV Park**, N. Hwy. 85, $15.22 w/hookups, tel. 387-6962 (NAPA); or **Del Sur RV Park**, 2050 N. Hwy. 85, $14.95 w/hookups, tel. 387-6907.

**Copper Kettle Shop**, on the downtown plaza, serves Mexican-American food. **Ice Cream/Etc.,** also on the plaza, serves snacks from breakfast through dinner—as well as ice cream. **Claudia's Cafe** is southeast of the plaza, across the road. Other restaurants lie north on the high-

way: **Pizza Hut,** 627 N. Second Ave., tel. 387-6842; **Señor Sancho's,** Mexican-American, 663 N. Second Ave., tel. 387-6226; **Bamboo Village,** Chinese, 1810 N. Second Ave., tel. 387-7536; and **Dairy Queen,** 1304 N. Second Ave., tel. 387-7407.

## Recreation and Information
The **Ajo Country Club** has a nine-hole golf course and a restaurant, seven miles northeast of town via Well and Mead Roads; tel. 387-5011. A public **swimming pool** opens in summer and **tennis courts** are next to the high school on Well Road. Ajo's **public library** and **post office** are by the plaza. The **Ajo District Chamber of Commerce** is on the main highway near the plaza at 321 Taladro, Ajo, AZ 85321; it's open Mon.-Fri. 8:30 a.m.-4:30 p.m., also Saturday 10 a.m.-3 p.m. in the cooler months if staffing permits; tel. 387-7742. A small but select inventory of books on the region is at **Si Como No,** 207 Taladra, at the south edge of the plaza facing the highway.

## CABEZA PRIETA NATIONAL WILDLIFE REFUGE

The 860,000 acres of desert wilderness west of Organ Pipe Cactus National Monument haven't changed much since white people arrived. There are no facilities, no paved roads, no running water.

Desert bighorn sheep, for which the refuge was founded in 1939, and the endangered Sonoran pronghorn are protected here. Much of the refuge is designated as wilderness. Twelve small mountain ranges rise above the desert floor. Wildlife and vegetation are similar to those in Organ Pipe Cactus National Monument, but the climate is harsher. Cabeza Prieta's annual rainfall averages about nine inches in the east and three inches in the west. Some areas go more than a year without rain.

Only jeep tracks and remnants of the old El Camino del Diablo (Devil's Highway) cross the landscape. Allow at least two days to cross the refuge on the roads between Ajo and Wellton; distance is 124 miles one-way, 59 miles in the refuge. You can undertake a shorter trip to the Growler Mountains, 20 miles west of Ajo via

Charley Bell Road. You can visit this land with a permit, a suitable vehicle, and supplies for desert travel. Summer conditions can be downright dangerous.

Cabeza Prieta doubles as a gunnery range for Luke Air Force Base and the Marine Corps Air Station, so you'll want to time your visit carefully. The military makes its schedules available by the first of each month to the refuge headquarters in Ajo. Permits are required for entry and you must sign a liability release.

Four-wheel-drive vehicles are required; anything else will get stuck in the loose sand. Vehicles must stay on designated roads. Be aware that Cabeza Prieta's rough roads can be very hard on vehicles; also, heavy brush can scratch up vehicle paint. Carry plenty of extra water. Be

sure to talk with a refuge officer before your trip to find out current conditions.

Contact the Cabeza Prieta Wildlife Refuge office of the U.S. Fish and Wildlife Service at 1611 N. Second Ave. (Ajo, AZ 85321), on the highway just north of town; it's open Mon.-Fri. 7:30 a.m.-noon and 1-4:30 p.m.; tel. 387-6483.

A permit for Cabeza Prieta allows travel on specified roads through surrounding military land, but you may not leave these roads; to explore any areas controlled by the military, you must obtain military permission. To visit the Tinajas Atlas Mountains and other areas west of the refuge, for example, obtain a Range Permit from: Commanding Officer, Range Management Department, Yuma, AZ 85369-9220; tel. 341-2216/3402.

# SOUTH FROM TUCSON TO MEXICO

Mexico lies at the end of a short drive south from Tucson via I-19, just 63 miles or 100 km—all of I-19 is signed in metric. Except for the speed limits, that is—the Highway Patrol doesn't want motorists feigning confusion at the sight of 100 kph signs.

You'll follow the Santa Cruz River Valley, one of the first areas in Arizona colonized by the Spanish. The Jesuit priest Eusebio Francisco Kino began mission work at Guévavi and Tumacacori in 1691, then moved to San Xavier and other sites. Livestock, new crops, and the new religion introduced by Kino and later padres greatly changed the lives of the Indians. You may want to stop at some of the many historic and scenic sights on the way.

## MISSION SAN XAVIER DEL BAC

The mission often lacked a resident priest and suffered many difficulties during its early years. Pima Indian revolts in 1734 and 1751 caused serious damage. Raiding Apache harassed residents and stole livestock. The oldest surviving part of the mission dates from 1757-63, when the Jesuit Father Alonso Espinosa built a large, flat-roofed adobe church. This structure was later moved and butted up against the east bell tower of the present church, and is now part of the south wing of the mission.

Franciscan missionaries began construction of the present church in about 1778. San Xavier is a marvelous example of Mexican folk baroque architecture. Shortage of materials and skilled artisans resulted in the folksy character of the building. There was no marble, so the main altar was painted to look like marble; no glazed tiles, so the dadoes were painted to look like tiles; and few chandeliers for lighting, so they were painted onto the walls.

A bit of mystery surrounds the church. No one knows for sure who designed it, or why the east bell tower and other parts were left unfinished. Records, however, indicate that friars ran short of construction funds.

You're welcome to step inside the church, where a recorded message tells its history and identifies the many saints and symbols. Above the altar, a statue of St. Francis Xavier is the central figure; above him stands the Virgin of the Immaculate Conception; highest of all is a figure representing the Catholic God. Flash photos are permitted unless a service is in progress. The church is still a spiritual center for the Tohono O'odham. Masses are held Sunday at 8 a.m., 9:30 a.m., 11 a.m., and 12:30 p.m.; and weekdays at 8:30 a.m.

The small hill to the east features a replica of the Grotto of Lourdes. To the west stands a former mortuary chapel where two early Franciscan friars

*San Xavier del Bac*

lie buried. Major celebrations are the San Xavier Pageant and Fiesta (first Friday after Easter), the Feast of St. Francis of Assisi (October), and the Feast of St. Francis Xavier (December).

The mission **museum** offers very good history exhibits with architectural plans, photos, religious art, priests' vestments, and furnishings; open Saturday and Sunday 8 a.m.-4 p.m.; a **gift shop** on the east side is open daily. **San Xavier Plaza** across from the mission includes the **Wa:k (Valley) Snack Shop** (Mexican, Indian, and American food) and shops selling Tohono O'odham, Zuni, Hopi, and Navajo crafts. Indians sometimes set up food stalls outside, especially on Sunday and religious holidays.

Mission San Xavier del Bac is open daily 8 a.m.-6 p.m., donations accepted; tel. 294-2624. It's 10 miles south of downtown Tucson; take I-19 south to Exit 92 and follow signs 0.8 mile west and north.

## SANTA RITA MOUNTAINS

Birdwatchers flock to Madera Canyon in the Santa Rita Mountains, 38 miles south of Tucson. The Santa Ritas, surrounded by a sea of desert, are home to unusual wildlife, of which the coppery-tailed trogon bird *(Trogon elegans)* is the star attraction. During summer this colorful, parrot-like bird flies in from Mexico to nest in tall trees in the canyon bottoms. More than 200 other bird species have been spotted in Madera Canyon. April and May are best for birdwatching, though hummingbirds are most numerous in both spring and summer. Bear, deer, mountain lion, coatimundi, and javelina also share the spring-fed canyon.

A 16-mile paved road from I-19 Exit 63 crosses the Santa Cruz Valley, then enters Madera Canyon. You'll leave the mesquite, ocotillo, and cacti of the desert behind as you drive through forests of juniper, oak, and pine. Obtain maps and trail information from the Forest Service in Tucson (tel. 670-4552) or Nogales (tel. 281-2296). The *Hiking Guide to the Santa Rita Mountains,* by Bob and Dotty Martin, and *Arizona Trails,* by David Mazel, offer detailed trail descriptions and maps.

### Hiking

The Santa Ritas include over 70 miles of hiking trails, many suitable for horseback riding. Most of the highest mountains lie within the **Mt. Wrightson Wilderness.** Mount Wrightson (elev. 9,543 feet) crowns the range and makes a challenging roundtrip hike. Two trails to the summit

*left: Grotto of Lourdes replica on Hill of the Cross; right: altar inside San Xavier del Bac*

start near Madera Canyon's Roundup Picnic Area (elev. 5,400 feet): **Old Baldy Trail #372** and **Super Trail #134.** Allow a full day (10 hours) or backpack overnight. Old Baldy Trail is shorter (nine miles roundtrip), more steep, and offers lots of shade through much of the day. Super Trail's incline is easier on the body, but it's longer (16.2 miles) and offers little shade. Many hikers go up one trail and descend the other or even make a figure-eight loop. The trails cross at Josephine Saddle, where other trails can be accessed. Mountain bikes are not an option for the entire route as 3.9 miles of Old Baldy and 7.6 miles of the Super Trail are in the wilderness area where mountain bikes are prohibited.

A popular day-hike is the 4.5-mile loop from Bog Springs Campground to Bog Springs and Kent Spring. Trail elevations range from 5,100 feet at the campground to 6,620 feet at Kent Spring. You can avoid the campground fee by

parking off the main road opposite the campground turnoff (elev. 4,820 feet), adding one mile to the roundtrip distance. For topo maps, see the 7.5-minute Mt. Wrightson quadrangle or the Southern Arizona Hiking Club's 1:62,500-scale Santa Rita map.

More leisurely hikes involve the 4.2-mile trail through Madera Canyon between Proctor Parking Area at the mouth of the canyon and Roundup Picnic Area at the end of the road; maps here and at several access points along the way show the trail segments. The 0.6-mile lower section of trail and two short loops, between Proctor Parking and White House Picnic Area, are paved and graded for wheelchair travel.

## Campground and Accommodations

**Bog Springs Campground** (elev. 5,600 feet) is open all year with water for $5 per site for day use or camping; trailers to 22 feet okay in some sites. **Santa Rita Lodge** in Madera Canyon has 12 rental units with kitchenettes and a gift shop; $71.25-88.58 d; HC 70, Box 5444, Sahuarita, AZ 85629; tel. 625-8746.

## Whipple Observatory

The Smithsonian Institution studies the heavens with the Multiple Mirror Telescope (one of the world's largest) and a variety of other telescopes on Mt. Hopkins. Six-hour tours begin at the observatory's office near Amado, 35 miles south of Tucson, from March to November. After a short video presentation at 9 a.m., you take a bus up a mountain road to the observatories.

Be prepared for temperatures 15-20° cooler than in the valley, possible summer showers, and the thin air at Mt. Hopkins' 8,550-foot summit. Call up to four weeks in advance for the schedule, directions, and required reservations; tel. 670-5707. Tours cost $7 adults, $2.50 children 6-12; children under six not permitted.

## GREEN VALLEY

Green Valley is a retirement area with a population of 23,500 nestled in rolling hills overlooking the Santa Cruz Valley. The town features several fine restaurants. **Best Western Inn** is at 111 S. La Canada Dr.; rates are $79.38-90.53 s, $101.18-111.83 d up in winter high season, tel. 625-2250 or (800) 221-2222.

**Green Valley Chamber of Commerce** can provide information on the area and various services; it's open Mon.-Fri. 9 a.m.-5 p.m. and Saturday 9 a.m.-noon (closed Saturday in July and August); drop by the office at 270 W. Continental Rd., adjacent to the Continental Shopping Plaza just west of I-19 Exit 63; Box 566, Green Valley, AZ 85622; tel. 625-7575. Green Valley is 25 miles south of Tucson; take I-19 Exits 69, 65, or 63.

## Sierrita Mine

This active copper mine lies west of Green Valley. You can see the massive terraces of waste rock from many miles away. The Sierrita pit measures 6,800 feet long, 6,000 feet wide, and 1,400 feet deep. Cyprus Minerals Company occasionally offers tours of the operation; tel. 648-8608.

## Titan II Missile Museum

You may think that you're trespassing on a top-secret military installation—official Air Force vehicles, helicopter, giant antenna, and refueling equipment look ready for action. But what once was top secret has thrown open its heavy doors to the public.

One-hour tours depart daily (except Christmas and Thanksgiving) 9 a.m.-4 p.m. from November 1 to April 30, then Wed.-Sun. 9 a.m.-4 p.m. the rest of the year. The last tour of the day begins at 4 p.m. Call 625-7736 first for reservations. Admission is $6 adults, $5 seniors and military, $3 ages 10-17. The museum is about 20 miles southeast of Tucson near Green Valley; take I-19 to Duval Mine Rd. Exit 69, then turn west three-quarters of a mile to the entrance.

## TUBAC

After the Pima Indian Revolt in 1751, the Spanish decided to protect their missions and settlers in this remote region. In order to accomplish this goal Tubac Presidio, the first European settlement in what's now Arizona, was founded the following year. Apache raids and political turmoil in following decades made life unbearable at times, and Tubac's citizens fled on eight occasions.

When the United States took over after the 1854 Gadsden Purchase, Tubac was nothing but a pile of crumbling adobe ruins. Prospectors and adventure-seekers, fired by tales of old Spanish mines, soon poured in. Mines were found, and by 1859 Tubac had become a boomtown, with Arizona's first newspaper, the *Weekly Arizonan.* The Civil War brought the good times to an end; the troops guarding the town headed east to fight. Apache once again raided the settlement, and the inhabitants once again had to flee. Tubac recovered after the Civil War, but the boom days were over.

Much later, when an art school opened in 1948, Tubac began a slow transformation into an artists' colony. Today, the village of Tubac features about 100 studios and galleries displaying modern jewelry, ceramics, woodcarvings, prints, batiks, paintings, and other works. The Tubac motto: Where Art and History Meet. During the weeklong Tubac Festival of the Arts

# COLD WAR DEFUSED—TITAN MISSILE MUSEUM

When the SALT treaty called for the deactivation of the 54 Titan missiles buried deep below ground in Arizona, Kansas, and Arkansas, the people at Pima Air and Space Museum asked that one site remain open for public tours. After complex international negotiations, the request was granted. And so today the Green Valley complex of the 390th Strategic Missile Wing has been declassified and opened to the public.

Here you can experience a harrowing tape of an Air Force crew preparing to launch a nuclear missile; in less than an hour its 460,000 pounds of thrust could take it from its blastproof Arizona silo to its Russian target 8,000 miles away.

The hardened command center is mounted on springs to withstand anything but a direct hit. You can sit behind the consoles where two officers once waited for the command that would tell them to use two sets of keys in two combination locks to retrieve launch codes that would incinerate millions of people. You'll pass through a pair of 6,000-pound blast doors to approach the missile itself—110 feet tall, weighing 170 tons when fully fueled and ready to fly.

in February, residents and visiting artists celebrate with exhibitions, demonstrations, and food. Pick up a copy of the *Monthly Arizonan* to learn what's going on in Tubac; tel. 398-3153. Tubac lies 45 miles south of Tucson; take I-19 Exit 34.

## Tubac Center of the Arts
This gallery, on Plaza Rd. near the entrance to Tubac, displays a variety of excellent work by local artists Tues.-Sat. 10 a.m.-4:30 p.m. and Sunday 1-4:30 p.m. from late September to late May; admission is free; tel. 398-2371.

## Tubac Presidio State Historic Park
A museum just east of the artists' colony recounts Tubac history since its founding in 1752.

The printing press used for Arizona's first newspaper is here and you can buy a reproduction of the first issue, dated March 3, 1859. Exhibits tell the stories of the people who've lived here. Models illustrate how the presidio appeared in the early years. Stairs lead underground to excavations of the original foundation and wall. The schoolhouse behind the museum dates from 1885—Tubac opened Arizona's first school in 1789.

**Anza Days Cultural Celebration** commemorates the 1775-76 trek to settle what is now the city of San Francisco. Held in October and hosted by Tubac Presidio State Park, the festival features entertainers, historic craft demonstrators, food vendors, and historic re-enactments.

The historic park, established in 1959 as Arizona's first state park, is open daily 8 a.m.-5 p.m.; admission is $2 ages 18 and over, $1 ages 12-17. A mesquite-shaded picnic area lies across the street; no camping.

**Juan Bautista de Anza National Historic Trail**
You can walk along a historic 4.5-mile trail from Tubac Presidio State Park to Tumacacori National Historic Monument. This trail is part of a planned 600-mile-long historic trail from Culiacán, Sinaloa, Mexico, to San Francisco, California, along the route followed in 1775-76 by Tubac Presidio Captain Juan Bautista de Anza when he commanded an immigration column of 240 colonists to start a settlement in Northern California. The only other section of the trail open is a short section in Anza-Borrego State Park in California. You may start at either the Tubac or Tumacacori end; in either case you will cross the Santa Cruz River after 1.25 miles. The river may be too high to cross safely or it may be dry. Never drink the river water—always carry a lot of your own, especially in hot weather. Do not stray from the trail as it crosses private land.

**On the Road in Tubac**
**Tubac Golf Resort,** one mile north, offers rooms starting at $109.70 d and casitas at $141.65 in winter with lower prices in the off season. Its **Montura Restaurant** serves American and continental food for breakfast, lunch, and dinner. The resort also has an 18-hole golf course, tennis court, pool, and jacuzzi; take I-19 Exit 40; tel. 398-2211 or (800) 848-7893.

**Burro Inn,** at Exit 40 off I-19, has rooms starting at $103.93 and serves American and Mexican food, including mesquite-cooked selections; tel. 398-2281. **Tubac Trailer Tether** has RV spaces on Burruel St. in town; $14.85 w/hookups; tel. 398-2111. **Mountain View RV Park** features sites for tents and RVs north on the I-19 frontage road between Exits 42 and 48; $14.85 no hookups, $18.09 w/hookups; pool and showers; tel. 398-9401.

**Tosh's Hacienda de Tubac** serves Southwestern and Mexican cuisine for lunch and dinner Mon.-Sun.; it's at the corner of Camino Otero and Burrell St.; tel. 398-3008. **Mom's Place** serves sandwiches and pizza for lunch on Tubac Plaza everyday except Sunday.

The **public library** is in a courtyard at the corner of Calle Baca and Plaza Road.

# TUMACACORI NATIONAL HISTORICAL PARK

This massive adobe ruin evokes visions of Spanish missionaries and devout Indian followers. Father Kino first visited the Pima village of Tumacacori in 1691, saying Mass under a brush shelter. Kino's successors continued their mission

*Tumacacori Mission*

work, teaching, converting, and farming, but work didn't begin on the present church until 1800.

Franciscan Father Narciso Gutierrez, determined to build a church as splendid as San Xavier del Bac, supervised the construction by Indian laborers. Work went slowly, and although never quite finished, the building was in use by 1822. Then the new Mexican government restricted funds for mission work and began to evict all foreign missionaries. Tumacacori's last resident priest, Father Ramon Liberos of Spain, was hauled off in 1828.

Indians continued to care for the church and received occasional visits by missionaries from Mexico, but raiding Apache made life hard. The last devout Indians finally gave up in 1848, packing up the church furnishings and moving to San Xavier del Bac.

Tumacacori fell into ruins before receiving protection as a national monument in 1908, then as a national historical park in 1990. Today, a museum recalls the history of the Indians and Spanish, shows architectural features, and displays some of the mission's original wooden statues. A self-guided tour includes details of the circular mortuary chapel, graveyard, storeroom, and other ruined structures. The grounds feature picnic tables, but no camping is permitted. The Patio Garden offers herbs, shade trees, and flowers; a booklet available at the visitor center explains their uses. Mexican or Indian craft demonstrations take place on Saturday and Sunday. Books, slides, postcards, and videos are sold in the visitor center. The **Tumacacori Fiesta** features Indian dances, crafts, and food on the first Sunday in December.

Two other Spanish mission ruins were recently added to the national historical park— Calabazas (11 miles south) and Guévavi (15 miles south). Check with park staff for opening dates. Tumacacori is open daily 8 a.m.-5 p.m.; admission is $2 ages 16 and over. Call ahead if you'd like to arrange a guided tour; tel. 398-2341. It's 48 miles south of Tucson near I-19 Exit 29, or just three miles south of Tubac on the east frontage road.

**On the Road in Tumacacori**
**Tumacacori Mission Restaurant,** across the street from the mission, serves Greek and Mexi-

can food. **Wisdom's Cafe,** 0.3 mile north, has Mexican and American food.

## PENA BLANCA LAKE AND VICINITY

A scenic, 52-acre lake in the hills 16 miles northeast of Nogales, Pena Blanca (Spanish for "White Rock") is named for light-colored bluffs overlooking the water. Anglers come to catch bass, bluegill, crappie, catfish and, from November to March, rainbow trout. At an elevation of 4,000 feet, the lake is a bit cooler than Tucson. A trail leads around the lakeshore.

**Pena Blanca Resort** beside the water includes a motel ($29.68 d, $42.40 family, $47.70-72.08 kitchenette), restaurant, boat rentals (motel guests get free use of a rowboat), groceries, and fishing supplies. Reservations are recommended, especially on weekends; tel. 281-2800. To reach the lake and lodge, take I-19 Ruby Rd. Exit 12 and drive west 11 miles on AZ 289, a paved road.

**White Rock Campground** is in Pena Blanca Canyon upstream from the lake. There's drinking water year-round and room for trailers to 22 feet; $5. Turn left 0.1 mile onto Forest Route 39 at Milepost 10, one mile before the lodge.

### Atascosa Lookout Trail
Forest Trail #100 climbs steeply from 4,700 feet through desert vegetation, oaks, juniper, and piñon pine to the summit at 6,255 feet. Allow a half day for the six-mile roundtrip. The trailhead is five miles west of Pena Blanca Lake on Forest Route 39, a dirt road. Look for a parking area on the south side of the road; the unsigned trailhead is on the north side.

From the top, you can see mountain ranges in Mexico to the south, Pena Blanca Lake and Nogales to the east, the Santa Ritas and Rincons to the northeast, the Santa Catalinas to the north, and the Baboquivaris to the west. The trail is included on the 7.5-minute Ruby topo map. Hike year-round except after snowstorms.

### Sycamore Canyon Trail
This trail is rough in spots, but you can follow it downstream all the way to the Mexican border, a distance of six miles one-way. The scenic

canyon contains plants and wildlife rarely found elsewhere in the United States. The trail crosses both the **Goodding Research Natural Area,** named for a prominent Arizona botanist, and the **Pajarita Wilderness.** The first 1.3 miles is easy walking; after that, boulder-hopping and wading are necessary. Toward the end, the canyon opens up and you'll see saguaro on the slopes. A barbed-wire fence marks the Mexican border.

The trailhead is about 10 miles west of Pena Blanca Lake on Forest Route 39; turn left a quarter mile on Forest Route 218 to Hank and Yank Historical Site. These adobe ruins were part of a ranch started in the 1880s by two former Army scouts.

Hiking in Sycamore Canyon is good all year. Elevation ranges from 4,000 feet at the trailhead to 3,500 feet at the border. Depending on how far you go, the hike can be an easy two-hour stroll for the first mile or so, or a long (10-hour) 12-mile roundtrip day-hike all the way to Mexico; see the Ruby topo map. No camping allowed along the trail.

### Arivaca Lake
This is a beautiful 90-acre lake, 24 bumpy miles west on Forest Route 39 from Pena Blanca Lake. Anglers catch largemouth bass, bluegill, and catfish while enjoying the solitude of this remote spot. Facilities are minimal: just parking areas, a boat ramp, and outhouses.

The best road in is from Amado (I-19 Exit 48, 37 miles south of Tucson) to the village of Arivaca, 20 miles (paved). From Arivaca go south five miles on Forest Route 39 (gravel), then left 2.5 miles to the lake.

The other route travels from Pena Blanca Lake on Forest Route 39; go 21 miles west from the lake, then turn right and drive 2.5 miles. This route winds through the Atascosa Mountains past the ghost towns of Ruby (fenced off) and Oro Blanco.

# NOGALES

Nogales, astride the U.S. and Mexican border, is a truly international city. Many visitors to Mexico have shopping on their minds, and Nogales offers a huge selection of handicrafts. You'll also find fine restaurants and serenading mariachi bands. Mexicans too, like to cross the border to shop and sample foreign culture.

### History
Indians used Nogales Pass for at least 2,000 years for migration and trade. The Hohokam came through on their way to the Gulf of California to collect shells prized as bracelet and necklace material. Pima, possibly descended from the Hohokam, settled and traveled in the Santa Cruz River Valley and Nogales area after A.D. 1500. During the Spanish era, missionaries, soldiers, ranchers, and prospectors also passed through. Apache used the pass on raiding forays well into the 19th century. Traders on the Guaymas-Tucson route knew the spot as Los Nogales (Spanish for "The Walnuts"). A survey team marked the international line here in 1855, one year after the Gadsden Purchase.

The town—or rather, the two towns, one in each country—was started, appropriately enough, by two men. In 1880, Juan José Vásquez established a roadhouse on the Mexican side, and some months later Jacob Isaacson set up a trading post on the American side. The first railroad line to cross the border between

Gen. Fierro  Gen. Villa  Gen. Ortega

ROCHLIN ARCHIVES

*Pancho Villa (center) and associates, 1915*

the U.S. and Mexico came through Nogales in October 1882. Trade, silver mining, and ranching contributed to the growth of the twin towns. In 1898 the 1,500 population on the U.S. side made it the fifth-largest city in Arizona.

When Pancho Villa threatened Nogales in 1916, the worried U.S. Army established Camp Little on the edge of town. Relations between the two halves of Nogales remained good despite the political turmoil in Mexico, and Camp Little closed in 1933. Tourists discovered Nogales in the 1940s, and tourism, along with trade, keeps the border busy today.

## Sights

The **Pimeria Alta Historical Society Museum** provides a good introduction to Nogales. Artifacts and old photos illustrate the long and colorful history of southern Arizona and northern Sonora. The building, raised in 1914 to house the Nogales City Hall and police and fire departments, is itself an attraction. You can see the old jail, human-powered water pump, law office, and other exhibits. The society's research library and archives offer a wealth of books on regional history as well as an extensive collection of historic photographs and is open to the public. The museum and library are open Tues.-Fri. 10 a.m.-noon and 1:30-5 p.m., and Saturday 10 a.m.-4 p.m.; admission is free; tel. 287-4621. You'll find the distinctive mission-style building on the corner of Grand Ave. and Crawford St., a quarter mile north of the border.

The square granite structure with a shiny aluminum dome, on the hillside to the northeast, is the former **Santa Cruz County Courthouse**, built in 1904. Local artists display their work in the **Hilltop Art Gallery;** it's open daily noon-4:30 p.m. Sept.-May; free admission; Hilltop Dr.; tel. 287-5515.

## Accommodations

Places to stay in town, listed from north to south, include **Rio Rico Resort & Country Club,** with golf, tennis, pool, and horseback riding; it's 12 miles north of town near I-19 Exit 17; rates are $127.26-159.08 s or d with breakfast; tel. 281-1901. You can also try **Super 8 Motel** on I-19 and Mariposa Rd. for $47.75 s, $51.08-59.97 d, tel. 281-2242 or (800) 800-8000; **Motel 6,** 141 Mariposa Rd. at Grand Ave., $33.30 s, $39.97 d,

---

**NOGALES**

1. Chamber of Commerce
2. Denny's Restaurant
3. Hilltop Art Gallery
4. Pizza Hut
5. War Memorial Park
6. public library
7. Las Vigas Steak Ranch
8. Consulado de Mexico
9. post office (Arizona)
10. old Santa Cruz County Courthouse
11. Pimeria Alta Historical Society Museum
12. bus station (Arizona)
13. Federal Building (U.S. Immigration and Customs)
14. border crossing
15. Hotel Fray Marcos de Niza
16. post office (Mexico)
17. La Roca Restaurant
18. Hotel Olivia
19. Hotel Granada

---

tel. 281-2951; **El Dorado Motel,** 945 N. Grand Ave., closed for remodeling, was to reopen in 1996; **Best Western Time Motel,** 921 N. Grand Ave., $42.20-54.41 s, $46.64-58.86 d, tel. 287-4627 or (800) 528-1234; and **Mission Motel,** also scheduled to reopen in 1996, tel. 287-2472.

Other accommodations include **Best Western Siesta Motel,** 673 N. Grand Ave., $46.64-53.30 s, $48.86-66.63 d, tel. 287-4671 or (800) 528-1234; and **Americana Motor Hotel,** 639 N. Grand Ave., $61.08 s, $72.18 d, tel. 287-7211 or (800) 874-8079.

About a dozen hotels lie on the Mexican side; prices usually run US$20-60. **Hotel Fray Marcos de Niza** has luxury rooms on Av. Obregón one block south of the border. **Hotel Plaza Nogales** offers luxury accommodations at Km 7.5.

## Campgrounds

**Mi Casa RV Park** is 4.5 miles north of the border at 2901 N. Grand Ave.; rates are $5 tent (it does not have tent spaces but will accommodate tenters when it has excess space), $15.40 RV w/hookups; tel. 281-1150. Campgrounds with and without hookups are also available at **Pena Blanca Lake** and **Patagonia Lake State Park.**

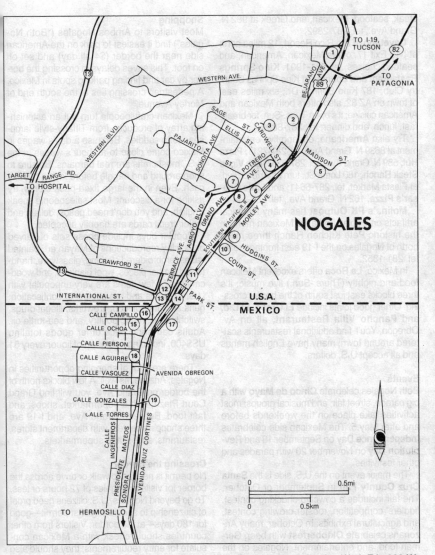

## NOGALES

**Food**

Most of the restaurants on the Arizona side lie along Grand Avenue. Except for Chinese, pizza, and fast-food places, nearly all offer both Mexican and American food. From north to south, you'll find **Mr. C's Supper Club,** featuring live

entertainment and dancing Wed.-Fri., 282 W. Viewpoint Dr., tel. 281-9000; **Grand China Restaurant,** Mandarin and Szechuan cuisine, 1997 N. Grand Ave. in Mariposa Shopping Center, tel. 281-2888; **Denny's,** 683 N. Grand Ave., tel. 287-4572; and **Zulas Papachoris',** with steak, seafood, Mexican, and Greek at 982 N. Grand Ave., tel. 287-2892.

**Cayetano** at Rio Rico Resort, 12 miles north at I-19 Exit 17, offers Mexican, American, and seafood choices; tel. 281-1901. **Kino Springs Restaurant and Lounge,** at Kino Springs Country Club, 187 Kino Springs Dr., six miles east of town on AZ 82, also offers both Mexican and American cuisine; it's open Tues.-Sun. for breakfast, lunch, and dinner; tel. 287-8800.

Try also **Americana,** offering live entertainment at 8639 N. Grand Ave., tel. 287-7211; **Pizza Hut,** 589 N. Grand Ave., tel. 287-9257; **Las Vigas Steak Ranch,** 180 Loma St., turn off Arroyo Blvd. at Fiesta Market, tel. 287-6641; and **Little Caesar's Pizza,** 162 N. Grand Ave., tel. 287-4144.

**Molina's PK Outpost** has many historical artifacts on display and a full Mexican menu in the historic Pete Kitchen Ranch three miles north of Nogales on the I-19 east frontage road; tel. 281-1852.

In Mexico, **La Roca** offers excellent Mexican food and nightly (Thurs.-Sun.) live music; it's three blocks east just south of the border crossing. Other good joints include **El Greco, El Cid,** and **Pancho Villa Restaurant,** all on Av. Obregón. You'll find additional restaurants scattered around town; many have English menus and all accept U.S. dollars.

## Events

Both Nogales celebrate **Cinco de Mayo** with a big parade, street fair, and musical groups; most activities take place on the weekends before and after May 5. The Mexican side celebrates **Independence Day** on September 16 and **Revolution Day** on November 20 with parades and other festivities.

The major event on the U.S. side is the **Santa Cruz County Fair** in September or October. The fair includes a cowchip-chucking contest, fiddlers' competition, rooster-crowing contest, and agricultural exhibits. In October, many Arizonans celebrate **Oktoberfest** with beer, German food, and entertainment. Nogales on the Arizona side sponsors a **Christmas Parade** in late November or early December.

**Bullfighting** is popular on the Mexico side in the Guadalupe Plaza de Toros; contact the Nogales-Santa Cruz Chamber of Commerce for dates.

## Shopping

Most visitors to Ambos Nogales ("Both Nogales") find it easiest to park on the American side near the border ($4 all day) and set off on foot. This saves delays in crossing the border by car and finding parking spots in Mexico. A pedestrian crossing lies at the south end of Morley Avenue.

Mexican craftspeople turn out an astonishing array of products, from Tiffany-style lampshades to saddles. Because a day's wages in Mexico come close to an hour's wages in the U.S., most crafts are real bargains. Be sure to shop around and haggle before laying out any cash. Even in the large fixed-price stores, try asking for a discount. Most salespeople speak English, and you don't need pesos; dollars and major credit cards are happily accepted.

Popular buys include chess sets of carved onyx, clay reproductions of Mayan art, painted vases, embroidered clothing, glassware, handtooled leather pieces, wool blankets, and woodcarvings. A few items are very unpopular with U.S. Customs and are subject to confiscation: guns and ammunition, fireworks, illegal drugs, switchblades, meat, poultry, and sea-turtle oil. Adults can bring back other goods totaling US$400, including one quart of liquor every 31 days.

There are a lot of shopping opportunities in Nogales, Arizona, as well. A few blocks north of the border on Grand Ave. you will find Grand Court Plaza, with a supermarket, shops, and fast food. Between Grand Ave. and I-19 are three shopping centers with department stores, restaurants, shops, and supermarkets.

## Crossing the Border

No permit is needed to walk or drive across the border for visits in Nogales of 72 hours or less. To go beyond Nogales, U.S. citizens need proof of citizenship to secure a tourist permit—good for 180 days—at the border. Visitors from other countries should check with a Mexican consulate for entry requirements; they should also see U.S. Immigration about re-entry before stepping across. In Nogales, Arizona, the Consulado de Mexico is at 480 Grand Ave.; tel. 287-2521.

A separate permit is needed for driving a car in Mexico beyond Nogales. Pick it up at the bor-

Nogales, Mexico

der or any Mexican consulate by showing proof of car ownership. Large vehicles and trailers can cross more easily at the commercial crossing west of the main crossing; take Mariposa Rd. (AZ 189).

You also need to buy Mexican auto insurance. Numerous agencies in Nogales, Arizona, advertise Mexican insurance, with daily and longer rates.

You don't need to change money in Nogales; dollars or pesos are welcomed on both sides of the border. For longer trips into Mexico, local currency is essential. Shop for pesos at money-changers near the border on the U.S. side; Safeway and other stores near the border almost always have a surplus of Mexican currency and will sell it at a good rate.

## Services

The **post office** lies just east of the border station. **Carondelet Holy Cross Hospital** is west of town at 1171 W. Target Range Rd.; tel. 287-2771. You'll find a public **swimming pool** and **tennis courts** near the War Memorial Park on Madison Street. Golfers can play at **Rio Rico Golf Course** (18 holes, 1410 Rio Rico Dr., 12 miles north near I-19 Exit 17, tel. 281-8567) and **Kino Springs Country Club** (18 holes, six miles northeast on AZ 82, Patagonia Rd., tel. 287-8701).

## Information

The **Nogales-Santa Cruz Chamber of Commerce** is very helpful with information on both the local area and travel in Mexico. A video program presents a visual tour of Santa Cruz County sights, plus info on crossing the border and visiting Mexico. It's open Mon.-Fri. 8 a.m.-5 p.m.; write Kino Park, Nogales, AZ 85621; tel. 287-3685. When entering Nogales from the north on Grand Ave. (US 89), turn right on the street just past the Patagonia Rd. interchange (AZ 82). The Mexicans also have a **tourist office** just south of the Grand Ave. border crossing.

The **Nogales Ranger Station** of the U.S. Forest Service recently relocated, and plans are to create extensive displays in the new lobby. It's open Mon.-Fri. 8 a.m.-4:30 p.m. at 303 Old Tucson Rd. (Nogales, AZ 85621); from I-19 north of Nogales take the Ruby Rd. exit east to the frontage road and head south 0.3 mile to Old Tucson Rd.; tel. 281-2296. Nogales, Arizona, has a **library** at 748 Grand Ave.; tel. 287-3343.

## Tours and Transport

**Citizen Auto Stage** sends eight to 10 buses daily to Tucson ($6.50 one-way). The trip to Tucson takes 1.75 hours and stops at Green Valley and other locations along the way. Citizen Auto Stage is just two blocks from the border at 35 N. Terrace

Ave., next to Safeway; tel. 287-5628. On the Mexican side, **Transporte Norte de Sonora (TNS)** and **Transportes del Pacífico** provide extensive bus services at low cost. Each departs from the bus terminal 4.5 km (2.8 mi) south of the border; the easiest way there is by taxi.

An express **train** leaves every afternoon for Mexico City (42 hours) via Hermosillo (four hours) and Guadalajara (28 hours); only coach seating is available. Pick up tickets at the office in the Mexican customs building near the border. The train station itself is about 4.5 km (2.8 miles) south, across from the bus station; take a taxi or the Av. Obregón bus. The Nogales-Santa Cruz Chamber of Commerce can advise on car, bus, and train travel to Mexico.

The nearest major **airports** are at Tucson (64 miles north) and Hermosillo (280 km/174 miles south). Nogales has a small international airport on Patagonia Road.

# PATAGONIA AND VICINITY

The rolling hills of grass and woodlands surrounding Patagonia make up some of the state's best cattle and horse land. Patagonia, 19 miles northeast of Nogales, lies on the alternate route to Tucson. Many people like to make a loop between the two cities by driving through Sonoita and Patagonia in one direction (I-10, AZ Hwys. 83 and 82) and the Santa Cruz Valley (I-19) in the other.

## Patagonia Lake State Park
Head here for a pleasant place to picnic, camp, boat, and fish. The 265-acre reservoir offers largemouth bass, crappie, sunfish, bluegill, catfish, and, in winter, rainbow trout. The marina has a boat ramp, gas, rentals (rowboat, paddleboat, and canoe), and camping and fishing supplies; it's open daily 8 a.m.-6 p.m. in summer, then daily except Wednesday the rest of the year; closed in December.

The west half of the lake is open for waterskiing, jet-skiing, and similar water sports Mon.-Fri. in summer and daily in the off season; the east half of the lake is a no-wake area. Swim at Boulder Beach (no lifeguard).

**Sonoita Creek Trail** begins at the east end of the east campground and winds to the mouth of Sonoita Creek, 1.2 miles roundtrip. Petroglyphs on the far side of the lake are accessible by boat or on foot.

At an elevation of 3,750 feet, the park stays open all year; the best time to visit is early spring through autumn. The campground, with showers, normally fills by Friday afternoon in summer. Picnic areas will also fill up on summer weekends; it's a good idea to call ahead. Boaters can use primitive sites around the lake and on a number of islands. Park fees are $10 per vehicle ($15 w/hookups) for camping or $5 per vehicle for day use; tel. 287-6965. From Nogales, go 12 miles northeast on AZ 82, then turn left at the sign and drive four miles on a paved road. The park gate is closed 10 p.m.-4 a.m.

## Patagonia-Sonoita Creek Preserve
The Nature Conservancy maintains 312 acres along Sonoita Creek as a wildlife preserve. Year-round water and a variety of habitats attract a number of birds; more than 275 species have been identified. White-tailed deer, *chulo* (coati), javelina, bobcat, and other animals live in the thickets and woods. The public is welcome to visit, but no picnicking, camping, or pets are allowed. It's open Wed.-Sun. 7:30 a.m.-3:30 p.m. all year.

Nature walks begin at 9 a.m. on Saturday from the entrance; no reservation needed. Summer visitors should apply insect repellent to keep off chiggers. Drop by the visitor center, near the entrance, for information, tel. 394-2400, or contact the **Nature Conservancy** at 300 E. University Blvd., Suite 230, Tucson, AZ 85705; tel. 622-3861. To reach the preserve, in Patagonia turn northwest off AZ 82 onto Fourth Ave., then turn left and drive 0.9 mile on Pennsylvania Avenue. The pavement ends and you'll have to drive across a creek; don't cross if you can't see the bottom. Then you're in the preserve.

## Empire-Cienega Resource Conservation Area
The landscape of much of Arizona is drastically changed from what it was in the late 1800s

when extensive grazing by domestic cattle expanded to the point that native grasses were severely depleted. The conservation area is still used for grazing, as it has been used for nearly 300 years, but grazing is now regulated and the grass grows as high as six feet. Fifteen inches of annual rainfall, at an average elevation of 4,500 feet, permits growth of some of the best examples of native grasslands in the state. Within the 45,000 acres of the conservation area you'll find large cottonwood trees lining the banks of Cienega Creek, oaks and junipers clinging to the hills, and mesquite trees scattered throughout the range.

The conservation area is open to individual visitors and campers without permits, but group activities require a permit. Camping is limited to 14 days within a six month period. Campfires are allowed but only dead wood lying on the ground may be collected. Access is via two entrances: one is on the east side of Hwy. 83, seven miles north of Sonoita, where a well maintained dirt road gives access to Empire Ranch and both South Road and Ranch Road; the other is via a less well maintained dirt road on the north side of Hwy. 82, five miles east of Sonoita. There are no paved roads within the conservation area, nor camping or picnicking facilities. However, visitors can enjoy bird watching, hiking, horseback riding, bicycling, hunting, camping (limited to 14 days), and many other outdoor activities. For more information and road conditions call the office in Tucson, tel. 722-4289; Sierra Vista, tel. 458-3559; or Safford, tel. 428-4040.

### Cave of the Bells
A variety of minerals and an underground lake attract experienced spelunkers to this undeveloped "wild" cave in the Santa Rita Mountains to the north. Obtain gate key and directions from the Forest Service office north of Nogales or the supervisor's office in Tucson.

### Ghost Towns
Decaying houses, piles of rubble, cemeteries, and old mine shafts mark deserted mining camps in the Patagonia Mountains to the south. You'll need the topo or Forest Service maps to find these old sites. In a 45-mile loop drive, you can visit Harshaw, Mowry, Washington Camp, and Duquesne. You can also drive east to the Huachuca Mountains, Parker Lake, or Coronado National Memorial on back roads. Most are dirt and should be avoided if it has recently rained or snowed.

### Accommodations, Food, and Recreation
The **Stage Stop Inn** (Box 777, Patagonia, AZ 85624) sits in the middle of sedate Patagonia; rates are $44.75 s, $55.95 d, $67.20 d kitchenette, $89.80 d suite; tel. 394-2211. The restau-

adobe ruins near
Harshaw

rant next door serves Mexican and American food daily 7 a.m.-10 p.m. **Rothrock Cottage and Adobe** (P.O. Box 526, Patagonia, AZ 85624) also offers accommodations close to downtown for $75 s or d including breakfast; tel. 394-2952. You'll find a couple of other restaurants, a bakery, a post office, a small library, and art galleries in town too.

**Richardson Park** has picnic tables and a playground.

**Circle Z Ranch,** a working cattle ranch, features horseback riding, swimming, hiking, birding, and tennis. The season runs Nov. 1-May 15; per-adult rates run $138.21-167.75 per day (three-day minimum stay) and $775.43-974.82 per week including lodging, food, and activities; add an optional 15% for gratuities. It's five miles southwest of Patagonia; write for details at Box 194 ATH, Patagonia, AZ 85624; tel. 287-2091.

# ALONG THE COCHISE TRAIL

Chief of the Chiricahua Apache, Cochise earned great respect from whites and Indians alike for his integrity and leadership skills. He never lost a battle. The southeast corner of Arizona was named Cochise County in his honor in 1881, despite his having waged war against Anglo troops and settlers from 1861 to 1872. Many historic sites of the Old West lie along a 206-mile loop through this varied country. Tourist offices call this drive the Cochise Trail.

## TOMBSTONE

When prospector Ed Schieffelin headed out this way in March of 1877, friends told him the only thing he'd find among the Apache and rattlesnakes would be his own tombstone. But he set out anyway, alone, and staked a silver claim, puckishly proclaiming it Tombstone. When Ed struck it rich at an adjacent site, his brother Al said, "You're a lucky cuss." And so the Lucky Cuss Mine became one of Arizona's richest. Other claims bore equally descriptive monikers: Contention, Tough Nut, and Goodenough.

The town incorporated in 1879 and contained as many as 10,000 souls just five years later. It was said that saloons and gambling halls made up two of every three buildings in the business district. The famous OK Corral gunfight took place here in 1881; historians still debate the details. Shootings and hangings in the 1880s kept Boot Hill Graveyard busy. Fires nearly wiped out Tombstone on two occasions, but it was flooding of the mines in 1886-87 that sent the town into a swift decline. Still, Tombstone, "the town too tough to die," managed to survive, and now attracts throngs of visitors seeking a peek into the old Wild West.

### Gunfights
Guns still blaze and bodies hit the dust in staged gunfights and barroom brawls. The action, portrayed by the Vigilantes, takes place in the Helldorado Outdoor Amphitheater, south end of Fourth Street, on the second, fourth, and fifth Sundays of each month at 2 p.m. At 2 p.m. on the first and third Sundays of the month the Wild Bunch works out at the OK Corral, culminating in a re-creation of the famous shootout. The Boot Hill Gunslingers stage shootouts daily in the Helldorado Outdoor Amphitheater. All events require a small admission fee.

### Boot Hill Graveyard
Lying here are Dutch Annie, a widely admired prostitute; the losers of the OK Corral shootout; hanging/lynching victims; and assorted gunslingers. Many of the estimated 276 graves are unmarked; those bearing messages have much to say about life in old Tombstone. Boot Hill lies just off AZ 80 on the north edge of town; enter free of charge through the Boot Hill Gift Shop; it's open daily 7:30 a.m.-6 p.m.

### St. Paul's Episcopal Church
Built in 1881, St. Paul's is the oldest standing Protestant church in Arizona; it's at the corner of Third and Safford.

### Tombstone Courthouse State Historic Park
Dating from 1882, this red-brick building has witnessed many emotional trials. Although some of the convicted were hanged in the courtyard to

**TOMBSTONE**

1. Boot Hill Graveyard
2. Top O' the Hill Restaurant
3. Stampede RV Ranch
4. Wells Fargo RV Park
5. St. Paul's Episcopal Church
6. Hacienda Huachuca Motel
7. Tombstone City Hall
8. Bella Union Restaurant
9. Schieffelin Hall
10. Larian Motel
11. Tombstone Motel
12. Adobe Lodge Motel
13. OK Cafe
14. city park (picnic tables)
15. OK Corral; Historama
16. Visitor Information Center;
    Tombstone Art Gallery
17. Crystal Palace Saloon
18. Tombstone *Epitaph*
19. Big Nose Kate's Saloon
20. Longhorn Restaurant
21. Cactus Rose Cafe
22. post office
23. Silver Nugget store
24. Bird Cage Theatre
25. Tombstone Courthouse State Historic Park
26. public library
27. Rose Tree Inn
28. Nellie Cashman's Restaurant
29. Old Firehouse

the northwest, not everyone had the benefit of the courthouse gallows. John Heath, reportedly the brains behind a robbery and murder in Bisbee, was taken from jail and lynched by a mob in 1884. The six-man coroner's jury later declared the unlucky fellow had died "... from emphysema of the lungs—a disease common to high altitudes—which might have been caused by strangulation, self-inflicted or otherwise."

Officials abandoned Tombstone's courthouse in 1931 when the county seat moved to Bisbee. The courthouse has been restored and now houses a museum of artifacts and photos of the old days. A gift shop offers books on Arizona history. The site is open daily 8 a.m.-5 p.m.; $2 adults 18 and over, $1 ages 12-17; tel. 457-3311; Third and Toughnut Streets.

### The OK Corral

The Earps and Doc Holliday shot it out with the Clanton cowboys on this site in October 1881. Markers and life-size figures show how it all happened—or at least one version of the story. Other sights to see include the studio and photos of Camilius S. Fly, old stables, carriages, a hearse that carried many a passenger to Boot Hill, and even a red-light district shack. Visitors can "walk where they fell" daily 8:30 a.m.-5 p.m. for $2 admission, children under six free. Located off Allen St. between Third and Fourth Streets.

### Historama

This 30-minute show re-creates the major events of Tombstone with movies and animated figures. Presentations take place hourly 9 a.m.-4 p.m.; $2, under six free. It's next door to the OK Corral entrance.

### Schieffelin Hall

Major theatrical companies of the day performed in this large adobe building dating from 1881. John Sullivan and a company of boxers gave exhibitions here. It's on the corner of Fremont and Fourth Streets, but not currently open to the public.

### Rose Tree Inn

A rose root sent from Scotland to comfort a homesick bride in the spring of 1885 has grown to cover an amazing 8,000 square feet. The rose tree, believed to be the world's largest, and listed in the *Guinness Book of Records,* is a Lady Banksia. Its sweet-scented white blossoms usually appear in early April. Rooms exhibit a collection of antique furnishings belonging to a pioneer who arrived by wagon train in 1880; the inn is open daily 9 a.m.-5 p.m.; $2 adults (under 14 free); Fourth and Toughnut Streets.

### Crystal Palace Saloon

Built in 1879, this watering hole and gambling house was the height of luxury in early Tomb-

ARIZONA STATE ARCHIVES

stone. As many as five bartenders stood on duty to serve thirsty customers round the clock. The clientele has changed over the years, but the saloon still serves up drinks. The interior has been restored quite accurately; pieces of the original wallpaper were used as a model to manufacture the current replacement. Fifth and Allen Streets.

## Tombstone *Epitaph*

As one story goes, the town's newspaper got its name when its founder, John P. Clum, took the stagecoach home from Tucson and asked passengers for appropriate suggestions. Ed Schieffelin happened to be on board, and he replied, "Well, I christened the district Tombstone; you should have no trouble furnishing the *Epitaph.*" Clum started the *Epitaph* in 1880 and it's still in business. You can visit the office to see the original press and other printing exhibits; open daily 9 a.m.-5 p.m.; admission is free. Souvenir copies are sold. It's on Fifth St. between Fremont and Allen Streets.

## Bird Cage Theatre

This 1881 dance hall, gambling house, saloon, brothel, and theater was the favored hangout of local characters and desperados. During its first eight years, the doors never closed. Birdcage-like stalls suspended from the ceiling gave the place its name. See if you can find some of the estimated 140 bullet holes in the walls and ceiling. The well-preserved building is open daily 8 a.m.-6 p.m.; admission is $3.50 adults, $3 seniors, and $1 children 8-12; Allen and Sixth Streets. Five additional display rooms that were sealed more than 100 years ago will be opened to view and the admission fee will be increased; call 457-3421 for details.

## ON THE ROAD IN TOMBSTONE

### Accommodations

**Adobe Lodge** ($48.65 s, $60 d) occupies the corner of Fifth and Fremont Streets; tel. 457-2241. **Larian Motel** (starting at $36) is at 410 E. Fremont St. (AZ 80); tel. 457-2272. **Tombstone Motel** ($45.40 s, $51 d) is at 502 E. Fremont St.; tel. 457-3478. The Best Western **Lookout Lodge** starts at $62.67 s, $73.47 d; 0.7 mile

north on AZ 80, with pool; tel. 457-2223 or (800) 652-6772.

Bed and breakfasts include the **Tombstone Boarding House** ($54-75.60 s, $64.80-86.40 d) at 108 N. 4th St., tel. 457-3716; and **Priscilla's B&B** ($42.32 s, $59.66 d) at 101 N. Third. St., tel. 457-3844.

### Campgrounds

**Wells Fargo RV Park** ($17.83 tent or RV no hookups, $21.07 RV w/hookups), right in town at Third and Fremont Streets, has a laundromat and showers; tel. 457-3966. **Stampede RV Ranch** ($17.28 RV w/hookups) at 201 W. Allen St. also provides a laundromat and showers; tel. 457-3738. **Tombstone KOA** lies one mile north of downtown on AZ 80; $18.36 tent, $19.44 RV no hookups, $23.22 RV w/hookups, $29.16 kamping kabin; it features a pool, laundromat, showers, and store; tel. 457-3829.

### Food

Not surprisingly, most restaurants feature western decor and food. **Nellie Cashman's Restaurant** is Tombstone's oldest, established in 1882; it's open daily for breakfast, lunch, and dinner at Fifth and Toughnut Streets; tel. 457-2212. **Longhorn Restaurant,** offering Mexican, American, and a few Italian items, is open daily for breakfast, lunch, and dinner at Fifth and Allen Streets; tel. 457-3405. **Bella Union** is open daily for breakfast, lunch, and dinner with steak, chicken, and seafood at the corner of Fourth and Fremont Streets; tel. 457-3656.

Pull in at the **OK Cafe** for breakfast or lunch; it's open daily at the corner of Allen and Third Streets; tel. 457-3980. **Cactus Rose Cafe** features pizza, pasta, and sandwiches at 150 S. Fifth St.; tel. 457-3850. **Top O' the Hill Restaurant** serves Mexican and American meals; it's open daily for breakfast, lunch, and dinner; north on AZ 80 near Boot Hill; tel. 457-3461. Tombstone has no major grocery stores in Tombstone.

### Events

**Shootouts** take place every day throughout the year when weather permits. **Helldorado Days,** Tombstone's biggest celebration, features three days of shootouts, parades, dances, and other lively entertainment beginning on the second Friday of October.

Smaller-scale festivities include **Territorial Days** (first weekend in March), **Cinco de Mayo** (May 5), **Wyatt Earp Days** (Memorial Day weekend), **Father's Day Parade** (third Sunday in June), **July 4, Vigilante Days** (second weekend in August), **Nellie Cashman Day** (August), **Rendezvous of the Gunfighters** (Labor Day weekend), and **Emmet Kelly, Jr. Days** (second weekend in November).

**Shopping, Services, and Information**

Many shops along Allen Street sell Old West souvenirs, rocks and minerals, books, clothing, jewelry, and crafts. Some also feature small museums, usually free, that may be worth a look. Tombstone Association of the Arts supports the **Tombstone Art Gallery** next to the Visitor Information Center, Fourth and Allen Streets. The **post office** is on Allen St. between Fifth and Sixth Streets.

The **Visitor Information Center** is open Mon.-Sat. 9 a.m.-5 p.m. and Sunday afternoons; corner of Fourth and Allen Streets; Box 268, Tombstone, AZ 85638; tel. 457-3929 or (800) 457-3423. The **public library** is at Fourth and Toughnut Streets.

# VICINITY OF TOMBSTONE

**Ghost Towns**

Ghost-town enthusiasts may want to explore remnants of former mining towns. **Gleeson,** 18 miles east on a graded gravel road, flourished around a copper mine from 1909 until the 1930s. Operations ended in 1955. You can see ruins of the jail, cemetery, school, adobe hospital, and other buildings. Mine tailings and machinery rest on the hillside.

**Courtland,** now occupied solely by ghosts, lies one mile east and three miles north of Gleeson on good gravel roads. A jail and numerous foundations remain. Watch out for open mine shafts in the area.

At the site of **Pearce,** nine miles north of Courtland, Jimmie Pearce found gold in 1894. The Commonwealth Mine was a success, and the town's population reached 1,500 before the mine closed in the 1930s. Reminders of the past include the old store, cemetery, post office, Pearce Church, abandoned houses, and

Commonwealth Mine ruins. You can also reach Pearce from I-10; take Exit 331 and head south 22 miles on US 191.

**San Pedro Riparian National Conservation Area**

Residents of this choice wildlife habitat—one of the richest in the United States—include 350 bird species, 82 mammal species, and 45 reptile and amphibian species. The San Pedro River, though only a trickle at times, nourishes willows, cottonwoods, and other streamside vegetation. From its beginning in Sonora, Mexico, the river flows north to join the Gila near Winkelman.

The riparian area, run by the Bureau of Land Management, is one to three miles wide and stretches for 36 miles from the Mexican border to near St. David. Visitors enjoy birdwatching, nature walks, and horseback riding. You can camp with a permit from the San Pedro Conservation Area office; $2 per person per night but no facilities.

Archaeologists have unearthed bones of extinct mammoths, bison, and camels killed by ancient hunters at Murray Springs and Lehner Mammoth Kill Site. Spear tips and butchering tools identify these people as members of the Clovis Man culture, which existed about 11,000 years ago.

**Santa Cruz de Terrante** was established as a presidio in 1775 by Colonel Hugo O'Conor for the Royal Spanish Army. Its purpose was to serve as a fort protecting the northern reaches of New Spain. By 1780 two captains and over 80 soldiers had been killed by Apache raids, which in turn largely prevented the cultivation of crops. After less than five years of use the site was abandoned. Today, all that remains of this presidio are a few weathered adobe walls and stone foundations. Excavations by the Amerind Foundation in the early 1950s have provided archaeologists with a plan of the presidio. Pick up a copy of the BLM brochure on the presidio before visiting the site.

For information, contact the local San Pedro Project Office in Sierra Vista (1763 Paseo San Luis, Sierra Vista, AZ 85635, tel. 458-3559); the Safford District office (711 14th Ave., Safford, AZ 85546, tel. 428-4040); or the Tucson Resource Office (12661 E. Broadway Ave., Tucson, AZ

5748, tel. 722-4289). These offices are open Mon.-Fri. 7:45 a.m.-4:15 p.m.

## FORT HUACHUCA

When raiding Apache threatened settlers and travelers in the San Pedro Valley in 1877, the Army set up a temporary camp near the Huachuca (wa-CHOO-ka) Mountains. In 1886, Fort Huachuca became the advance head-quarters for the campaign against Geronimo. Although the Army later closed more than 50 forts and camps in the territory, it retained Huachuca to deal with outlaws and renegade Indians near the Mexican border. World Wars I and II and the Korean War saw new duties for the fort; finally, in 1954, it converted to its current task of testing electronics and communications gear and serving as an information center and intelligence school.

### Fort Huachuca Museum
The museum's large collection of photos, Indian artifacts, dioramas, and memorabilia date from Apache-fighting days to the present. One room honors the fort's black troops, known as Buffalo Soldiers. Barracks and administrative buildings from the 1880s line the parade ground outside.

The museum and gift shop are open week-days 9 a.m.-4 p.m. and weekends 1-4 p.m.; ad-

mission is free; tel. 533-5736. The collection is housed in two buildings on either side of Hunger-ford at Grierson. It's about 2.5 miles from the main gate in Sierra Vista. Be sure to pick up a free visitor's pass at one of the gates; you may need to show a driver's license, vehicle regis-tration, and proof of vehicle insurance.

## SIERRA VISTA

The town of Sierra Vista grew up outside the gates of Fort Huachuca as a service center. Many Army retirees have settled here; they like the climate and social and recreational oppor-tunities, and can continue to use base facilities. Sierra Vista (pop. 37,500) now includes Fort Huachuca and is the largest and fastest growing community in Cochise County.

### Accommodations and Food
When driving toward Sierra Vista, you have a choice of taking the bypass route or going down-town via Fry Blvd. and Garden Avenue. Fry Blvd. has a good selection of motels and restau-rants, including a plethora of fast-food places. RV parks lie scattered around town.

### Events
Runners test themselves in the **Mule Moun-tain Marathon** on the first weekend in May.

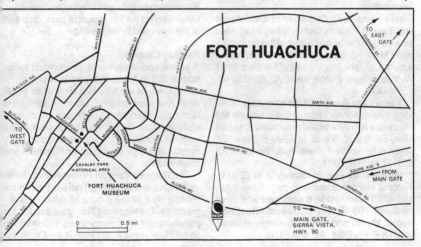

**Fireworks** light the sky during the July 4th celebration. **Art in the Park** attracts artists and craftspeople from all over the West on the first weekend of October. Balloons take to the air for the **Festival of Color Balloon Rally** on the last weekend in October. The **Christmas Parade** starts off the holiday season on the first Saturday in December. The local chamber of commerce maintains a listing of sports events and other area happenings.

### Recreation and Services
The **city park** features an outdoor pool, picnic tables, playground, basketball court, and horseshoe pits at 3025 E. Fry Blvd.; tel. 458-7922. Play golf at the 18-hole **Pueblo del Sol Golf Course,** 2770 Saint Andrews Dr., off S. Hwy. 92; tel. 378-6444. Fort Huachuca has made several on-site attractions open to non-service personnel including the **Mountain View Golf Course,** tel. 533-7092, and the **Buffalo Soldier Corral Stables,** tel. 533-5220. To go on post you must present a valid driver's license, vehicle registration, and proof of insurance. Catch a movie at **Uptown 3 Theatre,** 4341 S. Hwy. 92; tel. 378-2858. The **post office** is at 2300 E. Fry Blvd.; tel. 458-2540. **Sierra Vista Community Hospital** is at 300 El Camino Real, south off E. Fry Blvd.; tel. 458-4641.

### Information
**Sierra Vista Area Chamber of Commerce and Tourist Visitors Center** offers information about the sights and services of the region; it's open Mon.-Fri. 8 a.m.-5 p.m. and Saturday 9 a.m.-1 p.m., one block south of Fry Blvd. at 21 W. Wilcox Ave. (Sierra Vista, AZ 85635); tel. 458-6940.

**Sierra Vista Ranger Station** provides recreation information for national forest lands in the Huachuca and Whetstone mountains; it's open Mon.-Fri. 8 a.m.-5 p.m. at 5990 S. Hwy. 92, seven miles south of Sierra Vista (Hereford, AZ 85615); tel. 378-0311.

**Sierra Vista Public Library** is at 2950 E. Tacoma in the northeastern part of town; tel. 458-4225. **Livingston's** sells new and used books at 100 W. Fry Boulevard. **Hastings Books, Music, and Video** offers regional books at 3758 E. Fry Blvd.; tel. 459-8130.

### Transportation
**Sierra Vista Public Transit System** runs bus service along two routes in Sierra Vista; tel. 459-0595. **Bridgewater Transport** offers bus service to Tucson, Bisbee, and Douglas from the station at 28 Fab Ave., south off W. Fry Blvd.; tel. 458-3471. **America West Express** flies to Phoenix; tel. 459-8575 or (800) 235-9292.

# HUACHUCA MOUNTAINS

The Huachucas, south of Sierra Vista, present many hiking possibilities and a number of scenic drives. **Miller Peak Wilderness** contains much of the high country between Coronado National Memorial and Fort Huachuca. **Reef Townsite Campground,** at the site of a former mining camp, and **Ramsey Vista Campground,** a half mile away, lie in Carr Canyon on the eastern slopes; both are open all year, though only Reef has water; fees are $2 for trailhead parking, $3 day use, $5 camping. Both campgrounds are over 7,000 feet in elevation and can be cool in summer and cold the rest of the year. Contact the **Sierra Vista Ranger Station** of the Coronado National Forest for information on exploring the Huachucas.

The Army controls the northern part of the range—secret electronic installations cap some of the mountaintops. The road through the fort between Sierra Vista and Canelo passes over the northern foothills and offers some fine views. Upon entering the fort, pick up a pass; drop it off at the other end when leaving.

### Ramsey Canyon
A year-round stream and an elevation range from 4,200 to 9,466 feet provide habitats for many kinds of wildlife, including white-tailed deer, coati, and javelina. Up to 14 species of hummingbirds congregate here from spring to early autumn. Butterflies also appear in the warmer months. The Nature Conservancy owns a 300-acre sanctuary for hummers and other wildlife.

The **Ramsey Canyon Preserve** bird observation area and **Hamburg Trail** are open to the public daily 8 a.m.-5 p.m.; a $5 donation is appreciated. The Hamburg Trail goes through the preserve one mile, then continues a short way to an overlook (elev. 6,380 feet) in the Coronado

National Forest.

Visitors should first register at the visitor center. A gift shop sells hiking maps and an excellent selection of natural history and regional books. Call to obtain a parking reservation. April, May, and August can be crowded even on weekdays. Groups should always obtain advance permission; the small parking area cannot accommodate RVs or trailers. Don't bring pets. No picnicking or camping. The preserve is four miles up Ramsey Canyon Rd. from AZ 92; the turnoff is six miles south of Sierra Vista.

Ramsey Canyon Preserve offers six comfortable housekeeping cabins along Ramsey Creek; one bedroom at $75 s or d, two bedrooms at $85 s or d; tel. 378-2785.

**Ramsey Canyon Inn Bed & Breakfast,** just outside the preserve, offers rooms starting at $90 d and housekeeping units starting at $95; they offer free homemade pie made fresh from their orchard's produce for afternoon enjoyment; tel. 378-3010.

### Coronado National Memorial

Francisco Vásquez de Coronado marched through this area in 1540 in search of the mythical Seven Cities of Cíbola. Although his backers judged the quest a failure, Coronado's was the first major European expedition into the American Southwest. Both this park in the Huachuca Mountains and the adjacent national forest are named in his honor.

The visitor center, staffed by National Park Service rangers, features history, plant, and wildlife exhibits; it's open daily 8 a.m.-5 p.m.; tel. 366-5515. A nature walk outside introduces local flora. There's a picnic area nearby but no campground. The turnoff for Coronado National Memorial lies about midway between Sierra Vista and Bisbee on AZ 92. The visitor center is 4.5 miles in; Montezuma Pass is another 3.2 miles and 1,345 feet higher on a dirt road. You can also take the back roads—mostly dirt or gravel—from Patagonia or Nogales. Snowstorms occasionally close the pass in winter.

Outstanding views of Arizona and Mexico stretch to the horizon from the top of 6,864-foot Coronado Peak, reached by the half-mile **Coronado Peak Trail** from Montezuma Pass. The path ascends 290 feet with many shaded benches for resting. Signs describe Coronado's ex-

pedition and the natural features of the Huachuca Mountains. **Joe's Canyon Trail,** 3.1 miles one-way, connects Montezuma Pass with the visitor center in the valley below; elevation change is 1,345 feet.

You can reach Miller Peak (9,466 feet), the highest point in the Huachuca Mountains, on the **Miller Peak Crest Trail,** a 12-mile roundtrip hike north from Montezuma Pass. This is the southernmost section of the **Arizona Trail,** which continues generally northward across the state.

**Coronado Cave Trail** starts across the cattleguard at the northeast end of the Montezuma Pass parking area and winds up the hillside behind the visitor center (obtain the required free permit first) to a limestone cave with some formations; the first quarter mile is gentle, followed by a steep half mile to the cave entrance; elevation gain is 470 feet. The cave is over 600 feet long, up to 20 feet in height and up to 70 feet wide with several crawl areas; carry a spare flashlight in case you drop one; stout footwear and a canteen are also useful.

### Parker Canyon Lake

This 130-acre fishing lake west of the Huachucas is a rarity in a land of little surface water. Trout are stocked in the cooler months to join the year-round population of bass, bluegill, sunfish, and catfish. The water also attracts many birds and other wildlife. The **Arizona Trail** reaches mile 20 from the Mexican border here.

**Lakeview Campground** (elev. 5,400 feet) is open all year with drinking water but no showers or hookups; $5 day use, $8 camping. A **marina** features groceries, fishing supplies, licenses, boat ramp, and boat rentals. You can rent a rowboat, or boat with electric motor; tel. 455-5847. A 4.5-mile hiking trail goes around the lake. Parker Canyon Lake lies 28 miles south of Sonoita on AZ 83, 23 miles southwest of Sierra Vista, and 15 miles northwest of Coronado National Memorial.

## BISBEE

Squeezed into Mule Pass Gulch, the old mining town of Bisbee is one of Arizona's most unusual settlements. A tiny mining camp in 1877, Bisbee grew into a solid and wealthy town by 1910;

*early Bisbee smelter*

ARIZONA STATE ARCHIVES

the fine Victorian houses built in the boom years remain. Brewery Gulch, a side canyon with more than 50 saloons in the early 1900s, earned a reputation for the best drinking and entertainment in the territory. Bisbee's riches, mostly copper ore, came from underground chambers and giant surface pits. Bisbee is in the Mule Mountains, 24 miles south of Tombstone and 95 miles southeast of Tucson.

## History

The story of Bisbee began over 100 million years ago, when a giant mass of molten rock deep in the earth's crust expelled great quantities of steam and hot water. These mineral-rich solutions slowly worked their way upward, replacing the overlying limestone rock with rich copper ores.

While looking for silver in 1875, Hugh Jones became the first person to discover minerals here, but, annoyed to find only copper, he soon left. Two years later, Jack Dunn, an Army scout, also found ore. He couldn't leave his Army duties to go prospecting, so he and his partners made a deal with George Warren to establish a claim and share the profits. Warren, a tough old prospector and heavy drinker, lost Dunn's grubstake in a saloon while on his way to the Mule Mountains. Warren quickly found new back-

ers—Dunn and his partners not among them—and filed claims. Two years later he recklessly put his share on a wager that claimed he could outrun a man on horseback; he lost everything. Warren died penniless, but the suburb south of downtown Bisbee takes its name from him.

New electrical industries needed copper, and investors were interested in Warren's camp. Judge DeWitt Bisbee and a group of San Francisco businesspeople bought the Copper Queen Mine in 1880, though the judge never did visit the mining community named for him. From the east, Dr. James Douglas of the Phelps Dodge Company also came to Arizona, buying property near the Copper Queen. After the two companies discovered the richest ores lay on the property boundary, they merged rather than fight it out in court.

Soon a smelter filled the valley with smoke and the clatter of machinery. Streets were paved and substantial buildings went up. Labor troubles between newly formed unions and mine management culminated in the infamous Bisbee Deportation. In July 1917, more than 1,000 striking miners were herded at gunpoint into boxcars and shipped out of the state. Working conditions improved in the following years, but Bisbee's economic life rolled with copper prices. The giant Lavender Pit closed in 1974, when the rich ore bodies finally ran out, and underground mining ended the following year. The district had provided more than eight billion pounds of copper.

The town didn't dry up and blow away, however. People liked it here—the climate (elev. 5,300 feet), the scenery, the character. Bisbee today is popular with visitors and retired people. The City of Bisbee consists of the historic district and the communities of Lowell, Warren, San Jose, and Naco. Although mining has ended, a small leaching and precipitation operation continues to recover copper from waste ore.

## SIGHTS

You can learn the history of the many early 1900s buildings in town with the chamber of commerce *Bisbee Walking Tour* pamphlet.

### Bisbee Mining and Historical Museum

Mining dioramas, old photos, minerals, and artifacts illustrate life during Bisbee's early years in a national award-winning display. A major theme of the display is that Bisbee was an urban environment with trolleys and other conveniences considered modern at the time. It's open daily 10 a.m.-4 p.m.; $3 adults, $2.50 seniors, free for ages 18 and under; tel. 432-7071. The Shattuck Memorial Archival Library offers extensive material on local history. The museum and library are housed in the former Phelps Dodge General Office Building (1897) in Copper Queen Plaza downtown.

### Queen Mine Tour

Don a hard hat, lamp, and yellow slicker for a ride deep underground on a mine car. A guide—himself a miner—will issue the equipment and lead you through the mine. He'll explain history,

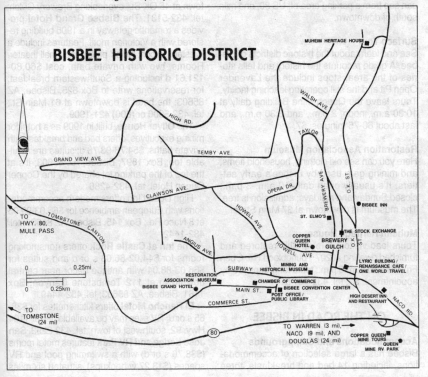

# BISBEE HISTORIC DISTRICT

MUHEIM HERITAGE HOUSE

WALSH AVE.

HIGH RD.

GRAND VIEW AVE.

TEMBY AVE.

TAYLOR

OPERA DR.

BREWERY AVE.

O.K. ST.

CLAWSON AVE.

HOWELL AVE.

BISBEE INN

ST. ELMO'S

THE STOCK EXCHANGE

TOMBSTONE CANYON

TO HWY. 80, MULE PASS

ANGIUS AVE.

HOWELL AVE.

COPPER QUEEN HOTEL

BREWERY GULCH

O.K. ST.

LYRIC BUILDING / RENAISSANCE CAFE / ONE WORLD TRAVEL

0.25mi
0.25km

SUBWAY

RESTORATION ASSOCIATION MUSEUM

BISBEE GRAND HOTEL

MINING AND HISTORICAL MUSEUM

CHAMBER OF COMMERCE

MAIN ST.

POST OFFICE / PUBLIC LIBRARY

BISBEE CONVENTION CENTER

HIGH DESERT INN AND RESTAURANT

NACO RD.

TO TOMBSTONE (24 mi)

COMMERCE ST.

80

TO WARREN (3 mi), NACO (9 mi), DOUGLAS (24 mi)

COPPER QUEEN MINE TOURS

QUEEN MINE RV PARK

drilling tools, blasting methods, ore loading, and other mining features in the stope (work area) and tunnels.

The mine, in use for more than 60 years, shut down in 1943. Its four levels have 147 miles of passageways; the whole district boasts over 2,000 miles. The tour is highly recommended; bring a sweater or jacket as it's cold inside (47° F). There are some steps to the stope area but the rest of the short walk is level. The 60- to 75-minute tour leaves daily at 9 a.m., 10:30 a.m., noon, 2 p.m., and 3:30 p.m.; $8 adults, $3.50 children 7-11, and $2 children three to six; tel. 432-2071. Reservations recommended. Buy tickets at the Queen Mine Building just south of downtown off AZ 80.

### Lavender Open Pit
A total of 380 million tons of ore and waste has been scooped out of this giant hole, which you can see from a parking area off US 80, one mile south of downtown.

### Surface Tour
See and learn about the historic districts of Bisbee. A guide recounts the history and tells stories of the area; stops include the Lavender Open Pit and the still operating leaching facility. Tours leave the Queen Mine Building daily at 10:30 a.m., noon, 2 p.m., and 3:30 p.m., and last about 60-75 minutes; $7.

### Restoration Association Museum
Here you can see old clothing, household items, and mining gear used by Bisbee's early settlers. It's usually open daily 10 a.m.-3 p.m., closed Sunday and holidays; admission is free. The museum is downtown at 37 Main Street.

### Muheim Heritage House
Tours lead visitors through this restored and furnished dwelling at 207 Youngblood Hill. Open Fri.-Mon. 10 a.m.-5 p.m.; tours for groups are by appointment; $2; tel. 432-7071.

## ON THE ROAD IN BISBEE

### Accommodations and Campgrounds
Bisbee has a large selection of accommodations, including 14 bed and breakfasts, three hotels, three motels, two overnight apartments, and four RV parks. The chamber of commerce can supply a list, including prices.

The **Copper Queen Hotel** has been the place to stay since its construction in 1902 by the Copper Queen Mining Company. Rooms differ in size and features; some have been attractively restored and furnished in a 1940s style. The old-fashioned hotel features a saloon, dining room, and swimming pool. Rooms cost $74.07-127.13 d; for reservations write to Box Drawer CQ, Bisbee, AZ 85603, or call 432-2216 or (800) 247-5829 in state. This elegant four-story hotel sits downtown on Howell Ave., behind the Mining and Historical Museum.

The **Bisbee Inn** offers bed and breakfast in a restored hotel, formerly the LaMore, opened in 1917. Baths are shared; $32.06 s, $43.11 d; no smoking, no pets upstairs. Make reservations at Box 1855, Bisbee, AZ 85603; the inn is downtown at 45 OK St., overlooking Brewery Gulch; tel. 432-5131. The **Bisbee Grand Hotel** provides a romantic getaway in a 1906 building restored with a Victorian motif. Features include a Western saloon, ladies' parlor, and small theater. Rooms, two with private bath, cost $60.80-121.61 d including a Southwestern breakfast; for reservations write to Box 825, Bisbee, AZ 85603; the hotel is downtown at 61 Main St.; tel. 432-5900 or (800) 421-1909.

The **Oliver House,** built in 1909 as a hotel for mining executives, offers bed and breakfast with private baths; $54.78-93.78 d; suites are available too; Box 1897, Bisbee, AZ 85603; it's at the top of the parking lot shared by the Copper Queen Hotel; tel. 432-4286.

High Desert Inn offers modern accommodations with European ambience for $66.03-99.05 at 8 Naco Rd.; Box 145, Bisbee, AZ 85603; tel. 432-1442.

The **Inn at Castle Rock** offers nonsmoking rooms for $44.02-66.03 s or d and suites for $66.03-88.04 with antique decor near central downtown at 112 Tombstone Canyon; Box 1161, Bisbee, AZ 85603; tel. 432-4449.

**El Rancho Motel** offers kitchenettes for $38-65 s or d; RV sites may be available; it's at 1104 Hwy. 92, southwest of town; tel. 432-2293. **San Jose Lodge and RV Park** features motel rooms ($38.70 s or d) with a swimming pool and RV spaces ($13.27 w/hookups), situated six miles

*a faro game running full blast at Bisbee's Orient Saloon in 1903*

southwest of Bisbee at 1002 Naco Hwy.; tel. 432-5761. **Queen Mine RV Park** features great views and a central location; RVers can stay for $15 (w/hookups); showers. Take the road to Copper Queen Mine Tours and continue a short way up the hill; tel. 432-5006. **Shady Dell RV Park** has sites for tents ($10) and RVs ($15 w/hookups), as well as showers at 1 Douglas Rd., behind the Chevron station near the traffic circle; tel. 432-3567.

    **Turquois Valley Golf Course** has an RV park ($14 w/hookups and showers) off the Naco Hwy., 4.5 miles south of AZ 92; tel. 432-3091. **Double Adobe Trailer Park** offers tent spaces for $5 s, $7 d and RV sites for $12.60 w/hookups; showers are available. Take AZ 80 east four miles toward Douglas, then turn left four miles on Double Adobe Rd.; tel. 364-4000.

### Food
The **Copper Queen Hotel** restaurant has continental and American cuisine for breakfast, lunch, and dinner; tel. 432-2216. **Café Roka** serves upscale north Italian cuisine for dinner only Wed.-Sat. at 35 Main; tel. 432-5153. **Renaissance Cafe,** next to the Lyric Building, offers sandwiches and subs; tel. 432-4020.

    **Café Maxi** serves American fare for breakfast, lunch, and dinner daily in the Bisbee Convention Center, across from the Mining and Historical Museum; tel. 432-7063. **High Desert Inn** serves contemporary American cuisine for lunch and dinner Wed.-Sun. plus Sunday brunch at 8 Naco Rd.; tel. 432-1442.

    Buy natural foods at **Bisbee Food Co-op** downtown at 22 Main Street. **Safeway** supermarket is out of town at the Naco turnoff.

### Shopping
Bisbee's mines have also yielded turquoise and other beautiful copper minerals. Several shops downtown sell stones set in silver as well as loose and rough stones. Another shop sits at the Lavender Pit overlook. See paintings, ceramics, and other work of local artists in art shops downtown.

### Entertainment
Contact the chamber of commerce to find out what's playing in town. The **Bisbee Grand Theater** offers Murder Mystery Weekends; tel. 432-5900. The **Copper Queen Hotel Saloon** offers live easy-listening music Thurs.-Sat. evenings. **St. Elmo's** in Brewery Gulch has country and rock music on some weekends. The **Stock Exchange** in Brewery Gulch also sometimes hires acoustic bands on weekends.

### Events
**La Vuelta de Bisbee** is a challenging multistage bicycle race held in April. Runners tackle the **Mule Mountain Marathon**'s full 26-mile distance from Bisbee to Fort Huachuca or run shorter lengths in May. Arizona's oldest **July 4th Celebration and Parade** includes entertainment and mining contests.

    A nationally known **Poetry Festival** is held in August. Participants have an excellent opportunity for exercise in October—the **Thousand Step Stair Climb.** Also in October rockhounds come to town for the **Bisbee Mineral Show.** The **Bisbee Historic Home Tour** and the **Festival of Lights** mark the start of the holiday season on the weekend after Thanksgiving. Art festivals and other special events take place through the year; check with the Bisbee Chamber of Commerce for dates.

**Recreation, Services, and Information**
**Turquois Valley Golf Course** has nine holes, a restaurant, and a RV park off the Naco Hwy., 4.5 miles south of AZ 92; tel. 432-3091. **Copper Queen Community Hospital** is at Bisbee Rd. and Cole Ave., three miles south in Warren; tel. 432-5383. The **post office** and **city library** are at 6 Main St. in downtown Bisbee. The **Bisbee Chamber of Commerce** is at 7 Main St. (Box BA, Bisbee, AZ 85603); it's open Mon.-Fri. 9 a.m.-5 p.m. and Saturday and Sunday 10 a.m.-3 p.m.; tel. 432-5421.

**Transport**
**Bridgewater Transport** provides bus service to the Tucson airport and Greyhound station and to Sierra Vista and Douglas; purchase tickets from One World Travel on OK St. near the Lyric Building; tel. 432-5359. For a taxi, call **Sun Arizona** at 432-5757.

**Vicinity of Bisbee**
Bisbee is the geographic center of one of America's best birding areas. Good places include the San Pedro Riparian Area, the Huachuca Mountains, and the Chiricahua Mountains.

**Naco** is a sleepy Mexican border town just nine miles south of Bisbee. There's little to see or do here; the Mexican side is much like the rural communities of interior Mexico. **Transporte Norte de Sonora (TNS)** buses will take you to Hermosillo, Juárez, Nogales, Casas Grandes, and other Mexican destinations.

## DOUGLAS AND AGUA PRIETA

The prettiest sight in Douglas, some residents used to say, was the billowing steam and smoke from the giant copper smelter just west of town. The busy ore-processing plant meant jobs.

In 1900, the Phelps Dodge Company, finding Bisbee's smelter too small and inconvenient to handle ores from recently purchased mines in Mexico, began looking for a new smelter site in Sulphur Springs Valley. They chose this spot and named the new town for Dr. James Douglas, president of the company.

Douglas and its sister town in Mexico, Agua Prieta, boomed when prices of copper shot high and suffered when they dropped low. Mexican government troops battled it out in Agua Prieta with revolutionaries Captain "Red" Lopez in 1911 and Pancho Villa in 1915. Pancho Villa even made threats against the town of Douglas before eventually retreating. An international airport—part of the runway lies in the United States, part in Mexico—opened here in 1928.

Smokestacks of the Phelps Dodge smelter puffed their last in January 1987, but the two cities have diversified into other industries. American companies operate manufacturing plants in Agua Prieta under the "twin plant" concept, using Mexico's inexpensive labor to assemble American products. With these new opportunities, Agua Prieta's population has tripled in the last 10 years to more than 75,000.

Douglas (pop. 15,000) and Agua Prieta have few sights, but many visitors and retired people choose Douglas as a base to explore historic and scenic areas in Arizona and Mexico. The chamber of commerce has a self-guided driving-tour leaflet highlighting the historic sites of Douglas. The **Cochise County Historical Society** has pioneer and Indian artifacts in various displays around Douglas. Visit their offices and research library in Two-Flags Mall at 1012 G Ave., next door to the Gadsden Hotel; tel. 364-5226. To see the only city block in the U.S. with a church on each corner visit **Church Square** between 10th and 11th Streets and D and E Avenues. The old Southern Pacific Depot has been restored to its grandeur of the early 20th century and can be visited a couple of blocks north of the chamber of commerce.

**Accommodations**
The massive five-story **Gadsden Hotel** dominates downtown Douglas. Built in 1907 and rebuilt in 1928, the hotel calls itself "the last of the grand hotels." The lobby features massive marble columns decorated with 14-karat gold leaf,

*lobby of the Gadsden*

supporting a vaulted ceiling with stained-glass panels. A Tiffany stained-glass mural 42 feet long decorates one wall of the mezzanine, reached by an Italian white marble staircase. Over 200 authentic cattle brands embellish the walls of the Saddle and Spur Tavern, just off the lobby. Rooms cost $32-115; 1046 G Ave., Douglas, AZ 85607; tel. 364-4481. Douglas also contains a **Motel 6,** $28.73 s, $35.36 d, 111 16th St., tel. 364-3998; a **ThriftLodge,** $32.07 s, $40.91 d, 1030 19th St., tel. 364-8434; **Border Motel,** $28 s, $33.17 d, 1725 19th St., tel. 364-8491; and **Family Crest Bed and Breakfast,** $45.85 s, $70.56 d, 910 E. Ave., tel. 364-3998.

**Price Canyon Ranch,** a working cattle ranch on the southeastern slopes of the Chiricahuas (elev. 5,600 feet), features horseback riding. Guests stay in bunkhouses ($100 s or d including meals and riding) or the campground ($6 tent, $10 RV w/hookups); pack trips in the mountains can be arranged with at least one month's notice. Other activities include fishing, hiking, and bird-watching. Price Canyon Ranch is 37 miles northeast on AZ 80, then left seven miles on Price Canyon Rd. (Box 1065, Douglas, AZ 85608); open year-round; tel. 558-2383.

### Campgrounds

RV parks, all with hookups, on the north side of town include **Saddle Gap RV Park,** at Hwy. 80 and Washington, $10, tel. 364-5863; **Doug-**las Golf and Social Club, on Leslie Canyon Rd., $12, tel. 364-3722; and **Double Adobe Trailer Park,** $12.60, also tent spaces $5 s, $7 d, 17.5 miles northwest, head west 8.5 miles on Double Adobe Rd. from US 191, tel. 364-4000. **Plantation RV Park** is on the west end of town off Hwy. 80 at Plantation Rd.; $8.50 RV w/hookups, $4 tents; tel. 364-4637.

### Food

The **Gadsden Hotel** has a Mexican-American restaurant, 1046 G Ave.; tel. 364-4481. Another choice for Mexican-American food is **Grand Cafe** at 1119 G Ave.; tel. 364-2344. **La Fiesta Cafe** is famed for its fine Mexican food, 524 Eighth St.; tel. 364-7020.

Several other Mexican restaurants are scattered around town, and Agua Prieta has even more. **Barrigan's Fine Food & Spirits** offers steak, seafood, and pasta at 1711 9th St.; tel. 364-5454. **Lai-Lai Restaurant** offers a variety of Chinese cuisines, 1341 F Ave.; tel. 364-8898. You'll pass Burger King, McDonald's, and Pizza Hut on the west side of town on AZ 80.

### Events

The **July 4th Celebration** includes entertainment, parade, car show, games, dances, and fireworks at Veteran Park. The **Labor Day Golf Tournament** in September has been running longer than any other invitational golf tournament in the state. **Douglas Fiestas Celebration** in mid-September honors Mexican independence with ballet folklorico, mariachis, talent show, games, and food at Veteran Park. **Cochise County Fair** presents intercollegiate rodeo, livestock exhibits, carnival, and other entertainment on the third weekend of September at Cochise County Fairgrounds on Leslie Canyon Road.

**Two Flags International Festival of the Arts** on the third weekend in October features a parade, art exhibits, entertainment, food, a grand ball, and other events. The Christmas Parade **Holiday Night Lights** is an evening event of lighted floats held the last Saturday of November. Many of these activities center on **Castro Park** between 9th and 10th Streets and between D and E Avenues.

### Shopping
Shops just across the border in Agua Prieta sell **Mexican crafts,** but on a much smaller scale than in Nogales. The Douglas Chamber of Commerce promotes this as "leisurely shopping," because nearly everything is fixed in price.

### Recreation and Services
**Veterans Park** features picnic tables, playground, outdoor pool, tennis, basketball, and ball fields at Dolores Ave. and Sixth St.; tel. 364-7038. **Causey Park** is a smaller area with picnic tables and playground at 15th St. and Carmelita, near a pair of water towers. **Douglas Golf and Social Club** features nine holes northeast of town off Leslie Canyon Rd.; tel. 364-3722.

The **post office** sits on the corner of 10th St. and F Avenue. The **Southeast Arizona Medical Center** is four miles west of town on AZ 80, then north on County Rd. N; tel. 364-7931.

No permits are needed to visit Agua Prieta; for longer trips into Mexico, obtain papers at the border station. Mexican auto insurance is sold by **Sanborn's** (San Xavier Insurance Agency), 533 11th St., tel. 364-2411; and by **Jones Associates,** 561 10th St. at F Ave., tel. 364-8496.

### Information
People at the **Douglas Chamber of Commerce** are very helpful and stock a good selection of maps and brochures. The office is at 1125 Pan American Ave. at 12th St. (Douglas, AZ 85607) and open Mon.-Fri. 9 a.m.-5 p.m.; tel. 364-2477.

Folks at **Douglas Ranger Station** in the Coronado National Forest can tell you about camping, hiking, and back roads of the Chiricahua and Dragoon mountains; it's open Mon.-Fri. 7:30 a.m.-4:30 p.m.; RR 1, Box 228R, Leslie Canyon Rd., Douglas, AZ 85607. From AZ 80 just northeast of town, turn north on Leslie Canyon Rd., then take the first right; tel. 364-3468. The **public library** is at 625 10th St., between E and F Avenues; tel. 364-3851.

### Transport
The American Red Cross offers **Dial-a-Ride** to anywhere within Douglas for $1 Mon.-Fri., 9 a.m.-5 p.m.; tel. 364-4474. **Bridgewater Transport** buses run several times daily to Tucson's airport and Greyhound station with stops en route at Bisbee and Sierra Vista; 538 14th St. between G and F avenues; tel. 364-2233. In Agua Prieta, **Transporte Norte de Sonora (TNS)** heads out to Cananea, Nogales, Hermosillo, Ciudad Obregón, Tijuana, Guadalajara, and Mexico City. A train also goes to Nogales, but the bus is easier and faster. For taxi service, call **Gadsden Taxi** at 364-5555.

# VICINITY OF DOUGLAS

### Douglas Wildlife Zoo
Established for propagation of exotic animals and birds, this collection is now open to the public. Drop in to see parrots, peacocks, emus, deer, lemurs, apes, and other creatures from distant lands. It's open daily 10 a.m.-5 p.m. except major holidays; $3 adults, $2 children 3-12; tel. 364-2515. From Douglas, head west 2.5 miles on AZ 80 to just past the Ford dealership, then turn north 1.7 miles on Plantation Road.

### Slaughter Ranch
John Slaughter, a former Texas Ranger, wandered into southeast Arizona in 1884. He bought the 93,000-acre San Bernardino Ranch, then developed it during the next 30 years. His 1890s house, corral, and other structures have been restored to show what ranch life was like in territorial Arizona at the turn of the century. Rooms

*Geronimo (far right) and companions; photo by C.S. Fly of Tombstone, circa 1886*

feature period furniture and photo exhibits of Slaughter's colorful career. Another section of the ranch has become the 2,330-acre San Bernardino National Wildlife Refuge.

Ranch exhibits are open Wed.-Sun. 10 a.m.-3 p.m.; $3 adults, free under age 14; tel. 558-2474. From Douglas, head east 16 miles on 15th St., which becomes the Geronimo Trail, to the ranch gateway.

## CHIRICAHUA MOUNTAINS

Rising from dry grasslands, the Chiricahua (chee-ree-KAH-wah) Mountains are a wonderland of rock formations, spectacular views, diverse plant and animal life, and a variety of hiking trails. Volcanic rock, fractured by slow uplift of the region, has eroded into strangely shaped forms. Heavier weathering at the base of some columns leaves giant boulders balanced delicately on pedestals. The Chiricahuas harbor a unique mix of Sierra Madrean and Southwestern flora and fauna. Birders come to view coppery-tailed elegant trogons, hummingbirds, and many other species.

Chiricahua National Monument offers the most spectacular erosional features; a scenic drive and many trails provide easy access. Chiricahua Wilderness, to the south, protects the highest summits of the range, including 9,796-foot Chiricahua Peak. A narrow mountain road crosses the range from near the entrance of the national monument on the west side to Portal on the east side; not recommended for trailers and usually closed by snow in winter. Fort Bowie National Historic Site lies just north of the Chiricahuas; take the gravel road south from Bowie or northeast from AZ 186.

## CHIRICAHUA NATIONAL MONUMENT

In 1924, President Calvin Coolidge signed a bill making the most scenic part of the mountains a national monument. The entrance is 70 miles north of Douglas, 36 miles southeast of Willcox, and 120 miles east of Tucson. Be sure to fill up with gas before coming out, as there are no supplies near the monument.

### Visitor Center
A short slide show introduces the monument and its sightseeing possibilities. Exhibits illustrate area geology, ecology, and wildlife, as well as the lifestyles of the Chiricahua Apache and early ranchers. Rangers can answer questions and advise on road and hiking conditions. Campfire programs are held mid-March to mid-September; check for times. Other naturalist programs may be scheduled too. Books, prints,

Sugarloaf Mountain
(on left) from
Sara Deming
Canyon Trail

posters, videos, maps, and other items are sold. It's open daily 8 a.m.-5 p.m.; tel. 824-3560. A $4 car entry fee is collected at the entrance station.

### Bonita Canyon Drive

This six-mile paved mountain road from the visitor center climbs through Bonita Canyon to Massai Point (elev. 6,870 feet), where you'll encounter a geology exhibit and sweeping views. A short nature trail and longer day-hikes start here. Look north for the profile of Cochise Head. Winter storms can close the road, but snowplows emerge as soon as a storm is over.

### Hiking

The Chiricahuas are best appreciated on foot, whether on short nature trails or extended hikes. Pace yourself to allow for the altitude and rough terrain. Carry water on longer trips. Thunderstorms often strike in July and August; if caught, stay low and avoid exposed areas. Watch for rattlesnakes, too; this is their most active season, though they also slither about in spring and autumn.

You can hike any time of year, but conditions are usually ideal from March to May and October to November. Snow sometimes blocks trails from December to February. Monument trails are for day-hikes only; no permit needed. Camping is restricted to the campground near the visitor center, but many backpack trips are possible in the nearby Coronado National Forest. Horseback riding is permitted in the monument, but

rangers like to be told when horses are brought into the monument. Horse trailers should be parked at the Faraway Ranch Parking Lot. Dogs are not permitted on any trails except the Faraway Trail; they must be on leashes at all times within the monument.

Maps sold at the visitor center include a Chiricahua topo map with hiking trails, a geologic map, and a Coronado National Forest map. You can ride to the high country on the **hikers' shuttle,** then walk downhill back to the visitor center; the shuttle, supported by donations, operates once daily at 8:30 a.m. in the morning.

### Trails

The free monument brochure includes a map outlining all trails. **Faraway Meadow Trail** is an easy 1.2-mile walk between Faraway Ranch and the visitor center. The path winds through lush vegetation watered by a small seasonal stream; a good place for birdwatching. A short side trail leads to the campground.

The **Fire and Flood Trail** near the visitor center is a new nature trail designed to expose the visitor to the effects of fire and flood on the terrain. This short, easy trail is recommended for birding.

The most impressive scenery awaits hikers on the Echo Canyon Loop and Heart of Rocks trails. **Echo Canyon Trail** winds through spectacular rock formations in a 3.5-mile loop; begin from Echo Canyon parking lot or Massai Point trailheads, both near the end of Massai Point

Drive. **Heart of Rocks Trail** passes famous rock formations—Punch and Judy, Duck on a Rock, Big Balanced Rock, and others—on a seven-mile out-and-back trip from Massai Point. With a half day, you can make a nine-mile loop by returning on the **Sarah Deming** and **Echo Canyon** trails. **Inspiration Point** is a one-mile roundtrip excursion off Heart of Rocks Trail with views over the whole length of Rhyolite Canyon.

You could also hike all the way down to the visitor center via **Rhyolite Canyon Trail. Sugarloaf Mountain** (elev. 7,307 feet) is the highest peak in the monument, with excellent views of Arizona, New Mexico, and the Chiricahuas including the eroded remnants of the volcano that created the rock layers. It's a 1.8-mile roundtrip hike to the summit from the Sugarloaf trailhead. **Natural Bridge Trail,** off Bonita Canyon Dr., offers pleasant but less spectacular hiking to a small rock bridge—actually a fallen rock column—2.5 miles from the road.

**Faraway Ranch**

*an enormous balanced rock in Chiricahua National Monument*

Members of the Erickson family lived on this ranch for 91 years before its purchase in 1979 by the National Park Service. Rangers lead tours through the old ranch house daily offering tales of the family, ranch life, and the surrounding region. You're welcome to visit the grounds during daylight hours any time of the year; signs and a small exhibit building relate stories about the ranch and the people who lived here.

Faraway Ranch is 1.5 miles west of the visitor center by road, then a quarter mile in on foot, or you can take the 1.2-mile Faraway Meadow Trail from the visitor center or campground.

**Campgrounds and Services**
**Bonita Campground,** a half mile from the visitor center, costs $7 (no hookups or showers); trailers to 26 feet okay. Another possibility is to drive up Pinery Canyon Rd. into the Coronado National Forest. The turnoff for Pinery Canyon is just outside the monument. Look for a likely spot after about six miles; no water, facilities, or charge.

**El Dorado Trading Post,** one mile west of the park entrance, offers RV and tent campsites at $6 (no hookups or showers, both are planned) as well as groceries and camping supplies; tel. 824-3510. The next nearest supplies and accommodations are 26 miles southeast in Sunizona, at the junction of AZ 181 and US 191, or farther west in Sunsites, which has an RV park, several cafes, and the **Pearce-Sunsites Chamber of Commerce;** it's open Mon.-Fri. 9 a.m.-4 p.m. and Saturday 10 a.m.-2 p.m, tel. 826-3535. Willcox, 36 miles north of the monument, offers the nearest motels as well as restaurants, stores, and RV parks.

## CHIRICAHUA WILDERNESS AND VICINITY

The national forest includes many hiking and horseback trails. A scenic mountain road crosses the range through Pinery Canyon on the west to Onion Saddle (7,600 feet) and continues east to Cave Creek Canyon and Portal. The road is narrow, bumpy, and mostly unpaved, but passable for cautious drivers. Snow and fallen trees may close the road from December to April.

*kissing rocks, Heart of Rocks Trail*

A side road from Onion Saddle travels south along a ridge and climbs to Rustler Park (8,400 feet), usually closed in winter. From here, hikers can take the **Crest Trail** south to Chiricahua Peak (9,796 feet), a wilderness area and the highest point in the range. Many other trails branch off in all directions.

Forest trails in the Chiricahua Mountains total about 111 miles, but conditions differ greatly. Trail locations and lengths are depicted on the Chiricahua Mountains Trail and Recreation topo map (scale 1:62,500), available at Tucson hiking stores, some Forest Service offices, and Chiricahua National Monument. The Coronado National Forest (Douglas Ranger District) map shows trails but lacks contour lines and fine detail.

### Campgrounds

The Coronado National Forest has 15 campgrounds; see the national forest map for locations, seasons, and facilities. A $5-6 camp fee—half price for day use—is charged for sites with water; others are free. No permits are needed for backpacking or hiking.

## FORT BOWIE NATIONAL HISTORIC SITE

When the Butterfield Stagecoach line began to carry mail and passengers from Missouri to California in 1858, the company built a station at a spring near Apache Pass. Although it was in the middle of Indian country, Cochise and his Chiricahua Apache allowed the station and stage to operate unhindered. All this changed two and a half years later when Second Lieutenant George Bascom falsely accused Cochise of kidnapping and theft. Troops attempted to hold Cochise by treachery, but the Indian chief knifed through his tent-canvas prison and escaped. Both sides executed hostages, and the war was on. Cochise was determined to kill or drive all white people from the region. Unfortunately for white settlers, many Army troops left Arizona at this time to fight the Civil War in the east.

On July 15, 1862, Brigadier General James Carleton and his California Column were on their way to meet the threat posed by the Confederate invasion of New Mexico when an advanced detachment, under command of Captain Thomas Roberts, was attacked by Indians at Apache Pass. Roberts fended them off but suggested to Carleton the need for a fort. The original Fort Bowie was built within a month. Indian raids continued until 1872, when Cochise made peace with the Army in exchange for reservation land.

Bad management by the Indian Bureau, followed by the government's stealing back much of the reservation, angered many Apache. Cochise had died on the reservation, but Geronimo, the wily Apache leader, led bands of followers into Mexico in 1881 and began a new series of raids. Army cavalry and scouts from Fort Bowie sought out the elusive Indians. Geronimo's small band was the last to surrender, five years later, ending Arizona's Indian wars. The fort was abandoned October 17, 1894.

### Visiting the Fort

Modern highways bypass the area, and only crumbling ruins and fading memories remain. The National Park Service maintains the historic site and staffs a ranger station offering a few exhibits; it's open daily 8 a.m.-5 p.m. Signs identify fort buildings, the stage-station site, and battle and massacre locations. Old photos show how the fort appeared in its heyday.

To preserve the historic setting, visitors must approach the site by foot. A sign near the start of the trail describes the hike as easy but visitors not used to the elevation or the summer heat should consider both these factors. From the main road, follow a 1.5-mile, one-way trail past the stage-station site, a cemetery, the Battle of Apache Pass site, and Apache Spring to the extensive ruins of Fort Bowie. An optional return trail takes you to a ridgetop with scenic views while adding no distance. From the town of Bowie, on I-10, drive 12 miles south on a gravel road; parking is on the right, trailhead on the left.

From Willcox (22 miles west) or Chiricahua National Monument (25 miles south), take AZ 186 to Apache Pass Rd., drive over the pass, then look for the signed parking on the left. In bad weather, Apache Pass Rd. can become slippery and is not recommended. The fort site has water and a small ranger station with exhibits but no camping facilities. Picnic tables are at the trailhead and fort.

## WILLCOX

Started in 1880 as a construction camp for the Southern Pacific Railroad, Willcox became a supply and shipping point for local ranchers; agriculture is still the town's most important industry. Apples, peaches, cherries, grapes, pecans, and pistachios now supplement the mainstays of cattle, cotton, and small grains. Willcox (pop. 3,825), just off I-10, is a convenient base for visiting the scenic and historic sights of the area.

The **Willcox Chamber of Commerce** and **Museum of the Southwest** in the Cochise Visitor Center have history exhibits, an information desk, gift shop, and art gallery. Open Mon.-Sat. 9 a.m.-5 p.m. and Sunday 1-5 p.m.; free admission. Take I-10 Exit 340 (AZ 186), then turn northeast a half mile on Circle I Rd.; tel. 384-2272. **Stouts Cider Mill,** near the visitor center, sells products from local apple orchards.

### Rex Allen Arizona Cowboy Museum

Rex Allen grew up singing and playing the guitar on a homestead near Willcox. His musical skills led him into the recording industry, then into movies. *Arizona Cowboy,* released in 1950, was the first of his many films; he also starred in the TV series "Frontier Doctor." Inside the museum, you'll see photos, movie posters, guitars, saddles, sequined cowboy suits, and a buggy used in "Frontier Doctor." It's open Mon.-Sat. 10 a.m.-4 p.m. and Sunday 1-4 p.m.; admission is $2/individual, $3/couple, or $5/family; tel. 384-4583.

*Fort Bowie ruins*

The museum building, originally a turn-of-the-century saloon, is at 150 N. Railroad Ave.—Willcox's main street in the old days. You'll see other historic structures nearby. The **Willcox Commercial Store** (1881) on the corner is the oldest commercial building in Arizona still in use in its original location. Geronimo used to shop here.

### On the Road in Willcox

Willcox includes a good selection of motels, RV parks, and restaurants along the I-10 business route and off I-10 Exit 340 (AZ 186). **Rex Allen Days** honors Arizona's "Mr. Cowboy" on the first weekend of October with a PRCA rodeo, Western music and dances, golf tournament, and other activities. **Keillor Park** has picnic tables, playground, outdoor pool, and tennis courts; from I-10 Exit 340, take Rex Allen Dr. one block toward downtown, then turn right one block on Bisbee Avenue.

**Twin Lakes Country Club** has a nine-hole golf course south of downtown off Willcox Dr.; tel. 384-2720. The **post office** is at the corner of 200 S. Curtis Ave. and Grant Street. **Northern Cochise Community Hospital** is at 901 W. Rex Allen Dr.; tel. 384-3541. The **Wilcox Art Center** is at 207 West Maley St. and Curtis Avenue. The **public library** is on the corner of 400 W. Maley St. and Tucson Ave.; tel. 384-4271.

# VICINITY OF WILLCOX

### Frontier Relics

Orville Mickens has packed this small museum with historical artifacts from Fort Bowie and other areas of the Southwest. Its hours are irregular, so it's best to call first; tel. 384-3481. It's in Dos Cabezas about 14 miles southeast of Willcox on AZ 186, on the way to Chiricahua National Monument.

### Willcox Playa

This giant lake bed south of Willcox is visible from I-10 and covers 50-60 square miles. The playa is usually dry, but after heavy rains it becomes a shallow lake. You may see mirages on the surface in summer. As many as 10,000 sandhill cranes and smaller numbers of ducks and geese winter here.

### Cochise Stronghold Canyon

This canyon is set in a beautiful wooded area of towering pinnacles in the heart of the Dragoon Mountains, 30 miles southwest of Willcox. During the 15 years that the great Apache chief Cochise and about 250 warriors hid out here, no white person was safe in the valleys below. Cochise was never defeated in battle; he agreed to peace in 1872 only when land was promised for his tribe. The Dragoon Mountains take their name from the Third U.S. Cavalry Dragoons.

Today the mountains offer picnicking, hiking trails, and a campground with water from early April to mid-September; the campground costs $6 for day use or for an overnight stay. A self-guided nature trail, starting from the south end of the campground, explains the diverse plant life and other features of the area.

**Cochise Stronghold Trail** continues up the valley past Cochise Spring and Halfmoon Tank to Stronghold Divide, six miles roundtrip. It's also possible to continue down the other side of the range into West Stronghold Canyon. A rough but scenic 24-mile drive crosses the range to the south at Middlemarch Pass, connecting the ghost town of Pearce with Tombstone to the west. For Cochise Stronghold, turn west nine miles on Ironwood Rd. from US 191 on the north side of Sunsites; pavement ends after three-quarters of a mile.

### Amerind Foundation

Amateur archaeologist William Fulton started the foundation in 1937 to increase the world's knowledge of American Indian cultures. The name comes from a contraction of American and Indian. Especially active in research of Southwest and Mexican archaeology, the foundation has amassed an outstanding artifact collection; some can be seen here.

The museum features archaeological and ethnographic exhibits of the native peoples of the Americas. The Amerind's art gallery displays paintings and sculptures by Indian and Anglo-American artists of the 19th and 20th centuries. A museum store sells Native American artwork, crafts, and books. A picnic area is nearby. The museum is open daily 10 a.m.-4 p.m. Sept.-May (closed major holidays); it's a good idea to call for summer hours; rates are $3 adults, $2 ages 12-18, and seniors 60 and older; tel. 586-3666.

The foundation is housed in Spanish-colonial revival buildings among the rock formations of Texas Canyon, 64 miles east of Tucson between Willcox and Benson. Take I-10 Dragoon Exit 318, go southeast one mile, turn left at the sign and drive three-quarters of a mile.

# BENSON

Benson lies 36 miles west of Willcox and 45 miles east of Tucson. The Butterfield Stage crossed the San Pedro River nearby in the early 1860s, but the town didn't really get going until the railroad arrived in 1880, filling its saloons with cowboys, miners, Mexicans, and Chinese. The community is quiet now and offers motels, restaurants, and campgrounds for travelers. **Benson Chamber of Commerce** has information about the town and area; stop by Mon.-Fri. 9 a.m.-4 p.m. or Saturday 10 a.m.-3 p.m. at Oasis Court, 363 W. Fourth St. (Box 2255, Benson, AZ 85602); tel. 586-2842.

## San Pedro Valley Arts and Historical Museum
Photos and artifacts show life in the early railroad, mining, and ranching days. Local handmade crafts are sold. It's open Tues.-Sat. 10 a.m.-4 p.m., same days in summer 10 a.m.-2 p.m.; admission is free. From Fourth St., the main street through downtown, turn one block south on San Pedro to the museum; tel. 586-3070.

## San Pedro and Southwestern Excursion Train
Ride the excursion train along the San Pedro River to places no paved road goes. See ranches and mines and the site of a presidio from Spanish colonial days. Much of the terrain is barely touched by modern times. Enjoy the view from a panorama observation car or from a deluxe parlor car. Tickets cost $15 adult ($24 round trip), $12 senior ($21 round trip), $9 student ($16 round trip), or $40 family ($72 round

trip). The depot is 1.5 miles southeast of downtown Benson off Hwy. 80; tel. 586-2266.

## Kartchner Caverns State Park
Beautiful limestone formations, softly tinted yellow and red, decorate this pristine cave system. Magnificent columns up to 50 feet high, delicate "soda straws" (one is a quarter of an inch in diameter and 20 feet long), shields, stalactites, stalagmites, and nearly every other type of cave entity grow in this living cave.

Kartchner Caverns became Arizona's 25th state park in 1988. Because exceptional care is being taken to preserve the interior formations and environment as trails are constructed, the first sections of the 2.5-mile-long cave won't open until late 1997—and the date has already been pushed back several times. Campgrounds may open before the cave does; call or write for information about the current status of the park; Box 1849, Benson, AZ 85602; tel. 586-7257. The caverns are just off AZ 90 about nine miles south of I-10 Exit 302.

## Singing Wind Bookshop
This unique shop, on a ranch near Benson, carries an excellent selection of regional books and other titles. It's open daily 9 a.m.-5 p.m., including holidays; tel. 586-2425. Go north 2.3 miles on Ocotillo Rd. (I-10 Exit 304) from town, then turn right at the sign and drive a half mile. There's a gate halfway in.

## Holy Trinity Monastery
Experience the tranquility of a monastery by visiting Holy Trinity Monastery along the banks of the San Pedro River in the town of St. David just south of Benson. Attractions include a bird sanctuary trail, views of swans in Spirit Lake, a museum with artifacts from around the world with an impressive antique Bible collection, artifacts from the Civil War period, and a room dedicated to Southwestern Indian culture. You are also free to meditate in the church and retreat accommodations are available ($30 s, $55 d, including meals) but you should call ahead; tel. 720-4016.

# BOOKLIST

## DESCRIPTION AND TRAVEL

Aitchison, Stewart. *A Guide to Exploring Oak Creek and the Sedona Area.* RNM Press, 1989. A series of natural history driving tours with brief mentions of hiking trails.

Annerino, John. *Adventuring in Arizona: The Sierra Club Travel Guide to the Grand Canyon State.* San Francisco: Sierra Club Books, 1991. True to its name, this excellent guide lists backroad driving tours, hiking trails, river trips, and climbing routes through the state's most spectacular country. Includes history and travel tips.

*Arizona Great Outdoors.* P.O. Box 6243, Scottsdale, AZ 85261. Published quarterly, this free newsletter is found in many locations, including libraries. It lists outdoor clubs, how to contact them, and some outdoor events.

*Arizona Highways.* 2039 W. Lewis Ave., Phoenix, AZ 85009. Published monthly, this outstanding magazine features superb color photography with articles on the state's history, people, places, wildlife, back roads, and hiking.

Babbitt, Bruce, ed. *Grand Canyon: An Anthology.* Flagstaff: Northland Press, 1978. Twenty-three authors from the days of the Spanish to the present relate their experiences of the Grand Canyon.

Brown, Bonnie, and Carol D. Bracken. *The Complete Family Guide to Navajo-Hopi Land.* Self-published, 1986. Handy guide for visiting these tribes of the Four Corners region. Full of practical advice on where to stay and eat, shopping, and services.

Casey, Robert L. *A Journey to the High Southwest.* Chester, CT: Globe Pequot Press, 1990. Contains travel tips for southern Utah and adjacent Arizona, New Mexico, and Colorado.

Cook, James E. *Arizona 101.* Cocinero Press, Box 11583, Phoenix, AZ 85061, 1981. "Enroll" in this humorous and factual short study of Arizona.

Dutton, Allen A., and Diane Taylor Bunting. *Arizona Then and Now: A Comprehensive Rephotographic Project.* Phoenix: Ag2 Press. A photo album comparing old photographs with present-day scenes.

Fishbein, Seymour L. *Grand Canyon Country: Its Majesty and Its Lore.* Washington, DC: The National Geographic Society, 1991. Incredible color photography illustrates fine text.

Green, Stewart. *Arizona Scenic Drives.* Helena, MT: Falcon Press,1992. Twenty-nine scenic drives are described with maps and camping information.

Hammons, Lee. *Mineral and Gem Localities in Arizona.* Arizona Maps and Books, Box 1133, Sedona, AZ 86336, 1977. An introduction to the entire state, with 30 color maps showing locations of rocks, minerals, gems, and fossils. Written for both rockhounds and prospectors.

Hirsch, Bob, and Stan Jones. *Fishin' Lake Powell.* Sun Country Publications. Helpful advice on where and how to catch Lake Powell game fish.

Hoefer, Hans (and others). *American Southwest.* APA Insight Guides, 1984. Outstanding color photography illustrates this travel guide to Arizona, New Mexico, and adjacent areas.

Klinck, Richard E. *Land of Room Enough and Time Enough.* Peregrine Smith Books, 1958, 1984. The geography, legends, and people of Monument Valley.

Leydet, Francois. *Time and the River Flowing: Grand Canyon.* New York: Sierra Club-Ballantine Books, 1968. Essays on and color photos of the Grand Canyon.

Lockard, Peggy Hamilton. *This is Tucson, Guidebook to the Old Pueblo.* Pepper Publishing, 433 N. Tucson Blvd., Tucson, AZ 85716-4744, 1988. Excellent guide to the culture, sights, and restaurants of Tucson and vicinity.

Loving, Nancy J., and Tom Bean. *Along the Rim: A Road Guide to the South Rim of Grand Canyon.* Grand Canyon Natural History Assoc., 1981. Beautiful booklet on viewpoints, history, and ecology along the Rim Drive.

*Phoenix and Valley of the Sun Official Visitors Guide.* Phoenix and Valley of the Sun Convention and Visitors Bureau, One Arizona Center, 400 E. Van Buren St., Suite 600, Phoenix, AZ 85004; tel. (602) 254-6500. Free informative magazine revised twice annually.

Plate, Harry, and Trudy Plate. *100 Best Restaurants in Arizona.* Kelton Publishing Co., 1996 (revised annually). Handy guide to many of the best restaurants (163) in the Phoenix area, Tucson, Sedona, and other cities.

Sherman, James, and Barbara Sherman. *Ghost Towns of Arizona.* Norman, OK: University of Oklahoma Press, 1986. Brief histories of about 130 ghost communities. Well illustrated with black-and-white photos, but maps are poor.

Story Behind the Scenery series: *Grand Canyon; Grand Canyon-North Rim; Glen Canyon-Lake Powell; Canyon de Chelly; Petrified Forest; Lake Mead-Hoover Dam.* Las Vegas: KC Publications. Beautiful color photos.

Tegler, Dorothy. *Retiring in Arizona.* Gem Guide Books, Box 30555, Phoenix, AZ 85046, 1987. Full of facts to help you choose your area, then settle in.

Thollander, Earl. *Back Roads of Arizona.* Flagstaff: Northland Press, 1978. Attractive sketches illustrate this road guide to the scenic but seldom-traveled roads of the state. With an introduction by Edward Abbey.

*Tucson Official Visitors Guide.* Metropolitan Tucson Convention and Visitors Bureau, 130 S. Scott Ave., Tucson, AZ 85701; tel. (602) 624-

1817. An informative magazine updated twice yearly; free.

Varney, Philip. *Arizona's Best Ghost Towns: A Practical Guide.* Flagstaff: Northland Press, 1994. Explore the ruins of Arizona's boom-and-bust towns with this easy-to-use guide.

Wallace, Robert. *The Grand Canyon.* The American Wilderness Series. New York: Time-Life Books. A well-illustrated book covering the Canyon. Excellent photography by Ernst Haas.

Writers' Program of the WPA. *Arizona: A State Guide.* Tucson: Hastings House, 1940, 1956. Recently reprinted under the title *The WPA Guide to 1930's Arizona* by the University of Arizona Press. A classic guidebook that still makes good reading.

## HIKING, BICYCLING, AND SKIING

Aitchison, Stewart. *A Naturalist's Guide to Hiking the Grand Canyon.* New York: Prentice Hall, 1985. The author introduces you to Canyon climate, geology, "critters," and plants, then guides you on 30 hikes. Good maps.

Aitchison, Stewart, and Bruce Grubbs. *The Hiker's Guide to Arizona.* Helena, MT: Falcon Press, 1991. One of the best all-around hiking guides to the state; the 104 hikes include a wide variety of regions and terrain.

Annerino, John. *Hiking the Grand Canyon.* A Sierra Club Totebook. San Francisco: Sierra Club Books, 1993. Easily the most comprehensive guide to trails and routes within the canyon. A long introduction provides background on geology, natural history, Indians, and hike planning. The large fold-out topo map clearly shows trails and routes. River-runners will be pleased to find a section of trail descriptions beginning at the water's edge.

Annerino, John. *Outdoors in Arizona: A Guide to Hiking and Backpacking.* Phoenix: Arizona Highways, 1989. Descriptions of 48 hiking areas with maps and very nice color photos.

Arizona Atlas and Gazetteer. Freeport, ME: De Lorme Mapping, 1993. Mostly topographic maps covering the entire state. The scale is too small for really fine detail but the book is useful as a reference.

Arfield, Mike and Steve Wardell. Valley of the Sun Golf Guide. Tempe: Golf Guys, 1993. A review of the 50 best golf courses in Phoenix, Scottsdale, and the East Valley.

Bennett, Sarah. The Mountain Bikers Guide to Arizona. Helena, MT: Falcon Press, 1993. This handy guide describes 59 classic rides; includes maps and photographs.

Blair, Gerry. Rockhounder's Guide to Arizona. Helena, MT: Falcon Press, 1992. A guide to Arizona's natural wealth with descriptions of 75 hunting sites for turqoise, gold, agates, garnet, crystals, and fossils with maps and photographs.

Bowman, Eldon. A Guide to the General Crook Trail. Flagstaff: Museum of Northern Arizona Press and the Boy Scouts of America, 1978. Trail guide to Crook's historic military road. The route begins in Camp Verde and travels east 113 miles along the Mogollon Rim. The Boy Scouts cleared and re-marked this trail as a bicentennial project.

Brainard, Robert and Kamie Brainard. Trail-vision-Hiking Arizona, Vol. 1. Discovery Productions, 9187 E. Conquistadores Dr., Scottsdale, AZ 85255; tel. (800) 354-3004, 1995. This multimedia CD-ROM guide to more than 100 hiking trails throughout Arizona offers complete directions, elevation profiles, trail maps, more than 1,000 color photos of trails and surroundings, video clips, a wildflower guide, and more. Readers can search for trail features with keyword searches such as "aspens."

Bremner, Dugald. Ski Touring Arizona. Flagstaff: Northland Press, 1987. Tour descriptions of the beautiful snow-country of eastern, northern, and southern Arizona. Detailed topo maps.

Butchart, Harvey. Grand Canyon Treks: A Guide to the Inner Canyon Routes. La Siesta Press, 1976. The classic hiking guide to the Canyon; the most useful of Butchart's three books.

Butchart, Harvey. Grand Canyon Treks II: A Guide to the Extended Canyon Routes. La Siesta Press, 1975. Butchart describes rarely used trails and routes in Marble Canyon and the western Grand Canyon.

Butchart, Harvey. Grand Canyon Treks III: Inner Canyon Journals. La Siesta Press, 1986. Additional material expands upon his earlier books.

Carlson, Jack and Elizabeth Stewart. Hiking Guide to the Superstition Wilderness. Tempe: Clear Creek Publishing, 1995. More than 50 hikes are described in the Superstition Wilderness with trail maps, difficulty rating, and history and legends of the Superstitions including the Lost Dutchman Mine.

Fletcher, Colin. The Man Who Walked through Time. New York: Random House, 1989. Well-written adventure tale of Fletcher's two-month solo hike through the Grand Canyon. Fletcher was the first to travel the length of the park entirely on foot.

Freeman, Roger, and Ethel Freeman. Day Hikes and Trail Rides in and around Phoenix. Gem Guide Books, Box 30555, Phoenix, AZ 85046, 1991. The rugged Sonoran Desert that surrounds Arizona's biggest city offers excellent hiking and horseback riding. Detailed trail descriptions.

Ganci, Dave. Hiking the Southwest: Arizona, New Mexico, and West Texas. San Francisco: Sierra Club Books, 1983. A handy guide with a good introduction, practical hints, and information on a variety of trails.

Glending, Eber, and Pete Cowgill. Trail Guide to the Santa Catalina Mountains. Rainbow Expeditions, 915 S. Sherwood Village, Tucson, AZ 85710, 1987. Handy guide to trails and routes of this range north of Tucson.

Hancock, Jan. Horse Trails in Arizona. Phoenix: Golden West Publishers, 1994. Each of the 42 trails listed are given a description, location, length, elevation, plus locations of water sources, corrals, and trailer parking.

Kaibab National Forest. *Recreation Opportunity Guide (North Kaibab Ranger District).* Southwest Natural and Cultural Heritage Assoc., Drawer E, Albuquerque, NM 87103, 1989. Details trails, scenic drives, camp and picnic areas, history, and wildlife of the beautiful forest country north of the Grand Canyon.

Kaibab National Forest. *Visitors Guide: Kaibab National Forest Williams, Chalender & Tusayan Districts.* Southwest Natural and Cultural Heritage Assoc., 1990. Contains sections on trails, bike routes, scenic drives, camp and picnic areas, history, and wildlife near Williams and the Grand Canyon South Rim.

Kals, W.S. *Land Navigation Handbook.* San Francisco: Sierra Club Books, 1983. After reading this book you'll be able to confidently explore Arizona's vast backcountry. This handy pocket-guide not only offers details on using map and compass, but tells how to navigate using the sun, the stars, and an altimeter.

Kelsey, Michael R. *Canyon Hiking Guide to the Colorado Plateau.* Kelsey Publishing, 1991. One of the best guides to hiking in the canyon country. Geologic cross-sections show the formations you'll walk through. The book features descriptions and maps for hikes in Arizona, Utah, and Colorado. The author uses the metric system, but the book is otherwise easy to follow.

Kelsey, Michael R. *Hiking and Exploring the Paria River.* Kelsey Publishing, 1991. The classic Paria Canyon hike, with info on nearby Bryce Canyon and other geologically colorful areas. Includes histories of John D. Lee, ghost towns, ranches, and mining.

Kiefer, Don R. *Hiking Arizona.* San Marino, CA: Golden West Publishers, 1991. Fifty hikes, many little known, with tips for safe and enjoyable hiking.

Krause, Steve, and Teresa Henkle. *Sedona Guide: Day Hiking & Sightseeing Arizona's Red Rock Country.* Pinyon Publishing Co., Box 23809, Tempe, AZ 85285, 1991. Trail descriptions, viewpoints, maps, and illustrations covering the famous Red Rock Country and Oak Creek Canyon near Sedona.

Leavengood, Betty. *Tucson Hiking Guide.* Boulder: Pruett Publishing Co., 1991. A thorough guide to the hiking trails of the Tucson area.

Mangum, Richard K., and Sherry G. Mangum. *Flagstaff Hikes and Mountain Bike Rides.* Hexagon Press, 300 E. Bennett Dr., Flagstaff, AZ 86001, 1995. Handy guide to hiking trails and mountain bike routes near Flagstaff.

Mangum, Richard K., and Sherry G. Mangum. *Sedona Hikes and Mountain Bike Rides.* Flagstaff: Hexagon Press, 1992. A guide to 121 dayhikes, 15 mountain-bike rides, and five vortex sites, with maps and directions.

Martin, Bob, and Dotty Martin. *Arizona's Mountains: A Hiking & Climbing Guide.* Boulder: Pruett Publishing Co., 1991. A guide to hiking and climbing in Arizona; includes maps and charts.

Martin, Bob, and Dotty Martin. *Hiking Guide to the Santa Rita Mountains of Arizona.* Boulder: Pruett Publishing Co., 1986. A guide to mountains and canyons south of Tucson; topo maps, charts, and 52 hike descriptions.

Mazel, David. *Arizona Trails: 100 Hikes in Canyon and Sierra.* Berkeley: Wilderness Press, 1989. An excellent hiking guide to many of the designated wilderness areas of the state, including the Grand Canyon, Superstitions, Chiricahuas, and Mazatzals. Excellent maps.

Moran, Charles W. *Hiking Trails of the Huachuca Mountains.* Livingston's Books, Sierra Vista, AZ 85635, 1981. Useful guide to the peaks and canyons of the Huachucas in southeast Arizona.

Morris, Larry A. *Hiking the Grand Canyon and Havasupai.* Tucson: Aztex Press, 1981. Background on the Grand Canyon and Havasupai Indians; includes hiking tips and trail descriptions.

Nelson, Dick, and Sharon Nelson. *50 Hikes in Arizona.* Tecolote Press, 1981. A sampling of easy to difficult hikes, with trail descriptions and maps.

Ray, Cosmic. *Fat Tire Tales and Trails.* Self-published, 1994. Lots of way cool mountain-bike rides around Arizona . . . both summer and winter fun.

Sagi, G. J. *Fishing Arizona.* Phoenix: Golden West Publishers, 1992. Travel directions are given to 50 good fishing lakes with outline maps of the shorelines plus information about the types of fish found in each lake. A list of fish, by type, gives the state record.

Thybony, Scott. *Official Guide to Hiking the Grand Canyon.* Grand Canyon Natural History Assoc., 1994. Introduction and guide to the best-known trails of the Grand Canyon.

Waterman, Laura, and Guy Waterman. *Backwoods Ethics: Environmental Issues for Hikers and Campers.* Stone Wall Press, 1994. Thoughtful commentaries on how hikers can explore the wilderness with minimal impact. Case histories dramatize the need to protect the environment.

## RIVER-RUNNING AND BOATING

Abbey, Edward. *Down the River.* New York: E.P. Dutton, 1991. Abbey expresses joy and concern in a series of thoughtful, witty, and wide-ranging essays on the American West.

Belknap, Buzz. *Grand Canyon River Guide.* Westwater Books. Covers the 288 miles of Colorado River through Marble and Grand Canyons; begins at Lees Ferry and ends at Lake Mead.

Crumbo, Kim. *A River Runner's Guide to the History of the Grand Canyon.* Boulder: Johnson Books, 1981. Highly readable guide with a foreword by Edward Abbey.

Hirsch, Bob. *Houseboating on Lake Powell: First Class Adventure.* Self-published, 1988. Tips on operating and living aboard a houseboat; includes fishing and sightseeing information.

Jones, Stan. *Boating and Exploring Map: Lake Powell and Its 96 Canyons.* Sun Country Publications, 1985. Information-packed map show-ing natural features, marinas, Indian sites, hiking trails, and 4WD tracks. Map text describes points of interest, navigation, history, fishing, and wildlife.

Kelsey, Michael R. *Boater's Guide to Lake Powell.* Wasatch Book Distr., P.O. Box 1108, Salt Lake City, UT 84110, 1991. This comprehensive guide will help you explore the lake, whether traveling in a small inflatable raft, as the author did, or a more luxurious craft. Includes many maps, photos, and hiking descriptions.

Simmons, George C., and David L. Gaskill. *River Runner's Guide to the Canyons of the Green and Colorado Rivers: With Emphasis on Geologic Features, Vol. III.* Flagstaff: Northland Press, 1969. This volume covers Marble Canyon and Grand Canyon.

Slingluff, Jim. *Verde River Recreation Guide.* San Marino, CA: Golden West Publishers, 1990. River-running on the Verde and its tributaries; includes boating tips and natural history.

Stephens, Hal G., and Eugene M. Shoemaker. *In the Footsteps of John Wesley Powell: An Album of Comparative Photographs of the Green and Colorado Rivers, 1871-72 and 1968.* Boulder: Johnson Books and The Powell Society, 1987. Fascinating photo album of identical river views snapped nearly 100 years apart. Photos show how little—and how much—the forces of erosion, plants, and human beings have changed the Green and Colorado River Canyons. The text describes geologic features for each of the 110 pairs of photos. Maps show locations of camera stations.

Stevens, Larry. *The Colorado River in Grand Canyon: Comprehensive Guide to Its Natural and Human History.* Red Lake Books, 1986. Maps and concise guides to geology, Indian history, exploration, flora, and fauna.

## HISTORY

Cline, Platt. *They Came to the Mountain: The Story of Flagstaff's Beginnings.* Flagstaff: Northern Arizona University with Northland Press, 1976. Highly readable account of Flagstaff's founding and early years.

Coolidge, Dane. *Arizona Cowboys.* Tucson: University of Arizona Press, 1984. Working the range in the early 1900s.

Crampton, C. Gregory. *Land of Living Rock.* New York: Alfred A. Knopf, Inc., 1972. Story of the geology, early explorers, Indians, and settlers of the high plateaus in Arizona, Utah, and Nevada. Well illustrated with color and black-and-white photos, maps, and diagrams.

Crampton, C. Gregory. *Standing Up Country.* New York: Alfred A. Knopf, Inc., 1964. Illustrated historical account of the people who came to the canyon lands of Arizona and Utah—Indians, explorers, outlaws, miners, settlers, and scientists.

Dellenbaugh, Frederick S. *A Canyon Voyage: A Narrative of the Second Powell Expedition Down the Green-Colorado River from Wyoming, and the Expeditions on Land, in the Years 1871 and 1872.* Tucson: University of Arizona Press, reprinted 1984. Dellenbaugh served as artist and assistant topographer on the expedition.

Faulk, Odie B. *Arizona: A Short History.* Norman, OK: University of Oklahoma Press, 1979. Popular account of Arizona from the first days of European exploration through the territorial years and statehood.

Forrest, Earle R. *Arizona's Dark and Bloody Ground.* Tucson: University of Arizona Press, 1936, 1984. An account of the ruthless Pleasant Valley War between cattle owners and sheep owners.

"The Heart of Ambos Nogales." *The Journal of Arizona History.* Vol. 17, No. 2 (Summer 1976): page 161. The story of Nogales.

Hinton, Richard J. *The Handbook to Arizona: Its Resources, History, Towns, Mines, Ruins, and Scenery.* First published by Payot, Upham and Co. in 1878; reprinted by Arizona Silhouettes in 1954. This volume gives a clear picture of Arizona's early years.

Hughes, J. Donald. *In the House of Stone and Light.* Grand Canyon Natural History Assoc., 1978.

A well-illustrated history of the Grand Canyon from the early Indians to the modern park.

Johnson, G. Wesley, Jr. *Phoenix: Valley of the Sun.* Continental Heritage Press, 1982. Excellent text and photos trace the development of Phoenix from the ancient Hohokam to the modern metropolis.

Lavender, David. *River Runners of the Grand Canyon.* Tucson: University of Arizona Press, 1985. Descriptions of action-packed adventures on the river, beginning with Powell's trips in 1869 through the closing of Glen Canyon Dam in the early 1960s.

Lummis, Charles F. *Some Strange Corners of Our Country.* Tucson: University of Arizona Press, 1891, 1892, reprinted in 1989. Step back a century to visit the Southwest's Indian country, Grand Canyon, Petrified Forest, and Montezuma Castle.

Mitchell, John D. *Lost Mines of the Great Southwest.* Glorieta, NM: Rio Grande Press, 1933, 1984. Who isn't enthralled by legends of lost treasure? You'll reach for a pick and shovel after reading this one.

Parker, Lowell. *Arizona Towns and Tales.* Phoenix: Phoenix Newspapers, Inc., 1975. Entertaining tales of personalities and places of yesteryear.

Pattie, James Ohio. *The Personal Narrative of James O. Pattie.* Missoula: Mountain Press Publishing Co., 1988. Reprint of 1831 edition. An early fur trapper, who claimed to be the first white American to see the Grand Canyon, tells of his experiences in the wildlands of the West during the 1820s.

Powell, J.W. *The Exploration of the Colorado River and Its Canyons.* Mineola, NY: Dover Publications, reprinted 1961. Powell's 1869 expedition, the first running of the Colorado River through the Grand Canyon. Also contains a description of the 1870 Uinta Expedition.

Rusho, W.L., and C. Gregory Crampton. *Lees Ferry: Desert River Crossing.* Salt Lake City: Cricket Prods., 1992. A historical study of Lees Ferry, with over 135 rare and unusual photographs.

Sheridan, Thomas E. *Arizona: A History*. University of Arizona Press, 1995. This history starts with paleolithic times and goes to the 1990s examining in particular the transition of the state's economy from a dominance of mining and ranching, to the current dominance of tourism, outside business, and environmentalism.

Sikorsky, Robert. *Fools Gold: The Facts, Myths and Legends of the Lost Dutchman Mine and the Superstition Mountains*. San Marino, CA: Golden West, 1983. The history of the most famous lost mine of all.

Summerhayes, Martha. *Vanished Arizona*. Lincoln: University of Nebraska Press, 1979. Reprint of 1911 Salem Press second edition. In 1874 a young New England woman marries an Army officer; together they set out for some of the wildest corners of the West. Her accounts bring into sharp focus frontier Arizona life.

Trimble, Marshall. *Arizona: A Cavalcade of History*. Tucson: Treasure Chest Publications, 1989. Very comprehensive and well illustrated with historic photos.

Trimble, Marshall. *Arizona Adventure: Action-Packed True Tales of Early Arizona*. San Marino, CA: Golden West, 1982. Nineteen stories from Arizona's Old West.

Trimble, Marshall. *Roadside History of Arizona*. Missoula: Mountain Press Publishing Co., 1986. Fascinating tales, with many historic photos. Organized by region and highway.

Wagoner, Jay J. *Arizona Territory 1863-1912: A Political History*. Tucson: University of Arizona Press, 1970. Excellent history of the territorial years.

Woody, Clara T., and Milton L. Schwartz. *Globe, Arizona*. The Arizona Historical Society, 1977. Stories of early miners, pioneers, Indian battles, and the Graham-Tewksbury feud, also known as the Pleasant Valley War.

# ARCHAEOLOGY

Ambler, J. Richard. *The Anasazi: Prehistoric Peoples of the Four Corners Region*. Flagstaff: Museum of Northern Arizona, 1977. One of the best overviews of Anasazi history.

Grant, Campbell. *Canyon de Chelly: Its People and Rock Art*. Tucson: University of Arizona Press, 1978. The geology, archaeology, and history of the canyons, with many illustrations. Nearly half the text is devoted to a discussion of the wealth of petroglyphs and pictographs left by the Anasazi, Hopi, and Navajo.

Gregonis, Linda, and Karl Reinhard. *Hohokam Indians of the Tucson Basin*. Tucson: University of Arizona Press, 1979. Introduction to the prehistoric Hohokam Indians.

Lister, Robert, and Florence Lister. *Those Who Came Before: Southwestern Archaeology in the National Park System*. Tucson: University of Arizona Press, 1983. A well-illustrated guide to the history, artifacts, and ruins of prehistoric Indian cultures in the Southwest. Includes descriptions of the parks and monuments that contain these sites today.

McGregor, John C. *Southwestern Archaeology*. Champaign: University of Illinois Press, 1982. If you're curious why archaeologists like their work, and how they do it, this book presents the motivations and techniques of this special group of scientists. It also describes cultures and artifacts from the earliest known peoples to the present.

Noble, David Grant. *Ancient Ruins of the Southwest*. Flagstaff: Northland Publishing, 1991. Well-illustrated guide to the prehistoric ruins of Arizona, New Mexico, Colorado, and Utah.

Oppelt, Norman T. *Guide to Prehistoric Ruins of the Southwest*. Boulder: Pruett Publishing Co., 1989. An introduction to ancient cultures with descriptions of more than 200 sites in Arizona, New Mexico, Colorado, and Utah.

Patterson, Alex. *A Field Guide to Rock Art Symbols of the Greater Southwest.* Boulder: Johnson Books, 1992. A dictionary-style guide to petroglyphs and pictographs with many illustrations grouped by subject.

Viele, Catherine. *Voices in the Canyon.* Southwest Parks and Monuments Assoc., 1980. Highly readable and well-illustrated book about the ancient Anasazi and their villages of Betatakin, Keet Seel, and Inscription House.

## ARIZONA INDIANS OF TODAY

Courlander, Harold. *The Fourth World of the Hopis: The Epic Story of the Hopi Indians as Preserved in Their Legends & Traditions.* Albuquerque: University of New Mexico Press, 1987.

Courlander, Harold. *Hopi Voices: Recollections, Traditions, and Narratives of the Hopi Indians.* Albuquerque: University of New Mexico Press, 1982. A selection of 74 Hopi narrations explaining their mythology, history, exploits, games, and animal stories. One of the best books on Hopi culture.

Dedera, Don. *Navajo Rugs: How to Find, Evaluate, Buy and Care for Them.* Flagstaff: Northland Press, 1990. A history of Navajo weaving, including regional styles and practical advice.

Dittert, Alfred, Jr., and Fred Plog. *Generations in Clay: Pueblo Pottery of the American Southwest.* Flagstaff: Northland Press, 1980. An introduction to the pottery of the Pueblo Indians, both prehistoric and modern. Well illustrated, with black-and-white and color photos.

Dozier, Edward P. *Hano, A Tewa Indian Community in Arizona.* Orlando: Holt, Rinehart and Winston, 1966. A study of Tewa history, society, religion, and livelihood.

Dyk, Walter (recorded by). *Son of Old Man Hat: A Navajo Autobiography.* Lincoln: University of Nebraska Press, 1967, original copyright 1938. A Navajo relates his story of growing up in the late 1800s.

Evers, Larry, ed. *The South Corner of Time.* Tucson: University of Arizona Press, 1980. Stories and poetry by contemporary Indians of the Hopi, Navajo, Tohono O'odham, and Yaqui tribes.

Fontana, Bernard. *Of Earth and Little Rain.* Tucson: University of Arizona Press. Essays and photos on Tohono O'odham life.

Forrest, Earle. *The Snake Dance of the Hopi Indians.* Westernlore Press, 1961. A detailed look at Hopi mythology and ceremonies, illustrated with many old photos.

Gillmore, Frances, and Louisa Wetherill. *Traders to the Navajos.* Albuquerque: University of New Mexico Press, 1934, 1983. The Wetherills lived in and explored the Monument Valley region, trading with the Navajo. These are some of their stories about lost mines, early travelers, and the Navajo people.

Gilpin, Laura. *The Enduring Navajo.* Austin: University of Texas Press, 1989. An excellent book of photographs about the Navajo people, their homes, land, ceremonies, crafts, tribal government, and trading posts.

James, Harry C. *Pages from Hopi History.* Tucson: University of Arizona Press, 1974. Beginning with the tribe's mythological entrance into this world, Hopi history is traced through early migrations, encounters with the Spanish, difficulties with Mexicans and Navajo, resistance to U.S. authority, and their life today.

Kammer, Jerry. *The Second Long Walk: The Navajo-Hopi Land Dispute.* Albuquerque: University of New Mexico Press, 1980. Background on both sides of the long-running land dispute between the Navajo and the Hopi.

Locke, Raymond F. *The Book of the Navajo.* Los Angeles: Mankind Publishing, 1976, 1989. Navajo legends, art, culture, and history, from early to modern times.

Luckert, Karl W. *Coyoteway: A Navajo Holyway Healing Ceremonial.* Tucson and Flagstaff: The

University of Arizona Press and Museum of Northern Arizona Press, 1979. A rare look at an important Navajo ceremony. It requires nine days and involves chanting, fire-making, sandpainting, and other rituals. Photos and chant translations provide a peek into intricate Navajo beliefs.

Mooney, Ralph. "The Navajos." *National Geographic Magazine.* (Dec. 1972): page 740. Describes the Navajo people and how they have balanced their traditions with life in 20th-century America.

Mullet, G.M. *Spider Woman Stories.* Tucson: University of Arizona Press, 1979. Selected stories from Hopi mythology.

Page, Jake. "Inside the Sacred Hopi Homeland." *National Geographic Magazine.* (Nov. 1982): page 607. A rare look at the spiritual life of the Hopi.

Page, Susanne, and Jake Page. *Hopi.* New York: Harry N. Abrams, Inc., 1982. Records details of Hopi spiritual life. Everyday life, ceremonies, and sacred places rarely seen by outsiders are described and illustrated with large color photos.

Simmons, Leo, ed. *Sun Chief: The Autobiography of a Hopi Indian.* New Haven: Yale University Press, 1963. A Hopi tells of his experiences growing up in both the Hopi and white worlds, then returning to traditional ways.

Suntracks, Larry Evers. *Hopi Photographers/Hopi Images.* Tucson: University of Arizona Press, 1983. Features photography of the Hopi, 1880-1980, including historic photos by Anglos and modern work by Hopi photographers; black-and-white and color.

Titiev, Mischa. *Old Oraibi: A Study of the Hopi Indians of Third Mesa.* Albuquerque: University of New Mexico Native American Studies, 1992. Detailed account of Hopi society and ceremonies.

Webb, George. *A Pima Remembers.* Tucson: University of Arizona Press, 1959 (reprinted 1982). Traditional stories of the Pima Indians.

Wright, Barton. *Hopi Kachinas: The Complete Guide to Collecting Kachina Dolls.* Flagstaff: Northland Press, 1977. Dolls from clowns to ogres illustrated and explained.

Wright, Margaret. *Hopi Silver.* Flagstaff: Northland Press, 1989. History and examples of Hopi silversmithing.

Yava, Albert. *Big Falling Snow.* Albuquerque: University of New Mexico Press, 1992. A Tewa-Hopi discusses the history and traditions of the Tewa and Hopi, including conflicts with missionaries and government officials who tried to Americanize the tribes.

Zolbrod, Paul G. *Diné bahanè: The Navajo Creation Story.* Albuquerque: University of New Mexico Press, 1988. Deities, people, and animals come to life in this translation of Navajo mythology.

# NATURAL SCIENCES

Arnberger, Leslie P., and Jeanne R. Janish. *Flowers of the Southwest Mountains.* Southwest Parks and Monuments Assoc., 1982. Descriptions and illustrations of flowers and common trees found at 7,000 feet and above.

Barnes, F.A. *Canyon Country Geology for the Layman and Rockhound.* Wasatch Publishers, Inc., 1978. Geologic history and guide to rockhounding; emphasis on southeast Utah and adjacent Arizona.

Bowers, Janice Emily. *100 Desert Wildflowers of the Southwest.* Southwest Parks and Monuments Assoc., 1989. A general introduction with brief descriptions, including a color photo for each flower.

Bowers, Janice Emily. *100 Roadside Wildflowers of Southwest Woodlands.* Southwest Parks and Monuments Assoc., 1989. Brief descriptions and color photos for 100 flowers found above 4,500 feet.

Chronic, Halka. *Roadside Geology of Arizona.* Missoula: Mountain Press Publishing Co.,

1983. Well illustrated with photos, maps, and diagrams. Organized along major highway routes; also covers the national parks and some national monuments.

Cunningham, Richard L. *50 Common Birds of the Southwest*. Southwest Parks and Monuments Assoc., 1990. Each bird is represented by a color photo and description of migration, feeding, and nesting habits. Includes Spanish and Latin names.

Dodge, Natt N. *Poisonous Dwellers of the Desert*. Southwest Parks and Monuments Assoc., 1981. Describes creatures to watch out for—poisonous insects, snakes, and the Gila monster. Includes advice on insecticides and bite treatment. Some nonvenomous animals often mistakenly believed to be poisonous are listed as well.

Dodge, Natt N., and Jeanne R. Janish. *Flowers of the Southwest Deserts*. Southwest Parks and Monuments Assoc., 1985. Desert plant and flower guide for elevations under 4,500 feet.

Doolittle, Jerome. *Canyons and Mesas*. The American Wilderness Series. New York: Time-Life Books, 1974. Text and photos give a feel for the ruggedly beautiful country of northern Arizona and adjacent Utah and Colorado.

Earle, W. Hubert. *Cacti of the Southwest*. Phoenix: Desert Botanical Garden, 1980. Lists the 152 known species of cacti in the Southwest, with black-and-white and color photos.

Elmore, Francis H., and Jeanne R. Janish. *Shrubs and Trees of the Southwest Uplands*. Southwest Parks and Monuments Assoc., 1976. Color-coded pages help locate plants and trees found above 4,500 feet.

Fischer, Pierre C. *70 Common Cacti of the Southwest*. Southwest Parks and Monuments Assoc., 1989. Each cactus is represented by a color photo and description.

Halfpenny, James, and Elizabeth Biesiot. *A Field Guide: Mammal Tracking in Western America*. Boulder: Johnson Books, 1986. No need to guess

what animal passed by. This well-illustrated guide shows how to read the prints of creatures large and small. More determined detectives can sample the intriguing scatology chapter.

McKee, Edwin D. *Ancient Landscapes of the Grand Canyon Region*. Flagstaff: Northland Press, 1982. Brief account of the geologic history of the Grand Canyon.

Manning, Reg. *What Kinda Cactus Izzat?* Reganson Cartoon Books, 1969. A fun book on the cacti and other desert plants in the Southwest.

Nations, Dale, and Edmund Stump. *Geology of Arizona*. Dubuque: Kendall/Hunt Publishing Co., 1981. Learn how time and geologic processes have formed the state's remarkable natural features. A comprehensive introduction to geology with good photos and illustrations.

Nelson, Dick, and Sharon Nelson. *Easy Field Guide Series of Arizona: Snakes, Insects, Birds, Mammals, Cactus, or Trees*. Primer Publishers. Easy-to-carry mini-guides.

Olin, George. *House in the Sun*. Southwest Parks and Monuments Assoc., 1977. A guide to the Sonoran Desert—why it exists, and how life has adapted to it. Also tells how *you* can adapt to the sometimes harsh conditions there, enjoying the desert in safety. Many color photos.

Olin, George, and Dale Thompson. *Mammals of the Southwest Deserts*. Southwest Parks and Monuments Assoc., 1982. Well illustrated with black-and-white and color drawings.
Peterson, Roger Tory. *A Field Guide to Western Birds*. Boston: Houghton Mifflin, 1990. Well illustrated with drawings.

Powell, Lawrence Clark, and Michael Collier. *Where Water Flows: The Rivers of Arizona*. Flagstaff: Northland Press, 1980. Essays and beautiful color photos about seven of Arizona's rivers.

Smith, Robert L. *Venomous Animals of Arizona*. Tucson: University of Arizona Press, 1982. Ever wonder about a scorpion's love life? Good descriptions of poisonous insects and animals, with medical notes.

Sweet, Muriel. *Common Edible and Useful Plants of the West*. Happy Camp, CA: Naturegraph Publishers, 1976. Nontechnical descriptions of plants and trees with food, medicinal, and other uses. Most of these helpful rooted creatures were first discovered by Native Americans and later used by pioneer settlers.

Whitney, Stephen. *A Field Guide to the Grand Canyon*. New York: William Morrow, 1982. Excellent, well-illustrated guide to the Canyon's geology, early Indians, flowers, trees, birds, and animals. Most of the information also applies to other canyons on the Colorado Plateau. Includes practical advice for visiting and hiking in the Grand Canyon.

## ONWARD TRAVEL

Barnes, F.A. *Utah Canyon Country*. Utah Geographic Series, Inc., no. 1, 1986. Stunning color photos illustrate this book about the land, people, and natural history of southern Utah. The text also describes parks, monuments, and practicalities of travel.

Castleman, Deke. *Nevada Handbook*. Chico, CA: Moon Publications, 1995. Castleman captures the soul of Nevada's glittering cities, mixed with info on wilderness, history, and small backcountry towns. Hundreds of insider's tips.

Cummings, Joe. *Baja Handbook*. Chico, CA: Moon Publications, 1994. Thorough, engaging guide to Mexico's "forgotten peninsula." Special emphasis on sidetrips for travelers eager to trek off the beaten path.

Cummings, Joe. *Northern Mexico Handbook*. Chico, CA: Moon Publications, 1994. Excellent reference for travelers intent on tackling some of North America's most unexplored turf.

Cummings, Joe and Chicki Mallan. *Mexico Handbook*. Chico, CA: Moon Publications, 1996. A user friendly and comprehensive guide offering practical travel information as well as an insight into the Mexican culture.

Franz, Carl. *The People's Guide to Mexico*. Santa Fe: John Muir Publications, 1990. This hefty guide is crammed with useful advice on driving, public transport, accommodations, cantinas, markets, and staying healthy.

Harris, Richard. *22 Days in the American Southwest*. Santa Fe: John Muir Publications, 1991. Itineraries and suggested schedules to help you cover the highlights in a short time. Not for leisurely or serendipitous touring.

Metzger, Stephen. *Colorado Handbook*. Chico, CA: Moon Publications, 1996. Colorado calls you to Mesa Verde National Park, beautiful canyon country, and the heart of the magnificent Rocky Mountains.

Metzger, Stephen. *New Mexico Handbook*. Chico, CA: Moon Publications, 1996. Explore the landscapes, ancient pueblos, Spanish sites, wilderness areas, art, and cities of New Mexico with this informative guidebook.

Weil, Mary. *The Rocky Point Gringo Guide— A Travel Guide to Puerto Peñasco-Mexico*. Tempe: Frontier Travel Adventures, 1992. A useful source of information for the traveler to the Puerto Penasco area offering advice on crossing the border, recreation, entertainment, shopping, beaches, dining, hotels, and safety.

Weir, Bill and Robert Blake. *Utah Handbook*. Chico, CA: Moon Publications, 1995. Explore the magical canyon country north of Arizona with this handy and comprehensive guide. Learn about Utah's unique history, city sights, mountains, and deserts.

Whipperman, Bruce. *Pacific Mexico Handbook*. Chico, CA: Moon Publications, 1995. In addition to comprehensive travel information this book offers an excellent overview of life along the Pacific Coast.

## REFERENCE

Comeaux, Malcolm L. *Arizona: A Geography*. Geographies of the United States series. Boulder: Westview Press, 1981. A 336-page volume full of info on Arizona geography, settlement, population, resources, and agriculture.

Walker, Henry P., and Don Bufkin. *Historical Atlas of Arizona*. Norman: University of Oklahoma Press, 1986. Clear maps and concise text cover the geography, Indian tribes, exploration, and development of Arizona.

## CUISINE

Fischer, Al, and Mildred Fischer. *Arizona Cook Book*. San Marino, CA: Golden West, 1983. A culinary guide to the state, including Indian, Western, and barbecue cuisine. Learn how to prepare your own cactus jelly.

Furey-Werhan, Carol. *Grand Canyon Pioneers Society Cookbook*. Grand Canyon: Grand Canyon Pioneers Society, 1988. Some recipes go back to pioneer days; others are more modern.

Kavena, Juanita Tiger. *Hopi Cookery*. Tucson: University of Arizona Press, 1980. Learn how to make piki bread, bake a prairie dog, fix squash and fresh corn casserole, and make a yucca pie.

# HIKING TRAILS INDEX

*Italicized* page numbers indicate information in captions, charts, illustrations, maps, or special topics.

# INDEX

Page numbers in **boldface** indicate the primary reference to a given topic. *Italicized* page numbers indicate information in captions, charts, illustrations, maps, or special topics.

# ABOUT THE AUTHORS

## BILL WEIR

Back in school, Bill Weir always figured he'd settle down to a career job and live happily ever after. Then he discovered traveling. After graduating with a B.A. degree in physics from Berea College in 1972, Bill found employment as an electronic technician in Columbus, Ohio. But the very short vacation breaks just didn't provide enough time for the trips he dreamed of.

So in 1976 he took off on his trusty bicycle, Bessie, riding across the United States from Virginia to Oregon with Bikecentennial '76. The following year he took off on an even longer bicycle trip—from Alaska to Baja California. Then came the ultimate journey—a bicycle cruise around the world. Bill pedaled the globe from 1980 to 1984, spending most of his time in the South Pacific and Asia. Naturally he used Moon's excellent *South Pacific Handbook* and *Indonesia Handbook*. Correspondence with the authors led to the idea of writing a guidebook of his own. Bill returned to his home base of Flagstaff, Arizona, and set to work researching and writing *Arizona Traveler's Handbook.*

As soon as the labor on that book came to an end, Bill headed north across the Grand Canyon to the Beehive State to create the *Utah Handbook.* Bill continues to explore Arizona and Utah, always discovering new places and learning more about the old. Between books, Bill enjoys trips to Asia, which, he says, "add to life's richness of experiences."

## ROBERT BLAKE

Robert Blake was born at Pensacola Naval Air Station, the son of a U.S. Naval aviator. By the time he finished first grade, he'd lived in seven places—including all four corners of the country.

With a keen interest in astronomy, Robert attended Pensacola Junior College, University of Arizona, and Northern Arizona University in the mid- to late 1960s. Robert was drafted into the army in 1970. He served first as a guard in northern Italy, within sight of the Alps, then as an optical engineer at Night Vision Labs in Fort Belvoir, Virginia.

In the years since, Robert has taught college astronomy, physics, and math. He rose from teacher to lecturer, instructor, and finally assistant professor at Odessa College, where he directed the college planetarium.

Active in hiking, caving, and astronomy, Robert has enjoyed the Flagstaff area for 25 years. He met Bill Weir at a Flagstaff Hiking Club meeting; the two soon agreed to collaborate on future editions of *Arizona Traveler's Handbook.*

# MOON TRAVEL HANDBOOKS
### THE IDEAL TRAVELING COMPANIONS

**M**oon Travel Handbooks provide focused, comprehensive coverage of distinct destinations all over the world. Our goal is to give travelers all the background and practical information they'll need for an extraordinary travel experience.

Every Handbook begins with an in-depth essay about the land, the people, their history, art, politics, and social concerns—an entire bookcase of cultural insight and introductory information in one portable volume. We also provide accurate, up-to-date coverage of all the practicalities: language, currency, transportation, accommodations, food, and entertainment. And Moon's maps are legendary, covering not only cities and highways, but parks and trails that are often difficult to find in other sources.

Below are highlights of Moon's North America and Hawaii Travel Handbook series. Our complete list of Handbooks covering North America and Hawaii, Mexico, Central America and the Caribbean, and Asia and the Pacific, are listed on the order form on the accompanying pages. To purchase Moon Travel Handbooks, please check your local bookstore or order by phone: (800) 345-5473 Monday-Friday 8 a.m.-5 p.m. PST.

## MOON OVER NORTH AMERICA
## THE NORTH AMERICA AND HAWAII TRAVEL HANDBOOK SERIES

> "Moon's greatest achievements may be the individual state books they offer. . . . Moon not only digs up little-discovered attractions, but also offers thumbnail sketches of the culture and state politics of regions that rarely make national headlines."
>
> —*The Millennium Whole Earth Catalog*

### ALASKA-YUKON HANDBOOK
by Deke Castleman and Don Pitcher, 460 pages, **$14.95**
"Exceptionally rich in local culture, history, and reviews of natural attractions. . . . One of the most extensive pocket references. . . . An essential guide!" — *The Midwest Book Review*

### ALBERTA AND THE NORTHWEST TERRITORIES
by Nadina Purdon and Andrew Hempstead, 466 pages, **$17.95**
"*Alberta and the Northwest Territories Handbook* provides strong coverage of one of the most rugged territories in Canada."
—*The Bookwatch*

### ARIZONA TRAVELER'S HANDBOOK
by Bill Weir and Robert Blake, 448 pages, **$17.95**
"If you don't own this book already, buy it immediately"
—*Arizona Republic*

## ATLANTIC CANADA HANDBOOK

by Nan Drosdick and Mark Morris, 436 pages, **$17.95**
Like a corner of Europe, Canada's eastern seacoast provinces boast Irish brogue, Scottish kilts, Highland flings, and a rich heritage of British influence. *Atlantic Canada Handbook* provides extensive coverage of this region, including New Brunswick, Nova Scotia, Newfoundland, and Prince Edward Island. While there are many guides to Canada, none offers the detailed regional coverage of this comprehensive handbook.

## BIG ISLAND OF HAWAII HANDBOOK

by J.D. Bisignani, 349 pages, **$13.95**
"The best general guidebooks available"          —*Hawaii Magazine*

## BRITISH COLUMBIA HANDBOOK

by Jane King, 375 pages, **$15.95**
"Deftly balances the conventional and the unconventional, for both city lovers and nature lovers."
          —*Reference and Research Book News*

## COLORADO HANDBOOK

by Stephen Metzger, 470 pages, **$18.95**
"Hotel rooms in the Aspen area, in the height of winter sports season, for $20-$30? . . . who but a relentless researcher from Moon could find it?"          —*The New York Daily News*

## GEORGIA HANDBOOK

by Kap Stann, 350 pages, **$17.95**
". . . everything you need to know to enjoy a journey through Georgia."          —*Southern Book Trade*

## HAWAII HANDBOOK

by J.D. Bisignani, 1004 pages, **$19.95**
Winner: Grand Excellence and Best Guidebook Awards, Hawaii Visitors' Bureau
"No one since Michener has told us so much about our 50th state."          —*Playboy*

## HONOLULU-WAIKIKI HANDBOOK

by J.D. Bisignani, 365 pages, **$14.95**
"The best general guidebooks available."          —*Hawaii Magazine*

## IDAHO HANDBOOK

by Bill Loftus, 282 pages, **$14.95**
"Well-organized, engagingly written, tightly edited, and chock-full of interesting facts about localities, backcountry destinations, traveler accommodations, and cultural and natural history."
          —*Sierra Magazine*

## KAUAI HANDBOOK

by J.D. Bisignani, 274 pages, **$13.95**
"This slender guide is tightly crammed. . . . The information provided is staggering."          —*Hawaii Magazine*

## MAUI HANDBOOK
by J.D. Bisignani, 393 pages, **$14.95**
Winner: Best Guidebook Award, Hawaii Visitors' Bureau
"*Maui Handbook* should be in every couple's suitcase. It intelligently discusses Maui's history and culture, and you can trust the author's recommendations for best beaches, restaurants, and excursions." —*Bride's Magazine*

## MONTANA HANDBOOK
by W.C. McRae and Judy Jewell, 466 pages, **$17.95**
"Well-organized, engagingly written, tightly edited, and chock-full of interesting facts about localities, backcountry destinations, traveler accommodations, and cultural and natural history."
—*Sierra Magazine*

## NEVADA HANDBOOK
by Deke Castleman, 473 pages, **$16.95**
"Veteran travel writer Deke Castleman says he covered more than 10,000 miles in his research for this book and it shows."
—*Nevada Magazine*

## NEW MEXICO HANDBOOK
by Stephen Metzger, 322 pages, **$14.95**
"The best current guide and travel book to all of New Mexico"
—*New Mexico Book League*

## NORTHERN CALIFORNIA HANDBOOK
by Kim Weir, 779 pages, **$19.95**
"That rarest of travel books–both a practical guide to the region and a map of its soul." —*San Francisco Chronicle*

## OREGON HANDBOOK
by Stuart Warren
and Ted Long Ishikawa, 520 pages, **$16.95**
". . . perhaps the most definitive tourist guide to the state ever published." —*The Oregonian*

## TEXAS HANDBOOK
by Joe Cummings, 598 pages, **$17.95**
"Reveals a Texas with a diversity of people and culture that is as breathtaking as that of the land itself."
—*Planet Newspaper,* Australia

"I've read a bunch of Texas guidebooks, and this is the best one."
—Joe Bob Briggs

## UTAH HANDBOOK
by Bill Weir and Robert Blake, 458 pages, **$16.95**
"What Moon Publications has given us—at long last—is a one-volume, easy to digest, up-to-date, practical, factual guide to all things Utahan. . . . This is the best handbook of its kind I've yet encountered." —*The Salt Lake Tribune*

## WASHINGTON HANDBOOK

Don Pitcher, 630 pages, **$18.95**

"Departs from the general guidebook format by offering information on how to cope with the rainy days and where to take the children. . . . This is a great little book, informational, fun to read, and a good one to keep."     —*Travel Publishing News*

## WYOMING HANDBOOK

Don Pitcher, 495 pages, **$14.95**

"Wanna know the real dirt on Calamity Jane, white Indians, and the tacky Cheyenne gunslingers? All here. And all fun."     —*The New York Daily News*

### Hit The Road With Moon Travel Handbooks

## ROAD TRIP USA

### Cross-Country Adventures on America's Two-Lane Highways

by Jamie Jensen, 800 pages, **$22.50**

This 800-page Handbook covers the entire United States with 11 intersecting routes, allowing travelers to create their own cross-country driving adventures. Of the featured routes, six run west to east from coast to coast, and five run north to south from Canada to Mexico.

Packed with both practical information and entertaining sidebars, *Road Trip USA* celebrates the spontaneity and culture of the American highway without sacrificing the essential comforts of bed and bread. In addition to engaging commentary on literally thousands of sights and diversions, readers will find such essential information as the locations of diners with the best apple pie and the call letters of good radio stations on lonely stretches of road.

The World Wide Web edition of *Road Trip USA* has been generating excitement on the Internet for over a year. The *Road Trip* exhibit includes a map with hundreds of original entries and links to local Internet sites. WWW explorers are encouraged to participate in the exhibit by contributing their own travel tips on small towns, roadside attractions, regional foods, and interesting places to stay. Visit *Road Trip USA* online at: **http://www.moon.com/rdtrip.html**

## MOONBELT

A new concept in moneybelts. Made of heavy-duty Cordura nylon, the Moonbelt offers maximum protection for your money and important papers. This pouch, designed for all-weather comfort, slips under your shirt or waistband, rendering it virtually undetectable and inaccessible to pickpockets. It features a one-inch high-test quick-release buckle so there's no more fumbling around for the strap or repeated adjustments. This handy plastic buckle opens and closes with a touch but won't come undone until you want it to. Moonbelts accommodate traveler's checks, passports, cash, photos, etc. Size 5 x 9 inches. Available in black only. **$8.95**

## Travel Matters

Travel Matters is Moon Publications' free newsletter, loaded with specially commissioned travel articles and essays that get at the heart of the travel experience. Every issue includes:

**Feature Stories** covering a wide array of travel and cultural topics about destinations on and off the beaten path. Past feature stories in *Travel Matters* include Mexican professional wrestling, traveling to the Moon, and why Germans get six weeks vacation and Americans don't.

**Transportation** tips covering all forms of transportation by land, sea, and air. Transportation topics covered recently have included driving through Baja California, new Eurail passes, trekking in Tibet, and biking through Asia.

**Health Matters,** by Dirk Schroeder, author of *Staying Healthy in Asia, Africa, and Latin America,* focusing on the most recent medical findings that affect travelers. Learn about hepatitis A and B, critical travel supplies, and how to avoid common ailments.

**Book and Multimedia Reviews** providing informed assessments of the latest travel titles, series, and support materials. Recent reviews include The Rough Guide to *World Music, Passage to Vietnam* CD-ROM, and *I Should Have Stayed Home: The Worst Trips of Great Writers.*

**The Internet** page, which provides updates on Moon's WWW site, online discussions, and other travel resources available in cyberspace. A wide range of topics have been covered in this column including how to go online without going crazy, the Great Burma Debate, and details on Moon's *Road Trip USA* project.

**Fellow Traveler,** a reader question and answer column for travelers written by an international travel agent and world traveler.

To receive a free subscription to *Travel Matters,* call (800) 345-5473,
e-mail us at travel@moon.com, or write to us at:

Moon Publications
P.O. Box 3040
Chico, CA 95927-3040

Please note: Subscribers who live outside of the United States will be charged $7 per year for shipping and handling.

# MOON TRAVEL HANDBOOKS

## NORTH AMERICA AND HAWAII

Alaska-Yukon Handbook (0161) . . . . . . . . . . . . . . . . . . . $14.95
Alberta and the Northwest Territories Handbook (0676) . . . . . $17.95
Arizona Traveler's Handbook (0714) . . . . . . . . . . . . . . . . $17.95
Atlantic Canada Handbook (0072) . . . . . . . . . . . . . . . . . $17.95
Big Island of Hawaii Handbook (0064) . . . . . . . . . . . . . . . $13.95
British Columbia Handbook (0145) . . . . . . . . . . . . . . . . . $15.95
Colorado Handbook (0447) . . . . . . . . . . . . . . . . . . . . . $18.95
Georgia Handbook (0390) . . . . . . . . . . . . . . . . . . . . . $17.95
Hawaii Handbook (0005) . . . . . . . . . . . . . . . . . . . . . . $19.95
Honolulu-Waikiki Handbook (0587) . . . . . . . . . . . . . . . . $14.95
Idaho Handbook (0617) . . . . . . . . . . . . . . . . . . . . . . . $14.95
Kauai Handbook (0013) . . . . . . . . . . . . . . . . . . . . . . . $13.95
Maui Handbook (0579) . . . . . . . . . . . . . . . . . . . . . . . $14.95
Montana Handbook (0498) . . . . . . . . . . . . . . . . . . . . . $17.95
Nevada Handbook (0641) . . . . . . . . . . . . . . . . . . . . . . $16.95
New Mexico Handbook (0153) . . . . . . . . . . . . . . . . . . . $14.95
Northern California Handbook (3840) . . . . . . . . . . . . . . . $19.95
Oregon Handbook (0102) . . . . . . . . . . . . . . . . . . . . . . $16.95
Road Trip USA (0366) . . . . . . . . . . . . . . . . . . . . . . . . $22.50
Texas Handbook (0633) . . . . . . . . . . . . . . . . . . . . . . . $17.95
Utah Handbook (0684) . . . . . . . . . . . . . . . . . . . . . . . $16.95
Washington Handbook (0455) . . . . . . . . . . . . . . . . . . . $18.95
Wyoming Handbook (3980) . . . . . . . . . . . . . . . . . . . . . $14.95

## ASIA AND THE PACIFIC

Australia Handbook (0722) . . . . . . . . . . . . . . . . . . . . . $21.95
Bali Handbook (0730) . . . . . . . . . . . . . . . . . . . . . . . . $19.95
Bangkok Handbook (0595) . . . . . . . . . . . . . . . . . . . . . $13.95
Fiji Islands Handbook (0382) . . . . . . . . . . . . . . . . . . . . $13.95
Hong Kong Handbook (0560) . . . . . . . . . . . . . . . . . . . . $15.95
Indonesia Handbook (0625) . . . . . . . . . . . . . . . . . . . . . $25.00
Japan Handbook (3700) . . . . . . . . . . . . . . . . . . . . . . . $22.50
Micronesia Handbook (0773) . . . . . . . . . . . . . . . . . . . . $13.95
Nepal Handbook (0412) . . . . . . . . . . . . . . . . . . . . . . . $18.95
New Zealand Handbook (0331) . . . . . . . . . . . . . . . . . . . $19.95
Outback Australia Handbook (0471) . . . . . . . . . . . . . . . . $18.95
Pakistan Handbook (0692) . . . . . . . . . . . . . . . . . . . . . $22.50
Philippines Handbook (0048) . . . . . . . . . . . . . . . . . . . . $17.95

Southeast Asia Handbook (0021)..................... $21.95
South Korea Handbook (3204).......................... $14.95
South Pacific Handbook (0404)......................... $22.95
Tahiti-Polynesia Handbook (0374)...................... $13.95
Thailand Handbook (0420).............................. $19.95
Tibet Handbook (3905) ................................. $30.00
Vietnam, Cambodia & Laos Handbook (0293) ......... $18.95

## MEXICO

Baja Handbook (0528) ................................. $15.95
Cabo Handbook (0285).................................. $14.95
Cancún Handbook (0501) ............................... $13.95
Central Mexico Handbook (0234)........................ $15.95
Mexico Handbook (0315)................................ $21.95
Northern Mexico Handbook (0226)...................... $16.95
Pacific Mexico Handbook (0323) ....................... $16.95
Puerto Vallarta Handbook (0250)....................... $14.95
Yucatán Peninsula Handbook (0242) ................... $15.95

## CENTRAL AMERICA AND THE CARIBBEAN

Belize Handbook (0307) ............................... $15.95
Caribbean Handbook (0277)............................ $16.95
Costa Rica Handbook (0358) ........................... $18.95
Jamaica Handbook (0706) ............................. $15.95

## INTERNATIONAL

Egypt Handbook (3891) ................................ $18.95
Moon Handbook (0668)................................. $10.00
Moscow-St. Petersburg Handbook (3913) .............. $13.95
Staying Healthy in Asia, Africa, and Latin America (0269) .. $11.95
The Practical Nomad (0765)............................ $13.95

---

### PERIPLUS TRAVEL MAPS
All maps $7.95 each

| | | |
|---|---|---|
| Bali | Jakarta | Phuket/S. Thailand |
| Bandung/W. Java | E. Java | Sabah |
| Bangkok/C. Thailand | Java | Sarawak |
| Batam/Bintan | Kuala Lumpur | Singapore |
| Cambodia | Ko Samui/S. Thailand | Vietnam |
| Chiangmai/N. Thailand | Lombok | Yogyakarta/C. Java |
| Hong Kong | N. Sumatra | |
| Indonesia | Penang | |

# WHERE TO BUY MOON TRAVEL HANDBOOKS

**BOOKSTORES AND LIBRARIES:** Moon Travel Handbooks are sold worldwide. Please contact our sales manager for a list of wholesalers and distributors in your area.

**TRAVELERS:** We would like to have Moon Travel Handbooks available throughout the world. Please ask your bookstore to write or call us for ordering information. If your bookstore will not order our guides for you, please contact us for a free catalogue.

> Moon Publications, Inc.
> P.O. Box 3040
> Chico, CA 95927-3040 U.S.A.
> tel.: (800) 345-5473
> fax: (916) 345-6751
> e-mail: travel@moon.com

# IMPORTANT ORDERING INFORMATION

**PRICES:** All prices are subject to change. We always ship the most current edition. We will let you know if there is a price increase on the book you order.

**SHIPPING AND HANDLING OPTIONS:** Domestic UPS or USPS first class (allow 10 working days for delivery): $3.50 for the first item, 50 cents for each additional item.

**EXCEPTIONS:** *Tibet Handbook, Mexico Handbook,* and *Indonesia Handbook* shipping $4.50; $1.00 for each additional *Tibet Handbook, Mexico Handbook* or *Indonesia Handbook.*

Moonbelt shipping is $1.50 for one, 50 cents for each additional belt.

Add $2.00 for same-day handling.

UPS 2nd Day Air or Printed Airmail requires a special quote.

International Surface Bookrate 8-12 weeks delivery: $3.00 for the first item, $1.00 for each additional item. Note: Moon Publications cannot guarantee international surface bookrate shipping. Moon recommends sending international orders via air mail, which requires a special quote.

**FOREIGN ORDERS:** Orders that originate outside the U.S.A. must be paid for with either an international money order or a check in U.S. currency drawn on a major U.S. bank based in the U.S.A.

**TELEPHONE ORDERS:** We accept Visa or MasterCard payments. Minimum order is US$15. Call in your order: (800) 345-5473, 8 a.m.-5 p.m. Pacific standard time.

# ORDER FORM

Prices are subject to change without notice. Be sure to call (800) 345-5473 for current prices a▮ editions or for the name of the bookstore nearest you that carries Moon Travel Handbooks • 8 a.m.–5 p.m. PST. (See important ordering information on preceding page.)

Name: _____ Date: _____

Street: _____

City: _____ Daytime Phone: _____

State or Country: _____ Zip Code: _____

| QUANTITY | TITLE | PRICE |
|---|---|---|
|  |  |  |
|  |  |  |
|  |  |  |
|  |  |  |
|  |  |  |
|  |  |  |
|  |  |  |
|  |  |  |

Taxable Total _____

Sales Tax (7.25%) for California Residents _____

Shipping & Handling _____

**TOTAL** _____

Ship: ☐ UPS (no P.O. Boxes)　☐ 1st class　☐ International surface mail

Ship to: ☐ address above　☐ other _____

_____

Make checks payable to: **MOON PUBLICATIONS, INC.**, P.O. Box 3040, Chico, CA 95927-3040 U.S.A. We accept Visa and MasterCard. **To Order**: Call in your Visa or MasterCard number, or send a writ- ten order with your Visa or MasterCard number and expiration date clearly written.

Card Number: ☐ **Visa**　☐ **MasterCard**

☐ ☐ ☐ ☐ ☐ ☐ ☐ ☐ ☐ ☐ ☐ ☐ ☐ ☐ ☐ ☐

**Exact Name on Card:** _____

Expiration date: _____

Signature: _____

# THE METRIC SYSTEM

| | |
|---|---|
| 1 inch | = 2.54 centimeters (cm) |
| 1 foot | = .304 meters (m) |
| 1 mile | = 1.6093 kilometers (km) |
| 1 km | = .6124 miles |
| 1 fathom | = 1.8288 m |
| 1 chain | = 20.1168 m |
| 1 furlong | = 201.168 m |
| 1 acre | = .4047 hectares |
| 1 sq km | = 100 hectares |
| 1 sq mile | = 2.59 square km |
| 1 ounce | = 28.35 grams |
| 1 pound | = .4536 kilograms |
| 1 short ton | = .90718 metric ton |
| 1 short ton | = 2000 pounds |
| 1 long ton | = 1.016 metric tons |
| 1 long ton | = 2240 pounds |
| 1 metric ton | = 1000 kilograms |
| 1 quart | = .94635 liters |
| 1 US gallon | = 3.7854 liters |
| 1 Imperial gallon | = 4.5459 liters |
| 1 nautical mile | = 1.852 km |

To compute celsius temperatures, subtract 32 from Fahrenheit and divide by 1.8. To go the other way, multiply celsius by 1.8 and add 32.

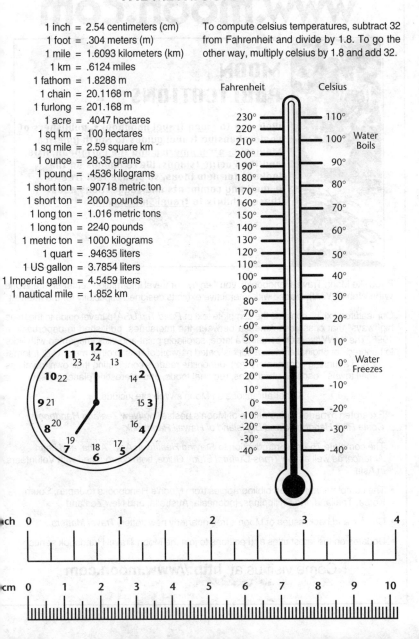